Mental Health Care
Issues in America

Mental Health Care Issues in America

AN ENCYCLOPEDIA

VOLUME ONE: A–M

Michael Shally-Jensen,
Editor

 ABC-CLIO

Santa Barbara, California • Denver, Colorado • Oxford, England

Copyright 2013 by ABC-CLIO, LLC

Library of Congress Cataloging-in-Publication Data

Mental health care issues in America : an encyclopedia / Michael Shally-Jensen, editor.

v. cm.

Includes bibliographical references and index.

ISBN 978–1–61069–013–3 (hard copy : alk. paper) — ISBN 978–1–61069–014–0 (ebook)

1. Mental health—United States—Encyclopedias. 2. Mental health services—United States—Encyclopedias. 3. Psychiatry—United States—Encyclopedias. 4. Mental illness—United States—Encyclopedias. I. Shally-Jensen, Michael.

RC437.M46 2013

362.19689003—dc23   2012023911

ISBN: 978–1–61069–013–3
EISBN: 978–1–61069–014–0

17 16 15 14 13   1 2 3 4 5

This book is also available on the World Wide Web as an eBook.
Visit www.abc-clio.com for details.

ABC-CLIO, LLC
130 Cremona Drive, P.O. Box 1911
Santa Barbara, California 93116-1911

This book is printed on acid-free paper ∞

Manufactured in the United States of America

Contents

Alphabetical List of Entries

Topical List of Entries

Children and Youth

Adolescence and Mental Health

Attention Deficit/Hyperactivity Disorder

Autism Spectrum Disorders

Campus Life and Mental Health

Children and Mental Health

Depression

Drug Abuse and Mental Health

Eating Disorders

Family and Mental Illness

Gender Identity Disorder

Genetics and Mental Health

Impulse Control Disorders

Intellectual Disability

Internet Gaming Addiction

Learning Disabilities

Lesbian, Gay, Bisexual, and Transgender (LGBT) Mental Health Issues

Residential Treatment for Young People

School Mental Health

Self-Injury and Body Image

Suicide and Suicide Prevention

Ethnicity, Race, and Culture

African Americans and Mental Health

American Indian and Alaskan Native Mental Health

Asian American and Pacific Islander Mental Health Issues

Culturally Competent Mental Health Care

Latinos and Mental Health

Institutions, Settings, and Social Contexts

Campus Life and Mental Health

Community Mental Health

Creativity and Mental Health

Disasters and Mental Health

Psychiatry, Psychology, and Pharmaceuticals

The Public Sphere

Therapies and Approaches

Introduction

Estimates vary, but in the 1950s, at the height of the era of the large psychiatric hospital, the number of inpatients nationwide is thought to have stood at nearly 560,000. By 1965 it had dropped to 475,000, and 15 years later it stood at about 150,000. More recently, it has fluctuated between that figure and estimates as low as 60,000 (Dowbiggin 2011; Grob 1994; Lamb & Weinberger 2001). Over this same period, of course, a significant increase (about 70%) occurred in the general population of the United States, making all the more dramatic the scale of the shrinkage of the inpatient population and the elimination of state psychiatric institutions. These changes took place not as a result of improved mental health among the American populace but as a consequence of a shift of approach toward the mentally ill and their treatment. No longer were long-term care and, in the best of cases, comprehensive therapy the default modes of treatment in serious cases. Instead, emphasis came to be placed on drug therapy and community-based mental health centers. This transition from the old regime to the new is commonly referred to as deinstitutionalization.

Some observers would insist that this shift from high-minded institutional management of cases to community outpatient clinics and greater freedom of choice on the part of mental health consumers (including their right to refuse treatment) was and continues to be purely a good thing. And, to be sure, there have been many positive developments as a result of this shift, including a generally more humane, less patronizing approach to people living with mental illness. On the other hand, there are those who would argue with equal vigor that allowing millions of Americans with mental disabilities to go untreated or cycle in and out of hospital emergency rooms is nothing short of systematic neglect. Which of the two points of view is right, if such a stark choice can be made, cannot be decided definitively here. Rather, the goal of the present work is to provide an overview of this and other issues in order to allow readers to draw their own conclusions.

Even at the height of the era of the large mental hospital, such institutions served only a small portion of the many millions of people with depression, bipolar disorder, crippling anxieties, schizophrenia, and other ailments. The hospitals tended to take primarily people who were in the throes of a psychotic episode (i.e., separation from reality), discharging them when they responded to treatment, improved on their own, or were able for one reason or another to return to their lives on the outside—with or without external supports. In addition to housing patients living with chronic, serious mental illness, then, mental hospitals served a sizeable population of patients who experienced single instances of mental distress or perhaps recurring episodes of mental illness.

Today, of course, we know that the work done by the traditional mental hospitals was far from perfect. There were serious problems with everything from who was admitted and why to the type and amount of care (if any) patients received. The archives and library shelves are filled with testaments to the effect that patients were sometimes simply warehoused and forgotten or subject to restraints and left in confinement. The system was patriarchal and hierarchical to the extreme, with patients treated less as individuals with lives and rights of their own than as inmates in a quasi-penal institution run by a select group of (male) psychiatric wizards. Doctor-to-patient (and nurse-to-patient) ratios were unsustainable. Yet despite their many failings, the public mental hospitals stood with their doors open as places to which people experiencing mental and emotional difficulties could go for care.

This is no longer the case, for better or for worse. While those fortunate enough to hold full-time jobs with comprehensive health care benefits are able to access the mental health care system to one degree or another, and while there continue to be public community mental health resources available for those in need, the scope and range of care, and the number of persons served, are not what they used to be. Today there are far fewer full-service institutions available for those needing help, and there is a general shortage of qualified health care professionals to handle cases. This is unfortunate in that it is, above all, help and shelter, shelter and care, that people living with mental illness require. As the writer Alex Beam explained when asked why he should devote his time to the study of a historic mental hospital (McLean Hospital outside of Boston),

> Life is impossible ... Who can't understand the need for shelter? And who can't sympathize with the people who seek that shelter? ... This is a book [i.e., Beam's *Gracefully Insane*] about the men and women who needed shelter more than most of us, or who, in some cases, were more honest about their need for protection than we are. (Beam 2001, 14–15)

Shelter and care continue to be the touchstones of contemporary mental health care (along with drug therapy); and yet even at McLean, one of the nation's premier mental institutions, the standard six-week stay of former times has by now become, under the best of circumstances, a five-day period of observation and release, with pressure to reduce the time even more. In the public sphere (McLean is private), the situation is even worse. The place of last resort is no longer the mental hospital but, often, the criminal justice system, where millions of homeless mentally ill and other individuals are assigned to jails and prisons and offered minimal or nonexistent psychiatric care.

In the course of emptying out the mental hospitals during the deinstitutionalization era, a variety of new laws were enacted making it illegal to commit psychiatric patients against their will—unless they posed an immediate threat to themselves or to others. Court decisions steadily built on such laws. By and large, the emergence of these laws can be viewed as a positive development in the history of mental health and patients' rights. Through them, the individual has gained priority over impersonal bureaucracy. Patients themselves, not third parties, have the right to choose what is best as far as their own health and well-being goes. And yet at the same time, this development can be regarded as having come at the expense, in many cases, of the long-term mental health outlook of the individual or individuals involved. It appears to be a case of one step forward and one step back.

One problem is that most patients with serious mental illness, particularly those prone to psychotic breaks, display what psychiatrists call "poor insight" into their condition. They don't think they are ill; they don't feel they need their medications; they don't trust that doctors or other mental health professionals have their best interests at heart. They would prefer to stay the course and see where it leads them rather than authorize others to assume responsibility for them or have a say in whether they might be better served in an institutional setting—if only temporarily.

The case of journalist Pete Earley and his son is exemplary in this regard. In *Crazy: A Father's Search through America's Mental Health Madness* (Earley 2006), Earley describes his attempts to help his college-age son, Mike, after he becomes ill with bipolar disorder and is arrested. That Mike was off his medications and experiencing a psychotic episode when he broke into a neighbor's house plays no part in his criminal case, for according to the applicable state laws Mike is first and foremost a criminal offender. Moreover, his father has no say in the matter because Mike is of legal age. Worse, even in the midst of the crisis Mike is not inclined to go back on his medications, as he feels he is better off without them. Earley makes clear that his son is not really *seeing* the crisis for what it is, and yet he (Earley) is helpless to do anything about it. After release from jail, Mike eventually returns to his medication and therapy—to good effect—only to lapse again into psychosis and trouble when he decides that he has had enough.

Earley also describes a year he spent talking with officials and inmates at the Miami-Dade County Jail, where he followed the cases of persons with mental disorders. He looks at their time in jail, their lives out in the community, and, in many cases, their return to jail or alternative forms of punishment. At every turn, he found an array of incompatible laws and practices concerning patient's rights and the criminal justice system, a confused bureaucracy that allowed only for the most expedient solution at any given moment. Earley's book was one of two finalists for the Pulitzer Prize in 2007 and has won awards from the National Alliance on Mental Illness, Mental Health America, and the American Psychiatric Association.

In addition to socio-legal issues, closing the mental hospitals has created issues that our general hospitals must now confront. Not specializing in handling mental patients, and burdened by high costs, general hospitals typically follow the practice of "assess and release" (or "in and out"). That is, they are inclined, given the legal and financial considerations involved, to forgo admitting mental patients, including those with severe problems; and when they do admit them they often quickly discharge them. Even hospitals with dedicated mental health wings commonly hold patients only long enough to provide brief evaluation and a course of medication. Long-term planning and treatment are thus supplanted by ad hoc decisions and temporary fixes, resulting in a mixed form of care that often contravenes the intents of the family members most closely involved in the patient's life and well-being.

If they cannot or will not make use of the hospitals, what are those with serious mental and emotional difficulties to do? Where are they to go? Many, of course, make use of community health clinics, but such clinics are not ideal venues by any means and, in any case, they are dwindling in number. Clearly, many individuals without personal supports in place will end up homeless or in jail, and some of them may also commit suicide. Others could possibly cause public disturbances, even potentially dangerous ones. Most, however, simply fall below the radar and are ignored by society. Whatever the result, it is useful to know the scope of the problem. Is the state of mental health care in the United States a cause for alarm or is the matter largely under control? Is there reason for us as citizens to be concerned about it? How many people have severe mental illness? How many are treated and thus able to carry on with their lives, and how many are left untouched by the health care system? What kinds of problems—behavioral, social, and other—are we talking about? What needs to be done to address them?

Dimensions of the Problem

The first question we should ask, then, is how many Americans have mental illness? According to the most widely cited source on the subject, the National Comorbidity Study Replication (NCS-R), serious mental illness affects 6 percent of the adult population (age 18 and above) in the United States (Kessler et al. 2005a). With the total adult population standing at nearly 235 million, that means that more than 14 million people are considered to be living with severe mental illness. Perhaps more alarming, more than 25 percent of Americans experience a mental disorder of either the acute or chronic variety in a given year, one quarter of them experiencing severe symptoms and the rest experiencing moderate or mild symptoms (Substance Abuse and Mental Health Services Administration [SAMHSA] 2010). Estimates of lifetime prevalence rates for the various types of disorders show anxiety disorders to be the most common, at 28.8 percent of affected adults, followed by mood disorders (20.8%) and substance use disorders (14.6%). About half of all cases involve more than one diagnosis, which most often is a substance use disorder. Detailed estimates of children and youth with serious mental illness are not presented by the NCS-R, but other studies reveal that about 5 percent of children aged 4 to 17 experience serious emotional or behavioral difficulties, and just over 8 percent of adolescents (aged 12 to 17) experience major depression (SAMHSA 2010).

Although mental disorders occur across the life span, affecting all people regardless of race, ethnicity, gender, education, or socioeconomic status, the majority of people with mental disorders do not receive treatment; indeed, nearly half of those with a *severe* mental illness do not do so (Regier et al. 1993). Ronald Kessler and colleagues, who conducted the NCS-R study, estimate that half of all Americans will experience some form of mental disorder during their lifetime, with first onset usually occurring in childhood or adolescence (Kessler et al. 2005b). Failure to address such occurrences early, of course, can lead to more serious problems later on and increase the personal and societal costs involved, including the risk of suicide. As for geographic distribution, the prevalence of mental illness is roughly the same in urban and rural areas, but access to services is generally better in urban areas. Of the approximately 2 million homeless persons in the United States, an estimated one-quarter of them live with a serious mental illness and another quarter have milder forms of psychiatric disorder.

Uneven Coverage and Backward Trends

The health care system in the United States continues to be bifurcated, or split in two: lower-income people rely on the public sector for care and higher-income people turn to the private sector. Millions of people who are uninsured or who have inadequate insurance coverage are unable to pay for mental health services on their own. For them, the public mental health system remains the principal provider of services—and, it should be noted, "public mental health system" means *state* mental health system, because there is no national mental health system in place. The missions and operations of state mental health agencies vary significantly, but most are centered on the treatment of more severe and persistent cases of mental illness. In many rural areas, the majority of patients must make do without access to a trained psychiatrist.

Researchers have identified an association between poverty and higher rates of mental disorder. Data from the National Health Interview Survey indicate that

6.6 percent of economically disadvantaged children (those whose family income was less than the poverty threshold) aged 4 to 17 had definite or severe emotional or behavioral difficulties, compared with 4.2 percent of children of the same age whose family income was at least twice the poverty threshold (see SAMHSA 2010).

People with substantial personal income, in contrast, and with good medical insurance, are able to make use of private mental health providers, ranging from private psychotherapists to rooms in dedicated psychiatric facilities. Even in this case, however, insurance plans typically limit the number of behavioral health visits available to patients. Primary care physicians remain the lynchpins of the mental health system, providing up to 40 percent of basic mental health care services to the general population and serving as initial points of reference for cases requiring specialists. The approach in the medical community to people with less serious emotional disorders is that of outpatient services, often through prescription medications and monthly or quarterly 15-minute med checks. Employee assistance programs help employees in the workplace with the assessment of mental health issues and referrals to appropriate treatment sources.

In other words, significant divides continue to mark mental health care in the United States today. Even where formal coverage exists the services available may be limited, difficult to access, or inadequate to the task. This situation, together with the fact that millions of Americans continue to go untreated, is part of what led the President's New Freedom Commission on Mental Health to conclude that "the mental health treatment system in America is in shambles" (President's New Freedom Commission on Mental Health 2003). This is a strong condemnation, and yet there is little that has happened in the 10 years since it was issued to lead one to believe that the situation has improved or will improve anytime soon.

Indeed, the trend in spending runs in the opposite direction—at least when compared to spending on general health care. National expenditures for the treatment of mental disorders amounted to $100 billion in 2003, the most recent year for which national estimates are available. It is projected to reach $203 billion in 2014. However, spending for all health care conditions has been increasing at a higher rate than spending on mental health conditions. In 1986, for example, mental health spending was 7.5 percent of all health care spending. In 2003 that share was 6.2 percent, and in 2014 it is projected to be 5.9 percent (SAMHSA 2010). Also, most of the increase in recent and projected spending is in the area of medications, not services. As another measure of spending, one can note that the number of mental health organizations with 24-hour hospital/residential treatment settings decreased from 3,512 to 2,891 between 1986 and 2004 and is expected to continue to decline (SAMHSA 2010). Such gaps in the system create problems elsewhere in society. As one pair of experts have noted, the system, at best, is "better but not well" (Frank & Glied 2006).

Homelessness

Consider homelessness. There is no single answer as to why a sharp increase in homelessness has occurred over the past several decades, but a major contributing factor in the view of many observers is the deinstitutionalization movement that began in the 1950s. Community-based mental health programs that were supposed to fill the gap simply could not meet the challenge, and as a result millions of former inpatients became homeless and more visible to the public. If someone released from a hospital and suffering from major depression, bipolar disorder, or schizophrenia is unable to cope with reality (i.e., is actively psychotic), he or she very likely will soon exhaust any resources available to him or her, including the attentions of family members or other interested parties—to the extent they exist. Such persons will frequently end up homeless and with little or no chance that his or her mental condition is going to improve on its own.

It is significant, too, that in many cases mentally ill homeless persons became homeless *because of* their mental illness, not because a lack of housing caused them to become mentally ill. This, at least, is the conclusion of the U.S. Conference of Mayors (2011) and scholars such as E. Fuller Torrey (1997). Illnesses such as schizoaffective disorder are considered to have led such individuals to miss whatever opportunities they may have had to exploit personal resources and forced them to become homeless. The fact is that such persons require treatment in order to give them a chance to manage their affairs and maintain a home. The idea that housing alone will address the problem is misguided, although housing is a central part of the equation.

The reverse situation is not entirely absent, either. That is, homelessness can and does create stressors that contribute to or in some sense "cause" mental illness. Today, as more and more children and families face removal from their homes for nonpayment of mortgages or rent, it is important to realize that virtually anyone could become homeless. The happily employed can suddenly become the unemployed homeless, and the life of the unemployed homeless is a life of unending difficulty, peril, and discouragement. Substance abuse, nutritional issues, physical health problems, street crime victimization, and the stigma of being homeless take a toll on one's mental health. It is hardly surprising that many homeless individuals become unhinged and require a visit to the emergency room or seek suicide as an option. Either that or they end up in jails as "mentally disturbed persons," in the jargon of law enforcement.

Suicide

The presence of a mental disorder, even in its early stages, together with other risk factors such as substance abuse, family history of illness, poor living conditions, and so on, are a potent mix that can lead to suicidal ideation. Overall, about

35,000 Americans kill themselves each year, making it the 10th leading cause of death. The rate is even higher among older people, particularly men over the age of 65. Further, for every 1 person who suicides, 10 more try and fail. Research shows that 90 percent of all those who commit suicide are struggling with a mental disorder of some kind—most commonly, depression and substance abuse—at the time of their death. Approximately 12 percent of people living with schizophrenia, 13 percent of those living with an anxiety disorder, and 16 percent of those diagnosed with bipolar disorder succeed in taking their own lives (Hobson & Leonard 2002; National Institute of Mental Health 2010).

Remarkably, a majority of these cases are not handled by mental health professionals. Rather, primary care physicians are the ones who most commonly encounter suicide victims in the period preceding their death—if, that is, the victim sees a professional in the first place. General and family practitioners are to be lauded for the frontline medical care they provide, but at the same time many of them are not equipped to detect and diagnose mental and emotional problems in their patients during routine office visits. The problem of suicide and suicidal ideation is compounded by the fact that insurers and hospitals maintain strict rules about coverage and admissions for any "suspected" condition or "preliminary" diagnosis, and also by the fact that suicides typically occur precisely when the individual is in crisis and least likely to have the wherewithal to seek help from a professional.

Where such individuals do obtain help, when it is available, is from intimate friends, parents, or relatives. If, however, one considers, again, that 10 times the number of people who do commit suicide *attempt* to commit suicide, and that a very high percentage of those who follow this path suffer from an acute mental disorder, it becomes clear that more is needed in these situations than the counsel of family and friends. Mental health professionals have a clear role to play here, as do policy makers and the public in making all of us more aware of the issue and coming up with better ways to address it.

Racial and Ethnic Disparities

In the mental health field, research shows that institutionalized discrimination and differential treatment of ethnic and racial minorities are present. The Surgeon General's supplemental mental health report (Office of the Surgeon General 2001) states that four main points of disparity have been identified. First, minorities do not have the same access to mental health services as European Americans; sometimes these services are not only less accessible to minorities but less available. Second, persons belonging to minority populations receive fewer needed mental health services overall as compared to European Americans. Third, when members of minority populations do receive mental health services, they are typically of poorer quality than those received by their counterparts. And finally, more research is needed on the topic of minorities and mental health.

The Surgeon General notes that the discrimination and racism experienced by minorities can and do affect their mental health, which in turn adversely impacts their socioeconomic conditions. The kind of institutionalized discrimination involved is a pattern of disparate treatment stemming from organizational policy rather than from overtly racist acts. Such covert discrimination may result from either organizational practices or subtle biases against individuals on the part of mental health professionals.

Criminal Justice System

Over the past few decades, the role of jails in housing the mentally ill has increased. The rise seems to be related, in part, to heightened awareness of and public concern over disorderliness, alcoholism, drug addiction, crime, violence, and suicide. It is also related to continuing cutbacks in mental health funding at the state and municipal levels. Thus the penal system must step in to compensate for the absence of viable community mental health systems. Efforts to rid the city streets of mentally ill homeless persons and others generally have had the effect not of improving the situation but merely of pushing the problem to the margins or making it someone else's (another municipality's) problem. At the same time, such efforts substantially expand the mentally ill population in jails and prisons.

The results are by now clear. As one newspaper headline recently noted, "Ripple Effects of [Community] Center Closings Will Continue for Many Years" (Warren 2011). The accompanying story, which describes a scenario common to an increasing number of municipalities, reports that in Chicago, for instance, fewer community health centers and an increase in the number of uninsured persons seem likely to produce "more desperate souls seeking shelter with their families, more children whose conditions go undiagnosed, more patients than John H. Stroger Jr. Hospital [a general hospital] can deal with, more disturbed offenders shuttled off to Cook County Jail, and more homeless people."

In line with this development, studies of inmate populations have found a disproportionate percentage of severely mentally ill individuals behind prison walls. A 1999 Department of Justice study reported that about 16 percent of prison and jail inmates had some form of mental illness (Ditton 1999). A 2006 study by the Department of Justice reported that more than half of all prison and jail inmates had a mental health problem (Glaze & James 2006). Roughly one-quarter of state prisoners, 14 percent of federal prisoners, and 21 percent of jail inmates reported a recent history of mental health problems. These results are consistent with other prisoner studies that have found between 16 and 25 percent of the prisoners surveyed to have a severe mental illness (Lamb & Weinberger 2005).

Virtually all mental health professionals today would agree that people with mental illness do not belong in jail solely because of their illness, and virtually all corrections experts would agree that having people with mental illness in jails and prisons creates additional problems. Severely mentally ill inmates pose challenges in terms of prison order and discipline, and these individuals often end up as the targets of bullying and violence from other prisoners. In jails, of course, which hold offenders for shorter periods of time, incarceration is merely a temporary fix. These institutions become revolving doors whereby the mentally ill are processed and soon leave—untreated—or, at best, find themselves "diverted" to alternative programs that are based on crisis intervention models. Neither the criminal justice system nor persons living with mental illness are well served by these developments, although some diversion programs, at least, have proved useful.

Public Violence

In recent years there have been several high-profile cases of mass violence involving guns and gun users with mental illness. One of the most recent (2012) was the killing in Aurora, Colorado, of 12 people and the wounding of 58 others in a movie theater by a one-time graduate student with a recent history of mental problems. Before that (2011) came the shooting in Tucson, Arizona, of U.S. Representative Gabrielle Giffords and 18 other people by a young man who was subsequently diagnosed with schizophrenia, although people familiar with the man were aware of his erratic behavior before the shooting. Six people, including a nine-year-old girl, were killed. Another historic case was the 2007 shooting on the campus of Virginia Tech in Blacksburg, Virginia. In that case, a student previously diagnosed with a severe anxiety disorder and showing signs of increasingly troubled behavior, stalked and killed 32 people and wounded 25 others. Serious questions were raised afterward about his access to guns, given his medical history, and what could have been done to prevent the tragedy. In between these two events at least two other similar incidents occurred. One was the 2009 mass killing that took place on the Fort Hood Army Base in Texas, and the other was the shooting at an American Civic Association immigration center in Binghamton, New York, in the same year. In these two cases the question of mental illness on the part of the perpetrators has not yet been definitively resolved, and, indeed, the Fort Hood shooting is notable for having been committed by an army psychiatrist. Still, mental health professionals, generally speaking, are inclined to accept that anyone undertaking to perform such heinous acts is likely to be in a tenuous psychological state, to say the least, and to appreciate that such persons likely could have benefited from professional intervention at an earlier stage.

Of course, for every front-page story about mass murder there are numerous other instances of singular acts of violence carried out by people living with mental illness or subject to severe expressions of anger. Often these acts affect not strangers or members of the public at large but rather domestic partners, other family members, or even colleagues from work. These are cases that, similarly, perhaps could have been prevented if public awareness and sensitivity were greater than they are, if consumer outreach efforts were more substantial, and if access to resources was greater. That is a lot of ifs, but if as concerned citizens we hope to make the best use of our energies, it is necessary both to look back on what might have been and to project forward about the future of mental health care in the United States.

Stigma

The traditional stigma attached to mental illness may be waning in some respects but in others it is still alive and well, unfortunately. In a number of basic areas of living—employment, education, relationships and marriage, health care, and even participation in houses of worship—people living with mental illness continue to encounter difficulties and to be treated with less than full measures of trust and respect. As a result, many continue to experience, unnecessarily, a sense of shame and fear and to seek ways to hide or keep secret their condition. In this sense, mental health consumers face a battle on two fronts: the first against their own medical and health issues and the second against society and its biases. While such maltreatment has led many to become mental health advocates who organize and speak out on behalf of fellow consumers, most persons living with mental health problems simply muddle through and hope for the best. Indeed, the Surgeon General concluded more than a decade ago that stigma represents the "foremost obstacle" to the recovery of mental health consumers (U.S. Department of Health and Human Services 1999). If the situation has perhaps changed since then, this has been mostly a qualitative change, not a radical change in underlying perceptions.

Prescription Drugs and the Medical Model

One of the most important changes in mental health practice over the past 15 or 20 years has been the rise in the use of psychotropic medications (i.e., mind-altering drugs). In 1996, for example, there were 121 million prescription fills for this type of medication; in 2006, there were 274 million fills. The rate of antidepressant treatment almost doubled from 1996 to 2005, with one type of antidepressant in particular, selective serotonin reuptake inhibitors (SSRIs), more than doubling and continuing to climb today. Dramatic increases were also reported in psychotropic medication use among preschool-age children, particularly for stimulant medication. A recent study comparing youth Medicaid enrollees in two states showed that nearly one-third of young people using psychotropic medication were receiving multiple medications (SAMSHA 2010).

The medical model of mental illness, which holds that psychological and behavioral problems result from chemical imbalances in the brain, remains largely unproven and yet is central to the practice of modern psychiatry. To a lesser extent this same model influences the mental health profession at large, although many of those working outside of psychiatry employ other approaches. The focus under the medical model is not social or "environmental" factors as contributors to mental illness, but rather neural dysfunction and genetics. The emphasis is placed on clinical diagnosis and treatment using medications. Nonpsychiatrists, on the other hand, generally augment or even supplant medications with other forms of treatment, such as psychotherapy. Recent data show that in many cases psychotherapy, often in combination with drugs, can be just as or even more effective than medications alone. Equally helpful in most cases, of course, are supports in the community, including family, housing, employment, and social services.

Thus we have a great divide in the mental health field regarding the very understanding of its subject and the preferred way to deal with individual cases. On the one hand, the pharmaceutical industry spends billions of dollars every year in developing and marketing drugs to psychiatrists and consumers—with great success, one might add. And on the other hand, as critics point out, the underlying premise of such drugs is faulty, we are greatly "overmedicated" as a society, and serious, long-term damages can result from the use of psychiatric medicines. Meanwhile, practitioners must locate themselves somewhere along a philosophical continuum ranging from full faith in the biomedical model to appreciating the need to combine drugs and therapy to complete rejection of the medical model and reliance instead on counseling, therapy, and social supports. In truth, there are far fewer purists or extremists at the ends of the continuum than there are pragmatic professionals in the middle who want to make available the best resources for their clients. But as a point of difference, it should be noted that the medical model currently commands the overwhelming majority of those resources, at least as measured by commercial transactions, insurance policies, and the flow of research dollars. Whether or not this is as it should be remains an open question.

Contents of This Encyclopedia

Each of the topics noted above, and many more besides, are taken up in the *Mental Health Care Issues in America: An Encyclopedia*. The encyclopedia is arranged alphabetically in order to allow users to easily locate entries and to provide a well-rounded view of the overall topic, which includes not only mental disorders and therapies but also social and cultural factors, institutional settings and contexts, legal and ethical issues, and issues of broad public interest or concern. A list of entries by broad topic is provided in the front pages of the work to allow users to focus their research efforts on certain topics. The index at the end of the work also provides access.

Whereas most other reference works in the field focus on one or two specific areas, *Mental Health Care Issues in America: An Encyclopedia*, drawing on increasing public awareness of the topic and a growing body of scholarly literature, takes the broadest possible view of its subject. It offers an objective look at the state of mental health care in the United States and of the mental health field itself. As a library reference work, the encyclopedia should be of interest to students in the health sciences, psychology, counseling, social work, social studies/sociology, American studies, public policy, law and medicine, and social history.

Each of the 115 entries includes a definition or statement of the issue it examines along with a review of its scope and history. Because of the wide range of topics covered, the specific format or structure of an entry depends largely on the subject matter, but in general key facts are laid out along with a description of current thinking in the field and efforts to address the issue. Where appropriate, recent or current public controversies surrounding a topic are noted. A conclusion and/or statement of future prospects is provided in most of the entries as needed.

The contributors come from a wide range of disciplines and include psychologists, psychiatrists, public health experts, counseling professionals, social workers, criminal justice experts, ethnic studies scholars, media specialists, social historians, scholars of law and ethics, education specialists, and other social scientists and researchers. Each has been asked to provide a short, effective survey of the topic about which he or she is writing. The aim has been to provide a balanced treatment overall, one that presents both consensus views and more critical perspectives.

While all of the entries draw on scholarly research, they have been written so that a reasonably diligent upper-level high school student or undergraduate or other layperson can follow the discussion and findings. As much as possible, specialized terms are used only selectively and are defined in text wherever necessary. Subheadings help break down the topics into more easily understandable parts. An additional feature, employed in selected entries, is the use of sidebars, or text boxes, to cover topics of interest related to the main topic of the entry but not necessarily integral to it. Each entry ends with a targeted bibliography including references used by the writer as well as related sources. A general bibliography of useful books, articles, and online sources is provided at the end of the encyclopedia.

It is hoped that the encyclopedia will inspire conversations among students and teachers as well as serve a practical function for student researchers and members of the general public. It is certainly the case that the subject deserves our attention and that the way we approach it says something about who we are and how we see ourselves as a society. That, at least, is the most important lesson that can be taken away from this work.

—*Michael Shally-Jensen*

Bibliography

Beam, Alex. 2001. *Gracefully Insane*. New York: Public Affairs.

DHHS Steering Committee on the Chronically Mentally Ill. 1980. *Toward a National Plan for the Chronically Mentally Ill*. Washington, DC: U.S. Public Health Service.

Ditton, Paula M. 1999. *Mental Health and the Treatment of Inmates and Probationers*. U.S. Department of Justice, Bureau of Justice Statistics. Retrieved from http://bjs.ojp.usdoj.gov/index.cfm?ty=pbdetail&iid=787.

Dowbiggin, Ian. 2011. *The Quest for Mental Health: A Tale of Science, Medicine, Scandal, and Mass Society*. New York: Cambridge University Press.

Earley, Pete. 2006. *Crazy: A Father's Search through America's Mental Health Madness*. New York: Putnam.

Frank, Richard G., and Sherry A. Glied. 2006. *Better but Not Well: Mental Health Policy in the United States since 1950*. Baltimore: Johns Hopkins University Press.

Glaze, Lauren E., and Doris J. James. 2006. *Mental Health Problems of Prison and Jail Inmates*. U.S. Department of Justice, Bureau of Justice Statistics. /Retrieved from http://bjs.ojp.usdoj.gov/index.cfm?ty=pbdetail&iid=789.

Grob, G. N. 1994. *The Mad among Us: A History of the Care of America's Mentally Ill*. New York: Free Press.

Hobson, J. Allan, and Jonathan A. Leonard. 2002. *Out of Its Mind: Psychiatry in Crisis—a Call for Reform*. New York: Basic Books.

Kelly, Timothy A. 2009. *Healing the Broken Mind: Transforming America's Failed Mental Health System*. New York: New York University Press.

Kessler, Ronald C., Olga Demler, Richard G. Frank, et al. 2005a. "Prevalence and Treatment of Mental Disorders, 1990 to 2003." *New England Journal of Medicine* 352: 2515–2523. Retrieved from: http://www.nejm.org/doi/full/10.1056/NEJMsa043266#t=articleDiscussion.

Kessler, Ronald C., Wai Tat Chiu, Olga Demler, and Ellen E. Walters. 2005b. "Prevalence, Severity, and Comorbidity of Twelve-month DSM-IV Disorders in the National Comorbidity Survey Replication (NCS-R)." *Archives of General Psychiatry* 62: 617–627. Retrieved from: http://www.ncbi.nlm.nih.gov/pmc/articles/PMC2847357/.

Lamb, H. R., and L. E. Weinberger, eds. 2001. *Deinstitutionalization: Promise and Problems*. San Francisco: Jossey-Bass.

Lamb, H. R., and L. E. Weinberger. 2005. "The Shift of Psychiatric Inpatient Care from Hospitals to Jails and Prisons." *Journal of the American Academy of Psychiatry and the Law* 33: 529–534.

National Institute of Mental Health. 2010. "Suicide in the U.S.: Statistics and Prevention." Retrieved from http://www.nimh.nih.gov/health/publications/suicide-in-the-us-statistics-and-prevention/index.shtml.

Office of the Surgeon General. 2001. *Mental Health: Culture, Race, and Ethnicity*. Rockville, MD: U.S. Department of Health and Human Services, U.S. Public Health Service.

President's New Freedom Commission on Mental Health. 2003. *Achieving the Promise: Transforming Health Care in America*. Washington, DC: U.S. Government Printing Office.

Regier, D. A., W. Narrow, D. S. Rae, R. W. Manderscheid, B. Z. Locke, and F. K. Goodwin. 1993. "The De Facto U.S. Mental and Addictive Disorders Service System: Epidemiologic

Catchment Area Prospective 1-Year Prevalence Rates of Disorders and Services." *Archives of General Psychiatry* 50: 85–94.

Substance Abuse and Mental Health Services Administration (SAMHSA). 2010. *Mental Health, United States, 2008*. Rockville, MD: Center for Mental Health Services, SAMHSA.

Torrey, E. Fuller. 1997. *Out of the Shadows: Confronting America's Mental Illness Crisis*. New York: Wiley.

U.S. Conference of Mayors. 2011. *Hunger and Homelessness Survey*. Washington, DC: U.S. Conference of Mayors.

U.S. Department of Health and Human Services. 1999. *Mental Health: A Report of the Surgeon General*. Rockville, MD: U.S. Department of Health and Human Services, Substance Abuse and Mental Health Services Administration, Center for Mental Health Services.

Warren, James. 2011. "Ripple Effects of Center Closings Will Continue for Many Years." *New York Times*, December 24.

A

Addiction

See Alcohol Abuse, Alcoholism, and Mental Health; Drug Abuse and Mental Health; Gambling Addiction; Internet Gaming Addiction

Adolescence and Mental Health

Linda Wilmshurst

In 1906 G. Stanley Hall published *Adolescence*, recognizing this as a unique period of transition between childhood and adulthood dominated by what he called "storm and stress." More recently, this perception has been modified to include cultural variations, with adolescents in the West said to experience more stress than those in more traditional cultures (Arnett 1999). Youth in nonindustrial societies also tend to experience the transition as brief, while those in industrial societies experience it within a more protracted time frame. Regardless of the culture, the period of adolescence marks the transition between childhood and adulthood and brings with it significant changes in physical, cognitive, social, and emotional development.

Although all youth will experience the same physiological changes during adolescence, the rate and nature of these changes can vary with living conditions and the geographical region, such that the onset of menarche (first menstruation) can occur as early as 12 years of age to as late as 18 years of age (Eveleth & Tanner 1990). Universally, the onset of menarche results in increased production of adiposity (fat in the arms, legs, and trunk) and, in North America, often coincides with increased body dissatisfaction in females. By contrast, adolescent males experience decreases in fat and increases in muscle strength that can also cause body dissatisfaction relative to stereotypical male ideals. Disorders such as body dysmorphic disorder, previously rare, are now being diagnosed in 1 to 2 percent of Western males (Pope, Phillips, & Olivardia 2000). Preoccupation with increased muscularity, or muscle dysmorphia (also referred to as the "Adonis complex"), is on the rise in Western males (Pope, Phillips, & Olivardia 2000).

Adolescents are capable of problem solving using hypothetical deductive reasoning; however, an increase in self-consciousness and self-reflection can result in a resurgence of egocentrism (Elkind 1994), evident in distortions in thinking such as the "imaginary audience" (the belief that one is the center of attention and scrutiny) and the "personal fable" (the belief in one's own uniqueness). The latter belief can in some cases produce a sense of vulnerability and thus place adolescents at increased risk for depression, suicidal ideation, and increased risk-taking behaviors (Aalsma, Lapsley, & Flannery 2006).

Adolescents spend increasing time with their peers, and yet the parent-child relationship remains one of the strongest predictors of positive mental health, since family cohesion can help buffer against feelings of alienation and depression (Wilmshurst 2009). The authoritative parenting style (high on nurturance and acceptance) has been associated with positive outcomes in adolescence. At the same time, researchers have recognized that in some environments (high-risk neighborhoods) the *authoritarian parenting style* (high on coercive control and low on granting autonomy) can reduce antisocial behaviors and increase academic success (Steinberg, Blatt-Eisengart, & Cauggman 2006). Peers can be instrumental in influencing dropout rates, delinquency, and criminal behavior—for better or for worse (Blum et al. 2000).

Disorders and Treatment

Internalizing Disorders (Anxiety and Mood Disorders)

While prevalence rates for internalizing disorders do not differ by gender in childhood, in adolescence female prevalence rates (15.7%) are significantly higher than rates for males (3.9%).

Anxiety Disorders   Anxiety disorders with likely onset in adolescence include obsessive-compulsive disorder (OCD), social phobia (social anxiety disorder), panic disorder, acute stress disorder, and posttraumatic stress disorder (PTSD).

While the majority of children outgrow their desire to engage in ritualized behaviors, youth with obsessive-compulsive disorder experience persistent and recurring thoughts (obsessions) and behavior patterns (compulsions) daily, for at least an hour. The most common OCD thoughts and behaviors are fear of contamination (excessive hand washing, cleaning), safety concerns (checking locks), hoarding (collecting), and orderliness/symmetry issues (aligning, balancing, the need to have things "perfect").

There is increasing support for a biological and neurological basis for OCD (serotonin malfunction, overactivity of the orbital region of the frontal cortex and caudate nuclei); and yet exposure-based cognitive-behavioral therapy (CBT), rather than medication, is the treatment of choice for youth (Wilmshurst 2009). The FOCUS program (Freedom from Obsessions and Compulsions Using Special Tools), a manualized CBT program, has been highly successful in treating adolescents with OCD (Barrett, Healy-Farrell, & March 2004).

The adolescent's self-conscious tendencies can trigger onset of social phobia, a pervasive fear of embarrassment in public that can include concerns over speaking, eating, or even writing in public. Treatments for social phobia are similar to those used for specific phobias and include such behavioral methods as modeling (demonstration), reinforced practice, and social skills training (Wilmshurst 2009).

When forced to face the object of his or her anxieties, a young person (like other persons) may experience a panic attack, which is an overwhelming feeling lasting for up to 10 minutes that can include physiological (heart palpitations, sweating, dizziness) as well as mental symptoms (feeling trapped, fears of going crazy, sense of losing control). Repeated attempts to avoid having panic attacks may result in a diagnosis of panic disorder, which in some cases is accompanied by agoraphobia (particularly when fear of panic results in the individual becoming homebound). Panic Control Treatment for Adolescents (PCT-A; Hoffman & Mattis 2000) is a successful CBT program that includes educational (awareness of physiological symptoms) as well as behavioral (desensitization) components.

An individual who experiences or witnesses a traumatic and life-threatening event (natural disasters, war, extreme violence) resulting in feelings of intense fear, helplessness, and horror, may develop acute stress disorder (in cases where symptoms last for less than one month) or posttraumatic stress disorder (PTSD; in cases where symptoms persist beyond one month). Symptoms of PTSD involve three different areas, including (1) reexperiencing the event (flashbacks, dreams); (2) avoidance of stimuli associated with the event, and numbing; and (3) persistent symptoms of increased arousal (problems with sleeping, concentration, anger control; American Psychiatric Association [APA] 2000, p. 467). Adolescents with PTSD may demonstrate increased risk-taking behaviors and loss of a sense of purpose while also experiencing issues around identity formation (Wilmshurst 2009).

Mood Disorders   Adolescents who experience a pervasive depressed mood and loss of interest in day-to-day activities may be diagnosed with major depressive disorder (MDD) in cases where symptoms last for less than two weeks; or dysthymic disorder (DD), a less severe though persistent condition (symptoms must last a year or more for the diagnosis to be applicable). Mood disorders can involve a variety of symptom types, including vegetative (weight loss/gain, insomnia or hypersomnia), cognitive/affective (feelings of worthlessness, guilt, problems concentrating, recurrent suicidal ideation), and behavioral/ psychomotor symptoms (agitation, or loss of energy/fatigue). While depression is relatively rare in childhood (2%), the risk increases significantly in adolescence, with 4 to 7 percent of teens experiencing a depressive episode (Costello et al. 2002). The U.S. Food and Drug Administration (FDA) has issued a so-called black box warning about the dangers of prescribing antidepressants for youth owing to the potential of increased suicide risk. However, based on results of their extensive review of research, Bridge and colleagues (2007) state that the benefits of antidepressants such as fluoxetine (Prozac) far outweigh any potential risks. The most common form of treatment for adolescents, either in isolation or as an adjunct to medication, are behavioral, learning-based programs, including CBT.

When depressed states are offset by manic episodes, a diagnosis of bipolar disorder (BD) is possible. The prevalence of BD in adolescence has increased significantly in recent years, with one study reporting a 53.2 percent increase in the diagnosis between 1994 and 2004 (Brotman et al. 2006). Biological and genetic causes have linked the disorder to low levels of serotonin, high levels of norepinephrine, and low levels of glutamate (Wilmshurst 2009). Manic states involving elevated or irritable mood can be accompanied by such symptoms as grandiose thoughts and actions, decreased need for sleep, pressured speech, increased goal-directed behaviors, and engagement in high-risk behaviors (APA 2000). Forty-two percent of adolescents with BD do not graduate on time and experience chronic stress and interpersonal problems (Kutcher 2005). Mood stabilizers such as lithium, or antipsychotics such as resperidone or olanzapine, can be effective in treating BD in adolescence; however, the side effects of these medications (nausea, weight gain, tremors) often result in problems with compliance in their administration (Wilmshurst 2009).

Suicide Risk and Prevention   Suicide rates increase dramatically after 14 years of age, and several risk factors have been identified in this connection. These include teen pregnancy, exposure to suicide (contagion effect), and trouble with school or the law. The Signs of Suicide (SOS) prevention program (SOS) has been adopted in over 675 schools and is effective in reducing suicide attempts. The program trains high school students to be aware of the signs of suicide among their peers and equips them to respond as if an immediate medical emergency was evident using the ACT (acknowledge, care, and tell) protocol (Aseltine & DeMartino 2004).

Externalizing Disorders

Conduct Disorder (CD)   Prevalence rates for conduct disorder (CD) range between 6 and 16 percent for males and between 2 and 9 percent for females (APA 2000). Although oppositional defiant disorder (ODD) is more common in younger children, onset for CD is usually in adolescence. Youth with CD show a persistent pattern of behavior that involves the violation of social norms or the rights of others, as evident in acts of aggression (bullying, cruelty), property destruction (vandalism), deceit/theft, or rule violations (truancy, running away). While 75 percent of children with ODD do not go on to develop CD, 90 percent of those with CD were initially diagnosed with ODD (Wilmshurst 2009). CD can be caused by an interaction between genetic and environmental factors.

In recent years, community-based treatment alternatives such as multisystemic therapy (MST; Henggeler & Borduin 1998) have replaced residential treatment centers (RTCs) as the treatment of choice for CD. The Oregon Social Learning Center (OSLC) has been successful in placing youth in specialized foster care programs while training their parents in behavioral methods prior to reuniting the youth with their families (Chamberlain & Reid 1998).

Disordered Eating and Eating Disorders   Almost 30 percent of youth surveyed reported body dissatisfaction (CDC 2009). This tendency was higher in females (33%) than in males (28%), and was highest among 12th-grade females (36%, as compared to 32% among 9th-grade females). Nationally, 44 percent of adolescents have reported "trying to lose weight" through such methods as eating less or eating low-calorie foods (39%), exercise (61%), fasting for 24 hours (11%), taking diet pills (5%), or using laxatives or vomiting (4%). According to the tripartite influence model, body image dissatisfaction is a function of three main influences—peers, parents, and the media—and places girls at increased risk for eating disorders (Wilmshurst 2009). There are two main categories of eating disorders: anorexia nervosa (AN) and bulimia nervosa (BN).

Individuals diagnosed with AN maintain a weight that is less than 85 percent of the minimum expected weight for their age and have an intense fear of gaining weight or becoming fat. They also have a distorted sense of body proportion and experience amenorrhea (absence of three consecutive menstrual cycles). Weight restriction is maintained by either limiting intake (restricting subtype) or eliminating excess intake through acts of purging, such as overexercising or self-induced vomiting (binge eating/purging subtype). AN is predominantly a female disorder (90%) with onset between 14 and 18 years of age. It affects approximately 1 percent of the population.

Individuals with BN share the same preoccupation with food and fear of weight gain, but they are not able to maintain weight loss, often fluctuating from being underweight to overweight. Feelings of tension and irritability lead to binge eating, followed by guilt and compensatory purging (self-induced vomiting, laxatives, diuretics, fasting, or exercise). Individuals with BN engage in binge-purge cycles at least twice weekly over the course of three months. Onset of BN occurs in later adolescence or early adulthood.

Individuals with eating disorders (EDs) seldom seek assistance willingly, and relapse rates are high. Treatment for AN focuses on medical concerns (restoration of weight lost, and electrolyte balance), reframing maladaptive thinking (CBT), and enhancing self-esteem and interpersonal relationships. Individuals with BN may also require medical intervention if excessive purging has caused damage to the esophagus, teeth, and digestive system. Similar to AN, the most widely used treatment for BN is CBT focusing on maladaptive thoughts about body dissatisfaction, self-esteem, and enhancement of interpersonal relationships. Integrating a relapse-prevention component is highly important to the success of treating any ED.

Prevention programs aimed at assisting young females to develop a healthier and more positive attitude about their body image are not without their own inherent risks. For example, Carter and colleagues (1997) found at six-month follow-up that dieting had rebounded to a higher level than prior to intervention, leading them to question potential iatrogenic effects (clinically caused symptoms) inherent in prevention programs targeting EDs.

Substance Use and Abuse   The *Diagnostic and Statistical Manual of Mental Disorders* (*DSM*) recognizes two broad categories of substance disorders: substance use disorders (SUDs), which includes substance dependence (compulsive use, increased tolerance, and withdrawal symptoms), and substance abuse disorders (recurrent and adverse consequences of taking drugs). The *DSM* provides information on the various types of substance intoxication that can result from drugs that act as depressants (alcohol), stimulants (amphetamines), and hallucinogens/cannabis (LSD, marijuana).

Youth in grades 9 through 12 reported recent usage of substances at the following rates: 26 percent tobacco, 42 percent alcohol, and 21 percent marijuana. In addition, 24 percent admitted to binge drinking (five or more drinks in a row), while 20 percent had used a prescription medication (e.g., Oxycontin, Vicodin) without a prescription. Methamphetamine use was reported at 4 percent while inhalants were used by 12 percent. Nationally, 23 percent of students stated that they procured illegal drugs on school property (Centers for Disease Control and Prevention [CDC] 2009).

There are many theories concerning how exposure to drugs can cause addictions in some individuals. From a biological perspective, genetic factors such as abnormal dopamine receptors have been found in the majority of individuals with alcohol dependence and in about half of those addicted to cocaine (Lawford et al. 1997). Other theorists have cited the gateway hypothesis, which suggests that early and initial drug use paves the way for heavy drug usage later on (Wilmshurst 2009). However, others believe that it is the environmental context that is most influential in drug use, including exposure opportunities and peer influences. On the other hand, parental monitoring of youth activities can have a protective effect.

Similar to EDs, there have been concerns about the relative merit of individual versus group programs, given the potential iatrogenic effects of deviancy training in residential treatment facilities (where youth sharing similar substance problems are aggregated). The need to address relapse prevention is also an essential issue, since about half of those enrolled in programs will relapse within three months (Pagliaro & Pagliaro 1996). The most widely used programs for SUDs are 12-step models (e.g., Alcoholics Anonymous and similar youth versions), CBT, and family-based treatment (Henggeler & Bourduin 1990). Although the Drug Abuse

Resistance Education Program (DARE) has been widely used in middle schools, it has been found ineffective in preventing drug use. The LifeSkills Training program (LST), consisting of fifteen 45-minute lessons, has been found to reduce alcohol, tobacco, and inhalant use in at-risk students enrolled in over 30 inner-city schools in New York (Griffin et al. 2003).

Ethical Issues and Treatment Concerns

Working with adolescents who experience mental health issues can present a number of ethical challenges, including knowing the age of majority in the state of practice and the state's definitions of conditions of emancipated minors and mature minors. Underage youth may claim status as an emancipated minor in some states if they are financially independent, married, or in the armed services. As a mature minor, an adolescent can receive treatment without consent from a caregiver for such conditions as drug abuse and sexually transmitted diseases.

The age of majority can range from 18 to 21 years of age, depending on the state, and represents the time when youth are legally entitled to the same confidentiality privileges as adults. Treating an adolescent who is a minor can be problematic because parents can legally have access to information regarding treatment sessions and any reports generated. As a result, it is often prudent to discuss and negotiate rules of confidentiality with parents, enlisting their support for withholding information from the sessions until a trusting relationship can be developed with the adolescent.

See also Alcohol Abuse, Alcoholism, and Mental Health; Bipolar Disorder; Campus Life and Mental Health; Children and Mental Health; Culturally Competent Mental Health Care; Depression; Drug Abuse and Mental Health; Eating Disorders; Family and Mental Illness; Internet Gaming Addiction; Obsessive-Compulsive Disorder; Panic Disorder; Preventative Mental Health Programs; Residential Treatment for Young People; Self-Injury and Body Image; Social Anxiety Disorder; Suicide and Suicide Prevention

Bibliography

Aalsma, M. C., D. K. Lapsley, and D. J. Flannery. 2006. "Personal Fables, Narcissism, and Adolescent Adjustment." *Psychology in the Schools* 43: 481–491.

American Psychiatric Association. 2000. *The Diagnostic and Statistical Manual of Mental Disorders* (4th ed., text rev.). Washington, DC: American Psychiatric Publishing.

Arnett, J. J. 1999. Adolescent Storm and Stress, Reconsidered. *American Psychologist* 54: 317–326.

Aseltine, R. H., Jr., and R. DeMartino. 2004. "An Outcome Evaluation of the SOS Suicide Prevention Program." *American Journal of Public Health* 94: 446–451.

Barrett, P. M., L. Healy-Farrell, and J. S. March. 2004. "Cognitive-Behavioral Family Treatment of Childhood Obsessive-Compulsive Disorder: A Controlled Trial." *Journal of the American Academy of Child & Adolescent Psychiatry* 43: 46–62.

Blum, R., T. Beuhring, M. Shew, L. Bearinger, R. Sieving, and M. Resnick. 2000. "The Effects of Race/Ethnicity, Income, and Family Structure on Adolescent Risk Behaviors." *American Journal of Public Health* 90(12): 1879–1884.

Bridge, J. A., S. Iyengar, C. Salary, P. Barbe, B. Birmaher, H. A. Pincus, L. Ren, and D. A. Brent. 2007. "Clinical Response and Risk for Reported Suicidal Ideation and Suicide Attempts in Pediatric Antidepressant Treatment." *Journal of the American Medical Association* 297: 1683–1696.

Brotman, M. A., M. Schmajuk, B. A. Rich, D. P. Dickstein, A. E. Guyer, E. J. Costello, H. L. Egger, A. Angold, D. S. Pine, and E. Leibenluft. 2006. "Prevalence, Clinical Correlates and Longitudinal Course of Severe Mood Dysregulation in Children." *Biological Psychiatry* 60: 991–997.

Carter, J., D. Stewart, V. Dunn, and C. Fairburn. 1997. "Primary Prevention of Eating Disorders: Might It Do More Harm Than Good?" *International Journal of Eating Disorders* 22: 167–172.

Centers for Disease Control and Prevention. 2009. *Youth Risk Behavior Surveillance— United States, 2009*. Morbidity and Mortality Weekly Report. Retrieved from http://www.cdc.gov/mmwr/preview/mmwrhtml/ss5905a1.htm.

Chamberlain, P., and J. Reid. 1998. "Comparison of Two Community Alternatives to Incarceration for Chronic Juvenile Offenders." *Journal of Consulting and Clinical Psychology* 66: 624–633.

Cheng, K., and K. M. Myers. 2011. *Child and Adolescent Psychiatry: The Essentials* (2nd ed.). Philadelphia: Kluwer/Lippincott.

Costello, J., D. Pine, C. Hammen, J. March, P. M. Plotsky, M. M. Weissman, J. Biederman, H. H. Goldsmith, J. Kaufman, P. M. Lewinsohn, M. Hellander, K. Hoagwood, D. S. Koretz, C. A. Nelson, and J. F. Leckman. 1998. "Development and Natural History of Mood Disorders." *Biological Psychiatry* 52: 529–542.

Elkind, D. 1994. *A Sympathetic Understanding of the Child: Birth to Sixteen* (3rd ed.). Boston: Allyn & Bacon.

Eveleth, P. B., and J. M. Tanner. 1990. *Worldwide Variation in Human Growth* (2nd ed.). Cambridge: Cambridge University Press.

Griffin, K. W., G. Botvin, T. R. Nichols, and M. M. Doyle. 2003. "Effectiveness of a Universal Drug Abuse Prevention Approach for Youth at High Risk for Substance Use Initiation." *Prevention Medicine* 36: 1–7.

Henggeler, S. W., and C. M. Borduin. 1990. *Family Therapy and Beyond: A Multisystemic Approach to Treating the Behavior Problems of Children and Adolescents*. Pacific Grove, CA: Brooks/Cole.

Hoffman, E. C., and S. G. Mattis. 2000. "A Developmental Adaptation of Panic Control Treatment for Panic Disorder in Adolescence." *Cognitive and Behavioral Practice* 7: 253–261.

Kutcher, S. 2005. "ADHD/Bipolar Children and Academic Outcomes." *Directions in Psychiatry* 25: 111–117.

Lawford, B., R. Young, J. A. Rowell, J. N. Gibson, G. F. Feeney, T. L. Ritchie, K. Syndulko, and E. P. Noble. 1997. "Association of the D2 Dopamine Receptor A1 Allele with Alcoholism: Medical Severity of Alcoholism and Type of Controls." *Biology and Psychiatry* 41: 386–393.

Pagliaro, A. M., and L A. Pagliaro. 1996. *Substance Use among Children and Adolescents*. New York: Wiley.

Pope, H. G., K. A. Phillips, and R. Olivardia. 2000. *The Adonis Complex: The Secret Crisis of Male Body Obsession*. New York: Free Press.

Steinberg, L., L. Blatt-Eisengart, and E. Cauggman. 2006. "Patterns of Competence and Adjustment among Adolescents from Authoritative, Authoritarian, Indulgent and Neglectful Homes." *Journal of Research on Adolescence* 16: 47–58.

Wilmshurst, L. 2009. *Abnormal Child Psychology: A Developmental Perspective*. New York: Routledge.

African Americans and Mental Health

Alma J. Carten

American-born blacks, whose experiences in the United States are shaped by a history of slavery and systemic discrimination sanctioned in law and custom, are no longer the country's dominant ethnic group of African descent. Changes in immigration law, globalization, and shifting world populations have increased the ethnic, linguistic, cultural, and religious diversity of communities of African descent within the continental United States. The country's oldest black immigrants, who have historically come from the Anglophone Caribbean and identify as "West Indians," and those from continental Africa where dominating countries have been Ghana, Nigeria, Liberia, and Ethiopia, are being joined by the newest arrivals who are coming from more than 50 African nations, Haiti, Latin and South American countries, Canada, France, and England (U.S. Census Bureau 2001).

The extensive demographic and cultural heterogeneity within and among people of African descent requires varied treatment approaches that capture the nuanced experiences of these highly diverse and culturally rich communities. For the newest arrivals, attention must be given to the effects of exposure to personal violence, trauma, and dislocation associated with the immigrant and refugee experience. For native-born African Americans, the population of concern in this entry, attention must be given to the legacy of racism and discrimination that has had a significant impact of their experience in the nation's mental health system.

The Historical Foundation

Historically, mental health services in the United States have been undertaken from a Eurocentric perspective that embraced doctrines of white supremacy. Beliefs about the inherent superiority of whites and the inferiority of blacks resulted in the entrenchment of empirically unfounded assumptions about the behavior and mental capabilities of blacks, and served as the theoretical basis for scientific racism that informed mental health policy and practice well into the 20th century (Carten 2006; Thomas & Sillen 1979). Concomitantly, these assumptions promoted the favoring of a "deficit model" that pathologized normative and adaptive behaviors of blacks and led to the flourishing of untested theories about their ability for psychological change and suitability for the various psychotherapies.

The residual effects of such "scientific racism" for understanding etiology and shaping interventions with African Americans are reflected in findings reported in the Supplement to the Surgeon General's Report on Mental Health (2001), which identifies striking racial and ethnic disparities in mental health outcomes for Americans. In addition to barriers involving cost, service fragmentation, and stigma, the report asserts that these disparate outcomes are attributable in part to past and current racism and discrimination, which has slowed the development of adequate mental health theory necessary for the creation of sound, evidence-based practice with African Americans (U.S. Department of Health and Human Services 2001).

Current Status and Continuing Barriers

The experience of African Americans in the United States is paradoxical in that it can be viewed either as a cup half full or a cup half empty. The United States has provided a wealth of opportunity that has allowed a growing number of native-born blacks to move into mainstream society and into the ranks of an increasingly robust black middle class. Despite notable gains, statistical data also reveal that blacks are relatively poorer, and they experience more hardships than other ethnic and racial groups. In the field of mental health, there is a preponderance of research documenting the considerable obstacles confronted by African Americans in accessing quality care (Algeria et al. 2002; Snowden 2001; Snowden & Pingitore 2002; U.S. Department of Health and Human Services 2001).

According to the Office of Minority Health (U.S. Department of Health and Human Services 2012), African Americans comprise 12.9 percent of the U.S. population, yet they are 20 percent more likely to report serious psychological distress and a greater persistence and severity of mental illness. Recent years have seen a dramatic rise in suicide rates for young males, and a disproportionate presence of African Americans among populations with high susceptibility to mental health problems, including the homeless and prison populations, children and youth in the foster care and juvenile justice systems, and individuals living in shelters with co-occurring problems of chemical dependency.

Despite the extensiveness of need, data from the National Institute of Mental Health report that only one out of three African Americans who need mental health care receives it, and African Americans are less likely to be retained in treatment or to receive follow-up care. Significant barriers to service access and retention include a mistrust of formal mental health systems, reinforced by clinician stereotyping. Also contributing are a bias in standardized psychological tests, the clinical interview, and other forms of institutional racism (U.S. Department of Health and Human Services 2001; Whaley 2001; Snowden 2001; Trierweiler et al. 2000). Some behavioral and attitudinal barriers are related to the effects of low educational attainment among blacks, which makes for a limited understanding of mental illness and a resultant poor use of preventive care; in consequence, there is a tendency to minimize feelings and emotions that may be early symptoms of serious mental health problems.

Prevalence, Risk, and Protective Factors

Prevalence of mental illness among blacks is found to be similar to that of the general population (Bresnahan et al. 2007; Williams et al. 2007) African Americans are, however, more likely to receive inequitable treatment and are generally poorly served by the mental health system (Snowden & Pingitore 2002; U.S. Department of Health and Human Services 2001; Williams, Gonzalez, & Neighbors 2007). The inability of clinicians to differentiate behavioral symptoms of paranoia associated with racial discrimination and prejudice from psychopathology remains a continuing theme of past and recent research findings (Hu & Snowden 1991; Snowden 2001; Thomas & Sillen 1979). Clinicians continue to assign more severe diagnostic labels to African Americans and continue to have limited understanding of the implications of cultural influences on the presentation of symptoms. Consequently, African Americans are overdiagnosed for schizophrenia and underdiagnosed for affective disorders (mood disorders), and have higher rates of psychiatric hospital admissions (Smedley, Stith, & Nelson 2003; Trierweiler et al. 2000; U.S. Department of Health and Human Services 2001). These are among some of the occurrences contributing to a distorted view of the nature and scope of mental illness within the African American community, and they mask environmental conditions or causes that have implications for understanding the incidence of mental illness and the need for services.

African Americans have historically interacted within economic, political, and social environments characterized by pervasive inequalities, placing them at increased risk for social problems found to have measurable effects on the rates of mental illness (U.S. Department of Health and Human Services 2001). They are exposed to environmental stressors, such as high levels of job-related racial harassment, that increase risk for psychosocial distress, and they are more likely to experience subtle forms of racism or micro-aggression that are no less damaging in their effects (Franklin-Jackson & Carter 2007; Sue 2003).

Despite the bleak statistical picture, African Americans exhibit resilience and as a community are characterized by attributes that serve as protective factors, helping to mitigate the adverse effects of environmental and psychosocial stressors. Spirituality, self-help, a reliance on extended kin and informal helpers—all are enduring characteristics of black culture (Billingsley 1968; Hill 1971). These traditions support coping and adaptive behaviors and also account for a preference to look to the faith community and prayer as sources of healing rather than to professional mental health providers (Neighbors & Jackson 1984; Taylor & Chatters 1991).

New approaches to culturally competent mental health services are capitalizing on these natural helping networks within the African American community. One example is new funding opportunities available under the faith-based initiatives of the federal government. These initiatives have increased the presence of community-based church-affiliated programs that have made significant inroads into changing attitudes in order to reduce the stigma typically associated with mental illness, a major barrier to the utilization of professional care. Further, community-based programs encouraging the involvement of family and extended kin result in a number of added benefits, not the least of which are psychosocial benefits for family members who themselves are impacted by a diagnosis of mental illness in a loved one. Families and extended kin also serve as a critical extension of the "treatment team" by supporting a mentally ill family member's retention in therapy and his or her compliance with treatment.

Promising Best Practices

Emergent best practices are being shaped by new trends that encourage comprehensive definitions that view mental health as existing along a dynamic continuum; the integration of new understandings about the role of culture in shaping beliefs about the causes and cures of mental illness; and recognition of the role of oppressive systems in contributing to the emotional distress felt by marginalized populations. New approaches are anchored in the values of the community mental health and the more recent recovery movements. Generally, these trends indicate a move beyond psychodynamic models focused on individual psychopathology and embrace instead concepts from ecological and systems perspectives that view people as being in reciprocal interaction with interrelated networks of environmental, social, economic, and political systems. These approaches draw on theories from behavioral and cognitive psychology and encourage the use of evidence-based approaches anchored in concepts of resilience, strength, self-efficacy, empowerment, competency, and skill building.

Holistic Approaches to Health and Wellness

An ecological perspective and public health approach are vital to effective mental health practice in communities of color. Both Healthy People 2000 (U.S. Department of Health and Human Services 2000) and the World Health Organization adopt definitions of mental health that incorporate a holistic perspective, one that considers the individual in the context of his or her functioning within larger societal and institutional structures and his or her ability to cope with and manage the demands of changing life conditions and transitions. The World Health Organization, for example, defines mental health as an overall state of well-being in which the individual realizes his or her own abilities, can cope with the normal stresses of life, can work productively and fruitfully, and is able to make a contribution to the larger community. Similarly, the Report to the Surgeon General on Mental Health takes a "wide-angle lens" that gives consideration to both mental illness and wellness and encourages the use of a public health model, that is, one that is concerned with the health of the population in its entirety and acknowledges the link between health and the physical and psychosocial environment (U.S. Department of Health and Human Services 1999).

Integrating Culture into the *Diagnostic and Statistical Manual*

The *Diagnostic and Statistical Manual of Mental Disorders* (*DSM-IV-TR*), published by the American Psychiatric Association (1994), is the most widely used system for the classification of mental disorders nationally and internationally. The manual has been revised four times since it was initially published in the early 1950s. With growing awareness about the significance of race and ethnicity for understanding mental illness, increasing attention has been given to the role of culture in diagnosis and treatment (Kutchins & Kirk 1997; Mezzich 1997). Thus, since 1994 the *DSM* has included a listing of culture-bound syndromes, or clusters of symptoms that are more common to some cultures than to others. The forthcoming *DSM-5*, due out in 2013, will give further attention to the classification of symptoms of posttraumatic stress syndrome, which may be especially useful for appreciating trauma resulting from the cumulative effects of racism and discrimination and also the effects of the immigration and refugee experiences.

Undoing Racism Approaches

An antiracism model is emerging as a promising practice for uncovering the more subtle forms of institutional racism and personal bias that contribute to mental distress, and for accounting for the persistence of racial disparities in wellness outcomes observed across virtually all fields of practice in the health and human services. The primary goal of this model is to raise awareness about the effects of the insidious and often invisible forms of institutional racism that contribute to poor patient outcomes. Anchored in critical race theories, as well as cognitive and behavioral change theories, the antiracism model encourages an examination of the implications of racism for society as a whole. Mental illness exacts a high cost on society when one considers the suffering endured by families and the large share of public resources consumed for rehabilitation and the lowering of workforce productivity (Fellin 1996). The emerging model encourages whites to weigh the benefits and gains accrued from "white privilege" against these larger human, economic, and societal costs and losses. Recent research findings provide an added rationale for this approach by illuminating the psychological costs of racism for the mental health of whites. Findings suggest that the passive acceptance or failure to question the underlying assumptions of unearned privilege promotes feelings of guilt, unwarranted suspiciousness, psychological dissonance, and unintentionally contribute to the perpetuation of institutional racism (Harvey & Oswald 2000; Neville, Worthington, & Spanierman 2001; Spanierman et al. 2006; Utsey et al. 2002).

Conclusions

The nation's commitment to improving mental health services for African Americans and other people of color is reflected in a number of new initiatives. The National Institute for Mental Health is providing support for research on minority populations; the Council on Social Work Education has received funding to increase the presence of minorities in leadership roles in the mental health field; the Office of Minority Health was created to encourage health policies that eliminate racial and ethnic disparities and to oversee the implementation of Healthy People 2010 (U.S. Department of Health and Human Services 2000); and the Supplement to the Surgeon General's Report on Mental Health (U.S. Department of Health and Human Services 2001) was a groundbreaking report that focused national attention on the failures of the mental health system in meeting the needs of African Americans and other people of color.

These efforts are being matched in the private sector and include initiatives developed by the National Alliance on Mental Illness (NAMI), in the form of the a Multicultural Action Center, and by the Black Mental Health Alliance, which provides linkages to clinicians of varied disciplines as well as other resources. The Association of Black Psychologists and the Association of Black Psychiatrists are national professional membership organizations that have had a historical presence in promoting initiatives to improve clinical practice with people of color. These developments, combined with the rise in research on evidence-based practice with diverse populations in need of mental health services, undoubtedly will have a positive impact over time.

See also Culturally Competent Mental Health Care; *Diagnostic and Statistical Manual of Mental Disorders (DSM)*; Evidence-Based Practice and Outcome Measurement; Poverty, Unemployment, Economic Inequality, and Mental Health; Public Health Perspectives; Recovery Movement; Religion, Spirituality, and Mental Health; Stigma; Trauma

Bibliography

Algeria, M., G. Canino, R. Rios, J. Calderón, D. Rusch, and A. N. Ortega. 2002. "Inequalities in Use of Specialty Mental Health Services among Latinos, African Americans, and non-Latino Whites." *Psychiatric Services* 53: 1547–1555.

American Psychiatric Association. 1994. *Diagnostic and Statistical Manual of Mental Disorders* (4th ed.). Washington, DC: American Psychiatric Publishing.

Arminio, J. 2001. "Exploring the Nature of Race-Related Guilt." *Journal of Multicultural Counseling and Development* 29: 239–252.

Billingsley, A. 1968. *Black Families in White America*. Englewood Cliffs, NJ: Prentice-Hall.

Bresnahan, M., M. D. Begg, A. Brown, A. Schaefer, N. Sohler, B. Insel, and E. Susser. 2007. "Race and Risk of Schizophrenia in a US Birth Cohort: Another Example of Health Disparity?" *International Journal of Epidemiology* 36: 751–758.

Carten, A. J. 2006. "African Americans and Mental Health." In J. Rosenfeld and S. Rosenfeld, eds., *Community Mental Health: Direction for the 21st Century* (pp. 125–138). New York: Routledge.

Fellin, R. 1996. *Mental Health and Mental Illness: Policies, Programs, and Services*. Itasca, IL: Peacock.

Franklin-Jackson, D., and R. T. Carter. 2007. "The Relationship between Race-Related Stress, Racial Identity, and Mental Health for Black Americans." *Journal of Black Psychology* 33: 5–26.

Harvey, R. D., and D. L. Oswald. 2000. "Collective Guilt and Shame as Motivation for White Support of Black Programs." *Journal of Applied Social Psychology* 30: 1790–1811.

Hill, R. B. 1971. *The Strengths of Black Families*. New York: National Urban League.

Iyer, A., C. W. Leach, and F. J. Crosby. 2003. "White Guilt and Racial Compensation: The Benefits and Limits of Self-Focus." *Personality and Social Psychology Bulletin* 29: 117–129.

Kutchins, H., and S. A. Kirk. 1997. "The Enduring Legacy of Racism in the Diagnosis of Mental Disorders." In S. A. Kirk, ed., *Making Us Crazy: DSM: The Psychiatric Bible and the Creation of Mental Disorders* (pp. 200–237). New York: Free Press.

Mezzich, J. E. 1997. "The Place of Culture in *DSM-IV*." *Journal of Nervous and Mental Disease* 187(8): 457–464.

Neighbors, H. W., and J. S. Jackson. 1984. "The Use of Informal and Formal Help: Four Patterns of Illness Behavior in the Black Community." *American Journal of Community Psychiatry* 12(6): 629–644.

Neville, H. A., R. L. Worthington, and L. B. Spanierman. 2001. "Race, Power, and Multicultural Counseling: Understanding White Privilege and Color-Blind Racial Attitudes." In J. G. Pontretto, J. M. Casas, L. A. Suzuki, and C. M. Alexander, eds., *Handbook of Multicultural Counseling* (2nd ed., pp. 257–288). Thousand Oaks, CA: Sage.

Ponterotto, J. G. 1991. "The Nature of Prejudice Revisited: Implications for Counseling Intervention." *Journal of Counseling and Development* 70: 216–224.

Sillings, J. H., and J. E. Dobbins. 1991. "Racism as a Disease: Etiology and Treatment Implications." *Journal of Counseling and Development* 70: 206–212.

Smedley, B. D., A. Y. Stith, and A. R. Nelson. 2003. *Unequal Treatment: Confronting Racial and Ethnic Disparities in Health Care*. Washington, DC: National Academies Press.

Snowden, L. R. 2001. "Barriers to Effective Mental Health Services for African Americans." *Mental Health Services Research* 3: 181–187.

Snowden, L. R., and D. Pingitore. 2002. "Frequency and Scope of Mental Health Service Delivery to African Americans in Primary Care." *Mental Health Services Research* 4: 123–130.

Spanierman, L. B., V. P. Poteat, A. M. Beer, and P. I. Armstrong. 2006. "Psychological Costs of Racism to Whites: Identifying Profiles with Cluster Analysis." *Journal of Counseling Psychology* 53: 434–441.

Sue, D. W. 2003. "What Is White Privilege?" In D. W. Sue, *Overcoming Our Racism: The Journey to Liberation* (pp. 23–44). San Francisco: Jossey-Bass.

Taylor, R. J., and L. M. N. Chatters. 1991. "Religious Life." In J. S. Jackson, ed., *Life in Black America* (pp. 105–123). Newbury Park, CA: Sage.

Thomas, A., and S. Sillen. 1979. *Racism and Psychiatry*. New York: Citadel Press.

Trierweiler, S. J., W. W. Neighbors, C. Munday, S. E. Thompson, V. J. Binion, and J. P. Gomez. 2000. "Clinician Attributions Associated with Diagnosis of Schizophrenia in African Americans and Non-African Patients." *Journal of Counseling Psychiatry* 68: 171–175.

U.S. Census Bureau. 2001. *The Black Population in the United States*. Washington, DC: U.S. Census Bureau.

U.S. Department of Health and Human Services. 1999. *Mental Health: A Report of the Surgeon General*. Rockville, MD: U.S. Department of Health and Human Services, Substance Abuse and Mental Health Services Administration, Center for Mental Health Services.

U.S. Department of Health and Human Services. 2000. *Healthy People 2010*. Rockville, MD: U.S. Department of Health and Human Services.

U.S. Department of Health and Human Services. 2001. *Mental Health: Culture, Race and Ethnicity—a Supplement to Mental Health: A Report of the Surgeon General*. Rockville, MD: U.S. Department of Health and Human Services, Substance Abuse and Mental Health Services Administration.

U.S. Department of Health and Human Services. 2012. Office of Minority Mental Health. "Mental Health and African Americans." April 24. Retrieved from http://minorityhealth.hhs.gov/templates/content.aspx?lvl=3&lvlID=9&ID=6474.

Utsey, S. O., E. McCarthy, R. Eubanks, and G. Adrian. 2002. "White Racism and Suboptimal Psychological Functioning among White Americans: Implications for Counseling and Prejudice Prevention." *Journal of Multicultural Counseling and Development* 30: 61–95.

Whaley, A. L. 2001. "Cultural Mistrust: An Important Psychological Construct for Diagnosis and Treatment of African Americans." *Professional Psychology: Research and Practice* 32: 555–562.

Williams, D. R., H. H. Gonzales, H. Neighbors, R. Nesse, J. M. Abelson, J. Sweetman, and J. S. Jackson. 2007. "Prevalence and Distribution of Major Depressive Disorder in African Americans, Caribbean Blacks, and Non-Hispanic Whites." *Archives of General Psychiatry* 64: 305–315.

Alcohol Abuse, Alcoholism, and Mental Health

T. Em Arpawong and Steve Sussman

Public Impact of Alcohol Use Disorders in the United States

Tremendous individual and public health costs arise from alcohol use disorders (AUDs). According to the Centers for Disease Control and Prevention (CDC), alcohol-related deaths are the third leading type of preventable death as well as the leading risk factor for serious injury in the United States (CDC 2009). Collectively, alcoholism and alcohol abuse disorders cause over 79,000 deaths annually in the United States with approximately one-third of those being car-related accidents and nearly one-half being homicides. Among college students alone (ages 18–24) approximately 600,000 are injured each year because of alcohol-related incidents (Hingson, Zha, & Weitzman 2009). Alcohol-related incidents cause approximately 30 percent of all hospital admissions and are one of the top 10 causes of disability-adjusted life years (DALYs), a measure of disease burden and injury (Michaud et al. 2006). AUDs contribute to educational failure, loss of productivity, increased health care costs, deterioration of relationships, and higher crime rates. Overall, the costs of alcohol-related morbidity and mortality, including the costs of treatment for alcohol-related crime and traffic collisions, come to $184.6 billion annually (Harwood 2000). Physical symptoms may occur from AUDs since prolonged problem use of alcohol damages the brain, liver, heart, lungs, gastrointestinal system, pancreas, immune system, muscle, and peripheral nerves. Further, problem drinking increases one's risk for various cancers (e.g., liver and breast). Alcohol is the number one preventable cause of birth defects with mental deficiency. It contributes to 1 in 100 children being diagnosed with fetal alcohol syndrome, among the offspring of female alcoholics. (Fetal alcohol syndrome disorder is characterized by several diagnostic criteria: central nervous system impairment, pattern of facial dysmorphology [e.g., low nasal bridge, small midface, wide-set eyes, small head circumference], growth deficiencies, and learning and behavioral problems.)

Symptoms of Alcohol Use Disorders

Alcohol-related problems negatively affect not only the life of the drinker but also the health and well-being of family and friends as well as society as a whole. Denial is common among those who abuse alcohol (Dare & Derigne 2010). Often, alcoholics blame their drinking on situations or other people. While stressful events or aggressive urging by others may precede their alcohol consumption, alcoholics frequently drink at other times as well (e.g., on celebratory occasions), and achieve intoxication when drinking. The recurrent intoxication is often a symptom of AUD recognized by friends and family. Significant others often see that alcoholics fail to meet personal responsibilities, demonstrate increased irritability, or heightened emotional sensitivity, and may engage in deceitful practices to conceal their drinking. It is the repeated state of intoxication (in continuous or binging drinking patterns) that often disables an alcoholic from maintaining relationships or a stable sense of identity. Therefore key symptoms that may be identified by others are the alcoholic's "change in personality" (e.g., from a "Dr. Jeckyl" to a "Mr. Hyde"; Altschuler & Wright 2000) along with the deteriorating relationships with friends, family, partners, children, and coworkers. Alcoholics also demonstrate intrapersonal problems such as shame and guilt. Alcoholics may gradually become more antisocial or asocial in order to drink freely while in isolation.

When individuals who are physically dependent on alcohol abstain from drinking temporarily, they experience symptoms of withdrawal, often manifested by "the shakes." This withdrawal syndrome likely happens soon after one wakes, compelling him or her to begin drinking in the morning in order to relieve those symptoms. Also, because some degree of tolerance occurs in all alcoholics, another indication of alcoholism is the need to progressively consume larger quantities of alcohol in order to achieve the desired effect of intoxication.

Alcohol Abuse versus Alcohol Dependence Disorders

Alcoholism is a complex and heterogeneous disease. The most widely used diagnostic criteria for AUDs are published in the *Diagnostic and Statistical Manual of Mental Disorders* (*DSM*), by the American Psychiatric Association (APA). Currently, the *DSM-IV-TR*, or fourth edition of the manual, is being used by health care professionals to set standards when diagnosing a patient as having either alcohol abuse or alcohol dependence disorders (APA 2000).

Alcohol abuse is characterized by repeated use of alcohol despite experiencing adverse consequences from it. One who is diagnosed with an AUD has developed a maladaptive pattern of alcohol consumption that has resulted in significant impairment or negative consequences such as (1) poor work performance or school suspension (e.g., due to alcohol-related absences), (2) finding oneself in hazardous situations (e.g., driving an automobile while under the influence of alcohol), (3) getting into legal trouble for alcohol-related disorderly conduct, or (4) continued alcohol use despite recurrent social problems with others (e.g., neglecting one's children due to inebriation) due to the effects of alcohol. One does not need to be physically dependent on alcohol in order to abuse it.

If an individual is physically dependent on alcohol, he or she is referred to as alcohol dependent. Physical dependence is the need to consume alcohol in order to ward off withdrawal symptoms. It is characterized by (1) an uncontrollable compulsion to drink, despite a desire to diminish alcohol use, and (2) tolerance, or the need to consume increasing amounts of alcohol in order become intoxicated. Reports of three or more of seven symptoms are diagnostic of alcohol dependence disorder according to the *DSM-IV-TR*: neglect of other activities,

---

The Dopamine, or "Pleasure Molecule," Connection

"Researchers now postulate that addiction requires two things. First is genetic vulnerability, whose variables may include the quantity of dopamine receptors in the brain. . . . Second, repeated assaults to the spectrum of circuits regulated by dopamine, involving motivation, expectation, memory and learning . . . appear to fundamentally alter the brain's working."

—Abigail Zugar

Source: Abigail Zugar, "A General in the Drug War," *New York Times,* June 14, 2011, D4.

excessive use, impaired control, persistence of use, large amounts of time spent doing alcohol-related activities, withdrawal, and tolerance (APA 2000).

Both alcohol abuse and dependence disorders are debilitating conditions; in both cases the drinker may be referred to as being an "alcoholic." The fifth edition of the *Diagnostic and Statistical Manual* outlining criteria for mental disorders, the *DSM-5*, is expected to be completed in 2013 and plans to combine both alcohol abuse and alcohol dependence disorders into a single diagnosis of "alcohol use disorder." (Proposed revisions to the *DSM-5* may be accessed at: http://www.dsm5.org/ProposedRevisions/Pages/proposedrevision.aspx?rid=452.)

The primary impediment to the diagnosis of AUD is denial by the alcoholic. Second, there is generally a low level of suspicion of AUD held by most physicians since up to 72.9 percent of Americans have reported regular use of alcohol, with the majority never having problems that escalate to problem use (Kalaydjian et al. 2009). Indicators of AUD may include any of the aforementioned symptoms, or clinical symptoms such as unaccounted-for tremor, gastritis, hepatitis, blackouts, fatty liver, cirrhosis, or abnormal laboratory values detected from blood draws. (Abnormal values include both elevated mean corpuscular red blood cell volume and serum gamma-glutamyl transferase level, or elevated carbohydrate-deficient transferrin level without simultaneous hepatic disease.)

Prevalence in the United States

The National Institute on Alcohol Abuse and Alcoholism (NIAAA) houses data from the National Epidemiologic Survey on Alcohol and Related Conditions (NESARC). The most recent NESARC data was collected through face-to-face interviews between 2001 to 2002 with 43,093 Americans in order to estimate the prevalence of alcohol abuse and dependence as defined by the *DSM-IV*. Results show that, among adults, 4.7 percent (9.6 million) suffer from alcohol abuse and 3.8 percent (7.9 million) suffer from alcohol dependence in any 12-month period (Grant et al. 2004). Both alcohol abuse and dependence among all age groups tend to be higher for males than for females, although this trend remains true only for certain race/ethnic groups including whites, blacks, and Hispanics. Alcohol abuse tends to be more prevalent among whites (5.1%) compared to Hispanics (4.0%), blacks (3.3%), and Asians (2.1%). Alcohol dependence tends to be more frequent among Native Americans (6.4%), Hispanics (4.0%), and whites (3.8%) and less frequent among Asians (2.4%).

When either alcohol abuse or dependence is evaluated by age group (12–17, 18–29, 30–44, 45–65, and 65+ years), each successively older age group exhibits decreases in the prevalence (Grant et al. 2004). However, patterns of alcohol use may differ by age group. For example, research has shown that adolescents (ages 12–17 years) are more likely to engage in heavy episodic or "binge" drinking.

(The National Advisory Council defines binge drinking as "a pattern of drinking alcohol that brings blood alcohol concentration [BAC] to 0.08 gram percent or above. For the typical adult, this pattern corresponds to consuming 5 or more drinks [male] or 4 or more drinks [female] in about two hours" [NIAAA National Advisory Council].)

Estimates find that 1.47 million adolescents (5.9% of adolescents) met the criteria for an AUD in 2003 (National Household Survey on Drug Abuse). Emerging adults (ages 18–24 years) are most at risk for alcohol problems as they are most likely to drink heavily regardless of gender or ethnicity. Those who are not students and nonmilitary personnel in this age group tend to continue dangerous drinking patterns into later adulthood. One reason for this may be that these individuals do not have access to mental health services, making them more susceptible to problems associated with psychiatric conditions such as depression and anxiety. Individuals in midlife (ages 30–59 years) are most likely to seek treatment for their alcohol disorder as well as experience the consequences of heavy drinking (e.g., alcoholic liver disease, alcohol pancreatitis, disorders of the heart and circulatory system, alcohol-related brain disorders, endocrine and immune function problems). Although senior adults drink less than other age groups, studies show that people born in more recent years drink more than those from older generations. This forecasts that as the current generation ages, drinking in older age groups will rise (NIAAA 2008).

Recent evidence suggests there may be subtypes of alcoholics, categorized by clusters of the following physiological, behavioral, and cognitive factors: family history of alcoholism, age of onset of regular drinking and problems with alcohol, symptom patterns of AUDs, the coexistence of mood/anxiety or antisocial personality disorders, or other substance use disorders (Gunzerath et al. 2010). Based on NESARC data, there are five subtypes that have been identified and defined by the NIAAA (2007). Table on p. 21 provides a summary of the alcoholic typology as well as prevalence of each subtype among U.S. alcoholics.

Comorbidity of Psychiatric and Mental Health Disorders

According to the National Comorbidity Survey, alcoholics with comorbid disorders had suffered from a mood or personality disorders for up to 10 years prior to developing a diagnosed alcohol problem (Petrakis et al. 2002). Research suggests that dysregulation in the brain's stress system, or limbic-hypothalamic-pituitary-adrenal (LHPA) axis, may be the common link to both alcohol and psychiatric comorbidities. The mood disorders that most frequently occur with an AUD are posttraumatic stress disorder (PTSD), schizophrenia, anxiety, major depressive disorder (MDD), bipolar, and panic (with or without agoraphobia) disorders. In particular, symptoms of depression co-occur in up to 80 percent of those who

NESARC-Based Alcoholic Typologies

	Young Adult Subtype	Young Antisocial Subtype	Functional Subtype	Intermediate Familial Subtype	Chronic Severe Subtype
Percentage of U.S. alcoholics	31.5%	21.1%	19.4%	18.8%	9.2%
Age group	Young adults	Young adults	Middle aged	Middle aged	Middle aged
Duration of onset of alcohol dependence from drinking initiation	2.8 years	2.9 years	18.4 years	15.0 years	13.2 years
Multigenerational familial alcoholism	Low	Medium	Medium	Medium	High
Antisocial personality disorder	Low	Medium	Low	Medium	High
Mood disorders	Low	High	Low/Medium	Low/Medium	High
Anxiety disorders	Low	High	Low	Medium	High
Regular smoking	Medium	High	Medium	High	High
Other substance use disorders	Low	High		Low	High

Note: Low indicates 25 percent or less. Medium indicates approximately 50 percent. High indicates 75 percent or greater.
Source: Gunzerath, Hewitt, Li, and Warren. 2010; NIAAA, http://www.nih.gov/news/pr/jun2007/niaaa-28.htm.

are alcohol-dependent with 30 to 40 percent suffering from full MDD (Shivani, Goldsmith, & Anthenelli 2002).

Individuals with alcohol dependence, specifically, have a higher likelihood of suffering from mental health comorbidities than those with alcohol abuse disorder. For example, the odds of having a general anxiety disorder (GAD) in one's lifetime are 2.6 times greater (95% confidence interval: 2.0 to 3.5) for those with alcohol dependence compared to those without. However, the odds of having GAD in one's lifetime are slightly less at 1.8 times greater (95% confidence interval: 1.4 to 2.4) for those diagnosed with alcohol abuse than compared to those without (Vesga-López et al. 2008). As shown by NESARC data in table on p. 22, rates for nearly all psychiatric and personality disorders were greatest among those diagnosed with alcohol dependence compared to those suffering from alcohol abuse, both of which were greater than those not suffering from an AUD. Although rates are shown for males and females combined, some differences do occur by gender. Of the personality disorders specifically, antisocial personality disorder tends to

Prevalence of Psychiatric[a] and Personality[b] Disorders in Adults[c] with Alcohol Abuse, Alcohol Dependence, and without Any Alcohol Use Disorder (AUD)

Disorder	Alcohol Abuse		Alcohol Dependence		No AUD Present	
	Rate per 1,000 Population	S.E.	Rate per 1,000 Population	S.E.	Rate per 1,000 Population	S.E.
Major depressive disorder	81.53	7.38	204.82	14.35	66.49	2.31
Bipolar (manic) disorder	22.31	3.80	76.27	8.33	13.61	0.92
General anxiety disorder (GAD)	19.00	3.86	56.86	7.11	19.09	1.16
Panic disorder without agoraphobia	12.39	2.75	46.99	6.29	14.18	0.94
Panic disorder with agoraphobia	7.74	2.20	18.40	5.16	4.51	0.45
Social phobia	26.08	4.19	62.48	8.54	26.19	1.42
Antisocial personality disorder	73.89	7.42	183.28	12.15	11.01	0.91
Avoidant personality disorder	19.79	3.66	76.70	8.56	31.58	1.64
Dependent personality disorder	2.66[d]	1.29	24.61	5.35	3.25	0.46
Obsessive-compulsive personality disorder	94.76	8.98	152.12	11.04	81.50	2.89
Paranoid personality disorder	55.48	7.37	158.18	11.28	39.45	1.78
Schizoid personality disorder	24.92	3.99	81.67	9.75	29.00	1.42
Histrionic personality disorder	30.73	4.70	103.29	9.48	16.81	1.07

[a]Psychiatric (mood and anxiety) disorders are past-year diagnoses.
[b]Personality disorders are lifetime diagnoses.
[c]Rates of psychiatric and personality disorders per 1,000 population for people aged 18+ in the United States.
S.E.: standard error.
[d]Unreliable estimate with relative standard error > 0.3.
Source: Alcohol Epidemiologic Data System 2006 (National Institute on Alcohol Abuse and Alcoholism).

have higher prevalence in alcoholics who are male whereas borderline personality disorder has higher prevalence in alcoholics who are female.

Etiology: Causes of Alcohol Use Disorders

Alcohol abuse and dependence develop as the result of many complex biological, developmental, and social environmental factors. Studies on twins, conducted in Sweden and Finland, have explored the heritability of alcoholism and found that genetics may account for 49 to 64 percent of the risk for alcoholism (Köhnke 2008). This genetic inheritance may be due to an association with certain polymorphisms (genetic variations) involved. (Suspected polymorphisms involved include those at the genes for dopamine D2 receptor, serotonin transporter, or neuropeptide Y.) Thus identical twins (who share 100% of their genes) have a greater concordance rate for alcoholism than fraternal twins (who share approximately 50% of their genes), who in turn have a greater concordance rate than nontwin siblings. Further, the lower rate of AUDs among some Asian subgroups is related to the inheritance of a polymorphism that encodes the enzyme aldehyde dehydrogenase (ALDH2). In the normal metabolic pathway, alcohol (i.e., ethanol) is broken down into the by-product acetaldehyde, which in turn is metabolized by ALDH2 into acetic acid. Most Asians, however, have slower-acting forms of the ALDH2, such that accumulation of the by-product acetaldehyde causes an unpleasant reaction (e.g., blushing or red flush, headache, tachycardia). Hence, because individuals who inherit the slower-acting aldehyde dehydrogenase are less likely to confer euphoric or pleasant effects of intoxication, they are less likely to become alcoholics.

Aside from genetics, other biological and developmental characteristics may impact one's risk for developing an AUD. Individuals who begin drinking at an early age, as well as males, or those who abuse other substances are more likely to abuse alcohol or become dependent. Known risk factors include having a psychiatric or behavioral disorder such as anxiety (i.e., panic disorder or social phobia), MDD, PTSD, bipolar disorder, or schizophrenia. Some research evidence suggests that certain personality characteristics may place one at higher risk for alcoholism such as having excessively high expectations of oneself, a low tolerance for frustration, thrill-seeking and impulsive tendencies, and feeling inadequate or unsure of one's role. Children diagnosed with attention deficit hyperactivity disorder (ADHD) are at greater risk for alcoholism in adulthood, particularly when coupled with conduct disorder.

Rates of alcoholism are higher among individuals who have grown up in environments in which parents, other family members, or close friends have encouraged or tolerated drinking. Twin studies have shown definitive examples of this where identical twin pairs who were separated by adoption at a very young age demonstrate alcoholism discordance (Dick et al. 2001). Also, research shows that teens who have a low level of parental supervision, higher levels of family conflict, or inconsistent or severe parental discipline have a higher likelihood for developing an AUD. Cultural factors may play a large role. For example, the higher rate of AUDs among Native Americans tends to vary greatly by tribe although elevated risks have been attributed to a combination of established social norms regarding alcohol use, Native identity, accessibility, and multigenerational transmission of cultural practices (Yuan et al. 2010).

Prevention of Alcohol Use Disorders

Prevention of AUDs is relatively difficult among substances of abuse. This is due to several reasons. First, because moderate levels of drinking have been found to be good for one's health, it may be difficult to decipher the point at which drinking becomes problematic and requires attention. Second, individuals have differing levels of tolerance to alcohol such that, outside of monitoring symptoms closely over time, there is no simple way to tell when someone drinks too much or too often. Third, each person has a differing level of vulnerability for alcoholism including family history, genetics, social influences, stress, and intrapersonal predisposition (e.g., anxiety, lack of self-confidence, poor coping resources). Thus prevention efforts tend to focus on targeting those who may have multiple risk factors for problem drinking, or on a general population (10% of whom may develop an AUD).

Owing to the deleterious consequences of alcohol problem use, implementing evidence-based prevention interventions is crucial. Generally, prevention programming falls into four categories: family-focused, school-based, multidomain, and environmentally focused intervention programs. Family-focused interventions revolve around strengthening parenting skills and parent-child relationships, decreasing aggressive behaviors, and improving social and psychological readiness for school. Most are aimed at younger children or youth (under age 15) with several having shown effectiveness in delaying initiation of drinking as well as reducing alcohol consumption in adolescence (Perry et al. 2002).

School-based programs focus primarily on decreasing individual demand and use of alcohol by helping youth to resist social pressure to use alcohol. The most effective school-based programs are typically social influences and comprehensive life skills programs. Social influences programming provides normative information (e.g., to correct alcohol-related beliefs on peer acceptance and prevalence norms) and skill instruction (e.g., refusal assertion skill instruction, making a public commitment not to use). Comprehensive life skill programming augments social influences programming by adding life skills training (e.g., general life skills and/or competence to deal with social pressures to drink, or alternative methods to deal with stress) (Sussman 2005). Most studies have not followed students long enough to evaluate long-term effects, although two recent programs targeted at high school youth have been shown to be effective (Spoth, Greenberg, & Turrisi 2008) and, in general, some effects appear to have been maintained at least five years postprevention program among two-thirds of programs implemented prior to 2003 with long-term follow-ups (Skara & Sussman 2003).

Because most alcoholics begin drinking in adolescence and alcohol is the most frequently used substance by this age group (Johnston et al. 2009), school-based prevention work is vital to public health prevention efforts. Further, because youth often begin experimenting with many drugs other than alcohol during this time period, alcohol prevention programs are often subsumed under comprehensive substance use prevention programs. Although the predominant modality for delivering substance use prevention programs among adolescents is in classrooms, over the course of multiple sessions, a few programs incorporate a community component to utilize approaches from environmentally focused prevention efforts (Skara & Sussman 2003). Programs that incorporate multiple components (e.g., individual, family, school, community/environment) are considered a third category of prevention programs, called multidomain interventions. Such programs generally target younger adolescents. While promising, these programs may be difficult to implement due to the extensive resources needed to deploy them.

Environmentally focused prevention efforts intervene primarily through limiting the accessibility of alcohol, making alcohol consumption less acceptable, and creating a social environment that is more supportive to nonuse (Sussman 2005). These programs tend to impact older adolescents as well as the general public. Historically, this has been achieved through the following: (1) policy mechanisms, such as raising the minimum drinking age, levying higher taxes on alcohol, requiring traffic safety and driver training education, mandating warning labels; (2) community involvement, including actions of coalitions, collaborations between community leaders and businesses; or (3) mass media, such as through public service announcements. Some research demonstrates that policy-based approaches have been effective at reducing the rates of underage drinking, car accidents, and fatalities (NIAAA 2008).

Cessation Treatment or Therapy for Alcohol-Use Disorders

Despite there being nearly 18 million people ages 18 and older who suffer from AUDs (Grant et al. 2004), only about 25 percent receive any form of treatment or help (including clinical treatment or participate in support groups such as Alcoholics Anonymous or AA) during their lifetime. Further, alcoholics with psychiatric comorbidities are less likely to find treatment that addresses both illnesses. Only within the past two decades have studies begun investigating integrated treatments for comorbid alcoholics. Nevertheless, the ultimate goal of treating alcoholism is for the drinker to achieve abstinence. When an alcoholic makes attempts to continue drinking in a controlled fashion, rarely does he or she succeed. Those who tend to be less successful in achieving recovery tend to have a network of alcohol-consuming friends, began drinking heavily at a younger age, and imbibe relatively larger quantities of alcoholic beverages (Dawson et al. 2005).

Cessation approaches for alcoholism fall into two categories: psychosocial and pharmacologic treatments. Although combining both approaches is usually more effective in treating alcoholics with comorbidities, psychosocial treatments may be preferred for four reasons. First, for some conditions using pharmacologic treatments for alcoholism may have higher risks than benefits due to the type of disorder and potential reaction to medication. Second, psychosocial approaches are able to address functional deficits that result from the disorder (e.g., poor or atrophied coping skills). Third, psychosocial approaches may garner better compliance to treatments, or enhance compliance with psychiatric disorder medications. And, fourth, since worsening symptoms of a psychiatric disorder from alcohol abstinence may functionally debilitate the alcoholic (e.g., PTSD, depression, mania from bipolar disorder, frequent panic attacks), psychosocial treatments may best help individuals cope with the symptoms of the psychiatric disorder.

Psychotherapeutic Approaches

Most psychotherapeutic approaches to AUD treatment focus on behavioral therapy approaches including cognitive-behavioral therapy (CBT), 12-step facilitation, motivational enhancement therapy (also called motivational interviewing [MI]), community reinforcement, contingency management, behavioral couples and/or family therapy, brief behavioral intervention, and aversion therapy. The below table

Overview of Psychotherapeutic Principles and Approaches to the Treatment of Alcohol Abuse Use Disorder

Psychotherapy	Approaches
Cognitive-behavioral therapy	Focus on coping in the here and now; examining and change irrational thoughts that lead to distress or increase risk for relapse; skill building for coping with risk situations; also includes cue exposure with response prevention to extinguish association between alcohol cues and alcohol seeking.
12-step facilitation	Acceptance of addiction as a disease requiring abstinence to recover; willingness to engage fully in 12-step programs such as Alcoholics Anonymous; use of positive reinforcement (e.g., by recognizing abstinence anniversaries) and behavioral modeling (e.g., by having a sponsor).
Motivational enhancement	Focus on addressing ambivalence and barriers to change; enhancing motivation to change; relies on the behavioral principles of reinforcement and modeling.
Community reinforcement	Eliminating positive reinforcement for drinking and increasing positive reinforcement for sobriety.
Contingency management	Providing explicit incentives (e.g., money) for abstinence and for participating in treatment; uses reinforcing and punishing consequences, based on operant conditioning, to alter alcohol use behavior.
Behavioral couples and/or family therapy	Evaluates and treats relationship factors that contribute to alcohol use to help a significant other or family members provide support for abstinence (e.g., monitoring medication administration) by incorporating positive activities, communication skills training, and identification of potential relapse triggers.
Brief behavioral intervention	Assesses alcohol use and provides personalized feedback; focus on providing a menu of strategies for change, goal setting, empathy, and enhancing self-efficacy.
Facilitated self-change	Relies on assessment and feedback, motivation information and self-help materials focused on goal setting, problem-solving skills, and self-monitoring.
Aversion therapy	Pairs alcohol cues (i.e., sight, taste, or other cue) with an unpleasant experience (including nausea-inducing drugs and electric shock); uses covert sensitization imagery of aversive scenes paired with imagery of drinking alcohol.

Source: Adapted from Willenbring 2010; Witkiewitz and Marlatt 2011.

provides a summary of these commonly used behaviorally based psychotherapies and their principal techniques. The Substance Abuse and Mental Health Services Administration (SAMHSA) maintains a searchable database of effective treatment programs, the National Registry of Evidence-Based Programs and Practices, at http://www.nrepp.samhsa.gov.

Research has found these behaviorally based therapies to be among the most effective treatments for AUDs. Studies have attempted to decipher the key elements common to many of the programs. These may include social support; structure and goal direction; provision of rewards and rewarding of activities; normative models for successful abstinence; enhancement of self-efficacy; and teaching of coping skills (Moos 2007). Therefore identifying the specific therapeutic approach for specific individuals may be less important than identifying the specific elements appropriate for the alcoholic in his or her given situation.

Treatments for alcoholics with comorbidities are the most difficult to implement. Usually these dually diagnosed patients require a modification of standard modalities addressing alcohol abuse, as well as more close monitoring to ensure their safety. For instance, alcoholics with serious mental illness may experience suicidal ideation in response to treatment. Thus clinicians that treat dually diagnosed patients need to be keenly aware of the means by which both the psychiatric and alcohol disorders influence each other during cessation treatment.

Twelve-step facilitation programming tends to be one of the most popular treatment protocols, incorporating many of the active ingredients of effective programs. AA-related programming is embedded into up to two-thirds of alcohol inpatient programming, and is the most widely available community-based support system for alcoholics. The 12 steps provide a protocol for an alcoholic to become teachable, to become aware of his or her impact on self or others, to make amends, and to be better able to cope with life and be of service to others. AA is an abstinence-oriented, multidimensional, nonprofit, humanistic, voluntary, and supportive mutual-help fellowship for individuals for whom alcohol use is problematic. The essential component of AA is that alcoholics help one another to stay sober. An important adjunct to the program is self-selecting a sponsor who provides support and helps guide the individual in the program. In some cases, these 12-step programs may be beneficial for dually diagnosed patients, although efficacy may be contingent upon regular attendance at program meetings. However, some comorbid patients with severe psychiatric disorders may find the programs alienating and thus ineffective.

Particularly for adolescents, psychotherapeutic cessation programs are important because pharmacologic approaches are rarely implemented for youth. Youth cessation programs are typically offered through three primary modalities. First, and most common, are the individual or classroom-based behavioral interventions that focus on identifying intrinsic and extrinsic stimuli that trigger or enable alcohol use, and teach refusal skills, relaxation or stress-reduction techniques, and behavioral management techniques. Second are the family-based programs (including MST, integrated family and CBT, multidimensional family therapy, brief strategic family therapy) in which attempts are made to both change youth behavior and reduce risk factors for alcohol use that are present within the family or other social system (e.g., peers, school, or community). Third are the MI approaches, which help youth to recognize that the behavior is a problem and to build an internal motivation to change (Tripodi et al. 2010).

Pharmacologic Approaches

Pharmacologic approaches may be effective only as part of a comprehensive treatment plan that includes patient education and tandem psychotherapy. Pharmacologic therapies are particularly important options for the treatment of dually diagnosed patients for three reasons. First, some patients may be diagnosed with a comorbid mental disorder such that they would be uncomfortable and therefore less compliant in their attendance at psychosocial or group treatment sessions. Second, those with a comorbid mental disorder may have cognitive impediments that may diminish their ability to concentrate and thus weaken their motivation to learn new material in lessons required in psychosocial treatment sessions. Third, because most were initially diagnosed with the mental disorder prior to developing their alcohol problem, they may already be taking regular medications and hence can easily incorporate additional ones for the AUD.

Generally, medications for alcoholism exclusively work through one or several of the following mechanisms: to block cravings, to induce aversive side effects to alcohol consumption, to treat withdrawal symptoms, to treat associated psychiatric comorbidities or other drug abuse. Currently, three medications have been approved by the U.S. Food and Drug Administration (FDA) to treat alcoholism—disulfiram, naltrexone, and acamprosate—although they have not been as widely used for dually diagnosed patients. Disulfiram (or Antabuse) acts through producing a toxic by-product of alcohol metabolism (acetaldehyde) and thereby induces aversive reactions to drinking such as shortness of breath, nausea and vomiting, headache, flushing, and tachycardia. The idea is that patients will cease to drink in order to avoid such ill effects in the future. The second medication is Naltrexone (or ReVia), a competitive opiate antagonist that works by blocking the key chemical (opioid) in the brain to reduce cravings and the pleasurable effect from consuming alcohol. In turn, this results in reduced consumption by amount and/or frequency, limits risk for relapse, and enhances ability for one to remain abstinent. It has been shown to be very effective in the management of alcohol dependence when coupled with intense behavioral psychotherapy. Last, much evidence points toward the efficacy of acamprosate (or Campral) in helping to reduce withdrawal symptoms, and thus encouraging abstinence. Extensive evaluation of acamprosate for side effects, efficacy, and impact on psychiatric comorbidities is still pending.

Summary

Alcoholism and alcohol abuse pose tremendous cost to individual health as well as to public health. However, signs and symptoms of an AUD may be difficult to recognize without consistent and long-term monitoring. While genetics may contribute approximately 50 percent of the predisposition for alcoholism, the progression of AUDs is tractable through social, cultural, and other environmental influences. However, in order for prevention of AUDs to be successful, early intervention is necessary. The diagnosis of an AUD may occur up to 20 years after an individual has initiated heavy-drinking behavior. In addition, the physical and mental deterioration due to problem drinking develop over many years. Further, more often than not, AUDs co-occur with a mood or personality disorder that existed years before individuals report heavy-drinking behavior. The presence of such psychiatric disorders may help to characterize the alcoholic subtype present. Thus treatment for alcoholism and the associated disorder must be carefully tailored to the individual given their history of alcohol consumption as well as type of comorbidity. A combination of both psychotherapeutic and pharmacologic treatment modalities are preferred in order to achieve abstinence although continued evaluation of these cessation efforts is needed, particularly for dually diagnosed individuals.

See also Adolescence and Mental Health; Criminalization and Diversion Programs; Drug Abuse and Mental Health; Peer Support Groups; Preventative Mental Health Programs; Public Health Perspectives

Bibliography

Alcohol Epidemiologic Data System. Chen, Chiung M., Hsiao-ye Yi, Daniel E. Falk, Frederick S. Stinson, Deborah A. Dawson, and Bridget F. Grant. 2006. "Alcohol Use and Alcohol Use Disorder in the United States: Main Findings from the 2001–2002 National Epidemiologic Survey on Alcohol and Related Conditions (NESARC)." *U.S. Alcohol Epidemiologic Data Reference Manual 8, Number 1*. Bethesda, MD: National Institute on Alcohol Abuse and Alcoholism. Retrieved from http://www.niaaa.nih.gov/Resources/DatabaseResources/QuickFacts/MentalPhysicalHealth/Documents/psychcnd4.txt.

Alcoholics Anonymous. http://www.aa.org.

Altschuler, Eric L., and Daniel Wright. 2000. "Dr. Jekyll and Mr. Hyde: A Primer on Substance Dependence." *American Journal of Psychiatry* 157: 484.

American Psychiatric Association. 2000. *Diagnostic and Statistical Manual of Mental Disorders* (4th ed., text rev.). Washington, DC: American Psychiatric Publishing.

Centers for Disease Control and Prevention. 2009. "Implement Measures to Decrease Leading Causes of Death 2009." Retrieved from http://www.cdc.gov/about/stateofcdc/html/implement.htm.

Dare, Patricia A. S., and Leaanne Derigne. 2010. "Denial in Alcohol and Other Drug Use Disorders: A Critique of Theory." *Addiction Research and Theory* 18: 181–193.

Dawson, D. A., B. F. Grant, F. S. Stinson, P. S. Chou, B. Huang, and W. J. Ruan. 2005. "Recovery from DSM-IV Alcohol Dependence: United States, 2001–2002." *Addiction* 100(3): 281–292.

Dick, Danielle M., Richard J. Rose, Richard J. Viken, Jakko Kaprio, and Markku Koskenvuo. 2001. "Exploring Gene-Environment Interactions: Socioregional Moderation of Alcohol Use." *Journal of Abnormal Psychology* 110: 625–632.

Grant, Bridget F., Deborah A. Dawson, Frederick S. Stinson, Patricia Chou, Mary C. Dufour, and Roger P. Pickering. 2004. "The 12-Month Prevalence and Trends in *DSM-IV* Alcohol Abuse and Dependence: United States, 1991–1992 and 2001–2002." *Drug and Alcohol Dependence* 74: 223–234.

Gunzerath, Lorraine, Brenda G. Hewitt, Ting-Kai Li, and Kenneth R. Warren. 2010. "Alcohol Research: Past, Present, and Future." *Annals of the New York Academy of Sciences* 1216: 1–23.

Harwood, Henrick J. 2000. *Updating Estimates of the Economic Costs of Alcohol Abuse in the United States: Estimates, Update Methods, and Data.* Report prepared by the Lewin Group for the National Institute on Alcohol Abuse and Alcoholism. Rockville, MD: National Institutes of Health.

Hasin, Deborah S., Frederick S. Stinson, Elizabeth Ogburn, and Bridget F. Grant. 2007. "Prevalence, Correlates, Disability, and Comorbidity of *DSM-IV* Alcohol Abuse and Dependence in the United States: Results from the National Epidemiologic Survey on Alcohol and Related Conditions." *Archives of General Psychiatry* 64: 830–842.

Hingson, Ralph, Wenxing Zha, and Elissa R. Weitzman. 2009. "Magnitude of and Trends in Alcohol-Related Mortality and Morbidity among U.S. College Students Ages 18–24, 1998–2005." *Journal of Studies on Alcohol and Drugs* Suppl. 16: 12–20.

Johnston, Lloyd D., Patrick M. O'Malley, Jerald G. Bachman, and John E. Schulenberg. 2009. "Monitoring the Future: National Results on Adolescent Drug Use—Overview of Key Findings, 2008." National Institute on Drug Abuse. Rockville, MD: National Institutes of Health.

Kalaydjian, Amanda, Joel Swendsen, Wai-Tat Chiu, Lisa Dierker, Louisa Degenhardt, Meyer Glantz, Kathleen R. Merikangas, Nancy Sampson, and Ronald Kessler. 2009. "Sociodemographic Predictors of Transitions Across Stages of Alcohol Use, Disorders, and Remission in the National Comorbidity Survey Replication." *Comprehensive Psychiatry* 50: 299–306.

Köhnke, Michael D. 2008. "Approach to the Genetics of Alcoholism: A Review Based on Pathophysiology." *Biochemical Pharmacology* 75: 160–177.

Michaud, Catherine M., Matthew T. McKenna, Stephen Begg, Niels Tomijima, Meghna Majmudar, Maria T. Bulzacchelli, Shahul Ebrahim, Majid Ezzati, Joshua A. Salomon, Jessica G. Kreiser, Mollie Hogan, and Christopher J. L. Murray. 2006. "The Burden of Disease and Injury in the United States 1996," *Population Health Metrics* 4: 1–49.

Moos, Rudolph H. 2007. "Theory-Based Active Ingredients of Effective Treatments for Substance Use Disorders." *Drug and Alcohol Dependence* 88: 109–121.

Myers, P. L., and R. E. Isralowitz. 2011. *Alcohol.* Santa Barbara, CA: Greenwood.

National Institute on Alcohol Abuse and Alcoholism. 2007. "Researchers Identify Alcoholism Subtypes." Retrieved from http://www.nih.gov/news/pr/jun2007/niaaa-28.htm.

National Institute on Alcohol Abuse and Alcoholism. 2008. "Five Year Strategic Plan FY08-13: Alcohol Across the Lifespan." Retrieved from http://pubs.niaaa.nih.gov/publications/StrategicPlan/NIAAASTRATEGICPLAN.htm.

Perry, Cheryl L., Carolyn L. Williams, Kelli A. Komro, Sara Veblen-Mortenson, Melissa H. Stigler, Karen A. Munson, Kian Farbakhsh, Resa M. Jones, and Jean L. Forster. 2002. "Project Northland: Long-Term Outcomes of Community Action to Reduce Adolescent Alcohol Use." *Health Education Research* 17: 117–132.

Petrakis, Ismene L., Gerardo Gonzalez, Robert Rosenheck, and John H. Krystal. 2002. "Comorbidity of Alcoholism and Psychiatric Disorders: An Overview." *Alcohol Research and Health* 26: 81–89.

Shivani, Ramesh, R. Jeffrey Goldsmith, and Robert M. Anthenelli. 2002. "Alcoholism and Psychiatric Disorders: Diagnostic Challenges." *Alcohol Research & Health* 26: 90–98.

Skara, Silvana, and Steve Sussman. 2003. "A Review of 25 Long-Term Adolescent Tobacco and Other Drug Use Prevention Program Evaluations." *Preventive Medicine* 37(5): 451–474.

Spoth, Richard, Mark Greenberg, and Robert Turrisi. 2008. "Preventive Interventions Addressing Underage Drinking: State of the Evidence and Steps toward Public Health Impact." *Pediatrics* 121 (Suppl. 4): S311–S336.

Substance Abuse and Mental Health Services Administration. http://www.samhsa.gov.

Sussman, Steve. 2005. "Prevention of Adolescent Alcohol Problems in Special Populations." *Recent Developments in Alcoholism* 17: 225–253.

Tripodi, Stephen J., Kimberly Bender, Christy Litschge, and Michael G. Vaughn. 2010. "Interventions for Reducing Adolescent Alcohol Abuse: A Meta-Analytic Review." *Archives of Pediatric and Adolescent Medicine* 164: 85–91.

Vesga-López, Oriana, Franklin R. Schneier, Samuel Wang, Richard G. Heimberg, Shang-Min Liu, Deborah S. Hasin, and Carlos Blanco. 2008. "Gender Differences in Generalized Anxiety Disorder: Results From the National Epidemiologic Survey on Alcohol and Related Conditions (NESARC)." *Journal of Clinical Psychiatry* 69: 1606–1616.

Willenbring, Mark L. 2010. "The Past and Future of Research on Treatment of Alcohol Dependence." *Alcohol Research & Health* 33: 55–63.

Witkiewitz, Katie, and G. Alan Marlatt. 2011. "Behavioral Therapy Across the Spectrum," *Alcohol Research & Health* 33: 313–319.

Yuan, Nicole P., Emery R. Eaves, Mary P. Koss, Mona Polacca, Keith Bletzer, and David Goldman. 2010. " 'Alcohol Is Something That Been with Us like a Common Cold': Community Perceptions of American Indian Drinking." *Substance Use & Misuse* 45: 1909–1929.

Alternative Treatments

See Mind and Body Approaches to Mental Health; Therapeutic Community and Milieu Therapy

Alzheimer's Disease and Other Dementias

Kyle S. Page, Bert Hayslip Jr., and Kellye S. Carver

The term "dementia" is widely known and used, but often without an appreciation for its actual meaning. Broadly speaking, dementia refers to a progressive decline in cognitive functioning resulting in a significant impairment in daily living. In our society, dementia has become synonymous with forgetfulness and memory problems; however, there are many causes and manifestations of such cognitive impairment. Dementia must be understood with an emphasis on its societal, cultural, familial, and individual impact.

Alzheimer's Disease

Alzheimer's disease (AD) is the most common cause of dementia and has been deemed an urgent national health priority (National Institutes of Health 2010). This concern seems warranted considering the estimated 2.4 million to 5.3 million Americans currently diagnosed with the disease (Alzheimer's Association 2010; National Institutes of Health 2010). Alzheimer's disease ranks as the seventh leading cause of death in the United States (Alzheimer's Association 2010). While adults over the age of 65 comprise the vast majority of those affected, one should not necessarily equate AD with those only of an advanced age. Sadly, every 70 seconds someone in the United States develops AD, with 11 million to 16 million people predicted to have the disease by 2050 (Alzheimer's Association 2010).

Social demographics help to explain the recent push in our investigative efforts. Recently, the first members of the "baby boomer" generation (those born between 1946 and 1964) turned 65. Moreover, people are living longer than ever before, meaning that more adults will reach "older age" and stay there for a longer period of time (Federal Interagency Forum on Aging-Related Statistics 2010). Understanding these societal changes plays an important role in understanding AD and other dementias. As one in eight older adults are diagnosed with AD (Alzheimer's Association 2010) and with the current trend of an expanding population of older adults, there is real concern that the number of those affected with AD or any other form of dementia will greatly increase.

The impact of the disease is felt on a financial level. Worldwide, the estimated cost of dementia care is $279.3 billion. When one includes the cost of informal care, as when a caretaker assists with basic daily activities (hygiene, meals, etc.), the cost of care rises substantially, to $421.6 billion (Wimo, Winbald, & Jönsson 2010). In the United States alone, direct cost of dementia care is estimated to be $76.8 billion, an increase over estimates at the beginning of the decade. On a per person basis, the cost of care in North America remains the highest in the world, with an average of $26,700 spent annually (per person) on dementia care (Wimo, Winbald, & Jönsson 2010).

For the person with AD, the impact of the disease is great. Dementia will lead to a decrease in life span and progressively subtract from his or her quality of life. The cognitive and functional impairments that persons experience may be a safety risk, requiring close personal supervision. It is not uncommon for someone with AD to be placed in a long-term care facility. Family members and friends may experience grief or anticipatory grief, knowing that their loved one is slowly declining. There is a loss of functioning, interactions, and relationships (Doka 2004). The amount of stress the families can endure, and more so for those functioning as caregivers, can be detrimental to one's physical health, mental health, and quality of life (Montgomery, Rowe, & Kosloski 2007).

Risk Factors

One of the greatest risk factors for AD is age (Alzheimer's Association 2010). The number of people with AD doubles for every five-year age interval after the age of 65 (U.S. Department of Health and Human Services 2008), with those over 85 being at the highest risk (National Institutes of Health 2010). For those individuals developing the disease after the age of 65, it is referred to as "late-onset" AD. A diagnosis before the age of 65, sometimes as early as 35, is commonly referred to as "early-onset" AD (American Psychiatric Association 2000).

Gender is another risk factor for AD. Women outnumber men with the disease, largely due to the longer life expectancy for females (Alzheimer's Association 2010). There is some conflicting evidence suggesting that the decrease in estrogen after menopause plays a role in the increased risk for older women (Brinton 2001; Rodriques et al. 2010). Evidence for a racial difference is mixed, with most research, however, indicating that African Americans and Hispanic individuals are a higher risk, while Japanese and Chinese individuals show the lowest risk for developing this disease (Hannay et al. 2004).

Mild cognitive impairment (MCI) is a condition often believed to be a risk factor for the later development of AD (Albert et al. 2011; Sperling et al. 2011), although not everyone exhibiting this form of impairment will develop AD (Manning & Ducharme 2010). MCI is present when there is objective evidence of impairment in one or more cognitive domains, but not to an extent severe enough to cause significant impairment in everyday living. Other factors such as traumatic brain injury may cause mild impairment, which is a potential risk factor for AD (Hannay et al. 2004).

Much funding has focused on genetic and biomarker research for understanding, indentifying, and treating AD (National Institutes of Health 2010). Through these efforts, both past and present, we now recognize the vital role family history plays in determining one's risk for the disease. Compared to those families without a history of AD, having a first-degree relative with the disease will double one's chances of developing Alzheimer's (Hannay et al. 2004). Particular chromosomes are associated with the rare early-onset type of AD. Mutations found in the genes of chromosomes 21, 14, and 1 cause the formation of abnormal proteins. Containing any of these abnormal proteins will drastically increase the likelihood of developing the early-onset type of AD (U.S. Department of Health and Human Services 2008).

Work has been done to understand the genetic risk factors for late-onset dementia as well, primarily focusing on the gene apolipoprotein (ApoE) found on chromosome 19 (although a number of other genes are beginning to receive more attention). This naturally occurring gene serves a role in transporting cholesterol throughout the body (Hannay et al. 2004). However, one of the gene's forms, ApoE ε4, is believed to have a hand in the development of a later-in-life onset of AD (U.S. Department of Health and Human Services 2008). Inheriting one of these genes places an individual at an increased risk of developing the disease, but does not guarantee the development of AD (Alzheimer's Association 2010) as it is present in only about 40 percent of all persons diagnosed with AD (U.S. Department of Health and Human Services 2008). It is useful to keep abreast of the biological and genetic developments in AD research, as it is constantly and rapidly evolving.

Diagnostic Criteria—Past, Present, and Future

The distinctive pattern of AD that we now recognize today is by no means a recent discovery. What was once long believed to be an inevitable part of the aging process was recognized in 1904 as an unusual nature of the brain by Dr. Alois

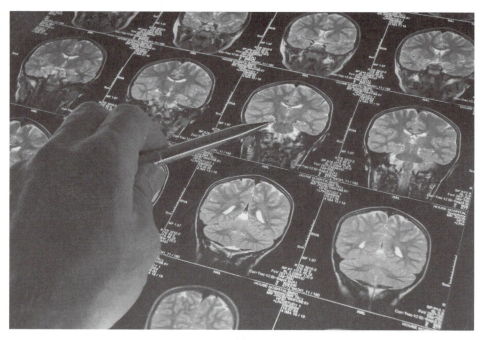

A brain MRI (magnetic resonance imaging) scan provides structural images of the brain by using radio waves and a magnetic field and is used in diagnosing Alzheimer's to exclude other medical conditions that can potentially cause the person's symptoms. (iStockPhoto.)

Alzheimer, a German psychiatrist (Cipriani et al. 2011). Diagnostically, there are certain considerations for a health professional when examining for the presence of AD. Before a diagnosis is made, several others must be "ruled out" as their presentations may appear similar. For example, normal age-related cognitive decline, depression, delirium (an acute confusional state), drug abuse, medication side effects, other diseases, and other causes of dementia must be considered. This makes AD a diagnosis of exclusion (Hannay et al. 2004).

According to the *Diagnostic and Statistical Manual of Mental Disorders* (American Psychiatric Association 2000), a diagnosis of AD is made in the presence of cognitive deficits and subsequent impairment in one's daily activities. There must be at least two cognitive impairments present, one of which must be memory impairment (defined as an "impaired ability to learn new information or recall previously learned information") (American Psychiatric Association 2000). Furthermore, one or more of the following cognitive deficits must be present: a disturbance in language abilities, impairment in carrying out motor activities, an inability to recognize objects, or a disturbance in executive functioning (such as planning ability, abstract thoughts, organizing, etc.). The impairment in motor activities and recognition of objects must occur despite intact motor and sensory functioning (American Psychiatric Association 2000). Lastly, these cognitive and functional changes are characterized by a slow onset and an unquestionable worsening of symptoms.

To date, the diagnosis of AD is based on the criteria established in 1984 by the National Institute of Neurological and Communicative Disorders and Stroke (NINCDS) and the Alzheimer's Disease and Related Disorders Association (ADRDA). We now know much more about AD and other dementias, particularly in the realm of biomedical research. New evidence suggests that not every patient with the AD has severe memory impairment, challenging the hallmark symptom of AD (McKhann et al. 2011). The changes and processes occurring in the person's life and brain may also occur long before an actual diagnosis of AD is warranted (Albert et al. 2011; Sperling et al. 2011). The National Institute on Aging and the Alzheimer's Association Workgroup recommend that for those individuals with biological evidence of AD but not the characteristic severe memory decline ("nonamnestic presentation"), language, visuospatial (visual perception of spatial relationships), and executive dysfunctions must also be observed. When these criteria are met, a diagnosis of "probable" AD dementia may be made (McKhann et al. 2011).

Course of the Disease

A major hallmark of AD is the impairment observed in memory functioning, usually for recent events. On formal testing, individuals will display rapid forgetting for newly learned information. Therefore delayed memory, or the recall of information after a delay, is a good indicator of AD, but may also implicate other cognitive concerns. Difficulties in expressive language (i.e., speaking), everyday judgment, and executive functioning will also begin to emerge. Persons with AD may have difficulty finding the right word for items and, as an example, may refer to a pencil as a "writing instrument" to circumvent this deficiency. In addition, they may demonstrate poor judgment, such as with financial decisions, planning activities, and performing tasks. Interestingly, many individuals may be unconcerned or unaware of their memory loss and errors in judgment as the disease worsens. Such individuals may deny or cover up the difficulties they are having, or find ways of compensating for the memory, decision-making, or attention problems they are experiencing (Hayslip, Patrick, & Panek 2011; Welsh-Bohmer & Warren 2006).

As the disease progresses, individuals experience a loss of memory for all remembered and learned information. Cognitive impairments become increasingly global and pervasive, disrupting the daily life of all those individuals involved in dementia care. For example, there are more pronounced difficulties in expressive speech, language comprehension, and motor abilities. Delusions and hallucinations are also common among the later stages of the disease. Personality changes, such as a disregard for manners, mood swings, or paranoia are not uncommon. In the late stages, the disease has a great impact on the functional abilities of the individual. Walking becomes impaired, appetite may decrease, and there will be an overall inability to satisfactorily perform daily activities of living (bathing, dressing, toileting). The Alzheimer's patient becomes increasingly difficult for others to relate to, understand, and care for, taking an emotional toll on the family and friends involved. Acting out, such as refusing care, being irritable or aggressive, and wandering may be difficult challenges to manage. At this point, AD is virtually indistinguishable from other forms of dementia (Welsh-Bohmer & Warren 2006).

Other Causes of Dementia

In order to give a diagnosis of AD, several other causes of dementia must first be ruled out. Taking a complete history from the person affected and his or her family, and using brain imagery (such as a CT scan), can be useful in determining cause and trajectory. Vascular dementia, the second most common cause of dementia, is an abrupt impairment brought on by cerebrovascular disease, such as a series of strokes. There may be a partial or complete blockage of blood vessels that can do considerable damage to the brain and a person's functioning (Manning & Ducharme 2010). Cognitive impairment is likely to be in executive functioning; however, the impairment caused largely depends on the location and severity of the brain tissue affected (Cato & Crosson 2006; Manning & Ducharme 2010). The co-occurrence of a cerebrovascular accident with AD can complicate the picture as well and is quite common. As a general rule, vascular dementia comes on suddenly, and over the course of time is characterized by ups and downs in functioning (termed *scalloping*), in contrast to Alzheimer's disease, whose onset is gradual and where declines are progressive and cumulative in nature.

Another cause of dementia is frontotemporal disorders that occur as the result of damage to nerve cells in the frontal and temporal lobes of the brain, and may be associated with earlier brain injury. Frontotemporal disorder is caused by various neurodegenerative diseases (such as Pick's disease) and can be identified only by brain autopsy after death (National Institute on Aging 2010). The manifestations of frontotemporal disorders include a progressive behavioral and personality decline, a progressive language decline, or a progressive motor decline. The frontal and temporal lobes touched by the disease causes impairment in planning, prioritizing, and multitasking. Furthermore, these people may have difficulty with forming sentences, movement, recognizing emotions, and responding in an appropriate manner, while memory functioning may not be affected (National Institute on Aging 2010).

Another category of dementias are those that are due to other medical conditions. These dementias impair cognitive functioning and disrupt daily life, but stem from various etiologies. For instance, a decline in cognitive functioning may be the result of the human immune-deficiency virus (HIV), Parkinson's disease, Huntington's disease, Creutzfeldt-Jakob's disease, Wernicke-Karsakoff syndrome, or repeated blows to the head (as with boxers). Impairments in executive functioning, the capability to make sound judgments, memory problems, language deficits, behavioral changes, and visual hallucinations are not uncommon. Careful screening and medical testing are needed to identify the cause, specific impact, and trajectory of the disease process (American Psychiatric Association 2000; Attix & Welsh-Bohmer 2006; Welsh-Bohmer & Warren 2006).

Interventions

A wealth of information exists to assist family members and professionals with nonmedical interventions for AD. While these interventions will not prevent or cure the disease, they can help manage, support, and maintain quality of life. For instance, to assist the memory-impaired person, a technique known as spaced retrieval (Camp 2006) can allow these persons to learn and maintain basic new information over time. In addition, environmental changes around the home can reduce the risk of injuries and promote staying in a familiar environment longer (National Institute on Aging 2009). When being placed in a long-term care facility, making the nursing home room reflect a homelike atmosphere with personal artifacts and decorations can ease some anxiety for the AD patient.

After conducting a conference on the prevention of AD and cognitive decline, the National Institutes of Health (Daviglus et al. 2010) stated, "Firm conclusions cannot be drawn about the association of any modifiable risk factor with cognitive decline or Alzheimer's disease" (2). This, of course, does not mean there are no promising interventions, but rather that further studies are needed involving randomized controlled trials of such interventions. However, evidence suggests that individuals may minimize their risk of cognitive decline by maintaining their physical health (diet, exercise, not smoking, etc.), engaging in cognitively stimulating and complex activities (puzzles, games, brain teasers, etc.), and maintaining good mental health (social interactions, support, etc.) (Williams et al. 2010).

A number of medications are currently available for the treatment of AD. However, at present no medication can cure or prevent this disease. Tacrine (Cognex), donepezil (Aricept), rivastigmine (Excelon), and galantamine (Reminyl) are designed to inhibit the breakdown of the neurotransmitter acetylcholine, which is implicated in the functioning of our memory. Overall, these medications may be used during the mild to moderate stages, and in varying degrees have been shown effective in slowing the process of cognitive decline for up to two years (Hayden & Sano 2006). Memantine (Namenda), on the other hand, works to block uptake of glutamate at NMDA receptor sites and is approved for moderate to severe stages of AD (Hayden & Sano 2006). Other medications may be used to treat aggression, depression, anxiety, hallucinations, and trouble sleeping that may accompany AD (National Institute on Aging 2009).

See also Elder Abuse and Neglect; Memory and Disorders of Memory

Bibliography

Albert, Marilyn S., Steven T. DeKosky, Dennis Dickson, Bruno Dubois, Howard H. Feldman, Nick C. Fox, Anthony Gamst, David M. Holtzman, William J. Jagust, Ronald C. Petersen, Peter J. Snyder, Maria C. Carrillo, Bill Thies, and Creighton H. Phelps. 2011. "The Diagnosis of Mild Cognitive Impairment Due to Alzheimer's Disease: Recommendations from the National Institute on Aging and Alzheimer's Assocaition Workgroup." *Alzheimer's & Dementia* 7(3): 270–279.

Alzheimer's Association. 2010. "2010 Alzheimer's Disease Facts and Figures." *Alzheimer's & Dementia* 6(2): 158–194.

American Psychiatric Association. 2000. *Diagnostic and Statistical Manual of Mental Disorders* (4th ed., text rev.). Arlington, VA: American Psychiatric Publishing.

Attix, Deborah K., and Kathleen A. Welsh-Bohmer. 2006. *Geriatric Neuropsychology.* New York: Guilford Press.

Brinton, Roberta Diaz. 2001. "Cellular and Molecular Mechanisms of Estrogen Regulation of Memory Function and Neuroprotection against Alzheimer's Disease." *Learning and Memory* 8(3): 121–133.

Camp, Cameron. 2006. "Spaced Retieval." In Deborah K. Attix and Kathleen A. Welsh-Bohmer, eds., *Geriatric Neuropsychology: Assessment and Intervention* (pp. 275–292). New York: Guilford Press.

Cato, M. Allison, and Bruce A Crosson. 2006. "Stable and Slowly Progressive Dementias." In Deborah K. Attix and Kathleen A. Welsh-Bohmer, eds., *Geriatric Neuropsychology* (pp. 89–102). New York: Guilford Press.

Cipriani, Gabriele, Cristina Dolciotti, Lucia Picchi, and Uhaldo Bonuccelli. 2011. "Alzheimer and His Disease: A Brief History." *Neurological Sciences* 32(2): 275–279.

Daviglus, M. L., C. C. Bell, W. Berrettini, P. E. Bowen, E. S. Connolly, N. J. Cox, J. M. Dunbar-Jacob, E. C. Granieri, G. Hunt, K. McGarry, D. Patel, A. L. Potovsky, E. Bush-Sanders, D. Silberberg, and M. Trevisan. 2010. *NIH State-of-the-Science Conference Statement on Preventing Alzheimer's Disease and Cognitive Decline.* Washington, DC: U.S. Department of Health and Human Services.

Doka, Kenneth J. 2004. *Living with Grief: Alzheimer's Disease.* Washington, DC: Hospice Foundation of America.

Federal Interagency Forum on Aging-Related Statistics. 2010. *Older Americans 2010: Key Indicators of Well-Being.* Washington, DC: U.S. Government Printing Office.

Hannay, H. Julia, Diane B. Howieson, David W. Loring, Jill S. Fischer, and Muriel D. Lezak. 2004. "Neuropathology for Neuropsychologists." In Muriel D. Lezak, Diane B. Howieson, and David W. Loring, eds., *Neuropsychological Assessment* (4th ed., pp. 157–285). Oxford: Oxford University Press.

Hayden, Kathleen, and Mary Sano. 2006. "Pharmacological and Other Treatment Strategies for Alzheimer's Disease." In Deborah K. Attix and Kathleen A. Welsh-Bohmer, eds., *Geriatric Neuropsychology: Assessment and Intervention* (pp. 414–455). New York: Guilford Press.

Hayslip, Bert, Julie H. Patrick, and Paul E. Panek. 2011. *Adult Development and Aging* (5th ed.). Malabar, FL: Krieger.

Lezak, Muriel D., Diane B. Howieson, and David W. Loring. 2004. *Neuropsychological Assessment.* Oxford: Oxford University Press.

Lu, L. C., and J. H. Bludau. 2011. *Alzheimer's Disease.* Santa Barbara, CA: Greenwood.

Manning, Carol A., and Jamie K. Ducharme. 2010. "Dementia Syndromes in the Older Adult." In Peter A. Lichtenberg, ed., *Handbook of Assessment in Clinical Gerontology* (pp. 155–178). New York: Academic Press.

McKhann, Guy M., D. S. Knopman, H. Chertkkow, B. T. Hyman, C. R. Jack Jr., C. H. Kawas, W. E. Klunk, W. J. Koroshetz, J. J. Manly, R. Mayeux, R. C. Mohs, J. C. Morris, M. N. Rossor, P. Scheltens, M. C. Carillo, B. Thies, S. Weintraub, and C. H. Phelps. 2011. "The Diagnosis of Dementia Due to Alzheimer's Disease: Recommendations from the National Institute on Aging and the Alzheimer's Association Workgroup." *Alzheimer's & Dementia* 7(3): 263–269.

Montgomery, Rhonda J., Jeannine M. Rowe, and Karl Kosloski. 2007. "Family Caregiving." In James A. Blackburn and Catherine N. Dulmus, eds., *Handbook of Gerontology: Evidence-Based Approaches to Theory, Practice, and Policy* (pp. 426–454). Hoboken, NJ: Wiley.

National Institute on Aging. 2009. *Caring for a Person with Alzheimer's Disease: Your Esay-to-Use Guide from the National Institute on Aging.* Washington, DC: U.S. Department of Health and Human Services.

National Institute on Aging. 2010. *Frontotemporal Disorders: Information for Patients, Families, and Caregivers.* Washington, DC: U.S. Department of Health and Human Services.

National Institutes of Health. 2010. *2009 Progress Report on Alzheimer's Disease: Translating New Knowledge.* Washington, DC: U.S. Department of Health and Human Services.

Rodriques, Mark A., Jonathan K. Foster, Guiseppe Verdile, Karen Joesbury, Richad Prince, Amanda Devine, Pankaj Mehta, John Beilby, and Ralph N. Martins. 2010. "Predicting Memory Decline as a Risk Factor for Alzheimer's Disease in Older Post-Menopausal Women: Quad Erat Demonstrandum?" *International Psychogeriatrics* 322(2): 332–335.

Sperling, Reisa A., Paul S. Aisen, Laurel A. Beckett, David A. Bennett, Suzanne Craft, Anne M. Fagan, Takeshi Iwatsubo, Clifforde R. Jack, Jeffrey Kaye, Thomas J. Montine, Denise C. Park, Eric M. Reiman, Christopher C. Rowe, Eric Siemers, Yaakov Stern, Kristine Yaffe, Maria C. Carrillo, Bill Thies, Marcelle Morrison-Bogorad, Molly V. Wagster, and Creighton H. Phelps. 2011. "Toward Defining the Preclinical Stages of Alzheimer's Disease: Recommendations from the National Institute on Aging and the Alzheimer's Assocaition Workgroup." *Alzheimer's & Dementia* 7(3): 280–292.

U.S. Department of Health and Human Services. 2008. *Alzheimer's Disease: Unraveling the Mystery.* Washington, DC: U.S. Department of Health and Human Services.

Welsh-Bohmer, Kathleen A., and Lauren H. Warren. 2006. "Neurodegenerative Dementias." In Deborah A. Attix and Kathleen A. Welsh-Bohmer, eds., *Geriatric Neuropsychology: Assessment and Intervention* (pp. 56–88). New York: Guilford Press.

Williams, John W., Brenda L. Plassman, James Burke, Tracey Holsinger, and Sophiya Benjamin. 2010. *Preventing Alzheimer's Disease and Cognitive Decline.* Evidence Report 193. Rockville, MD: Agency for Healthcare Research and Quality.

Wimo, Anders, Bengt Winbald, and Linus Jönsson. 2010. "The Worldwide Societal Costs of Dementia: Estimates for 2009." *Alzheimer's & Dementia* 6(2): 98–103.

American Indian and Alaskan Native Mental Health

William E. Hartmann and Joseph P. Gone

The topic of American Indian (AI) and Alaska Native (AN) mental health is a vital component of mental health dialogues today. Although AI/AN communities account for less than 1 percent of the U.S. population and raise particularly difficult challenges to popular mental health research and treatment paradigms, they merit the attention of mental health professionals for several reasons. Top among these reasons are the gravity of the mental health disparities these communities continue to face and the unfulfilled legal obligations established in treaties that guarantee the provision of adequate health care. Owing to the complexity of issues surrounding AI/AN mental health, a historical approach serves best to understand the context of AI/AN mental health problems today and the multiple perspectives on causes and potential solutions to their mental health disparities.

Historical and Cultural Overview

Prior to European contact, the territory now claimed by the United States was populated by over 7 million inhabitants speaking over 300 different languages, many as linguistically disparate as modern English and Chinese are today

(U.S. Department of Health and Human Services 2001). These Native inhabitants were organized into complex social networks based on kinship (i.e., genealogical lineage), known as tribes. In contrast to European states that exercised sovereignty over subjects and a geographically bounded region, North American indigenous tribes afforded roles to community members according to kinship networks and a reciprocal relationship with the land in a specific geographic region. Understanding that, as a people, they were created and sustained from their tribal lands, relationships between land and tribe were maintained by following ritual protocols, maintaining good relations with other beings that inhabited the land, and performing ceremonies of renewal (Kidwell, Noley, & Tinker 2001). As a result of North America's immense geographic diversity, the harmony established between land and tribe led to significant variations in lifestyle between regions. Whereas the fertile Southwest supported several corn-based agricultural communities, the Great Plains supported nomadic lifestyles based on game migrations and seasonal change, and the numerous small islands and inlets of the Northwest coast supported communities built around sea travel and fishing. In this way, indigenous tribes adapted their lifestyles to regional climates and strove to exist in harmony with the gradual seasonal change of the land on which they lived.

Despite the adaptive abilities of Native communities, European and Euro-American colonization of North America led to extended periods of violent oppression and jarring cultural change that have taken their toll on the health and welfare of Indigenous peoples. Beginning with the formation of selective alliances and declarations of war between colonizing European forces and indigenous tribes, the establishment of an independent United States of America with ideals of Euro-American cultural superiority quickly led to policies of displacement and containment for Native peoples. As political tactics adapted to shifts in power and societal values across the centuries, racially motivated genocide via massacres and death marches evolved into cultural genocide in the forms of forced sedentarization of tribal communities on reservations, where cultural practices were suppressed by religious organizations, attendance at off-reservation boarding schools aimed at "killing the Indian in the child" were mandated, and other governmental policies designed to make traditional lifestyles untenable were implemented (U.S. Department of Health and Human Services 2001). While these processes were fairly ubiquitous among tribes of the mainland United States, the experiences of Indigenous tribes in modern-day Alaska were somewhat distinct in that they managed to retain larger portions of their traditional lands due to decreased interest of Euro-American colonizers. At the same time, they suffered to a much greater extent from epidemics of tuberculosis, which led to frequent and extended relocations of infected community members to distant sanitariums (U.S. Department of Health and Human Services 2001).

It was in the wake of these and other horrific experiences at the hands of the U.S. government that indigenous communities assumed additional identities as American Indian and Alaska Native, which defined them both as a distinct ethno-racial category sharing similar cultural features and legacies of adversity and a political identity with rights to guarantees made by the U.S. federal government. Although reduced to only 250,000 individuals by the early nineteenth century, AI/AN communities have since flourished following a marked change in governmental policy instigated by the Self-Determination and Education Assistance Act of 1975. After this turning point, policies of active oppression shifted toward acknowledging many AI/AN tribes as sovereign "domestic dependent nations" with rights established by treaty to equal and adequate mental health care, among other entitlements (Gone & Trimble 2011). Although these more favorable conditions have allowed the AI/AN population to demonstrate its resiliency by growing to include nearly 2 million members of federally recognized tribes (U.S. Bureau of Indian Affairs 2011), the damage done to families, communities, and cultural support systems over centuries of violent oppression has left its mark on the mental health of many of these communities.

Key Mental Health Issues

Having evolved as a way of coping with forced abandonment of many traditional ways of life on reservations, widespread alcohol dependence has gradually spread to become a serious concern for many AI/AN communities (Hicks 2007). Despite significant variation in the prevalence between and within communities, the negative impact of alcohol dependence extends far beyond AI/AN individuals through increased family violence, risk-taking behaviors (e.g., drunk driving, unprotected sex), and many other mental and physical problems associated with excessive drinking. Also following from feelings of hopelessness that developed with the advent of reservation life, suicide has become a serious problem for many AI/AN communities facing conditions that promote continued feelings of hopelessness owing to disintegrated community support systems, confused and belittled cultural identities, and meager opportunities for success by either Western or traditional standards. Some communities have managed long stretches without seeing completed suicides (as well as increased positive indicators of physical and mental health) through a strengthening of ethno-cultural identity, community support systems, and political empowerment (Chandler & Londale 1998). Nevertheless, others continue to be plagued by frequent suicide completions.

AI/AN children also feel the effects of community-wide distress and the grim prospects they face growing up in these disadvantaged communities, often expressing their frustration by acting out. At school, these children are more frequently diagnosed with behavioral problems by school clinicians and demonstrate extremely high rates of school dropout.

A final problem area for AI/AN mental health has been the increased prevalence of posttraumatic stress disorder (PTSD). PTSD is a condition in which individuals experience extreme levels of anxiety that cause significant social, occupation, and/or interpersonal distress following a psychologically traumatic event (e.g., near-death experiences, rape, physical abuse). In addition to serving in the U.S. armed forces at the highest rate of any ethnic group in the country, AI/AN individuals are also disproportionately exposed to other traumatic non-war-related events associated with racism among members of the dominant society, various forms of alcohol-related violence, and life in extreme poverty (Gone & Trimble 2011; U.S. Department of Health and Human Services 2001).

Mental Health Services

To the surprise of many mental health professionals, despite experiencing such high levels of distress, very few AI/AN individuals seek help for their mental health problems, and when they do, they drop out of treatment at the highest rate of any cultural group in the United States (Sue, Allen, & Conaway 1978). Many mental health researchers suggest that part of the disconnect between AI/AN need and use (i.e., underutilization) of mental health services has been lack of access. Since its founding as a branch within the Department of Health and Human Services in 1955, the Indian Health Service (IHS) has become the primary provider of subsidized health services for AI/AN individuals. Unfortunately, chronic underfunding by the federal government has restricted the number of clinics IHS can support, and geographic isolation on reservation settings (only 34 urban IHS clinics exist) has severely limited access to the vast majority of today's AI/AN population, which lives in urban settings (Castor et al. 2006). Since poverty and unemployment are equally characteristic of urban Natives as those living on reservations, access to private mental health services is all but out of the question for most AI/AN individuals.

Although lack of access to services seems to play a key role in deterring help seeking among AI/AN communities, it does little to explain why even those who enter into mental health treatment programs drop out at such high rates. Subjective reports point to differences between the culture of the typical Western mental health clinic and that of AI/AN communities (U.S. Commission on Civil Rights 2004). Indeed, an AI/AN individual receiving mental health services must confront cultural discordance at the levels of the service provider and the intervention itself. Because of a shortage of AI/AN mental health practitioners, it is almost always the case that AI/AN individuals that make it through the door of a mental health clinic are presented with a non-Native, usually white counselor or clinician. As such, the development of mutual understandings and supportive client-therapist relationships proves exceedingly challenging and requires traversing vast differences in life experience, cultural norms of interaction, and understandings about how the world works.

In addition to being asked to share intimate life details with someone with whom they struggle to relate, AI/AN individuals can also experience Western mental health interventions as awkward, confusing, or even potentially undermining of their Native culture. Western therapies invariably carry both implicit and explicit assumptions about how a person is defined and how the world works—healing included. Evolving out of Western individualism, or egocentric views of the person as isolated and independently autonomous from their environment, mental health interventions have predominantly focused on problems or disorders of individuals. Whether implemented through one-on-one or small-group therapy sessions, the individualistic self of Western therapy leads to emphasis being placed on getting the client to understand how he or she has developed a problem (e.g., the individual attempts suicide because he or she is unable to see alternatives to feeling hopeless) and what he or she can do to resolve it (e.g., the person might challenge him or herself to take notice of hopeful opportunities). For many AI/AN individuals, on the other hand, selfhood is understood and experienced as a web of relations extending to family members, sacred lands, and other-than-human beings (e.g., spirits) in both the past and the present. As a result, individual-focused Western therapies seem to miss the bigger picture of how the context in which Native people exist heavily influences their behavior (e.g., a person attempts suicide because his or her ancestors suffered violent colonization that still affects living family members, sacred lands, and the tribe itself insofar as AI/AN cultures are constantly delegitimized by Western society). Such therapies also miss how problems experienced by an individual from an AI/AN community can be addressed (e.g., the person might restore harmony to his or her relations by reviving cultural practices).

Identifying Solutions

Solutions to these problems have long been called for but only recently begun to be explored in earnest (U.S. Commission on Civil Rights 2003). Perhaps most straightforward among them is the need for increased funding of mental health initiatives for AI/AN communities, a reasonable request considering that governmental appropriations for these communities equate to less than 40 percent per capita the allocations for the general population (IHS 2011). Increased funding could allow for the training of more AI/AN mental health professionals as well as the establishment of new IHS clinics for expanding AI/AN communities, whose only access to mental health services currently may be through admittance to an emergency room or prison. In addition to improving access to mental health services, funding could also support the development and assessment of solutions aimed at overcoming cultural barriers to mental health treatment.

Currently, the momentum among mental health researchers concerned with cultural barriers to treatment has coalesced behind adapting Western therapies to better fit AI/AN cultures, and "cultural competency" training for counselors and clinicians. These two strategies suggest that Western therapies can be adapted for use in AI/AN communities, often by incorporating Native cultural symbols (e.g., the medicine wheel) or by providing additional culturally salient components to therapy (e.g., an optional sweat lodge after a group therapy session). They also suggest that therapists can be educated to better understand and communicate with their AI/AN clients. Although some support has been found for improved outcomes as a result of cultural adaptations of therapy for AI/ANs (and other minority groups), and training in cultural competence would almost certainly improve counselor-minority client relationships, it is far from clear how such practices would apply to multicultural settings in which most AI/AN individuals now live. (One may ask, for example, for how many cultural groups would it be feasible to adapt therapies and train therapists to serve competently?) Furthermore, without additional funding, such changes are unlikely to help administrators of reservation-based clinics recruit and retain quality mental health professionals, a chronic problem in these isolated settings. Finally, concerns have also been raised among some researchers and AI/AN cultural leaders that many of the discordant beliefs and values embedded in Western therapies will not be addressed by simply adjusting their presentation or by teaching therapists more culturally appropriate ways of conveying their messages.

Those raising this final concern offer an alternative path to restoring AI/AN wellness that remains to be assessed of its potential effectiveness. Developed from the understanding gained through collaborative exchanges between mental health professionals and respected AI/AN community members, this approach adopts local worldviews by relying on community stakeholders such as AI/AN health center administrators, service providers, and respected leaders to develop local visions for overcoming barriers to their community's wellness. As such, it recognizes Euro-American colonization as the origin of AI/AN mental health disparities and promotes cultural revitalization according to local community healing traditions as the best means of returning to health. Such traditional healing practices might likely include performing various ceremonies, sharing traditional teachings, and/or increasing involvement in community activities. In focusing on cultural revitalization, this approach champions "culture as cure" for what is often described as a "cultural wound" inflicted over centuries of historical oppression (Gone & Trimble 2011).

Conclusion

Although elevated levels of distress among many AI/AN communities is evident, what is less clear are the best means by which the U.S. federal government can fulfill its treaty obligations to ameliorate such mental health disparities. The modestly improved outcomes from efforts to adapt Western therapies according to AI/AN cultural norms, and from training clinicians to be better versed in AI/AN cultures, suggest that this strategy of developing cultural variations within the Western mental health community is one potential route forward. Following this path will likely help to meet the needs of those AI/AN individuals interested in Western interventions but not comfortable negotiating the explicitly Western ecologies of mental health treatments. At the same time, the promise of empowering local AI/AN communities to develop and evaluate their own interventions involving traditional means of healing is heartening. The potential yield of this alternative route via healing and empowerment at the community level makes the thorough exploration of this option an imperative, in the eyes of many. Finally, increasing financial resources to remove barriers to accessing mental health services, to train members of AI/AN communities to become mental health professionals themselves, and to fund research that will propel forward efforts to adapt established interventions and support local strategies is essential. In light of the U.S. government's primary role in creating and sustaining these AI/AN mental health disparities over centuries of oppression, the obligation to meet AI/AN mental health needs is both a legal and ethical one.

See also Alcohol Abuse, Alcoholism, and Mental Health; Culturally Competent Mental Health Care; Posttraumatic Stress Disorder; Poverty, Unemployment, Economic Inequality, and Mental Health; Rural Mental Health Services; Suicide and Suicide Prevention

Bibliography

Castor, M. L., M. S. Smyser, M. M. Taualii, A. N. Park, S. A. Lawson, and R. A. Forquera. 2006. "A Nationwide Population-Based Study Identifying Health Disparities between American Indians/Alaska Natives and the General Populations Living in Select Urban Counties." *American Journal of Public Health* 96(8): 1478–1484.

Chandler, M. J., and C. Lalonde. 1998. "Cultural Continuity as a Hedge against Suicide in Canada's First Nations." *Transcultural Psychiatry* 35(2): 191–219.

Gone, J. P., and J. P. Trimble. 2011. "American Indian and Alaska Native Mental Health: Diverse Perspectives on Enduring Disparities." Unpublished manuscript.

Hicks, J. 2007. "The Social Determinants of Elevated Rates of Suicide among Inuit Youth." *Indigenous Affairs* 4: 30–37.

Indian Health Service. 2011. "IHS Year 2011 Profile," Retrieved from http://www.ihs.gov/PublicAffairs/IHSBrochure /Profile2011.asp.

Indian Self-Determination and Education Assistance Act of 1975, 25 U.S.C. Secs. 450f *et seq.*

Kidwell, C. S., H. Noley, and G. E. Tinker. 2001. " Creation." In *A Native American Theology* (pp. 34–35). Maryknoll, NY: Orbis Books.

Sue, S., D. B. Allen, and L. Conaway. 1978. "The Responsiveness and Equality of Mental Health Care to Chicanos and Native Americans." *American Journal of Community Psychology* 6(2): 137–146.

U.S. Bureau of Indian Affairs. 2011. "What We Do." Retrieved from http://www.bia.gov/WhatWeDo/index.htm.

U.S. Commission on Civil Rights. 2003. *A Quiet Crisis: Federal Funding and Unmet Needs in Indian Country.* Washington, DC: U.S. Commission on Civil Rights.

U.S. Commission on Civil Rights. 2004. *Broken Promises: Evaluating the Native American Health Care System.* Washington DC: U.S. Commission on Civil Rights, Office of the General Counsel.

U.S. Department of Health and Human Services, Office of the Surgeon General. 2001. "Mental Health: Culture, Race, and Ethnicity—a Supplement to Mental Health: A Report of the Surgeon General." Rockville, MD: U.S. Department of Health and Human Services, Center for Mental Health Services.

Anger and Aggression

Kathleen E. Darbor and Heather C. Lench

Burt and Linda Pugach appear to have the perfect marriage, but their romance did not start out so happily in the late 1950s. When they started dating, Burt was married to another woman. He refused to divorce his wife, and Linda finally left him and became engaged to another man. Burt did not take this well. In 1959, he hired someone to throw acid in Linda's face when she answered her door. The attack left Linda blind and disfigured, a condition that Burt regrets to this day. Burt describes himself as simply overcome with anger. While it is incredible that Linda would then marry Burt in 1973 after he was released from prison for this crime, the more critical issue is the anger that motivated Burt to hurt her, and how his actions might have been prevented. Although this may be an extreme (though true) case, many other people also experience problems in their daily lives as a result of anger. A man might become physically violent whenever he perceives a slight to his honor or might refuse to speak to his children when they do not accept his advice. A woman might throw objects during disputes with her husband or spread malicious rumors about a talented colleague. In each case, actions that resulted from anger can cause social or professional problems.

Anger is a normal and common emotional experience. In some cases, however, anger can become dysfunctional because its intensity or duration impairs people's ability to function at work or home. There has been a dramatic upsurge in the number of people referred for anger management treatment in the last few decades. Despite recognition that many people suffer from problems related to anger that require therapy, there are no guidelines for diagnosis or treatment because anger is not currently recognized as a disorder by the mental health field.

What Is Anger?

Anger is experienced when someone or something blocks the attainment of an important goal. For example, a spouse may prevent one from feeling valued by making demeaning comments; a computer crash may prevent one from finishing a course paper. Whether a goal is still attainable with additional effort determines whether people feel angry or sad when they fail. In one study, children judged that a boy with an injured leg that prevented him from playing with his friends would feel sad if his injury was permanent, but angry if it was not permanent and could be overcome after resting the leg (Levine 1995). Experiencing anger when a goal is blocked can motivate people to exert more effort to attain their goal. For example, if a student's computer crashes while he is working on a course paper, feeling angry might motivate him to have the computer immediately repaired. He might also be more careful to back up his work in the future.

Anger has a number of effects on the mind and body (Eckhardt & Deffenbacher 1995). Anger is usually accompanied by physical arousal, causing the heart to beat faster, adrenaline to release, and the body to prepare for action. Anger is also associated with changes in cognition (how people think about the world around them). When angry, people tend to focus on and remember information related to their anger. Consider the man who hung up on his child. During their argument he likely noticed that the child was not listening to what he had to say. He would remember all the other times this happened during previous arguments with his child. As a result of these thoughts, he would become even angrier, and would finally hang up. Anger is also expressed behaviorally, through aggressive facial expressions, actions, and verbalizations. These behavioral manifestations are often what observers use to identify whether someone is angry, and include a glowering look, physical aggression, offensive gestures, yelling, and cursing. Men and women are equally likely to experience intense anger, but men are more likely to aggress directly against people or objects, while women are more likely to aggress indirectly (e.g., gossiping, excluding people from groups).

Anger Disorders

Anger is a central component of one psychiatric disorder in the *Diagnostic and Statistical Manual of Mental Disorders* (*DSM-IV-TR*), which is the official manual used by clinicians for the diagnosis of mental disorders (American Psychiatric Association 2000). Intermittent explosive disorder is an impulse control disorder characterized by discrete episodes of aggression out of proportion to the situation. Irritability and rage are mentioned as potential symptoms, but are not required. Outbursts of anger and aggression are also mentioned as criteria for several personality disorders, including paranoid personality disorder, antisocial personality disorder, and borderline personality disorder. Problematic anger is often conceptualized as a subtype of existing mood disorders. For example, a person with frequent episodes of anger and aggression who is also suffering from depression would be diagnosed as having a depressive disorder "not otherwise specified." There is evidence, however, that people may experience dysfunctional anger without simultaneous symptoms of anxiety or depression. The next edition of the DSM (fifth edition) will include temper dysregulation disorder with dysphoria. This disorder is characterized by severe recurrent temper outbursts in response to common stressors within a background of chronic irritable mood and an onset in childhood.

Others have proposed multiple comprehensive categories for anger disorders similar to those in place for depressive and anxiety disorders. These diagnoses would differentiate anger disorders that involve (a) acute reactions to temporary stresses, (b) patterns of intense anger out of proportion to the situation, and (c) chronic anger, and could help to identify and treat anger problems *before* the individual develops a serious illness (Eckhardt & Deffenbacher 1995). These include adjustment disorder with angry mood (characterized by disproportionate angry mood, but little aggression or interference with daily life, in response to specific stressors), situational adjustment with/without aggression (characterized by consistent and intense reactions to specific events, which results in disruption of social, work, or school activities), and general anger disorder with/without aggression (characterized by chronic and pervasive anger that interferes with daily life). Early identification of these disorders could help to reduce the financial and moral burdens of anger disorders on society. More research is needed, however, to determine whether these potential diagnoses would capture important aspects of people's experiences with dysfunctional anger.

Are Anger and Aggression Always Bad?

Anger has long been blamed for incidents of tragic violence and many other societal ills. In ancient times, anger was seen as a form of madness, and outbursts were condemned. In contrast, Aristotle regarded properly controlled anger as useful under certain circumstances because it motivates people to prevent injustice. One of the benefits of anger is that it motivates additional effort toward goals and behavioral changes, possibly because anger makes people feel empowered and in control. In fact, angry people and the targets of anger report that anger often leads to positive outcomes, including conflict resolution (Averill 1983).

It is possible for a person to be angry without being violent or aggressive, just as it is possible for a person to be aggressive without first being angry. For example, someone can be aggressive in pressuring others to behave in a way that suits him or her, but the person doing so may not be acting out of anger. In fact, aggression rarely follows episodes of anger. Averill (1983) asked a large number of people to describe angry episodes in their lives. They reported physical aggression in only 10 percent of angry episodes, and verbal aggression in only half of angry episodes. Both types of aggression were reported less often than was talking about the problem and doing something to calm down. Aggression is thus only one of the behaviors that can follow anger, and may be an attempt to deal with blocked goals when other, more adaptive attempts prove unsuccessful.

How Does One Tell If Anger Is Dysfunctional?

Anger is often adaptive and undeserving of its bad reputation, but it can precipitate violence and aggression. Anger can cause people to remember things that made them angry in the past, and prime them to respond aggressively (Anderson & Bushman 2002). It can also reduce normal restraints and make aggressive responses feel more justified. In addition, anger may strain the cognitive resources required to control behavior. Consider a man who becomes angry over an insult. He is cognitively distracted by his anger and thus is less likely to suppress his urge to shove or punch the person who maligned him. In addition, anger causes physiological arousal, which can facilitate physical aggression.

Anger can be considered dysfunctional when it is out of proportion to the situation, experienced too frequently, or chronically elevated to the extent that responses impair the person (Eckhardt & Deffenbacher 1995). Such impairments may include damage to social relationships through physical or emotional harm to loved ones, which can lead to increased conflict and eventual dissolution of marriages or close friendships. They may also include less satisfaction with and more changes in jobs, and increased legal difficulties.

Whether intense, frequent, or chronic anger impairs a person often depends on his or her response to an angry episode. Anger is functional when it results in attainment of the blocked goal in a way that maintains relationships with others, and is dysfunctional when it results in failure to attain the blocked goal or behaviors that have negative social or legal consequences. Consider a man who wants to spend time with his girlfriend, but she wants to have a night out with her friends. His goal of spending time with her has been blocked and he becomes angry. He could discuss the matter with her and reach a compromise that allows both people to attain their goals. Or he could attempt to make her feel guilty every time she wants to spend time with anyone else, resulting in arguments and an end of the relationship, putting him even further from his original goal. In the first case, anger was functional in that it motivated a resolution; in the latter case, anger was chronic and dysfunctional because it resulted in goal failure and harm to a social relationship.

Another approach for identifying dysfunctional anger includes looking at whether or not expressions of anger are inappropriate. The uncontrolled expression of anger is generally considered inappropriate and conflicts with societal norms, although these norms vary by gender and culture. For example, acts of physical aggression are perceived to be less appropriate when committed by women. In the same vein, acts of physical and verbal aggression are viewed more negatively in some cultures than others. Some anger and aggression is valued in Western cultures in order to preserve independence and "stick up" for oneself; other cultures view anger as destructive and people who express anger are ostracized from social groups (Briggs 1998).

A final approach to determine if anger is dysfunctional is to look at its effect on the health of the individual. Feelings of anger toward the self and others are associated with higher rates of mental and physical ailments (Keinan et al. 1992). Anger has consistently been linked to hypertension and coronary problems, along with increased release of adrenaline and other hormones. People with chronic anger also tend to be slower to recover from blood pressure increases while feeling angry, which may put undue stress on the body. Anger may also influence health indirectly, through an increase in unhealthy habits associated with attempts to cope with intense emotion, such as smoking.

What Causes Dysfunctional Anger?

There is a tendency, by both clinicians and the general public, to dismiss anger as a problem. The assumption often is that there is some other, deeper issue (such as depression) that causes problematic anger. In contrast, no one would ever ask what was "really" causing someone's depression; instead, they accept that intense and chronic sadness is a problem that results from biological predispositions and negative experiences. This may lead individuals with anger disorders to feel misunderstood and decrease the likelihood that they will seek and adhere to treatment regimens.

As anger is not currently recognized as a disorder, its potential causes have not been systematically studied. The experience of problematic anger, and referrals to anger management, are associated with poor social and coping skills, which are likely necessary to deal with anger in an effective and socially acceptable way. Individuals lacking in social skills have difficulty accurately processing social events and the intentions of others. For example, they may interpret an ambiguous situation as being overly hostile, and react with anger out of proportion to the situation (Lochman et al. 2010). A lack of effective coping skills may also increase problematic anger as people repeatedly fail to resolve a problem. Over time, they are likely to experience even more frequent and intense anger as they struggle to find a way to overcome obstacles to their goals. Further, ineffective attempts at coping may affect their social and professional relationships as they may react in negative or inappropriate ways to stress.

When faced with stress, people with effective coping skills take steps to change the situation or how they perceive the situation in ways that result in positive emotions. Examples of effective coping strategies include problem solving, looking for positive results ("seeing the silver lining"), and finding positive meaning from events (Lench 2004). In contrast, people with ineffective coping skills tend to make a problem worse because the situation remains unresolved. Examples of ineffective coping strategies include less of a focus on problem solving and the use of more aggressive and antisocial actions, such as retaliation (Lench 2004). For example, Jennifer becomes angry when one of her coworkers gets a promotion before her. If she employs effective coping strategies, she will learn from the situation and work to develop the skills necessary to stand out to her boss in the future. If she employs ineffective coping strategies, she may spread rumors about the coworker, causing Jennifer to ruminate on the failure and potentially leading to disciplinary action when her actions are exposed. People with problematic anger also report that they have fewer positive ways to express their anger. They use less reciprocal communication and are less likely to take time to calm down, and generally report an inability to control their reactions in situations that trigger anger (Denson et al. 2011). This lack of control over impulsive behavior may explain many of the problems experienced by people with problematic anger, including physical assault on other people or objects, verbal assault, and nonverbal actions such as glaring or giving the finger (Lench 2004). Interventions targeting increased control over impulses might therefore prove beneficial.

Treatments for Anger and Aggression

What is anger management therapy? Unfortunately, because anger is not currently recognized as a mental disorder, it can mean many things and there are no guidelines for what kind of therapy should be given for different anger problems, whom it should be given to, or who should administer the therapy. Despite the lack of guidelines, anger management therapy can effectively lower angry individuals' blood pressures and improve their behavioral control (Larkin & Zayfert 1996). Reviews of the potential therapies to treat anger suggest that multiple types of therapy may be effective, especially those that target a variety of components of anger at one time (Edmondson & Conger 1996; Tafrate 1995). One such multicomponent treatment that has shown success is stress inoculation therapy. This therapy focuses on addressing the cognitive, emotional, and behavioral aspects of anger through cognitive preparation, skill acquisition, and practice of these skills in mildly stressful situations (Tafrate 1995). For example, a man becomes angry whenever his son's soccer coach does not play him. In therapy, this man would learn to identify situations that lead to dysfunctional anger, and to change his thoughts so that they do not result in inappropriate behavior. He might also learn relaxation techniques and practice them during increasingly stressful role-played or imagined situations. Other promising therapeutic approaches include techniques to increase the ability to tolerate physical and emotional distress and family therapy approaches.

In addition to the cognitive-behavioral therapies described above, there is some evidence that dysfunctional anger may be reduced by medication. Individuals suffering from "anger attacks" (brief episodes of intense anger, similar to the anxiety during panic attacks) experienced fewer attacks while taking low doses of antidepressant drugs that target the neurotransmitter serotonin (Fava, Anderson, & Rosenbaum 1990). Other studies have found that medications, including mood stabilizers and antipsychotics, are helpful in treating dysfunctional anger (Mercer, Douglass, & Links 2009).

Conclusion

Dysfunctional anger is a growing problem in today's society. The news is filled with examples of violence and aggression committed by people who are angry at some insult or stressful situation. Unfortunately, anger problems often go unrecognized and untreated. Burt Pugach is a prime example of the problems that can be caused by dysfunctional anger—he caused the permanent disfigurement of the woman he loved because his response to anger was out of proportion. If he had received treatment to improve his ability to cope with stress and express anger appropriately, just consider how different Linda Pugach's life might have been. She would still be able to see. Anger is a normal emotional experience that can become problematic and disrupt the lives of many individuals. Hopefully, there will one day be ways to identify and treat such anger before it results in harm to the self or others.

See also Mental Health Counseling; Peer Support Groups; Preventative Mental Health Programs; Self-Help; Stress and Stress Management

Bibliography

American Psychiatric Association. 2000. *Diagnostic and Statistical Manual of Mental Disorders* (4th ed., text rev.). Washington, DC: American Psychiatric Publishing.

Anderson, C. A., and B. J. Bushman. 2002. "Human Aggression." *Annual Review of Psychology* 53: 27–51.

Averill, James R. 1983. "Studies on Anger and Aggression: Implications for Theories of Emotion." *American Psychologist* 38: 1145–1160.

Briggs, Jean L. 1998. "Never in Anger: Portrait of an Eskimo family." In Jennifer M. Jenkins, Keith Oatley, and Nancy Stein, eds., *Human Emotions: A Reader* (pp. 45–54). Malden, MA: Blackwell.

Denson, Thomas F., Miriam M. Capper, Megan Oaten, Malte Friese, and Timothy P. Schofield. 2011. "Self-Control Training Decreases Aggression in Response to Provocation in Aggressive Individuals." *Journal of Research in Personality* 45: 252–256.

DiGuiseppe, Raymond, and Raymond C. Tafrate. 2007. *Understanding Anger Disorders*. New York: Oxford University Press.

Eckhardt, Christopher I., and Jerry L. Deffenbacher. 1995. "Diagnosis of Anger Disorders." In Howard Kassinove, ed., *Anger Disorders: Definition, Diagnosis, and Treatment: Series in Clinical and Community Psychology* (pp. 27–47). Philadelphia: Taylor & Francis.

Edmondson, Christine B., and Judith C. Conger. 1996. "A Review of Treatment Efficacy for Individuals with Anger Problems: Conceptual, Assessment, and Methodological Issues." *Clinical Psychology Review* 16(3): 251–275.

Fava, Maurizio, Keith Anderson, and Jerrold F. Rosenbaum. 1990. " 'Anger Attacks': Possible Variants of Panic and Major Depressive Disorders." *American Journal of Psychiatry* 147: 867–870.

Keinan, Giora, Hasida Ben-Zur, Michal Zilka, and Rafael S. Carel. 1992. "Anger In and Out, Which Is Healthier? An Attempt to Reconcile Inconsistent Findings." *Psychology and Health* 7: 83–98.

Larkin, Kevin T., and Claudia Zayfert. 1996. "Anger Management Training with Mild Essential Hypertensive Patients." *Journal of Behavioral Medicine* 19: 415–433.

Lench, Heather C. 2004. "Anger Management: Diagnostic Differences and Treatment Implications." *Journal of Social and Clinical Psychology* 23: 512–531.

Levine, Linda J. 1995. "Young Children's Understanding of the Causes of Anger and Sadness." *Child Development* 66: 697–709.

Lochman, John E., Tammy Barry, Nicole Powell, and Laura Young. 2010. "Anger and Aggression." In Douglas W. Nangle, David J. Hansen, Cynthia A. Erdley, and Peter J. Norton, eds., *Practioner's Guide to Empirically Based Measures of Social Skills* (pp. 155–166). New York: Springer.

Mercer, Deanna, Alan B. Douglass, and Paul S. Links. 2009. "Meta-Analysis of Mood Stabilizers, Antidepressants and Antipsychotics in the Treatment of Borderline Personality Disorder: Effectiveness for Depression and Anger Symptoms." *Journal of Personality Disorders* 23(2): 156–174.

Tafrate, Raymond C. 1995. "Evaluation of Treatment Strategies for Adult Anger Disorders." In Howard Kassinove, ed., *Anger Disorders: Definition, Diagnosis, and Treatment* (pp. 109–129). Philadelphia: Taylor & Francis.

Tafrate, Raymond C., and Howard Kassinove. 2009. *Anger Management for Everyone: Seven Proven Ways to Control Anger and Live a Happier Life*. Atascadero, CA: Impact.

Anorexia

See Eating Disorders

Antisocial Personality

See Psychopathy and Antisocial Personality Disorder

Anxiety Disorders

See Obsessive-Compulsive Disorder; Panic Disorder; Phobias; Posttraumatic Stress Disorder; Social Anxiety Disorder

Art and Mental Health

See Creativity and Mental Health

Asian American and Pacific Islander Mental Health Issues

Anne Saw and Stanley Sue

Attending to the mental health needs of Asian Americans and Pacific Islanders (AAPIs) requires an understanding of the diversity of the AAPI population, help-seeking patterns and psychiatric prevalence rates, the influences of culture on the experience and expression of mental illness, and structural influences on the mental health needs of AAPIs. These factors influence how practitioners can effectively meet the mental health needs of Asian Americans and Pacific Islanders. The review of AAPI mental health issues provided is based on available research and theoretical literature; however, it should be noted that although advances have been made to include minorities in research in the United States, AAPIs—particularly certain Asian ethnic groups such as South and Southeast Asian Americans and Pacific Islanders—continue to be underrepresented in psychological science.

Diversity within the AAPI Population

AAPIs represent a heterogeneous group comprised of individuals from over two dozen distinct ethnic/cultural groups. Asian Americans and Pacific Islanders comprise 4.8 percent and 0.2 percent, respectively, of the U.S. population (Hume, Jones, & Ramirez 2011). According to the 2000 U.S. Census, the six largest Asian ethnic groups are: Chinese, Filipino, Indian, Korean, Japanese, and Vietnamese (Reeves & Bennett 2004). The six largest Pacific Islander groups are: Native Hawaiian, Samoan, Guamanian, Tongan, Fijian, and Marshallese (Harris & Jones 2005). There is tremendous heterogeneity with the AAPI population as a whole and within ethnic subgroups. Two-thirds of Asian Americans were born outside of the United States (Reeves & Bennett 2004). In contrast, 89 percent of Pacific Islanders are native to the United States (Harris & Jones 2005). AAPIs also vary along many other demographic, cultural, and linguistic characteristics.

Help-Seeking Patterns and Psychiatric Prevalence Rates

It has been well documented that AAPIs underutilize mental health services relative to the general population. Data from the Collaborative Psychiatric Epidemiological Surveys (CPES) suggest that only 8.6 percent of Asian Americans seek help for mental health issues (Abe-Kim et al. 2007) compared to 17.9 percent of the general population. Among individuals most in need of mental health services (i.e., with a past-year probable psychiatric diagnosis), 34 percent reported seeking such services (Abe-Kim et al. 2007). In contrast, 41.1 percent of those with a past-year probable psychiatric diagnosis in the general population reported seeking mental health services (Wang et al. 2005). Furthermore, utilization rates among AAPIs varied depending on gender and generation status such that women and those born in the United States utilized mental health services at higher rates that men and immigrants (Abe-Kim et al. 2007). Data from a more recent epidemiological study (Substance Abuse and Mental Health Services Administration [SAMHSA] 2010) revealed that Asian Americans had the lowest utilization rate for mental health services compared to other racial/ethnic groups. Large-scale epidemiological data on mental health service use among Pacific Islanders are not available, and smaller community or mental health system studies tend to group Pacific Islanders with Asian Americans. These studies indicate that Pacific Islanders also underutilize mental health services compared to the general population (Ta et al. 2008; Zhang, Snowden, & Sue 1998).

It has been suggested that Asian Americans are reluctant to seek mental health treatment and tend to delay treatment until symptoms reach crisis levels (Sue & Sue 1999). Among AAPIs who seek mental health services, severity of psychiatric disturbance tends to be much higher compared to non-Hispanic whites (Durvasula & Sue 1996; Yeh et al. 2002). Barriers to help seeking for mental health issues include cultural conceptions about mental illness that are incongruent with Western beliefs, beliefs about treatment (e.g., shame or stigma, face concerns), lack of financial resources, culturally unresponsive services (e.g., lack of bilingual and bicultural therapists), and the preference among some AAPIs for complementary or alternative therapies (U.S. Department of Health and Human Services 2001).

Epidemiological data suggest that AAPIs have much lower lifetime and past-year prevalence rates for psychological disorders compared to the general U.S. population, but that heterogeneity exists within the population. SAMHSA (2010) found the past-year prevalence rates of mental disorders for individuals aged 18 and older were: 15.5 percent among Asians, 16.7 percent among Native Hawaiians or Other Pacific Islanders, 17.8 percent among Hispanics, 17.9 percent among African Americans, 20.7 percent among non-Hispanic whites, and 21.6 percent among American Indians or Alaska Natives. Using CPES data, Takeuchi and colleagues (2007) found that for Asian Americans, the lifetime prevalence of any psychiatric disorder was 17.3 percent and the past-year prevalence of any psychiatric disorder was 9.19 percent. For the general population, the lifetime and past-year prevalence rates were 46.4 percent (Kessler et al. 2005) and 26.2 percent (Kessler et al. 2005), respectively. Takeuchi et al. (2007) found that prevalence rates for different psychiatric disorders varied for Asian Americans according to gender, nativity status, and ethnicity. For example, second-generation Asian American women had higher prevalence rates for lifetime and past-year disorders compared to other Asian American groups.

Finally, considerable variability may exist among AAPIs so that some groups have high rates while others have low rates. Southeast Asians, particularly refugees, appear to be at high risk for mental disorders. In a study of Cambodian refugees who had lived in Cambodia during the Khmer Rouge regime and immigrated to the United States before 1993, Marshall, Schell, Elliott, Berthold, and Chun (2005) assessed the prevalence, comorbidity (i.e., rates of co-occurring disorders), and correlates of psychiatric disorders two decades after resettlement in the United States. This study was based on a random sample of households from the Cambodian community in Long Beach, California, the city with the largest single concentration of Cambodian refugees in the United States. Results indicated that the vast majority of the respondents had been exposed to trauma and violence before immigration (e.g., 99% experienced near death due to starvation; 96 percent reported forced labor; 90 percent reported having a family member or friend murdered; and 54 percent reported having been tortured). In terms of mental health status, 62 percent of the respondents had posttraumatic stress disorder (PTSD) and 51 percent had major depression in the past 12-months. However, low rates of alcohol use disorder (4%) were found. Significant correlates of PTSD and major depression included older age, having poor English-speaking proficiency, unemployment, being retired or disabled, and living in poverty. Both premigration and postmigration trauma exposure were positively associated with 12-month PTSD and major depression.

Cultural Considerations and Structural Influences

Prevalence studies such as the CPES are based on psychiatric diagnostic systems (namely, the *Diagnostic and Statistical Manual* [*DSM*] of the American Psychiatric Association). These systems have been criticized for being biased toward Western concepts of psychology and psychopathology (Lewis-Fernandez & Kleinman 1994). Culture may therefore impact accurate estimates of prevalence rates, resulting in underreporting the prevalence of mental illnesses for AAPIs and other ethnic minorities (McGuire & Miranda 2008). Therefore many cultural psychologists and psychiatrists have proposed that when studying psychiatric phenomena among ethno-cultural minorities, one must consider the cultural contexts within which individuals are embedded.

In addition to criticisms over the appropriateness of the diagnostic system, other problems also hinder an accurate assessment of the prevalence of mental disorders among Asian Americans. One involves the possibility that AAPIs have culture-bound syndromes that affect prevalence but are often undetected in prevalence studies. Culture-bound syndromes are disorders that are largely limited to specific societies or cultures and are influenced by local folk traditions. For example, the culture-bound syndrome of neurasthenia is found among Chinese individuals. It is defined as a mental and physical exhaustion marked by chronic fatigue, weakness, aches, and pains. Neurasthenia had been listed in previous versions of *DSM* but was removed in part because of its lower prevalence in the United States and because of the belief that the disorder was actually masked depression. In a study of Chinese Americans in Los Angeles, Zheng, Lin, Takeuchi, Kurasaki, Wang, and Cheung (1997) found that 6.3 percent of a random sample of respondents met the criteria for neurasthenia. Of these, over half had neurasthenic symptoms in the absence of symptoms of other *DSM* disorders, raising doubt that neurasthenia is simply another disorder (e.g., depression) in disguise. Thus although Chinese Americans are likely to experience neurasthenia, mental health professionals using the standard U.S. diagnostic system may fail to identify this disorder and the need for mental health care.

AAPI Cultural Beliefs Relevant to Mental Health

Although the AAPI population is extremely diverse, AAPIs share some similar cultural concepts, such as interdependence of self in relation to others (Markus & Kitayama 1991). Two concepts with important implications for mental health are somatization and face.

Although somatization, or the presentation of psychiatric symptoms in bodily form, is often thought of as a culturally mediated expression of emotional distress among individuals from non-Western cultures, more recent evidence suggests that somatization is one of the most common expressions of psychological distress worldwide (Kirmayer & Young 1998). For AAPIs, somatization may be a culturally appropriate means of experiencing and expressing distress. For example, in many AAPI cultures, the suppression rather than expression of emotion is valued. Therefore expressing distress using physical metaphors may be considered more appropriate (Cheung 1982).

Face refers to a complex set of socially sanctioned judgments about an individual or group's character and integrity that influence how the person or group behaves. Concern for face impacts help-seeking behaviors and choice of intervention for AAPIs with mental illness (e.g., Gong, Gage, & Tacata 2003). One proposed approach for addressing face concerns is to provide mental health education for individuals, their families, and communities impacted by mental illness (e.g., Lau & Wong 2008; Yang et al. 2007). Others have suggested that mental health practitioners must be more sensitive to the cultural value systems of their patients and provide culturally appropriate interventions (e.g., Sanchez & Gaw 2007).

Structural Influences on Mental Health

In addition to cultural influences, the mental health of AAPIs is also affected by their experiences in the United States and, for many AAPIs who are immigrants or refugees, by their experiences prior to migration. As such, it is important to consider the historical, sociopolitical, and environmental challenges faced by AAPIs who migrate to the United States.

For AAPIs who migrate directly from other countries, the process of adjustment can be challenging. Upon their arrival in the United States, immigrants and refugees often need to learn a new language, secure housing and employment, navigate complex economic and political systems, and develop new social relationships. They may experience acculturative stress when the demands of adjustment to U.S. culture exceed their available coping resources (Berry 1997). Acculturative stress can take different forms, such as confusion about their identity, marginalization or alienation, or psychopathology (Berry & Annis 1974).

Some AAPIs emigrate from countries that have experienced war, political conflict, and colonization. As mentioned earlier, the effects of premigration trauma and violence experienced by many Hmong Americans living in Cambodia during the Khmer Rouge regime has resulted in elevated rates of PTSD and major depression in this population. Several Asian countries, including the Philippines and India, and Pacific Islands, including Guam and Samoa, have experienced European and/or American colonialism. In a series of studies, David (see David 2011, for a summary) found that some Filipino Americans have *colonial mentality*, a perception of cultural inferiority that is negatively related with ethnic identity and collective self-esteem and positively related to depression symptoms. His research and that of others suggest that colonization influences mental health, even for those who were not directly colonized (Okazaki, David, & Abelmann 2007).

AAPIs have experienced a long history of racism and prejudice. Examples of the systematic racism and discrimination experienced by AAPIs include laws preventing miscegenation, land ownership, and citizenship, and the internment of Japanese Americans during World War II (Takaki 1994). Stereotypes of different AAPIs have also persisted throughout the course of American history (Wu 2002). Findings from NLAAS suggest that discrimination is related to an elevated risk for psychiatric disorders (Gee et al. 2007). Both blatant and subtle discrimination also impact the ethnic identity, self-esteem (Osajima 1993), and performance (Cheryan & Bodenhausen 2000).

Conclusion

The AAPI population represents one of the fastest-growing, most diverse ethnic/racial groups in the United States. The heterogeneity of this population presents challenges and opportunities for practitioners and researchers.

The research indicates that AAPIs have mental health needs that are often over-looked or inadequately addressed. To better address these needs through research and practice, we must consider cultural and structural factors that influence the mental health of AAPIs.

See also Culturally Competent Mental Health Care

Bibliography

Abe-Kim, J., D. T. Takeuchi, S. Hong, N. Zane, S. Sue, M. S. Spencer, H. Appel, E. Nicdao, and M. Alegría 2007. "Use of Mental Health-Related Services among Immigrant and US-Born Asian Americans: Results from the National Latino and Asian American Study." *American Journal of Public Health* 97: 91–98.

Berry, J. W. 1997. "Immigration, Acculturation, and Adaptation." *Applied Psychology: An International Review* 46: 5–68.

Berry, J. W., and R. C. Annis. 1974. "Acculturative Stress: The Role of Ecology, Culture, and Differentiation." *Journal of Cross-Cultural Psychology* 5: 382–406.

Cheryan, S., and G. V. Bodenhausen. 2000. "When Positive Stereotypes Threaten Intellectual Performance: The Psychological Hazards of 'Model Minority' Status." *Psychological Science* 11: 399–402.

Cheung, F. M. 1982. "Psychological Symptoms among Chinese in Urban Hong Kong." *Social Science and Medicine* 16: 1339–1344.

David, E. J. R. 2011. *Filipino-/American Postcolonial Psychology: Oppression, Colonial Mentality, and Decolonization*. Bloomington, IN: Authorhouse.

Durvasala, R., and S. Sue. 1996. "Severity of Disturbance among Asian American Outpatients." *Cultural Diversity and Mental Health* 2: 43–51.

Gee, G. C., M. Spencer, J. Chen, T. Yip, and D. T. Takeuchi. 2007." The Association between Self-Reported Racial Discrimination and 12-Month *DSM-IV* Mental Disorders among Asian Americans Nationwide." *Social Science & Medicine* 64: 1984–1996.

Gong, F., S. L. Gage, and L. A. Tacata Jr. 2003. "Help-Seeking Behavior among Filipino Americans: A Cultural Analysis of Face and Language." *Journal of Community Psychology* 31: 469–488.

Harris, P. M., and N. A. Jones. 2005. *We the People: Pacific Islanders in the United States, CENSR-26*. Washington, DC: U.S. Census Bureau.

Hume, K. R., N. A. Jones, and R. R. Ramirez. 2011. *Overview of Race and Hispanic Origin: 2010, C2010BR-02*. Retrieved from http://www.census.gov/prod/cen2010/briefs/c2010br-02.pdf.

Kessler, R. C., P. Berglund, O. Demler, R. Jin, K. R. Merikangas, and E. E. Walters. 2005. "Lifetime Prevalence and Age-of-Onset Distributions of *DSM-IV* Disorders in the National Comorbidity Survey Replication." *Archives of General Psychiatry* 62: 593–602.

Kessler, R. C., W. T. Chiu, O. Demler, K. R. Merikangas, and E. E. Walters. 2005. "Prevalence, Severity, and Comorbidity of 12-Month *DSM-IV* Disorders in the National Comorbidity Survey Replication." *Archives of General Psychiatry* 62: 617–627.

Kim, B. S. K., P. H. Yang, D. R. Atkinson, M. M. Wolfe, and S. Hong. 2001. "Cultural Value Similarities and Differences among Asian American Ethnic Groups." *Cultural Diversity and Ethnic Minority Psychology* 7: 343–361.

Lau, Y., and D. F. K. Wong. 2008. "Are Concern for Face and Willingness to Seek Help Correlated to Early Postnatal Depressive Symptoms among Hong Kong Chinese Women?

A Cross-Sectional Questionnaire Survey." *International Journal of Nursing Studies* 45: 51–64.

Leong, F. T. L., A. G. Inman, A. Ebreo, L. H. Yang, L. Kinoshita, and M. Fu. 2007. *Handbook of Asian American Psychology* (2nd ed.). Thousand Oaks, CA: Sage.

Lewis-Fernandez, R., and A. Kleinman. 1994. "Culture, Personality, and Psychopathology." *Journal of Abnormal Psychology* 103: 67–71.

Markus, H. R., and S. Kitayama. 1991. "Culture and the Self: Implications for Cognition, Emotion, and Motivation." *Psychological Review* 98: 224–253.

Marshall, G. N., T. L. Schell, M. N. Elliott, S. M. Berthold, and C.-A. Chun. 2005. "Mental Health of Cambodian Refugees 2 Decades after Resettlement in the United States." *JAMA* 294: 571–579.

McGuire, T. G., and J. Miranda. 2008. "New Evidence Regarding Racial and Ethnic Disparities in Mental Health: Policy Implications." *Health Affairs* 27: 393–403.

Okazaki, S., E. J. R. David, and N. Abelmann. 2007. "Colonialism and Psychology of Culture." *Social and Personality Compass* 1: 1–17.

Osajima, K. 1993. "The Hidden Injuries of Race." In L. Revilla, G. Nomura, S. Wong, and S. Hune, eds., *Bearing Dreams, Shaping Visions: Asian Pacific American Perspectives*. Pullman, pp. 81–91. WA: Washington State University Press.

Reeves, T., and C. Bennett. 2004. *We the People: Asians in the United States, CENSR-17*. Retrieved from http://www.census.gov/prod/2004pubs/censr-17.pdf.

Sanchez, F., and A. Gaw. 2007. "Mental Health Care of Filipino Americans." *Psychiatric Services* 6: 810–815.

Substance Abuse and Mental Health Services Administration. 2010. *Results from the 2009 National Survey on Drug Use and Health: Mental Health Findings* (Office of Applied Studies, NSDUH Series H-39, HHS Publication No. SMA 10-4609). Rockville, MD: Substance Abuse and Mental Health Services Administration.

Sue, D. W., and D. Sue. 1999. *Counseling the Culturally Different: Theory and Practice*, 3rd ed. New York: Wiley.

Ta., V. M., H. Juon, A. C. Gielen, D. Steinwachs, and A. Duggan. 2008. "Disparities in Use of Mental Health and Substance Use Services by Asian and Native Hawaiian/Other Pacific Islander Women." *Journal of Behavioral Health Services Research* 35: 20–36.

Takaki, R. 1994. *Strangers from a different shore: A history of Asian Americans*. New York: Back Bay.

Takeuchi, D. T., N. W. Zane, S. Hong, D. H. Chae, F. Gong, G. C. Gee, E. Walton, E., Sue, S., and M. Alegría. 2007. "Immigration-Related Factors and Mental Disorders among Asian Americans." *American Journal of Public Health* 97: 84–90.

U.S. Department of Health and Human Services. 2001. *Mental Health: Culture, Race, and Ethnicity—A Supplement to Mental Health: A Report of the Surgeon General*. Rockville, MD: U.S. Department of Health and Human Services, Substance and Mental Health Services Administration, Center for Mental Health Services.

Wang, P. S., M. Lane, M. Olfson, H. A. Pincus, K. B. Wells, and R. C. Kessler. 2005. "Twelve-Month Use of Mental Health Services in the United States." *Archives of General Psychiatry* 62: 629–640.

Watters, E. 2010. "The Americanization of Mental Illness." *New York Times Magazine*, January 8.

Wu, F. H. 2002. *Yellow: Race in America beyond Black and White*. New York: Basic Books.

Yang, L. H., A. Kleinman, B. G. Link, J. C. Phelan, S. Lee, and B. Good. 2007. "Culture and Stigma: Adding Moral Experience to Stigma Theory." *Social Science and Medicine* 64: 1524–1535.

Yeh, M., K. McCabe, M. Hurlburt, R. Hough, A. Hazen, S. Culver, A. Garland, and J. Landsverk. 2002. "Referral Sources, Diagnoses, and Service Types of Youth in Public Outpatient Mental Health Care: A Focus on Ethnic Minorities." *Journal of Behavioral Health Services Research* 29: 45–60.

Zhang, A. Y., L. R. Snowden, and S. Sue. 1998. "Differences between Asian and White Americans' Help Seeking and Utilization Patterns in the Los Angeles Area." *Journal of Community Psychology* 26: 317–326.

Zheng, Y. P., K. M. Lin, D. Takeuchi, K. S. Kurasaki, Y. X. Wang, and F. Cheung. 1997. "An Epidemiological Study of Neurasthenia in Chinese-Americans in Los Angeles." *Comprehensive Psychiatry* 38: 249–259.

Asperger's Syndrome

See Autism Spectrum Disorders

Attention Deficit/Hyperactivity Disorder

Carolyn Pender and Bradley Smith

Attention deficit/hyperactivity disorder (ADHD) is a common, chronic, impairing disorder characterized by developmentally inappropriate levels of inattention and/or hyperactivity/impulsivity in addition to significant deficits in functioning across multiple settings (American Psychiatric Association 1994). This condition is arguably one of the most heavily researched disorders affecting children, and advances have been made over a relatively short period of time in the understanding of symptoms, course of the disorder, and commonly co-occurring problems.

Historically, there has been controversy in the field about whether ADHD is a "real" disorder. Consistent with all mental health disorders, ADHD is socially defined since there is no single medical test to define the condition. Thus diagnosis relies on identifying symptoms that are extreme in comparison to other individuals in society. Currently, there is no scientific proof that ADHD can be prevented, and typically management of symptoms over the long term is appropriate (Barkley 2006). Thus ADHD should be regarded as a chronic condition with emphasis on managing the impairments related to ADHD in the most efficient, least intrusive manner.

Some researchers argue a biological basis to ADHD, and it is plausible that an objective medical test may be available for diagnosis of ADHD in the future (Smith, Barkley, & Shapiro 2006). The complexity of the biology/environment interaction may help to explain why symptoms of ADHD can be so variable across individuals, ages, and settings.

Not all individuals with ADHD show the same symptoms or level of severity. Moreover, ADHD-related impairments can be inconsistent and unstable with tremendous variability across and within settings. In many cases, persons with ADHD can attend to intrinsically interesting or novel activities for extended periods of time but rapidly lose interest in tedious activities. Thus it may appear as though the ability to pay attention in some situations and not others is an issue of willpower or motivation; however, this is not the case.

Outline of ADHD

Individuals with ADHD show deficits in attention and/or impulsivity when compared to same age and gender peers. Common issues include difficulties with sustaining attention, inhibiting responses (i.e., refraining from being impulsive), persisting on boring or repetitive activities, and putting forth consistent levels of 3effort (Smith, Barkley, & Shapiro 2006). Many, but not all, children with ADHD are more active, restless, and fidgety than normal children, which is commonly referred to as hyperactivity/impulsivity. Hyperactivity declines significantly across the elementary school years while problems with attention and impulsivity persist at relatively stable levels during this same period of development (Barkley 2006).

Recently, researchers have focused on identifying gender differences in impairments associated with ADHD. Some findings suggest girls with ADHD inattentive subtype, show greater impairments in academics and peer relationships (Elkins et al. 2011). Inattentive girls were viewed as less popular and more likely to be bullied than their non-ADHD peers. Interestingly, these researchers found the pattern did not hold true for inattentive boys. Researchers have also identified neurobiological differences between boys and girls with ADHD. Mahone and Wodka (2008) reviewed sex differences in typical brain development and among children diagnosed with ADHD and found discrepant patterns for males and females.

School-age children with ADHD earn significantly lower grades (Frazier et al. 2007), score lower on standardized achievement tests, and experience more frequent placement in special education, retention, and dropout (Molina et al. 2009). A recent study of adolescents diagnosed with ADHD found that improvements in school performance require direct targeting and measurement through proximal measures such as homework as opposed to distal measures such as standardized achievement tests (Langberg et al. 2011).

Evolution of ADHD

The current term used to describe this condition is attention deficit/hyperactivity disorder (ADHD) (American Psychiatric Association 1994) with three subtypes used to specify symptom concerns (i.e., inattention, hyperactivity/impulsivity, or a combination of both).

Prior to usage of the term ADHD, the same cluster of symptoms was referred to as attention deficit disorder with hyperactivity (ADD-H) or without hyperactivity (ADD), and this label first appeared in the American Psychiatric Association's *Diagnostic and Statistical Manual of Mental Disorders*, third edition (*DSM-III*), published in 1980 (American Psychiatric Association 1980). Some of the terms used prior to the ADD label include minimal brain damage, minimal brain dysfunction, hyperkinetic reaction of childhood, and hyperactive child syndrome.

In the 1940s, Strauss and Lehtinen (1947) attributed restless behavior and inattention to brain damage. They argued that such youth were thought to have sustained brain injuries, which caused the resultant behaviors of inattention and restlessness, and thus the term minimal brain damage emerged to describe these children.

In the 1960s, deficits in functioning were largely attributed to a higher rate of motor activity across time and settings that exceeded levels typical of normal children (Chess 1960). Researchers began to conclude with less frequency that restless and inattentive behavior resulted from actual brain damage and a shift in terminology occurred from the term "minimal brain damage" to "minimal brain dysfunction." This advance set the stage for the link between attention and brain damage to be completely removed from the diagnostic label and the disorder became known as hyperactive child syndrome or hyperkinetic reaction of childhood (Chess 1960).

By the mid-1970s, researchers argued deficits in sustained attention and impulse control characterized behavior and that the disorder consisted of impairments in investment, organization, and maintenance of attention; the inhibition of impulsive responding; the modulation of arousal levels to meet situational demands; and a strong tendency to seek immediate reinforcement (Douglas 1972).

In the late 1980s, the disorder was renamed attention defici-thyperactivity disorder in the *DSM-III-R* (American Psychiatric Association 1987), as a result of hyperactivity being considered a central feature to the condition. Also during this time, scientists began to identify executive function skills (i.e., self-regulation and governance) as being deficient in children with ADD (Douglas 1983).

In 1994, revisions to the *DSM* included the ability to subtype children into those presenting primarily with attention deficits (ADHD-I), hyperactivity/impulsivity (ADHD-H/I), or a combination of both symptom clusters (ADHD-C) (American Psychiatric Association 1994). Limitations to the *DSM-IV* criteria include multiple interpretations of the concept of developmentally inappropriate behavior, a lack of cultural sensitivity in the diagnostic sample, a lack of impulsivity items, and an arbitrary age of onset.

Currently, research findings are being used to consider changes in the diagnostic criteria for the *DSM-5*, which is scheduled for publication in May 2013. Proposed changes under review include retaining current symptoms for diagnosis but removing subtyping and adding a severity moderator. The inattention category may undergo refining or redefinition. Four new impulsivity symptoms have been developed. The onset of the disorder may be raised from 7 years of age to 12 years and may be based on symptom presence instead of impairment. Finally, the number of symptoms to indicate the presence of adult ADHD may be reduced from six to three (Anastopoulos 2011).

Diagnosis of ADHD

The most widely used criteria to diagnose ADHD is from the American Psychiatric Association's (APA) *Diagnostic and Statistical Manual*, fourth edition (*DSM-IV*; APA 1994). At least six symptoms of either inattentive behavior and/or hyperactive/impulsive behavior must be present to be diagnosed with ADHD. The symptoms must be considered developmentally inappropriate, be present in a minimum of two different settings, have been present for at least six months, and result in significant impairment in major life activities. Also, symptoms must not be better explained by other mental health disorders.

The *DSM-IV* inattention symptoms are as follows: (1) fails to give close attention to details, (2) shows difficulty sustaining attention, (3) does not seem to listen to when spoken to directly, (4) does not follow through on instructions, (5) has difficulty organizing tasks or activities, (6) avoids tasks that require sustained mental effort, (7) often loses things necessary for completion of tasks, (8) is easily distracted, and (9) is forgetful in daily activities.

The *DSM-IV* hyperactive/impulsive symptoms include: (1) fidgets with hands or feet or squirms in seat, (2) leaves seat in situations where it is considered inappropriate to do so, (3) runs about or climbs excessively, (4) has difficulty playing quietly, (5) is often "on the go" or acts as though "driven by a motor," (6) talks excessively, (7) blurts out answers before questions are completed, (8) has difficulty awaiting their turn, and (9) interrupts or intrudes on others.

A comprehensive ADHD evaluation includes a multimethod approach including a diagnostic interview, medical examination, information from multiple informants to capture symptoms across settings, use of multiple measures and methods to compensate for psychometric test weaknesses, standardized ADHD behavior rating scales, and other types of psychometric testing selected by the clinician depending on the individual's presenting symptoms (e.g., screening for depression or anxiety), and collection of sufficient information to develop an individualized treatment plan for the individual (Anastopoulos 2011).

Requesting multiple persons to document ADHD symptoms and related impairment is of critical importance in making an accurate ADHD diagnosis because individuals with ADHD are known to have limited insight into their symptoms. In a study examining deficits associated with ADHD among young adults, the diagnosis rate was approximately 5 percent of the sample. In contrast, when data from parents, spouses, or roommates were considered, the diagnosis rate was estimated to be around 65 percent (Barkley, Gordon, & Goldstein 2002). A second consideration in information collection involves the level of functioning of the informant. For example, when a stressed or depressed individual provides the information for an assessment, it may be clouded by their biased perspective (e.g., bad mood or hopelessness).

Unfortunately, most individuals do not undergo state-of-the-art evaluations for ADHD (Smith, Barkley, & Shapiro 2006). Consequently, ADHD is frequently misdiagnosed and sloppy assessment has been partially responsible for adding to the controversial nature of this disorder. At minimum, an ADHD screening should be based on the following information: a count of clinically significant symptoms of ADHD that shows extreme levels of impairment compared to same age peers (e.g., in the 95th percentile or higher), collection of information from multiple persons, documentation of significant impairment in multiple settings, evidence that the symptoms have been present for a long time, preferably since early childhood (e.g., before seven years of age), and a rule-out of competing explanations for the impairment, including medical and psychiatric conditions.

Prevalence of ADHD

According to the *DSM-IV*, between 3 and 5 percent of school-age children meet criteria for ADHD in the United States. Other researchers have suggested rates ranging from as low as 1.6 percent to as high as 16 percent (Anastopoulos 2011). Reasons for such wide ranges in prevalence include differences in methods used to diagnose the condition, age and gender of the research sample, and differences in the nature of the population (e.g., urban vs. rural samples).

Males are three times more likely to be diagnosed with ADHD than are females (Mahone & Wodka 2008). In clinical samples (e.g., groups of children seen in a research setting), males tend to meet criteria for a diagnosis of ADHD five to nine times more often than females. ADHD is more common among children than adults and is more likely to be seen in middle to lower-middle social classes. Further, there is increased diagnosis of ADHD in population-dense areas. To date, there is no evidence that ADHD prevalence varies by ethnicity after social class and urban/rural lifestyle have been accounted for. As summarized by Barkley (2006), research has shown that ADHD exists across the world, with children meeting *DSM-IV* diagnostic criteria in other countries such as Germany, Japan, Netherlands, New Zealand, and Canada.

Mental Health Disorders Commonly Co-occurring with ADHD

Russell Barkley (2006), a leading expert in ADHD research, has suggested that at least 80 percent of children with ADHD show evidence of a second disorder while 60 percent or more children have two or more comorbid disorders. Examples of commonly comorbid *DSM-IV* disorders include major depression, oppositional defiant disorder, conduct disorder, anxiety disorders, tics and/or Tourette's syndrome, and learning disabilities.

Accommodations for ADHD

Appropriate accommodations are those that are effective, efficient, and do not inadvertently reinforce the problem behavior (Smith et al. 2000). Accommodations should be individualized, evidence based, and sustainable over extended periods of time. There are many accommodations for ADHD that are helpful in managing symptoms. Licensed psychologists are trained to teach, model, and develop protocols to manage ADHD symptoms and should be consulted if symptoms are negatively impacting functioning.

ADHD across the Life Span

There is growing evidence that ADHD can be reliably and validly diagnosed among preschool children (Mahone 2011). Impulsive preschoolers run the risk of being rejected by peers due to inappropriate interpersonal behavior such as aggression and rule-breaking behaviors. Inattentive children may be neglected by their peers but are not usually actively rejected. Parents may notice that these children become bored easily and require a high level of attention of structure.

A common age for detecting ADHD symptoms is during first grade, when children are typically introduced to more rigorous academic requirements. Presenting problems at this age typically include academic difficulties, discipline problems at school and home, and conflict with peers. Limited insight is shown into problems and interventions need to be implemented and managed by adults.

Research studies have found that teens with ADHD are more likely to experience car accidents and receive speeding tickets, are less likely to graduate from high school, and are at greater risk for teenage pregnancy (Barkley 2006). College students with elevated symptoms of inattention have been found to display different deficits in functioning compared to students with high levels of impulsivity (Pender, Smith, & Dowd 2005). Specifically, first-year college students with high levels of inattention reported more difficulties with social relationships, conduct problems, alcohol-related problems, and depression. In contrast, students who were impulsive showed greater deficits in academic performance, increased difficulties with social relationships, and a greater number of hours spent consuming alcohol.

As adults, individuals with ADHD show greater interpersonal problems, problems with traffic violations and accidents, vocational difficulties, and a higher rate of smoking than the general population (Barkley, Gordon, & Goldstein 2002).

Treatment for ADHD

A multimodal approach (i.e., combining various treatment approaches) to treatment of ADHD symptoms is recommended as the best way to treat the disorder (Smith, Barkley, & Shapiro 2006). That is, to fully address symptoms characteristic of ADHD it is necessary to provide treatment in a variety of ways, which may include a combination of medicine, educational, behavioral, and psychological interventions.

Medicines

Although the first treatments that should be used with ADHD are behavioral, currently most children with moderate to severe ADHD are treated with medication (Molina et al. 2009). Over the past 30 years, methylphenidate, which is the active ingredient in Ritalin, has been the most commonly prescribed drug for ADHD. Many other stimulants are on the market; and Adderall, which is a mixture of amphetamine salts, has become commonplace in addressing ADHD symptoms. Straterra may achieve its effects in a method somewhat different than stimulants but can be equally effective. Most physicians agree that the stimulant drugs noted above, especially long-acting versions that are taken once a day (e.g., Concerta and Adderall XR), are the first-choice medications for ADHD because they continue to show effect throughout the day without the need for a "booster dose." Classic stimulants are considered rapid acting and produce effects within 30 to 45 minutes following oral ingestion, peaking in their effectiveness within two to four hours. To maintain a consistent medication level in the individual's system, it is often necessary to administer medication two to three times a day.

Studies suggest that providing low doses of behavioral interventions (e.g., daily report cards) with medication allow for lower doses of medication to be clinically effective. This avoids many of the dose-dependent side effects of medication and allows for a more varied and sustainable intervention/medication treatment plan. Controlled trials or drug "holidays" can be tried occasionally to see if medication is still needed, with a well-implemented behavior plan providing clinically meaningful information as well as therapeutic support.

Unproven or Disproven Treatments

Treatments for ADHD can be categorized as either evidence based, untested, or disproven. While experts researching the treatment and management of ADHD have identified several empirically proven forms of treatment for the disorder, many organizations and specialists continue to promote untested or even disproven therapies in the treatment of ADHD. Implementing non-evidence-based treatment for ADHD symptoms often results in a failure to reduce impairment and may actually result in a worsening of symptoms.

Disproven treatment approaches for ADHD include elimination diets (e.g., the removal of sugar, additives, or dyes from the individual's food intake), megavitamins and minerals, sensory integration training, chiropractic skull manipulation, play therapy, biofeedback, and self-control therapies.

Conclusion

ADHD affects millions of individuals across the United States, and diagnosis, treatment, and management of this disorder should be conducted by professionals with specialization in the area. While much progress has been made in understanding ADHD, many questions remain. Scientists are currently researching the origins of ADHD, including working toward a better understanding of the genetics of ADHD and the effect of various environments on shaping the expression of ADHD symptoms. Individualized treatment responses are also being examined to help streamline intervention. The long-term effects of treatment for children with ADHD is another popular area of study.

See also Adolescence and Mental Health; Children and Mental Health; *Diagnostic and Statistical Manual of Mental Disorders* (*DSM*); Family and Mental Illness; Learning Disabilities; Neurodiversity; School Mental Health

Bibliography

American Psychiatric Association. 1980. *Diagnostic and Statistical Manual of Mental Disorders* (3rd ed.). Washington, DC: American Psychiatric Association.

American Psychiatric Association. 1987. *Diagnostic and Statistical Manual of Mental Disorders* (3rd ed., rev.). Washington, DC: American Psychiatric Association.

American Psychiatric Association. 1994. *Diagnostic and Statistical Manual of Mental Disorders* (4th ed.). Washington, DC: American Psychiatric Association.

Anastopoulos, A. D. 2011. "Evidence-Based Assessment of Attention-Deficit/Hyperactivity Disorder in Children and Adolescents." Symposium conducted at the meeting of the North Carolina Psychological Association, Chapel Hill, February.

Barkley, R. A. 2006. *Attention Deficit Hyperactivity Disorder* (3rd ed.). New York: Guilford Press.

Barkley, R. A., M. Gordon, and S. Goldstein. 2002. "Research on Comorbidity, Adaptive Functioning, and Cognitive Impairment in Adults with ADHD: Implications for a Clinical Practice." In Sam Goldstein and Anne Teeter Ellison, eds., *Clinician's Guide to Adult ADHD: Assessment and Intervention* (pp. 43–69). San Diego, CA: Academic Press.

Chess, S. 1960. "Diagnosis and Treatment of the Hyperactive Child." *New York State Journal of Medicine* 60: 2379–2385.

Douglas, V. I. 1972. "Stop, Look, and Listen: The Problem of Sustained Attention and Impulse Control in Hyperactive and Normal Children." *Canadian Journal of Behavioural Science* 4: 259–282.

Douglas, V. I. 1983. "Attention and Cognitive Problems." In M. Rutter, ed., *Developmental Neuropsychiatry* (pp. 280–329). New York: Guilford Press.

Elkins, I., S. Malone, M. Keyes, W. Iacono, and M. McGue. 2011. "The Impact of Attention-Deficit/Hyperactivity Disorder on Preadolescent Adjustment May Be Greater for Girls Than for Boys." *Journal of Clinical Child and Adolescent Psychology* 40(4): 532–545.

Frazier, T., E. Youngstrom, J. Glutting, and M. Watkins. 2007. "ADHD and Achievement: Meta-Analysis of the Child, Adolescent, and Adult Literatures and a Concomitant Study with College Students." *Journal of Learning Disabilities* 40(1): 49–65.

Langberg, J., B. Molina, L. Arnold, J. Epstein, and M. Altaye. 2011. "Patterns and Predictors of Adolescent Academic Achievement and Performance in a Sample of Children with Attention-Deficit/Hyperactivity Disorder." *Journal of Clinical Child and Adolescent Psychology* 40(4): 519–531.

Mahone., E. M. 2011. "Study of Preschool Children with ADHD Finds Brain Differences Linked to Symptoms." Retrieved from http://add.about.com/od/researchstudies/a/Study-Of -Preschool-Children-With-Adhd-Finds-Brain-Differences-Linked-To-Symptoms.htm.

Mahone, E. M., and E. L. Wodka. 2008. "The Neurobiological Profile of Girls with ADHD." *Developmental Disabilities Research Reviews* 14: 276–284.

Molina, B., S. Hinshaw, J. Swanson, L. Arnold, B. Vitiello, P. Jensen, J. Epstein, B. Hoza, L. Hechtman, H. Abikoff, G. Elliott, L. Greenhill, J. Newcome, K. Wells, T. Wigal, R. Gibbons, K. Hur, P. Houck, and MTA Cooperative Group. 2009. "The MTA at 8 Years: Prospective Follow-Up of Children Treated for Combined Type ADHD in a Multisite Study." *Journal of the American Academy of Child and Adolescent Psychiatry* 48: 454–500.

Pender, C. 2005. "*DSM-IV* ADHD Dimensions of Inattention and Hyperactivity/Impulsivity as Predictors of Functioning in First-Year College Students." Unpublished master's thesis, University of South Carolina, Columbia.

Pender, C., B. Smith, and H. Dowd. 2005. *DSM-IV AD/HD Dimensions of Inattention and Hyperactivity/Impulsivity as Predictors of Functioning in First Year College Students.* Unpublished manuscript.

Smith, B., R. Barkley, and C. Shapiro. 2006. "Attention-Deficit/Hyperactivity Disorder." In E. Mash and R. Barkley, eds., *Treatment of Childhood Mental Disorders* (3rd ed., pp. 65–132). New York: Guilford Press.

Smith, B., D. Waschbusch, M. Willoughby, and S. Evans. 2000. "The Efficacy, Safety, and Practicality of Treatments for Adolescents with Attention-Deficit/Hyperactivity Disorder." *Clinical Child and Family Psychology Review* 3: 243–267.

Strauss, A. A., and L. E. Lehtinen. 1947. *Psychopathology and Education of the Brain-Injured Child.* New York: Grune & Stratton.

Resources

American Academy of Child and Adolescent Psychiatry. http://www.aacap.org.

American Academy of Pediatrics. ADHD. http://www2.aap.org/healthtopics/adhd.cfm.

American Psychological Association. ADHD. http://www.apa.org/topics/adhd/index.aspx.

Attention Deficit Disorder Association (ADDA). http://www.add.org.

Centers for Disease Control and Prevention (U.S.). Attention Deficit Hyperactivity Disorder (ADHD). http://www.cdc.gov/ncbddd/adhd.

Children and Adults with Attention Deficit/Hyperactivity Disorders (CHADD). http://www.chadd.org.

National Institute of Mental Health. ADHD. Retrieved from http://www.nimh.nih.gov/healthinformation/adhdmenu.cfm.

National Research Center on ADHD. (A Program of CHADD). http://www.help4adhd.org.

Autism Spectrum Disorders

Ruth E. Cook

Given the media attention it receives today, it is astonishing to realize that autism was once thought to be a rare disorder. It received little attention until 1943 when psychiatrist Leo Kanner identified the unique features of this disorder in each of 11 children he observed at Johns Hopkins Hospital in Baltimore. Since then, our knowledge of autism, or what are now termed autism spectrum disorders (ASDs), has expanded considerably. Even so, scientists, parents, teachers, and therapists continue to be baffled about the causes of the apparent increased prevalence of these pervasive developmental disorders. Fortunately, research is finding that early and intensive intervention leads to improvement in development.

Autism Spectrum Disorders: What Are They?

Autism spectrum disorders (ASDs) range from a severe form, called autistic disorder, to a milder form, Asperger syndrome. When reading about these disorders, one should keep in mind that the term "autism" is often used either specifically to refer to autistic disorder or more generally to denote ASD. No two individuals with ASD have identical symptoms. A symptom may be mild in one person and severe in another, with wide variations in abilities. Some individuals demonstrate near- or above-average intellectual and communication abilities while others are severely developmentally delayed and totally lack spoken language skills. Therefore the term "autism spectrum disorders"(ASDs) is used to refer to the broad range of subtypes and levels of severity that fall into the category of pervasive developmental disorders (PDDs).

According to the American Psychiatric Association (APA 2000, 69), all pervasive developmental disorders are characterized by "severe and pervasive impairment in several areas of development: reciprocal social interaction skills, communication skills, or the presence of stereotyped behavior, interest, and activities." These pervasive developmental disorders range in severity, are usually diagnosed in childhood, are prevalent throughout life, and affect people from all

Autism Redefined?

Experts working on the forthcoming fifth edition of the *Diagnostic and Statistical Manual of Mental Disorders* (DSM), which identifies and describes all mental health disorders for both children and adults, are considering revising the definition of autism. The definition is important because a diagnosis of autism can open up access to services and treatment for affected individuals.

The changes being considered would narrow the definition of autism and eliminate Asperger syndrome as a separate diagnosis, folding it into autism where appropriate but also limiting its scope so that some persons now living with Asperger would no longer be considered to have a mental disorder. The changes would also drop "pervasive developmental disorder not otherwise specified" from the diagnosis. If set in place, the new definition would likely remove tens of thousands of people from the roles of those diagnosed with autism.

Some experts, including Dr. Allen Frances, who coauthored the current edition of the DSM, have stated that the broadened definitions of autism, attention-deficit hyperactivity disorder, and bipolar disorder included in that edition were mistakes with negative social consequences. Frances and others feel that the current definitions have contributed to the making of "epidemics" of these disorders and that tightening the criteria by which one qualifies for a diagnosis is merely a corrective, of sorts. In any case, a changed diagnosis will likely change people's lives as well, for better or for worse.

—*Editor*

Source: Benedict Carey, "New Definition of Autism Will Exclude Many, Study Suggests," *New York Times*, January 19, 2012, A1; K. J. Dell'Antonio, "Experts Consider Changing the Definition of Autism," *New York Times*, January 20, 2012, http://parenting.blogs.nytimes.com.

socioeconomic and ethnic backgrounds throughout the world (Simpson et al. 2005). PDD is the diagnostic category heading under which the five specific diagnoses described below are listed.

Autistic Disorder

The term "autistic disorder" refers to individuals, usually males, who exhibit these impairments prior to 36 months of age and are moderately to severely intellectually impaired. Diagnostic criteria for autistic disorder fall into three main categories: (1) qualitative social interaction impairments, (2) qualitative communication impairments, and (3) repetitive and restricted stereotyped patterns of behavior, activities, and interests (Simpson et al. 2005).

As infants, these children show little interest in being held and may not be soothed by physical closeness with caregivers. They demonstrate significant limitations in eye contact, social smiling, and interactive play. As young children, they prefer to be alone and may not show anxiety when separated from family members. However, they may become anxious when there are changes to their environment or routine. They often repeat the words they hear, demonstrate repetitive motor behavior, and have strong attachments to objects. Such children commonly demonstrate delays in or total lack of spoken language development. As they grow older, they rarely share pleasure or excitement with others and have limited social interactions. They develop few or no friendships and often exhibit persistent and repetitive ritualistic speech or behaviors.

Childhood Disintegrative Disorder

According to the *Diagnostic and Statistical Manual of Mental Disorders* (*DSM-IV-TR*; APA 2000), children diagnosed with childhood disintegrative disorder behave similarly to those of children with autism disorder. However, children within this classification grow and develop normally for a period of time. They show typical social and communicative interactions and behavior for at least two years. Then, usually between three and four years of age, they begin to display "a clinically significant loss of previously acquired social skills or adaptive behavior, bowel or bladder control, play or motor skills" (APA 2000, 77). This rare disorder occurs more often in males who may have seizures and display very low intellectual functioning. While their disintegration is progressive, they do eventually stabilize. Some are able to recover previously attained developmental skills.

Rett's Disorder

Another very rare disorder, which occurs almost exclusively in females, is Rett's disorder. After a period of apparently normal development, between 6 and 24 months, autism-like symptoms begin to appear. Head growth decelerates, motor skills deteriorate, stereotypic hand wringing and washing may begin, and she becomes socially and communicatively unresponsive. These individuals demonstrate severe impairments in language development and severe to profound mental retardation. Serious medical concerns include seizures, respiratory problems, and risk of sudden cardiac death.

Asperger Syndrome

In 1944, this syndrome was named after Dr. Hans Asperger, a Viennese physician (Gillberg 1998). The children described by Asperger had many of the same characteristics discussed by Kanner a year earlier. However, Asperger described children who were higher functioning and whose impairments were, primarily, within the area of social interaction. Asperger syndrome (AS) was generally ignored until the 1990s when the APA added the syndrome to its list of pervasive developmental disorders.

This disorder can be especially puzzling to parents and professionals as these children tend to exhibit average to above-average intelligence. These children, usually males, are often misunderstood and their behavior is misinterpreted, making it extremely difficult to diagnose. The characteristics of children and youth with AS are most easily seen in situations that are often missed in a medical setting. Such settings include (1) interactions with peers, (2) stressful situations, (3) environments where the schedule or the routine is not predictable, (4) situations where sensory stressors are apparent, and (5) entirely new situations (Myles 2005). Medical professionals need to seek information from caregivers who observe their young patients in a variety of settings over time.

Pervasive Developmental Disorder—Not Otherwise Specified (PDD-NOS)

PDD-NOS is a somewhat vaguely defined diagnostic classification that includes children who demonstrate "severe and pervasive impairment in the development of reciprocal social interaction or verbal and nonverbal communication skill" (APA 2000, 77). Children and youth within this category do not meet the criteria for the other categories and generally fall at the higher functioning end of the ASD continuum. Their impaired verbal and nonverbal communication skills and/ or stereotyped behaviors or interests do, however, interfere with development of social skills.

There is often confusion between Asperger syndrome and PDD-NOS. However, individuals with Asperger syndrome typically do not have language delays and may read precociously or have extraordinarily rich vocabularies. Nevertheless, children with Asperger syndrome still struggle with the social aspects of language and nonverbal communication. Individuals with either classification, whose behaviors are less of a determent to their daily lives, are often referred to as having "high-functioning autism."

How Prevalent Is ASD and What Are Its Causes?

The question of how many people have ASD today cannot currently be answered accurately. In fact, statistics related to prevalence are constantly changing owing to both changes in diagnostic techniques and increased public awareness. The Centers for Disease Control (CDC) estimate that approximately 1 in 110 children may have ASD (CDC 2010). Clearly, service providers are reporting dramatic increases in the numbers of children and families seeking services (Ryan et al. 2011). National organizations cite figures suggesting that, currently, ASD is the fastest-growing developmental disability.

As for causes, experts do not know exactly what lies behind ASDs. They do, however, know that an earlier theory of causation, whereby autism and related

---

Nature or Nurture?

A recent study of twins highlights the importance of environmental factors, including conditions inside the womb, for understanding autism and its causes. Such factors may be, etiologically speaking, as significant as genes.

In the study, 77 percent of male identical twins and 50 percent of female identical twins were found to fall within the autism spectrum when one of the twins was already identified as having the disorder. The comparable rates among fraternal twins, were lower; among this group, 31 percent of males and 36 percent of females were found to fall within the spectrum.

The more unusual finding, however, was that only 38 percent of the autism cases identified could be attributed to genetic factors, whereas a full 58 percent could be attributed to shared environmental factors. Previous studies had suggested a genetic cause in as much as 90 percent of the cases. Because of this unexpected finding, and because rates of autism among non-twin siblings are far lower than those for fraternal or identical twins, researchers surmise that conditions inside the womb must play a key role in the development of the disorder.

Source: Laurie Tarkan, "Autism Study Finds Link to Environment," *New York Times*, July 5, 2011, A11.

---

disabilities were said to be caused by cold and unresponsive caregivers ("refrigerator mothers"), is demonstrably false.

The basis of vulnerability to ASD appears to be neurophysiological. Through brain scans, researchers have found abnormalities in brain structure and function. Although the search for specific autism genes is under way, scientists believe that genetic inheritance is not the sole contributor to autism. In fact, ASD is generally believed to involve a complex interaction between genes and environmental factors (Alterogt, Hanson, & Leshner 2008; Steenhuysen 2011).

The numerous causative or complicating factors currently being investigated include allergies to food and medicines, gastrointestinal abnormalities, and maternal exposure to mercury or antidepressants. Even the ages of fathers as well as mothers at conception are considered as possible contributing factors. Since autism is considered to be a spectrum of disorders, it is likely that there are multiple causes. It is encouraging to realize that a wide range of causative possibilities is being researched.

How Are Autism Spectrum Disorders Diagnosed?

While the causes of what appears to be a dramatic rise in the number of children and youth with ASD are the subject of much debate and study, experts are in agreement on one thing: early diagnosis and intervention are crucial to the possibility of a good prognosis.

There is currently no single test to diagnose ASD. There are no definitive biological signs or symptoms of ASD. In fact, as the name "autism spectrum disorder" suggests, ASDs cover a wide range of behaviors and abilities. Children with ASD develop at different rates in different areas of growth. They might show lags in language, social skills, and cognitive skills while their motor skills might be on target. Some children with ASD can learn a hard skill before they learn an easy one. Although they may be good at things like putting puzzle pieces together, they might have trouble with developing a skill that is easy for others, like talking with other children.

ASD is diagnosed through careful observation/assessment of behavior and knowledge of the individual's developmental history. Parents and pediatricians who suspect that a child might have a pervasive developmental disorder are encouraged to seek further evaluation from qualified professionals such as neurologists and psychiatrists who are familiar with this group of disorders.

Early Clues

In infancy, signals for formal developmental evaluation include no babbling, pointing, or other gestures by 12 months of age, no single words by 16 months of age and no two-word spontaneous phrases by 24 months of age. Loss of previously learned language or social skills is an important high-risk signal at any age.

Behavioral Criteria

To receive a diagnosis of autism or a related disorder, children must meet a certain number of the behavioral criteria as described in the *DSM-IV-TR* (APA 2000). As these criteria are more applicable to children around the age of three or older, diagnosis at an earlier age is difficult. In general, even though ASDs involve a wide spectrum of symptoms, individuals do have three common areas of deficit: communication problems, impaired social relationships, and unusual patterns of behavior. Communication skills and social interactions are not simply delayed or similar to that of a younger child. Instead, they are often unusual or even bizarre. The behaviors and communication cues of children with ASD are frequently very difficult to interpret.

To identify conditions of ASD as soon as possible, screening in infancy is essential (Ozonoff, Rogers, & Hendren 2003). Clinicians should pay particular attention to young children who do not look at faces and avoid eye contact, who do not attempt to imitate others, who do not respond when called by their name, who do not attempt to show objects to others by pointing at things, and who do not, in general, show interest in others. To focus on such behavioral symptoms, collaboration with caregivers is essential. While language delays are the symptom that most commonly captures the attention of parents, problems in other areas of development hold the key to being able to recognize behavioral signs at earlier and earlier ages. As children become preschoolers, parents may notice that children line up toys rather than play with them, and may become obsessive about watching and rewatching segments of a particular DVD. Older children who are verbal may obsess in talking about particular topics of interest.

Once high-risk signals have been recognized, children must be referred for more intensive evaluation that should include a formal audiological assessment and screening for lead poisoning. A complete evaluation is a comprehensive multidisciplinary process usually beginning with the pediatrician who ensures that a thorough family history and medical and neurological evaluation are completed. In addition to the pediatrician and audiologist, this multidisciplinary process can include one or more of the following professionals: psychologists, neurologists, speech-language pathologists, child psychiatrists, occupational therapists, and physical therapists as well as special educators. Included below are some of the areas of focus for these specialists who must be clinically knowledgeable of the unique characteristics of autism spectrum disorders.

Speech-Language and Communication Evaluations   Comprehensive assessment of both preverbal and verbal individuals should include both receptive and expressive language and communication, voice and speech production, and in verbal individuals, a collection and analysis of spontaneous language samples to augment scores on formal language tests. Specific attention will be paid to whether or not available speech and language skills are functional and appropriate.

Cognitive and Adaptive Behavior Evaluations   Cognitive instruments used by trained psychologists should provide a full range of standard scores that do not depend on social ability and should include independent measures of verbal and nonverbal abilities. A measure of adaptive functioning such as the Vineland Adaptive Behavior Scales (Sparrow, Cicchetti, & Balla 2005) should be included.

Sensorimotor and Occupational Therapy Evaluations   Experienced occupational or physical therapists assess fine and gross motor development, sensory processing abilities, tactile sensitivity, unusual or stereotyped mannerisms, and the impact of these elements on the individual's life. Occupational therapists should be concerned with how well the individual can function with daily life requirements including those of play or leisure activities, self-care, or work tasks.

Neuropsychological, Behavioral, and Academic Assessments   These assessments should be performed as needed and should include social skills and relationships, educational functioning, learning style, motivation and reinforcement, and self-regulation. Knowledge from such assessment is absolutely necessary to those who select services and planning appropriate intervention/instructional activities.

The Importance on Screening and Diagnosis

As young children with ASD can respond to their environment in both positive and negative ways and with behavior that is inconsistent, a common mistake is often made. That mistake comes from the "wait and see" mentality. Because early intervention can be effective, it is essential that professionals and parents avoid any delay in treatment. Parents' concerns should not be dismissed.

Which Disorders Most Commonly Accompany ASD?

Accompanying or comorbid disorders often have medical implications and treatment needs separate from those for the general characteristics of ASD. For example, a high percentage of individuals with ASD have some form of sleeping disorder. Lack of sleep and the resulting fatigue can exacerbate symptoms. It is important to be aware of the side effects of medications and the effect of the caffeine found in sodas and chocolate.

A significant portion of children with ASD also suffer from a seizure disorder such as epilepsy. Even if seizures are not serious, they can increase anxiety and heighten communication difficulties. As there are medications that can control seizures, it is essential that medical assistance be acquired immediately when seizures present themselves. Other medical conditions that can co-occur with ASD are fragile X syndrome, neurofibromatosis, tuberous sclerosis, and phenylketonuria. Close collaboration with medical practitioners is essential in handling conditions of comorbidity.

Although children with ASD have been found, as a group, to hear as well as other children, they may have auditory processing problems. Such processing problems may prevent them from understanding the meaning of sounds they hear, or distinguishing sounds in the foreground from sounds in the background. These problems may have a negative impact on academic performance and should be considered when assigning seats in the classroom or setting up the environment for a child expected to complete his or her homework.

Children with ASD have a high rate of pica, or the tendency to eat inappropriate substances such as soil, paint, and paint chips (Tierney 2004). This tendency can lead to bowel obstruction and the possibility of overexposure to lead. Thus the importance of tests for lead poisoning during screening and diagnosis is obvious. Other conditions of comorbidity include depression and anxiety disorders, especially with Asperger syndrome. Gastrointestinal disorders, higher rates of food allergies, and problems with attention and concentration are often reported by parents. Surprisingly, whether a tendency toward attention deficit hyperactivity disorder is a symptom of ASD or a separate disorder is yet to be determined.

Many autistic children have unusual sensitivities to sounds, sights, touch, taste, and smells. High-pitched intermittent sounds, such as fire alarms or school bells, may be painful to autistic children. Sensitivity to tactile and auditory stimuli may be responsible for the child's withdrawal or avoidance of social interaction, as well as difficulty tolerating certain sounds and processing speech. This avoidance, in turn, can interfere with the processes of attachment and development of social skills, as well as with the development of communication skills.

Putting together the comprehensive puzzle of causality and the implications of disorders as complicated as those of ASD is not easy. Future discoveries may make it possible for clinicians to break these disorders into more discrete elements that lend themselves more readily to effective treatment.

What Educational Interventions and Strategies Are Effective?

Even though every individual diagnosed with a spectrum disorder may be different, the families of these individuals all face the same overwhelming challenge of finding the best treatment or intervention for each complex condition. This dilemma was underscored by the National Research Council's report published in 2001 in which a committee of experts who were charged with the task of integrating the scientific, theoretical and policy literature concluded "there are virtually no data on the relative merit of one model (of intervention) over another" (Lord & McGee 2001, 171–172).

Nevertheless, there are a number of intervention approaches that are showing positive changes in children who receive intensive services from an early age. It is important to note that these interventions tend to focus on various aspects of the disorders, and on different developmental domains. Because of the variability in the targeted skill areas, the underlying theoretical assumptions, and the strategies employed, the selection of a particular approach (or combination of approaches) should depend on the needs and characteristics of each individual with ASD, and the concerns and preferences of family members.

Although research does not conclude that there is one best model of intervention, it does suggest that "several features shared by most efficacious treatments, regardless of model, philosophy, or type, have been identified: *they begin early, are intensive (at least 25 hours a week), are individualized and developmentally appropriate, and are family centered, involving parents at every level*" (Ozonoff, Rogers, & Hendren 2003, 23; emphasis added). The best programs are those that incorporate a variety of multidisciplinary best practices based on individual needs.

Features of Program Effectiveness

To promote scientifically validated methods of instruction for children and youth with ASD, the Committee on Educational Interventions for Children with Autism, Division of Behavioral and Social Sciences and Education, National Research Council provided a list of program features that the committee found to be critical to the effectiveness of the early intervention experience for young children (Lord & McGee 2001). These include:

- Entry into the program as soon as possible after diagnosis
- Active engagement in intensive instructional programming for the equivalent of a full school day, five days a week with full-year participation available depending on age/developmental level
- Repeated, planned teaching opportunities organized around relatively brief periods of time
- Sufficient amounts of adult attention in one-to-one and small-group settings to meet individualized goals
- Inclusion of a family education component
- Low student/teacher ratios (no more than two young children per adult)
- Strategies for ongoing program evaluation and assessment of individual children's progress, with program adjustments made accordingly

The committee also prioritizes six foci of interventions. These include focus on functional, spontaneous communication; social instruction that is delivered throughout the day in various settings; the teaching of interactive play skills; instruction that facilitates the development and transfer of cognitive skills; positive, contextual behavioral support; and focus on functional academic skills.

In an attempt to assist parents in recognizing when educational practices are linked to scientifically based research, Simpson and colleagues (2005) published a critique of the most commonly used interventions and treatments for individuals with autism-related disabilities. This and future publications designed to foster the implementation of evidence-based interventions will be an invaluable assistance in helping parents and professionals choose effective intervention approaches while avoiding various fads and "quick-fix" solutions.

See also Attention Deficit Hyperactivity Disorder; Children and Mental Health; Chronic Mental Illness; Creativity and Mental Health; Genetics and Mental Health; Neurodiversity

Bibliography

Alterogt, B. M., S. L. Hanson, and A. I. Leshner. 2008. "Autism and the Environment: Challenges and Opportunities for Research." *Pediatrics* 121: 1225–1229.

American Psychiatric Association. 2000. *Diagnostic and Statistical Manual of Mental Disorders* (4th ed., text rev.). Washington, DC: American Psychiatric Publishing.

Bazelon, E. 2007. "What Autistic Girls Are Made Of." *New York Times Magazine*. August 5. Retrieved from http://www.nytimes.com/2007/08/05/magazine/05autism-t .html.

Bernier, R., and J. Gerdts. 2010. *Autism Spectrum Disorders: A Reference Handbook*. Santa Barbara, CA: ABC-CLIO/Greenwood.

Centers for Disease Control and Prevention. 2010. "Prevalence of Autism Spectrum Disorders." MMWR Surveillance Summaries, 56 (SS-1). Retrieved from http://www.cdc.gov/mmwr/indss_2007.html.

Gillberg, C. 1998. "Asperger Syndrome and High Functioning Autism." *British Journal of Psychiatry* 172: 200–209.

Kanner, Leo. 1943/1985. "Autistic Disturbances of Affective Contact." *The Nervous Child* 2: 217–250. Reprinted in A. M. Donnellan, ed., *Classic Readings in Autism* (pp. 11–53). New York: Teachers College Press.

Lord, Catherine, and James P. McGee. 2001. *Educating Children with Autism.* Washington, DC: National Academy Press.

Myles, Brenda Smith. 2005. *Children and Youth with Asperger Syndrome.* Thousand Oaks, CA: Corwin Press.

National Autism Association. http://www.nationalautismassociation.org.

Ozonoff, S., S. J. Rogers, and R. L. Hendren. 2003. *Autism Spectrum Disorders: A Research Review for Practitioners.* Washington, DC: American Psychiatric Publishing.

Public Law 107-110. Washington, DC: U.S. Government Printing Office.

Ryan, J. B., E. M. Hughes, A. Katsiyannis, M. McDaniel, and C. Sprinkle. 2011. "Research-Based Educational Practices for Students with Autism Spectrum Disorders." *Teaching Exceptional Children* 20: 56–64.

Simpson, Richard L., S. R. deBoer-Ott, D. E. Griswold, B. S. Myles, S. E. Byrd, J. B. Ganz, K. T. Cook, K. L. Otten, J. Ben-Arieh, S. A. Kline, and L. G. Adams, L. G. 2005. *Autism Spectrum Disorders.* Thousand Oaks, CA: Corwin Press.

Sparrow, S., D. Cicchetti, and D. Balla. 2005. *Vineland Adaptive Behavior Scales (Vineland II).* San Antonio, TX: Pearson/PsychCorp.

Steenhuysen, Julie. 2011. "Environment, Not Just Genetics, at Play in Autism," Retrieved from http://www.reuters.com/article/2011/07/04/us-autism-environment -idUSTRE7634Y220110704.

Tierney, E. "Co-Morbidity in Autism." 2004. *The Exceptional Parent* 34: 60–63.

B

Behavioral Theories and Therapies

Nicole A. Adamson, Matthew J. Paylo, Leah Gongola, and Victoria E. Kress

Behavioral theory is a classic psychotherapeutic approach that focuses on analyzing and altering human behaviors based upon a pattern of actions and related consequences. This theory operates under the basic premise that human behavior is learned (Corey 2009). Thus through the use of proven techniques, undesirable behavior can be replaced by teaching new, more desirable behaviors. Several behavioral therapies are commonly accepted as effective treatments for a wide range of mental health needs, including (but not limited to) disruptive child and adolescent behavior, spousal abuse, irrational fears and phobias, and mood disorders such as anxiety and depression (Corey 2009; Lazarus 1997; Vargas 2009).

Key Concepts

All behavioral therapies have certain elements or characteristic in common. First, all such therapies rely on models of behavior change that are based upon empirically supported learning principles. Learning theory asserts that changes in thinking can alter internal processes, and overt behaviors will consequently be altered (Vargas 2009). This process occurs through respondent or operant conditioning. Respondent conditioning describes the process whereby behaviors are completed in response to a stimulus. Operant conditioning refers to the process by which a behavior is completed in anticipation of an often desirable consequence.

Second, behavioral therapists reject the idea that mental health issues and daily difficulties are the result of a disease. In fact, they place no emphasis on why or how problems develop; they care only about factors that currently influence a behavior and its continuation. Behavioral therapists do not believe it is fruitful to work on developing a client's insight. They believe that with behavior change alone, people will begin to feel better and that as they do, greater self-awareness may be developed. Thus insight is never a goal of behavioral therapy because even without insight, people are generally able to make required changes to their behavior.

All behaviorists have a commitment to the scientific method and value its use in helping clients change their behaviors. They also believe in the use of the scientific method as a means of assessing the efficacy of treatments and specific interventions. In other words, specific behaviors are targeted for change, and applied interventions are used to overcome these behaviors with a constant eye toward evaluating their effectiveness.

Additionally, behavioral therapists believe that the counseling relationship is necessary to create enduring client change. In other words, without a strong client-counselor relationship, a foundation for change is not present and clients may not optimally benefit from treatment interventions. However, behavioral therapists do not believe that enduring client change is achieved solely through the therapeutic relationship; rather, this relationship is only a vehicle for change to occur. Through this relationship, behavioral therapists believe that clients come to trust the mental health counselor, and thus they are open to their interventions. Especially since behavioral therapy requires clients to be active and complete assigned homework, a solid client-counselor relationship is important.

Related to this idea, behavioral therapies are active; they require clients to be active participants in the counseling process. Clients need to be participatory and learn new skills and ways to create behavioral changes. Clients need to track and monitor their behaviors and apply skills and new behaviors learned in session to situations outside of the session.

Classical Conditioning

Classical conditioning (i.e., respondent conditioning) was first demonstrated by Russian physiologist Ivan Pavlov in 1927. Pavlov's initial research on the digestive system of dogs switched to focus on salivation after he observed that the dogs began to salivate every time a laboratory assistant opened the door to feed them.

Behaviorism's Emergence

John Watson, the early twentieth-century American psychologist, is given the most credit for founding behaviorism. He was dissatisfied with the psychology of the time, complaining that psychology was slipshod compared to other sciences such as physics, chemistry, and biology. Watson was disenchanted with two aspects of psychology: the subject matter and the methods of study or research. In 1913, Watson published a paper titled "Psychology as the Behaviourist Views It," which is nicknamed the "Behaviorist Manifesto." The paper outlined his vision of the field, stating that only behavior should be the object of study in psychology (the study of emotions, thoughts, etc., would be the realm of another field such as philosophy) and study procedures should be objective. He added a third goal for the field: research in psychology should always be applied; that is, when a psychologist pursues a research question, he or she should have a particular application in mind for the research rather than studying simply for curiosity's sake.

—Gretchen Reevy

As a result, Pavlov conducted a series of experiments that showed how respondent behavior such as salivation occurs in response to a specific stimulus such as food (Vargas 2009). To begin the experiments, Pavlov presented a neutral stimulus (e.g., a bell) to the dogs and found that this had no effect on their salivation. Next, he paired the sound of the bell (i.e., neutral stimulus) along with the unconditioned stimulus (UCS) of food, which elicited the unconditioned response (UCR) of salivation. After pairing the bell and food for several trials, the dogs began salivating in response to the bell. As a result the bell became a conditioned stimulus (CS), and the conditioned response (CR) of salivation was established.

Operant Conditioning

Operant conditioning, traditionally associated with B. F. Skinner (1976), is the conceptual underpinning of applied behavior analysis (ABA) and refers to the process and effects of consequences (i.e., reinforcement or punishment) behavior. A functional consequence is a result that follows a given behavior and alters the frequency of that behavior in the future. If the future frequency of a behavior has increased, positive or negative *reinforcement* has taken place. Positive reinforcement occurs when a stimulus (or "reward") is added to the environment immediately following a behavior, while negative reinforcement occurs when a stimulus (particularly an undesirable stimulus) is removed from the environment immediately following a behavior. By contrast, if the future frequency of a behavior has decreased, positive or negative *punishment* has taken place. Generally, operant conditioning is most often referred to as the strengthening of behavior and should focus on the use and effects of reinforcement.

Therapeutic Techniques

Applied Behavior Analysis

Applied behavior analysis (ABA) is a science in which the principles of behavior are applied to improve socially significant behavior to a meaningful degree (Cooper, Heron, & Heward 2007). The framework of ABA encompasses many interventions, including reinforcement, prompting, stimulus control, shaping, and fading (Dunlap et al. 2008). ABA methods are used to teach new skills, to reinforce and maintain already learned skills, and to restrict or minimize conditions under which interfering behaviors occur. In addition, data are continuously collected and analyzed to evaluate intervention effectiveness and to formulate treatment decisions.

Relaxation Training

The essence of relaxation training is that an individual cannot be anxious and relaxed at the same time. Therefore relaxation training is the gradual tensing and

Experimental psychologist B. F. Skinner trains a rat in a Skinner Box, which illustrates the principle of reinforcement by rewarding the rats with food when they press a lever; Harvard University, 1964. (Nina Leen/Time & Life Pictures/Getty Images.)

relaxing of major muscle groups (i.e., legs, stomach, chest, shoulders, arms, neck, and face) combined with deep breathing in an attempt to become increasingly more relaxed. These techniques are often taught to individuals experiencing more than expected amounts of stress, fear, and/or anxiety. Relaxation training can be done as a stand-alone intervention or in conjunction with the process of systematic desensitization.

Systematic Desensitization

Systematic desensitization is a behavioral treatment grounded in classical conditioning that is used for fears, anxieties, and phobias. To begin the process, a client must identify a hierarchy of situations from least to most fearful in conjunction with being taught relaxation and coping strategies. Next, the client is prompted to imagine anxiety-producing situations beginning with the least fearful. The goal of the systematic desensitization process is for the client to use relaxation and coping strategies to gradually extinguish anxiety-producing fears. Client treatment traditionally begins with visualization procedures and gradually progresses to in vivo ("live") situations.

In Vivo Exposure

In vivo exposure, also called flooding, refers to the re-creation of a situation that occurs in an individual's actual environment and that creates a great deal of anxiety, fear, and/or stress. The individual desires to overcome the debilitating nature of these situations, and through the aid of a mental health clinician can do so through the re-creation of that situation in a controlled environment. There are two types of in vivo exposure: (1) gradual exposure, and (2) direct exposure (i.e., flooding). In the gradual approach, individuals learn and practice relaxation techniques as they are gradually exposed to stressful or anxiety-provoking things or situations. This process systematically builds up to the anxiety-provoking situations or things over the course of many sessions. In direct exposure (i.e., flooding), the individual is presented all at once with the stressful or anxiety-provoking stimulus. The rationale for this approach is that an individual's anxiety level will reach an apex and then dissipate. This realization will provide the individual with an experience for overcoming his or her fear, stress, or anxiety.

Social Skills Training

The central aim of social skills training is to facilitate and improve an individual's ability to communicate and interact with other human beings. Behaviorists contend that since social skills are learned behaviors, individuals can improve and correct those patterns of behaving (i.e., socialization) through operant conditioning, modeling, and role plays. The intention behind utilizing social skills training is that if individuals correct their maladaptive behaviors in social situations, they can reduce their level of stress and anxiety and begin to resolve their social interaction problems. Such training is used, for example, in cases of social anxiety disorder (social phobia).

Strengths and Limitations of Behavioral Therapies

Behavioral theory is a classic psychotherapeutic approach with empirically supported value in the mental health community. Behavioral therapies are effectively used to analyze and alter undesirable human behaviors. All behavioral therapies are based upon learning theory and share a similar foundation. Behavioral theory can be applied in a variety of settings and is effective with a broad range of mental health difficulties ranging from mood disorders to antisocial behaviors. However, behavioral therapy is most effective in the presence of a trusting therapeutic relationship and it does not address past events or insights that may be important to the client's success. Overall, behavioral theory is commonly accepted as a valuable addition to the mental health field and continues to be regarded as holding promise for future improvement.

See also Clinical Psychology; Cognitive-Behavioral Therapy; Mental Health Counseling; Psychotherapy

Bibliography

Cooper, J., T. Heron, and W. Heward. 2007. *Applied Behavior Analysis* (2nd ed.). Upper Saddle River, NJ: Prentice-Hall.

Corey, G. 2009. *Theory and Practice of Counseling and Psychotherapy* (8th ed.). Monterey, CA: Brooks/Cole.

Dunlap, G., E. G. Carr, R. H. Horner, J. R. Zarcone, and I. Schwartz. 2008. "Positive Behavior Support and Applied Behavior Analysis: A Familial Alliance." *Behavior Modification* 32(5): 682–698.

Lazarus, A. A. 1997. *Brief but Comprehensive Psychotherapy.* New York: Springer.

Mills, J. A. 1998. *Control: A History of Behavioral Psychology.* New York: New York University Press.

Skinner, B. F. 1976. *About Behaviorism.* New York: Vintage.

Vargas, J. 2009. *Behavior Analysis for Effective Teaching.* New York: Routledge.

Bipolar Disorder

Linda Wasmer Andrews

Bipolar disorder—formerly known as manic depression—is a mental disorder that causes unusual shifts in mood, energy, and ability to function. People with bipolar disorder alternate between moods that are overly low (depression) and overly high (mania). The shifts are more serious and disabling than the normal ups and downs that everyone experiences in day-to-day life.

Left untreated, bipolar disorder can damage relationships and wreak havoc with life at home, work, or school. People with the disorder have an increased risk of suicide and substance abuse. During manic periods, many also engage in self-destructive behaviors, such as reckless driving, unsafe sex, and spending sprees. In severe cases, some people even experience psychotic symptoms, such as delusions (distorted beliefs that are seriously out of touch with reality) and hallucinations (sensory perceptions of things that are not really there).

The dramatic mood swings of bipolar disorder can last for weeks or months, creating chaos not only for the person with the illness, but also for family and friends. Even once the person gets better, the disorder tends to recur, and without treatment, it usually gets worse with time.

Fortunately, effective help is available. In most cases, proper treatment can reduce the frequency and severity of bipolar episodes and help people lead happier, healthier lives. But like diabetes and asthma, bipolar disorder is a chronic condition that requires long-term treatment. Often, that means lifelong attention to managing the disorder.

Having an Episode

The overly high and low periods seen in bipolar disorder are known as episodes. These episodes can take four different forms: mania, hypomania, major depression and mixed.

Mania

During an episode of mania, people experience an excessively high, grandiose, or irritable mood that lasts for at least a week. (This time requirement is waived if the symptoms are severe enough to necessitate hospitalization.) When the person's mood is high or grandiose, at least three of the following symptoms must be present: (1) inflated self-esteem or exaggerated ideas about oneself, (2) decreased need for sleep, (3) unusual talkativeness or a feeling of pressure to keep talking, (4) racing thoughts or abrupt changes of topic when speaking, (5) easy distractibility, (6) increased activity or restlessness, and (7) excessive involvement in pleasurable but high-risk activities, such as sexual indiscretions or risky investments. If the person's mood is only irritable, at least four of these seven symptoms must occur. The symptoms cause marked problems in daily life or personal relationships, reach psychotic proportions, or require hospitalization to prevent harm to self or others.

Hypomania

The symptoms of hypomania are the same as those for mania, but they have to last only a minimum of four days. Also, although the person's mood is clearly

Bipolar Financial Markets

Psychologist Alden Cass has examined the ups and downs of financial markets and the parallel ups and downs of the stockbrokers involved in them. Cass discovered a kind of feedback loop between the markets and the moods of the traders. When the traders were depressed, they made fewer sales calls to potential investors, causing the market to decline, or become "sad," in effect. When the traders were "up," on the other hand, they made more sales calls and attracted more new money to the market, further pushing up share prices. In fact, observes Cass, in times of market highs the brokers showed symptoms of mania: they slept less, they harbored delusions of grandeur, they took greater risks, and they abused drugs at an increased rate. They felt that they could do no wrong. During market lows, in contrast, testing by Cass showed that symptoms of clinical depression were evident in 23 percent of the traders he studied, as compared with 7 percent of men in general.

—Editor

Source: Joshua Chaffin, "How Brokers with the Blues May Add to Market Miseries: Clinical Depression on Wall Street Can Affect Share Prices," *Financial Times*, March 8, 2002, 20.

different from usual, the change is not drastic enough to seriously impair functioning, necessitate hospitalization, or lead to psychotic symptoms. In fact, the milder burst of energy associated with hypomania may feel good to the person and lead to greater productivity. Even when family and friends come to recognize the mood swings as a problem, the person may deny that anything is wrong. Without treatment, however, hypomania sometimes turns into more severe mania or switches into depression.

Major Depression

In an episode of major depression, people have one or both of two core symptoms: (1) a low mood nearly all the time and (2) loss of interest or enjoyment in almost everything. At the same time, they may experience associated problems: (3) changes in weight or appetite, (4) trouble sleeping or oversleeping, (5) restless activity or slowed- down movements, (6) constant tiredness or lack of energy, (7) feelings of worthlessness or inappropriate guilt, (8) difficulty concentrating or making decisions, and (9) recurring thoughts of death or suicide. All told, at least five of the nine symptoms must be present for a minimum of two weeks. The symptoms are serious enough to cause significant distress or problems in daily life.

Mixed

During a mixed episode, a person simultaneously experiences the symptoms of both mania and major depression nearly every day for at least one week.

The person may be in a very down, hopeless mood while at the same time feeling highly energized. Common features of a mixed state include restlessness, trouble sleeping, changes in appetite, thoughts of suicide, and psychotic symptoms.

Criteria for Diagnosis

The symptoms of bipolar disorder are defined by the *Diagnostic and Statistical Manual of Mental Disorders*, fourth edition, text revision (*DSM-IV-TR*), a diagnostic guidebook published by the American Psychiatric Association and widely used by mental health professionals from many disciplines. According to the *DSM-IV-TR*, there are three types of bipolar disorder: bipolar I, bipolar II, and bipolar disorder not otherwise specified.

Bipolar I

This is the classic form of bipolar disorder, characterized by the occurrence of at least one manic or mixed episode. Often, but not always, there also has been an episode of major depression.

Bipolar II

In this form of bipolar disorder, the person has never had a full-fledged manic or mixed episode. Instead, there has been at least one episode of hypomania as well as at least one of major depression.

Bipolar Disorder Not Otherwise Specified

This catchall category includes other forms of bipolar illness that cause problems serious enough to need treatment but do not meet all the criteria for bipolar I, bipolar II, or cyclothymia (a disorder characterized by moods that alternate between hypomania and relatively mild depression). For example, some people have all the symptoms of mania or major depression, but they move so quickly from one mood to the other that they do not fulfill the time requirements. Others have repeated episodes of hypomania without alternating periods of depression. And many children and young adolescents develop a mixture of mania and depression that is disruptive but does not quite qualify as a mixed episode.

Course of the Illness

Bipolar disorder can start at any age from childhood to late life. However, it typically begins in late adolescence or early adulthood. At first, it may not be recognized as an illness, and people may suffer for years before they finally get proper diagnosis and treatment.

Bipolar I

More than 90 percent of people who have a first episode of mania go on to have another one in the future. Most people with bipolar I disorder are free of symptoms between episodes, but 20 to 30 percent have some residual mood symptoms. Even those whose mood seems to return to normal often continue to have problems getting along at work, school, or in relationships.

The interval between episodes tends to shorten as time goes on. About 5 to 15 percent of people with bipolar I disorder display rapid cycling, which means they have four or more mood episodes in a single year. For some, it reaches the point of multiple episodes in a single week or even within the same day. Rapid cycling is more common in women than in men.

Bipolar II

The course of bipolar II is similar to that of bipolar I. But only about 15 percent of those with the disorder continue to have some mood symptoms and problems in daily life between episodes. Within five years, 5 to 15 percent of people with bipolar II have a manic episode, which changes their diagnosis to bipolar I.

Causes and Risk Factors

Almost 3 percent of U.S. adults have bipolar disorder in any given year, according to the National Institute of Mental Health. The occurrence rate in older adolescents seems to be similar. And the first signs of the disorder may appear even earlier, often starting out as major depression, cyclothymia, or dysthymia (a relatively mild but quite long-lasting form of depression).

Genetic factors seem to play a role. Studies of identical twins, who share the same genes, have found that if one twin has bipolar disorder, the second twin is more likely than other siblings to also develop the illness. However, even the identical twin of someone with bipolar disorder does not always become ill, indicating that genes are not the whole story.

Environmental factors that may contribute to bipolar disorder include significant losses and high stress. Some people with the disorder also may have circadian rhythms (daily biological rhythms) that are out of sync with the outside world. These circadian disruptions could help explain the sleep disturbances seen in mania and depression. It is also possible that abnormal circadian rhythms do not cause the illness but do make it worse once it starts.

Brain imaging has shown that the brains of people with bipolar disorder tend to differ from the brains of healthy individuals. For instance, bipolar disorder has been associated with a decreased number of nerve cells in part of the hippocampus, a brain structure that plays a role in learning, emotion, and memory. The disorder also has been linked to a decreased number and density of support cells in the prefrontal cortex, the part of the brain involved in higher thought, problem solving, short-term memory, and emotion.

Abnormalities in certain chemicals that act as messengers within the brain may come into play as well. Two brain chemicals that seem to play key roles in depression are serotonin and norepinephrine. The biochemical changes involved in mania are less well understood.

Treatment of Bipolar Disorder

With proper treatment, most people with bipolar disorder—even those who are severely affected—start to feel considerably better. Treatment helps even out mood swings and relieve symptoms. A combination of medication and psychotherapy is usually most effective.

Pharmacological Approaches

Medications called mood stabilizers are prescribed to help keep moods on a more even keel. Lithium, the oldest and best-known mood-stabilizing drug, is still widely prescribed. However, other medications called anticonvulsants, originally developed to help prevent seizures, also help regulate moods. For maximum effect, anticonvulsant medications may be combined with lithium or with each other. When these medications alone do not provide enough relief, newer antipsychotics, originally designed to prevent or relieve psychotic symptoms, may help slow down racing thoughts to a more manageable speed.

Antidepressants were once commonly used to treat the depression phase of bipolar disorder. However, their use is now controversial, due to evidence that they may sometimes trigger a sudden switch to mania. When insomnia is a problem, a sedative may be prescribed.

Her True Self

"One painful truth about being bipolar is that I can't excuse my manic behavior by saying 'I wasn't myself.' My true self is all over the place. I am myself when I hear voices and I am also myself when I am balanced, centered, with or without the help of medication. Medication doesn't change who I am; it simply keeps me in one place for a longer stretch of time. Being here is as vital to my creativity as being anywhere else on the continuum."

—Ren Powell

Source: Ren Powell, "My Name Is Not Alice," in Richard M. Berlin, ed., *Poets on Prozac: Mental Illness, Treatment, and the Creative Process* (Baltimore: Johns Hopkins University Press, 2008), 53.

Psychological Approaches

Psychotherapy can provide emotional support and teach useful skills to people with bipolar disorder and their families. Research has shown that appropriate psychotherapy can improve mood stability, reduce hospitalizations, and enhance the ability to get along in daily life.

Two types of psychotherapy that may be particularly helpful are cognitive-behavioral therapy (CBT) and interpersonal and social rhythm therapy. CBT helps people with bipolar disorder learn to recognize and change dysfunctional thought and behavior patterns that are contributing to their illness. Interpersonal and social rhythm therapy helps people improve their relationships and regularize their routines. Regular daily routines and sleep schedules may help ward off future episodes of mania.

Psychoeducation can help people with bipolar disorder learn how to manage their illness at home and recognize signs of a relapse so any necessary changes can be made early, before symptoms become too severe. Family therapy can help reduce the stress and conflict in family life that often results from or contributes to bipolar symptoms.

Bipolar disorder is a challenging condition to live with. Yet proper treatment can help smooth out extreme peaks and valleys in mood and behavior. With ongoing treatment, most people with bipolar disorder can look forward to a much-improved quality of life.

See also Creativity and Mental Health; Depression

Bibliography

American Psychiatric Association. 2000. *Diagnostic and Statistical Manual of Mental Disorders* (4th ed., text rev.). Washington, DC: American Psychiatric Publishing.

Evans, Dwight L., and Linda Wasmer Andrews. 2005. *If Your Adolescent Has Depression or Bipolar Disorder: An Essential Resource for Parents.* New York: Oxford University Press.

Healy, David. 2008. *Mania: A Short History of Bipolar Disorder.* Baltimore: Johns Hopkins University Press.

Jamison, Kay Redfield. 1993. *Touched with Fire: Manic-Depressive Illness and the Artistic Temperament.* New York: Free Press.

Martin, Emily. 2007. *Bipolar Expeditions: Mania and Depression in American Culture.* Princeton, NJ: Princeton University Press.

Mayo Clinic. 2010, January 5. "Bipolar Disorder." Retrieved from http://www.mayoclinic.com/health/bipolar-disorder/DS00356.

Miklowitz, David J. 2010. *The Bipolar Disorder Survival Guide* (2nd ed.). New York: Guilford Press.

Newman, Cory F., Robert L. Leahy, Aaron T. Beck, Noreen Reilly-Harrington, and Laszlo Gyulai. 2002. *Bipolar Disorder: A Cognitive Therapy Approach.* Washington, DC: American Psychological Association.

Simeonova, Diana I., Kiki D. Chang, Connie Strong, and Terence A. Ketter. 2005. "Creativity in Familial Bipolar Disorder." *Journal of Psychiatric Research* 39: 623–631.

Borderline Personality Disorder

Gretchen Reevy

People with borderline personality disorder (BPD) exhibit persistent instability in mood, interpersonal relationships, and self-image and engage in frequent impulsive behavior. These characteristics largely deteriorate one's personal, social, and occupational functioning. People with BPD have emotional lability (mood swings) accompanied by episodes of anger, depression, and anxiety, lasting anywhere from a few hours to a few days; they are also prone to physical aggression and impulsivity. They tend to direct their anger inward, leading to a high rate of self-injury. Self-destructive behaviors in individuals with BPD include substance abuse (e.g., drugs or alcohol), binge eating, unsafe sex, reckless driving, and self-cutting. Past research indicates that 60 to 80 percent of people with BPD have attempted suicide at least once in their lifetime, while 10 percent of them die of suicide (James & Taylor 2008). Risk factors for people with BPD completing suicide include those with comorbid major depressive disorder, those with antisocial personality disorder, and those who are older with children, have less education, and have a family history of substance use (Soloff et al. 2005). Many of those with BPD suffer from deep feelings of emptiness, boredom, and confusion about their identity.

Examining the Disorder

Many people may be misdiagnosed with BPD, especially adolescents or young adults who use psychoactive substances (e.g., drugs or alcohol) or have identity problems. These individuals may temporarily display behaviors associated with BPD. According to the *Diagnostic and Statistical Manual of Mental Disorders* (fourth edition, text revision; American Psychiatric Association 2000),

---

Facts about Borderline Personality Disorder

- Approximately 30 to 40 percent of suicides are committed by people with personality disorders; individuals with borderline and antisocial personality disorders account for a large majority of these. Two-thirds of individuals who commit suicide have a diagnosable substance abuse disorder (James & Taylor 2008).

- Outpatients with borderline personality disorder make an average of three suicide attempts during their lifetime (Soloff et al. 2005).

- *Girl, Interrupted* is an Academy Award–winning film adapted from the memoir by Susanna Kaysen. In the 1993 book, Kaysen relates her true experiences as a patient with borderline personality disorder in a psychiatric hospital in the 1960s.

a description of mental health disorders used primarily in the United States, women account for about 75 percent of the patients diagnosed with BPD. The frequency of BDP is higher than that of schizophrenia or bipolar disorder (manic depression), though BDP is less familiar than these other disorders. BPD is estimated to occur in about 2 percent of the general population, in about 10 percent of people seen in outpatient mental health clinics, and in about 20 percent of psychiatric inpatients (American Psychiatric Association 2000). Individuals differ in the course of the disorder. However commonly, the instability and the risk of suicide reach their peak during young adulthood and, as people get older, seem to decrease.

People with BPD usually form unstable relationships with others. They often develop intense attachments to others even if their feelings are not mutual. Since people with BPD are highly sensitive of rejection, they tend to display intense anger when their relationship is different from their expectations. Typically, they experience increased distress during short-term separations from others. Self-destructive behaviors take place along with these disappointments and the fears of rejection. In addition, impulsive behaviors such as drinking a large amount of alcohol and binge eating are common in BPD.

Past studies suggest that both environmental and biological factors contribute to the onset of BPD. Many people with BPD report that as young children they were neglected or rejected by their parents. Additionally, people with BPD often report an unstable childhood environment that may involve witnessing violence or physical or sexual abuse (Sansone, Songer, & Miller 2005). Biological characteristics associated with BPD include lower serotonin (a chemical messenger in the brain) activity, which has been found in people with BPD who exhibit high impulsivity (Norra et al. 2003). One way of viewing BPD is through a *biosocial model* (Linehan, Cochran, & Kehrer 2001). First, an internal factor, such as difficulty identifying and controlling one's emotions or abnormal serotonin activity, may create vulnerability, then social factors contribute to development of the disorder. For instance, parents may interpret a child's intense emotionality as overdramatization or an attempt to manipulate, then may punish or trivialize the emotions of the child. The child then devalues or doubts his own emotions and never learns how to recognize and cope with intense emotional reactions.

Interventions

Group and individual psychotherapy are commonly used as treatments for BPD. In recent years, dialectical behavioral therapy has been used to treat BPD, and it receives more empirical support than any other treatment (Lieb et al. 2004). Dialectical behavior therapy involves a combination of cognitive and behavioral techniques and humanistic philosophy. The therapist plays a supportive role, listening and empathizing. She identifies the accurate perceptions of the client and helps the client to think about alternative ways of viewing situations and of responding emotionally to particular events. Social skills training may also be involved, sometimes in group therapy settings, where clients can learn new ways of interacting with others.

Antidepressant, mood-stabilizing, antianxiety, and antipsychotic drugs are also sometimes used to treat people with BDP, although medication treatment is controversial given the high rate of suicide attempts among those suffering from BPD. Over the past two to three decades, treatments for BPD have improved, and many sufferers can live productive lives.

See also Depression; Suicide and Suicide Prevention

Bibliography

American Psychiatric Association. 2000. *Diagnostic and Statistical Manual of Mental Disorders* (4th ed., text rev.). Washington, DC: American Psychiatric Publishing.

Films Media Group. 2004. *Should I Live or Should I Die? Understanding Borderline Personality Disorder* (DVD). New York: Films Media Group.

James, L. M., and J. Taylor. 2008. "Associations between Symptoms of Borderline Personality Disorder, Externalizing Disorders, and Suicide-Related Behaviors." *Journal of Psychopathology and Behavioral Assessment* 30: 1–9.

Lieb, K., M. C. Zanarini, C. Schmahl, M. M. Linehan, and M. Bohus. 2004. "Borderline Personality Disorder." *Lancet* 364: 453–461.

Linehan, M. M., B. N. Cochran, and C. A. Kehrer, C. A. 2001. "Dialectical Behavior Therapy for Borderline Personality Disorder." In D. H. Barlow, ed., *Clinical Handbook of Psychological Disorders* (3rd ed., pp. 470–522). New York: Guilford Press.

National Education Alliance for Borderline Personality Disorder. http://www.borderline personalitydisorder.com/.

National Institute of Mental Health. 2009. *Borderline Personality Disorder*. May 13. Retrieved from http://www.nimh.nih.gov/publicat/bpd.cfm.

Norra, C., M. Mrazek, F. Tuchtenhagen, R. Gobbelé, H. Buchner, H. Sass, and S. C. Hepertz. 2003. "Enhanced Intensity Dependence as a Marker of Low Serotonergic Neurotransmission in borderline Personality Disorder." *Journal of Psychiatric Research* 37: 23–33.

Reiland, R. 2004. *Get Me Out of Here: My Recovery from Borderline Personality Disorder*. Center City, MN: Hazelden.

Sansone, R. A., D. A. Songer, and K. A. Miller. 2005. "Childhood Abuse, Mental Healthcare Utilization, Self-Harm Behavior, and Multiple Psychiatric Diagnoses among Inpatients with and without a Borderline Diagnosis." *Comprehensive Psychiatry* 46: 117–120.

Soloff, P. H., A. Fabio, T. M. Kelly, K. M. Malone, and J. J. Mann. 2005. "High-Lethality Status in Patients with Borderline Personality Disorder." *Journal of Personality Disorders* 19: 386–399.

Bulimia

See Eating Disorders

C

Campus Life and Mental Health

Jake J. Protivnak, Kyoung Mi Choi, and Victoria E. Kress

Increasingly, students are entering colleges and universities with complicated mental health issues. These problems are not only related to relationship and developmental issues, as students are also struggling with suicidal ideation, personality disorders, and issues secondary to sexual and violent assaults on campus (Benton et al. 2003). In recent times, the incidence of depression is believed to have doubled, the rate of suicidality in students has tripled, and the number of sexual assault cases presented at college counseling centers has quadrupled (Benton et al.). In addition to the documented rise in severe mental illness on college campuses, high-profile media cases such as the 2007 Virginia Tech massacre, where a student gunned down 32 people and wounded 25 others before committing suicide, have highlighted the importance of counselors and prevention programs on college campuses.

Mental Health Issues on College Campuses

College students are navigating a number of developmental issues (e.g., separation from home, relationship difficulties, financial issues, identity development, multicultural issues, career/major choice) and mental health concerns (e.g., depression, anxiety, eating disorders) that college mental health staff professionals must address (Schwitzer & Choate 2007). Unaddressed mental health and developmental issues can lead to serious academic, career, and personal/social difficulties as well as potential disruptions to a campus community. According to the 2010 National Survey of Counseling Center Directors, 91 percent of the respondents reported college students having greater numbers of severe psychological problems than in previous years (Gallagher 2010). College counseling center directors reported an increase in the need to respond to crisis issues, psychiatric medication issues, learning disability concerns, alcohol and drug abuse, self-injurious behavior, sexual assault, and eating disorder-related issues (Gallagher 2010).

The 2010 National College Health Assessment (NCHA), a national survey of over 30,000 college students, found that students identified several mental health and developmental issues that decreased their academic performance (American College Health Association [ACHA] 2011). Students reported stress (25.4%), sleep difficulties (17.8%), anxiety (16.4%), concern for friend or family member (10.1%), depression (10%), relationship difficulties (9.6%), finances (6.3%), death of a friend or family member (5.1%), roommate difficulties (4.9%), and alcohol use (3.7%) as being the most significant factors in decreased academic performance (ACHA 2011). Three percent of college students reported other factors (e.g., physical or sexual assault, chronic pain, discrimination, drug use, eating disorder, and gambling) as also disrupting their academic success (ACHA 2011).

College students reported that they were treated by a mental health professional for the following mental health diagnoses: anxiety (9.2%), depression (8.3%), panic attacks (4.6%), attention deficit and hyperactive disorders (4.2%), insomnia (3.0%), obsessive-compulsive disorder (2.0%), other sleep disorders (1.8%), bipolar disorder (1.3%), phobia and substance abuse (1.0%; ACHA 2011). Less than 1 percent of college students self-reported treatment for anorexia, bulimia, and schizophrenia (ACHA 2011). The 2010 NCHA found that 5.1 percent of students reported that they intentionally self-injured during the past 12 months.

Suicide is the second leading cause of death among college students, and depression is a major contributing factor of students who commit suicide (ACHA 2011). The most concerning result of this study was the finding that in the prior 12-month period, 6 percent of college students seriously considered suicide and 1.3 percent attempted suicide (ACHA 2011). The aforementioned findings highlight the importance of campus-wide preventive programs to increase awareness of students who are in crisis due to mental health issues. While the majority of research and attention is focused on the traditional college student population, Hyun, Quinn, Madon, and Lustig (2006) reported a need for increased attention on the mental health issues of graduate students. It is critical for all college staff and other students to identify and seek campus mental health supports for undergraduate and graduate students who are known to have or suspected of having mental health issues.

Campus Mental Health Services

In the late nineteenth and early twentieth centuries, campus mental health services focused on vocational guidance and career development. Expectations and focuses of college mental health staff have expanded to more developmental, preventive, and campus community-focused services. Changes in mental health services on campus have evolved over the years in order to best meet the unique needs of college students. While the severity of the psychopathology and diversity of the student population on campus has increased (Much, Wagener, & Hellenbrand 2010), the majority of college students who received mental health-related services were Caucasian, female, and undergraduate, even as the percentage of students who use campus mental health services remains relatively low. Outreach, preventative, and psychoeducational programs, web-based resources, and peer support can help in reaching underserved populations (Harrar, Affsprung, & Long 2010).

Campus mental health services utilize brief and time-limited models of therapy, group work, self-help materials, and other programming to meet the high demands of the campus population and to balance between developmental and clinical approaches. While there is great variability in the number of counseling sessions provided to college students by campus staff, students are typically provided with about six individual counseling sessions. Campus mental health services regularly utilize community mental health resources so as to provide wide-ranging services to the campus community, and as referrals for individual students. In order to maintain competence, campus mental health staff engage in continuing education specific to college students in areas such as evidence-based treatment, multiculturalism, eating and mood disorders, sexual abuse, sexual orientation, and substance abuse (Stone, Vespia, & Kanz 2000).

Counseling-related services on campuses are provided through counseling centers, sexual assault services, alcohol education and prevention offices, health centers, and other settings. The mental health services delivered are based on the types and severity of the mental health needs of the college students, and vary depending on the size and type of institution and the philosophy regarding the importance of counseling services on campus. Often the base of the delivery of campus mental health services is in counseling centers. However, mental health education is also being delivered by student affairs professionals working in other functional areas such as residence halls, academic advising, career centers, and multicultural centers providing informal screening/assessment of students who are in need of additional mental health services. In fact, collaborative work relationships with other student affairs areas on campus are important in addressing the mental health issues of college students who are often underserved by college mental health staff (Much, Wagener, & Hellenbrand 2010).

Conclusion

Mental health services on college campuses are influenced by various internal factors (e.g., stereotyping, sexism, racism, stigmatization) and external factors (e.g., economic conditions, technological change, family issues). With decreased funding to higher education institutes, it is imperative that college mental health staff demonstrate accountability for the services they provide to address the mental health issues of college students. College counselors can help decrease the stigmatization of mental health issues and counseling by engaging in professional advocacy and campus outreach to educate people about mental health issues and about where those in need can go to receive services.

See also Adolescence and Mental Health; Alcohol Abuse, Alcoholism, and Mental Health; Culturally Competent Mental Health Care; Disasters and Mental Health; Drug Abuse and Mental Health; Eating Disorders; Mental Health Counseling; Preventative Mental Health Programs; Psychotherapy; School Mental Health; Stigma

Bibliography

American College Health Association. 2011. *American College Health Association-National College Health Assessment II: Reference Group Executive Summary Fall 2010.* Linthicum, MD: American College Health Association.

Benton, S. A., J. M. Robertson, W. Tseng, F. B. Newton, and S. L. Benton. 2003. "Changes in Counseling Center Client Problems across 13 Years." *Professional Psychology: Research and Practice* 34: 66–72.

Gallagher, R. P. 2010. *National Survey of Counseling Center Directors 2010.* Alexandria, VA: International Association of Counseling Services.

Harrar, W. R., E. H. Affsprung, and J. C. Long. 2010. "Assessing Campus Counseling Needs." *Journal of College Student Psychotherapy* 24: 233–240.

Hyun, J. K., B. C. Quinn, T. Madon, and S. Lustig. 2006. "Graduate Student Mental Health: Needs Assessment and Utilization of Counseling Services." *Journal of College Student Development* 47(3): 247–266.

Jampel, J. B. 2006. "Reading, Writing, and Therapy: Mental Health Issues among College Students." In T. G. Plante, ed., *Mental Disorders of the New Millennium: Vol. 1. Behavioral Issues* (pp. 209–225). Westport, CT: Praeger.

Kadison, R., and T. F. DiGeronimo. 2005. *College of the Overwhelmed: The Campus Mental Health Crisis and What to Do about It.* San Francisco: Jossey-Bass.

Much, K., A. M. Wagener, and M. Hellenbrand. 2010. "Practicing in the 21st Century College Counseling Center." *Journal of College Student Psychotherapy* 24: 32–38.

Peterson, Andrea. 2011. "A Serious Illness or an Excuse?" *The Wall Street Journal,* December 13, D1, D4.

Schwitzer, A., and L. Choate. 2007. "College Student Needs and Counseling Responses." *Journal of College Counseling* 10: 3–5.

Stone, G. L., K. M. Vespia, and J. E. Kanz. 2000. "How Good Is Mental Health Care on College Campuses?" *Journal of Counseling Psychology* 47: 498–510.

Vye, C., K. Scholljegerdes, and I. D. Welch. 2007. *Under Pressure and Overwhelmed: Coping with Anxiety in College.* Westport, CT: Praeger.

Child Abuse

See Children and Mental Health; Forensic Psychology; Sexual Disorders and Dysfunctions; Social Work

Children and Mental Health

Linda Wilmshurst

Historical Background

The beginning of the twentieth century ushered in a movement of social reform focusing on child protection, child labor laws, and opening the doors to mandatory public education. In France, anticipating an influx of "child laborers" into the schools, Alfred Binet (1857–1911) and Théodore Simon (1872–1961) were commissioned to develop scales to identify children with mental retardation for purposes of remedial education. The Binet-Simon scales were translated and standardized for American children, and over the next 60 years countless children in the United States were identified and placed in institutions for the mentally retarded. Also at this time, William Healey, an English-born psychiatrist, opened up the first child guidance clinic to treat juvenile delinquents using Sigmund Freud's (1856–1939) psychoanalytic methods. By 1933, there were 42 child guidance clinics located in juvenile detention centers, courts, hospitals, schools, and universities. Although the clinics were initially developed to deal with problems of child delinquency, eventually the focus shifted to the identification of overprotective or rejecting mothers (Horn 1984).

Roadblocks, Resistance, and Forward Movement

The testing movement brought a shift in attitude from prevention and treatment to identification and placement, resulting in overcrowded institutions and deplorable conditions that steadily worsened until the deinstitutionalization movement of the 1970s returned the focus to issues of intervention and treatment by providing special education resources within community-based schools. Another obstacle to progress was the prevailing attitude that children were either too young to experience mental disorders, or if they did, they would exhibit the same symptoms as adults. As a result, clinical child psychology was initially seen as a replica of adult psychopathology.

In the mid-1980s, Sroufe and Rutter (1984) launched the journal *Development and Psychopathology*, creating a major shift away from viewing abnormal child behavior as a static state and toward conceptualizing atypical behavior as lying along a continuum. The latter is defined by what is considered normal for a child at a particular stage of development as well as deviations from that norm (based on the frequency, intensity, and duration of a behavior).

Developmental Issues in Children's Mental Health
Risks and Protective Factors

Certain child characteristics (genetics, temperament) and environmental factors (family, peers, schools) can interact to place a child at greater risk for psychopathology or buffer a child from harm. Adding additional risks can have a *multiplier effect*. In a classic longitudinal study, Rutter (1979) found that children exposed to two risk factors were four times more likely to have a disorder, while those with four risk factors increased their risk 10-fold. Some common risk factors include: difficult temperament, low birth weight, harsh parenting style, history of parent pathology, negative peer influences, poor-quality schools and neighborhoods, and low socioeconomic status. Factors that can serve a protective function, include: intelligence, social competence, resilient temperament, positive parenting, positive peer influences, and quality schools (Wilmshurst 2009, 68).

Issues in Clinical Decision Making

The *Diagnostic and Statistical Manual of Mental Disorders* (fourth edition, text revision [*DSM-IV-TR*]; American Psychiatric Association [APA], 2000) is the most common system for diagnostic classification in North America. The *DSM-1* (1952) contained only two disorders of childhood: adjustment reaction and childhood schizophrenia. Currently, the *DSM-IV* (APA 2000) contains over 20 different disorders under the category of disorders "usually first diagnosed in infancy, childhood, or adolescence."

The *DSM* is a categorical system that specifies when a disorder is present or absent based on clinical judgment of whether symptoms meet the required criteria. There are several criticisms regarding the appropriateness of the *DSM* for diagnosing child disorders, including the fact that (1) the majority of field trials have been based on adult populations; (2) adult criteria for some disorders are not appropriate for child symptoms (Scheeringa, Wright, & Hunt, as cited in Wilmshurst 2009, 241); and (3) the *DSM* does not recognize the unique nature of symptoms at different stages of development.

As a result, some clinicians favor a "dimensional" system of classification that views behavioral deviance as situated on a continuum. The dimensional system uses statistical methods to determine symptom presentations in clinical populations (i.e., clients or patients) versus nonclinical populations based on responses to behavioral rating scales completed by parents and teachers, such as the Achenbach System of Empirically Based Assessment (ASEBA; Achenbach & Rescorla 2002). The rating scales provide a profile that allows for comparison of child behaviors with what is normally expected for a child of that age and gender.

While both of these systems—the *DSM* one and the dimensional system—classify child problems with the goal of targeting interventions to improve mental health, children who have disabilities may also be protected under federal laws if these disabilities interfere with their ability to perform major life activities (in which case antidiscrimination laws, such as Section 504 of the Rehabilitation Act of 1973 and Americans with Disabilities Act Amendments Act [ADAAA] of 2008 may apply), or if their ability to learn is impeded (in which case the Individuals with Disabilities Education Improvement Act [IDEA] of 2004 may apply).

Under Section 504, accommodations can be implemented in the school environment to provide equal opportunities to learn (e.g., note takers, extra time for tests). In addition, children can qualify for special education and related services (such as, counseling, speech or occupational/ physical therapy) if they meet criteria for one of the 13 categories under IDEA (2004) and if the disability interferes with learning. In addition to physical and sensory disabilities, the categories of autism, mental retardation, traumatic brain injury, and emotional disturbance are also recognized by IDEA.

Disorders and Treatment

Internalizing Disorders (Anxiety and Mood Disorders)

Internalizing problems are "within the self, such as anxiety, depression, somatic complaints, without known medical cause and withdrawal from contact" (Achenbach & Rescorla 2001, 93). In young children (ages 4 to 11), the prevalence rate for internalizing disorders is similar for boys (7%) and girls (9%). However, this is not the case for adolescents, where significantly more females are vulnerable to internalizing disorders than are males. High rates of comorbidity (co-occurrence) exist among these disorders, especially in young children. Evidence suggests that negative affect (emotional distress) and low positive affect (anhedonia) may be characteristics that are inherited and can be stable over time (Anthony et al. 2002).

Anxiety Disorders   The *DSM* currently lists six different types of anxiety disorders, including specific phobia, separation anxiety disorder, generalized anxiety disorder, obsessive-compulsive disorder, social phobia, panic disorder, acute stress disorder, and posttraumatic stress disorder (PTSD). In the present entry, the focus is on earlier occurring disorders; later-occurring anxiety disorders are a problem of adolescence and are discussed in that entry.

Although fears are common in childhood, some children develop *specific phobias*, a persistent and irrational fear of an object, situation, or place. The most common phobias include: animals, natural environment (thunder, lightning), blood/injection, or situations (flying, school). A child with a phobia responds to the fearful event in a highly anxious state that could trigger a panic attack. Children with *separation anxiety disorder* (SAD) experience intense fears of separation from a caregiver, often resulting in significant social and academic impairment. Anticipating a separation may cause symptoms of fear of harm from the caregiver, a refusal to attend school, and a reluctance to sleep alone. Seventy-five percent of those with SAD will demonstrate school refusal (APA, 2000). Children with *generalized anxiety disorder* (GAD), or "free-floating anxiety," on the other hand, worry excessively about a number of perceived threats. These highly anxious children may display a number of physical symptoms, such as restlessness, irritability, sleep difficulties, fatigue, and muscle tension.

There are several treatments for anxiety disorders for young children, including various combinations of cognitive and behavioral techniques. The Coping Cat

Program, for example, has been successful in individual and group therapy with children as young as seven years of age (Kendall & Southam-Gerow 1996).

Mood Disorders Depression in young children often appears as a pervasive mood of irritability or loss of pleasure or interest in day to day activities. The feelings can be mild and long lasting, up to a year (*dysthymic disorder*), or acute and debilitating (*major depressive disorder*). Symptoms can include problems with sleeping, eating, concentration, low energy levels, and feelings of hopelessness. Luby, Sullivan, Belden, Stalets, Blankenship, and Spitznagel (2006) discovered that preschoolers can exhibit one of two forms of depression, *hedonic depression* (a reactive form) or *anhedonic depression* (melancholic form), the latter being more severe and associated with a family history of depression and higher levels of cortisol (the stress hormone). Fluoxetine (Prozac) is the only medication for depression that the Food and Drug Administration (FDA) has approved for children eight years and older. However, 30 to 40 percent of all cases do not respond to the drug (Emslie et al., as cited in Wilmshurst 2005, 279). Cognitive-behavioral treatment (CBT) programs have been successful in helping children reframe negative thoughts into more positive coping statements and have been administered to school-aged children, individually, in groups, and with parents (Stark et al. 1996).

A mood disorder that meets criteria for both a major depressive episode and a manic, mixed, or hypomanic episode is called *bipolar disorder* (BD). Symptoms of manic episodes can include expansive and elevated moods, feelings of grandiosity, decreased need for sleep, pressured speech, flight of ideas, distractibility, and engagement in high-risk behaviors (APA 2000). In young children, BD is difficult to diagnose because the symptoms resemble those of attention deficit hyperactivity disorder (ADHD) and posttraumatic stress disorder (PTSD). Children with BD often exhibit rapid "cycling," as evident in wide mood swings over a relatively short period of time (e.g., daily). Children with BD can become violent and aggressive if given medication for ADHD. Bipolar tendencies are highly heritable, and a family history of them is an important diagnostic tool. Resperidone and lithium are medications that have been effective in managing symptoms of the disorder in children.

Externalizing Disorders

Childhood Aggression Although most children show a decline in aggressive behaviors with age, some "early starters" continue to display aggression as a stable characteristic throughout childhood and adolescence (Vitaro et al. 2006). Researchers have isolated two variants of aggression: (1) *cold-blooded*, or *proactive, aggression*, as evident in bullies who victimize; and (2) *hot-blooded*, or *reactive, aggression*, as evident in children who lack emotion regulation and control (Connor et al. 2003).

Oppositional Defiant Disorder (ODD) Children with ODD demonstrate persistent hostile and defiant patterns of behavior toward authority figures, as evident in: a loss of temper, irritability, lack of compliance, deliberate attempts to annoy, and being argumentative, spiteful, and vindictive. Children with ODD often experience problems at home and at school. Treatment often involves training parents in the consistent use of behavioral methods aimed at rewarding increases in compliance and punishing negative consequences in order to reduce inappropriate behaviors (Webster-Stratton 1990).

Conduct Disorder (CD) Children who demonstrate one symptom of CD prior to age 10 are considered to have *childhood-onset CD*. The disorder is diagnosed much later than ODD, is more serious in nature, and involves a persistent pattern of behaviors that violate social norms or the rights of others. (CD is discussed in more detail in the entry on adolescence and mental health.)

Disorders of Attention and Learning

Attention Deficit Hyperactivity Disorder (ADHD) Throughout development, children develop an increasing ability to concentrate and problem solve based on increased maturity in memory strategies, attention span, and self-control. However, 3 to 7 percent of the school-age population will demonstrate a persistent pattern of inattention, impulsivity, and hyperactivity. There are three types of ADHD: (1) predominantly inattentive type; (2) predominantly hyperactive-impulsive type; and (3) a combined type that meets the criteria for both. About 1 in 10 children diagnosed with ADHD will have the hyperactive-impulsive type, because it is far more obvious and visible. Many with the inattentive type go undiagnosed because the symptoms are more subtle (poor attention to details, problems sustaining attention over time, poor organization, forgetful, easily distracted, does not seem to listen). Given the nature of the disability, children with ADHD often encounter problems academically and socially. Of children diagnosed with the disorder, 30 percent repeat a grade (Barkley 1998).

Treatment with stimulant medications, such as Dexedrine, Ritalin, and Cylert, has been successful in increasing the number of catecholamines (i.e., "fight of flight" hormones) in the brain (Barkley 1998). Functional behavioral assessments have been helpful in developing behavioral intervention plans, while parent-training programs have also been instrumental in increasing parent awareness and child management strategies (Barkely 1998).

Specific Learning Disabilities (SLD)   Individuals with SLD often have average or above-average intelligence but demonstrate significant processing problems when they execute specific tasks such as reading/spelling (dyslexia), writing (dysgraphia), fine motor skills (dyspraxia), or mathematics (dyscalculia). Most studies support a genetic cause for SLD. Dyslexia is the most common type of SLD, accounting for 80 percent of all cases and affecting 5 to 17 percent of the school-age population (Shaywitz 1998).

For children with SLD, early identification and intervention can help prevent a child from developing more serious academic, social, and emotional problems. Many children with SLD also suffer from social skills deficits, lower self-esteem, and other comorbid disorders (e.g., ADHD).

Intellectual Disabilities and Pervasive Developmental Disorders

Intellectual Disabilities (ID)   Some children may have developmental delays (being slow to talk or walk) and catch up after a period of time. However, approximately 2 percent of the population has an intellectual level that is significantly below average (an IQ of 70 or below). In order to meet a diagnosis of intellectual disability (formerly mental retardation), an individual must also have deficits in two areas of adaptive functioning (self-help skills, communication, etc.) and have onset prior to 18 years. The majority of individuals with ID (85%) have a mild form of the disability and may master academic skills up to a grade 6 level and work in supervised settings. There are many causes for ID, including genetic defects responsible for syndromes such as Down, Prader-Willi, Angelman, and Williams, or environmental toxins (taratogens) caused by maternal substance use/abuse (fetal alcohol syndrome) or exposure to lead-based paint, along with exposure to rubella or birth trauma. Prevention and early intervention are critical to enhancing the quality of life.

Pervasive Developmental Disorders (PDDs)   The autistic spectrum disorders (ASDs) are part of the PDDs characterized by functional and qualitative impairments in three areas: (1) impaired social interaction, (2) impaired communication, and (3) a restricted range of activity (stereotypical, repetitive and nonfunctional routines). There is a wide range of functioning within this continuum, from very high-functioning individuals with Asperger syndrome who may have an IQ in the average or above-average range and present with odd behaviors (pragmatic speech problems, perseveration on topics), to those with autism who have an IQ in the intellectual disability range (the majority), evidence minimal communications skills, and have problems with social reciprocity and involvement with self-stimulation (spinning parts of objects, hand flapping, etc.).The category of pervasive developmental disorder—not otherwise specified (PDD-NOS) is reserved for those atypical cases that do not meet criteria for autism or Asperger. This category has come under criticism because it can significantly inflate the prevalence rate for ASD, as was evident in the most recent Centers for Disease Control and Prevention (CDC) report (2009) in which rates were seen to increase from "2 to 20 cases per 10,000" (APA 2000) to 1 case in every 110 children (CDC 2009).

What causes autism is not clear, although links to the once-suspected MMR vaccine (measles, mumps, rubella) have been conclusively ruled out (Jick & Kaye 2003). Currently, studies are focusing on uncovering possible causes from genetic transmission, brain chemistry (elevated serotonin levels), and brain function (corpus callosum, amygdala, and fusiform gyrus). Although most symptoms of ADD are visible before a child's third birthday, researchers with a trained eye can detect signals of the disorder in infancy (Gray & Tonge 2001), which is extremely important since the earlier the intervention, the more promising the outcome. Intense interventions using highly structured behavioral approaches (15 to 40 hours a week) have been successful in eliminating deficits (attention, compliance) and in enhancing adaptive and social behaviors and engaging parents as cotherapists (Hurth et al. 1999)

Ethical Issues in Research and Practice

Professional bodies develop ethical standards for working with children in various capacities. The most recent revisions of the American Psychological Association standards (2002, 2010) incorporate a number of safeguards for minors involved in research or practice. The safeguards stress the importance of explaining research, assessment, or treatment in language that is within the child's ability to comprehend; obtaining consent from the custodial parent for the child's participation; and obtaining the child's assent and willingness to participate. In cases of divorce, separation, or child custody, it is essential to determine who is the custodial parent for purposes of granting permission for the child's involvement, for gaining access to confidential reports, and for granting permission to release confidential reports to a third party.

See also Adolescence and Mental Health; Attention Deficit Hyperactivity Disorder; Autism Spectrum Disorders; Bipolar Disorder; Depression; Dissociative Disorders; Family and Mental Illness; Genetics and Mental Health; Learning Disabilities; Neurodiversity; Preventative Mental Health Programs; School Mental Health

Bibliography

Achenbach, T. M., and L. A. Rescorla. 2001. *Manual for the ASEBA School-Age Forms & Profiles*. Burlington: University of Vermont, Research Center for Children, Youth & Families.

American Psychiatric Association. 2000. *The Diagnostic and Statistical Manual of Mental Disorders* (4th ed., text rev.). Washington, DC: American Psychiatric Publishing.

American Psychological Association. 2002. "Ethical Principles of Psychologists and Code of Conduct." *American Psychologist* 57: 1060–1073.

American Psychological Association. 2010. "Ethical Principles of Psychologists and Code of Conduct: 2010 Amendments." Retrieved from http://www.apa.org/ethics/code/index.aspx.

Anthony, J. L., C. J. Lonigan, E. S. Hooe, and B. M. Phillips. 2002. "An Affect-Based, Hierarchical Model of Temperament and Its Relations with Internalizing Symptomatology." *Journal of Clinical Child and Adolescent Psychology* 31: 480–490.

Barkley, R. A. 1998. *Attention Deficit Hyperactivity Disorder* (2nd ed.). New York: Guilford Press.

Centers for Disease Control and Prevention. 2009. "Prevalence of Autism Spectrum Disorders." Autism and Developmental Disabilities Monitoring Network. United States, 2006. Surveillance Summaries. *MMWR* 58(SS 10; December 19): 1–20.

Connor, D. F., R. J. Steingard, J. Cunningham, J. Anderson, and R. H. Melloni. 2004. "Proactive and Reactive Aggression in Referred Children and Adolescents." *American Journal of Orthopsychiatry* 74: 129–136.

Gray, K. M., and B. J. Tonge. 2001. "Are There Early Features of Autism in Infants and Preschool Children?" *Journal of Pediatrics & Child Health* 37: 221–226.

Horn, M. 1984. "The Moral Message of Child Guidance, 1925–1945." *Journal of Social History* 18: 25–36.

Hurth, J., E. Shaw, S. G. Izeman, K. Whaley, and S. J. Rogers. 1999. "Areas of Agreement about Effective Practices among Programs Serving Young Children with Autism Spectrum Disorders." *Infants and Young Children* 12(2): 17–26.

Jick, H., and J. Kaye. 2003. "Epidemiology and Possible Causes of Autism." *Pharmacotherapy* 23: 1524–1530.

Kendall, P. C., and M. Southam-Gerow. 1996. "Long-Term Follow-Up of a Cognitive-Behavioral Therapy for Anxiety Disordered Youths." *Journal of Consulting and Clinical Psychology* 64: 724–730.

Luby, J. L., J. Sullivan, A. Belden, M. Stalets, S. Blankenship, and E. Spitznagel. 2006. "An Observational Analysis of Behavior in Depressed Preschoolers: Further Validation of Early Onset Depression." *Journal of the American Academy of Child and Adolescent Psychiatry* 45: 203–212.

Rutter, M. 1979. "Protective Factors in Children's Responses to Stress and Disadvantage." In M. Whalen and J. E. Rolf, eds., *Primary Prevention of Psychopathology: Vol. 3. Social competence in children* (pp. 49–79). Hanover, NH: University Press of New England.

Shaywitz, S. E. 1998. "Current Concepts: Dyslexia." *New England Journal of Medicine* 338(5): 307–312.

Sroufe, L. A., and M. Rutter. 1984. "The Domain of Developmental Psychopathology." *Child Development* 55: 17–29.

Stark, K. D., S. Swearer, C. Kurkowski, D. Sommer, and B. Bowen. 1996. "Targeting the Child and Family: A Holistic Approach to Treating Child and Adolescent Depressive Disorders." In E. D. Hibbs and P. S. Jensen, eds., *Psychosocial Treatments for Child and Adolescent Disorders: Empirically Based Strategies for Clinical Practice* (pp. 207–238). Washington, DC: American Psychological Association.

Vitaro, F., E. D. Barker, M. Boivin, M. Brendgen, and R. E. Tremblay. 2006. "Do Early Difficult Temperament and Harsh Parenting Differentially Predict Reactive and Proactive Aggression?" *Journal of Abnormal Child Psychology* 34: 685–695.

Webster-Stratton, C. 1990. "Long-Term Follow-Up of Families with Young Conduct Problem Children: From Preschool to Grade School." *Journal of Clinical Child Psychology* 19(2): 144–149.

Wilmshurst, L. 2009. *Abnormal Child Psychology: A Developmental Perspective.* New York: Routledge.

Chronic Mental Illness

Richard C. Tessler

In public policy discourse, the term "chronic mental illness" (CMI) invokes images of a patient population that can be distinguished by a serious psychiatric disorder, long duration or recurring episodes of mental illness, and residual disabilities undermining social and role functioning. Although schizophrenia is the most prevalent example of chronic mental illness, it is not the only relevant diagnosis, and even some cases of schizophrenia would not meet the duration and disability criteria for CMI (Harding, Zubin, & Strauss 1987).

The key to identification of CMI is the illness trajectory and a high level of need for services rather than diagnosis per se. In fact, most cases involve multiple diagnoses. Persons with CMI tend to experience frequent episodes requiring treatment, although in the current era not necessarily hospitalization. As a result of their disorders, they are often unmarried, unemployed, and dependent on Medicaid and other entitlement programs for income, health care, and housing. Although prognosis varies, CMI tends to have a major negative impact on social relations, family life, work, and independent living in general. Deinstitutionalization (i.e., the closing of asylums beginning in the mid-twentieth century) has brought increased visibility to this patient population while increasing both risks and opportunities associated with community living.

Population Size and Characteristics

Estimates of the size of the chronically mentally ill population range widely from 2 to 5 million people, depending on the criteria used for case definition and whether cases of only moderate severity are included along with more severe conditions. While the estimates are relatively soft, they nonetheless suggest the magnitude of the problem and give it a point of reference in public policy discourse. Barriers to identifying cases are numerous and make calculating the proportion of the American household population with CMI difficult. Finding cases outside of household settings has been somewhat more successful. In 1989, researchers from the National Institute of Mental Health (NIMH) estimated that there were approximately 200,000 homeless persons with CMI, more than a million in nursing homes, about 50,000 in mental hospitals, and another 50,000 in state prisons.

While the terminology suggests that the chronically mentally ill are a homogeneous group, clearly this is not a valid descriptor. In fact, the chronically mentally ill are a heterogeneous population with distinct subgroups dispersed across different living circumstances. Their needs for supportive care vary according to condition, circumstance, and cohort or group (Mechanic 2008).

The chronically mentally ill today are made up of different cohorts, each with its own social characteristics and clinical histories. The cohorts of most current concern are not the same as those from the early years of deinstitutionalization. For one, they are younger and better educated than previous cohorts owing to demographic changes in the age structure of the American population. They are also a larger group owing to increases in the numbers of individuals at risk for disorders such as schizophrenia with early adult onset. Moreover, the chronically mentally ill today lack the institutional histories of previous cohorts, although this does not suggest more positive illness trajectories or outcomes.

Despite being younger and better educated, the chronically mentally ill of the present era present numerous challenges to mental health professionals who try to engage them in treatment. Some reject psychiatric help, mingle with other disaffected and alienated young adults, are homeless at least episodically, abuse illegal substances, and behave in ways that alarm community residents. Raised in middle-class families, it is sometimes difficult for them to accept the chronicity of their psychiatric problems and their long-term dependence on public sources of care. In response, some displace their frustration and anger onto family, friends, and strangers. Some first come to the attention of mental health professionals through the criminal justice system.

Background

The history of the chronically mentally ill has been described as a series of cycles of reforms. In the United States, there have been at least three major reform movements (Tessler & Goldman 1982). The first introduced moral treatment and the asylum (eighteenth and nineteenth centuries), a second generated the mental hygiene movement and the psychopathic hospital (late nineteenth and early twentieth centuries), and the third created deinstitutionalization and the community mental health centers (mid-twentieth century). Each reform movement championed an innovative type of facility, and began with high expectations and the promise of preventing long-term disability. Each met with early success in treating acute cases but failed to contain the increasing numbers of patients who were incurable. In each cycle of reform, disappointment over failed expectations led to pessimism, retrenchment, and neglect of persons living with CMI.

In recent decades, the mental health system in the United States has been transformed from one that was dominated by state mental hospitals to one that is now more community based. During the 1960s and 1970s, the process of deinstitutionalization gave new visibility to the chronically mentally ill, as many thousands of long-stay patients were discharged to the community or transferred to nursing homes. Others who would have been admitted to state hospitals in earlier eras were denied admission under the new policy, or admitted only for brief hospital stays. In hindsight, the expansion of community mental health services tended to benefit persons with acute care needs more than those with chronic needs. In contrast to many other users of the community mental health centers, the chronically mentally ill tended to present multiple needs extending well beyond what the centers were prepared to offer, including needs for social rehabilitation, income maintenance, housing, health care, employment, social supports, and assistance in activities of daily living. Motivation to seek care and to comply with treatment regimens further challenged treatment planning.

Cycles of reform and neglect have also been evident in recent decades. There was a resurgence of interest in the chronically mentally ill during the Carter administration (1977–1981), which made them a centerpiece of the Mental Health Systems Act, and authorized the NIMH to launch the Community Support Program (CSP) and cooperate with other federal agencies in formulating a national plan for the CMI. Federal advocacy on behalf of the CMI ebbed during the Reagan years (1981–89), but the CMI were to benefit nonetheless from an expansion of Social Security Entitlement Programs. In recent years, a coalition of family advocacy groups and private foundations has joined with reform-minded state mental health authorities to take up the gauntlet once again. Their initiatives have incorporated several promising approaches and points of leverage for improving quality of life for the chronically mentally ill. A number of these are examined in the sections that follow.

System Integration and Managed Care

Caring for the chronically mentally ill in the community has been challenging because their needs span many different categorical programs. Recognition of this problem has led to a variety of efforts under the banner of *services integration*. The basic idea of services integration is to forge linkages between independent programs and to fix administrative responsibility in order to improve comprehensiveness, efficiency, and economy of scale. Recent examples of service integration strategies are (1) the Robert Wood Johnson Foundation Program on Chronic Mental Illness, which feature local mental health authorities; and (2) the ACCESS demonstration, cosponsored by a coalition of federal agencies, which included intensive case management for homeless veterans with mental disorders. Evaluation findings from these (and related) initiatives leave little doubt that with appropriate resources it is possible to improve system integration and coordination. However, the larger goal of improving psychiatric outcomes and functioning remains elusive (Morrissey 2000; Rosenheck et al. 2002).

In recent years, managed care has begun to shape how mental health services are accessed and utilized by persons with CMI. Mental health and substance abuse benefits for the chronically mentally ill, whose expected utilization is far higher than population averages, are increasingly being *carved out* of general operating budgets and outsourced to behavioral health companies who assume both the responsibility and the risk. The basic idea is to control costs through prospective budgeting (aka capitation, or fixed per-person fees) and by regulating use of services (aka utilization review). Costs are contained mainly through reductions in hospital admissions and length of stay. While direct costs to managed care companies and subcontractors are thereby reduced, indirect costs to other stakeholders may actually increase. To the extent that managed care companies ration not only unnecessary but also needed services, there will be consequences for family, community, as well as the criminal justice system.

Housing and Homelessness

Housing for the chronically mentally ill is now widely recognized to require the active involvement of mental health professionals. Program managers have more tools for accessing housing in contrast to the 1980s when housing entitlements were poorly coordinated with mental health services. Different views prevail about what kind of housing is best for the chronically mentally ill. Some professionals advocate for structured, supervised residences while others call for more independent living arrangements when possible. In practice, disruptive behaviors causing interpersonal conflict with landlords and neighbors tend to limit the available options (Carling 1993). Most professionals agree that the first priority is to find long-term housing and then to access needed support services.

The homeless chronically mentally ill are a major public policy concern. Estimates of this subgroup range from 20 to 35 percent depending on criteria for case identification and methods of case finding (Tessler & Dennis 1992). Chronic mental illness is clearly a risk factor for homelessness. Conversely, homelessness also exacerbates chronic mental illness. Combating homelessness among the chronically mentally ill is a continuing challenge requiring active engagement with family and friends especially during the transition from homeless shelter to community residence (Susser et al. 1997).

Work and Employment

Sheltered work has a long history both during the era of the large state mental hospitals and during deinstitutionalization. However, the nature of the work was often well below the capabilities of the patients, failing to engage their interest or to generate opportunities to transition to nonsheltered, competitive employment. New approaches featuring *supported employment* emerged in recent years.

The basic idea is to use program funds to help patients find jobs, and to provide on-the-job support to both patients and employers.

Supported employment programs have had notable successes, suggesting that with proper accommodation some patients can be productively employed even as they continue to cope with symptoms and disability (Salyers et al. 2004). Additional support for these approaches comes from the Americans with Disabilities Act, which requires employers to make reasonable accommodations to people with psychiatric (and other) disabilities. These are all hopeful signs. However, the majority of chronically mentally ill still lack paid employment, or work in marginal jobs and in undesirable work environments (Mechanic, Bilder, & McAlpine 2002).

Family Role and Involvement

Probably as many as a third of patients with CMI live with their parents at a time when most in their age cohort have left home and established independent residences. The family burden may include assistance in personal hygiene, shopping and preparing meals, household chores and laundry, and transportation. Less often, parents also have to cope with behavioral problems that disrupt household routines and alarm neighbors. Stigma may limit social activities and contribute to a profound isolation from neighbors, friends, and even other relatives (Tessler & Gamache 2000).

Increasingly, mental health professionals recognize the important role families play and are seeking their cooperation within a caregiving triad. This is in contrast to earlier epochs when at best family members were uninformed, excluded, and sometimes blamed for the illness. Reductions in family burden are increasingly viewed as desirable outcomes, and as an indicator (among many others) of the cost-effectiveness of mental health services and treatments. A variety of useful measures of family burden are now available for evaluators to use (Schene et al. 2001).

Rehabilitation and Education

In recent years, psychiatric rehabilitation has emerged as an adjunct and, in some cases, an alternative to traditional approaches to treating CMI. The basic idea is that even it medical knowledge is inadequate to cure the illness, there is still much to be gained by minimizing disability. Psychiatric rehabilitation is based on careful assessment of the social context of the illness and barriers to social and role functioning. Rehabilitation therapists work with the chronically mentally ill in pragmatic ways to find reasonable accommodations that have the potential to enhance independent living, and improve social relationships and work.

Rehabilitation often requires the therapist adopt an educational approach. This may involve encouraging the patient to reevaluate life circumstances, develop problem-solving strategies, and mobilize effort and motivation to achieve. Effective performance, rather than symptom remission, becomes the main criterion for evaluating the impact of psychiatric rehabilitation (Mechanic 2008).

Conclusions

Few topics in mental health are as emotionally charged as the topic of chronic mental illness. By the same token, few mental health topics are as central to public policy discourse. The recent designation of *serious and persistent mental illness* has only put different words to describe the same population without a significant change in the content of the discourse. Lay stereotypes tend to obscure real differences within the population of concern and to propagate distorted stereotypic images of the chronically mentally ill as dysfunctional and dangerous. On the other side of the ledger are exaggerated claims by reformists about the susceptibility of chronic mental illness to environmental control. Neither set of images will help to improve prospects for the chronically mentally ill.

For more than 200 years, the fate of the chronically mentally ill has depended on the social and political context for leveraging public resources on their behalf. Reforms have tended to occur in period when resources were ample and political resolve robust. The chronically mentally ill have not fared as well during periods of austerity and suspicions about big government. The *new federalism* of the early 1980s resulted in large numbers of persons with CMI losing Social Security income supports and becoming homeless. The current era of deficit reduction and threatened cutbacks in federal entitlement programs leading to an erosion of the safety net are cause for much concern for the chronically mentally ill along with other vulnerable populations.

See also Community Mental Health; Criminalization and Diversion Programs; Disability Rights; History of Mental Health Care; Hospitalization; Insurance and Parity Laws; Public Policy Issues; Rehabilitation Services; Undiagnosed Mental Illness

Bibliography

Carling, Paul J. 1993. "Housing and Supports for Persons with Mental Illness: Emerging Approaches to Research and Practice." *Hospital and Community Psychiatry* 44: 439–449.

Harding, Courtenay M., Joseph Zubin, and John S. Strauss. 1987. "Chronicity in Schizophrenia: Fact, Partial Fact or Artifact?" *Hospital and Community Psychiatry* 38: 477–486.

Mechanic, David. 2008. *Mental Health and Social Policy: Beyond Managed Care* (5th ed.). Boston: Pearson.

Mechanic, David, Scott Bilder, and Donna D. McAlpine. 2002. "Employing Persons with Serious Mental Illness." *Health Affairs* 21: 242–253.

Morrissey, Joseph P. 1999. "Integrating Service Delivery Systems for Persons with a Severe Mental Illness." In A. V. Horwitz and T. L. Scheid, eds., *A Handbook for the Study of Mental Health: Social Contexts, Theories, and Systems* (pp. 449–466). New York: Cambridge University Press.

Rosenheck, Robert A., Julie Lam, Joseph P. Morrissey, Michael O. Calloway, Marilyn Stolar, and Frances Randolph. 2002. "Service Systems Integration and Outcomes for Mentally Ill Homeless Persons in the ACCESS Program." *Psychiatric Services* 53: 958–966.

Salyers, Michelle P., D. R. Becker, R. E. Drake, W. C. Torrey, and P. F. Wyzik. 2004. "A Ten-Year Follow-Up of a Supported Employment Program." *Psychiatric Services* 55: 302–308.

Schene, A., R. Tessler, G. Gamache, and B. van Wijngaarden. 2001. "Measuring Family or Caregiver Burden in Severe Mental Illness: The Instruments." In G. Thornicroft and M. Tansella, eds., *Mental Health Outcome Measures* (pp. 48–71). London: The Royal College of Psychiatrists, Gaskell Publications.

Susser, Ezra, E. Valencia, S. Conover, A. Felix, W. Y. Tsai, and R. J. Watt. 1997. "Preventing Recurrent Homelessness among Mentally Ill Men: A 'Critical Time' Intervention after Discharge from a Shelter." *American Journal of Public Health* 87: 256–262.

Tessler, Richard, and Deborah L. Dennis. 1992. "Mental Illness among Homeless Adults: A Synthesis of Recent NIMH-Funded Research." In James R. Greenley and Phillip Leaf, eds., *Research in Community and Mental Health* (Vol. 7, pp. 1–51). Greenwich, CT: JAI Press.

Tessler, Richard, and Gail M. Gamache. 2000. *Family Experiences with Mental Illness*. Westport, CT: Auburn House.

Tessler, Richard, Howard H. Goldman, and Associates. 1982. *The Chronically Mentally Ill: Assessing Community Support Programs*. Cambridge, MA: Ballinger.

Clinical Psychology

Richard P. Halgin and Alessandro Piselli

Clinical psychology is a field that "integrates science, theory, and practice to understand, predict, and alleviate maladjustment, disability, and discomfort as well as to promote human adaptation, adjustment, and personal development. Clinical psychology focuses on the intellectual, emotional, biological, psychological, social, and behavioral aspects of human functioning across the life span, in varying cultures, and at all socioeconomic levels" (Society of Clinical Psychology, Division 12 of the American Psychological Association, http://www.div12.org/).

With the birth of the field dating back more than a hundred years, the profession of clinical psychology has evolved dramatically to a point at which clinical psychologists now engage in a range of roles including positions as psychotherapists, diagnosticians, researchers, educators, consultants, and administrators. It is instructive to look at both the history of the field and the nature of the roles it encompasses.

Emergence and Growth of the Discipline

The field of clinical psychology emerged at the turn of the last century primarily in the realms of psychotherapy and psychological testing. The term "clinical psychology" was first used by Lightner Witmer who in 1896 established a clinic at the University of Pennsylvania to study and treat children with learning and school problems. Witmer emphasized a criterion for this new field, which has been maintained to the present day—interventions with clients should be based on scientific methods and research. The history of psychological testing dates back to the pioneering work of scholars such as James McKeen Cattell who in 1890 coined the term "mental tests," and Alfred Binet who in the early 1900s developed the first IQ test.

Around the time that science and practice were being integrated in the realm of psychological testing, there was an emergence of interest in psychopathology and psychotherapy. The innovative and controversial work of Sigmund Freud as well as the contributions of two American psychologists, G. Stanley Hall and William James, introduced fresh approaches to understanding human development. The academic setting nurtured these creative theoretical explorations, so it was natural that these ideas would be put into practice on university campuses. By 1914, many university campuses had established psychological clinics, and psychologists expanded their efforts to new settings, including mental hospitals and facilities for developmentally and physically disabled people.

World War I was particularly important in the evolution of this new field. A group of psychologists accepted the U.S. Army's challenge to develop intelligence tests, known as *Army Alpha* and *Army Beta*, which could be administered to large groups for the purpose of efficient and economical screening of military recruits. Group intelligence testing was soon followed by group testing of soldiers for emotional problems.

During the 1920s and 1930s, the limited role of the clinical psychologist as an expert in psychological testing was reinforced. However, a major shift in professional activity took place during World War II and shortly thereafter. When the directors of the Veterans Administration (VA) and the U.S. Public Health Service were faced with large numbers of emotionally disturbed soldiers, they turned to psychology for assistance in treating these impaired individuals. The VA provided considerable financial support for training clinical psychologists, and played major roles in the expansion of the field of clinical psychology, and the recognition of clinical psychologists as leaders in the health field.

The VA defined the work of the clinical psychologist to include diagnosis, psychotherapy, and research. This dramatic expansion of the role of clinical psychology permanently changed the nature of the field. Clinical psychologists were no longer limited to the activities of testing and research but were accorded responsibilities that covered a range of clinical activities. This evolution of professional role was also accompanied by an increase in prestige and educational requirements, including the expectation that clinical psychologists hold a doctoral degree.

In the middle of the twentieth century, the American Psychological Association (APA) recognized the importance of establishing curriculum requirements for the field, and called a training conference in Colorado. The 1949 Boulder Conference provided a definition of "clinical psychologist" that would hold relatively constant for more than two decades: the clinical psychologist was to be a "scientist-practitioner," with training and expertise in both science and practice.

In 1973 at a conference in Vail, Colorado, an alternative training model emerged for clinical psychology: "practitioner-scholar." These professionals would continue to be trained in research methods, but with a greater emphasis on the acquisition of clinical skills. In the decades to follow, dozens of professional schools of psychology were established, such that concerns have been expressed about the possibility that the number of psychologists being trained could exceed the number of employment opportunities.

Professional Roles

The professional work of clinical psychologists spans many contexts and realms. In addition to their traditional roles as psychotherapists and experts in psychological assessment, clinical psychologists work as consultants, researchers, educators and administrators.

Psychotherapist

Psychotherapy is a process in which a helping professional works with a client who wishes to resolve some emotional problem, change some troublesome behavior, or develop increased self-understanding. The client may be an individual adult, adolescent or child, or may be a couple, family, or group. Psychological problems cover a wide continuum, ranging from minor adjustment difficulties (such as homesickness) to severe forms of psychological disturbance (such as suicidal depression). Consequently, the methods of intervention differ from case to case.

Psychotherapists adhere to a variety of psychotherapeutic models, each with its own theory and techniques. Traditionally, the psychotherapeutic models with the greatest number of followers have included psychodynamic, cognitive, humanistic-existential, family systems, and psychopharmacological. Although psychology textbooks present these as discrete approaches, most clinicians have a foundation theory for their work, but integrate aspects of different models depending on the presenting problem and needs of each client.

Psychotherapists who are psychodynamically oriented derive their techniques from Freudian theory, and view early life experiences as the primary determinants of current problems. They believe that many conflicts reside in a person's unconscious and that the resolution of current difficulties must be achieved through exploration of the unconscious. Although Freud emphasized the role of sexuality in human development, some of his later followers moved away from that view. In recent decades, psychodynamic psychotherapists have focused more on the role of early life relationships, sometimes called *object relations*, in the development of personality.

Clinical psychologists who describe their approach as cognitive (or cognitive-behavioral) are not concerned with the unconscious. Rather, they believe that current troubled behavior results from maladaptive learning and thinking, and that the resolution of difficulties lies in the learning of more effective thoughts and actions. In contrast to their more narrowly behavioral predecessors, who were criticized for focusing exclusively on observable behaviors, cognitive-behavioral therapists expanded their focus to include concern with cognitive processes. For example, cognitive therapists who treat depressed people would help their clients identify depressing thoughts (e.g., "I'm not good enough.") and replace such negative thoughts with more positive ones.

Reacting to what they believe are the dehumanizing aspects of the psychodynamic and behavioral approaches, adherents to a humanistic-existential approach focus on the more positive aspects of human existence. Because humanistic-existential psychotherapists believe that abnormal behavior results from the blocking of personal development, therapy involves the fostering of self-awareness, personal growth, and responsibility for one's decisions. These psychotherapists believe that it is important for the clinician to be warm and accepting of the client. Rather than focusing on conflicts and inadequacies that clients may feel, the clinician looks for ways to help clients reach their fullest potential in life. Although relatively few clinical psychologists currently self-identify as humanistic-existential clinicians, most incorporate aspects of this model through their efforts to be supportive and empathic.

Clinicians who employ a family systems approach see some psychological problems as caused by disturbances in the patterns of interactions and relationships within the family. Although there are distinct theories within the family perspective, all share a focus on family dynamics, the interactions among family members.

As understanding has increased about the role of neurochemistry in causing and aggravating psychological problems, more attention has been given to psychopharmacological interventions. Traditionally, the prescription of medications has been limited to physicians and allied health professionals. However, in some geographical regions and contexts the paucity of prescribers has been problematic, and has led to the granting of prescription privileges to psychologists with sufficient training and experience (e.g., state of New Mexico, U.S. Department of Defense). Efforts to expand prescribing privileges to clinical psychologists continue on the national and state levels. Because of their traditional training in psychotherapy, most prescribing psychologists use medication as only one component of a multipronged intervention.

Expert in Psychological Assessment

Psychological testing covers a broad range of measurement techniques, all of which use scorable information to yield inferences about psychological functioning. The information may concern intellectual abilities, personalities, emotional states, attitudes, and behaviors. Traditionally, psychologists with expertise in psychometrics have been the developers of such instruments, ensuring that the tests meet rigorous standards of validity and reliability.

With the historical roots of clinical psychology in the field of intelligence testing, clinical psychologists (and their colleagues in school psychology) continue to play a central role in administering and interpreting IQ tests such as the Wechsler scales, which have been revised several times over the past half century.

Clinical psychologists are also experts in personality testing, which is used for various purposes including diagnostic assessment and personnel screening. The most common personality assessment instruments involve self-report inventories, such as the Minnesota Multiphasic Personality Inventory-2 (MMPI-2), which provides information about aspects of an individual's personality on 10 clinical scales covering variables such as depression, hypochondriasis, and paranoia. Clinical psychologists may also use projective techniques such as the Rorschach Inkblot Test or the Thematic Apperception Test, both of which are techniques in which the responses of the test taker presumably disclose features of his or her personality or concerns that are not easily accessible through more overt techniques.

Behavioral assessment is conducted by some clinical psychologists to identify problem behaviors, to understand what maintains these behaviors, and to develop and refine appropriate interventions to change these behaviors. Techniques may include behavioral self-report (e.g., keeping a diary about the timing and intensity of an unwanted behavior), or behavioral observation (e.g., documenting the acting-out behavior of a hyperactive child).

Neuropsychological assessment is the process of gathering information about a client's brain functioning on the basis of performance on psychological tests, the best-known of which is the Halstead-Reitan Neuropsychological Test Battery, which measures sensorimotor, perceptual, and speech functions. Neuropsychological tests are used to assess a variety of conditions including brain damage, dementia, and learning disabilities.

Consultant

Many clinical psychologists are asked to apply their human relations expertise in contexts other than psychotherapy. When a clinical psychologist acts in the role of consultant, there is still a client, but the client in this case is often an organization. The consulting role depends on specialty areas of the clinical psychologist and on the needs of the organization. For example, a clinical psychologist may consult with human service agencies, possibly assisting their efforts to develop more effective treatment programs for clients. Another clinical psychologist may specialize in consulting to businesses or municipal groups, possibly assisting a company or a police department in the development of a stress reduction program. In the realm of consulting, various subspecialties have arisen, as clinical psychologists have carved out specializations in contexts such as forensics, sports, and organizational systems.

Clinical psychologists are recruited as consultants because they have been trained in three relevant areas: assessment, intervention, and research. *Assessment* training equips the clinical psychologist with the knowledge needed for defining the problem. *Intervention* skills enable psychologists to solve systemic problems by using techniques similar to those employed in family therapy. Lastly, *research* skills enable the consultant to evaluate the effectiveness of an intervention and offer informed recommendations.

Research

Research conducted by clinical psychologists is quite diverse, usually focusing on some facet of clinical diagnosis or treatment. For example, a psychopathologist may study the relationship between experiences of child abuse and subsequent emotional adjustment as an adult. Or, a psychotherapy researcher may study the differential effectiveness of various treatment programs for a particular emotional problem. The field of health psychology has expanded tremendously in recent decades, as psychologists have used their methodological expertise to conduct research on health-related behaviors and interventions aimed at improving physical functioning. For example, the field of behavioral medicine uses an interdisciplinary approach rooted in learning theory to address medical conditions affected by psychological factors.

Educator and Administrator

In addition to teaching in traditional classroom contexts, many clinical psychologists provide clinical supervision either in individual or in group meetings. Clinical supervision involves teaching trainees or unlicensed clinicians how to conduct psychotherapy, administer psychological testing, or provide consultation services. Clinical psychologists who engage in administrative work customarily work in mental health settings, as administrators of mental health clinics, treatment centers, or units in larger health care facilities. Clinical psychologists are often hired for such positions because they have knowledge and experience in several relevant spheres. For example, a clinical psychologist may be hired as the administrator of a community mental health center where the job description calls for a professional who is knowledgeable about psychopathology, psychotherapy, research, and organizational issues.

Becoming a Clinical Psychologist

Entrance into the field requires intensive training in a clinical psychology graduate program. Programs adhering to the Boulder model, which are usually located at research universities, emphasize research training to a considerable extent. Alternatively, professional schools of psychology, which offer either a PsyD (Doctor of Psychology) or a PhD, usually place greater emphasis on clinical training. Either type of program can be accredited by the American Psychological Association (APA), an important criterion for graduates seeking licensure and credentialing.

Programs accredited by the APA usually require four years of graduate courses and clinical practicum programs accompanied by a year-long internship at a health care facility. Academic studies involve the completion of various courses spanning the field of general psychology, with particular emphasis on clinical psychology. Additionally, students are involved in research to varying degrees depending on the philosophy of the doctoral program. Research-oriented programs require the student to complete a master's thesis and a doctoral dissertation. Following completion of the doctorate, the clinical psychologist must become licensed in order to practice independently. Licensing laws differ from state to state, but most states require a minimum of two years of full-time supervised work in the field, a passing grade on a standardized examination in general psychology, and possibly an additional assessment such as an oral examination, a clinical case presentation, or a jurisprudence examination.

Recent Trends and Future Possibilities

Recent trends in clinical psychology have emerged in response to changes in the health care marketplace. Many clinicians who entered the field because of idealistic aspirations to help people now find that they are competing in a business atmosphere to stay afloat financially. New approaches to health care, such as managed care, group practices, and contracting with businesses to provide mental health care for employees, have reduced the number of solo private practitioners.

In recent years, greater emphasis has been placed on *evidence-based practice* in psychology, which fosters the philosophy of integrating the best available research with clinical expertise in the context of client characteristics, culture, and preferences. While debate continues about what constitutes evidence within each of these realms, the evidence-based criterion influences most aspects of clinical research, training, and practice. For example, the increasing endorsement by managed care companies of cognitive approaches to psychotherapy is due in part to the proliferation of published studies pointing to the effectiveness of these techniques.

The increase in the number of doctoral program graduates during the past several decades presents the field with some challenges. Predoctoral internships have become increasingly difficult to obtain, as have jobs in traditional settings such as clinics and psychiatric hospitals. In recent years, financial pressures have pushed clinical psychologists to consider ways of expanding or shifting their practice to make their services more sustainable, marketable, and accessible. Some clinical psychologists have pursued specialized training in a narrow field so that they can carve out a niche such as the treatment of eating disorders, sexual dysfunction, sexual deviance, child behavior problems, physical pain, substance dependence, and so on. Some have pursued opportunities to integrate psychotherapy practices into medical settings and primary care. Supporters of this shift believe that clinical psychologists and medical professionals can do more to help clients when they collaborate to provide care. Some clinical psychologists have tapped the technological advances of the past two decades to expand their work into the realm of what is now called telehealth (e.g., the use of online and telephonic communication) to offer psychological services to clients in other parts of the country or the world.

Clinical psychologists are offered a variety of opportunities and seemingly countless possibilities. In addition to the personal enrichment that most clinical psychologists find in their work, most clinical psychologists derive satisfaction from the opportunity to have a positive impact on individuals, communities, and society.

See also Behavioral Theories and Therapies; Cognitive-Behavioral Therapy; Evidence-Based Practice and Outcome Measurement; Humanistic Theories and Therapies; Psychodynamic Psychotherapy; Psychotherapy; School Mental Health; Workplace Issues in Mental Health

Bibliography

Barlow, David H. 2011. *The Oxford Handbook of Clinical Psychology.* New York: Oxford University Press.

Benjamin, Ludy T. 2005. "A History of Clinical Psychology as a Profession in America (and a Glimpse at Its Future)." *Annual Review of Clinical Psychology* 1: 1–30.

Halgin, Richard P., and Susan Krauss Whitbourne. 2009. *Abnormal Psychology: Clinical Perspectives on Psychological Disorders* (6th ed.). New York: McGraw-Hill.

Kramer, Geoffrey P., Douglas A. Bernstein, and Vicky Phares. 2009. *Introduction to Clinical Psychology* (7th ed.). Upper Saddle River, NJ: Prentice-Hall.

Society of Clinical Psychology, Division 12 of the American Psychological Association. http://www.div12.org/.

Cognitive-Behavioral Therapy

Rebecca M. Ametrano and Michael J. Constantino

Cognitive-behavioral therapy (CBT) is one of the "Big Three" psychotherapy orientations along with psychoanalytic/psychodynamic and client-centered/humanistic approaches (Goldfried & Castonguay 1992). The roots of CBT can be traced to behavior therapy, an approach based on learning theory in which psychotherapists treat psychopathology by reinforcing desired behaviors and extinguishing undesired behaviors (Hollon & DiGiuseppe 2011). In the 1960s and 1970s, though, some behaviorists began to question the effectiveness of their strictly behavioral methods. For example, in his seminal book, *Principles of Behavior Modification*, Albert Bandura (1969) was one of the first theorists to question whether conditioning was the primary mechanism through which human learning, and thus psychotherapeutic change, occurred. Other influential thinkers (e.g., Beck, Ellis, Goldfried, Mahoney, Meichenbaum—see Bibliography) had similar perspectives, specifically suggesting that cognition was an essential component of the change process.

Background

Despite some initial resistance to cognitive models, an increasing number of behaviorists began to concede that there were limits to their existing interventions. For example, so-called token economies, an intervention model that relied solely on the use of positive reinforcement to increase the occurrence of desired behaviors, were difficult to generalize to novel situations outside of the therapy setting. The same could be said for assertiveness training and modeling. Ultimately, the realization that behavioral strategies alone would not be effective in all clinical cases prompted the integration of the newer cognitive interventions into existing behavioral therapies.

Reflecting this integration, Albert Ellis organized the first conference on cognitive-behavioral therapies in 1976. Ellis, a clinical psychologist and CBT pioneer, had developed Rational Emotive Behavior Therapy (REBT; Ellis 1962) over a decade earlier. Building on more traditional psychoanalytic principles, REBT was among the first formal CBT systems in that Ellis advocated belief change as a means to emotional and behavioral change (Hollon & DiGiuseppe 2011). Along with Ellis, Aaron Beck, a psychiatrist, also shaped the early CBT movement with his *cognitive therapy* (CT; A. Beck 1970). CT was initially used in the treatment of depression (A. Beck et al. 1979); however, it was ultimately adapted for a range of emotional disorders (e.g., anxiety disorders: Beck, Emery, & Greenberg 1985; personality disorders: A. Beck & Freeman 1990).

Central Tenets

The main tenet of all cognitively oriented approaches is that the way in which people think about or perceive situations has a direct influence on how they feel. In other words, emotional experiences are a function of the *perception* or *appraisal* of the situation, not simply the situation itself (A. Beck 1964; Mahoney 1974; Meichenbaum 1977). These emotions, in turn, lead people to behave in

Albert Ellis, speaking in New York on February 18, 1973. Ellis invented what is known as rational emotive behavior therapy, which stresses that patients can improve their lives by taking control of self-defeating thoughts, feelings, and behaviors. (AP Photo/ Jim Wells.)

certain ways. It follows then that certain thoughts may *negatively* influence one's psychological functioning. Consider the example in which students A, B, and C all receive poor grades on their exam. Student A thinks, "I studied so hard for this exam, I must be really stupid to have received such an awful grade." Student A feels depressed (negative emotion as a function of a negative thought) and withdraws from friends (maladaptive behavior as a function of negative emotion). Student B thinks, "I really needed a good grade; now I may not be able to pass the course." Student B feels anxious and studies intensely for subsequent exams. Finally, student C thinks, "I knew all of the material on this exam so well, the exam must have been unfairly graded." Student C feels angry and schedules an appointment to question the exam's fairness with the instructor. As one can see, the poor grade was constant across all three students' test results; however, their varying interpretations of the grade resulted in disparate emotions and behavioral responses. This perspective forms the basis of cognitive models of health and psychopathology.

From Ellis's rational-emotive perspective, beliefs can be either rational or irrational. To Ellis, psychologically healthy individuals base their beliefs on logic and empirical evidence, and recognize that the world is not always fair or perfect. On the other hand, psychologically unhealthy individuals often make catastrophic and illogical assumptions about the world, as well as about their worth and competence, which lead to negative emotional consequences. Ellis attributed another key aspect of health to flexibility of thought, with extreme beliefs emanating from rigidity of thought. Ellis also noted that because people can become upset about their own feelings, emotions could trigger additional negative or illogical thoughts, thus creating a vicious cycle.

Beck's cognitive model also highlighted dysfunctional thinking as being at the root of psychopathology. In his 1967 book, *Depression: Clinical, Experimental, and Theoretical Aspects*, Beck posited that individuals become depressed because of a propensity to perceive the world in a negative and biased way, which he labeled a *schema*. Schemata are "organized knowledge systems that bias the way information is processed in the direction of maintaining existing beliefs" (Hollon & DiGiuseppe 2011, 222). Based on the schema concept, cognitive theorists have identified three levels of thinking that are progressively "deeper" in one's belief structure.

At the deepest level are the *core beliefs* or core schemata (the terms are used interchangeably) about oneself. Core beliefs are developed early in childhood and become so ingrained in the psyche that people are often unaware of them. Instead, people tend to regard core beliefs as unchangeable personal traits. Examples of central core beliefs according to Beck's cognitive model include, "I am unlovable," "I am helpless," "I am a failure," and "I am incompetent."

At the middle level are the *intermediate beliefs*, which are attitudes, rules, and assumptions that are born from one's core beliefs. For example, the core belief "I am a failure" might lead to an intermediate belief of "If I am not perfect, then I am a perfect failure." The core belief "I am incompetent" might be connected to an intermediate belief "If I am not working excessively at all times, then I am worthless and lazy."

Finally, the most easily accessible belief level comprises *automatic thoughts*, which are negative views about the self, the world, and the future (what Beck termed the *cognitive triad*). Automatic thoughts are posited to color virtually automatically one's perceptions and interpretations of many or even most situations or stressors, thus enhancing or maintaining a negative mood. Often, automatic thoughts reflect *cognitive distortions*, which result from faulty information processing or errors in logic. Several common cognitive distortions include: all-or-nothing thinking, mind reading, overgeneralizing, catastrophizing, personalizing, and discounting positives. If a student thought, "What a failure I am, I can't believe I got a B on my exam," he or she would be engaging in all-or-nothing thinking, a type of cognitive distortion in which the student believes that anything less than an A equals personal failure (for this person there would be no "shades of gray"). Further, this automatic thought would be related to the intermediate belief that being perfect is the only way not to be a failure, which in turn relates to the core belief that he or she is a failure.

Therapeutic Dimensions

Based on cognitive-behavioral theories of psychopathology, the general process of CBT encompasses several key components. First, CBT is structured, focused, and time limited. CBT clients can expect to be in therapy anywhere from several sessions to a year depending on the nature of their presenting problem and the specific treatment plan. Generally speaking, the treatment plan outlines phases of therapy, including preparation for termination and relapse prevention, in a concrete manner. Thus therapy typically does not continue indefinitely. In fact, another central principle underlying CBT is to assist clients in developing skills and coping strategies to use on their own outside of therapy and after therapy ends. In essence, CBT clinicians help clients become their own therapist.

During therapy, CBT therapists have many cognitively and behaviorally oriented techniques at their disposal. However, all of these techniques are related to one overriding principle, namely, that *everything can be interpreted in multiple ways*. Related to this idea, CBT focuses on four overarching goals. The first goal involves the client and therapist working collaboratively to monitor and to identify, in successive order, automatic thoughts, cognitive distortions, intermediate beliefs, and core schemata. The second goal involves therapists helping clients link their automatic thoughts to their negative emotions. Once clients understand the connection between their thoughts and emotions, the third therapy goal is to challenge these maladaptive thoughts and to consider alternative ways of thinking about and interpreting situations. The fourth goal then involves replacing maladaptive thoughts with more adaptive, and often more logical and realistic, thoughts while tracking related changes in mood. Such changes are often amplified with behavioral experiments in which clients engage either during session or between sessions for homework.

As noted, CBT therapists have many techniques on which they can draw; however, virtually all courses of CBT will involve the use of *Socratic dialogue* and some form of a *dysfunctional thought record* (DTR). Socratic dialogue, or *questioning*, involves the clinician leading clients toward personal discovery through a tactful progression of questions. Although the question format preserves a client's sense of autonomy, the therapist also exerts a strong degree of influence over the client in the manner in which the questions are asked. Common generic

Socratic questions include: "What is the evidence that the thought is true?"; "What is the worst thing that could happen?"; "What is the most realistic outcome?"; and "What would I tell my friend to do if he or she was in the same situation?" A more specific dialogue might include asking the client to think about alternate explanations for why an event occurred (e.g., "Other than him not loving you, why might your boyfriend have forgotten to call you yesterday?") or to produce evidence to support more adaptive thought processes (e.g., "I understand you are concerned about failing your exam on Monday. Can you tell me how many algebra exams have you failed in the past?"). This type of questioning gently pushes the client to see situations from new, more adaptive perspectives while at the same time allowing the client to come to the answers to the questions on his or her own, which helps lead to a sense of personal mastery.

DTRs, which were initially developed by Aaron Beck in the late 1970s, are a structured form for helping clients respond more effectively to their triggering situations and related maladaptive thoughts (see also J. Beck 1995). DTRs usually contain five columns including: the distressing situation, automatic thought(s) (during that situation), emotion(s) (during that situation), alternative response (upon reflecting on the situation), and outcome (after considering alternative responses to the situation). Using the DTR, clients monitor situations that trigger unpleasant emotions, record the accompanying automatic thoughts, and document their corresponding emotions. Then, initially in collaboration with their therapist, clients attempt to produce more adaptive responses to the situation (based heavily on the use of Socratic questioning). Finally, after working through potential adaptive responses, clients record how much they believe their initial automatic thought, how strongly they feel the initial corresponding emotion, and how much they believe the new, more adaptive response. Ideally, the client will experience a decrease in the intensity of the negative emotion, and a stronger belief in the adaptive versus the maladaptive thought. The therapist can then emphasize for the client that the situation never changed; rather, it was the client's interpretation of the situation that changed, which resulted in the decrease in negative emotion. Over time, clients can use DTRs on their own, either formally with the form or informally in their head.

As can be seen from the various techniques discussed, CBT clients take an active role in their own treatment, relying on the therapist predominantly as a guide or a teacher. The therapeutic relationship in CBT is one of *collaborative empiricism* where the client and therapist work together to resolve the client's distress. Clients are taught to be scientists who view thoughts as ideas to be tested as opposed to established and immutable truths. As Judith Beck (another influential figure in the field, and daughter of Aaron Beck) has noted, the therapist will likely take a more active role at the start of the therapy, but as the client's symptoms reduce and he or she has a better grasp of therapeutic process, the responsibility balance will shift toward the client (J. Beck 1995). Unlike some other forms of therapy, empathy and warmth on the part of therapist are viewed as neither necessary nor sufficient for psychotherapeutic change; however, many CBT therapists will certainly aspire toward these relationship elements, as they might help to support the primary change mechanism—cognitive modification.

Research and Evaluation

Over the past several decades, CBT has been one of the most widely researched forms of psychotherapy. Early on, Beck and colleagues demonstrated that cognitive therapy was at least as efficacious as medication in the treatment of depression (Kovacs et al. 1981). These positive findings have been frequently replicated; for example, DeRubeis and colleagues (2005) showed cognitive therapy to be as effective as medication treatment for severely depressed clients when implemented by experienced cognitive psychotherapists. Research has also consistently revealed that CBT has more enduring effects in the treatment of depression than psychopharmacological treatments (Hollon, Stewart, & Strunk 2006). Results supporting the use of CBT also extend beyond depression. CBT is considered an empirically supported treatment for conditions such as panic disorder, obsessive-compulsive disorder, posttraumatic stress disorder, eating disorders, pain disorders, and even some personality disorders.

Despite the empirical support and popularity of CBT, limitations exist. First, although CBT may successfully treat acute symptoms, it does not always promote the client's inner growth and development. In this vein, it is possible that CBT addresses the symptoms, but not necessarily the cause of a given psychological problem. Furthermore, CBT, with its here-and-now, problem-oriented focus, might not be well suited for clients presenting with vague concerns (e.g., existential issues). Finally, some critics also contend that CBT might be viewed as manipulative and controlling, and that distressing thoughts are not always irrational or maladaptive!

It is unlikely to think that any psychological treatment will be effective for all individuals across all conditions, and CBT is no exception. Limitations notwithstanding, CBT has become a major force in psychotherapy over the past few decades. Hollon and DiGiuseppe (2011) outlined several possible factors that led CBT to its current state of prominence in the field: (1) CBT represents a compromise between the psychoanalytic and behavioral traditions; (2) CBT has developed and maintained a strong commitment to research; and (3) both REBT and cognitive therapies tend to be relatively brief, which is valuable in an era of cost-effectiveness and limited insurance coverage. Whatever the reasons, cognitive and behavioral therapies are empirically viable, and often a first line choices in the treatment of a range of psychological conditions.

See also Behavioral Theories and Therapies; Clinical Psychology; Humanistic Theories and Therapies; Psychodynamic Psychotherapy; Psychotherapy

Bibliography

Bandura, A. 1969. *Principles of Behavior Modification.* New York: Holt, Rinehart & Winston.

Beck, Aaron T. 1964. "Thinking and Depression: II. Theory and Therapy." *Archives of General Psychiatry* 10: 561–571.

Beck, Aaron T. 1967. *Depression: Clinical, Experimental, and Theoretical Aspects.* New York: Hoeber.

Beck, Aaron T. 1970. "Cognitive Therapy: Nature and Relation to Behavior Therapy." *Behavior Therapy* 1: 184–200.

Beck, Aaron T., Gary Emery, and Ruth Greenberg. 1985. *Anxiety Disorders and Phobias: A Cognitive Perspective.* New York: Basic Books.

Beck, Aaron T., and Arthur M. Freeman. 1990. *Cognitive Therapy of Personality Disorders.* New York: Guilford Press.

Beck, Aaron T., A. John Rush, Brian F. Shaw, and Gary Emery. 1979. *Cognitive Therapy of Depression.* New York: Guilford Press.

Beck, Judith S. 1995. *Cognitive Therapy: Basics and Beyond.* New York: Guilford Press.

DeRubeis, Robert J., Steven D. Hollon, Jay D. Amsterdam, Richard C. Shelton, Paula R. Young, Ronald R. Salomon, John P. O'Reardon, Margaret L. Lovett, Madeline M. Gladis, Laurel L. Brown, and Robert Gallop. 2005. "Cognitive Therapy vs. Medications in the Treatment of Moderate to Severe Depression." *Archives of General Psychiatry* 62: 409–416.

Ellis, A. 1962. *Reason and Emotion in Psychotherapy.* New York: Lyle Stuart.

Goldfried, Marvin R., and Louis G. Castonguay. 1992. "The Future of Psychotherapy Integration." *Psychotherapy* 29: 4–10.

Hollon, Steven D., and Raymond DiGiuseppe. 2011. "Cognitive Theories of Psychotherapy." In John C Norcross, Gary R. VandenBos, and Donald K. Freedheim, eds., *History of Psychotherapy: Continuity and Change* (pp. 203–241). Washington, DC: American Psychological Association.

Hollon, Steven D., Michael O. Stewart, and Daniel Strunk. 2006. "Enduring Effects for Cognitive Behavior Therapy in the Treatment of Depression and Anxiety." In Susan T. Fiske, Alan E. Kazdin, and Daniel L. Schacter, eds., *Annual Review of Psychology* (pp. 285–315). Palo Alto, CA: Annual Reviews.

Kovacs, Maria, John A. Rush, Aaron T. Beck, and Steven D. Hollon. 1981."Depressed Outpatients Treated with Cognitive Therapy or Pharmacotherapy: A One-Year Follow-Up." *Archives of General Psychiatry* 38: 33–39.

Mahoney, Michael J. 1974. *Cognition and Behavior Modification.* Oxford: Ballinger, 1974.

Meichenbaum, Donald. 1977. *Cognitive Behavior Modification: An Integrative Approach.* New York: Plenum.

College Mental Health Issues

See Campus Life and Mental Health

Community Mental Health

Jessica Rosenberg

"Community mental health" is a broad term that encompasses historical and contemporary issues related to the treatment of persons with serious mental illness. Such persons occupy a special niche in society, by virtue of their disability, and also because of stigma and social marginalization. Considerable advances in treatment and civil rights have been achieved since the brutal beginnings of mental health care that enable people who were heretofore warehoused, often for life, to live full lives and to participate freely in society with dignity and independence.

The development of successful treatments such as Thorazine, the first effective psychotropic, as well as a civil rights movement that won significant gains in fighting discrimination toward the mentally ill, brought about reforms in mental health policy and improved access to treatment. Nonetheless, persons with serious mental illness continue to contend with numerous challenges, chiefly, insufficient psychosocial resources, a societal trend toward the criminalization of the mentally ill, and the impact of damaging co-occurring disorders, such as addiction. Central to the obstacles confronting the development of community mental health care is pervasive and persistent societal stigma toward mental illness, an issue that was highlighted by the Surgeon General as a tragic barrier that deprives people of their full participation in society (U.S. Department of Health and Human Services 1999).

History

While society has always had members who manifest characteristics associated with mental illness, such as delusional thinking or bizarre behavior, an organized humane response to such ills has been elusive. During the American colonial period, people with mental illness were labeled "lunatics" and kept out of the public view by their family. The prevailing belief was that they were possessed by the devil, and several barbaric methods were employed to rid them of evil spirits, such as being immersed in an ice bath until unconscious, and bloodletting, sometimes to the point of death (Leupo n.d.; U.S. Department of Health and Human Services 1999).

Two major factors provided the foundation for the development of the public mental hospitals, and made it possible for American society to move from a reliance on familial care to a system of institutional care: (1) The industrial era of the 1880s, which involved a rural-to-urban migration that led to overcrowded cities and urban crime; and (2) a huge influx of immigration that provided many benefits, such as cultural diversity and a skilled workforce, but also contributed to social problems that needed to be attended to. These powerful demographic changes provided an impetus for society to develop a system to care for its dependent and disabled, partly motivated by the desire to stabilize urban growth. The first public mental institution in the United States, Eastern State Hospital in Williamsburg, Virginia, was founded in 1773, and by 1935, it housed approximately 2,000 psychiatric patients (Wacksman 2003). During the 1880s, mental hospitals rapidly grew in number. By the late 1880s, approximately 139 mental institutions had been built in the United States, with a patient population estimated to be close to 41,000 (Grob 1991).

American mental asylums functioned as total intuitions characterized by rigid and highly stratified rules that governed all aspects of an individual's existence (Goffman 1961). While the term "mental asylum" is closely associated in the public's imagination with huge gothic walls behind which barbaric and terrifying conditions existed, their development occurred within the context of social reforms, and were part of the humanistic ideals of a school of thought termed "moral management mental health," an approach based on the work of the French psychiatrist Philippe Pinel (1745–1826), which emphasized compassion, kindness, and respect as essential to the treatment of the mentally ill (Weissmann 2008). During the first half of the twentieth century, the number of mental hospitals increased significantly despite a decrease in public funding, and as a result, the conditions of care deteriorated. Overcrowded wards included a mix of violent offenders, vagrants, alcoholics, and other socially marginalized groups. The focus was on long-term custodial care; the use of invasive procedures that could control the inpatient population, such as lobotomies (severing parts of the brain) and electro-convulsive therapy, were common; and the ideals of treatment, were essentially abandoned (Grob 1991; Klein forthcoming).

Deinstitutionalization

By the 1970s, through the process of deinstitutionalization, a term used to describe the massive discharge of people with serious mental illness from mental hospitals to the community, approximately 500,000 individuals were discharged to the community. Between 1955 and the mid-1970s, the number of patients hospitalized in state mental hospitals decreased by more than 60 percent (Rosenberg & Rosenberg 2006; Talbot 2004). Several multifaceted factors propelled the shift from institutionally based care to community care: (1) President Kennedy's commitment to issues of mental health treatment, perhaps influenced by his personal experience with his sister, a victim of a lobotomy; (2) the passage of the Community Mental Health Act of 1963, a federal act passed under the Kennedy administration that provided funding for community mental health centers; (3) the development of a new generation of psychotropic medications, starting with Thorazine (which was developed in 1950); and (4) the passage of Medicare and

Medicaid in 1965, legislation that provided a funding stream for community mental health (Rosenberg & Rosenberg 2006).

Deinstitutionalization, which involved discharging inpatients who were accustomed to life in a "total institution" to the community, was poorly implemented. It occurred in the absence of adequate support for the psychosocial needs of the patients, especially with regard to housing and the access to treatment, and resulted in a marked increase in ranks of the homeless. Numerous other societal problems, substance abuse and criminal behaviors among the most pernicious, have been linked to deinstitutionalization and to society's failure to deliver on the promise of community mental health (Rosenberg & Rosenberg 2006).

Stigma

In the classic text *Asylums: Essays on the Social Situation of Mental Patients and Other Inmates* by Erving Goffman (1961), stigma is conceptualized as an "attribute that is deeply discrediting" and that reduces the bearer "from a whole and usual person to a tainted, discounted one" (3). Persons who are stigmatized possess characteristics that position them outside of the expectations established by socially accepted norms. Stigma represents a relational attribute, a "mark," that connects him or her to negative stereotypes. Stigma is not only a label but, rather, suggests that the person is inherently tainted. In the process, stigma victims are blamed for "being" socially unacceptable. Whereas an individual diagnosed with cancer is referred to as "having cancer," a person diagnosed with schizophrenia is viewed as "being schizophrenic" (Corrigan & Lee forthcoming; Link & Phelan 2001; Rosenberg et al. 2006).

A comprehensive report on mental health issues by the Surgeon General found that nearly two-thirds of people with a diagnosable psychiatric condition do not seek treatment, and identifies stigma as a central barrier that prevents individuals from seeking help. The negative portrayals of people who are psychiatrically disabled in the media, for example, as depraved, dangerous and violent, inhibit people from self-identifying as mentally ill, and tragically lead to the loss of self-esteem and hope for the future (U.S. Department of Health and Human Services 1999).

The Consumer Movement

The consumer movement is a civil rights movement that developed in opposition to the brutal and dehumanizing treatment of people with serious mental illness. It dates back to the nineteenth-century expansion of the asylum and opposed brutal and coercive treatment, such as lobotomies and the forced institutionalization of the psychiatrically disabled. It is primarily comprised of people who have been personally involved with the mental health system, and who define themselves as "consumers" of mental health care (as opposed to patients), who seek to win full rights and participation in society for the psychiatrically disabled, and who fight for humane treatment.

The consumer movement owes much of its ideologically orientation to the civil rights movement. In the 1960s and 1970s, as deinstitutionalization proceeded, psychiatric inpatients protested the substandard treatment and conditions of institutions. In the wake of community-based care, treatment models that are designed and delivered by consumers began to gain acceptance in mainstream mental health care, such as peer-run community mental health programming, mutual support groups, and the use of peer advocates. A national survey examining the extent of consumer-run mental health in the United States found 7,467 treatment groups that met the criteria of consumer-run, which was comparatively larger than the number of traditional mental health organizations (4,546) in the United States (Goldstrom et al. 2006). The success of the consumer movement in promoting the rights of the psychiatrically disabled and in controlling their own treatment is evident in the proliferation and mainstream acceptance of these models (Corrigan et al. 2007; Pulice & Miccio 2006)

Recovery

The strength of the consumer movement and the move from institution to community-based care is rooted in a philosophical orientation that embraces the concept of recovery. Recovery is a perspective that stands in juxtaposition to antiquated and destructive notions that view mental illness as a chronic condition. Recovery challenges mental health policy and practice that dehumanize the mentally ill, rob them of their civil rights, subject them to barbaric interventions, and deny them full participation in society. Recovery is rooted in hope and optimism, in the conviction that persons with serious mental illness can achieve full participation in society (Corrigan & Lee forthcoming; U.S. Department of Health and Human Services 1999).

Community Mental Health Treatment Models

Assertive Community Treatment

Assertive community treatment (ACT) is widely recognized as an effective treatment for persons with serious mental illness. It is designed to treat people who have significant difficulty with everyday functioning, and has been shown to reduce rehospitalizations. The ACT model is a mobile treatment program that delivers psychiatric services to the client in his or her community. Staffed by a multidisciplinary team that typically includes a psychiatrist, a nurse, and a case manager, ACT provides a broad range of therapeutic services, including medication management, crisis intervention, and individual supportive therapy. Major features of the program are: (1) The team travels to the client where he or she resides; (2) services are available 24 hours/seven days a week; (3) caseloads are small and shared among team members; and (4) treatment plans are flexible and tailored to meet client needs (Burns & Firn 2002; McLaughlin forthcoming).

Case Management

Case management (CM) is a treatment framework that works with seriously mentally ill clients and links them with needed services. There are a number of different models that provide case management services, and while their orientation may differ, the following core components of CM are well established: (1) outreach, (2) assessment, (3) case plan development, (4) service referral/procurement, (5) monitoring and advocacy, and (6) evaluation (Thomas 2006).

Family Psychoeducation

Family psychoeducation (FPE) is an effective family treatment model that has been shown, based on decades of research, to improve outcomes for persons with severe mental illness through stabilizing family functioning. FPE departs from earlier views of the family that "blamed" mental illness on family dysfunction, and, in contrast, is based on the assumption that families cope with having an ill member as best as they can. FPE validates the family's experience of grief, loss and fear and provides them with support and education, typically in group modalities, such as multifamily groups (Lynch, Mason, & McFarlane forthcoming; McFarlane 2002).

Community Mental Health: Challenges for the Twenty-First Century

Deinstitutionalization was founded on principles of social reform and in recognition of the civil rights of psychiatrically disabled. The public awareness that it was not acceptable to force the mentally ill to live in substandard conditions and that participation in the community could be achieved propelled deinstitutionalization forward. However, for large numbers of inpatients who were discharged from institutions, many of whom had spent years institutionalized, there was no adequate community system of care in place for them. The failure of community mental health subsequent to the passage of the Community Mental Health Act of 1963 is the absence of a coordinated community infrastructure to meet the complex and multifaceted needs of the psychiatrically disabled. Persons with serious mental illness were discharged from institutional care without adequate housing, social supports, or community mental health treatment centers. Many became homeless, became involved in substance abuse, were vulnerable to criminals, were targets of violence and exploitation, or were jailed (Fakhoury & Priebe 2007).

Coordinated and comprehensive systems of care require a unified approach wherein policy promotes treatment, which in turn is supported by funding. However, the history of community mental health illustrates that public policy too often lags behind knowledge expansion and best practice treatment models, while funding is frequently inconsistent and inadequate.

See also Criminalization and Diversion Programs; Disability Rights; History of Mental Health Care; Homelessness and Mental Illness; Mental Health Advocacy; Peer Support Groups; State Mental Health Agencies; Stigma; Therapeutic Community and Milieu Therapy

Bibliography

Burns, T., and M. Firn. 2002. *Assertive Outreach in Mental Health: A Manual for Practitioners.* New York: Oxford University Press.

Corrigan, P. W., and E. Lee. Forthcoming. "Recovery and Stigma in People with Serious Mental Illness." In J. Rosenberg and S. Rosenberg, eds., *Community Mental Health: Challenges for the 21st Century* (2nd ed.). New York: Routledge.

Corrigan, P. C., K. T. Mueser, G. R. Bond, R. E. Drake, and P. Solomon. 2007. *Principles and Practice of Psychiatric Rehabilitation: An Empirical Approach.* New York: Guilford Press.

Fakhoury, W., and S. Priebe. 2007. "Deinstitutionalization and Reinstitutionalization: Major Changes in the Provision of Mental Healthcare." *Psychiatry* 6(8): 313–316.

Goffman, E. 1961. *Asylums: Essays on the Social Situation of Mental Patients and Other Inmates.* New York: Anchor Books.

Goldstrom, I. D., J. Campbell, J. A. Rogers, D. B. Lambert, B. Blacklow, M. J. Henderson, and R. W. Manderscheid. 2006. "National Estimates for Mental Health Mutual Support Groups, Self-Help Organizations, and Consumer-Operated Services." *Administration and Policy in Mental Health and Mental Health Services Research* 33(1): 92–103.

Grob, G. N. 1991. *From Asylum to Community: Mental Health Policy in America.* Princeton, NJ: Princeton University Press.

Klein, E. Forthcoming. "Community Mental Health Policy." In J. Rosenberg and S. Rosenberg, eds., *Community Mental Health: Challenges for the 21st Century* (2nd ed.). New York: Routledge.

Leupo, K. n.d. "The History of Mental Illness." Retrieved from http://www.toddlertime.com/advocacy/hospitals/Asylum/history-asylum.htm.

Link, B. G., and J. C. Phelan. 2001. "Conceptualizing Stigma." *Annual Review of Sociology* 27: 363–385.

Lynch, S., N. Mason, and W. McFarlane. Forthcoming. "Family Psychoeducation in the Treatment of Mental Illness: Historical Context, Current Practice and Future Directions." In J. Rosenberg and S. Rosenberg, eds., *Community Mental Health: Challenges for the 21st Century* (2nd ed.). New York: Routledge.

McFarlane, W. R. 2002. *Multifamily Groups in the Treatment of Severe Psychiatric Disorders.* New York: Guilford Press.

McLaughlin, J. J. Forthcoming. "Assertive Community Treatment: An Evidence-Based Practice and Its Continuing Evolution." In J. Rosenberg and S. Rosenberg, eds., *Community Mental Health: Challenges for the 21st Century* (2nd ed.). New York: Routledge.

Pulice, R. T., and S. Miccio. 2006. "Patient, Client, Consumer, Survivor: The Mental Health Consumer Movement in the United States." In J. Rosenberg and S. Rosenberg, eds., *Community Mental Health: Challenges for the 21st Century* (pp. 7–14). New York: Routledge.

Rosenberg, J., and S. Rosenberg, eds. 2006. *Community Mental Health: Challenges for the 21st Century.* New York: Routledge.

Rosenberg, J., S. Rosenberg, C. Huygen, and E. Klein. 2006. "Stigma, Sexual Orientation and Mental Illness: A Community Mental Health Perspective." In J. Rosenberg and

S. Rosenberg, eds., *Community Mental Health: Challenges for the 21st Century* (pp. 117–123). New York: Routledge.

Talbott, J. A. 2004. "Deinstitutionalization: Avoiding the Disasters of the Past." *Psychiatric Services* 55: 1112–1115.

Thomas, P. 2006. "The Practice Effectiveness of Case Management Services for Homeless Persons with Alcohol, Drug, or Mental Health Problems." In J. Rosenberg and S. Rosenberg, eds., *Community Mental Health: Challenges for the 21st Century* (pp. 181–194). New York: Routledge.

U.S. Department of Health and Human Services. 1999. *Mental Health: A Report of the Surgeon General—Executive Summary.* Rockville, MD: U.S. Department of Health and Human Services, Substance Abuse and Mental Health Services Administration, Center for Mental Health Services, National Institutes of Health, National Institute of Mental Health.

Wacksman, J. 2003. "A Most Curious Choice: The Mystery Surrounding the Establishment of the Eastern State Hospital in Williamsburg." Retrieved from http://www.resnet.wm.edu/~jjwack/history.html.

Weissmann, G. 2008. "Citizen Pinel and the Madman at Bellevue." *The FASEB Journal* 22(5): 1289–1293.

Complementary and Alternative Medicine

See Mind and Body Approaches to Mental Health

Consumers' Movement

See Advocacy Groups; Recovery Movement; Rights of Patients with Mental Conditions

Counseling

See Mental Health Counseling

Creativity and Mental Health

Daphne Algaze, Dennis K. Kinney, and Ruth Richards

For thousands of years, people have reported an apparent association of creative genius with psychopathology and, more generally, with mental suffering. Aristotle, for example, wrote that all of the greatest creators of his time seemed to suffer from periods of mental illness. Some writers have even suggested that experiencing the extreme psychological symptoms and suffering associated with severe mental illness may be a necessary "price" one must pay for great creativity. But is this really true? Recent psychological research suggests that it may not be, and that it is *not* the severe symptoms of mental illness that facilitate creativity but rather certain traits associated with liability for (or proneness to) some mental illnesses. That is, milder, or even subclinical, traits associated with liability for some severe mental disorders may be what is conducive to creative work, whereas severe symptoms and suffering may actually interfere with creativity (Kinney & Richards 2011; Richards 1981; Runco & Richards 1998).

With everyday creativity defined in terms of the two criteria of *originality* and *meaningfulness*, it has been hypothesized that increased creative potential might be an advantage to genes that also increase susceptibility to certain mental illnesses. That is, enhanced creativity may be a biological advantage to certain genes, one that offsets the biological disadvantages associated with severe mental illness. This compensatory advantage may help explain why some severe mental illnesses—and the genes that increase risk for them—may persist at relatively high rates in the general population. There is a precedent for this idea in the case of severe medical disorders such as sickle cell anemia, where the sickle cell gene persists at high levels in areas where malaria is endemic, because the gene provides the compensatory advantage of increased resistance to malaria (e.g., Kinney & Matthysse 1978; Richards, Kinney, Lunde, Benet, & Merzel 1988; Runco & Richards 1998).

In this entry, we review relevant research, including related topics, such as the potential appeal of creative activity for persons at risk for some major mental disorders. Also considered is whether creative activity may lead to mental illness—or alternatively, to mental health. We conclude with practical implications of creativity research for issues such as nurturing creative talent and reducing the symptoms and stigma of mental illness.

Research on Creativity and Major Mental Disorders

A direct and simple association between major mental illness and eminent creativity—i.e., creativity that has achieved major social or professional acclaim—would appear, at first glance, to be supported by research that has found high rates of mental illness among eminent creators, particularly in artistic fields (a collection of key studies is found in Runco and Richards's edited volume, 1998). Ludwig (1995), for example, studied 1,000 eminent creators about whom a major biography had been written between 1960 and 1990, finding that those in artistic professions were much more likely to have suffered a mental illness than those in nonartistic professions. Andreasen (1987) studied eminent creative writers in the United States and found that 80 percent of them had suffered from a mood disorder at some point in their lives. But eminent creators are not typical, and they show certain strengths by virtue of their success. What, then, can be said about the general population?

These and related findings on eminent creativity (e.g., Kinney & Richards 2011; Richards 1981; Runco & Richards 1998) raise questions about associations between creativity and psychopathology. Does mental illness trigger creativity, or is it only part of a more complex relationship? What specific types of psychopathology or genetic liability for mental illness are likely to lead to enhanced creativity, and what psychological mechanisms mediate this effect? Does it matter if one considers eminent versus everyday creators?

Creativity and Favorable Traits Associated with Liability for Mental Illness

Several studies (see Kinney et al. 2000–2001; Runco & Richards 1998) have investigated creativity among the close biological relatives of patients with schizophrenia or bipolar disorder. These studies found the highest creativity, on average, was not among the patients with severe mental illness but rather among their *relatives*, who had either milder symptoms or no evidence of any psychopathology at all. This is consistent with the concept of compensatory advantage. For example, Richards, Kinney, Lunde, Benet, and Merzel (1988) compared ratings of vocational and avocational creativity in several groups: (1) patients diagnosed with bipolar disorder or with cyclothymia (a disorder with milder but more frequent mood swings); (2) their "psychiatrically normal" first-degree relatives; and (3) a control group with neither a personal nor a family history of a major mood disorder, cyclothymia, or schizophrenia. Unlike the studies of eminent creators in special areas (e.g., writing, visual arts), these studies chose subjects based on their psychiatric diagnoses, then evaluated them for their creativity using *The Lifetime Creativity Scales* (Richards et al. 1988), which allowed assessment of real-life, everyday creativity as the dependent (or outcome) variable. This approach allows for generalization of study findings to the population at large.

In this study, the "index" group, composed of patients and their relatives (all those carrying risk for bipolar disorders), had a significantly higher mean creativity rating, overall, than the control group. *Within* the index group, however, the cyclothymes had a higher mean creativity score than the two other groups combined. The mean creativity rating for bipolar disorder patients was no higher than that for controls, whereas the patients' psychiatrically *healthy* relatives had the highest creativity mean of any group. Thus healthier mental status combined with genetic risk for bipolar disorder was a much better predictor of elevated creativity than the disorder itself. In other words, both personal and family history need to be considered in understanding creativity-psychopathology associations.

These results, as well as those from complementary studies that have asked patients with mood disorders to describe what psychological states characterized their most creative periods, suggest that there is an "inverted-U" relationship between elevated mood and creativity (Kinney & Richards 2011; Richards et al. 1988; Richards & Kinney 1998) consistent with the idea of compensatory advantage. That is, *milder* mood elevation seems to facilitate creativity, whereas extreme moods inhibit it. Jamison (1993) noted that individuals with genetic liability for bipolar disorder tend to have certain personality traits that may help them achieve recognition for their creative talent and products. Moderately elevated mood, as in hypomania or even subclinical mood elevation, is associated, for example, with increased confidence, risk taking, extroversion, persuasiveness, energy, and productivity—all qualities that can help innovators obtain ideas, energy, attention and support for their creative endeavors. Richards and Kinnney (1998) found related patterns. Richards (1981) argued for potential advantages for creativity of mild mood elevation's effect on cognition, affect, and motivation. In full-blown mania, by contrast, such psychological features tend to balloon into grandiose delusions, reckless behavior, and flight of ideas—severe symptoms that typically interfere with, rather than aid, creative work and recognition.

Further support for this view comes from a study (Richards et al. 1992) of everyday creativity in *depressed* individuals with a family history of bipolar disorders versus similar individuals without such a history. Creativity was significantly higher in depressives *with* the bipolar family history, suggesting that there is some subclinical (or even nonclinical) advantage for creativity running in families with bipolar disorder.

A complementary study of the "schizophrenia spectrum" (Kinney et al. 2000–2001) investigated the creativity of adoptees who had a biological parent with schizophrenia as well as adoptees with no family history of mental disorder. The results of this study were similar to those for the study of creativity and the "bipolar spectrum." That is, adoptees who did not have schizophrenia but *did* have milder symptoms that tend to be genetically linked to schizophrenia (either schizotypal disorder or multiple schizotypal signs; Kendler, Gruenberg, & Kinney 1994) were significantly more creative than other adoptees. Greater creativity was most strongly correlated with "positive" schizotypal traits, such as magical thinking or recurrent illusions. Thus the results of this research on the "schizophrenia spectrum" of disorders are consistent with the "inverted-U" pattern found in the bipolar spectrum, as well as with the presence of a genetically mediated compensatory advantage.

It is notable that psychological traits associated with genetic liability for schizophrenia, rather than symptoms of schizophrenia itself, are associated with higher creativity. Interestingly, while bipolar-spectrum individuals were more likely to manifest their creativity in vocational endeavors, those on the schizophrenia spectrum tended to manifest their creativity more in avocational, or unpaid, activities (Kinney et al. 2000–2001; Richards et al. 1988). The latter activities are less likely than work-related ones to be subject to competition and critical judgment, whereas avocational activities are perhaps more comfortable for individuals on the schizophrenia spectrum, who may tend to have more reticence and social anxiety.

In summary, research on everyday creativity in both the bipolar and schizophrenia spectra of disorders suggests that creativity is most enhanced not by severe psychiatric symptoms but rather by other characteristics associated with genetic liability for schizophrenia or mood disorders. These characteristics may include greater novelty seeking and increased access to unusual thoughts and perceptions—traits that may help generate novel ideas and products (Richards et al. 1988; Kinney 1992). Hence, increased creative potential may be a compensatory advantage of susceptibility genes for schizophrenia and bipolar disorder, an advantage that helps keep these genes—and the disorders themselves—at relatively high rates in the population (Kinney et al. 2011; Richards et al. 1988).

Important supportive evidence for these conclusions also comes from multiple studies of how creativity is related to mood and personal characteristics in *nonclinical* populations (see Runco & Richards 1998). For example, Schuldberg (2000–2001) and his colleagues examined creativity measures in college students along with clinical and subclinical traits that have been associated with the schizophrenia and/or bipolar spectra. Higher scores on a battery of creativity tests and questionnaires were positively correlated with measures of hypomania and positive schizotypal signs. The results of these studies thus complement the findings of an association between higher mean creativity and milder symptoms on the schizophrenia and bipolar spectra.

While some creative people have symptoms of psychopathology, they also tend to have healthy characteristics that allow them to adapt their work to practical, "real-world" ends and to flourish and achieve. For instance, in Barron's studies of eminent creators (see Richards 2007), although some creators were quite high on measures of psychopathology on the MMPI, they were also unusually high on one feature—ego strength—that usually is low. Barron saw this as reflecting the creator's adaptive use of unconscious material.

Creativity, Unconventional Thinking, and Liability for Mental Illness

Unconventional modes of thinking and perceiving are associated with creativity as well as with liability for both bipolar disorder and schizophrenia. At one extreme, these unconventional modes can take the form of the hallucinations and severe thought disorder seen in mania and schizophrenia, such as grandiose and paranoid delusions or incomprehensible speech. Formal thought disorder, a core feature of schizophrenia, can also be observed in mania, though it tends to manifest itself differently in schizophrenia, where it usually takes the form of poverty of content, illogicality, and circumstantiality. In contrast, manic patients tend to display pressured speech, flights of ideas, overinclusive thinking, and incongruent combinations of ideas (Schuldberg 2000–2001; Jamison 1993).

The severity and adaptiveness of unconventional thinking styles vary greatly across the bipolar and schizophrenia spectra. Studies of thought disorder by Philip Holzman, Deborah Levy, and colleagues of the healthier biological relatives of patients with schizophrenia or bipolar disorder have found that such relatives are much more likely than control subjects to display unconventional or disordered types of thinking, though in much less severe form than in those with mania or schizophrenia (see Runco & Richards 1998). While these milder forms are seen by some psychologists as types of thought disorder, from a different perspective they might be viewed as creative processes; the potential for a high score on the Torrance Tests of Creative Thinking has even been suggested. Once again the *adaptive* use of mental contents—rather than the contents themselves—may be the critical difference.

Jamison (1993), for example, concluded that the reduced inhibition and greatly increased quantity of ideas produced during hypomanic episodes give an individual more ideas to work with, along with a propensity to combine ideas in unconventional ways that can produce creative ideas that would not occur to other people. Richards (2010), in a review, cites literature linking latent inhibition to creativity, schizophrenia, faith in intuition, and openness to ideas.

In addition, shifting mental states may hold value for creativity. While hypomania tends to generate many novel ideas, depressed states (which often follow manic ones in bipolar disorder) often make people more self-critical—an effect that is conducive to critical editing of the many novel ideas generated during hypomanic episodes (separating the truly creative ideas from the bizarre or impractical ones). One should also note that *state* variables—i.e., actual mood—as well as *trait* variables—e.g., personal and family history—are associated with creativity in those with major illness. That is, individuals who have serious bipolar disorder (full-blown manic-depressive disorder) report that they are most creative during periods of *mild* mood elevation. This has been found to be the case for everyday creators (see Richards & Kinney 1998) as well as eminent ones (Jamison 1993).

Richards (2007) suggested that some types of psychopathology encourage a form of cognition that is on the "edge of chaos." Bipolar liability, in particular, may bring looser ideas and the confidence to entertain them. Living at the "edge of chaos" in some individuals can be a choice, not a necessity. People who are willing and able to produce divergent ideas have the potential to create valuable new insights. With sufficient ego strength, some individuals can work productively in this state, rather than descend into confused, even psychotic, thinking. Fodor and Laird (2004) theorized that people with an inclination toward bipolar disorder would behave more creatively in this "edge of chaos" state than others. To test this, they assigned subjects to either a play-therapy group or a control group. Half of each group was composed of subjects with a bipolar inclination, whereas the other half had no such inclination. In the experimental group, play therapy was used to induce a state approximating the "edge of chaos" in subjects, by introducing them to widely disparate perspectives. The play therapy was also designed to enhance mood. Each subject was then asked to write a haiku poem. Subjects exposed to play therapy were judged by the investigators to have written more creative poems. Moreover, main effects and an interaction effect showed that, within the experimental group, those with a bipolar inclination wrote the most creative poems, especially in the subgroup that experienced a higher mood elevation as the result of the play therapy.

Psychological Tension, Unease, and Creative Work

Yet what leads to success in the world? People with some degree of psychopathology may be drawn to creative fields for a variety of reasons. They may, for example, find that creative fields are more tolerant of their eccentric behavior and, in the case of the arts, sometimes even welcome it. Another factor may be relief of a sense of psychological unease. Eminent creators, according to Ludwig (1995), are more restless and apt to work through their own problems in their expressive work, and/or to create new problems to distract themselves. By challenging themselves with creative problem solving, they may relieve this disquiet, though only temporarily, so that they are constantly looking for new creative activities.

While good moods may encourage creative work, such work itself often has frustrating parts and can generate tension. Paradoxically, then, people in a good mood may sometimes be reluctant to engage in creative behavior, which they fear may end this good mood. Those who are accustomed to quickly changing moods—such as those with bipolar disorder, cyclothymia, or subclinical cases on a bipolar spectrum—may be less inclined to engage in mood maintenance, instead persisting in their creative work, even if it means temporarily exchanging positive mood for creative tension (Richards & Kinney 1998).

Therapeutic Effects of Creative Activity on Mood and Mental Health

Richards (2007) reviewed diverse literature on the healing power of "everyday" creativity. There is evidence that creativity can benefit both our physical and our psychological health; mental imagery, for example, can encourage relaxation and produce positive changes in immune and cardiovascular function. Creative expression can also help us bring certain difficult experiences to consciousness where they can be more rationally processed. The work of Pennebaker and colleagues (see Pennebaker, Kiecolt-Glaser, & Glaser 1998; Pennebaker & Seagal 1999) indicates that expressive writing can help people organize and process complex emotional experiences, thereby significantly improving emotional and physical health. Without structure, painful experiences can lead to unconscious distress, rumination, and more. Forming a coherent narrative may give people a sense of control over painful events in their lives, leading to resolution instead of unproductive defending. For instance, Pennebaker and Seagal (1999) had students in an experimental group write about a traumatic event for 15 minutes a day over four consecutive days. A control group wrote for the same amount of time about a nonemotional subject. While the moods of those who wrote about traumatic events actually worsened immediately after the writing task, when measured two weeks later the moods of those in the experimental group were now better than those of the control subjects. Experimental participants subsequently had fewer doctor visits, signaling improved health. In the study of Pennebaker, Kiecolt-Glaser, and Glaser (1998), the experimental group was also healthier on two measures of immune function.

Recent research has supported the claims made by art therapists about the healing power of artistic expression (De Petrillo & Winner 2005; Dalebroux, Goldstein, & Winner 2008). De Petrillo and Winner (2005) investigated whether and how artistic activity can improve mood. They first instilled a negative mood in all of their subjects, by introducing them to photos and videos depicting various tragedies. Participants then either (1) created expressive artwork or (2) engaged in a nonexpressive drawing task designed to distract them. Even when the distraction task was engaging, such as a puzzle, it had much less effect on mood than did the art making. By coding the content of the artwork, the experimenters found that some subjects used negative imagery to release their negative feeling, as a catharsis. Other subjects, in contrast, chose to create artwork with more positive themes, distracting themselves from negative rumination. Redirecting one's emotions in a more positive focus may serve therapeutic functions.

Dalebroux, Goldstein, and Winner (2008) then investigated which approach is more effective in regulating and repairing mood. They introduced three groups of subjects to a negatively valenced mood before assigning activities. The first group was instructed to draw something that expressed their current mood. A second group was asked to draw something that portrayed happiness. A third group engaged in a visual distraction task that involved scanning a page for symbols. The investigators found that having subjects draw something with positive content was most conducive to mood repair.

Art therapy is often used to treat patients suffering from stressful and painful medical illnesses. Mindfulness-based art therapy (MBAT) was developed as a group intervention for cancer patients designed to allow both verbal and nonverbal expression, in the hopes of decreasing stress. Monti et al. (2006) implemented a randomized, controlled trial to test the efficacy of this treatment, enrolling 111

Drug Therapy and Creative Individuals

Research on psychopharmacological treatment indicates that bipolar patients' nonadherence to their prescribed medication is a major cause of relapse. Noncompliance dramatically increases morbidity and mortality. It can also affect creativity. By some estimates, for example, more than half of bipolar patients fail to comply with their medication regimens in the year prior to or following a hospitalization. Noncompliance issues are also widespread among patients in the schizophrenia spectrum.

Because of widespread misunderstanding about the relation between creativity and mental illness, some creative but disturbed people actively avoid drug therapy, fearing it will dull their creativity. How ironic—and tragic—that the opposite is true! Research strongly suggests that appropriate treatment is actually likely to enhance rather than inhibit creativity. A clear understanding of this could dramatically increase medication compliance—and survival. The "creativity-psychopathology" link is widely misunderstood; the actual link is powerful testimony to the *healing* potential for patients when severe symptoms are controlled and creativity as compensatory advantage comes to the fore.

adult women diagnosed with cancer and comparing the women enrolled in the MBAT treatment with controls on a waiting list. The women in the intervention group had significantly decreased distress compared to the controls. Creative activities that encourage one to consciously express and act upon unresolved problems thus appear to have a major benefit for mood.

Practical Implications

The research evidence for an association of increased everyday creativity with liability (potentiality) for certain mental illnesses has a number of practical implications. For example, this evidence may boost the morale of patients and their families, as well as help reduce the stigma often associated with these illnesses and liability for them. It may also enhance patients' compliance with treatment, by showing them that treatment can bring about a mental state that is optimal for creativity—even for those with severe disorders, who may shine during better states of mood or cognition. The research evidence may also help prevent the development of severe mental illness by showing individuals who carry increased liability for bipolar of schizophrenic disorders that they can become more creative and function better with the right kind of treatment.

Moreover, the evidence for increased creative potential in individuals with genetic liability for illnesses such as schizophrenia and bipolar disorder has further implications for those in the helping professions—including therapists, counselors, educators, coaches, pastoral counselors, and other clinicians—who could help foster creativity in their students or clients. Clinicians and educators are often in an unusually good position to do this while helping patients manage or avoid psychiatric symptoms that may thwart their creative efforts (Kinney 1992).

Simplistic views linking creativity to "madness" do a major disservice to both individuals and society, by glamorizing painful illness and discouraging treatment compliance. In addition, such misguided views may discourage unaffected individuals from developing their own creativity for fear of developing psychological problems (Richards 2007). Such simplistic views undermine our essential humanity, and they ignore "the enormous discipline, will and rationality that are truly essential to creative work" (Jamison 1993, 97).

See also Bipolar Disorder; Genetics and Mental Health; Humanistic Theories and Therapies; Literary Works and Mental Illness; Media Portrayals of Mental Illness; Neurodiversity; Schizophrenia

Bibliography

Andreasen, Nancy C. 1987. "Creativity and Mental Illness: Prevalence Rates in Writers and Their First-Degree Relatives." *The American Journal of Psychiatry* 144(10): 1288–1292.

Brain and Behavior Research Foundation. http://bbrfoundation.org/.

Dalebroux, Anne, Thalia R. Goldstein, and Ellen Winner. 2008. "Short-Term Mood Repair through Art-Making: Positive Emotion Is More Effective Than Venting." *Motivation & Emotion* 32(4): 288–295.

De Petrillo, Lili, and Ellen Winner. 2005. "Does Art Improve Mood? A Test of a Key Assumption Underlying Art Therapy." *Art Therapy: Journal of the American Art Therapy Association* 22(4): 205–212.

Fodor, Eugene M., and Bobbi A. Laird. 2004. "Therapeutic Intervention, Bipolar Inclination, and Literary Creativity." *Creativity Research Journal* 16(2): 149–161.

Jamison, Kay Redfield. 1993. *Touched with Fire: Manic-Depressive Illness and the Artistic Temperament*. New York: Free Press.

Kendler, Kenneth S., Alan M. Gruenberg, and Dennis K. Kinney. 1994. "Independent Diagnoses of Adoptees and Relatives as Defined by *DSM-III* in the Provincial and National Samples of the Danish Adoption Study of Schizophrenia." *Archives of General Psychiatry* 51(6): 456–468.

Kinney, Dennis K. 1992. "The Therapist as Muse: Greater Roles for Clinicians in Fostering Innovation *American Journal of Psychotherapy* 46(3): 434–453.

Kinney, Dennis K., and Steven Matthysse. 1978. "Genetic Transmission of Schizophrenia." *Annual Review of Medicine* 29: 459–473.

Kinney, Dennis K., and Ruth L. Richards. 2011. "Bipolar Mood Disorders." In M. A. Runco and S. R. Pritzker, eds., *Encyclopedia of Creativity* (2nd ed., pp. 140–148). San Diego: Academic Press.

Kinney, Dennis K., Ruth L. Richards, Patricia A. Lowing, Deborah LeBlanc, Morris E. Zimbalist, and Patricia Harlan. 2000–2001. "Creativity in Offspring of Schizophrenic and Control Parents: An Adoption Study." *Creativity Research Journal* 13(1): 17–25.

Ludwig, Arnold M. 1995. *The Price of Greatness: Resolving the Creativity and Madness Controversy*. New York: Guilford Press.

Monti, Daniel A., Caroline Peterson, Elisabeth J. Shakin Kunkel, Walter W. Hauck, Edward Pequignot, Lora Rhodes, and George C. Brainard. 2006. "A Randomized,

Controlled Trial of Mindfulness-Based Art Therapy (MBAT) for Women with Cancer." *Psycho-Oncology* 15(5): 363–373.

Pennebaker, James W., Janice K. Kiecolt-Glaser, and Ronald Glaser. 1998. "Disclosure of Traumas and Immune Function: Health Implications for Psychotherapy." In Mark Runco and Ruth Richards, eds., *Eminent Creativity, Everyday Creativity, and Health* (pp. 287–302). Greenwich, CT: Ablex.

Pennebaker, James W., and Janel D. Seagal. 1999. "Forming a Story: The Health Benefits of Narrative." *Journal of Clinical Psychology* 55(10): 1243–1254.

Richards, Ruth. 1981. "Relationships between Creativity and Psychopathology: An Evaluation and Interpretation of the Evidence." *Genetic Psychology Monographs* 103: 261–324.

Richards, Ruth. 1997. "Conclusions: When Illness Yields Creativity." In Mark Runco and Ruth Richards, eds., *Eminent Creativity, Everyday Creativity, and Health* (pp. 483–491). Greenwich, CT: Ablex.

Richards, Ruth. 2007. "Everyday Creativity: Our Hidden Potential." In Ruth Richards, ed., *Everyday Creativity and New Views of Human Nature: Psychological, Social, and Spiritual Perspectives* (pp. 25–53). Washington, DC: American Psychological Association.

Richards, Ruth. 2010. "Everyday Creativity: Process and Way of life—Four Key Issues." In James C. Kaufman and Robert J. Sternberg, eds., *The Cambridge Handbook of Creativity* (pp. 189–215). New York: Cambridge University Press.

Richards, Ruth, and Dennis K. Kinney. 1998. "Mood Swings and Creativity." In Mark Runco and Ruth Richards, eds., *Eminent Creativity, Everyday Creativity, and Health* (pp. 137–156). Greenwich, CT: Ablex.

Richards, Ruth L., Dennis K. Kinney, H. Daniels, and K. Linkins. 1992. "Everyday Creativity and Bipolar and Unipolar Affective Disorder: Preliminary Study of Personal and Family History." *European Psychiatry* 2: 49–52.

Richards, Ruth L., Dennis K. Kinney, Inge Lunde, Maria Benet, and Ann P. Merzel. 1988. "Creativity in Manic-Depressives, Cyclothymes, Their Normal Relatives, and Control Subjects." *Journal of Abnormal Psychology* 97(3): 281–288.

Runco, Marc, and Ruth Richards, eds. 1998. *Eminent Creativity, Everyday Creativity, and Health*. Greenwich, CT: Ablex.

Schuldberg, David. 2000–2001. "Six Subclinical Spectrum Traits in Normal Creativity." *Creativity Research Journal* 13(1): 5–16.

Society for the Psychology of Aesthetics, Creativity, and the Arts. American Psychological Association Division 10. http://www.apa.org/divisions/div10/.

Criminalization and Diversion Programs

Patricia E. Erickson

One of the most significant social problems in American society is the criminalization of the mentally ill. The phrase "criminalization of the mentally ill" describes a process whereby agents of social control—legislators, police, district attorneys, and judges—impose a criminal rather than a psychiatric definition on an individual's behavior. Thus the social control apparatus used to manage the mentally ill becomes the criminal justice system rather than the mental health system. Instead of emphasizing a humane approach and medical intervention, criminalization of the mentally ill reflects an emphasis on a punitive approach as society's primary response.

In the United States, criminalization of the mentally ill occurred largely because of the deinstitutionalization movement—the process of moving severely mentally ill people out of large state mental hospitals into communities for treatment that began in the 1950s and 1960s but took firm hold in the 1970s. However, while community mental health treatment became the formal policy of the federal government, often the mentally ill did not receive or seek treatment. Lacking treatment and frequently homeless, mentally ill individuals committed crimes; prisons and jails became their places of confinement.

This entry examines the deinstitutionalization movement by exploring the social forces that shaped it. It then considers how the movement led to the criminalization of the mentally ill. Finally, the entry describes the emergence of diversions programs developed to provide alternatives to the incarceration of the mentally ill.

The Deinstitutionalization Movement

Deinstitutionalization of the mentally ill was first articulated as the direction for public policy by President John F. Kennedy in the early 1960s. In 1961, the Joint Commission on Mental Illness and Health's Action for Mental Health concluded that long-term stays in state hospitals, also referred to as asylums, produced institutionalized behavior and a tendency toward chronic illness. The commission recommended preventing hospitalization, curtailing its length when it was unavoidable, and returning patients to community life, where they would receive treatment through community-based services. In the late 1970s, President Jimmy Carter's Commission on Mental Health, reasoned that deinstitutionalization had "the objective of maintaining the greatest degree of freedom, self-determination, autonomy, dignity, and integrity of body, mind, and spirit for the individual while he or she participates in treatment or receive services" (Torrey 1997, 10–11).

Several social forces shaped the push for deinstitutionalization. First, the deplorable conditions in some state hospitals came to public attention. After World War II, Mennonites, the Brethren, and Quakers, who were given conscientious objector status during the war, worked in state mental hospitals and reported on the deplorable conditions of patients in the hospitals (Sareyan 1994). A 1945 *Life* magazine article, "The Shame of the States," revealed graphically the conditions in asylums; and a popular 1948 movie, *The Snake Pit*, dramatized the plight of a woman in a state hospital. This critique of the asylum continued into the 1960s and 1970s, two decades that witnessed the civil rights and women's movements. It found expression with the publication of Ken Kesey's very popular novel, *One Flew over the Cuckoo's Nest* (1962), followed by the 1975 movie by the same name.

Second, academic circles also claimed that the asylum was a repressive and an unneeded institution. Psychiatrist Thomas Szasz, a leader in the antipsychiatry movement, argued that mental illness was a myth, that it was a name given for problems in living rather than for an identifiable (i.e., biologically rooted) illness (Szasz 1961). French philosopher and historian Michel Foucault (1965) similarly maintained that the modern concept of madness was a cultural invention for social control of deviant behavior, while Scottish psychiatrist R. D. Laing (1960) claimed that the schizophrenic patient was often playing at being mad (through a kind of existential game). Sociologist Erving Goffman (1961) based his classic study and critique of asylums as oppressive institutions on his field work in St. Elizabeth's, a public mental hospital. The perspectives of academics found its way into public discourse and validated the view of the need to find an alternative to the state mental hospital.

Third, during the 1960s and 1970s, the hospitalized mentally ill and their advocates sought legal rights based on autonomy and an ideal of limited governmental regulation of behavior. They criticized the legal procedure of involuntary civil commitment, which was by far the most common procedure for hospital admission of the mentally ill. Involuntary civil commitment required patients to accept treatment, irrespective of the wishes of patients. But in the 1960s and 1970s, involuntary civil commitment laws and court decisions changed dramatically in favor of the rights of the mentally ill (Perlin 2000; Torrey 1997). Two U.S. Supreme Court decisions were especially important. In *O'Connor v. Donaldson* (422 U.S. 563 [1975]), the Court ruled that a finding of "mental illness" alone cannot justify a state's locking up a person against his will and keeping him indefinitely in custodial confinement. A state cannot, the Court held, constitutionally confine a nondangerous individual who is capable of surviving safely in freedom. In *Addington v. Texas* (441 U.S. 418 [1979]), the Court reset the standard of proof required to commit persons from the usual civil burden of "preponderance of evidence" to the higher standard of "clear and convincing evidence."

Fourth, support for deinstitutionalization of the mentally ill also occurred because of incentives provided by the federal government. The Community Mental Health Centers Act (CMHCA) (Pub. L. No. 88-164 [1963]) along with the Institutionalized Mental Disease (IMD) exclusion (42 U. S. C. § 1396d [a] [1994]) transformed the delivery of mental health services. The CMHCA provided a massive infusion of federal funds to state agencies to develop small mental health centers within the community. The IMD exclusion forbade federal Medicaid funds for state psychiatric hospitals. In 1972, through Social Security amendments, the federal government provided financial penalties on states not implementing effective programs for controlling unnecessary use of mental hospitals. In 1974, Congress also authorized the Supplemental Security Income (SSI) program (42 U. S. C. §§ 1381–1385f [1972]) designed to help the aged, blind, and disabled individuals who have little or no income, and in 1975 other legislation continued to stimulate community-based services (Rose 1979, 446).

Finally, optimism about releasing the mentally ill into the community also occurred because of the discovery of psychotropic drugs. In 1954, the Food and Drug Administration approved the use of a new tranquilizing drug, chlorpromazine, marketed under the trade name of Thorazine. State mental hospitals were the first to use the drug, and physicians were genuinely impressed with what they saw when they introduced Thorazine and other new psychotropic drugs into the hospital setting. Once hospitals established the effectiveness of the new psychotropic drugs, the pressures toward deinstitutionalization intensified and the medical establishment supported its implementation (Gronfein 1985).

The Unintended Consequences of Deinstitutionalization

It soon became apparent that optimism about deinstitutionalization was short-sighted as federal funding to support its implementation waxed and waned and successful integration of the mentally ill into communities proved difficult to achieve. Forgotten was how large state hospitals had provided not only treatment but also a supervised setting for the mentally ill. In the community, large numbers of the mentally ill were often homeless and frequently relied on illicit drugs and alcohol to help with cope with their symptoms. In addition, scientific research identified a manifestation of mental illness: people with serious mental illness often did not consider themselves mentally ill. In spite of their symptoms, people with severe mental illness frequently steadfastly believe that their symptoms represent normal reality (Amador et al. 1994). While psychotropic medications helped, individuals often stopped taking prescribed medications because of their side effects and/or the belief that they no longer needed medicine to function normally in society. Homelessness, the use of illicit drugs and alcohol, and the failure to take prescribed medications created the conditions for criminal behavior.

Thus the unintended consequence of deinstitutionalization became the "transcarceration" of the mentally ill—that is, the "transfer" of the mentally ill from confinement in asylums to incarceration in jails and prisons. A number of studies began to document this "transcarceration" phenomenon in the mid-1970s. Studies of jails reported a significant number of seriously mentally ill inmates who had formerly been state mental hospital patients (Torrey 1997, 28–29). By the early 1980s, researchers began to examine seriously the problem of mentally ill people in jails. Research by Teplin (1990) and Guy, Platt, Zwerling, and Bullock (1985) for example, found an alarmingly high incidence of serious mental illness such as schizophrenia and mania among jail inmates. A study conducted by the Public

Citizen Health Research Group and the National Alliance for the Mentally Ill (Torrey et al. 1992) mailed questionnaires to the directors of all county and city jails in the United States asking them to estimate the percentage of inmates who on any given day "appeared to have a serious mental illness." Overall, the jail directors estimated that 7.2 percent of inmates appeared to have a serious mental illness.

Studies of prisons also found a disproportionate percentage of severely mentally ill individuals behind prison walls (Torrey 1997, 30–31). A 1999 Department of Justice study (Ditton 1999) reported that roughly 16 percent of prison and jail inmates had some form of mental illness. A 2006 study by the Department of Justice (James & Glaze 2006) reported that at midyear 2005 more than half of all prison and jail inmates had a mental health problem. About 24 percent of state prisoners, 14 percent of federal prisoners, and 21 percent of jail inmates reported a recent history of a mental health problem. More than two-fifths of state prisoners (43%) and more than half of jail inmates (53%) met the criteria for mania. About 23 percent of state prisoners and 30 percent of jail inmates reported symptoms of major depression. An estimated 15 percent of state prisoners and 24 percent of jail inmates reported symptoms that met the criteria for a psychotic disorder.

Even more disconcerting was that once incarcerated, the mentally ill were not at all well served by prisons and jails ill-equipped to treat them or understand their behaviors. Investigations and lawsuits concerning the conditions of confinement of mentally ill prisoners documented the paucity of mental health treatment and the reliance on punishment as the primary response to their problematic behaviors. The American Psychiatric Association (2000, 4) concluded that prisoner access to mental health treatment was impeded by delays in transmitting prisoners' oral or written request for care, permitting unreasonable delays before patients are seen by mental health staff or outside consultants, and the imposition of fees that prevented or deterred prisoners from seeking care. The lack of treatment of the incarcerated mentally ill created a climate in which mentally ill inmates could repeatedly violate the rules of the prison because of their mental disorder. Moreover, correctional officers often lacked training in mental illness and frequently believed that mentally ill behaviors reflected manipulation or malingering rather than mental illness (Human Rights Watch 2003, 106–109). Consequently, research indicated that correctional officers often acted more aggressively than they should to restrain mentally ill prisoners because they did not know how to react to the often irrational and sometimes violent behavior of mentally ill prisoners (Human Rights Watch 2003, 80–81). Beginning in the mid-1980s, corrections departments increasingly chose to segregate or isolate mentally ill prisoners into solitary confinement cells (Human Rights Watch 2003, 141–147). Suicide and efforts of self-harm were particularly prevalent in segregated, high-security settings (Human Rights Watch 2003, 179–181).

Diversion Programs

Transcarceration of the mentally ill from asylums to prisons generated a great deal of publicity and public concern. In response, one of the most important developments was the development of diversion programs, also known as "jail diversion programs." These programs provide an alternative to criminal sanctions to persons with mental illness who have come into contact with the law. The objective of mental health diversion is to provide effective linkages to comprehensive community-based services to enable people with mental illnesses to receive treatment and live successfully in their communities without future offending. Communities often receive federal or state funding to implement diversion programs. There are several different kinds of diversion programs defined by the point in the criminal justice processing where diversion occurs and by the kind of services provided.

Prearrest Diversion Programs

Prearrest or precharge diversion programs attempt to divert mentally ill people from the criminal justice system to appropriate community-based mental health treatment programs before formal charges are filed. People with serious mental illness may come to the attention of law enforcement because of circumstances related to their illness. Often these individuals have a criminal record, past psychiatric hospitalizations, and co-occurring substance abuse. There are several different models of prearrest programs. One of the most widely used is the Crisis Intervention Team (CIT) model, a police-based model first implemented in Memphis, Tennessee. Officers who volunteer to be on the CIT team receive 40 hours of training in psychiatric disorders, substance abuse issues, and relevant legal issues. In addition to regular patrol duties, CIT officers respond to calls when there is an indication of a "mental disturbance" and they transport individuals to emergency services that have a no-refusal policy for police cases. In addition to the CIT model, other models of prearrest diversion include the San Diego Psychiatric Emergency Response Team (PERT) and the Community Services model (CSO) in Birmingham, Alabama (Bazelon Center for Mental Health Law n.d.). While police agencies using pre-arrest diversion report lower arrest rates for persons diverted, as yet there is no clear of what the long-term outcomes are for persons with mental illness who have experienced prearrest diversion (Steadman & Naples 2005; Hartford, Carey, & Mendonca 2006).

Postarrest Diversion Programs

Postarrest diversion programs provide the mentally ill person with access to appropriate mental health treatment outside of jail soon after arrest. Typically, these programs provide for an evaluation of by a mental health professional for the presence of mental illness and negotiation with appropriate members of the criminal justice system to provide for a mental health disposition instead of prosecution or a reduction in charges. Thresholds, Chicago, is an example of a model of postarrest diversion. Individuals incarcerated in the Cook County Jail who have a serious mental illness, a history of arrests, and a substance abuse problem are the focus of the program. Thresholds uses assertive community treatment (ACT) to provide services that include intensive case management, medication monitoring, housing and transportation assistance, and money management services. The program also provides long-term services, staying with clients through subsequent hospitalizations and arrests. Other models of postarrest diversion include Jail Diversion in Bernalillo County, New Mexico, and Montgomery County, Pennsylvania (Bazelon Center for Mental Health Law n.d.). As with prearrest diversion, while individual programs report decrease days spent in jail and lower arrest rates for persons diverted, additional research is needed to focus on what impact the specific services have on achieving mental health or quality-of-life improvements (Case, Steadman, Dupuis, & Morris 2009; Steadman & Naples 2005).

Court-Based Diversion Programs

Court-based programs target individuals with a mental illness who have been charged with misdemeanors or felonies. The intent is to move individuals into treatment as a condition for reduction in charges or community supervision. Court-based diversion programs are found in traditional criminal courts, such as Cases Nathaniel Project, in New York City, and Pre-Trial Diversion, in Hamilton County, Ohio (Bazelon Center for Mental Health Law n.d.). The development of mental health courts, i.e., federally funded specialty courts in which cases involving people with mental illness are handled through a special docket, is an increasingly visible form of a court-based diversion program. The structure of a mental health court differs significantly from a traditional criminal proceeding. Before a typical mental health session, a variety of representatives from various mental health agencies as well as the prosecutor and defense counsel gather in chambers to review with the supervising judge the appropriateness of new program participants, the progress of current participants, and strategies to deal with participants who are noncompliant with treatment or who cannot be located. As with other diversion programs, treatment within mental health courts often relies upon forms of outpatient treatment that provides for close supervision of the mentally ill and usually has intensive treatment programs already in place in the community. Since mental health courts are a relatively new development, little empirical evidence exists regarding their effectiveness. Research indicates that these courts may be effective in diverting individuals from jails and prisons, but little evidence exists concerning whether psychiatric symptoms improve for the individuals who participate in these courts (Boothroyd et al. 2003; Boothroyd et al. 2005; Christy et al. 2005; Griffin, Steadman, & Petrila 2002; Moore & Hiday 2006; Redlich et al. 2006).

Comprehensive Diversion Approaches

Comprehensive programs provide linkages between the mental health and criminal justice system at several points along the criminal justice continuum. Referrals of individuals can come from various sources including law enforcement, prisons, jails, attorneys, prosecutors, judges, and probation and parole officers. Project Link, in Rochester, New York, is an example of a comprehensive program. Its admission criteria include the presence of severe mental illness, a history of previous involvement with the criminal justice system, and a history of nonadherence with outpatient treatment. Project Link consists of a mobile treatment team and a mental illness and chemical treatment residence. Its staff includes a forensic psychiatrist and a nurse practitioner, a team of case advocates. The mobile treatment team brings treatment to clients in their natural environments rather than bringing clients to clinics. The treatment residence, for clients with mental illness and chemical dependency, offers four levels of care ranging from total supervision to acquisition of skills for independent living. Once treatment is completed, staff assists clients in finding subsequent housing. Staff members also assist their patients in courtroom and jail settings and work closely with parole and probation officers in the community. Project Link conducted an evaluation of the program with a subgroup of 44 clients who had completed one full year in the project. It found a significant reduction in hospital stays and jail days per client and an average reduction in direct service and residential costs per client (Lamberti et al. 2001).

Reentry Diversion Approaches

For people with mental illness, transition to the community after jail and prison is especially difficult because they need to access to mental health services as well as other supports in the community such as housing. Reentry programs seek to address these needs. Some programs may provide only specialized services while others are comprehensive. Patuxent Institution Community Integration Project, in Maryland, is an example of a comprehensive program. The Patuxent Correctional Institution, Baltimore Mental Health Services, Baltimore Intensive Case Programs, and Baltimore city mental health providers collaborate to provide the program. Its focus is on inmates with serious mental illnesses or dual diagnoses. Participation is voluntary. Three months prior to their release inmates meet with an intensive case manager to assess their needs and prepare community service plans for them. Other reentry diversion models include New York City Link,

Hamden County, Massachusetts, and Rensselaer County, New York (Bazelon Center for Mental Health Law n.d.). Little research exists on the effectiveness of these programs.

Conclusion

Criminalization of the mentally ill remains a serious social problem in American society. The GAINS Center estimates that approximately 800,000 persons with serious mental illness are admitted annually to U.S. jails (National GAINS Center n.d.). While the implementation of programs to divert individuals from the criminal justice system into treatment is an important recognition of the seriousness of the problem, the effectiveness of diversion programs needs further investigation in terms of both whether mentally ill individuals are diverted into appropriate treatment and whether such treatment decreases the numbers of mentally ill individuals who are diverted from the criminal justice system. In addition, a frequent criticism is whether participation in these programs is truly "voluntary" or whether they contain elements of coercion because often the choice is between incarceration and treatment.

See also Chronic Mental Illness; Community Mental Health; Disability Rights; Ethical Issues; History of Mental Health Care; Homelessness and Mental Illness; Involuntary Treatment; Neurodiversity; Prisons and Mental Health; State Mental Health Agencies

Bibliography

Books and Journal Articles

Amador, X. F., M. Flaum, N. C. Andreasen, D. H. Strauss, S. A. Yale, S. C. Clark, and J. M. Gorman. 1994. "Awareness of Illness in Schizophrenia and Schizoaffective and Mood Disorders." *Archives of General Psychiatry* 51(10): 826–836.

American Psychiatric Association. 2000. *Psychiatric Services in Jails and Prisons.* Washington, D.C: American Psychiatric Publishing.

Bazelon Center for Mental Health Law. (n.d.). A Better Way: Programs Offering Alternatives to Incarceration. Retrieved from http://bazelon.org.gravitatehosting.com/LinkClick.aspx?fileticket=4OYTGprsbs%3d&tabid=246.

Boothroyd, R. A., C. C. Mercado, C. Calkins, N. G. Poythress, A. Christy, and J. Petrila. 2005. "Clinical Outcomes of Defendants in Mental Health Courts." *Psychiatric Services* 56(7): 829–834.

Boothroyd, R. A., N. G. Poythress, A. McGaha, and J. Petrila. 2003. "The Broward Mental Health Court: Process, Outcomes and Service Utilization." *Journal of Law and Psychiatry* 26(1): 55–71.

Case, B., H. J. Steadman, S. A. Dupuis, and L. S. Morris. 2009. "Who Succeeds in Jail Diversion for Persons with Mental Illness? A Multi-State Study." *Behavioral Sciences and the Law* 27: 661–674.

Christy, A., N. G. Poythress, R. A. Boothroyd, J. Petrila, and S. Mehra. 2005. "Evaluating the Efficiency and Community Safety Goals of the Broward County Mental Health Court." *Behavioral Sciences & the Law* 23(2): 222–243.

Ditton, P. M. 1999. *Mental Health and the Treatment of Inmates and Probationers.* Washington, DC: U.S. Department of Justice, Bureau of Justice Statistics.

Earley, Pete. 2006. *Crazy: A Father's Search through America's Mental Health Madness.* New York: G. P. Putnam's Sons.

Erickson, Patricia E., and Steven K. Erickson. 2008. *Crime, Punishment, and Mental Illness: Law and the Behavioral Sciences in Conflict.* New Brunswick, NJ: Rutgers University Press.

Foucault, M. 1965. *Madness and Civilization: A History of Insanity in the Age of Reason.* New York: Vintage Books (reprint 1988).

Goffman, E. 1961. *Asylums: Essays on the Social Situation of Mental Patients and Other Inmates.* New York: Doubleday (reprint 1991).

Griffin, P. A., H. J. Steadman, and J. Petrila. 2002. "The Use of Criminal Charges and Sanctions in Mental Health Courts." *Psychiatric Services* 53(10):1285–1289.

Gronfein, W. 1985. "Psychotropic Drugs and the Origins of Deinstitutionalization." *Social Problems* 32 (5): 437–454.

Guy, E., J. J. Platt, I. Zwerling, and S. Bullock. 1985. "Mental Health Status of Prisoners in an Urban Jail." *Criminal Justice and Behavior* 12: 29–53.

Hartford, K., R. Carey, and J. Mendonca. 2006. "Pre-arrest Diversion of People with Mental Illness: Literature Review and International Survey." *Behavioral Sciences & the Law* 24: 845–856.

Human Rights Watch. 2003. *Ill-Equipped: U.S. Prisons and Offenders with Mental Illness.* New York: Human Rights Watch.

James, D. L., and L. E. Glaze. 2006. *Mental Health Problems of Prison and Jail Inmates.* Washington, DC: U.S. Department of Justice, Bureau of Justice Statistics.

Laing, R. D. 1960. *The Divided Self: An Existential Study in Sanity and Madness.* New York: Penguin.

Lamberti, J. S., R. L. Weisman, S. B. Schwarzkopf, N. Price, R. M. Ashton, and J. Trompeter. 2001. "The Mentally Ill in Jails and Prisons: Towards an Integrated Model of Prevention." *Psychiatric Quarterly* 72(1): 63–77.

Moore, M. E., and V. A. Hiday. 2006. "Mental Health Court Outcomes: A Comparison of Re-arrest and Re-arrest Severity between Mental Health Court and Traditional Court Participants." *Law and Human Behavior* 30(6): 659–674.

National GAINS Center. (n.d.). *What Is Jail Diversion?* Retrieved from http://gainscenter.samhsa.gov/html/jail_diversion/what_is_jd.asp.

Perlin, M. L. 2000. *The Hidden Prejudice: Mental Disability on Trial.* Washington, DC: American Psychological Association.

Redlich, A. D., H. J. Steadman, J. R. Monahan, P. Clark, and J. Petrila. 2006. "Patterns of Practice in Mental Health Courts: A National Survey." *Law and Human Behavior* 30(3): 347–362.

Rose, S. M. 1979. "Deciphering Deinstitutionalization: Complexities in Policy and Program Analysis." *Milbank Memorial Fund Quarterly/Health and Society* 57(4): 429–460.

Sareyan S. 1994. *The Turning Point: How Men of Conscience Brought About Major Change in The Care of America's Mentally Ill.* Washington, DC: American Psychiatric Publishing.

Slate, Risdon, and W. Wesley Johnson. 2008. *The Criminalization of Mental Illness: Crisis and Opportunity for the Justice System.* Durham, NC: Carolina Academic Press.

Steadman, H. J., and M. Naples. 2005. "Assessing the Effectiveness of Jail Diversion Programs for Persons with Serious Mental Illness and Co-occurring Substance Use Disorders." *Behavioral Sciences & the Law* 23: 163–170.

Szasz, T. 1961. *The Myth of Mental Illness: A History of Involuntary Mental Hospitalization*. New York: Harper & Row.

Teplin, L. A. 1990. "The Prevalence of Severe Mental Disorders among Male Urban Jail Detainees." *American Journal of Public Health* 80: 663–669.

Torrey, E. F. 1997. *Out of the Shadows: Confronting America's Mental Illness Crisis*. New York: Wiley.

Torrey, E. F., J. Stieber, J. Ezekiel, S. M. Wolfe, J. Sharfstein, J. H. Noble, and L. M. Flynn. 1992. *Criminalizing the Seriously Mentally Ill*. Washington, D.C: National Alliance for the Mentally Ill and Public Citizen Health Research Group.

Cases

Addington v. Texas, 442 U.S. 418 (1979).

O'Connor v. Donaldson, 422 U.S. 563 (1975).

Statutes

Community Mental Health Centers Act of 1963, Pub. L. No. 88-164, 77 Stat. 282 290-94 (1963).

Social Security Act, 42 U. S. C. § 1396d (a) (1994).

Supplemental Security Income for the Aged, Blind and Disabled, 42 U. S. C. §§1381-1385f (1972).

Culturally Competent Mental Health Care

Sandra DiVitale, Poonam Ghiya, David Jordan, Mary Montaldo, and Stanley Sue

Cultural competence is one of the most frequently discussed topics in the mental health field. There is growing realization that a qualified therapist or counselor must be culturally competent in order to work with diverse populations. Because of the multiethnic nature of American society and the frequent interactions with other cultural groups and societies throughout the world, skills must be developed to effectively work with people from different cultures. Indeed, local and national organizations have attempted to develop guidelines and standards for the provision of mental health services to ethnic minority populations.

History of Efforts toward Cultural Competence

Certain developments in psychology have provided the foundation for cultural competency. In the 1970s, the Association for Non-White Concerns (ANWC) in

Personnel and Guidance, a division of the American Personnel and Guidance Association (APGA), met extensively to address the issue of ethnic mental health disparities. A significant part of the organization's mission was to recognize the human diversity and multicultural nature of U.S. society. The ANWC strove to enhance the development, human rights, and the psychological health of all people as critical to the social, educational, political, professional, and personal reform in the United States (McFadden & Lipscomb 1985). The organization strived to identify and worked to eliminate conditions that create barriers to the provision of effective mental health treatment.

Subsequently, the Association for Multicultural Counseling and Development (AMCD) was established. As a division of the American Counseling Association, the AMCD brought further support for the development of multicultural treatment, including decreasing mental health disparities among diverse populations. A major goal of the AMCD was to design programs that could specifically improve ethnic and racial empathy and understanding in counselors and therapists as well as enhance the understanding of cultural diversity (M. L. Smith & Roysircar 2010).

Development of Organizational Guidelines and Practices

The American Psychological Association (APA) and its divisions have played a large role in recognizing ethnic and cultural considerations in professional practice. APA Division 17 (Counseling Psychology) and the National Institute for Multicultural Competence (NIMC) strongly advocated for cultural competency. The goal of this advocacy was twofold. These organizations advocated for transformative changes in the mental health and human service sectors. Furthermore, they promoted the principles and spirit of multiculturalism among mental health professionals and other human service providers. An attempt was made to have providers acquire the knowledge, skills, and awareness to work respectfully, effectively, and ethically among persons from diverse groups and backgrounds (D. W. Sue & Torino 2005).

APA Division 12 (Society of Clinical Psychology) established the section on the Clinical Psychology of Ethnic Minorities. This section's mission was to promote research on clinical interventions with American racial and ethnic minority populations. Furthermore, Division 12 fostered sensitivity training of all psychologists as to cultural, racial, and ethnic issues.

One of the most significant events was the adoption by APA of the 2003 *Guidelines on Multicultural Education, Training, Research, Practice, and Organizational Change for Psychologists*. The guidelines provided psychologists with the rationale for the importance of, and need for, devoting efforts toward multiculturalism and diversity. Importantly, they also gave principles and procedures to follow in education, training, research, practice, and organizational change

(American Psychological Association 2003). Soon after, other professional mental health organizations also established policies to enhance cultural competency. In 2004, the American Psychiatric Association's Steering Committee to Reduce Disparities in Access to Psychiatric Care created a plan to further cultural sensitivity and awareness and to diminish mental health disparities. Finally, the National Association of Social Workers developed standards and guidelines for social work practice designed to allow social workers to effectively serve multicultural populations (National Association of Social Workers 2007).

Definitions of Cultural Competency

Various definitions of cultural competency exist. Culturally competent care has been defined as a system or intervention that values and incorporates culture, considers assessment of the cross-cultural relations, and adapts interventions to meet culturally unique needs of clients (S. Sue et al. 2009). Chin views cultural competence as a set of behaviors, attitudes, and policies that allow a system, agency, or group of professionals to work effectively in cross-cultural situations (Chin 2000). A precise definition of cultural competency or adaptation was offered by T. B. Smith, Rodriguez, and Bernal (2011): the systematic modification of an evidence-based treatment (EBT) or intervention protocol to consider language, culture, and context so that it is compatible with the client's cultural patterns, meaning, and values. All of the definitions stress effective interventions that consider, or are compatible with, the culture, attitudes, values, behaviors, and social contexts of clients.

In examining cultural competence, it is important to distinguish between different levels in the provision of services. The first level is the provider or therapist level. The provider works one-on-one with clients usually in a treatment or case management role. Cultural competency at this level involves culturally appropriate interpersonal sensitivity, assessment, rapport building, therapeutic alliance, and credibility. This first level—i.e., cultural competency among therapists—has gained the most attention and research. The second level occurs within an organization or agency. Examination is made of the extent to which a mental health agency's organizational structure mental health programs are culturally responsive. These programs include the organizational hierarchy, hiring of staff, establishment of programs, program evaluation, outreach to communities, access and availability of service, utilization, costs and benefits, and quality of care for members of different cultural groups. The third level deals with systems of care within a community. The organization and structure of mental health services for different ethnic populations (e.g., health maintenance organizations, geographic areas served, and collaboration with community agencies, churches, schools, and law enforcement agencies) are of interest at this level.

Justification for the Focus on Culturally Responsive Care

The impetus for cultural competency came from the growing cultural and ethnic diversity of the United States and from the realization that disparities existed in the accessibility, availability, and quality of care given to members of ethnic minority groups. These disparities resulted in underutilization of services as well as poorer treatment outcomes. For example, compared to white Americans, ethnic minority groups were often found to underutilize services or prematurely terminate treatment. The National Survey on Drug Use and Health (Substance Abuse and Mental Health Services Administration 2010) revealed that African Americans, Hispanics, and Asian Americans were far less likely than non-Hispanic white Americans to use mental health services, even after controlling for prevalence of mental disorders.

The problems faced by ethnic minority populations have been recognized for decades. The President's Commission on Mental Health pointed to a number of difficulties encountered by ethnic minorities in the service delivery system (President's Commission on Mental Health 1978). It noted that racial and ethnic minorities are underserved and inappropriately served. More recently, the U.S. Surgeon General (2001) and the President's New Freedom Commission on Mental Health (2003) concluded that these problems persist in the provision of services to ethnic minority groups.

Given the disparities, important issues concerning equal justice or ethical grounds have also been raised. Ethnic or racial disparities in the quality of care violate notions of equity and fairness in the delivery of services. For instance, the American Psychological Association (2003) recommended that psychologists recognize that fairness and justice entitle all persons to access to and benefit from the contributions of psychology and to equal quality in the processes, procedures, and services being conducted by psychologists. Why do the disparities exist? Addressing this question is important because insights can be gained into the causes of disparities and into the means for reducing services inequities.

The sources of treatment disparities are complex, are based on historic and contemporary inequities, and involve many players at several different levels, including health systems, their administrative and bureaucratic processes, utilization managers, health care professionals, and patients (Smedly et al. 2003). The delivery of quality services to different populations is especially difficult because of cultural and institutional influences that determine the nature of services. Services often reflect the racism and biases found in the broader society. Moreover, the cultures of various minority groups have received little attention compared to that of the mainstream culture. While culture is only one relevant factor in providing effective mental health treatment, it is a critical one.

Culturally Competent Interventions

Considerable efforts have been expended in trying to develop specific interventions that are culturally responsive. As suggested by S. Sue, Zane, Nagayama Hall, and Berger (2009), components of treatments can be categorized on the basis of method of delivery, content, and specialized interventions (such as cognitive behavioral treatments, storytelling interventions, and family therapies). They believe that delivery can help to make an intervention more culturally consistent, enhance the credibility of the treatment or provider, or render the treatment understandable to ethnic minority clients. Common types of delivery include the use of bilingual therapists who can speak the ethnic language of clients (e.g., translating materials or having bilingual therapists), matching the ethnicity of therapists with clients, changing the interpersonal style of the intervention (e.g., showing *respeto* or culturally appropriate respect with Hispanics), or providing a cultural context for interventions. These modifications share a common feature in that they involve generic applications that can be implemented across most types of treatment (e.g., psychodynamic, behavioral, and cognitive-behavioral).

Culturally adapted content refers to introduction of issues in therapy that deal with cultural patterns, immigration, minority status, racism, and background experiences. The content may serve to increase understandability and credibility of the intervention and to demonstrate the pertinence of the intervention to the real-life experiences of clients. Finally, specialized interventions involve the discovery or specific treatments or modification of therapies that are more culturally compatible with clients or the incorporation of cultural rituals or practices in treatment.

Studies have supported the value of some of these strategies. When mental health services were designed specifically for the local context and provided in their own ethnic neighborhoods, Asian American clients living in Los Angeles were found to have better outcomes than their counterparts attending mainstream clinics (Yeh, Takeuchi, & Sue 1994). Using culturally relevant support services like community members, spiritual leaders, and extended family, better mental health outcomes have also been demonstrated. For instance, Latino children showed significant reductions in presenting symptoms after one year when their mothers were included in their treatment recounting cultural folk stories (Costantino, Malgady, & Rogler 1986).

Furthermore, historically disenfranchised groups tended to seek out and use mental health services when their cultural values match those addressed in the interventions provided. For example, African American clients tended to remain in treatment when mental health treatment included Afrocentric values (Banks et al. 1998; Oliver 1989). Likewise, using the ecological validity framework, Duarte-Velez, Bernal, and Bonilla (2010) demonstrated how a culturally adapted cognitive-behavioral therapy (CBT) could be flexibly adapted to incorporate client values, preferences and context while still retaining fidelity to its treatment protocol when addressing the needs of a gay Latino adolescent client. The authors cited a number of preexisting efficacy studies for CBT with built-in cultural flexibility, which are sometimes termed "living manuals."

Outcomes of Specific Cultural Competency Strategies

Ethnic Match

The literature on matching therapists and clients based on ethnicity has demonstrated mixed results. Some studies have found that when clients are matched to therapists by native language and ethnicity, they have tended to stay in treatment longer and to report satisfaction with treatment (Campbell & Alexander 2002). Generally, when therapist and client are ethnically matched, research shows that the client is less likely to drop out of therapy, with the possible exception of African American clients, and the clients attend more therapy sessions (Maramba & Nagayama Hall 2002; S. Sue et al. 1991). However, a recent meta-analysis of this research revealed that ethnic match did not produce any positive effects on treatment outcomes (Griner & Smith 2006). The reasons for the discrepancy between the results seen for length of treatment and outcome measures due to ethnic match are unclear. One hypothesis is that the ethnic match produces an initial attractiveness feature for the client, which causes him or her to stay in treatment longer but does not affect therapeutic results in the long run. It is also possible that ethnic or language match between clients and therapists is important in certain situations, as when clients are unacculturated and/or recent immigrants (S. Sue et al. 2009).

Language Match

Unlike the area of ethnic match, the research on matching therapists and clients in terms of their language spoken is very clear. Research demonstrates that matching clients with a therapists who speak their primary language (if other than English) greatly improves treatment outcomes (Meyer, Zane, & Cho 2008). In Griner and Smith's (2006) meta-analysis of 76 studies, treatment effectiveness was two times greater in matched than unmatched language dyads involving therapists and clients.

Overall Findings on the Effects of Culturally Based Interventions

Overall, studies show that therapy that is culturally adapted in some way is significantly more effective than treatments that are not culturally adapted. This effect was especially true when clients were older, Hispanic/Latino, or Asian American. Furthermore, the average effect size of culturally adapted treatments for less acculturated Hispanic/Latino(a) clients to be two times as large as the effect sizes for moderately acculturated Hispanic/Latino(a) participants.

Interestingly, the more cultural adaptations used in the treatment approaches, the better the outcomes for ethnic minority clients. The research is not clear as to which cultural adaptations are the most efficacious when several are used simultaneously.

Finally, a debate was introduced into the body of research about a possible need to reconceptualize the thinking on culturally adapted treatments (S. Sue 1988; S. Sue & Zane 1987). The suggestion was to begin studying variables that were more proximal—that is, of more immediate relevance—to therapeutic outcome than race or ethnicity. Some of the more proximal variables suggested were: therapist attitudes, values, knowledge, competency, etc. It was thought that this could explain some of the more conflicting findings in the research on the distal variables of race and ethnicity. Therefore some recent studies have examined the effect of proximal variables on therapeutic outcome.

A study by Meyer, Zane, and Cho (2011) found that college students' perceptions of match when listening to an audio recording of a session increased their perceptions of the therapist's credibility. They also found that the more attitudinally similar the participants perceived the therapist to be to themselves, the more support they felt, and the better the participants perceived their alliance to be with the therapist. This therefore indicates that attitudinal match may be more important than ethnic match in terms of therapeutic outcomes.

Other studies have examined cognitive matching in relation to its effects on therapeutic outcome (Zane et al. 2005). Such studies have found that therapist-client matching on perception of the goals of therapy produced positive therapeutic outcomes. Additionally, T. B. Smith, Domenech Rodriguez, and Bernal (2011) found that using metaphors or symbols that were congruent with the client's worldview explained a significant portion of the variance in effect sizes. Finally, clients who perceived similarity between themselves and their therapists on the expectations about the benefit of treatment felt more comfortable in later sessions and felt they got more out of sessions.

Conclusions

In terms of the clinical application of this research, there is an overwhelming consensus among researchers and clinicians alike that an urgent need exists for clinicians to integrate culturally adapted treatments into their practices. As the research indicates, the more cultural adaptations a clinician can integrate, the more effective his or her work with culturally diverse clients will be. Moreover, the data show a need for more therapists who speak languages other than English in order to meet the needs of the many clients who do not speak English as their primary language. However, the literature also demonstrates the myriad ways in which therapists can match their clients to make treatment more effective that go beyond their race or ethnicity. Research suggests that cognitive match between clinicians and their clients may also make treatment more effective, and suggests that these more proximal variables may have a greater impact on treatment. For the broader field of psychology, while there is a clear recognition of the need for culturally competent care, the research has not followed. More research is needed in order to clearly define what approaches to being culturally sensitive work and how established, empirically supported treatments can be adapted to work with diverse populations. Only when this much needed research is conducted can the findings be used to inform clinical practice and close the gap in the services offered to minority groups.

See also African Americans and Mental Health; American Indian and Alaskan Native Mental Health; Asian American and Pacific Islander Mental Health Issues; *Diagnostic and Statistical Manual of Mental Disorders* (*DSM*); Latinos and Mental Health;

Bibliography

American Psychological Association. 2003. "Guidelines on Multicultural Education, Training, Research, Practice, and Organizational Change for Psychologists." *American Psychologist* 58: 377–402.

Banks, R., A. Hogue, T. Timberlake, and H. Liddle. 1998. "An Afrocentric Approach to Group Social Skills Training with Inner-City African American Adolescents." *Journal of Negro Education* 65: 414–423.

Campbell, C. I., and J. A. Alexander. 2002. "Culturally Competent Treatment Practices and Ancillary Service Use in Outpatient Substance Abuse Treatment." *Journal of Substance Abuse Treatment* 22: 109–119.

Chin, J. L. 2000. "Culturally Competent Health Care." *Public Health Reports* 115(1): 25–34.

Costantino, G., R. G. Malgady, and L. H. Rogler. 1986. "Cuento Therapy: A Culturally Sensitive Modality for Puerto Rican Children." *Journal of Consulting and Clinical Psychology* 54: 639–645.

Duarte-Velez, Y., G. Bernal, and K. Bonilla. 2010. "Culturally Adapted Cognitive-Behavioral Therapy: Integrating Sexual, Spiritual, and Family Identities in an Evidence-Based Treatment of a Depressed Latino Adolescent." *Journal of Clinical Psychology: In Session* 66: 895–906.

Griner, D., and T. B. Smith. 2006. "Culturally Adapted Mental Health Interventions: A Meta-Analytic Review." *Psychotherapy: Theory, Research, Practice, Training* 43(4): 531–548.

Maramba, G. G., and G. C. Nagayama Hall. 2002. "Meta-Analyses of Ethnic Match as a Predictor of Dropout, Utilization, and Level of Functioning." *Cultural Diversity and Ethnic Minority Psychology* 8(3): 290–297.

McFadden, J., and W. D. Lipscomb. 1985. "History of the Association for Non-white Concerns in Personnel and Guidance." *Journal of Counseling & Development* 63(7): 444.

Meyer, O., N. Zane, and Y. I. Cho. 2011. "Understanding the Psychological Processes of the Racial Match Effect in Asian Americans." *Journal of Counseling Psychology.* Advance online publication.

National Association of Social Workers. 2007. *Indicators for the Achievement of the NASW Standards for Cultural Competence in Social Work Practice*. Washington, DC: National Association of Social Workers.

Oliver, W. 1989. "Black Males and Social Problems: Prevention through Afrocentric Socialization." *Journal of Black Studies* 20: 15–39.

President's Commission on Mental Health. 1978. *Report to the President*. Washington, DC: U.S. Government Printing Office.

President's New Freedom Commission on Mental Health. 2003. *Achieving the Promise: Transforming Mental Health Care in America. Report of the President's New Freedom Commission on Mental Health*. Rockville, MD: U.S. Department of Health and Human Services, Substance Abuse and Mental Health Services Administration.

Smedley, B. D., A. Y. Stith, and A. R. Nelson. 2003. *Unequal Treatment: Confronting Racial & Ethnic Disparities in Health*. Washington, DC: National Academy Press.

Smith, M. L., and G. Roysircar. 2010. "African American Male Leaders in Counseling: Interviews with Five AMCD Past Presidents." *Journal of Multicultural Counseling & Development* 38(4): 242–255.

Smith, T. B., M. Domenech Rodriguez, and G. Bernal. 2011. "Culture." *Journal of Clinical Psychology* 67(2): 166–175.

Substance Abuse and Mental Health Services Administration. 2010. *Results from the 2009 National Survey on Drug Use and Health: Mental Health Findings*. Office of Applied Studies, NSDUH Series H-39, HHS Publication No. SMA 10-4609. Rockville, MD: Substance Abuse and Mental Health Services Administration.

Sue, D. W., and G. C. Torino. 2005. "Racial-Cultural Competence: Awareness, Knowledge, and Skills." In R. T. Carter, ed., *Handbook of Racial-Cultural Psychology and Counseling: Training and Practice* (Vol. 2, pp. 3–18). Hoboken, NJ: Wiley.

Sue, S. 1988. "Psychotherapeutic Services for Ethnic Minorities: Two Decades of Research Findings." *American Psychologist* 43(4): 301–308.

Sue, S., D. C. Fujino, L. Hu, D. T. Takeuchi, and N. W. S. Zane. 1991. "Community Mental Health Services for Ethnic Minority Groups: A Test of the Cultural Responsiveness Hypothesis." *Journal of Consulting and Clinical Psychology* 59(4): 533–540.

Sue, S. and N. Zane. 1987. "The Role of Culture and Cultural Techniques in Psychotherapy: A Critique and Reformulation." *American Psychologist* 42(1): 37–45.

Sue, S., N. Zane, G. C. Nagayama Hall, and L. K. Berger. 2009. "The Case for Cultural Competency in Psychotherapeutic Interventions." *Annual Review of Psychology* 60: 525–548.

U.S. Surgeon General. 2001. *Mental Health: Culture, Race, and Ethnicity. A Supplement to Mental Health: A Report of the Surgeon General*. Rockville, MD: U.S. Department of Health and Human Services.

Walton, E., K. Berasi, D. Takeuchi, and E. S. Uehara. 2009. "Cultural Diversity and Mental Health." In T. L. Scheid and T. N. Brown, eds., *A Handbook for the Study of Mental Health: Social Contexts, Theories, and Systems* (2nd ed., pp. 439–460). New York: Cambridge University Press.

Watters, E. 2007. "Suffering Differently." *New York Times Magazine*. August 12. Retrieved from http://www.nytimes.com/2007/08/12/magazine/12wwln-idealab-t.html.

Yeh, M., D. T. Takeuchi, and S. Sue. 1994. "Asian American Children in the Mental Health System: A Comparison of Parallel and Mainstream Outpatient Service Centers." *Journal of Clinical Child Psychology* 23: 5–12.

Zane, N., S. Sue, J. Chang, L. Huang, J. Huang, S. Lowe, et al. 2005. "Beyond Ethnic Match: Effects of Client-Therapist Cognitive Match in Problem Perception, Coping Orientation, and Therapy Goals on Treatment Outcomes." *Journal of Community Psychology* 33: 569–585.

D

Dementia

See Alzheimer's Disease and Dementia

Depression

Rudy Nydegger

Depression profoundly impacts the life and health of millions of people around the world on a daily basis. Although each of us has occasionally experienced "mood swings" or has felt depressed for a few days or weeks as a result of a difficult or traumatic event, a significant disappointment, the loss of someone close, or a failed relationship, the term "clinical depression" is reserved for a person demonstrating a specific list of symptoms that have been present for a considerable length of time. However, situations that severely affect us emotionally and/or physically might eventually develop into depression, and therefore people who have experienced these types of events should be monitored for the possibility of depression. Of course most people who have dealt with very emotionally demanding situations do not develop true depression, but it is helpful to remember that when a negative mood does not go away in a reasonable amount of time, or continues to worsen, then professional help is warranted.

Diagnosing Depression

In the case of depression, it is important that the clinician recognize the subtle differences between a true depressive disorder and the moods that resemble depression. Some practitioners consider that all mood problems, including clinical depression, are varying degrees of the same disorder and should be listed on one continuum from very mild (mood swings) to very severe (major depression). Proponents of such a perspective conclude that when a person suffers from a depressed mood, they are at a higher risk for developing a depressive disorder later on (Hankin & Abramson 2001). This view is not universally accepted, and most practitioners and researchers hold that placing the qualitatively and quantitatively different clinical depression on the same continuum as other mood problems is like comparing apples to oranges.

Complicating the picture, it is also true that depression as not just a single disorder: there are many different types of depression as well as other distinct disorders that include a negative mood component (see Sidebar). Further, depression can frequently accompany other medical or psychological conditions, which can further complicate diagnosis and treatment planning. Those suffering from depression often experience emotional, motivational, behavioral, cognitive, and physical symptoms:

- Emotionally, patients may feel miserable, empty, sad, humiliated, and worthless.
- Motivationally, they may lack the desire to do anything, and experience a decreased interest in work, social activities, and anything that used to be enjoyable.
- Behaviorally, depressed people show decreased energy and activity levels, often isolate themselves, and may stay in bed far longer than they need to for normal sleep and rest.
- Cognitively, thinking patterns can include a negative view of self, pessimistic thoughts, as well as problems with short-term memory, attention, and concentration.
- Finally, people suffering from depression often complain of several physical symptoms that are sometimes vague and diffuse, such as headaches, indigestion, constipation, dizzy spells, general pain, and sexual dysfunction (Comer 2004).

Officially, the American Psychiatric Association in the *Diagnostic and Statistical Manual of Mental Disorders* (fourth edition, text revision; 2000) lists a set of symptoms that are used to diagnose clinical depression. Two of the basic, core characteristics of depression are depressed (*or dysphoric*) mood and a lack of interest or enjoyment in things formerly found to be enjoyable (*anhedonia*). In addition, depressed persons usually have difficulty falling asleep or staying asleep (*insomnia*), or routinely oversleep and are still tired and never feel as though they have had enough sleep (*hypersomnia*).

Other symptoms of depression can be expressed in extreme changes in nutrition and activity levels. Some depressed people have no appetite and cannot eat, often leading to weight loss, while others feed the depression, frequently with poor nutritional choices like sugars and simple carbohydrates, leading to weight gain. Reduced energy and activity levels are typical to most who are depressed, although some become either anxious or agitated (not to the same degree, however, as a manic state in bipolar disorder).

Negative feelings about self and things in general, as well as widespread pessimism, are typically found in depressed patients, and they often ponder death or suicide. Most patients explain that they do not necessarily want to die;

Forms of Depression and Depression-Related Illnesses

Depression as a concept covers a wide variety of symptoms, and these symptoms moreover are often present in various combinations. Furthermore, they frequently occur with symptoms associated with other psychiatric disorders, making depression one of if not the most variable of mental illnesses. (In this sense it echoes schizophrenia.) It is instructive, therefore, to consider the varieties of depression and depression-related disorders.

Major depression: Marked, sustained unhappiness or darkness of mood (also called clinical depression)

Bipolar disorder: Alternating episodes of depression and mania

Atypical depression: Depression associated with increased appetite and weight gain along with other symptoms

Eating disorders: Anorexia and bulimia often have a depression component

Drug and alcohol abuse: Behaviors that frequently involve depression

Obsessive-compulsive disorder (OCD): An anxiety disorder that can include depressive symptoms

Dysthymia: A less severe form of clinical depression

Cyclothymia: A mild form of bipolar disorder

Hypochondria: Hypochondriacs (i.e., those preoccupied with real or imagined health problems) often have symptoms of depression

Postpartum depression: Depression, ranging from moderate to severe, following childbirth

Premenstrual syndrome (PMS): Depression and/or other symptoms occurring prior to menstruation

Seasonal affective disorder (SAD): Depressive mood arising with the onset of winter

Adjustment disorder: Disturbance of mood (including depression) associated with specific psychosocial stressors (such as marital problems or work-related issues)

Social phobia (or social anxiety disorder): Persons living with social phobia may experience depression as well

Depressive personality disorder: A pervasive pattern of depressive cognitions and behaviors beginning by early adulthood

Psychotic depression: Delusions or hallucinations involving depressive themes (including persecution, hopelessness, and death)

—Editor

nevertheless, they can see no compelling reason to continue living either. Depressed people will also describe a lack of cognitive and intellectual efficiency and difficulty thinking clearly. Obviously, being depressed is not pleasant for anyone, and sufferers often report feeling miserable and finding no hope in the future. Two words that capture the nature of depression for many people are "helplessness" and "hopelessness." This is why depressed people tend to be annoyed or sink even deeper when others say to them, "Snap out of it!" or "Just go out and do things and you'll feel better!" The reality of the depressed person's condition is more complicated than that.

Since symptoms of depression are similar to those of other types of problems and diseases, an accurate diagnosis is sometimes difficult to make, and major depression is frequently misdiagnosed and often goes untreated for a long period of time. Many people do not seek professional help because of the stigma surrounding mental illness or because they do not believe anyone can help them. Many depressed people are so fatigued and discouraged that they cannot force themselves to go to an appointment. Interestingly, some people might not even know that they are depressed because they have felt so badly for so long it seems "normal" to them; they may not even be aware that they are actually experiencing symptoms of depression.

Depressed people are critical of and discouraged about themselves, usually report low self-esteem, and often believe that they do not *deserve* to feel good (depression is their punishment for being worthless). With this frame of mind, the depressed person will be unable to demonstrate the same level of mastery of his or her job as previously, and lacks the usual sense of pleasure in his or her relationships and in other activities. Owing to the difficult and cyclical nature of depression, growing feelings of worthlessness often lead to eventually just giving up and accepting the depression as inevitable and unending. Patients become so fatigued and tired of performing poorly that they choose not do anything rather than to continue failing. More precisely, depressed people will usually *perceive themselves* as failing, even if those around them do not agree. When this downward spiral begins, it is difficult to stop, and before long others will recognize the performance and behavioral problems. This then becomes a "self-fulfilling prophecy": if you truly believe that you are doing a bad job and that no one wants to be around you, and you consistently act on those feelings, eventually your performance *will* suffer and people really will not want to spend time with you because you are such a "downer" to be around.

Prevalence and Social Effects

During any given year, about 9.5 percent of the U.S. population, or about 20.9 million adults, suffer from some type of depression (National Institute of Mental Health 2011). This is a huge number, and yet it does not even include the millions of other depression sufferers whose illness is undiagnosed. According to some researchers (Druss, Rosenheck, & Sledge 2000), major depressive disorder (MDD) is the leading cause of disability in the United States. They point out that MDD results in more days of disability, lost workdays, and presenteeism (when a person shows up to work too sick, impaired, stressed out, or distracted to be productive) than many other medical or psychological conditions, creating a huge financial burden for employers. In terms of lost hours of work, medical costs, reduced effectiveness, and other related problems, the enormous expense of depression burdens all of us. Not only are employers affected, but other employees, customers, insurance carriers, family members, and friends are affected as well. Although cost estimates of depression in the United States will vary, the American Psychiatric Association (1998) estimates the impact of depression on general well-being and national prosperity, if one includes all of the direct and indirect costs, to be in excess of $80 billion per year, and it is likely much higher given the passage of time since the estimate came out.

Depression also affects those around the depressed person. One study (Glenn & Bergman 1997) suggests that depression is associated with excess disability, impaired health, lower quality of life, and lower well-being for patients *and* their significant others. They report that depression is one of the most serious emotional problems and that its total impact may exceed that of any other medical condition or psychiatric disorder. The study also points out that the true cost of depression must include those around the depressed patient who are affected in terms of their lives, their relationships, and their jobs.

Depression can also have a significant effect upon other psychological and medical conditions, and physicians and other health professionals do not always recognize depression as a major health risk. One set of studies followed depressed men and women for several years to record how their health status was affected by depression. Researchers found that, after controlling for confounding conditions (interfering factors), men with *minor* depression had a 1.80-fold higher risk of death. Women with minor depression, on the other hand, did not have a significantly increased mortality risk. However, both men and women with *major* depression had a 1.83-fold increased risk for mortality (Penning et al. 1999). Since this study did not spell out specific types of depression, it means that people with any diagnosed depression are almost twice as likely to die in a four-year time span as the controls who were not depressed. Depression is clearly one of the most pressing public health issues in the United States today (Depression and Bipolar Support Alliance 2006).

Although symptoms of depression are unpleasant and intrusive, it may seem odd that depression is still frequently missed or misdiagnosed. Why would a person who feels miserable resist available help? Many people, especially men, are reluctant to pursue professional help for something as "simple" as depression owing to the stigma of appearing "weak." Such people adhere to the "you can get through this on your own" school of thought. Others have inadequate knowledge about symptoms of depression and assume their depressed feelings are "normal" or "no big deal." In general, many are unaware that treatment is available or hold to the misconception that one must be "crazy" to be in need of professional help.

Getting Treatment

Support and encouragement from those who care is one of the best ways to get people who need professional care to see an appropriate professional. Treatment usually begins with seeing one's primary care physician (PCP) and eliminating any physical conditions that may present similar symptoms to depression. Since depression is most frequently seen initially in the primary care setting, most family practitioners and other PCPs are getting training in recognizing and initially treating depressive disorders. The first line of treatment for depression is usually psychotropic medications (Helpguide 2006), often prescribed by the PCP prior to a client's seeing a psychiatrist or psychopharmacologist. However, adequate treatment for depression must involve the appropriate mix of therapies, including psychological treatment as well as medication. If a person is receiving *only* medication from a non-mental health professional, and is not receiving psychotherapy, he or she is likely not receiving adequate treatment.

Clinical depression is frequently misdiagnosed or missed altogether by health professionals, and can be confused with other conditions. It is common for depressed persons to self-medicate and experience temporary symptom relief by using alcohol or nonprescription drugs. Alcohol acts as a depressant on the central nervous system (CNS) and can be problematic for two reasons: (1) it can produce symptoms similar to depression; and (2) it can mask the symptoms of depression, especially if the physician is unaware of the alcohol or drug abuse due to a patient hiding or denying it.

Another unfortunate reality of medical care today is that physicians are under pressure to see as many patients as possible, and often do not have the time to listen carefully in order to detect the subtle indicators of depression. For example, some of the aches and pains that a patient presents may actually be related to depression, but in the absence of other indicators, the physician simply may not recognize the depression. Finally, some people believe that all depression is transitory and that if you just leave it alone, it will go away by itself (Helpguide 2006). Fatigue and lack of motivation are common symptoms of depression, which often puts patients in the difficult position of not wanting to or not being able to do those things that may actually help them. It is becoming more common in primary care practices to routinely screen patients for depression using depression screening inventories, and this has led to much better recognition and treatment of depression at earlier and more treatable stages. This is particularly important in older adults who are more likely to present with physical symptoms of depression and may simply think that the symptoms are another medical condition or are just part of "getting old." When diagnosed and treated in a timely manner, depression is very treatable and most patients who are given adequate treatment will show significant improvement.

Current Status and Future Possibilities

It is tragic that many people do not receive treatment for depression and many other conditions because they simply do not have access to services owing to income/economics, logistics, or location. Society is making choices about health care, and specifically mental health care, and these choices prevent millions of people from receiving the help they need. Although there are many effective treatments available today, depression is often untreated (Ebmeier, Donaghey, & Steele 2006). This reality is not likely to change quickly, but we must remember that when conditions like depression are not treated appropriately they will typically result in more complicated psychological and medical problems later, and this will be more expensive and difficult to treat. Therefore trying to save money by *not* treating something like depression is very likely going to result in much higher expenses in the future.

See also Alcohol Abuse, Alcoholism, and Mental Health; Bipolar Disorder; Eating Disorders; Loss and Grief; Obsessive-Compulsive Disorder; Psychosomatic Disorders; Psychotherapy; Social Anxiety Disorder; Suicide and Suicide Prevention; Undiagnosed Mental Illness

Bibliography

American Psychiatric Association. 1998. *Let's Talk Facts about Depression*. Washington, DC: American Psychiatric Association.

American Psychiatric Association. 2000. *Diagnostic and Statistical Manual of Mental Disorders* (4th ed., text rev.). Washington, DC: American Psychiatric Publishing.

Andrews, L. W. 2010. *Encyclopedia of Depression*. Santa Barbara, CA: Greenwood Press.

Comer, R. J. 2004. *Abnormal Psychology* (5th ed.). New York: Worth.

Depression and Bipolar Support Alliance. 2006. The State of Depression in America. Retrieved January 15, 2007, from http://www.dbsalliance.org/pdfs/wpsearchable.pdf.

Druss, B. G., R. A. Rosenheck, W. H. Sledge. 2000. "Health and Disability Costs of Depressive Illness in a Major U.S. Corporation." *American Journal of Psychiatry* 157(8): 1274–1278.

Ebmeier, K. P., C. Donaghey, and J. D. Steele. 2006. "Recent Developments and Current Controversies in Depression." *Lancet* 367: 153–167.

Glenn, M. B., and S. B. Bergman. 1997. "Cardiovascular Changes Following Spinal Cord Injury." *Topics in Spinal Cord Injury Rehabilitation* 2: 45–53.

Hankin, B. L. E., and L. Y. Abramson. 2001. "Development of Gender Differences in Depression: An Elaborated Cognitive Vulnerability-Transactional Stress Theory." *Psychological Bulletin* 127(6): 773–796.

Helpguide. 2006. Depression in Older Adults and the Elderly: Signs, Symptoms, Causes and Treatments. Retrieved May 2, 2006, from http://www.helpguide.org/mental/depression_elderly.htm.

National Institute of Mental Health. 2011. Depression. Retrieved November 3, 2011, from http://www.nimh.nih.gov/health/publications/depression/complete-index.shtml.

Nydegger, R. 2008. *Understanding and Treating Depression: Ways to Find Hope and Help*. Westport, CT: Praeger.

Penning, B. W., S. W. Geerlings, D. J. Deeg, J. T. van Eijk, W. van Tilburg, and A. T. Beekman. 1999. "Minor and Major Depression and the Risk of Death in Older Persons." *Archives of General Psychiatry* 56(10): 889–895.

Developmental Disorders

See Attention Deficit/Hyperactivity Disorder; Autism Spectrum Disorders; Children and Mental Health; Intellectual Disability; Learning Disabilities

Diagnostic and Statistical Manual of Mental Disorders (DSM)

Matthew J. Paylo, Nicole A. Adamson, Carrie DeMarco, and Victoria E. Kress

The *Diagnostic and Statistical Manual of Mental Disorders* (fourth edition, text revision; *DSM-IV-TR*; American Psychiatric Association [APA] 2000) is a reference manual that is used by trained mental health clinicians (e.g., psychiatrists, psychologists, counselors, social workers, marriage and family therapists) to describe, classify, and relay information regarding mental health disorders. Mental health providers use the *DSM* system to compress an overwhelming amount of mental health information into a system of manageable diagnoses (Seligman, Walker, & Rosenhan 2001). Additionally, the *DSM* offers mental health professionals a common language to use in discussing and trying to understand mental illness. This language is utilized by researchers and clinicians alike, so that for each disorder there can be a reliable prognosis and an appreciation of its prevalence and course along with an understanding of the operable modes of treatment or intervention.

The *DSM* is currently divided into 17 different categories of mental disorders (e.g., Substance-Related Disorders, Mood Disorders, and Anxiety Disorders). These categories consist of disorders with similar symptoms and similar manifestation of those symptoms. Mental disorders in the *DSM* are further articulated according to when, how, and for how long these symptoms persist, the level of impairment of these symptoms on an individual's functioning, and the presence or absence of other mental disorders. In describing these mental disorders, each disorder is addressed with regard to the following considerations: the disorder's diagnostic features; the associated features of that disorder and the distinguishing specifiers for that disorders; a specific coding number; the specific culture, age, and gender features; prevalence, course, familial patterns; and differential diagnosis (i.e., the other disorders that could be considered given some or parts of the symptom presentation).

Although the *DSM* is a valuable resource for helping professionals, there are some setbacks to using this diagnostic tool. The *DSM* authors do not acknowledge the etiology ("causes") of the disorders. The authors do not address or recommend treatment approaches either; the manual's authors purport only to describe the symptoms associated with each mental disorder. Presently, the *DSM* is in its fourth edition. It has evolved significantly from its original roots.

The *DSM* assessment system is accepted as the most prominent communication system used in discussing and expressing mental health consumer (i.e., client or patient) difficulties, and it serves to reduce client-related information into a more manageable, digestible form (Seligman, Walker, & Rosenhan 2001). By categorizing people's psychological difficulties, the *DSM* aims to assist researchers and clinicians in comparing various treatment approaches to particular difficulties. Further, *DSM* classification provides researchers with a system for use in investigating underlying causal mechanisms and processes of particular diagnoses, which in turn may allow for prevention and improved control over the outcomes of psychiatric disorders (APA 2000; Hinkle 1999; Maniacci 2002; Mead, Hohenshil, & Singh 1997). Additionally, the *DSM* provides information about the course, prevalence, cultural, gender, and familial issues related to each diagnosis—information that may be helpful to counselors who are struggling to fully understand their clients' experiences. This understanding may enable effective referral and/or planning of counseling, psychotherapy, and other psychiatric treatment strategies (Duffy et al. 2002; Mead, Hohenshil, & Singh 1997; Waldo, Brotherton, & Horswill 1993).

History of the *DSM*

Initially, the *DSM* was created to provide a more accurate representation of the U.S. population for census purposes. Early census material was extremely rudimentary, and in 1840, the census had only one category for mental illness, "idiocy/insanity." By 1880, the U.S. census had evolved to inquire about seven designations, which included mania, melancholia, monomania, paresis, dementia, dyssomnia, and epilepsy. In 1917, the "Committee on Statistics" (now known as the American Psychiatric Association) along with the National Commission of Mental Hygiene created a manual outlining 22 diagnoses that were called the *Statistical Manual for the Use of Institutions for the Insane*. Several revisions of this manual and input from the New York Academy of Medicine led to the eventual completion of the U.S. medical guide, the *Standard Classified Nomenclature of Diseases*.

The Second World War forced large-scale involvement of mental health clinicians in the treatment of soldiers. This frontline treatment of soldiers created sweeping changes in the perception and classifications of mental disturbances and therefore paved the way for the first edition of the *Diagnostic and Statistical Manual of Mental Illness (DSM)*. Printed in 1952, this manual classified 106 mental disorders and was more comprehensive than other manuals in the past (Grob 1991). Subsequent changes were made to the original *DSM* over the following decades (i.e., *DSM-II*, 1968; *DSM-III*, 1980; *DSM-III-R*, 1987; *DSM-IV*, 1994; and *DSM-IV-TR*, 2000), including defining mental illness, new means to classify mental disorders, a multiaxial assessment approach (i.e., use of several axes that provide different information helpful to a clinician when diagnosing, treating, and predicting outcomes), and the addition and subtraction of specific mental disorders. As researchers, psychiatrists, and mental health clinicians began to understand mental disorders and mental illness, the *DSM* evolved in response to the most up-to-date research regarding mental illness. This present version of the *DSM*, the *DSM -IV-TR*, is 943 pages long, and identifies about 300 mental disorders.

Organization of the *DSM*

The current version of the *DSM* classifies mental illness into the following mental disorder groupings:

- *Disorders First Diagnosed in Infancy, Childhood, or Adolescence*, consisting of mental retardation; learning disorders; motor-skills disorders; communication disorders; pervasive developmental disorders; attention deficit and disruptive behavior disorders; feeding and eating disorders of infancy or early childhood; tic disorders; elimination disorders; and other disorders
- *Delirium, Dementia, and Amnestic and Other Cognitive Disorders*, or disorders resulting from deficits in cognition that produce significant change from a previous level of functioning
- *Mental Disorders Due to a General Medical Condition*
- *Substance-Related Disorders*, or disorders related to the use of alcohol, amphetamines, hallucinogens, inhalants, opioids, sedatives, or other substances
- *Schizophrenia and Other Psychotic Disorders*, or disorders marked by psychotic symptoms associated with schizophrenia and related disorders
- *Mood Disorders*, namely, depressive disorders and bipolar disorders
- *Anxiety Disorders*, or disorders involving uncontrollable panic or anxiety

- *Somatoform Disorders*, or disorders involving physical symptoms that suggest a general medical condition but not fully explained by the medical condition

- *Factitious Disorders*, or "faked" physical or psychological symptoms produced in order to assume the sick role

- *Dissociative Disorders*, or disturbance of consciousness, memory, identity, or perception

- *Sexual and Gender Identity Disorders*, consisting of sexual dysfunctions, paraphilias (atypical sexual behaviors as defined by culture and society), and gender identity disorders

- *Eating Disorders*, or severe disturbances in eating behavior

- *Sleep Disorders*, consisting of dyssomnias (trouble initiating or maintaining sleep, excessive sleepiness, or other disturbances), parasomnias (unusual behavioral events or physiological actions during sleep), and other sleep disorders

- *Impulse-Control Disorders*, or disorders involving the failure to resist the desire to perform a harmful act because it provides pleasure, gratification, or relief to the individual

- *Adjustment Disorders*, or disorders involving the inability to respond to identifiable stressors

- *Personality Disorders*, covering enduring patterns of inner experience that produce behaviors that significantly deviate from cultural expectations

- *Other Conditions*, including medication-induced movement disorder, relational problems, problems related to abuse or neglect, and so on (APA 2000)

Using the *DSM*
Multiaxial System

As stated earlier, one of the significant alterations of the *DSM* was the addition of the multiaxial system of diagnosing. This multiaxial assessment system, which includes five axes, each of which relates to a unique domain, is intended to help mental health providers conceptualize clients more holistically, apply interventions and treatments, and predict client outcomes that consider clinical, medical, and psychosocial impressions of that individual. These five axes are:

- *Axis I—Clinical Disorders and Other Conditions.* All of the mental disorders or conditions are listed on this axis, except for personality disorders and mental retardation.

- *Axis II—Personality Disorders and Mental Retardation.* Besides these two categories, prominent maladaptive personality features and prominent defensive mechanisms may also be listed on Axis II.

- *Axis III—General Medical Conditions*. Medical conditions that are potentially relevant to the understanding or management of the client's mental disorder are listed on Axis III.

- *Axis IV—Psychosocial and Environmental Problems*. Problems that may affect the diagnosis, treatment, or prognosis of a mental disorder—particularly, environmental events or deficiencies, life stresses, social or occupational problems, and so on—are listed on Axis IV.

- *Axis V—Global Assessment of Functioning*. This concerns the provider's judgment of the individual's overall level of functioning, expressed as a number between 1 and 100 (1 being the most impaired level and 100 the most optimal).

Cultural Considerations

The *DSM* addresses culture-bound syndromes, or syndromes that are found only in individuals living in certain areas of the world, which provides helpful information about the demographics of those who are typically affected by certain diagnoses and the course of manifestation that can be expected. Most of the behaviors and experiences of the individual are considered by others in that culture to represent illnesses, and most have local names. However, in a broader context, the same symptoms may have a different name or may not be considered to be part an illness at all.

An example of a culturally bound syndrome is *taijin kyofusho*, a culturally distinctive phobia seen in Japanese society. Symptoms of this syndrome include a fear that one's body and its functions displease, embarrass, or offend others by means of odor, appearance, movements, or facial expressions. In contexts outside of Japan, this may be known as a form of social anxiety disorder or it may be accepted as a reasonable response to interacting with others. The *DSM* takes care to identify the cultural context associated with over two dozen culture-bound syndromes.

Blueprint for Diagnosing

According to Morrison (2006), the following is the means or process employed by a mental health clinician in reaching a diagnosis using the DSM. The clinician must first work up a comprehensive history for the individual, drawing on information taken from the interview, other informants, psychological testing, and past medical and mental health records. During this process, the clinician documents the following:

- The course of the current illness
- Previous mental health difficulties and past treatments

- Personal, family, and social background information
- Medical history
- Results of a mental status exam (MSE)

An MSE is a structured or semistructured way of assessing an individual's level of functioning and self-presentation. The clinician usually evaluates the following domains in a comprehensive MSE: appearance, attitude, and activity; mood and affect; speech and language; thought process, thought content, and perception; cognition; insight and judgment; and finally, impulse control. The purpose of the MSE is to obtain a comprehensive evaluation of the individual's mental state and level of functioning, and to assist the clinician in the accurate diagnosis of a mental illness if a diagnosis is warranted.

As the clinician explores the history of the individual, he or she compiles a collection of symptoms that together point to an identifiable mental disorder. If warranted, the clinician will consider all the symptoms (e.g., including the lack of symptoms) and categorize them, producing a list of potential disorders that may explain the symptoms present. This is called "working through" the differential diagnosis by evaluating every option through considering the symptoms present or reported by the individual. Utilizing a *DSM* decision tree (i.e., a process for ruling in or out a diagnosis by responding to a group of yes/no questions), the clinician can arrive at a working diagnosis for that individual. At this point in the process, the clinician will need to consider any comorbid diagnoses (i.e., disorders that are often correlated with that diagnosis) and all relevant biopsychosocial information. In making a final diagnosis, the clinician will understand that it is not fixed or permanent but rather is fluid and can be reevaluated if new information, new testing, or specific responses to treatment become available.

The ability to diagnose varies depending on one's profession and the state or jurisdictions within which one practices. For example, in the state of Ohio, clinical counselors, independent social workers, independent marriage and family therapists, and psychologists can all diagnose and treat mental and emotional disorders as described in the *DSM*.

Limitations of the *DSM*

The *DSM* is not without limitations and criticism. There are many noteworthy drawbacks of the system. The *DSM* is just one diagnostic system (the World Health Organization utilizes the ICD-10, for example), and it can be argued that no one system can ever be entirely perfect; each one will excel in certain areas but have deficiencies in others. It would be difficult for any system to diagnose with perfect accuracy. Accordingly, mental health professionals might tentatively explore a number of diagnostic systems in order to have an objective diagnostic discussion with clients. The following sections discuss several key limitations.

The Medical Model

Some argue the *DSM* provides a simplistic view of mental health diagnoses that closely resembles the medical model of treatment. *DSM* diagnoses can *narrow a clinician's focus* by encouraging him or her to look only for behaviors that fit with a "medical model" understanding of the client's situation, effectively ignoring other, *contextual-* or *developmental-*focused sources (etiologies) (Eriksen & Kress 2005). The medical model of treatment assumes, for the most part, that there is one correct diagnosis for a particular health concern, and therefore a specific way to treat and even remedy such conditions. This idea of symptoms, causes, and treatments implies that there is some biological or physical cause for client problems. The model tends to assume that mental disorders occur in isolation of context, environment, and socio-emotional stressors.

The medical model has been criticized for being reductionistic, mechanistic, static, and linear (Eriksen & Kress 2006). *DSM* diagnoses reduce complex information into short diagnostic blurbs, which tend to be very general and even stereotypical. Although mental health symptoms are just one part of an overall person, the *DSM* often tends to generalize symptoms to explain other aspects of a person. As a result, clients often define themselves through their mental health diagnosis and can become cognitively and emotionally "stuck"—that is, they can experience feelings of helplessness in overcoming their difficulties. Diagnostic criteria set forth in the *DSM* also tend to be static and linear and do not account for the ever-changing circumstances of human life. Clinicians can work through this drawback by regularly completing reassessments and appreciating how mental health diagnoses can change over time.

Harm of Diagnosis

The issuance of a *DSM* diagnosis can potentially cause harm to clients, and diagnoses should be ascribed with care. An in-depth understanding of the risks associated with *DSM* diagnosis can allow mental health professionals to provide beneficial service to clients. Similarly, a client's understanding of the risks associated with mental health diagnosis can allow clients to consent in an informed manner and work toward counteracting potential harm.

DSM diagnoses can sometimes become self-fulfilling prophecies (Rosenhan 1973). If a diagnosis is viewed as static or unchanging, one might begin to feel hopeless or powerless over the mental health concerns. The client may begin to believe that there is no point in working toward change. Also, clients may begin to feel as though it is not necessary to change and that any behaviors or symptoms of mental illness are excusable and can be blamed on the mental illness. The client may choose not to work toward change and to succumb to the diagnosis, and the diagnostic symptoms will continue to manifest. This can also serve to minimize the individual's sense of uniqueness (Eriksen & Kress 2005).

Diagnostic labels are often stigmatized and held in shame by the general public. Mental health diagnoses tend to separate clients from mainstream populations and diagnosed populations may be treated differently in society. Some people may tend to blame people for their diagnoses or assume that they are incompetent or otherwise impaired by the symptoms associated with mental health diagnoses.

A mental health diagnosis can prove to be harmful to a client in the legal system as well. The privileged communication enjoyed between mental health professionals and clients can be broken if ordered by a judge. Mental health records can be held against an individual in court. For instance, a person who is trying to win custody of children could be seen as unfit owing to a stigmatizing mental health diagnosis.

Finally, with the inception of managed care, a *DSM* diagnosis is almost always required by third-party payers (e.g., insurance companies, Medicaid) to provide reimbursement of services to mental health clinicians. This requirement ensures third parties that appropriate treatment modalities are being employed in accordance with the client's diagnosis and the clinician's recommendations. In addition, third-party payers can regulate treatment length and frequency and stay informed of the client's progress through use of the *DSM*. Third-party providers often reimburse mental health services only for diagnosed conditions. This could potentially invite clients' exaggeration of symptoms in order to receive services and perhaps promote mental health professionals' exaggeration of client symptoms in order to issue a diagnosis for treatment.

A Ranking of Diagnostic Categories?

The trouble is that the *DSM-IV* is like a dictionary, intended to be broad and comprehensive and thus inclusive of every possible category of mental illness regardless of severity. It is an attempt to catalog and classify *all* pathological psychological experiences outside the "norm." Accordingly, it includes forms of mental illness that do not warrant the same level of attention as, say, schizophrenia or major depression. Pathological deviations from the norm included in the *DSM-IV* range from mild cases of simple caffeine intoxication to potentially suicidal cases of chronic major depression. This poses a challenge for insurers, whether private or governmental, who must set parameters for coverage eligibility. Should all 297 categories of mental illness listed in the *DSM-IV* be equally covered, or should some be prioritized over others?

—Timothy A. Kelly

Source: Timothy A. Kelly, *Healing the Broken Mind: Transforming America's Broken Mental Health Care System* (New York: New York University Press, 2009), 12.

Validity

The "science" of the *DSM* diagnostic process has been called into question by research showing that certain of the diagnoses (e.g., personality disorders) are not reliably or consistently applied among providers, and that the validity of some of the disorders (e.g., gender identity disorder) remains an issue (Eriksen & Kress 2005). It is important to evaluate the extent to which the *DSM* truly measures the constructs for which it was designed. Many factors could potentially limit the validity of the *DSM* depending upon the research used to create this diagnostic system, those who influence its content, and the populations for which it is used. The norming population must be very diverse in order to allow the findings in the *DSM* to be applied to a wide range of people, and sociopolitical influences or the agendas that various groups have in relation to what is and is not included in the *DSM* must also be considered.

Determining "Normal"   The process of creating mental health diagnoses inherently implies that certain mental health symptoms are *abnormal*—that is, they prevent healthy functioning in an individual. This is a concept that requires some sort of judgment or separation of people and behaviors; in order to determine what is abnormal, a definition of normal must first be determined. Due to the discriminating nature of such definitions, it is important to consider who typically constructs them and on what basis is it decided. These definitions are commonly adopted by the majority of society and the effects of such beliefs can be observed in many societal systems (e.g., employment decisions, popular-media portrayals, and even religious practices). Therefore it is imperative in using the *DSM* or similar systems to have a critical understanding of the context and historical influence of commonly held definitions of normal and abnormal with regard to mental health.

Cultural Bias   Historically, people who have not conformed to societal conventions have been ostracized. Homosexuals were diagnosable as mentally ill until 1973 (APA 1980). African Americans were in earlier eras considered less than fully human, so that any pursuit of human "rights" was considered abnormal and any slave's pursuit of freedom was at one time diagnosable as *drapetomania* (Szasz 2002). In the twentieth century, Christian Euro-Americans considered Native Americans and Asians who had different customs to be heathens or savages. These past perceptions support the continuing need for review and discussion of cultural norms and biases effecting mental health definitions in the present era.

By definition, each culture assigns unique meaning to personality, intelligence, difficulties, and illnesses. Castillo (1997), among others, found that culture clearly affects clients' and counselors' perceptions of reality. Such cultural realities effect the kinds of symptoms reported by clients (and understood by clinicians), how such symptoms are expressed, the meaning and etiology assigned to the symptoms, and how they are treated. All of these elements come into play in the doctor-patient (or client-counselor) situation and, beyond that, in the wider community.

Gender Bias   Gender bias impacts both men and women under the *DSM* diagnostic system. Diagnostic labels can be stigmatizing in themselves, but gender stereotypes add an additional stigma to certain diagnoses. It is typically noted in the *DSM*, for example, whether a diagnosis is more prevalent among males or females. This information is determined by professional working groups that synthesize research findings, literature reviews, and data analysis. Yet the sources of such research must be viewed as subject to continuing scrutiny and analysis if the effort to identify any lingering sexist assumptions is to be advanced. Although research does support the assumption that certain genders are more prone to certain mental health disorders, there are many factors that contribute to such findings. Plausible explanations for these findings include human (scientific) error, cultural bias, reliance on sociopolitical stereotypes, and even unstated political agendas.

Gender bias can lead to under- or overdiagnosis of certain diagnoses as well as the pathologizing of behaviors that may or may not be indicators of mental health concerns (Eriksen & Kress 2005). Women who express anger, for example, go against typical cultural stereotypes, and such behavior is sometimes pathologized as a maladaptive mental health condition. If a woman has a legitimate reason to be angry, of course, this could be harmful in two ways. She might be stigmatized for expressing her feelings, which can further frustrate her. And the source of the anger may never be successfully addressed and could fester and multiply until it is resolved. A number of similar scenarios can occur for males as well as. An ongoing discussion and analysis of such issues is needed to promote understanding and address any shortcomings.

Reliability

The reliability of the *DSM* is a function of its ability to produce consistent diagnoses among and between the people using it over time. The *DSM* cannot serve its intended use if it is unreliable; there is no way it can gauge what it is supposed to gauge if it produces a different diagnosis each time. On the other hand, simply because a diagnostic tool is reliable does not mean that it is valid; a diagnosis consistently applied in error is still a faulty diagnosis.

Evidence for the reliability of mental health professionals' diagnostic decisions is limited, especially for personality disorders (Widiger 2002). The *DSM* has been constructed by research groups whose members analyze and incorporate research findings from various published sources. Such findings often have biased samples, and therefore biased findings. Although researchers take care to control for extraneous variables, there is no perfectly reliable study. Logically, therefore, the *DSM* cannot be completely reliable, either.

Reliability of the *DSM-IV* is slightly better than that of its predecessors. Various studies have found that its reliability is especially high in the case of mental health professionals who have consulted with one another regarding specific cases. Conversely, reliability remains weak in the case of mental health professionals who have not consulted with one another (Zinbarg et al. 1994).

The very nature of the *DSM* suggests why its diagnostic reliability cannot be particularly high. The manual specifically states that mental health professionals should use the *DSM*'s diagnostic criteria as *guidelines* and make final decisions by means of their own clinical judgment (APA 2000). Although some have argued that this strategy contradicts the *DSM* developers' efforts to create a reliable tool, it can also be regarded as an indicator of the developers' realistic appreciation of the *DSM*'s limitations. In the end, mental health professionals must strive for increased reliability by consulting with other professionals regarding particular applications of the *DSM* criteria. Professionals can also work toward increased reliability through the use of highly structured diagnostic assessments.

Strengths of the DSM

Much of what was said in the initial sections of this article speaks to the utility of the *DSM* as a diagnostic tool. Any concerns about the *DSM* cannot overshadow the fact that there exist serious mental disorders that impact people's lives—disorders that greatly affect individuals, families, and society at large. The impact of these mental illnesses makes it critical for mental health professionals to continue seeking knowledge about these problems and their treatment. The *DSM* (and criticism of the *DSM*) is one tool in that campaign.

As noted above, the *DSM*'s multiaxial assessment system has become the primary language of communication regarding client problems, offering a way of reducing complex client-related information into a digestible form (Seligman, Walker, & Rosenhan 2001). Moreover, the *DSM*, by categorizing people's psychological problems, assists researchers and theorists in comparing and establishing treatment methods and prevention approaches. *DSM* diagnoses can also help clinicians to identify those clients whose problems extend beyond their areas of competence (Eriksen & Kress 2005).

Finally, the *DSM* may directly benefit clients. For example, some clients can benefit from a concrete explanation (e.g., a diagnosis) of their behavior and experiences. Labeling clients' lived experiences may offer them freedom from shame and guilt while normalizing their experiences (Eriksen & Kress 2005).

Future of the *DSM*

The *DSM* will continue to evolve. The next proposed change to the manual has an anticipated publication date of mid-2013. Significant changes are being considered, among them the possible inclusion of a system of symptom continuums (rather than an either-or system); restating the definition of a mental disorder; adding additional mental disorders (including "relational disorder," the first to involve not just an individual but a *relationship*); the collapsing of some current disorders into others in the same category (such as Asperger syndrome folded into autism spectrum disorder); a reworking of the personality disorders category (by incorporating it into Axis I); and the possible discontinuation of certain mental disorders. Whatever changes do occur in the latest, fifth edition of the *DSM*, the manual will continue to be an integral component of mental health diagnosing and clinical practice, reflecting the prevailing perceptions of our society toward mental illness and the field of mental health as a whole.

See also Clinical Psychology; Culturally Competent Mental Health Care; Medical Model of Mental Illness; Neurodiversity; Psychiatry; Stigma

Bibliography

American Psychiatric Association. 1980. *Diagnostic and Statistical Manual of Mental Disorders* (3rd ed.). Washington, DC: American Psychiatric Association.

American Psychiatric Association. 2000. *Diagnostic and Statistical Manual of Mental Disorders* (4th ed., text rev.). Washington, DC: American Psychiatric Publishing.

Castillo, Robert J. 1997. *Culture and Mental Illness: A Client-Centered Approach.* Pacific Grove, CA: Brooks Cole.

Duffy, M., S. E. Gillig, R. M. Tureen, and M. A. Ybarra. 2002. "A Critical Look at the *DSM-IV.*" *Journal of Individual Psychology* 58: 363–374.

Eriksen, Karen P., and Victoria E. Kress. 2005. *Beyond the DSM Story: Ethical Quandaries, Challenges, and Best Practices.* Thousand Oaks: CA: Sage.

Eriksen, Karen P., and Victoria E. Kress. 2006. "The *DSM* and Professional Counseling Identity: Bridging the Gap." *Journal of Mental Health Counseling* 28: 202–217.

Grob, M. C. 1991. Book Reviews. *Bulletin of the Menninger Clinic* 55: 113–114.

Hinkle, J. S. 1999. "A Voice from the Trenches: A Reaction to Ivey and Ivey (1998)." *Journal of Counseling and Development* 77: 474–483.

Maniacci, M. P. 2002. "The *DSM* and Individual Psychology: A General Comparison." *Journal of Individual Psychology* 58: 356–363.

Mead, M. A., T. H. Hohenshil, and K. Singh. 1997. "How the *DSM* System Is Used by Clinical Counselors: A National Study." *Journal of Mental Health Counseling* 19: 383–401.

Morrison, James 2006. *Diagnosis Made Easier: Principles and Techniques for Mental Health Clinicians.* New York: Guilford Press.

Rosenhan, D. L. 1973. "On Being Sane in Insane Places." *Science* 179: 250–258.

Seligman, M. E. P., E. F. Walker, and D. L. Rosenhan. 2001. *Abnormal Psychology.* New York: Norton.

Szasz, Thomas S. 2002. *Liberation by Oppression: A Comparative Study of Slavery and Psychiatry.* New Brunswick, NJ: Transaction.

Waldo, M., W. D. Brotherton, and R. Horswill. 1993. "Integrating *DSM-III-R* Training into School, Marriage and Family, and Mental Health Counselor Preparation." *Counselor Education and Supervision* 32: 332–342.

Widiger, T. A. 2002. "Values, Politics, and Science in the Construction of the *DSM*s." In J. Z. Sadler, ed., *Descriptions and Prescriptions: Values, Mental Disorders, and the* DSM*s* (pp. 25–41). Baltimore: Johns Hopkins University Press.

Zinbarg, R. E., D. H. Barlow, M. Liebowitz, L. Street, E. Broadhead, W. Katon, and H. Kraemer. 1994. "The *DSM-IV* Field Trial for Mixed Anxiety and Depression." *American Journal of Psychiatry* 151: 1153–1162.

Disability Rights

Susan Stefan

There are many federal statutes aimed at protecting people with disabilities from discrimination. There are also state and local statutes in virtually every state, but this entry will focus on federal statutes applicable in all states.

Each of the federal statutes discussed below includes psychiatric disabilities within its purview, despite efforts from some members of Congress to exclude such disabilities when the Americans with Disabilities Act (ADA) was passed in 1990 (Stefan 2001). Although the first federal law was passed in 1974, and new federal laws prohibiting disability discrimination have been passed in every decade since then, change has come slowly. In 1988, Congress prohibited discrimination in housing on the basis of disability in the Fair Housing Amendments Act. In 1990, it passed the Americans with Disabilities Act because of its disappointment with the ineffectiveness of prior antidiscrimination law. In 2008, the Americans with Disabilities Amendments Act was enacted because of congressional frustration with the way that courts were limiting the protections of the ADA. This entry will describe federal antidiscrimination laws, including eligibility requirements, and will discuss the most important cases that have been decided regarding the rights of people with psychiatric disabilities.

The Basic Structure of Antidiscrimination Law
The Definition of Disability

The basic structure of all of these statutes is similar. All federal laws protecting individuals from discrimination on the basis of disability have the same definition of disability. An individual is considered disabled for purposes of federal disability discrimination law if the person has a physical or mental impairment that substantially limits one or more major life activities, has a record of such an impairment, or is regarded as having such an impairment. In the realm of psychiatric disabilities, the last alternative is often the most important. For many people, experiences of discrimination stem from being regarded as too dangerous, or too unstable, to be given a job, granted a professional license, or benefit from services, simply on the basis of a psychiatric diagnosis. For this reason, many individuals do not disclose their psychiatric disability. In order to benefit from most (but not all) of the protections of disability discrimination law, however, the individual's disability must be disclosed or already known.

Psychiatric disabilities such as depression, anxiety disorder, schizophrenia, and other common diagnoses are clearly "impairments." In order to qualify as disabilities, they must substantially limit one or more major life activities. Examples of major life activities, recently expanded by Congress in the Americans with Disabilities Amendments Act, include concentration, learning, thinking, caring for oneself, reading, working, and communicating. The Americans with Disabilities Amendments Act added "interacting with others" as a major life activity, ending division among the courts regarding this issue. Courts have declined to identify driving as a major life activity.

The Definition of Discrimination

The definition of discrimination is also generally the same across federal statutes. There are two kinds of discrimination prohibited by these statutes. The first involves applying stereotypes or assumptions about a disability to treat a person adversely: e.g., refusing to hire a person to operate dangerous equipment simply because the individual was taking medication for a psychiatric condition (Equal Employment Opportunity Commission [EEOC] 1997). These stereotypes can be involved in screening or eligibility requirements, or in the ways in which an agency administers its programs. No party subject to antidiscrimination law can avoid its responsibilities under the law by contracting with other parties not covered by the law.

The second kind of discrimination involves refusing to make modifications or alterations to job or program requirements—"reasonable accommodations"—to enable a person to do the job or benefit from the program. An accommodation is not reasonable if it alters or modifies essential elements of a job or fundamental aspects of a program. For example, an employer might change a 9-to-5 workday into a 10-to-6 workday to enable an employee to see his or her therapist. However, in most cases, allowing an employee to work from home is not a reasonable accommodation. In addition, an employee might be required to obtain and maintain a security clearance; an employer cannot be sued if the federal government's discriminatory refusal to provide a security clearance makes a person ineligible for a job, and the federal government cannot be sued, except for employment discrimination in a federal job under Section 501 of the Rehabilitation Act.

The scope of protection from disability discrimination covered by these statutes is extremely broad, ranging from housing to employment to all state and local government programs, and virtually all public accommodations. These statutes prohibit discrimination against people with psychiatric disabilities in areas as diverse as voting, state Medicaid programs, education, and professional licensing.

The most important victory for people with psychiatric disabilities was the U.S. Supreme Court's recognition that unnecessary segregation, including institutionalization, constitutes discrimination on the basis of disability, and the requirement that services be provided in the most integrated setting appropriate to the needs of the individual (*Olmstead v. L.C.* 1999) This decision, applying the "integration mandate" regulation of the Americans with Disabilities Act, has been extraordinarily important in ensuring that people with psychiatric disabilities do not have to give up their liberty in order to receive the mental health services they need.

Although the federal antidiscrimination statutes share a definition of disability and a definition of discrimination, there are distinctions in coverage, scope, and available remedies as well as in the practices of the agency charged by law with regulating and enforcing the statute. These differences will be discussed in greater detail below.

Federal Laws Prohibiting Disability Discrimination
Sections 501 and 504 of the Rehabilitation Act (1974)

Section 501 of the Rehabilitation Act prohibits the federal government from discriminating in employment on the basis of disability and requires that it provide reasonable accommodations to disabled employees. Unlike all other disability discrimination statutes, Section 501 also requires that the federal government make affirmative efforts to hire employees with disabilities.

Section 504 of the Rehabilitation Act prohibits disability discrimination by any entity that receives federal funds. Unlike Section 501, it is not limited to employment discrimination. Generally, an individual who prevails in a Section 504 case may receive both money damages and injunctive relief (i.e., a court orders the defendant to take action to end ongoing discrimination).

Because of the wide range of entities receiving federal funds, the scope of Section 504 of the Rehabilitation Act is fairly broad, encompassing discrimination in employment, insurance, medical practices, schools, universities, and professional licensing boards. Each of the different cabinet-level agencies has distinct regulations implementing Section 504. The Department of Justice is the "coordinating agency" whose basic definitions of disability and discrimination apply to all other agencies. Each agency then formulates regulations to apply to its own distinctive area, such as transportation, labor, or education.

For example, the Department of Education prohibits discrimination on the basis of disability by educational institutions, including local school districts, receiving funds from the Department of Education. The Office of Civil Rights (OCR) of the Department of Education receives and investigates complaints regarding discrimination in education (Department of Education).

Many courts interpret the requirements of Section 504 as being identical to those of the Americans with Disabilities Act. Although many aspects of Section 504 are indeed identical to the ADA, there are some differences: Section 504 requires discrimination to be "solely" on the basis of disability, and requires that the defendant must in some way receive federal funds. Discrimination cases often include a Section 504 claim because it permits money damages, unlike Title III of the Americans with Disabilities Act (see below), and does not require a showing of intentional discrimination, as some courts require for damages to be awarded under Title II of the Americans with Disabilities Act.

The Fair Housing Amendments Act (1988)

The Fair Housing Act was amended in 1988 to prohibit discrimination on the basis of disability in housing, including sales of houses, rentals, and zoning decisions. In the first decade of the Fair Housing Amendments Act, it was used to strike down exclusionary zoning aimed at preventing the operation of group homes. In *City of Edmonds v. Oxford House* (1995), the Supreme Court held that the Fair Housing Amendments Act permits communities to limit the maximum number of persons in a dwelling, but not to use definitions of "family" to exclude group homes for persons with disabilities.

The FHAA also requires landlords to make reasonable accommodations in rules, policies, practices, or services, when such accommodations may be necessary so that people with disabilities have an equal opportunity to use and enjoy a dwelling. In the area of psychiatric disabilities, such accommodations have included permitting emotional support animals or devising accommodations for tenants whose behavior is disturbing, although not dangerous. It should be noted that the regulations of the Department of Housing and Urban Development on emotional support animals are broader than those of the Department of Justice, providing the right for a tenant with a disability to have animals that are "necessary as a reasonable accommodation to assist, support, or provide services to persons with disabilities."

The Americans with Disabilities Act (1990)

The Americans with Disabilities Act has an extremely broad scope. Its five titles prohibit discrimination in employment (Title I), by "public entities" such as state and local governments (Title II), and by "public accommodations" including hotels, restaurants, hospitals, private schools and universities, and doctors' offices (Title III). Title IV of the ADA is devoted to telecommunications and television access for people with hearing and speech impairments. Title V of the ADA contains miscellaneous provisions, discussed below.

Title I (Employment)   The ADA prohibits employers from asking job applicants any questions related to a potential disability until a conditional job offer is made (EEOC 2000). At that point, an employer can require an applicant to take a preemployment medical examination, as long as all new employees are required to take the same physical. This protection is undermined by an exception permitting employers to require an applicant to take a drug test. Most tests for illegal drugs also reveal the presence of prescription drugs, and some prescription drugs can even be reported as potentially illegal drugs on drug tests. Additionally, while medical testing of job applicants is forbidden until a job offer is made, some "personality" tests are permitted. The line between "personality" and "medical" tests is unclear, although the Seventh Circuit recently struck down the use of the MMPI-II (Minnesota Multiphasic Personality Inventory) as impermissible because it screened out people with psychiatric disabilities (*Karraker v. Rent-a-Center* 2005). The ADA also requires that any information an employer has about an employee's disability must be kept confidential and filed separately from other employment records.

The ADA also requires employers to give employees time off, or restructure their schedules, or other modifications of the work environment, if needed as a reasonable accommodation to accomplish essential job requirements (EEOC 1997). An employer may require an employee whose behavior causes concern that he or she cannot perform his or her job to undergo a psychiatric evaluation, although it must be limited to the employee's capacity to perform the job. Generally, an employer is not required to tolerate workplace misconduct that would not be tolerated in nondisabled employees, but if the causes of the misconduct can be addressed or ameliorated by providing a reasonable accommodation to a person with a disability, the employer should consider providing such an accommodation.

Title II (Public Entities)   This title of the ADA covers a broad range of activities, since it applies to all state and local entities. Title II prohibits discrimination by police, the state judiciary, state colleges and universities, prisons, jails, and state health systems. Title II operates to invalidate state statutes that discriminate on the basis of disability. Among statutes that have been struck down by the federal courts are the Maine constitutional amendment that permitted people under conservatorship to vote, unless their conservatorship was because of mental illness (*Doe v. Rowe* 2001); the Vermont statute permitting people to make enforceable advance directives, unless the advance directive dealt with psychiatric medication and was made by a person who had been civilly committed (*Hargrave v. Vermont* 2003); and the Florida statute granting people full rights to see their medical records, but only limited rights to see their psychiatric records (*Doe v. Stincer* 1997, 1999).

Title III (Public Accommodations)   Public accommodations are commercial establishments, including private hospitals, doctors' offices, hotels, restaurants, and insurance companies that offer services, products, or benefits to the public. These "public accommodations" are not permitted to discriminate on the basis of disability in their programs or services. Most of the cases involving people with psychiatric disabilities under Title III have been attempts to obtain relief from discriminatory insurance coverage, or denial of coverage. While insurance companies are covered as public accommodations under Title III, Title V contains a "safe harbor" provision that limits insurance company liability under certain circumstances. This is a complex provision requiring more space than is available here to explain (Stefan 2001). While there is a mixed record in these cases, other federal legislation such as the Patient Protection and Affordable Care Act (2010) and the Mental Health Parity and Addiction Equity Act (2008) may be better vehicles to pursue equitable treatment by insurance companies toward people with psychiatric disabilities.

Title V (Miscellaneous)   Title V of the ADA prohibits discrimination on the basis of association with a disabled person, prohibits retaliation for attempts to exercise rights under the ADA, and contains a number of exclusions inserted at the last minute by conservative members of Congress; the ADA thus explicitly excludes the following "conditions" from being considered "disabilities": homosexuality, bisexuality, transvestitism, transexualism, and (in the same provision) exhibitionism, pedophilia, and voyeurism, as well as pyromania, compulsive gambling, and kleptomania. More substantively, Title V also excludes people who are currently addicted to the illegal use of drugs, but creates an exception for those who are participating in supervised rehabilitation programs or have been successfully rehabilitated from past addiction. As mentioned above, Title V also contains protections from liability for disability discrimination for insurance companies who conform to certain requirements.

The Americans with Disabilities Amendments Act (2008)

After the passage of the ADA, the U.S. Supreme Court and lower courts gradually made it more and more difficult for individuals to prove they had a disability and thus to qualify for the statute's protection. In the area of psychiatric disability, courts had on occasion found plaintiffs with major depression, bipolar disorder, and even schizophrenia not to have a disability under the ADA (Stefan 2002). The ADAA lists conditions that will presumptively be considered disabilities, including major depression, bipolar disorder, posttraumatic stress disorder, obsessive-compulsive disorder, and schizophrenia.

In addition, courts interpreted the ADA limited protection for individuals whose disabilities were mitigated by medication, while also refusing to protect individuals who had refused to take medications, or whose disability (like many psychiatric disabilities) manifested itself only intermittently. These court rulings affected individuals with epilepsy, diabetes, cancer, emphysema, and numerous other disabilities. Finally, of greatest importance to people with psychiatric disabilities, courts had severely restricted the provision permitting individuals to sue because they were regarded as disabled.

In 2008, Congress passed the Americans with Disabilities Amendments Act, disapproving these past judicial interpretations of the ADA and instructing courts to construe the definition of disability in a far more liberal manner. In addition, Congress disapproved of the limitations courts had imposed on the "regarded as disabled" prong of the definition. The Americans with Disabilities Amendments Act took effect in 2009. In 2011, the EEOC issued the first regulations interpreting the Americans with Disabilities Amendments Act, underscoring the more liberal interpretation of 'disability' and the status of being regarded as disabled (Federal Register 2011). The Department of Justice has also joined a number of lawsuits seeking to enforce the right to receive services within the individual's community rather than in institutional settings (Department of Justice 2012). In 2012, the Department of Justice took the position, in a case called *Lane v. Kitzhaber*, that providing vocational rehabilitation services must ensure that, similarly, such services are provided in the most integrated setting appropriate to the needs of the individual (Department of Justice 2012).

See also Ethical Issues; Forensic Psychology and Psychiatry; History of Mental Health Care; Insurance and Parity Laws; Involuntary Treatment; Mental Health Advocacy; Public Policy Issues

Bibliography

Americans with Disabilities Act (1990), 42 U.S.C. 12101 *et seq.*

City of Edmonds v. Oxford House, 514 U.S. 725 (1995).

Department of Education, Office for Civil Rights Home Page. http://www2.ed.gov/about/offices/list/ocr/index.html.

Doe v. Rowe, 156 F.Supp.2d 35 (D.Me. 2001).

Doe v. Stincer, 990 F.Supp. 1427 (S.D.Fla. 1997), *vacated on other grounds*, 175 F.3d 879 (11th Cir. 1999).

Equal Employment Opportunity Commission. 1997. "Enforcement Guidance on the ADA and Psychiatric Disabilities." Retrieved from http://www.eeoc.gov/policy/docs/psych.html.

Equal Employment Opportunity Commission. 2000. "Enforcement Guidance on Disability-Related Inquiries and Medical Examinations of Employees under the Americans with Disabilities Act." Retrieved from http://www.eeoc.gov/policy/docs/guidance -inquiries.html.

Fair Housing Amendments Act (1988), 42 U.S.C. 3601 *et seq.*

Federal Register. 2011. "Regulations to Implement the Equal Employment Provisions of the Americans with Disabilities Act as Amended." 76 Federal Register 16978-17017 (March 25). Retrieved from https://federalregister.gov/a/2011-6056.

Hargrave v. Vermont, 340 F.3d 27 (2nd Cir. 2003).

Karraker v. Rent a Center, 411 F.3d 831 (7th Cir. 2005).

Mental Health Parity and Addiction Equity Act (2008), enacted as part of P.L. 110-343, 122 Stat. 3765.

Olmstead v. L.C., 527 U.S. 581 (1999).

Patient Protection and Affordable Care Act (2010), P.L. 111-148, 124 Stat. 119.

Rehabilitation Act (1974), 29 U.S.C. 791 and 794.

Stefan, Susan. 2001. *Unequal Right: Discrimination against People with Mental Disabilities and the Americans with Disabilities Act.* Washington DC: American Psychological Association Press.

Stefan, Susan. 2002. *Hollow Promises: Employment Discrimination against People with Mental Disabilities.* Washington DC: American Psychological Association Press.

U.S. Department of Justice. ADA Home Page. http://www.ada.gov.

U.S. Department of Justice. 2012. "Olmstead: Community Integration for Everyone." Retrieved from www.ada.gov/olmstead/.

Disasters and Mental Health

Joshua Miller

Every disaster is unique and yet we strive to learn from each one and seek to discern patterns, draw conclusions, make generalizations, and formulate theories that, hopefully, will guide us when future disasters occur. What is good about this process is that, over time, we have improved our ability to be helpful to people and communities and, with the aid of research and evaluation, have begun to learn which approaches are more helpful than others. And yet such formulations can also be seductive and misleading; a recipe book of responses is developed, based on prior disasters, that does not quite have the right ingredients or has not taken into account, as it were, the dietary habits and restrictions of the consumers when the next disaster occurs. Often the recipes assume that one diet suits all, with little attention to culture and sociocultural factors.

What Is a Disaster?

Disasters are usually clustered into different types, namely, natural, technological, and complex (e.g., terrorism, armed conflict, mass murder) (Halpern &

Tramontin 2007; Rosenfeld et al. 2005). Natural disasters include earthquakes, floods, mud slides, hurricanes, and tsunamis—events often referred to as "acts of God." Technological disasters comprise chemical spills, train and plane crashes, bridge, building, and damn collapses—the consequence of human negligence or omission. Complex disasters involve human intention, the desire to cause destruction, death and damage, such as the attacks in the United States on September 11, 2001 or the bombing of the federal building in Oklahoma City in 1995. Whenever there is a human component to the cause of the disaster—through either commission or omission—there are often accompanying feelings of anger and mistrust of officials, which are usually not as pronounced after natural disasters (Halpern & Tramontin 2007; Rosenfeld et al. 2005; Van den Eynde & Veno 1999).

At first glance, the Wenchuan earthquake in China in 2008 or Hurricane Katrina in the United States in 2005 could be categorized as natural disasters. But the distinctions between different types of disasters are not as clear-cut or simple as presented. Many disasters have elements of the various categories. For example, Hurricane Katrina involved a natural disaster, the hurricane, but there was also a technological disaster (Masozera, Bailey, & Kerchner 2007), e.g., the crumbling of inadequately built levees and the spilling of ineffectually stored chemicals. It can also be argued that it was a complex disaster, considering how some police, media, and government responded to African American victims in a hostile and at times violent way (Dreier 2006; Masozera, Bailey, & Kerchner 2007). And there were the ongoing social disasters of racism and poverty that plagued New Orleans and the Gulf Coast of Mississippi, which interacted with the catastrophic event of the hurricane (Dreier 2006; J. Miller 2012; Park & Miller 2006).

A disaster has a certain set of facts, but how these events are interpreted and constructed has a lot to do with the event's impact (Echterling & Wiley 1999; Van den Eynde & Veno 1999). There is often a political struggle to define the meaning of the event, and there are usually competing, multiple interpretations of what happened.. This leads to another aspect of disaster, the psychosocial consequences, which are a combination of the literal losses (e.g., death and destruction) as well as the meaning that people make of these consequences. Are these consequences part of a recurring cycle of natural storms and events, or are they new and therefore more threatening? Are they part of karma and unavoidable natural processes, or were they exacerbated and magnified by incompetence, corruption, or malfeasance? The stories of disasters that emerge encapsulate contested meanings about the causes and consequences, which in turn have an impact on how empowered and hopeful versus how disempowered and despondent people feel in the wake of disaster.

The Social Ecology of Disaster

Thus if disaster is a process that involves the social construction of the disaster, competing narratives, conflicting agendas, political struggles, social upheavals, and disrupted cultural norms and practices, then it is helpful to map out the social ecology of a disaster. The social ecology of disaster is the recursive relationship between the catastrophic event, geophysical conditions, sociohistorical and socio-political factors, culture, and the meaning of narratives that both tell the stories of the disaster and shape the reactions of affected people, responders, officials, and society at large (J. Miller 2012; Park & Miller 2006). Within this framework, there is always an emerging, fluid, interactive relationship between the precipitating event, the affected people, and the affected community.

The concept of social ecology of disaster offers a number of dimensions to consider. This includes what caused the disaster, the scale of its destruction, when the disaster began and ended, the impact on individuals and families, the consequences for social groups and communities, the balance between vulnerabilities and assets, and the rescue, response, and recovery effort. There are, in other words, the numbers or facts as well as the scars, thoughts, feelings, and narratives behind the numbers.

Negative Consequences and Sources of Resilience

It is useful to review what the literature says about negative consequences of disasters as well as the sources of resilience for the individual, the family, and the community.

Negative Consequences

There are consequences for individuals, families, social groups, communities, and in some cases society at large when a disaster occurs. We consider here the literature on common reactions at the individual, family, and community levels. In reality, all three of these interact and influence one another and should not be considered separately. With disasters, as Kaniasty and Norris (1999, 26) have put it, "individual suffering unveils itself within the parameters of other people's suffering."

Individual   There is a saying in the field of disaster mental health that people undergo "normal reactions in response to abnormal events." Normal or not, they are often experienced as being very distressing, overwhelming, debilitating, and destabilizing, particularly when there has been loss of life. This is even more profound when many children have died, as is the case with the Wenchuan earthquake in China. When considering individual reactions there are certain important questions and debates within the disaster mental health field. One is, "How much will symptoms subside on their own over time?" Another is, "How prevalent are clinical syndromes such as posttraumatic stress disorder (PTSD) or clinical depression?" One can also ask, "How much does culture influence reactions to disasters and are there some reactions that are universal across cultures?" There are many discussions and disagreements about how best to help people recover from a disaster.

A classic way of categorizing the "normal" reactions to disasters is by six dimensions: physical, cognitive, emotional, behavioral, spiritual, and interpersonal (Yassen 1995). The categories themselves bespeak certain cultural assumptions, as there are cultures that do not distinguish between physical and emotional stress. Under the category of physical reactions are hyperalertness, exhaustion, muscle tension, weakened immune system, headaches, sweating, and decreased sexual libido (Halpern & Tramontin 2007; Yassen 1995). Cognitive reactions include poor concentration, obsessive-compulsive thinking, rumination, memory lapses, and difficulty in thinking through and completing tasks that the person can usually manage (Halpern & Tramontin 2007; Yassen 1995). People report either that they cannot remember the events of the disaster and immediately afterward or that they can vividly recall every second of a sequence, as if it were happening in slow motion (J. Miller 2012). There is sometimes a sense of detachment, as if this is happening to someone else. The metaphors of "being in a dream" or "happening like in a movie" often come up. People directly exposed to the disaster may also have a hyperawareness of senses such as smell, sound, and taste that are associated with the disaster.

Physical reactions such as being hyperalert or in a depleted physical state, or cognitive reactions such as obsessive rumination about a disaster, can in turn cause strong emotional reactions. Typical emotional reactions include fear, anxiety, anger, and hostility (Yassen 1995). Sadness, guilt, remorse, and grief are common, particularly when there has been loss of life or of property and cherished possessions. Culturally, there are tremendous variations about what emotions are socially acceptable to express and how they are expressed. In some cultures, emotional reactions are often expressed as physical symptoms. All of this can have behavioral consequences: people may constantly scan for perceived threats, have difficulty sleeping or eating, use drugs or alcohol to excess, or engage in self-harmful behaviors such as self-mutilation or attempting suicide (Halpern & Tramontin 2007; Yassen 1995).

Whether a person is spiritual or religious or not, disasters can affect one's sense of the way of the world as core beliefs and assumptions are uprooted and challenged. People often reevaluate what is important to them, as disasters can also challenge their trust and faith in other people, society, or their governments (J. Miller 2012). There are also social consequences in reaction to disasters: people may withdraw from interactions with other people (Halpern & Tramontin 2007; Yassen 1995) or evince greater social mistrust and suspicion. At home, there can be less cohesion between family members, and sometimes one family member may become very controlling of others in the family (Halpern & Tramontin 2007). Children often feel less secure and less reassured by their parents

A woman deals with stress and depression after a hurricane in Florida.
(AP Photo/Steve Mitchell.)

(Rosenfeld et al. 2005), particularly if the parents are struggling emotionally and feel unsure about their ability to adequately protect their children. Disasters can also negatively affect workplace trust (Vineburgh et al. 2007) and the cohesion that exists between social groups. At the same time, disasters can bring family members, friends, and social and work groups closer together as they face a common threat.

Some individual reactions to disasters can be quite severe, particularly when people experience PTSD. The estimates of how many people will develop intractable PTSD in response to a traumatic event range from 2 to 29 percent (Ursano et al. 2007). People with PTSD find that they uncontrollably reexperience the traumatic event through recurring dreams, flashbacks, and intrusive thoughts. This leads to attempts to avoid anything that might trigger these reactions and is associated with high arousal rates, often manifested as hypervigilance, which can contribute to tension, sleep disorders, difficulties with concentrating, and difficulties with affect (mood) regulation. What can be confusing is that many of these symptoms are also part of the diagnoses of acute stress disorder (ASD). Unlike PTSD, however, ASD is usually resolved or substantially mitigated within weeks and certainly by two months (Benedek 2007). Responders, therapists, police, firefighters, and other helping professionals and volunteers can develop many of the symptoms associated with PTSD and ASD through what have been called "secondary trauma," "vicarious traumatization" (Pearlman & Saakvitne 1995), "compassion fatigue" (Figley 1995), and "disaster distress" (J. Miller 2012). Depression is another psychiatric consequence for some affected people and responders (Bendek 2007).

Family Reactions   In addition to individual reactions to disasters, there are consequences for families. Family structures are altered by separations, including death. The usual roles of family members can be undermined, including such roles as breadwinner, family spokesperson, or even who is head of the household. Children may be expected to assume more adult types of responsibilities. Disasters can affect family boundaries by placing the family in a unique and temporary situation where family members do not have their usual capacity to manage and negotiate issues like privacy or information that is usually the privilege of certain members of the family. The boundary between the family and the outside world and local community may also shift, as when families are grouped together in a shelter or relocated to internally displaced persons (IDPs) camps. Routines and rituals are displaced. Disasters place a burden of stress on family members, so that those who usually care for others may be themselves emotionally overwhelmed.

Community Consequences   Major disasters wreak havoc on a community's infrastructure. Homes, offices, roads, stores, banks, health facilities, and electricity, transportation, and communication systems are often damaged, destroyed, or incapacitated by a disaster. Government offices may also be overwhelmed or temporarily out of action. All of this leads to disruptions in the economy and fragmentation of the fabric of the community's social networks, weakening community cohesion. People lose their autonomy and capacity to care for themselves and their families, leading to a loss of social roles and community efficacy.

Such disruptions also occur between a community and their "transitional pathways"—the connections between a community's present and its history and cultural traditions (Landau 2007). Citizens may lose faith not only in their leader's ability to be helpful but also in their cultural and spiritual practices to offer answers and solutions to the dilemmas posed by the disaster. Breaches with the past and fractured social cohesion can lead to a collective sense of hopelessness and a dim view of what the future holds.

Sources of Resilience

Despite the scale of destruction and of psychological and social disruptions, individuals and families are resilient and the vast majority recover from disasters, often with a renewed sense of purpose and meaning. If we think of resilience as the adaptive capacity of people to regain meaningful life trajectories in the face of disruptive, overwhelming, or even life-threatening events (Bonano 2004), it is important to consider what contributes to this process. Resilience, like disasters, is a process that involves a synergistic interaction between the individual, family, and community.

On an individual level, it helps to be able to make sense of what happened, to be able to manage life after the disaster, to construct some kind of meaning about events, and to regain and sustain a sense of hope (Kabat-Zinn 1990; J. Miller 2012; Walsh 2007). Emotionally, it helps to be able to soothe oneself and eventually to be able to achieve positive emotions, such as joy, fun, and even humor (Seligman, Rashid, & Parks 2006; Tugade & Frederickson 2004)—despite the scale of losses. Such emotions increase when they are shared with others through social connections as well as through acts of altruism, such as helping others (Otake et al. 2006).

Within families, resilience is fostered by member's regaining their ability to care for one another, adapt to new situations, and reestablish some semblance of order and routine. This in turn connects with reconstructing communal interdependence so that family members can rely not only on one another but also on other families. This is why if people need to be relocated to shelters or displaced persons camps, that they are ideally placed close to people who they already know or who were their neighbors before the disaster. Lastly, it is helpful to collectively grieve and mourn losses and to reconnect with cultural practices and traditions that were disrupted by the disaster.

Helping Individuals, Families, and Communities to Recover from Disaster

In the immediate aftermath of a disaster, psychological first aid—which involves offering care and comfort, emotional validation, information, material supports, and brief psychological intervention and problem solving to individuals and groups—is a common mental health intervention (J. Miller 2012). Psychological first aid seeks to mitigate acute distress, normalize reactions, and help people to find their footing so that they can cope in the short term and have a foundation for long-term recovery.

In the short and midterm after a disaster, a psychosocial capacity building approach will reach more people and be more sustainable. Such an approach may be defined as "interventions provided by professional and nonprofessional people, both local and from the outside, that constitutes a multisystemic, culturally grounded, empowerment- and resiliency-oriented approach designed to help individuals, families, social groups, and communities recover from a disaster" (J. Miller 2012, 191). Psychosocial capacity building seeks to be sustainable over time and builds on a foundation of local capacities and resources. When employing a psychosocial capacity building approach, the role of a mental health responder is more that of consultant and partner than that of an expert who directly treats people. There is an emphasis on accessing and recovering local resources and capacities and collaboratively assessing needs and planning interventions. Groups that focus on tasks or activities are commonly used as they bring people together, help them to feel more socially connected, and foster social cohesion and a sense of collective efficacy.

It is useful to draw on Hobfoll et al.'s (2007) international meta-research, where they identified five areas that help people to recover from "mass trauma." Anything that responders can do to foster these processes is usually helpful. The first is that people need to feel a sense of safety—it is difficult to recover when one continues to feel insecure and unsafe. The second is achieving the ability to self-calm. Group activities, physical activity, or individual mindfulness exercises are examples of interventions that can work toward this goal. A third area is having a sense of efficacy. Individual efficacy is enhanced when there is collective and group efficacy (Landau 2007; J. Miller 2012) and thus groups and community activities that enhance a sense of competence and connection are helpful. A fourth area is feeling interpersonally and socially connected with others. And the fifth area is regaining a sense of hope, which, again, builds on feeling efficacious, connected with others, and having increasing control or agency over one's life as well as a greater acceptance of one's limitations.

Two other things are generally helpful—regaining a sense of place (Prewitt Diaz & Dayal 2008; J. Miller 2012) and reestablishing community cohesion, which is enhanced by a sense of fairness and social justice (J. Miller 2012; Weyermann 2007). A sense of place means having a base of operations for both personal and work life, even if temporary, as well as a sense of belonging to a community. And feelings of fairness and social justice are achieved when there is a collective perception that everyone is receiving help, that there is equity, and that relief efforts benefit all affected by the disaster, which in turn contributes to greater social cohesion and resiliency.

Conclusion

Good practice involves an interaction between helping professionals and the people and communities that they are trying to support. There is no substitute for flexibility and humility in the field, and there are no manuals that can tell responders what to do and how to do it in all circumstances with all people. At best, such manuals provide general guidelines and parameters for intervention. Helping professionals should consider approaching disasters with the confidence that outsiders have something to offer while retaining a sense of humility and commitment and trust in the resiliency and efficacy of the local people. It is only through working collaboratively and working in partnership with local citizens that we are able to appreciate the complexity and richness of human frailty and resilience in the face of disaster.

See also Culturally Competent Mental Health Care; Depression; Emergency Services; Family and Mental Illness; Loss and Grief; Mental Health Counseling; Peer Support Groups; Posttraumatic Stress Disorder; Religion, Spirituality, and Mental Health; Trauma

Bibliography

Benedek, David M. 2007. "Acute Stress Disorder and Post-Traumatic Stress Disorder in the Disaster Environment." In Robert J. Ursano, Carol S. Fullerton, Lars Weisaeth, and Beverley Raphael, eds., *Textbook of Disaster Psychiatry* (pp. 140–163). Cambridge: Cambridge University Press.

Bonanno, G. A. 2004. "Loss, Trauma, and Human Resilience: Have We Underestimated the Capacity to Thrive after Extremely Aversive Events?" *American Psychologist* 59(1): 20–28.

Dreier, Peter. 2006. "Katrina and Power in America." *Urban Affairs Review* 41: 528–549.

Echterling, Lennis G., and Mary Lou Wylie. 1999. "In the Public Arena: Disaster as a Socially Constructed Problem." In Richard Gist and Bernard Lubin, eds., *Response to Disaster: Psychosocial, Community and Ecological Approaches* (pp. 327–346). Philadelphia: Brunner/Mazel.

Figley, Charles R. 1995. "Compassion Fatigue as Secondary Traumatic Stress Disorder: An Overview." In Charles R. Figley, ed., *Compassion Fatigue: Coping with Secondary Traumatic Stress Disorder in Those Who Treat the Traumatized* (pp. 1–20). New York: Brunner/Mazel.

Halpern, James, and Mary Tramontin. 2007. *Disaster Mental Health: Theory and Practice*. Belmont, CA: Thomson Learning.

Hobfoll, Stevan E., Patricia Watson, Carl C. Bell, Richard A. Bryant, Melissa J. Brymer, Matthew J. Friedman, Merle Friedman, Berthold P. R. Gersons, Joop T. V. M. De Jong, Christopher M. Layne, Shira Maguen, Yuval Neria, Ann E. Norwood, Robert S. Pynoos, Dori Reissman, Josef I. Ruzek, Arieh Y. Shalev, Zahava Solomon, Alan M. Steinberg, and Robert J. Ursano. 2007. "Five Essential Elements of Immediate and Mid-Term Mass Trauma Intervention: Empirical Evidence." *Psychiatry* 70(4): 283–315.

Kabat-Zinn, Jon. 1990. *Full Catastrophe Living: Using the Wisdom of Your Body and Your Mind to Face Stress, Pain, and Illness*. New York: Delta.

Kaniasty, Krzysztof, and Fran Norris. 1999. "The Experience of Disaster: Individuals and Communities Sharing Trauma." In Richard Gist and Bernard Lubin, eds., *Response to Disaster: Psychosocial, Community, and Ecological Approaches* (pp. 25–61). Philadelphia: Brunner/Mazel.

Landau, Judith. 2007. "Enhancing Resilience: Communities and Families as Agents of Change." *Family Process* 41(1): 351–365.

Masozera, Michel, Melissa Bailey, and Charles Kerchner. 2007. "Distribution Impacts of Natural Disasters across Income Groups: A Case Study of New Orleans." *Ecological Economics* 63: 299–306.

Miller, Joshua. 2012. *Psychosocial Capacity Building in Response to Disasters*. New York: Columbia University Press.

Miller, Kenneth E., Madhur Kulkarni, and Hallie Kushner. 2006. "Beyond Trauma-Focused Psychiatric Epidemiology: Bridging Research and Practice with War-Affected Populations." *American Journal of Orthopsychology* 76(4): 409–422.

Otake, Keiko, Satoshi Shimai, Junko Tanaka-Matsum, Kanako Otsui, and Barbara L. Fredrickson. 2006. "Happy People Become Happier through Kindness: A Counting Kindness Intervention." *Journal of Happiness Studies* 7: 361–375.

Park, Yoosun, and Joshua Miller. 2006. "The Social Ecology of Hurricane Katrina: Rewriting the Discourse of 'Natural' Disasters." *Smith College Studies in Social Work* 76(3): 9–24.

Pearlman, Laurie Anne, and Karen W. Saakvitne. 1995. *Trauma and the Therapist: Countertransference and Vicarious Trauma in Psychotherapy with Incest Survivors.* New York: Norton.

Prewitt Diaz, Joseph O., and Anjana Dayal. 2008. "Sense of Place: A Model for Community Based Psychosocial Support Programs." *The Australasian Journal of Disaster and Trauma Studies* 2008(1). Retrieved December 16, 2009, from http://www.massey.ac.nz/~trauma/issues/2008-1/prewitt_diaz.htm.

Reyes, Gilbert, and Gerard A. Jacobs, eds. 2005. *Handbook of International Disaster Psychology.* Westport, CT: Praeger.

Rosenfeld, Lawrence B., Joanne S. Caye, Ofra Ayalon, and Mooli Lahad. 2005. *When Their World Falls Apart: Helping Families and Children Manage the Effects of Disasters.* Silver Springs, MD: NASW Press.

Seligman, Martin. E. P., Tayyab Rashid, and Acacia C. Parks. 2006. "Positive Psychotherapy." *American Psychologist* 61: 774–788.

Tugade, Michele M., and Barbara L. Fredrickson. 2004. "Resilient Individuals Use Positive Emotions to Bounce Back from Negative Emotional Experiences." *Journal of Personality and Social Psychology* 86(2): 320–333.

Ursano, Robert J., Carol S. Fullerton, Lars Weisaeth, and Beverley Raphael. 2007. "Individual and Community Responses to Disaster." In Robert J. Ursano, Carol S. Fullerton, Lars Weisaeth, and Beverley Raphael, eds., *Textbook of Disaster Psychiatry* (pp. 3–28). Cambridge: Cambridge University Press.

van den Eynde, Julie, and Arthur Veno. 1999. "Disastrous Events: An Empowerment Model of Community Healing." In Richard Gist and Bernard Lubin, eds., *Response to Disaster: Psychosocial, Community, and Ecological Approaches* (pp. 167–192). New York: Brunner/Mazel.

Vineburgh, Nancy T., Robert K. Gifford, Robert J. Ursano, Carol S. Fullerton, and David M. Benedek. 2007. "Workplace Disaster Preparedness and Response." In Robert J. Ursano, Carol S. Fullerton, Lars Weisaeth, and Beverley Raphael, eds., *Textbook of Disaster Psychiatry* (pp. 265–283). Cambridge: Cambridge University Press.

Walsh, Froma. 2007. "Traumatic Loss and Major Disasters: Strengthening Family and Community Resilience." *Family Process* 46(2): 207–227.

Weyermann, Barbara. 2007. "Linking Economics and Emotions: Towards a More Integrated Understanding of Empowerment in Conflict Areas." *Intervention* 5(2): 83–96.

Yassen, Janet. 1995. "Preventing Secondary Traumatic Stress Disorder." In Charles. R. Figley, ed., *Compassion Fatigue: Coping with Secondary Traumatic Stress Disorder in Those Who Treat the Traumatized* (pp. 178–208). New York: Brunner/Mazel.

Dissociative Disorders

Marlene E. Hunter

Perhaps the best-known dissociative disorder, dissociative identity disorder, or DID, used to be called multiple personality disorder (MPD). It was only a few decades ago that physicians and psychologists began to recognize an important factor:

the person who is diagnosed as "MPD" does not have "multiple personalities"; rather, he or she has a personality *structure* that is in compartments. This might seem a minor change in the way to describe the situation, but in fact it is important, as each section or compartment of that single personality structure can be viewed as referring to various experiences or situations to which the person always responds in a particular way. With DID, two or more conscious personas, or identities, control behavior, although usually only one of them operates at any given moment. Psychologically "splitting" in this way is how the individual manages to deal with his or her world.

Thus dissociative disorders can be described as creative (though highly problematic) ways to manage one's world, to make sense out of what seems to be nonsense, and—above all—to keep *safe*. In effect, dissociation means to "get away" via mental means. There are several ways in which such distancing can be accomplished. The main forms of dissociation are amnesia (loss of memory), fugue (altered state of consciousness), and depersonalization (loss of sense of self), as well as dissociative identity disorder. *Amnesia* may be caused by physical experiences such as trauma to the head, but in some cases it is caused by intrusive emotional situations. *Fugue*, in contrast, involves the person's moving about, even speaking, purposively but not being fully aware of the situation; some or all memories of the person's identity have become temporarily inaccessible (through psychological, not physical, mechanisms or causes). *Depersonalization*, on the other hand, involves the sensation of being away from one's body and one's thoughts—rather like observing oneself from the outside. Persons who experience depersonalization realize that things are not as they appear, but there is little they can do about it. Depersonalization may last a few minutes or go on more or less continually for years. Like the other dissociative disorders, depersonalization is often triggered by intense stress or traumatic events.

Dissociation, then, is a complex phenomenon that is associated in some cases (but not all) with the two principal stress disorders: acute stress disorder and posttraumatic stress disorder. It may be viewed as a kind of defense undertaken when a person experiences trauma. It is a way to postpone acknowledgment of the traumatic experience until the person is ready to accept it and integrate it into the self.

The present entry focuses primarily on dissociative identity disorder (DID), as it has received the most attention among nonspecialists and as it helps to illuminate aspects of the other disorders.

Dissociative Identity Disorder

As noted, DID has one very prominent characteristic: the young child, in order to make sense of what is happening to her, begins to form "parts" of herself (or himself). Such "compartmentalizing" can start at a very early age, often as young as two or three years. It invariably starts with abuse—verbal, sexual, physical, or some combination of the three. Because of such abuse, the child has to get away, so she does so through her imagination. She escapes mentally to "somewhere else." The child, that is, "leaves" or dissociates in order to feel safe. She can be somewhere safe, psychically speaking, somewhere where she can regain a sense of personal control. The situation is such that the abuse or trauma seems to be happening to "that girl down there" rather than to oneself.

To understand dissociation, it is useful to appreciate the various mental "states" occurring in human beings. We are born with five such states: two sleeping states (dreaming and not dreaming), two awake states (making sounds and not making sounds), and one crying state. Further states emerge as the child ages. Usually, by the age of eight, children have created a cohesive "whole" with respect to these five states and a growing range of other emotional and intellectual states. In the case of DID, however, some states, such as fear, remain *separate*—apart from the others. It is such compartmentalization that lies at the heart of dissociative identity disorder (Hunter 2004).

Also useful for an understanding of dissociation is awareness of the four main types of social functioning that can be difficult for people, of any age, to manage. The first type involves affect control, or control over the emotions. Children do not understand or learn affect control on their own; rather, they respond to what is going on around them. They see and experience adult anger or affection, for example.

The second type of social functioning is known as "impulse control," which is somewhat self-explanatory. People who suffer (and they *do* suffer) from an inability to control their impulses—touching, speaking, moving, etc.—frequently find themselves at odds with others around them and must deal with these unwanted intrusions into their own lives as well.

The third type involves the connection between mind and body. When that connection becomes disordered, the result is known as "somatization and biological dysregulation." In other words, some factors come to affect the person's psychophysical well-being, and she may find herself in a situation where normal experiences—physical, emotional, or both—become too intrusive. In these situations, emotional responses may lead to physical reactions, and ordinary events can begin to intrude on solid, positive emotional expression. An example would be anger overtaking argument, which in turn becomes rage—and the consequent headache that leads to physical disability for the next few hours.

Finally, there are what is known as disturbances in self-regulation. In such cases, the person cannot keep herself behaviorally in line with what are considered to be normal, useful ways of functioning. These disturbances include, for example, problems with food intake, social conduct, management of the intensity or duration of responses, and even cognition (control of thoughts).

> Over a hundred different secondary personalities (known as alters) associated with one physical body have been identified. A single body's alters may have consistent differences in handedness, facial expression, cerebral bloodflow and EEG recordings; up to 60 points' difference in IQ scores, with their own characteristic visual abilities, handwriting, vocabulary, speech patterns and immunological responses; they have diverse memories and personal and family histories, and different ages, genders, ethnicity and sexual orientations.
>
> —Roland Littlewood
>
> *Source*: Roland Littlewood, *Pathologies of the West* (Ithaca, NY: Cornell University Press, 2002), 166.

All of these areas of social functioning become that much more difficult to manage when one is living in an abusive or dysfunctional situation that interferes with one's usual ability to get on in the world. In extreme cases, the result can be the onset of dissociative identity disorder.

How Does It Begin?

The main "school" or site for the development of dissociative disorders is *the family*, particularly families in which there has been no teaching of normal affect or emotional regulation. In a normal, well-focused, and caring family, an adult can comfortably say to a child, "You're angry—what's wrong?" or "You look sad—what's the matter?" Hugs and understanding are always there. A child who is brought up in such a positive family will learn, at a very early age, that parents are there to help, to reaffirm the child's emotions or explain what those emotions are all about. Caring adults can help a child understand what is needed—physically or emotionally—and offer good suggestions as to how something can be realized. A child brought up in such a warm and understanding milieu will inevitably learn the positives of family life, and how to manage difficult situations such as disappointment.

The family, in other words, is there to help a child to form a positive, cohesive identity. It is important for the adults to know that good, productive relationships, and also the coming together of aspects of consciousness and awareness, are not automatically achieved. They are instead *developmental achievements*. The pattern goes like this:

- By the age of 12 months, the child has developed several separate emotional states that are recognizable by the parents, caretakers, and family physicians.
- By 18 to 24 months of age, one begins to see the blending of the various emotional states and the development of what are known as "megacognitive

capacities"—that is, how the child's brain is learning to think about and react to more than one situation at a time. These maturing capacities depend on the development and maturation of the part of the brain known as the orbitofrontal cortex (the front part of the brain) and other similar areas through which the brain begins to understand language, experience and emotions.

Even more important is that the development of those particular parts of the brain are directly related to what is known as the "attachment relationship" (Bretherton 1992). The child comes to realize that the adult cares for her—*or does not*. A young child is not necessarily able to put this into words, but at the emotional level it registers deeply. A child who has had negative experiences in this regard must find a way to escape, and this is the beginning of dissociation. Unless some personal healing has occurred—which is extremely rare—the child is on her way to developing DID.

Children with these experiences eventually find paths to "get away" in order to avoid the emotions, physical pain, and terror of abuse; but then other situations begin to intrude on their lives. For example, they become old enough to begin to go to school. This is a completely new and different experience for the child. She or he does not know how to manage it, and so, typically, another part or aspect of the child develops in order to do so. That part, or alter, may in fact do very well in school and be a top student. And often, by then, there are *three* parts of the child's personality structure: the child who feels safe in her imaginary realm, the child who is a student at school, and the child who must face her day-to-day dysfunctional situation.

In time, given an increasing number of differing experiences in these children's lives, they may develop many additional "parts" or alters. Each one has a role to play, and each needs to be accepted in varying situations. The various personas consider themselves as individuals, as indeed they are. In general, adults who have DID often come across to those around them as moody, annoying, or refusing to express any continuity of perspective across a range of situations. This is especially common when the person with DID works at a demanding job, for example.

How Does It End?

Many people who have, as adults, realized that DID has become an intrusive factor in their lives end up seeking professional help. The therapeutic process is a demanding one, as it must address every aspect of the client's complex identities. Each "part," or alter, of the person must be recognized and appreciated. It is not uncommon for the therapist to find that some alters are far more comfortable than others with the idea of coming out and therapeutically merging into what most people think of as a whole individual.

Recovered Memories and DID

Dissociative identity disorder (DID) is, or has been in the past, one of the more controversial psychiatric diagnoses. Beginning in the late 1970s, when the disorder was still known as multiple personality disorder (MPD), a marked increase in the number of reported cases occurred. Skeptics attributed the rise, in part, to the popularity of the film and book *Sybil* (1976), whose protagonist suffers from MPD. Many of the cases that subsequently emerged were said to be the result of terrible child abuse, often involving ritualistic cult practices or sexual victimization within the family.

A very different explanation has been proposed by academic researchers working within the mainstream of psychological science. As stated by Nicholas Spanos, for example, in his book *Multiple Identities and False Memories* (1996), DID is in large measure an iatrogenic condition. *Iatrogenic* comes from a Greek word meaning "physician-induced," that is, produced by a medical treatment or diagnostic procedure rather than by the usual sources of illness. Spanos states that DID has been "created by therapists with the cooperation of their patients and the rest of society." The authors of the American Psychiatric Association's diagnostic manual are somewhat noncommittal on the matter, writing only that the "sharp rise" in cases in recent years is subject to varying interpretations (APA 2000, 486).

In fact, in 2011, the very woman who inspired *Sybil* (her real name is Shirley Mason) announced that her therapy from several decades ago had been completely compromised by her therapist, who administered the so-called truth serum, sodium pentothal, to her but then steered her in the direction of creating false personalities (Nathan 2011).

—*Editor*

Bibliography

American Psychiatric Association. 2000. *Diagnostic and Statistical Manual of Mental Disorders* (4th ed.). Washington, DC: American Psychiatric Publishing.

Lilienfeld, S. O., and H. Arkowitz. 2011. "Can People Have Multiple Personalities?" *Scientific American Mind* September/October: 64–65.

Nathan, D. 2011. "A Girl Not Named Sybil." *New York Times Magazine*, October 14. Retrieved from http://www.nytimes.com/2011/10/16/magazine/a-girl-not-named-sybil.html.

Spanos, N. P. 1996. *Multiple Identities and False Memories: A Sociocognitive Perspective*. Washington, DC: American Psychological Association.

Thus the treatment method is primarily extended psychotherapy. Medications are not necessarily used except in the case of co-occurring (comorbid) disorders. Some therapists may deliberately respond only to a single identity at first, later incorporating the others into the process. As the process continues, more personalities come into play and are encouraged to show mutual awareness and to communicate. A productive treatment process, rather like family therapy, involves a firm commitment by all parties to reach the final goal.

See also Hypnosis and Hypnotherapy; Posttraumatic Stress Disorder; Trauma

Bibliography

Bretherton, I. 1992. "The Origins of Attachment Theory: John Bowlby and Mary Ainsworth." *Developmental Psychology* 28: 759–775.

Hacking, I. 1995. *Rewriting the Soul: Multiple Personality and the Sciences of Memory.* Princeton, NJ: Princeton University Press.

Hunter, M. E. 2004. *Understanding Dissociative Disorders: A Guide for Family Physicians and Health Care Professionals.* Bethel, CT: Crown House.

Lilienfeld, S. O., and H. Arkowitz. 2011. "Can People Have Multiple Personalities?" *Scientific American Mind* (September/October): 64–65.

Simeon, D., and J. Abugel. 2008. *Feeling Unreal: Depersonalization Disorder and the Loss of the Self.* New York: Oxford University Press.

Stout, M. 2002. *The Myth of Sanity: Divided Consciousness and the Promise of Awareness.* New York: Penguin.

Drug Abuse and Mental Health

Yue Liao and Steve Sussman

Basic Concepts

A drug is any substance that can alter the biomedical or physiological processes of tissues or organisms (World Health Organization 1994). Drugs can be used to prevent or cure diseases or enhance physical or mental well-being. When talking about drug misuse, the term "drug" often refers specifically to psychoactive drugs, which are substances that cross the blood-brain barrier and can affect mental processes (e.g., cognition or affect) when ingested. Sometimes, too, the term refers specifically to illicit drugs, which are produced, sold, or used illegally.

A drug may be injected (e.g., heroin and speed), smoked (e.g., crack cocaine and marijuana), sniffed (e.g., inhalants and cocaine), huffed (inhalants), or swallowed (e.g., pills; Sussman & Ames 2008). Table on p. 209 summarizes eight categories of drugs that are divided on the basis of their subjective and behavioral effects: (1) depressants, which slow down or relax an individual; (2) PCP, which has depressant and hallucinogen-like effects and may facilitate violence; (3) inhalants, which exert sedative effects with different administration (sniffed or huffed) from other depressants; (4) stimulants, which can make the individual nervous or more aware; (5) opiates, which relieve pain and may relax or demotivate the user; (6) hallucinogens, which expand cognitive perceptions and may lead to perceptual distortions and easily agitated behavior; (7) cannabis, which may alter one's perceptions (e.g., sense of time); and (8) others, which are new drugs of abuse that have short abuse histories (fewer than 20 years' duration; Sussman & Ames 2001).

Drug Categories Based on Health Promotion Subjective-Behavioral Scheme

Drug Category	Descriptions	Examples
Depressants	Generally taken orally and slow down the central nervous system. Intoxication may include slurred speech, deficient coordination, rapid eye movements, attention or memory impairment, sedation, and anxiety reduction.	Sedatives for relaxation, hypnotics to induce sleep anxiolytic to reduce anxiety, and anticonvulsants (e.g., barbiturates).
PCP (Phencyclidine)	Can be smoked or taken orally. Intoxication involves intense analgesia, delirium, stimulant and depressant actions, staggering gait, slurred speech, and vertical nystagmus. It can produce catatonia and paranoia, flushing, coma, violent behavior, and memory loss effects.	Street names include angel dust, hog, and rocket fuel.
Inhalants	Can be used through mouth (huffing), nose (fluting), or nose and mouth (bagging). Intoxication includes euphoria, headaches, dizziness, nausea, and fainting.	Solvents (e.g., glue, gasoline, and antifreeze), aerosols (e.g., spray paint and cooking spray), amyl and butyl nitrite (e.g., Rush, room deodorizers), and anesthetics (e.g., nitrous oxide, "laughing gas").
Stimulants	Can be taken orally, smoked, sniffed, or injected. Intoxication generally includes euphoria, fatigue reduction, restlessness, decreased appetite, and hypervigilance and can include irritability and paranoia.	Cocaine (such as freebase and crack), amphetamines (e.g., Dexedrine and Benzedrine), methamphetamine, caffeine, and amphetamine-like products (Preludin or Ritalin).
Opiates	Generally taken orally, smoked, or injected. Intoxication generally includes slurred speech, analgesia, slowed respiration, drowsiness, euphoria, and possibly itching.	Morphine, codeine, and thebaine (from natural origin); heroin, hydrocodone, hydromorphine, and oxycodone (semisynthetic); meperdine, fentanyl, and pentazocine (synthetic).
Hallucinogens	Generally taken orally. Intoxication generally includes sensory changes experienced as visual illusions and hallucinations, alteration of experience of external stimuli and thoughts, and an intermingling of senses and can involve paranoia and thoughts of losing one's mind.	Indole (serotonin-like) alkylamines (e.g., LSD, DMT, psilocybin ["magic mushrooms"]), catecholamine-like phenylalkylamines (e.g., mescaline and DOM), and anticholinergic antagonist psychedelics (e.g., sco-polamine).
Cannabis	Generally is smoked. Can produce a sense of well-being and relaxation, loss of temporal awareness, and impairment of short-term memory.	Marijuana, dried leaves from cannabis; street names include pot, weed, buddah, and herb. Hashish, the resin from cannabis; street names include hash, hash oil, finger and patties.

(continued)

Drug Categories Based on Health Promotion Subjective-Behavioral Scheme (*Continued*)

Drug Category	Descriptions	Examples
Others	Any other drugs that may not fit into one of the previous seven health behavior-related categories.	Steroids, generally are taken orally, can cause mood swings, depression, irritability, and aggressiveness. "Designer drugs" may have been newly synthesized, or have received renewed popularity in public circles, e.g., GHB and ketamine (special K).

Source: Sussman and Ames 2001.

Drug misuse often refers to drugs being used in a "nonmedical" manner, meaning either without a prescription or more frequently than prescribed (Huang et al. 2006), or not as directed, or in quantity such as to be likely to induce an intoxicated state (e.g., to incur a negative impact on oneself or others). The major guideline used for clinically assessing drug abuse disorder is provided by the American Psychiatric Association (APA). The APA's *Diagnostic and Statistical Manual of Mental Disorders* (*DSM-IV-TR*) defines substance abuse disorder as a maladaptive pattern of drug use leading to clinically significant impairment or distress, as manifested by one or more of the following (occurring within a 12-month period): (1) recurrent drug use resulting in failure to fulfill major life roles; (2) recurrent drug use in physically hazardous situations (e.g., when operating machinery or driving a car); (3) recurrent drug-related legal problems; and (4) continued drug use despite having persistent social or interpersonal problems (APA 2000). Substance dependence disorder is a more severe diagnosis that subsumes substance abuse disorder and is defined by three or more of the following: (1) tolerance—that is, there is either a need for markedly increased amounts of the drug to achieve the desired drug effect or a markedly diminished effect with continued use of the same amount of the drug; (2) withdrawal—that is, either a characteristic withdrawal syndrome occurs when one terminates using the drug, or the same or a similar drug is taken to relieve/avoid the syndrome; (3) the drug often is taken in larger amounts or over a longer period than was intended; (4) there is a persistent desire or unsuccessful effort to cut down or control drug use; (5) a great deal of time is spent on activities necessary to obtain the drug, use the drug, or recover from its effects; (6) important social, occupational, or recreational activities are given up or reduced because of drug use; and (7) drug use continues despite knowledge of having a persistent or recurrent physical or psychological problem that is likely to have been caused or worsened by the drug. In the proposed *DSM-5*, due out in 2013, substance abuse and dependence disorders will be combined, legal consequences will be removed from the diagnosis owing to low prevalence of the criterion, and craving will be added as a key diagnostic feature (APA 2010).

Prevalence and Scope of Problem Use

According to the Substance Abuse and Mental Health Services Administration (SAMHSA), an estimated 21.8 million Americans aged 12 or older were current (past month) illicit-drug users in 2009, which represents about 8.7 percent of that population. The overall rate of current illicit-drug use in 2009 among youths aged 16 or 17 was 16.7 percent; among young adults aged 21 to 25, 20.5 percent; and among adults aged 50 to 54, 6.9 percent. Results from epidemiological studies also indicate that the rate of current illicit drug use is higher for males than females, lowest among Asians and highest among American Indians or Alaska Natives, lower for college graduates, and higher for unemployed persons. In 2009, an estimate of 3.9 million persons aged 12 or older were classified with drug dependence or abuse in the past year, and 7.8 million persons needed treatment for drug use problem. However, only 19.1 percent of the persons who needed treatment received treatment at a specialty facility in 2009 (Substance Abuse and Mental Health Services Administration 2009).

A number of epidemiological studies have shown that one-third to one-half of all persons who have a mental health problem meet criteria for drug abuse or dependence at some point in their lives, and the odds of comorbid (co-occurring) mental disorders are elevated among drug-dependent individuals (Kessler & Wang

---

Abuse of Prescription Drugs

Prescription drug abuse has now surpassed the usual types of drugs taken illegally, such as cocaine and methamphetamine. Rates for both hospitalizations related to prescription drugs and for overdose deaths have risen steeply. High school students have reported that tranquilizers and prescription narcotics such as Oxycontin and Vicodin have far more recreational use among teenagers than cocaine or heroin do.

As Dr. Abigail Zuger notes:

Prescriptions written for potentially addictive pain medications [have] soared in the past decade, reaching more than 200 million in 2010. . . . Surveys asking teenagers where they get pills find that relatively few buy from strangers. Many have their own prescriptions, often from dental work. Even more are given pills by friends and relatives. . . .

—*Editor*

Source: Abigail Zugar, "A General in the Drug War," *New York Times*, June 14, 2011, D1, D4.

2008; RachBeisel, Scott, & Dixon 1999). The lifetime prevalence of substance use disorders among those with schizophrenia diagnoses are estimated to vary from 48 to 64 percent. The lifetime prevalence of substance use disorders among individuals suffering from any mood disorder is approximately 32 percent (56% bipolar and about 30% unipolar); among those with an anxiety disorder is estimated to be 24 percent (36% if a panic disorder is involved); and among those suffering from obsessive-compulsive disorder it is 33 percent. Substance abuse among individuals with diagnoses of mental disorders is of some concern since co-occurrence of mental disorders may lead to an increased risk of relapse for either or both disorders. Drug abuse can induce, mimic, or exacerbate an underlying mental illness. For example, cocaine use can cause and be a consequence of depression, and can lead to (or exacerbate) anxiety or psychosis. On the other hand, mental health problems may lead to drug abuse, which may, in turn, lead to more serious mental health problems (Crome 1999). Professionals face a particular challenge from mental health-drug use problems, the so-called "dual diagnosis," as they combine to produce a greater impairment of psychosocial function (e.g., disruptive behavior and violence), poorer health outcomes (e.g., HIV infection and medical noncompliance), and higher rates of utilization of acute services, leading to more costly care than a single diagnosis alone (Drake & Wallach 2000).

Etiology

Numerous studies have shown that the etiology (or "cause") of drug abuse involves a dynamic interplay between biological, environmental, and developmental factors over time (Sussman & Ames 2008). The search for specific genes that may account for the biological risk underlying drug use and abuse is challenging and ongoing. As a complex behavior, drug abuse is likely to be a function of many different genes rather than the effects of any single drug-abuse gene. Linkage and association studies point to polymorphisms (genetic variations) involved in neurological systems (e.g., brain reward) involved in the addiction process. Drugs of abuse target the mesolimbic (or central limbic) dopamine system in the brain, as well as other neurotransmitter systems (e.g., serotonin, norepinephrine). The interaction between drugs and individual-specific neural substrates (neurophysiology) leads to the development of drug abuse (Koob & Le Moal 2001; Piazza & Moal 1996).

Moreover, researchers have proposed that early involvement with drug use in adolescence increases the risk of later dependence by altering a person's normal developmental trajectory (Palmer et al. 2009). Drug use and abuse in adolescence increases the possibility of continued exposure to high-risk environments that may limit the attainment of adult roles, impair physical and mental health, and foster the development of antisocial behaviors (Jessor 1998). Other early life circumstances and processes, such as exposure to childhood sexual abuse, novelty-seeking personality, and affiliation with substance-using peers could put individuals at greater risk of drug abuse and dependence (Fergusson, Boden, & Horwood 2008). These adolescents may have relatively fewer life skills as well.

Among young teens, social influences (e.g., parents, peers, mass media) are very important predictors of drug use and abuse. Studies have repeatedly demonstrated that friend and peer use of drugs are among the strongest predictors of teen drug use. Affiliation with drug using groups influences the likelihood that one will experiment with drugs. This is because such peer groups tend to use drugs, offer drugs to each other within groups, and role model drug use (Sussman & Ames 2008).

The presence of co-occurring childhood psychopathology (mental disorder) is found to be another risk factor for the development of drug abuse disorders during adolescence or later in life (Weinberg 2001). For example, conduct disorder, attention-deficit/hyperactivity disorder, mood disorders, anxiety disorders, and learning disorders are some of the frequently identified mental disorders that are associated with drug use. Psychological dysregulation, such as delayed behavioral, emotional, or cognitive development, may explain a correlation between childhood mental disorders and drug use in adolescents (Tarter & Vanyukov 2002).

As shown in the below table, four general models have been proposed to summarize the etiological theories of the high prevalence of co-occurrence of drug use disorders in patients with severe mental illness (e.g., schizophrenia and bipolar

Etiological Models of Comorbidity of Mental Illness and Drug Abuse Disorder

Model	General Concepts	Examples
Common factor models	Some factors can independently increase the risk of developing both mental illness and drug abuse disorder.	Genetic factors, either shared genetic factors within individual family members or genetic factors between different relatives due to assortative mating; antisocial personality disorder and its childhood precursor, conduct disorder; lower socioeconomic status and poverty in general; and impairment in cognitive functioning are found to independently increase the vulnerability to both mental illness and drug abuse disorder.
Secondary drug abuse disorder models	Mental illness increases individuals' vulnerability to developing drug abuse disorder.	Psychosocial risk factor models, which assume that drug abuse disorder is secondary to mental illness, and include: (a) self-medication model, which denotes that individuals seek specific drugs to alleviate particular painful affects; and (b) alleviation of dysphoria model, which indicates that people

(continued)

Etiological Models of Comorbidity of Mental Illness and Drug Abuse Disorder (*Continued*)

Model	General Concepts	Examples
		with mental illness are prone to dysphoric experiences that make them also prone to use psychoactive drugs. Supersensitivity model, the biologically based model of increased sensitivity to the effects of drugs in persons with mental illness. Thus persons with mental illness may be more likely to experience negative consequences from using relatively small amount of drugs.
Secondary psychiatric illness models	The theory that drug abuse disorder can lead to mental illness.	Abuse of psychotomimetic drugs (e.g., stimulants, hallucinogens, and cannabis) can lead to long-term psychotic disorder due to behavioral sensitization (the increased sensitivity of response) and kindling (repeated stimulant administration reduces degree of increase in behavioral responses).
Bidirectional models	The ongoing, interactional effects between mental illness and drug abuse disorder.	Drug abuse disorder could trigger mental illness in a biologically vulnerable individual, which is then maintained by continued drug abuse due to socially learned cognitive factors, such as beliefs, expectancies, and motives for drug use.

Source: Mueser, Drake, and Wallach 1998; Sussman and Ames 2008.

disorder): (1) the common factor models, which suggest that high rates of comorbidity are the result of shared risk factors, including genetic and antisocial personality factors, for both drug abuse and mental illness; (2) the secondary drug abuse disorder models, which suggest that mental illness increases individuals' chance of developing drug abuse disorder; (3) the secondary psychiatric disorder models, which suggest that drug use facilitates mental illness in individuals who would otherwise not develop these disorders; and (4) the bidirectional models, which hypothesize that either disorder can increase vulnerability to the other disorder (Mueser, Drake, & Wallach 1998; Sussman & Ames 2008). Given the heterogeneous population of persons with co-occurring mental illness and drug abuse disorder, more than one model may apply for a given individual.

Prevention of Drug Misuse

Most drug use prevention programs have focused on adolescents, since initiation and experimentation with drugs increases dramatically during this critical period (Sussman et al. 1995). Moreover, as discussed above, early onset of drug use has also been shown to significantly correlate with developing drug dependence later in life. Universal preventions (i.e., delivered to an entire population regardless of risk status) are the most common drug use prevention programs.

Targeted preventions (tailored to higher-risk groups or individuals) have also been implemented, although relatively few such programs exist (Sussman et al. 2004). Both universal and targeted drug use prevention programs have been found to increase knowledge, decrease prodrug attitudes, and decrease drug use among adolescents. Research findings have suggested that the most effective prevention programs target salient risks and protective factors at the individual, family, and community levels, and are guided by relevant psychosocial theories regarding the etiology of drug use and abuse (Griffin & Botvin 2010). Moreover, prevention programs are most beneficial when an individual is developmentally able to learn the material, when the contents of the material are meaningful and relevant to the individual, when the material is provided in contexts that permit exposure to most of the material, and when implemented by highly trained facilitators (Sussman 2001).

Drug use prevention programs have been primarily implemented in school settings, since adolescents are a captive audience to this type of programming. Other effective forms of prevention program delivery include family-based home settings, community-based settings (e.g., Boys and Girls Clubs), and various media-based settings (e.g., computer based, television, print ads). Most drug use prevention approaches are designed to create awareness of social influences that promote drug use experimentation and to counteract these influences (Skara & Sussman 2003). Programs focusing on social influences and skills enhancement are two major psychosocial approaches being utilized. Social-influences programs are designed to correct social misperceptions (e.g., alter norms regarding the prevalence and acceptability of drug use) and build drug resistance skills. Skill-enhancement programs include general self-management and social competence skills training (e.g., listening and communication skills training, assertiveness training, social decision making, and activism skills training). Comprehensive social-influences/life-skills programs tend to include both types of approaches (Sussman & Ames 2008).

Applying prevention programs in social settings (e.g., in groups) is essential to inducing and maintaining change among adolescents, to help correct cognitive misperceptions and provide a venue for practicing newly learned behavioral skills with corrective input from educators and feedback from peers that may mimic real-world social situations. It is important to recognize the influence of the family unit because of the close and historical patterns of interaction within the unit. Parent- or family-targeted prevention programs include those that offer early childhood education, social support for parents, crisis management, parenting skills training, parent-child communication skills, and resource acquisition instruction or networking. Family involvement can lead to a 15 percent relative effect in compliant families (Sussman 2005). Examples of successful family-based prevention program include the Strengthening Family Program (SFP) and Family Matters (FM). SFP is a family skills training program for high-risk families to reduce problem behaviors and drug abuse in children and early teens age 6 to 16 years and to improve social competencies and school performance (http://www.strengthening familiesprogram.org/). FM mails booklets to parents with subsequent telephone contacts by health educators to encourage completion of the book and any included parent-child activities (http://familymatters.sph.unc.edu/).

Several drug prevention programs also target to enhance adolescent's mental health, such as to prevent stress and depression. For example, the Reconnecting Youth (RY) program focuses on youth at risk for dropout. It utilizes group support and providing life skill training with feedback to parents. Evaluation of RY program effects shows 18 percent improvement in grades, 54 percent decrease in drug use, and 32 percent decline in perceived stress (Sussman et al. 2004). Teen Intervention Project (TIP) provides group sessions for drug-misusing teens. In addition to substance abuse education, TIP also discusses stress prevention strategies (e.g., regular exercise, setting realistic goals, and learning how to relax) and stress coping strategies (e.g., problem solving and talking with others; Kortlander & Leon Morris 2001). Implementation of TIP showed a significant decrease in perceived stress at postintervention (Lowe 2006).

Assessment and Treatment

As described earlier, the major guideline used for clinically assessing drug abuse disorder is based on criteria provided by *DSM-IV*. Aside from a formal diagnostic interview, such as the Structured Clinical Interview for the *DSM-IV* (SCID), there are a variety of self-report screens for drug use and drug abuse disorder among teens and adults. For example, the Substance Abuse Subtle Screening Inventory (available in separate versions for adults and adolescents), the Drug Use Screening Inventory (documents the level of involvement with drugs and quantifies severity of consequences associated with drug use), the Personal Experience Screening Questionnaire (screens for the need for further assessment of drug abuse disorder and provides a brief overview of psychosocial problems, drug use frequency, and faking tendencies), and the Chemical Dependency Assessment Profile (assesses drug abuse and dependency problems; Miller 1999; SAMHSA 2009).

It is recommended that persons with severe mental illness should receive routine screening for any regular use of nonprescribed psychoactive drugs because (1) controlled use of psychoactive drugs by individuals with severe mental illness are likely to lead to a drug abuse disorder over time, (2) use of even a small amount of drugs is likely to be associated with negative outcomes among these individuals, and (3) individuals with severe mental illness are likely to be unaware of or confused about the consequences of their drug use (RachBeisel, Scott, & Dixon 1999).

Historically, people with co-occurring mental health and drug use problems received treatments from two different systems targeting either their mental health or drug use issues. This parallel treatment approach ignores the interactive nature of the comorbid disorders and the outcomes of the treatment are not very effective (Mangrum, Spence, & Lopez 2006). Recognition of this limitation led to the development of integrated treatment programs that acknowledge the unique needs of people with co-occurring disorders by providing coordinated psychiatric and drug abuse interventions, and enhanced case management to obtain adjunct services addressing other social problems common in these individuals. Studies of comprehensive integrated treatment programs indicated that participation in such treatments resulted in greater treatment engagement, decreased drug use, increased remission, and decreased hospitalization (Drake, Mercer-McFadden, Mueser, McHugo, & Bond 1998). Indeed, integrated treatments, along with stage-wise interventions, engagement strategies, motivational counseling, active treatment, relapse-prevention strategies, long-term program retention, and comprehensive services are found to be the essential principles for an effective treatment program for co-occurring mental illness and drug abuse disorder (Drake, Mueser, Brunette, & McHugo 2004; see below table).

Principles of Treatment for Dual Diagnosis

Principle	Descriptions	Examples
Integrated treatment	One clinical team provides appropriate mental health and drug abuse treatments in a coordinated way and guides the individual toward learning to manage intertwined illnesses. Each treatment component therefore helps people to manage both disorders.	Family psychoeducation interventions that address mental illness, drug abuse, and their interactions. Social skill training that emphasizes developing relationships and targets the need to avoid peer pressure and social situations that could lead to drug use.
Stage-wise interventions	Tailor programs to the individual's stages of treatment: (a) engagement—engaging a person in a collaborative and trusting relationship; (b) persuasion/motivation—helping the person to become motivated to participate in recovery-oriented programs; (c) active treatment—helping the person to learn skills for managing both illnesses and pursuing goals; and (d) relapse prevention—helping the person who is in stable remission to develop and use relapse prevention strategies.	Helping people move from the earlier stages of treatment toward active treatment stage by discussing drug use patterns, learning information about drug effects, verbalizing life goals, identifying pros and cons of drug use, and relating changes in drug use to achieving desired outcomes.

(*continued*)

Principles of Treatment for Dual Diagnosis   (*Continued*)

Principle	Descriptions	Examples
Engagement strategies	Engage people in the program by providing outreach, motivational counseling, flexibility, practical assistance, and culturally competent services.	Engage inner-city homeless people through outreach by street workers with same language and cultural background and provide help on housing and other practical matters.
Motivational counseling	Helps individuals identify their goals and then to recognize that drug use or an untreated mental illness interferes with attaining these goals.	Help people set specific, proximal, and attainable goals that require a reduction in drug use, and provide performance feedback. Then focus on achieving the goal rather than focusing on decreasing the drug use per se.
Active treatment	Help individuals acquire skills and supports needed to manage their illnesses.	Provide counseling to help promote adherence; provide cognitive and behavioral skill training to help recognize early warning signs and prevent relapse; provide social network and family interventions to strengthen the immediate social environment to promote recovery.
Relapse-prevention strategies	Prevents individuals from relapsing once they achieve stability, remission, or symptom control.	Encourage people to have a job in the community before leaving the residential treatment program.
Long-term pro-gram retention	Prolongs retention by flexibly managing relapses without dismissals.	Focus on providing appropriate supports in the community rather than on quick and intensive treatment programs.
Comprehensive services	Individualizes services according to needs and address illnesses broadly rather than narrowly as would a discrete treatment intervention.	Include peer supports, family interventions, vocational services, liaison with the criminal justice system, money management, trauma interventions, housing supports, and other supports for people who need them.

Source: Drake, Mueser, Brunette, and McHugo 2004.

Although abstinence from drug use for at least one month could help determine whether drug abuse disorder or the psychiatric diagnosis is primary, this approach may delay the decision to initiate psychotropic medications (Griswold, Aronoff, Kernan, & Kahn 2008). Therefore, referral to an adolescent psychiatrist should be concurrent with ongoing drug abuse treatment in adolescents with comorbidities. Drug abuse treatment should always be tailored to each adolescent's particular needs since no single approach is suitable for all individuals. A thorough assessment that evaluates adolescents' problems multidimensionally is critical to matching them to programs that are adolescent-specific and formulating treatments that are age-appropriate (Sanchez-Samper & Knight 2009).

The below table summarizes key approaches of drug abuse treatment for adolescents. In general, treatment of adolescents with drug abuse should involve not only involve professionals and therapeutic components but also family and peer support. Family support and strength building are a crucial part of adolescent drug abuse treatment. The two most common modalities of family therapy are Multidimensional Family Therapy (MDFT) and Multisystemic Therapy (MST). MDFT was designed to treat adolescents who have drug abuse and behavioral problems. Individual and family sessions are held up to four times a week, coupled with

Drug Abuse Treatments for Adolescents

Treatment	General Descriptions	Examples
Cognitive behavioral therapy	A structured, goal-oriented therapeutic approach designed to teach specific skills for maintaining abstinence by identifying and modifying thoughts and feelings that precede drug use. Can be used both in groups and with individuals.	Keeping a diary of significant events and associated feelings, thoughts, and behaviors. Try substituting risky behaviors with behaviors other than drug use or avoiding high-risk situations altogether.
Motivational enhancement therapy	A person-centered counseling approach for initiating behavior change that aims to help individuals resolve ambivalence about engaging in treatment and stopping drug use.	Therapists work closely with individuals on establishing decisional balances (the pros and cons of change), strengthening self-efficacy (confidence in the ability to change across problem situations), identifying situational temptations to engage in problem behavior, and modifying behaviors that are specific to the problem area.
Contingency management	Based on the behavioral principle that if a good behavior is rewarded, it is more likely to be repeated in the future. It uses reinforcement procedures systematically to modify behaviors of drug-abusing adolescents in a positive and supportive manner.	Individuals are called at random to provide urine specimens at least once a week, and rewards (such as vouchers that can be exchanged for gift certificates, clothing, and movie tickets) are provided for each negative test result for drugs.
12-step programs	The 12-step approach involves admitting that one cannot control one's addiction and recognizing a higher power that can give strength, examining past errors with the help of a sponsor and making amends for these errors, learning to live a new life with a new code of behavior and helping others who suffer from the same addiction.	Narcotics Anonymous, Cocaine Anonymous. Adolescents might benefit most by attending young people's meeting and obtain a sponsor who is aware of his or her individual developmental level when progressing through the 12 steps.

Source: Sanchez-Samper and Knight 2009.

interim phone contact and intensive advocacy with the adolescent's school (Deas & Thomas 2001). MST is an intensive four-month program developed to address the needs of high-risk adolescents. Therapists work closely with parents to identify the goals of treatment, ascertain the causes of drug abuse disorder, and implement solutions. It also includes comprehensive psychiatric and drug abuse services, with sessions held in the family's home (Liddle et al. 2002). Peer groups play a critical role in promoting abstinence from drugs and preventing drug abuse. While undergoing drug abuse treatment, adolescents need to be involved with new peer groups that can support one another in remaining abstinent.

There are several treatment strategies that can be effective for both youth and adults. The Minnesota approach is primarily inpatient or residential care that lasts for a few weeks to a few months. The Minnesota approach makes use of Alcoholics Anonymous (AA) concepts, resources, and precepts including "12 steps" central to recovery. Another approach involves the therapeutic community (TC); all clients and counselors serve as the primary therapist, generally in an inpatient setting. Clients are provided with increased responsibilities and privileges as they pass through structured phases of treatment within the TC. One-on-one counseling, remedial education, and occupational training (for older teens) also are provided. Behavioral and cognitive-behavioral approaches seek to decrease the frequencies of behaviors compatible with drug use and at the same time increase the frequency of behaviors incompatible with drug use. These approaches are used widely in inpatient and outpatient settings. They include instructions of a whole variety of behavioral techniques including assertiveness training (to instruct how one can better obtain their needs in social interactions), anger management, and environmental advocacy (how to get one's needs met within systems). Group therapy can address concerns about peer pressure, relationships, prevention of relapses, and other treatment issues. The dynamics of group therapy also leave room for interpersonal and intrapersonal growth and make adolescents and adults more involved with the encouragement and example of their peers (Sanchez-Samper & Knight 2009). The 12-step fellowships, such as the Narcotics Anonymous (NA) and Cocaine Anonymous (CA), represent one form of peer-based group therapy. Many adolescents start to attend NA/CA while they are in residential or inpatient care and are often encouraged to continue their attendance upon discharge (Sussman 2010), though over 95 percent of attendees are adults generally over 30 years of age.

Summary

Mental health and drug use problems continue to be a major public health challenge. Many people reporting drug abuse have experienced mental health problems at some point in their lives, and many individuals with severe mental health problems have a history of past or current drug abuse or dependence. Recently, researchers and clinicians have tried to understand the complex diagnostic and treatment issues posed by the co-occurrence of mental health and drug use problems among youth. The many common risk factors shared by mental health illness and drug abuse provide opportunities for comprehensive prevention programs to target both problems at the same time. And future studies could evaluate whether the prevention of one set of problems reduces the prevalence of comorbidity. Integration of mental health and drug abuse services is a promising way to enhance efforts to prevent drug abuse and to help dual diagnosis individuals to recover. Future policies not only should address integrated treatment but also create safe and protective environments with the opportunities for educational and social success.

See also Adolescence and Mental Health; Alcohol Abuse, Alcoholism, and Mental Health; Criminalization and Diversion Programs; Peer Support Groups; Preventative Mental Health Programs; Public Health Perspectives

Bibliography

American Psychiatric Association. 2000. *Diagnostic and Statistical Manual of Mental Disorders* (4th ed., text rev.). Arlington, VA: American Psychiatric Publishing.

American Psychiatric Association. 2010. "*DSM-5* Development: R Substance Disorder." Retrieved from http://www.dsm5.org/ProposedRevisions/Pages/proposedrevision .aspx?rid=431.

Crome, I. B. 1999. "Substance Misuse and Psychiatric Comorbidity: Towards Improved Service Provision." *Drugs: Education, Prevention, and Policy* 6(2): 151–174.

Deas, D., and S. E. Thomas. 2001. "An Overview of Controlled Studies of Adolescent Substance Abuse Treatment." *The American Journal on Addictions* 10(2): 178–189.

Drake, R. E., C. Mercer-McFadden, K. T. Mueser, G. J. McHugo, and G. R. Bond. 1998. "Review of Integrated Mental Health and Substance Abuse Treatment for Patients with Dual Disorders." *Schizophrenia Bulletin* 24(4): 589–608.

Drake, R. E., K. T. Mueser, M. F. Brunette, and G. J. McHugo. 2004. "A Review of Treatments for People with Severe Mental Illnesses and Co-Occurring Substance use Disorders." *Psychiatric Rehabilitation Journal* 27(4): 360–374.

Drake, R. E., and M. A. Wallach. 2000. "Dual Diagnosis: 15 Years of Progress." *Psychiatric Services* 51(9): 1126–1129.

Fergusson, D. M., J. M. Boden, and L. J. Horwood. 2008. "The Developmental Antecedents of Illicit Drug Use: Evidence from a 25-Year Longitudinal Study." *Drug and Alcohol Dependence* 96(1–2): 165–177.

Griffin, K. W. and G. J. Botvin. 2010. "Evidence-Based Interventions for Preventing Substance use Disorders in Adolescents." *Child and Adolescent Psychiatric Clinics of North America* 19(3): 505–526.

Griswold, K. S., H. Aronoff, J. B. Kernan, and L. S. Kahn. 2008. "Adolescent Substance use and Abuse: Recognition and Management." *American Family Physician* 77(3): 331–336.

Huang, B., D. A. Dawson, F. S. Stinson, D. S. Hasin, W. Ruan, T. D. Saha, S. M. Smith, R. B. Goldstein, and B. F. Grant. 2006. "Prevalence, Correlates, and Comorbidity of Nonmedical Prescription Drug use and Drug use Disorders in the United States: Results of the National Epidemiologic Survey on Alcohol and Related Conditions." *Journal of Clinical Psychiatry* 67(7): 1062–1073.

Jessor, Richard, ed. 1998. *New Perspectives on Adolescent Risk Behavior.* Cambridge: Cambridge University Press.

Kessler, R. C., and P. S. Wang. 2008. "The Descriptive Epidemiology of Commonly Occurring Mental Disorders in the United States." *Annual Review of Public Health* 29: 115–129.

Koob, G. F., and M. Le Moal. 2001. "Drug Addiction, Dysregulation of Reward, and Allostasis." *Neuropsychopharmacology* 24(2): 97–129.

Kortlander, S. E., and S. Leon Morris. 2001. "The Teen Intervention Project." In E. F. Wagner and H. B. Waldron, eds., *Innovations in Adolescent Substance Abuse Interventions* (pp. 189–203). Oxford: Elsevier Science.

Liddle, H. A., C. L. Rowe, T. J. Quille, G. A. Dakof, D. S. Mills, E. Sakran, and H. Biaggi. 2002. "Transporting a Research-Based Adolescent Drug Treatment into Practice." *Journal of Substance Abuse Treatment* 22(4): 231–243.

Lowe, J. 2006. "Teen Intervention Project—Cherokee (TIP-C)." *Pediatric Nursing* 32(5): 495–499.

Mangrum, L. F., R. T. Spence, and M. Lopez. 2006. "Integrated versus Parallel Treatment of Co-occurring Psychiatric and Substance Use Disorders." *Journal of Substance Abuse Treatment* 30(1): 79–84.

Miller, G. A. 1999. *The Substance Abuse Subtle Screening Inventory (SASSI) Manual* (2nd ed.). Springville, IN: SASSI Institute.

Mueser, K. T., R. E. Drake, and M. A. Wallach. 1998. "Dual Diagnosis: A Review of Etiological Theories." *Addictive Behaviors* 23(6): 717–734.

Newton, David E. 2010. *Substance Abuse: A Reference Handbook.* Santa Barbara, CA: ABC-CLIO/Greenwood.

Palmer, R. H., S. E. Young, C. J. Hopfer, R. P. Corley, M. C. Stallings, T. J. Crowley, and J. K. Hewitt. 2009. "Developmental Epidemiology of Drug Use and Abuse in Adolescence and Young Adulthood: Evidence of Generalized Risk." *Drug and Alcohol Dependence* 102(1–3): 78–87.

Piazza, P. V., and M. L. Moal. 1996. "Pathophysiological Basis of Vulnerability to Drug Abuse: Role of an Interaction between Stress, Glucocorticoids, and Dopaminergic Neurons." *Annual Review of Pharmacology and Toxicology* 36(1): 359–378.

RachBeisel, J., J. Scott, and L. Dixon. 1999. "Co-occurring Severe Mental Illness and Substance Use Disorders: A Review of Recent Research." *Psychiatric Services* 50(11): 1427–1434.

Sanchez-Samper, X., and J. R. Knight. 2009. "Drug Abuse by Adolescents: General Considerations." *Pediatrics in Review* 30(3): 83–92.

Skara, S., and S. Sussman. 2003. "A Review of 25 Long-Term Adolescent Tobacco and Other Drug Use Prevention Program Evaluations." *Preventive Medicine* 37(5): 451–474.

Substance Abuse and Mental Health Services Administration. 2009. *Screening and Assessing Adolescents for Substance Use Disorders: Treatment Improvement Protocol (TIP) Series 31.* Rockville, MD: U.S. Department of Health and Human Services.

Substance Abuse and Mental Health Services Administration. 2010. *Results from the 2009 National Survey on Drug Use and Health: Vol. 1. Summary of National Findings.* Rockville, MD: U.S. Department of Health and Human Services.

Sussman, Steve, ed. 2001. *Handbook of Program Development in Health Behavior Research and Practice.* Thousand Oaks, CA: Sage.

Sussman, S. 2005. "Risk Factors for and Prevention of Tobacco Use." *Pediatric Blood and Cancer* 44(7): 614–619.

Sussman, S. 2010. "A Review of Alcoholics Anonymous/Narcotics Anonymous Programs for Teens." *Evaluation & the Health Professions* 33(1): 26–55.

Sussman, Steve, and Susan L. Ames. 2001. *The Social Psychology of Drug Abuse.* Buckingham, UK: Open University Press.

Sussman, Steve, and Susan L. Ames. 2008. *Drug Abuse: Concepts, Prevention, and Cessation.* New York: Cambridge University Press.

Sussman, S., C. W. Dent, T. R. Simon, A. W. Stacy, E. R. Galaif, M. A. Moss, S. Craig, and A. C. Johnson. 1995. "Immediate Impact of Social Influence-Oriented Substance Abuse Prevention Curricula in Traditional and Continuation High Schools." *Drugs and Society* 8(3–4): 65–81.

Sussman, S., M. Earleywine, T. Wills, C. Cody, T. Biglan, C. W. Dent, and M. D. Newcomb. 2004. "The Motivation, Skills, and Decision-Making Model of Drug Abuse Prevention." *Substance Use & Misuse* 39(10–12): 1971–2016.

Tarter, R. E., and M. M. Vanyukov, eds. 2002. *Etiology of Substance use Disorder in Children and Adolescents: Emerging Findings from the Center for Education and Drug Abuse Research.* Binghamton, NY: Haworth Press.

Weinberg, N. Z. 2001. "Risk Factors for Adolescent Substance Abuse," *Journal of Learning Disabilities* 34(4): 343–351.

World Health Organization. 1994. *Lexicon of Alcohol and Drug Terms.* Geneva: World Health Organization.

Drug Companies

Fred Leavitt

The development of medicinal drugs has increased life expectancy, allowed diabetics to lead productive lives, prolonged the lives of people with heart problems, cured many formerly deadly infectious diseases, and made surgical operations bearable. When internists ranked the importance of 30 medical innovations in treating patients, 4 drugs were ranked in the top 10 and 11 in the top 20 (Fuchs 2001). Many of the important drugs were developed through research financed by drug companies.

Unfortunately for worldwide health, however, drug companies are also businesses beholden to their shareholders. Their bottom line therefore is making money and, in doing so, they have engaged in many ethically questionable and even, according to some, criminal behaviors. Marcia Angell (2009), a former editor-in-chief of the *New England Journal of Medicine*, has written that

> Over the past two decades the pharmaceutical industry has moved very far from its original high purpose of discovering and producing useful new drugs. Now primarily a marketing machine to sell drugs of dubious benefit,

this industry uses its wealth and power to co-opt every institution that might stand in its way, including the US Congress, the FDA [Food and Drug Administration], academic medical centers, and the medical profession itself.

The development of new drugs requires expensive laboratory research with uncertain results. Company spokespersons cite the cost of research to justify the prices they charge, which are far higher in the United States than in other industrialized countries. But several factors can be pointed to as weakening such arguments. First, companies often exaggerate their developmental costs. Second, much of their research goes toward developing drugs that differ only slightly from others already on the market; these "me-too" drugs typically offer little or no advantage over the ones already available. Third, much of the crucial basic research is done in academic institutions using money granted from the taxpayer-funded National Institutes of Health (NIH). Fourth, the drug industry gets many tax credits for research. Research and development costs are tax exempt and do not depreciate like other investments. The drug industry pays a lower tax rate than other industries—just 5.6 percent of its profits in taxes (Baker 2011; Guenther 1999).

Research Methodology

Research in the pharmaceutical industry is typically outsourced to commercial research organizations (CROs). Drug companies hire CROs for virtually all aspects of drug development, from conception to FDA approval and beyond. CROs craft the research protocols, conduct the research, report the results, prepare articles (on a "ghostwriter" basis) for medical journals, and create marketing campaigns. In 2008, drug companies spent approximately $20 billion for CRO services, or about 29 percent of their drug development budget (Akst 2009). The several hundred CROs in existence compete with each other for industry contracts, and those that report favorable results are, in general, more likely to receive future contracts. This gives them serious incentive to manipulate and even, in some cases, falsify data. In 1992, the Office of Research Integrity (ORI) was established to investigate allegations of scientific misconduct. In every year since, the ORI has found several cases, many related to drug development (see F. Leavitt 2003 for examples).

The law requires that drug companies submit all data collected to the FDA. Doctors, however, get their information from medical journals, not FDA filings; and a great deal of negative information never reaches the journals. Rising, Bacchetti, and Bero (2008), for example, found that studies on approved drugs that had positive outcomes were nearly five times as likely as those with negative outcomes to eventually be published. Furthermore, the conclusions in journals often differed from those reported to the FDA in ways that favored the drugs. In part to rectify this situation, the NIH, in association with the FDA, started a website, clinicaltrials.gov, on which all drugs trials must be registered in addition to being reported to the FDA.

In drug trials, test subjects are often recruited by their doctors, who are compensated by the drug companies for doing so. Top recruiters can earn more than $1 million a year—a monetary incentive powerful enough to have induced some doctors, at least, to persuade patients to take drugs for which they were not suited, sometimes with disastrous results (Eichenwald & Kolata 1999). Many trials with human subjects, in fact, are conducted in developing countries, because poor people are relatively easy to recruit and unlikely to litigate. In 2008, 6,485 trials were conducted in foreign countries of drugs intended for Americans; 78 percent of human test subjects were enrolled at foreign sites; and 80 percent of the applications submitted to the FDA for new drugs contained data from foreign trials (Alliance for Human Research Protection 2010). The experiments have occasionally been found to fall below the standards established by U.S. ethics committees.

In studies of psychiatric drugs, subjects are typically given a placebo and asked to return in several days. Then, placebo responders (i.e., those reacting favorably to the placebo) are excluded from further participation, which ensures that drug/placebo differences are maximized. Also excluded are people who have tried any other treatment for their condition, because they are considered refractory cases (even though such cases may more accurately reflect real conditions). These two policies ensure that drug effects are maximized, but they also raise questions about the general applicability of drugs tested in this way.

Lobbying Efforts

According to M. Asif Ismail (2005) of the nonpartisan Center for Public Integrity, the drug and health products industry spent more than $800 million in federal lobbying and campaign donations during the prior seven years. Industry representatives lobbied members of Congress and executives in several agencies, including the Department of Health and Human Services, the FDA, and the State Department. They also contributed $133 million to candidates running for federal and state offices. Their efforts helped them block attempts to contain drug prices by, for example, allowing U.S. citizens to import medicines from countries (such as Canada) that cap prescription drug prices.

The 2003 Medicare prescription drug plan is widely regarded as financially benefiting the pharmaceutical companies. Many of the people who were instrumental in developing the plan left Congress shortly afterward to become lobbyists for drug companies (Pierce, Shankman, & Larson 2009). Republican congressman

---

Drug Marketing and Free Speech

In promoting their products to doctors, drug companies have found that it is advantageous to know what drugs a doctor has prescribed in the past. To that end, the companies collect data from pharmacies on prescriptions, including the doctor's name, the drugs prescribed, and the dosages. They can then employ targeted marketing campaigns and generally increase sales.

Some states, such as Vermont, have sought to regulate such practices. In 2007, Vermont passed a law that prohibited the sale of such records by pharmacies and their use in marketing campaigns by drug companies. However, the U.S. Supreme Court, on June 23, 2011, ruled that the Vermont law is an unconstitutional restriction of free speech, thus making it more difficult for states to protect medical privacy.

Writing for the 6-to-3 majority, Justice Anthony Kennedy stated that the law violates First Amendment rights by imposing an unwarranted burden on speakers (drug marketers) and their speech (information about doctors and their prescriptions). The majority on the Court, in other words, treated commercial speech, which traditionally is subject to restriction, essentially the same as political speech, which is well protected under the Constitution.

In his dissent, Justice Stephen Breyer wrote that the speech in question in this case is "entirely commercial," and the only possible burden on speakers is that of limiting the use of data that can help "pharmaceutical companies create better sales messages."

—Editor

Source: New York Times, June 24, 2011, A22.

Walter Burton said of the legislation at the time that "the pharmaceutical lobbyists wrote the bill" (Hari 2009).

Strategic Alliances

It is not unknown for drug companies to sponsor organizations for patients with specific disabilities and then promote their own drug for treating the disability. According to one industry executive, patient groups help companies to "rapidly disseminate information about a product to patients" (Willis 1977). Speaking tours and television exposure are arranged for articulate, personable leaders of the patient groups. Weinstein (2009) has written, "As a veteran pharma marketer, I have witnessed that the most direct and efficient tool for driving long-term support for brands has been, and continues to be, a well-designed, advocacy-based public education program."

The nationwide nonprofit group Children and Adults with Attention Deficit Disorders (CHADD) is by many accounts an objective organization guided by the latest scientific findings. Yet, until recently, CHADD's basic message was that parents should strongly consider placing anyone diagnosed with the disorders on Ritalin. CHADD was originally created by, and received much of its financial support from, the manufacturer of Ritalin. Concerns about the lack of transparency regarding that relationship were raised in Congress, and today CHADD claims to make no endorsements or recommendations regarding specific psychiatric medications (CHADD 2012; Grassley 2010).

The National Alliance for the Mentally Ill (NAMI) bills itself as "a grassroots organization of individuals with brain disorders and their family members." According to one author, however, 18 drug firms gave NAMI a total of $11.72 million between 1996 and mid-1999 (Silverstein 1999). In 2004, NAMI opposed the warnings on containers for antidepressants regarding evidence that the drugs caused suicide in some users under 18 years of age. In 2006, NAMI opposed warnings on attention-deficit hyperactivity disorder (ADHD) drugs concerning evidence that they can cause heart attack, stroke, and sudden death in children (see F. Leavitt 2003 for more examples). At the same time, NAMI has been forthcoming about where it gets its funding (from industry and nonindustry sources alike; Grassley 2010).

The Citizens Commission on Human Rights (n.d.) scrutinized the advisory board members of the Depression and Bipolar Support Alliance. Seven board members, it was found, had been investigated by the Senate Finance Committee over conflicts of interest involving drug companies. Many others held stock in drug companies or received money from them for consulting, ghostwriting, or conducting research.

"Off-Label" Violations

Once a drug has been approved by the FDA for at least one use, doctors can prescribe it to treat any disease condition and patient population and at any dosage level. However, drug companies are legally barred from promoting drugs for other than the specific uses for which they have been approved. Nevertheless, drug companies in the last decade have pleaded guilty to criminal offenses and paid billions of dollars in penalties on the charge of deceptively marketing drugs for unapproved (or "off-label") uses. According to Wilson (2010), every major company selling antidepressant drugs either has settled recent government cases for hundreds of millions of dollars or is currently under investigation for possible health care fraud.

Evans (2010) offered a simple explanation for why so many companies are repeat offenders: the fines for being caught breaking the off-label law are tiny compared with the firms' annual revenues. For example, Pfizer paid $2.3 billion for improperly marketing Bextra and three other drugs; yet that amount represents only 14 percent of Pfizer's $16.8 billion in revenue from selling those drugs between 2001 and 2008. Zyprexa provided Lilly with $36 billion in revenue from 2000 to 2008—more than 25 times as much as the total in penalties Lilly has had to pay. It is understood that the companies consider the penalties a cost of doing business.

Creating Customers

Like most businesses, drug companies use several strategies to increase sales. They advertise to both physicians and laypeople. They organize nationwide campaigns to persuade patients to dispose of drugs once the expiration date has been reached—although, with a few exceptions such as tetracycline, most drugs remain safe and effective beyond the marked expiration date. One foundation funded by a drug company instituted a program of free height screening for schoolchildren and then wrote parents of children in the bottom fifth percentile for their age group about a potential treatment. The treatment, unsurprisingly, was a drug the company manufactured (F. Leavitt 2003). Yet, in any group of people, some individuals will be at the extremes. It does not necessarily mean that those persons have something wrong with them.

One major strategy within the industry is to broaden the definitions of existing diseases and create new ones for which drugs can be prescribed. Most medical conditions can be conclusively diagnosed by simple observation supplemented by blood tests, biopsies, CT scans, and the like. Psychiatric disorders cannot, which makes them especially vulnerable to what Lynn Payer (1992) called disease mongering (i.e., trying to convince essentially well people that they are sick, or slightly sick people that they are very ill). Moynihan, Doran, and Henry (2008) wrote of a three-day international conference during which several participants gave examples of the practice. Drug companies, for example, have exaggerated the prevalence of restless leg syndrome and have coined a new condition, female sexual dysfunction. Their efforts to promote diagnoses of bipolar disorder led to a 40-fold increase of that diagnosis in children and adolescents between 1997 and 2007 (Moreno et al. 2007). The companies encourage the prescription of drugs as first-line treatment for each condition.

The companies promote "awareness programs," ostensibly as a public service to educate people about problems they may have that have not yet been diagnosed. For example, one awareness campaign stated: "Depression is a disease that anyone can get. It can be cured by medicine. Early detection is important" (Batty 2007). Candidates for antidepressant treatment included anyone who had felt sad for two weeks, had an appetite change, had trouble sleeping, had a drop in libido, or experienced tiredness—symptoms that virtually all adults have had at some point in their lives. Other awareness campaigns have focused on anxiety and stress disorders, ADHD, and premenstrual dysphoric disorder. The campaigns increase the number of people who believe they have a psychiatric problem and need pharmacological help.

The TeenScreen program was developed to screen high school students and refer those at high risk for suicide for treatment. In 2003, the President's New Freedom Commission on Mental Health (NFC) recommended that TeenScreen be implemented for all American school children and adolescents (Citizens

Commission on Human Rights, n.d.). Most of the NFC members were consultants, spokespersons, or otherwise connected to the drug industry (TeenScreen n.d.). About 90 percent of children who see a psychiatrist are prescribed a drug (Stubbe & Thomas 2002), so the TeenScreen program resulted in a substantial increase in the number of children receiving prescriptions. While some teenagers will benefit from drugs, critics believe that too many are receiving unnecessary and possibly harmful medication.

Concluding Comments

Following the prevailing medical model of mental illness, ads for psychiatric drugs claim that medications work by correcting chemical imbalances in the brain. People who accept such an explanation are more unlikely to search for environmental factors that may contribute to, or in some cases be the sole cause of, their problems. Medications can and do help many individuals, but that does not mean that one cannot be skeptical of claims made by pharmaceutical industry representatives and seek additional information.

When trying to understand the actions of drug companies, those who are most critical of possible overmedication believe that money is the driving force behind decisions in the field. In approaches to research and development, advertising, promotions, ensuring consumer safety, lobbying, and forming alliances, there seem to be few important differences between the drug industry and other powerful industries. But whereas defective computers, clothing, and home entertainment systems are frustrating and lead to added expense, faulty or overprescribed medications can do harm and need to be understood in the context in which they were developed.

See also Ethical Issues; Marketing of Drugs; Medical Model of Mental Illness; Psychopharmacology

Bibliography

Akst, J. 2009. "Contract Research on the Rise." Retrieved from http://www.thescientist.com/blog/display/55878/.

Alliance for Human Research Protection. 2010. "Deadly Medicine: Foreign Clinical Trials-Vanity Fair." Retrieved from http://www.thenhf.com/article.php?id=2669.

Angell, M. 2009. "Drug Companies & Doctors: A Story of Corruption." Retrieved from http://www.nybooks.com/articles/archives/2009/jan/15/drug-companies-doctorsa-story-of-corruption/.

Baker, D. 2011. "The Trouble with Corporate Taxes." Retrieved from http://www.nytimes.com/roomfordebate/2011/02/01/the-trouble-with-corporate-taxes/to-overhaul-the-corporate-tax-code-start-with-drug-companies.

Batty, D. 2007. "Depression Is Overdiagnosed, Psychiatrist Claims." *The Guardian*, August 17. Retrieved from http://www.guardian.co.uk/lifeandstyle/2007/aug/17/world.health.

Bodenheimer, T. 2000. "Uneasy Alliance: Clinical Investigators and the Pharmaceutical Industry." *Health Policy Report* 342: 1539–1544.

CHADD (Children and Adults with Attention Deficit/Hyperactivity Disorder). 2012. "Mission Statement." Retrieved from http://www.chadd.org/Content/CHADD/AboutCH-ADD/Mission/default.htmCitizens Commission on Human Rights. n.d. Retrieved from http://www.cchrint.org/psycho-pharmaceutical-front-groups/dbsa-advisory-board/.

Eichenwald, K. and Kolata, G. 1999. "Drug Trials Hide Conflicts for Doctors." *The New York Times*, May 16.

Evans, D. 2010. "When Drug Makers' Profits Outweigh Penalties." *Bloomberg News*, March 21, G01.

Fuchs, V. 2001. "Physicians' Views of the Relative Importance of Thirty Medical Innovations." *Health Affairs* 30: 30–42.

Grassley, C. 2010. Letter to Ruth Hughes, Children and Adults with Attention Deficit/Hyperactivity Disorder (CHADD). May 4. Retrieved from http://www.grassley.senate.gov/about/upload/2011-05-04-CEG-Letter-to-CHADD.pdf.

Guenther, G. 1999. "Federal Taxation of the Drug Industry from 1990 to 1996." *Analyst in Business Taxation and Finance*, Congressional Research Service, December 13.

Hari, J. 2009. "The Horrifying Hidden Story Behind Drug Company Profits." Retrieved from http://www.huffingtonpost.com/johann-hari/the-horrifying-hidden-sto_b_251365.html.

Hilton, I. 2000. "A Bitter Pill for the World's Poor." Retrieved from http://www.guardian.co.uk/comment/story/0,3604,247568,00.html

Ismail, M. 2005. "Drug Lobby Second to None: How the Pharmaceutical Industry Gets Its Way in Washington." Retrieved from http://projects.publicintegrity.org/rx/report.aspx?aid=723.

Leavitt, F. 2003. *The REAL Drug Abusers*. Lanham, MD: Rowman & Littlefield.

Leavitt, J., and F. Leavitt. 2011. *Improving Medical Outcomes: The Psychology of Doctor/Patient Visits*. Lanham, MD: Rowman & Littlefield.

Moreno, C., G. Laje, C. Blanco, H. Jiang, A. B. Schmidt, and M. Olfson. 2007. "National Trends in the Outpatient Treatment of Bipolar Disorder in Youth." *Archives of General Psychiatry* 64: 1032–1039.

Moynihan, R., E. Doran, and D. Henry. 2008. "Disease Mongering Is Now Part of the Global Health Debate." *PLoS Medicine* 5: e106. doi:10.1371/journal.pmed.0050106.

Payer, L. 1992. *Disease-Mongers: How Doctors, Drug Companies, and Insurers Are Making You Feel Sick*. New York: Wiley.

Pierce, O., S. Shankman, and J. Larson. 2009. "Chart: Medicare Drug Plan Architects Now Drug Company Lobbyists." Retrieved from http://www.propublica.org/special/medicare-drug-plan-architects-now-drug-company-lobbyists-102009.

Rising, K., P. Bacchetti, and L. Bero. 2008. "Reporting Bias in Drug Trials Submitted to the Food and Drug Administration: Review of Publication and Presentation." *PLoS Medicine* 5: e217.

Silverstein, K. 1999. "Prozac.org: An Influential Mental Health Nonprofit Finds Its 'Grassroots' Watered by Pharmaceutical Millions." Retrieved from http://motherjones.com/politics/1999/11/prozacorg.

Stubbe, D. E., and W. J. Thomas. 2002. "A Survey of Early-Career Child and Adolescent Psychiatrists: Professional Activities and Perceptions." *Journal of the American Academy of Child and Adolescent Psychiatry* 41: 123–130.

TeenScreen. n.d. "The Key Players." Retrieved June 3, 2011, from http://www.teenscreentruth.com/teenscreen_key_players.html.

Weinstein, J. 2009. "Public Relations: Why Advocacy Beats DTC." Retrieved from http://pharmexec.findpharma.com/pharmexec/article/articleDetail.jsp?id=129300&sk=&date=&pageID=1.

Willis, J. 1977. "You and Patients Can Pull Together." *Pharmaceutical Marketing*, July, 26.

Wilson, D. 2010. "Side Effects May Include Lawsuits." Retrieved from http://www.nytimes.com/2010/10/03/business/03psych.html?emc=eta1.

Drug Therapy

See Psychopharmacology

E

Eating Disorders

Jennifer Couturier and James Lock

When most people think of eating disorders they think of celebrities who have suffered from them, including the singer-songwriter Karen Carpenter who eventually died from anorexia nervosa (AN) in 1983. Eating disorders are common conditions that have devastating effects on individuals and their families. According to the *Diagnostic and Statistical Manual of Mental Disorders* (American Psychiatric Association 2000), eating disorders are divided into three main categories consisting of anorexia nervosa (AN), bulimia nervosa (BN), and eating disorder not otherwise specified (EDNOS). The diagnostic symptoms of these disorders are presented in table in p. 234. Generally speaking, AN requires a low body weight, whereas BN affects individuals of normal weight but who have eating problems such as binge eating (eating large amounts of food in an uncontrolled way) and purging (vomiting, or using laxatives, or other means). Both disorders involve a restriction in food intake to various degrees, and a preoccupation with shape and weight. For a diagnosis of AN, there is a requirement that menstrual cycles have ceased for a period of three months. The third category, EDNOS, is reserved for those individuals who do not exactly fit into either of the other two diagnostic categories, but still have significant problems pertaining to eating and their thoughts or feelings about weight and shape. Often, children and adolescents fit into this category because they have been identified early and do not manifest all of the symptoms required, or they do not meet the duration of illness requirement for certain criteria for the diagnosis of AN (three months of amenorrhea) or BN (three months of binge eating and purging).

Problems Associated with Eating Disorders

In addition to behavioral symptoms, eating disorders have medical complications. Due to the effects of starvation in AN there can be problems with the heart, bones, and hormonal and fluid systems within the body, just to name a few examples. All muscles, including the heart muscle, can become weakened, causing the heart to beat irregularly or to fail completely. This can be a cause of death in AN. With starvation, menstrual cycles stop, and because of this, not enough calcium is deposited into the bones, leading to osteoporosis, a condition most often associated with older women who no longer menstruate. Future fertility can also be

Diagnostic Criteria for Eating Disorders

Anorexia Nervosa	Bulimia Nervosa	Eating Disorder Not Otherwise Specified
• Refusal to maintain body weight at or above a minimally normal weight for age and height • Intense fear of gaining weight or becoming fat • Body image disturbance, undue influence of weight or shape on self-evaluation, or denial of the seriousness of the current low body weight • Amenorrhea	• Recurrent episodes of binge eating, characterized by eating a large amount of food, and a sense of lack of control • Compensatory behavior to prevent weight gain (vomiting, laxatives, diuretics, fasting, exercise) • Binge eating and compensatory behaviors both occur about twice a week for three months • Self-evaluation is unduly influenced by shape or weight	• All of the criteria for AN are met, except for amenorrhea • All of the criteria for AN are met, except weight that despite significant weight loss, weight is in the normal range • All of the criteria for BN are met, except for the frequency and/or duration • Regular use of compensatory behavior after eating small amounts of food, when there is a normal body weight • Repeatedly chewing and spitting out food • Binge-eating disorder: recurrent episodes of binge eating that are not accompanied by compensatory behaviors

Specifications:
  Restricting or binge-eating/purging type
	Specifications:
	  Purging or nonpurging type	

Source: Adapted from the *DSM-IV-TR* (American Psychiatric Association 2000).

impacted by these hormonal changes. Fluid systems can be disrupted by dehydration, which can also cause death. Even the brain can be affected by starvation since not enough nutrients are taken in to nourish the brain. Brain scans have shown brain shrinkage during the illness. In children and adolescents, growth can be halted as there are not enough nutrients present to build muscle, bone, and tissue needed for growth. The mortality rate for AN is the highest of all psychiatric illnesses, and death is largely attributed to these medical complications, and to suicide (American Psychiatric Association Work Group on Eating Disorders 2000).

For BN, medical complications can be just as severe. These complications arise not from starvation but from binge eating and purging, which disrupt the delicate balance of chemicals in the body. For example, levels of potassium and sodium become out of balance. Since the heart relies on these elements to pump blood through the body, this leads to an inability of the heart to regulate its rhythm. As in AN, this can be a cause of death in BN. In addition, there can be severe damage to the teeth and the esophagus due to vomiting. Tears can occur in the esophagus, causing bleeding that can be very dangerous. Binge eating also has its dangers with the potential to cause the stomach to dilate and even rupture (Rome & Ammerman 2003).

In terms of the outcome or prognosis of eating disorders, there is still much to learn. Generally, for AN, the outcome appears to be good in about 50 to 70 percent of patients, with the others developing a more chronic illness that lasts many years and may lead to death. The course of AN is highly variable with some individuals recovering fully after a single episode, others experiencing many relapses and remissions, and still others chronically deteriorating over many years (American Psychiatric Association 2000). Estimated mortality rates are around 5 to 10 percent; there is, however, an approximate 1 percent increase in mortality risk for each year that the illness persists (American Psychiatric Association 2000; Steinhausen 2002). Outcome appears to be better for younger patients, for example, those who receive help for their illness in their teen years. Although many patients with AN recover in terms of weight restoration, enduring preoccupations about food and weight are common. In addition, of those initially diagnosed with AN, up to 40 percent go on to develop bulimic symptoms, and other psychological symptoms can persist including anxiety and depression. We know less about the long-term prognosis of BN. The overall success rate for patients receiving treatment is between 50 and 70 percent, although relapse rates are high (30–50%) (American Psychiatric Association Work Group on Eating Disorders 2000). Within clinic samples of patients with BN, symptoms appear to persist for at least several years. Often, patients are reluctant to seek treatment due to shame and embarrassment, and they may go untreated for many years. In any event, both AN and BN carry serious medical complications, and a significant proportion of individuals experience a chronic and debilitating course of illness.

How Common Are Eating Disorders?

Both AN and BN are much more common in females than in males, with over 90 percent of cases occurring in women. AN typically begins in mid- to late adolescence (American Psychiatric Association 2000). The average prevalence rate for AN is 0.3 to 0.5 percent for young females, and the incidence rate (number of new cases per year) is at least 8 per 100,000 people per year (American Psychiatric Association 2000). BN has a slightly later age of onset compared to AN, first occurring in late adolescence or early adulthood. The prevalence rate for BN is 1 to 3 percent, and the incidence rate is at least 12 per 100,000 people per year (American Psychiatric Association 2000). BN has been dramatically increasing in incidence since 1970, and there are actually no reports of BN prior to 1960. Gerald Russell (1979) first described this condition in the late 1970s. However, there is always a possibility that BN existed prior to 1960 in a hidden form of illness. There has been much debate over whether the incidence and prevalence of AN is increasing. Some reports indicate that the incidence rate of AN in 15- to 24-year-old females definitely increased over the past century, until the 1970s, while others suggest a modest increase in incidence in AN, after controlling for factors such as population size changes, female proportion of the population, and method of ascertainment of diagnosis. Agreement exists in the literature that AN was first described clearly by Gull in England and Lasegue in France almost simultaneously in the late nineteenth century. However, cases of self-starvation have been documented as early as the fifth and sixth centuries, but were attributed to demonic possession, and treated with exorcism.

Causes and Risk Factors

There has been much debate over the causes of eating disorders with many theories proposed, including dysfunctional families, the media's emphasis on appearance and the thin ideal, low self-esteem, and depression and anxiety, to name just a few. The bottom line is that we do not know what causes eating disorders. Dieting has long been associated with the development of eating disturbances and disorders. The evidence behind this theory comes from two sources. The first line of evidence is that patients who seek treatment for an eating disorder often report that dieting preceded the onset of their disorder, and the second comes from laboratory studies in which imposed dieting and restrained eating were related to the development of binge-eating behavior. The relationship between dieting and eating disorders appears to be the strongest for people who binge eat.

Historically, family dysfunction has been targeted as a cause of eating disorders. Families have been described as having poor structure and boundaries, being too close, too critical and conflictual, or too chaotic. However, in many of these studies, the timing of the family dysfunction in relation to the onset of the eating disorder has not been considered. It is now thought that these familial patterns of behavior might be a consequence of the presence of the illness rather than a cause. There are currently no longitudinal studies to determine the role of families as risk factors for eating disorders, and until these studies are completed, family dysfunction can be considered to be *related to* eating disorders—just as family dysfunction is related to many other types of chronic illnesses (Jacobi et al. 2004).

Biological factors may also be important in predisposing an individual to eating disorders. Although no genes have been identified as causative factors for eating disorders, it is thought that genetic vulnerability interacts with factors in the environment to culminate in an eating disorder. It is also thought that not only one gene is involved but that many genes contribute to the development of an eating disorder. A chemical found within the brain called serotonin has also been implicated as a potential causal factor in eating disorders. Serotonin abnormalities have been found in those patients currently ill with AN and BN and in those recovered from these illnesses. However, the time precedence of the serotonin abnormality has not been established, and it still remains unclear whether a serotonin abnormality was present before the illness developed.

Treatments

One of the difficulties in treating individuals with eating disorders is that very little research has been conducted, and there is only a small evidence base of treatment studies. Generally, there are two broad types of treatments that can be used: talking therapy, otherwise known as psychotherapy; and medication treatment, otherwise known as pharmacotherapy. There are also different types of settings in which these treatments are delivered: inpatient (in the hospital), outpatient (outside the hospital), and day treatment (partial hospitalization).

For adults with AN, there is actually very little data that provide clear support for any effective treatment. There is a slightly larger evidence base for treating adolescents with AN. For adolescents with AN, Russell, Szumkler, Dae, and Eisler (1987) found that those who had been ill for less than three years gained more weight with family therapy than with individual therapy. These benefits of family therapy were still apparent at the five-year follow-up point (Eisler et al. 1997). The type of family therapy used in this study, called "Maudsley Family Therapy" or "Family-Based Treatment" (Lock et al. 2001), views parents as capable of reintroducing food to their affected child and it also involves the siblings. This therapy goes against prior psychotherapeutic views of AN in which parents were viewed as too controlling and pathological, and instead views parents as the best resource for the ill child. The evidence base for family-based treatment for children and adolescents with AN is definitely growing, and this type of treatment has now been shown to be effective in several studies (Lock et al. 2005, 2010; Robin et al. 1999). In terms of medication treatment for AN, no rigorous clinical studies have shown medication to be of benefit in the acutely ill phase of AN.

For patients suffering from BN, the first line of treatment for which there is the most evidence is outpatient psychotherapy, with cognitive-behavioral therapy (CBT) specifically modified for patients with BN (Fairburn, Marcus, & Wilson 1993). Another type of psychotherapy, called interpersonal psychotherapy (IPT), has also been shown to be effective in patients with BN, but it may take longer to notice beneficial effects as compared to CBT (Agras et al. 2000). Whereas CBT focuses on cognitions or thoughts related to binge eating and purging, IPT focuses on relationships and feelings and their association with the eating disorder. Family therapy for adolescents with BN has also recently been shown to be effective (Le Grange et al. 2007). In terms of medication for BN, many studies have confirmed that antidepressants reduce binge frequency (Walsh & Klein 2003; Zhu & Walsh 2002). The FDA has approved the antidepressant fluoxetine for treating BN.

Eating Disorders and Society

The comprehensive costs of eating disorders to individuals, families, and society are difficult to summarize because costs are not reflected merely in the monetary expense of treatment but also in the years of productive life lost and the burden of illness shouldered by individuals and their families. In terms of treatment costs, AN is just as costly or even more costly than treatments for schizophrenia (Striegel-Moore et al. 2000). This is largely attributable to the use of hospitalization. In terms of societal burden, there is the cost to the health care system of hospitalization along with medical and psychiatric care. There is also the loss of productive years of life when patients are too ill to work or study, and from the elevated rates of premature death. With the advent of managed care in the United States, and the lack of empirically supported treatments for AN, treatment coverage under insurers has become difficult (Lock 2003). This increases the financial and emotional burden on families that may already be struggling to manage.

Future Research

Much more research is needed in the field of eating disorders. We currently know little about the causes of eating disorders, and longitudinal studies might aid in answering these questions. However, such studies are expensive to carry out and likely will not change the evolution of these disorders, as many risk factors are not modifiable. Much of the research currently being done with patients with eating disorders is focused on possible genetic links and examines families with two or more ED patients. It is hoped that common genes can be found. In addition, imaging studies looking at the structure and function of the brains of ill and recovered patients is providing new information about the neurochemistry involved in eating disorders. Studies focusing on those already ill within the early stages of the illness in adolescence appear most promising. When the illness becomes more chronic in adulthood, treatment compliance is even more problematic and prognosis is poor. Our best chance of intervention appears to be in adolescence, when the illness is developing and parents can have more of an impact in getting their child help.

See also Adolescence and Mental Health; Depression; Mind and Body Approaches to Mental Health; Preventative Mental Health Programs; Self-Injury and Body Image; Suicide and Suicide Prevention

Bibliography

Agras, W. S., T. Walsh, C. G. Fairburn, G. T. Wilson, and H. C. Kraemer. 2000. A Multicenter Comparison of Cognitive-Behavioral Therapy and Interpersonal Psychotherapy for Bulimia Nervosa. *Archives of General Psychiatry* 57(5): 459–466.

American Psychiatric Association. 2000. *Diagnostic and Statistical Manual of Mental Disorders* (4th ed., text rev.). Washington, DC: American Psychiatric Publishing.

American Psychiatric Association Work Group on Eating Disorders. 2000. "Practice Guideline for the Treatment of Patients with Eating Disorders (Revision)." *American Journal of Psychiatry* 157(1 Suppl): 1–39.

Eisler, I., C. Dare, G. F. Russell, G. Szmukler, D. le Grange, and E. Dodge. 1997. "Family and Individual Therapy in Anorexia Nervosa: A 5-Year Follow-Up." *Archives of General Psychiatry* 54(11): 1025–1030.

Fairburn, Christopher G., Marsha D Marcus, and G. Terence Wilson. 1993. "Cognitive-Behavioral Therapy for Binge Eating and Bulimia Nervosa: A Comprehensive Treatment Manual." In C. G. Fairburn and G. T. Wilson, eds., *Binge Eating: Nature, Assessment, and Treatment* (pp. 361–404). New York: Guilford Press.

le Grange, D., R. D. Crosby, P. J. Rathouz, and B. L. Leventhal. 2007. "A Randomized Controlled Comparison of Family-Based Treatment and Supportive Psychotherapy for Adolescent Bulimia Nervosa." *Archives of General Psychiatry* 64(9): 1049–1056.

Jacobi, C., C. Hayward, M. de Zwaan, H. C. Kraemer, and W. S. Agras. 2004. "Coming to Terms with Risk Factors for Eating Disorders: Application of Risk Terminology and Suggestions for a General Taxonomy." *Psychological Bulletin* 130(1): 19–65.

Lock, J. 2003. A Health Service Perspective on Anorexia Nervosa. *Eating Disorders* 11: 197–207.

Lock, J., W. S. Agras, S. Bryson, and H. C. Kraemer. 2005. A comparison of short- and long-term family therapy for adolescent anorexia nervosa. *Journal of the American Academy of Child and Adolescent Psychiatry* 44(7): 632–639.

Lock, J., D. le Grange, W. S. Agras, and C. Dare. 2001. *Treatment Manual for Anorexia Nervosa: A Family-Based Approach*. New York: Guilford Press.

Lock, J., D. Le Grange, W. S. Agras, A. Moye, S. W. Bryson, and B. Jo. 2010. "Randomized Clinical Trial Comparing Family-Based Treatment with Adolescent-Focused Individual Therapy for Adolescents with Anorexia Nervosa." *Archives of General Psychiatry* 67(10): 1025–1032.

National Eating Disorders Association. http://www.nationaleatingdisorders.org.

National Institute of Mental Health. 2011. "Eating Disorders." Retrieved from http://www.nimh.nih.gov/health/publications/eating-disorders/complete-index.shtml.

Robin, A. L., P. T. Siegel, A. W. Moye, M. Gilroy, A. B. Dennis, and A. Sikand. 1999. "A Controlled Comparison of Family versus Individual Therapy for Adolescents with Anorexia Nervosa." *Journal of the American Academy of Child and Adolescent Psychiatry* 38(12): 1482–1489.

Rome, E. S., and S. Ammerman. 2003. "Medical Complications of Eating Disorders: An Update." *Journal of Adolescent Health* 33(6): 418–426.

Russell, G. F. 1979. "Bulimia Nervosa: An Ominous Variant of Anorexia Nervosa." *Psychological Medicine* 9: 429–448.

Russell, G. F., G. I. Szmukler, C. Dare, and I. Eisler. 1987. "An Evaluation of Family Therapy in Anorexia Nervosa and Bulimia Nervosa." *Archives of General Psychiatry* 44(12): 1047–1056.

Steinhausen, H. C. 2002. "The Outcome of Anorexia Nervosa in the 20th Century." *American Journal of Psychiatry* 159(8): 1284–1293.

Striegel-Moore, R. H., D. Leslie, S. A. Petrill, V. Garvin, and R. A. Rosenheck. 2000. "One-Year Use and Cost of Inpatient and Outpatient Services among Female and Male Patients with an Eating Disorder: Evidence from a National Database of Health Insurance Claims." *International Journal of Eating Disorders* 27(4): 381–389.

Stryer, S. B. *Anorexia*. Westport, CT: Greenwood Press.

Walsh, B. T., and D. A. Klein. 2003. "Eating Disorders." *International Review of Psychiatry* 15(3): 205–216.

Zhu, A. J., and B. T. Walsh. 2002. "Pharmacologic Treatment of Eating Disorders." *Canadian Journal of Psychiatry* 47(3): 227–234.

Economic Issues

See Poverty, Unemployment, Income Inequality, and Mental Health; Public Policy Issues; State Mental Health Agencies

Elder Abuse and Neglect

Kellye S. Carver, Kyle S. Page, and Bert Hayslip Jr.

As compared to child abuse and domestic violence, the attention given to elder abuse is much more recent (Krienert, Walsh, & Turner 2009). Yet abuse of elders can take many forms, ranging from physical harm to neglect of care, and it is of particular concern because it affects persons who cannot often defend themselves against assault or exploitation. Understanding and awareness of elder abuse, however, allows for better recognition, reporting, and prevention of this inexcusable crime.

Defining Elder Abuse

Understanding elder abuse is challenging owing in part to a lack of recognition and underreporting of the crime (Acierno et al. 2010; Cyphers 1999) as well as to the phenomenon being underresearched (Lachs & Pillemer 1995). Recognition and research are further hampered by vague or inconsistent definitions, means of recording reported cases, and local legal requirements (Acierno et al. 2010; Choi & Mayer 2000; Jogerst et al. 2003; National Center on Elder Abuse [NCEA] 2007a).

Despite the lack of consensus on what actually constitutes abuse, there have been recent attempts to clarify and standardize definitions of elder abuse to address this problem. Generally speaking, elder abuse falls into three categories: domestic abuse, institutional abuse, and self-neglect/self-abuse (NCEA 2007a). The NCEA (2011) further identifies six different forms of elder abuse, although older adults are rarely subjected to just one type of abuse (Choi & Mayer 2000). We discuss these types of abuse below. Generally speaking, elder abuse is considered "elder" when it occurs in any person over the age of 65, although the age criteria can vary from state to state.

Physical abuse includes injuring elders, causing physical pain, or using medications improperly (e.g., denying needed medicine, overdosing; NCEA 2011). This type of abuse may result in bruises, lacerations, broken bones, cuts, sprains, burns, internal injuries, broken eyeglasses, or medication misuse, including the withholding of medication (Choi & Mayer 2000; Cyphers 1999; NCEA 2011). *Emotional or psychological abuse*, on the other hand, involves causing "mental pain" (NCEA 2011). This may occur verbally with threats, humiliation, insults, intimidation, or verbal harassment, as well as nonverbally, as with ignoring the elder, treating them like a child, or forcing them into social isolation (Choi & Mayer 2000; Cyphers 1999; Lachs & Pillemer 1995; NCEA 2011). Older adults may become irritated, withdrawn, embarrassed, or depressed as a result (NCEA 2011). Understandably, physical abuse is more readily recognized than is emotional or psychological abuse (Childs, Hayslip, & Radika 2000).

Sexual abuse includes any unwanted sexual contact that violates the elder, including touching, rape, forced nudity, and sexually explicit photography (Cyphers 1999; NCEA 2011). It may result in bruises or blood in genital areas, as well as diseases or infections (NCEA 2011). In addition, sexual and other types of abuse are not uncommon in nursing homes (Ulsperger & Knottnerus 2011). If the abuse of an older woman has been committed by a family member, available data suggest that it is typically a son, and thus is incestual in nature. If the victim is male, the abuser is more likely to be a friend, and in such cases, fondling is the most common form of sexual abuse, especially by facility staff in long-term care institutions. Though it is perhaps less common, spousal abuse is not unheard of, and may represent a long-standing pattern of domestic violence. When the family member is the abuser, it becomes increasingly difficult to convince the elder that it is best to separate from a son or husband, or have that person arrested. In such cases, feelings of profound betrayal and a loss of trust are paramount. Despite the often violent and intrusive nature of elder sexual abuse, abusers are indeed seeking sexual gratification from someone who is frail or cognitively impaired. These characteristics differentiate sexual abuse and other forms of elder mistreatment. Even when sexual abuse is long-standing in nature, older victims may not be fully examined by physicians, or their complaints and concerns may not be taken seriously not only by health care professionals but also, in some cases, by family members themselves. Importantly, the elder may have more physical and emotional difficulty in recovering from an attack, assault, or rape. Infection or breaking of bones may accompany such abuse, complicating matters further for both the elder and the family (see Baker, Sugar, & Eckert 2009; Burgess 2006; Ramsey-Klawsnik 2003).

Financial or material exploitation involves handling an elder's money, property, belongings, or other assets without permission or legal rights (NCEA 2011). Abusers may add their name to the elder's credit cards, combine bank accounts, transfer assets, forge the elder's signature, steal checks or possessions, or make unauthorized withdrawals. They may also make illegal use of the elder's property or belongings (Lachs & Pillemer 1995; NCEA 2011). In this respect, inconsistencies between the nature of an elder's living situation and socioeconomic status or income are often cues that some form of financial abuse or exploitation are present.

Abandonment occurs when a caregiver or responsible party (e.g., nurse) deserts an elder; this can and does take place in a wide variety of public and private settings, such as hospitals, nursing homes, or shopping malls (NCEA 2011). Similarly, *neglect* occurs when responsible parties such as legal guardians or caregivers fail to meet the basic needs of an elder (e.g., food, water, housing, medical care, personal safety; NCEA 2011). This includes not obtaining needed services or medications for the elder and/or not carrying them out appropriately, whether intentionally or unintentionally (Choi & Mayer 2000; Lachs & Pillemer 1995; NCEA 2011). As a result, elders may suffer from malnutrition, bed sores, unacceptable living conditions, or poor hygiene (NCEA 2011).

Self-neglect takes place when elders unknowingly place their own health or life in jeopardy and is most prevalent among women and the oldest elders (Cyphers 1999; NCEA 2011). Self-neglected elders present with many of the same symptoms as those who are neglected (NCEA 2011), although this is sometimes considered a form of elder abuse. Elders who are cognizant of their behaviors and aware of the dangers do not fall into this category (Cyphers 1999).

Prevalence of Elder Abuse

The National Elder Abuse Incidence Study estimated that almost 500,000 individuals endured elder abuse in 1996. This number increased by over 100,000 with the inclusion of self-neglect (Cyphers 1999). Among mistreated older adults, neglect was most prevalent, affecting almost half of the elders (49.9%), followed by emotional abuse (35%), financial exploitation (30%), physical abuse (26%), and abandonment (4%; Cyphers 1999).

More recent results indicate over 489,000 incidents of elder abuse and neglect among 35 states (some states were not included because of differences in state data collection and organization as well as the research design used), with rates believed to be higher when estimating the 15 remaining states' incidence of abuse (Jogerst et al. 2003). In addition, Acierno et al. (2010) interviewed almost 6,000 older adults across the United States and found that almost 5 percent of elders (age 60 and older) reported emotional abuse, almost 2 percent reported physical abuse, and around 1 percent reported sexual abuse. Considering that most studies use self-reported incidence or an examination of available records, the prevalence of abuse may be much higher than reflected in current work, affecting as many as 10 percent of elders (Santos & King 2010).

Elder abuse also occurs within hospitals and prisons (Lachs & Pillemer 1995, 2004; NCEA 2007a; Stojkovic 2007), although very little research has examined abuse in these environments (Ramsey-Klawsnik et al. 2008). Perhaps reflecting their greater vulnerability, older persons are sometimes abused sexually in nursing homes and assisted-living centers (see Ramsey-Klawsnik et al. 2008; Ulsperger & Knottnerus 2011), wherein perpetrators are frequently male (usually a facility staff or another resident) and are often easily identified when investigated. Severely impaired residents, particularly females, are at highest risk of being abused, and abusive acts include molestation and rape (Ramsey-Klawsnik et al. 2008; Teaster et al. 2007).

Risk Factors for Abuse: Characteristics of the Elder

Risk factors vary for each type of abuse; however, unemployment, exposure to prior trauma, and a history of domestic violence seem to be somewhat consistent risk factors (Acierno et al. 2010; NCEA 2007b). Most victims are white (Krienert, Walsh, & Turner, 2009; Ploeg et al. 2009). Not surprisingly, physical frailty and health problems may put elders at higher risk for abuse by others (see Lachs & Pillemer 1995; NCEA 2007b). Functionally impaired older adults who rely on others for care have a higher probability of being abused as well (Acierno et al. 2010; Choi & Mayer 2000; Cyphers 1999), although the evidence appears to be inconclusive (see Lachs & Pillemer 2004; NCEA 2007b). Living with the abuser is relatively common (see Krienert, Walsh, & Turner 2009; NCEA 2007b; Ploeg et al. 2009), although living alone increases the likelihood that an elder will neglect themselves or be financially exploited (Choi & Mayer 2000; see also Lachs & Pillemer 2004). Similarly, substance and alcohol abuse put elders at higher risk for self-neglect, as they are less able to look after themselves (Choi & Mayer 2000). Indeed, observing the behavior of an older person in the presence of a potential abuser is often revealing of such abuse; such persons are often fearful, rarely finish their sentences, or are uncharacteristically quiet.

Those elders who exhibit confusion, dementia, cognitive impairment, or mental illness (particularly depression) are also at a higher risk for abuse (Cyphers 1999; see also Lachs & Pillemer 1995, 2004). In these situations, characteristics of the caregiver (such as anxiety, depression, stress, less education) and the care recipient (physically assaultive or aggressive) are known to increase the risk for abuse (Wiglesworth et al. 2010). Cognitive impairment is particularly salient in cases of financial exploitation (Choi & Mayer 2000).

The roles of gender and age, however, are unclear. Cyphers (1999) found that women are victimized two to three times more often than men, particularly when considering emotional/psychological abuse and financial exploitation. Conversely, Acierno et al. (2010) found that neither gender was more likely than the other to suffer abuse with other factors being equal. Furthermore, the oldest cohort of older adults, often called the old-old (age 80+), may be much more likely to be abused (Cyphers 1999), while other researchers have found the young-old elders (between 60 and 70) to be most at risk (Acierno et al. 2010).

Prevalence rates of elder abuse among minority groups are also inconsistent. Some research reflects that African American elders may be overrepresented in certain types of abuse, whereas members of the Latino community and other minority groups seem to report less elder abuse (Cyphers 1999). Other research notes no differences between racial groups when other factors are equal (Acierno et al. 2010). Differential rates of elder abuse across minority groups may also reflect differences in cultural identity, perceptions of abuse, the role of family, ethnic or racial heritage, socioeconomic status, or country of birth (see Parra-Cardona et al. 2007; Tauriac & Scruggs 2006). According to Acierno et al. (2010), self-neglect was more prevalent among minority groups as well as older adults who had lower incomes, less social support, or declining health.

Risk Factors for Abuse: Characteristics of the Offender

Ramsey-Klawsnik (2000) posited that offenders fit into one of five categories: Some are overwhelmed with the stress of caregiving; others may be well intentioned but impaired and unable to give proper care; still others may be narcissistic, considering only their own needs and how an older adult can benefit them. Finally, two particularly dangerous types of offenders are those who are domineering or sadistic; these individuals are intentionally hurtful and controlling toward others, often feeling that the abuse is deserved (Ramsey-Klawsnik 2000).

Sometimes elder abuse is the result of domestic abuse that continues into old age (NCEA 2007b), or caregiver stress may become overwhelming for the abuser, leading to abusive behaviors (NCEA 2007b). The abuser may also have a mental illness, a history of violence, a substance abuse problem, or be dependent on the elder for financial support or housing (NCEA 2007b, 2007c; Ploeg et al. 2009; see also Lachs & Pillemer 1995, 2004). Ages of perpetrators vary, with many being middle aged (age 40 or older; Cyphers 1999; Krienert et al. 2009), although financial exploiters are often markedly younger (Cyphers 1999). For many victims (60–90%), the abuser comes from within his or her own family—usually a spouse or adult child (Cyphers 1999; Kreinert et al. 2009; NCEA 2007b, 2007c; Ploeg et al. 2009), particularly in cases of physical and psychological abuse (Choi & Mayer 2000). However, abuse by acquaintances is also common (Kreinert et al. 2009); financial exploitation may be the exception, wherein abusers are frequently strangers (Choi & Mayer 2000).

The role of the gender of the offender is unclear as a risk factor. Men and women may commit elder abuse relatively equally, although it may be expressed in different ways: some research has found that men are more likely to abuse elders, while women are more likely to neglect them (Cyphers 1999). Other research notes that perpetrators are male almost 75 percent of the time (Krienert, Walsh, & Turner 2009).

Reporting Elder Abuse

It may be difficult to recognize elder abuse, as the symptoms of abuse are often similar to those of age-related health problems (Lachs & Pillemer 2004). Unfortunately, screening techniques are largely ineffective (e.g., the victim may try to hide the abuse, unclear definitions of abuse within the health professions), and even successful screening or intervention may result in either no change or a worse situation for the victim. Instead, elder abuse awareness may provide the best chance for abuse recognition and prevention (Lachs & Pillemer 2004). In this respect, a lack of knowledge, stereotypically negative views about older persons, fear of retribution by the abuse, fear of being removed from their or of being institutionalized, embarrassment, or a fear of abandonment may all contribute to the underreporting of elder abuse.

By 1985, most states had initiated laws for elder abuse reporting, investigation, and penalties, although these laws were quite varied and inconsistent (see Jogerst et al. 2003). Even Adult Protective Service (APS) definitions of elder abuse can vary between states and make reporting or investigating elder abuse difficult (Choi & Mayer 2000). Most states now have mandatory reporting laws, meaning that anyone with knowledge of elder abuse is required to report the abuse to authorities, no matter what their relationship to the elder may be; in these cases, a failure to report leads to legal action (Jogerst et al. 2003; Teaster 2000). Thus being proactive and/or acting on a considered hunch or even casual observation is key to identifying abuse and/or preventing it from worsening or persisting.

Reports of elder abuse usually come from family members, hospital staff, police, friends/neighbors, or in-home service providers (Cyphers 1999). Agencies like APS or the Area Agency on Aging are responsible for following up on reports (Bergeron 2000; NCEA 2010). Unfortunately, these agencies are often underfunded, understaffed, and often, staff may be asked to follow unclear or inconsistent laws when conducting investigations, particularly between states (Bergeron 2000). For example, laws differ in who is covered under the law (e.g., only "incapacitated" or "vulnerable" elders instead of all elders), who is obligated to report abuse, reporting methods, what penalties are, and where final authority rests (Bergeron 2000; Bergeron & Gray 2003; Jogerst et al. 2003; NCEA 2007a). Jogerst et al. (2003) found that on average, almost half of reports (44.8%) appear to be substantiated. However, states also vary in how many reports are substantiated, depending on such factors as the number of elderly persons living in the state, mandates to report, clarity of elder abuse definitions/laws, report-tracking practices, and the level of public awareness (Jogerst et al. 2003).

Intervention and Treatment for Elder Abuse

Practitioners may be able to offer health, social, or legal services to victims (Bergeron 2000; Bergeron & Gray 2003; NCEA 2010), although intervention can be difficult. As an example, some states require the practitioner to gain the elder's permission before becoming involved (Bergeron 2000; Bergeron & Gray 2003). The older adult may also refuse any services recommended by APS. In these situations, it may be necessary for practitioners to examine the older adult's cognitive capabilities—an often difficult and complex assessment—or the presence of learned helplessness (i.e., the older adult is so fearful of their abuser, they are unable to make a decision; Bergeron 2000). If the elder is indeed able to make sound decisions but refuses help, clinicians must respect elders' rights to autonomy and simply provide the elder with information and alternatives as appropriate (Lachs & Pillemer 1995). In many cases, APS services also include interventions for the perpetrator in hopes of preventing further abuse (Bergeron 2000).

When offering alternatives or interventions, APS officials must consider cultural, socioeconomic, and other factors. For example, community resources for younger victims are often inappropriate for elders (e.g., domestic violence safe houses often exclude males or have no handicap access). Elders also have fewer options for earning an income, securing another residence, or obtaining more help by themselves (Bergeron 2000). Bergeron (2000) states that the unique needs of elders require a "creative" (44) service delivery approach, causing many frustrated APS agencies to appeal to the government for additional funding and support.

After systematically reviewing the available research, Ploeg, Fear, Hutchison, MacMillan, and Bolan (2009) noted a lack of research on interventions for elder abuse and "insufficient evidence to support any particular intervention" for the abused elder, perpetrators, or health care professional (206). Interventions involving community programs, religious or spiritual support, support groups, assessment, and case management may be beneficial but need to be subjected to further research (Brownell & Wolden 2002; Ploeg et al. 2009). It could be argued that any form of intervention, whether it be preventative or remedial, is beneficial. Indeed, understanding intervention at many levels (Danish 1981) is critical to preventing and treating both the offender and the abused older adult. Thus educating the public, providing respite care to stressed caregivers, and changing societal views about older persons are equally important in this respect, especially as the large group of baby boomers moves into old age.

See also Alzheimer's Disease and Other Dementias; Hospitalization; Social Work in Mental Health; State Mental Health Agencies

Bibliography

Acierno, Ron, Melba A. Hernandez, Ananda B. Amstadter, Heidi S. Resnick, Kenneth Steve, Wendy Muzzy, and Dean G. Kilpatrick. 2010. "Prevalence and Correlates of

Emotional, Physical, Sexual, and Financial Abuse and Potential Neglect in the United States: The National Elder Mistreatment Study." *American Journal of Public Health* 100(2): 292–297.

Baker, M., N. Sugar, and L. Eckert. 2009. "Sexual Assault of Older Women: Risk and Vulnerability by Living Arrangement." *Sexuality Research and Social Policy* 6: 79–87.

Bergeron, L. Rene. 2000. "Servicing the Needs of Elder Abuse Victims." *Policy and Practice* 58: 40–45.

Bergeron, L. Rene, and Betsey Gray. 2003. "Ethical Dilemmas of Reporting Suspected Elder Abuse." *Social Work* 48(1): 96–105.

Brownell, Patricia, and Agata Wolden. 2002. "Elder Abuse Intervention Strategies: Social Service or Criminal Justice?" *Journal of Gerontological Social Work* 40(1/2): 83–100.

Burgess, A. W. 2006. "Sexual Abuse, Trauma and Dementia in the Elderly: A Retrospective Study of 294 Cases." *Victims and Offenders* 1: 193–204.

Childs, H., B. Hayslip, and L. Radika. 2000. "Young and Middle Aged Adults' Perceptions of Elder Abuse." *The Gerontologist* 40: 75–85.

Choi, Namkee G., and James Mayer. 2000. "Elder Abuse, Neglect, and Exploitation: Risk Factors and Prevention Strategies." *Journal of Gerontological Social Work* 33(2): 5–25.

Cyphers, Gary C. 1999. "Out of the Shadows: Elder Abuse and Neglect." *Policy & Practice of Public Human Services* 57(3): 25–30.

Danish, S. 1981. "Life Span Development and Intervention: A Necessary Link." *The Counseling Psychologist* 9: 40–43.

Jogerst, Gerald J., Jeanette M. Daly, Margaret F. Brinig, Jeffrey D. Dawson, Gretchen A. Schmuch, and Jerry G. Ingram. 2003. "Domestic Elder Abuse and the Law." *American Journal of Public Health* 93(12): 2131–2136.

Krienert, Jessie L., Jeffrey A. Walsh, and Moriah Turner. 2009. "Elderly in America: A Descriptive Study of Elder Abuse Examining National Incident-Based Reporting System (NIBRS) Data, 2000–2005." *Journal of Elder Abuse & Neglect* 21(4): 325–345.

Lachs, Mark S., and Karl Pillemer. 1995. "Abuse and Neglect of Elderly Persons." *New England Journal of Medicine* 332(7): 437–443.

Lachs, Mark S., and Karl Pillemer. 2004. "Elder Abuse." *Lancet* 364: 1263–1272.

Nahmiash, D. 2006. "Abuse and Neglect of Older Adults: What Do We Know about It and How Can We Identify It?" In T. G. Plante, ed., *Mental Disorders of the New Millennium: Vol. 2: Public and Social Problems* (pp. 47–67). Westport, CT: Praeger.

National Center on Elder Abuse. 2007a. "Elder Abuse/Mistreatment Defined." Retrieved from http://www.ncea.aoa.gov/NCEAroot/Main_Site/FAQ/Basics/ Definition .aspx.

National Center on Elder Abuse. 2007b. "Risk Factors for Elder Abuse." Retrieved from http://www.ncea.aoa.gov/NCEAroot/Main_Site/ FAQ/Basics/Risk_Factors.aspx.

National Center on Elder Abuse. 2007c. "Who Are the Abusers?" Retrieved from http://www.ncea.aoa.gov/NCEAroot/Main_Site/FAQ/Basics/Abusers.aspx.

National Center on Elder Abuse. 2010. "The Community Response." Retrieved from http://www.ncea.aoa.gov/NCEAroot/Main_Site/FAQ/Basics/Who_Responds.aspx.

National Center on Elder Abuse. 2011. "Major Types of Elder Abuse." Retrieved from http://www.ncea.aoa.gov/NCEAroot/Main_Site/FAQ/Basics/Types_Of_Abuse.aspx.

Parra-Cardona, Jose R., Emily Meyer, Lawrence Schiamberg, and Lori Post. 2007. "Elder Abuse and Neglect in Latino Families: An Ecological and Culturally Relevant Theoretical Framework for Clinical Practice." *Family Process* 46(4): 451–470.

Ploeg, Jenny, Jana Fear, Brian Hutchison, Harriet MacMillan, and Gale Bolan. 2009. "A Systematic Review of Interventions for Elder Abuse." *Journal of Elder Abuse & Neglect* 21: 187–210.

Ramsey-Klawsnik, Holly. 2000. "Elder-Abuse Offenders: A Typology." *Generations* 24(2): 17–22.

Ramsey-Klawsnik, Holly. 2003. "Elder Sexual Abuse within the Family." *Journal of Elder Abuse and Neglect* 15: 43–58.

Ramsey-Klawsnik, Holly, Pamela B. Teaster, Marta S. Mendiondo, Jennifer L. Marcum, and Erin L. Abner. 2008. "Sexual Predators Who Target Elders: Findings from the First National Study of Sexual Abuse in Care Facilities." *Journal of Elder Abuse & Neglect* 20(4): 353–376.

Santos, E. J., and D. A. King. 2010. "The Assessment of Elder Abuse." In P. A. Lichtenberg, ed., *Handbook of Assessment in Clinical Gerontology* (pp. 229–243). San Diego, CA: Academic Press.

Stojkovic, S. 2007. "Elderly Prisoners: A Growing and Forgotten Group within Correctional Systems Vulnerable to Elder Abuse." *Journal of Elder Abuse & Neglect* 19(3–4): 97–117.

Tauriac, Jesse J., and Natoschia Scruggs. 2006. "Elder Abuse among African Americans." *Educational Gerontology* 32: 37–48.

Teaster, Pamela B. 2000. "A Response to the Abuse of Vulnerable Adults: The 2000 Survey of State Adult Protective Services." Washington, DC: National Center on Elder Abuse.

Teaster, Pamela B., Holly Ramsey-Klawsnik, Marta S. Mendiondo, Erin Abner, Kara Cecil, and Mary Tooms. 2007. "From Behind the Shadows: A Profile of the Sexual Abuse of Older Men Residing in Nursing Homes." *Journal of Elder Abuse and Neglect* 19(1–2): 29–45.

Ulsperger, J. S., and J. D. Knottnerus. 2011. *Rituals of Abuse in Nursing Homes: What You Can Do about It.* Boulder, CO: Paradigm.

Wiglesworth, Aileen, Laura Mosqueda, Ruth Mulnard, Solomon Liao, Lisa Gibbs, and William Fitzgerald. 2010. "Screening for Abuse and Neglect of People with Dementia." *Journal of the American Geriatrics Society* 58: 493–500.

Electroconvulsive Therapy

Timothy Kneeland

Electroconvulsive therapy (ECT) is the application of electrical current to the brain to induce a tonic-clonic (or "gran mal") seizure and ameliorate the symptoms of mental illness. After ECT was invented in 1938 by the Italian psychiatrist Ugo Cerletti, it became the most successful of the somatic medical remedies invented during the interwar years to combat the chronic and untreatable mental diseases of the era, which included schizophrenia, major depressions, acute manias, and paresis (a neurological disorder). At the time of the invention of ECT, and other somatic remedies, many patients were doomed to a live out their lives in the often inhumane conditions of state mental institutions, which were over-crowded and underfunded. The population of the chronic mentally ill had risen in the first years of the twentieth century, prompting both European and American physicians to seek a remedy for the public health crisis in new somatic inter-ventions or heroic measures to rescue patients from a life of insanity.

Emergence of ECT

The first significant somatic treatment was developed in 1917 when Julius Wagner von Jauregg (1857–1920) discovered that following a high fever some of his mental patients became calmer and more coherent. To induce fevers he began injecting patients with a benign strain of malaria that generated a therapeu-tic fever as high as 105°. Fever therapy became a standard treatment for patients suffering from paresis, the end stage of neurosyphilis, before the advent of anti-biotics. For his insight Wagner-Juaregg was awarded the Noble Prize in Medicine in 1927, and his treatment, called fever therapy, was utilized in at state institutions in the United States into the 1950s (Braslow 1997).

Manfred Sakel (1900–1957) discovered, through an accidental overdose, that placing patients with schizophrenia into an insulin coma could alleviate the psy-chotic symptoms of mental disease. Sakel experimented with insulin shock, as the treatment came to be called, until he discerned that the best practice was to induce a daily insulin coma, lasting for at least an hour, over a period of 10 days or longer. Following a course of treatments by insulin shock, Sakel claimed that patients evinced increased lucidity, a markedly friendlier attitude, and enhanced communicative skills. Sakel boasted that his intervention had an 88 percent suc-cess rate in treating schizophrenia. In the absence of other therapies, insulin shock was adopted in both Europe and the United States, but was abandoned in the early 1950s with the advent of ECT (Valenstein 1986).

Ladislas von Meduna (1896–1964) was a neuropsychiatric researcher who studied the brain. After conducting autopsies on the brains of both epileptics and schizo-phrenics, he concluded that schizophrenics had a deficiency of glia tissue in their hippocampus while epileptics had an overabundance. If schizophrenics could be given an artificial gran mal seizure, perhaps they would develop more tissue in this region and diminish the symptoms of schizophrenia? Thus he developed a new con-vulsive treatment for schizophrenia. After first trying and rejecting camphor in oil, he found pentylenetetrazol (Metrazol or Cardazol) more effective. Clinical trials with the convulsive treatment indicated that schizophrenics did show signs of remission after their convulsive treatments. From its first use in 1936 until the middle decade of the twentieth century, this treatment was used frequently on schizophrenics and showed good results for patients who had only recently fallen ill (Braslow 1997).

The Italian psychiatrist Ugo Cerletti (1877–1963) was well aware of the new heroic measures but was most interested in the effects of Metrazol to induce convulsions. Cerletti wanted an even more efficient and controlled method to induce seizures than Metrazol. He and his assistant, Lucio Bini, began experimenting on dogs to determine if a nonlethal dose of electricity could be applied directly to the brain. After a series of successful experiments on dogs, Cerletti tried Electroshock, his name for the procedure, on his first patient, a schizophrenic who had been brought to Cerletti's clinic by the local police. To send the patient into seizure Cerletti tried several combinations of electrical application until he found the proper voltage and duration of electricity to generate a convulsive seizure. The patient was given electroconvulsive treatments from April to May of 1938, and after only one month of electroconvulsive therapy he showed sufficient remediation of his symptoms that he was released from the hospital (Shorter & Healy 2007).

ECT in the United States

The procedure for electroconvulsive therapy has evolved considerably from Cerletti's time. Initially it consisted of sending 70–100 volts of electricity through the brain via two electrodes placed on the temples. The tonic-clonic seizures the electrical current induced sent the body into a thrashing convulsion and patients flailed about on the table, often breaking bones, biting their tongues, and involuntarily urinating, defecating, or ejaculating. Treatments were given daily for upwards of two weeks or more, and occasionally more than one treatment was given per day. Although of short duration the procedure was difficult for the untrained to watch, but the results far outweighed any concerns of that time. Treatment provided temporary respite from psychoses and neuroses and allowed institutionalized patients to return home. Thus ECT became a highly prized treatment that replaced nearly every other somatic approach available in the interwar years, including hydrotherapy, fever therapy, insulin shock, metrazol shock, and lobotomies. Despite fears that the technique caused brain damage and memory impairment, it was adopted for a wide variety of psychoses and neuroses, and for patients as young as 2 or as old as 100 (Kneeland & Warren 2008).

Invented on the eve of the Second World War, ECT was brought to the United States by psychiatrists fleeing the Nazis, including David Impastato, Victor Gonda, Renato Almansi, and Lothar Kalinowsky. Once it was established in the United States, ECT was used to treat a spectrum of illnesses from anxiety and depression to schizophrenia. The treatment was easy to use, was more effective than any competing treatment, and was quickly established as the leading treatment for nearly every mental disease, including such "diseases" as homosexuality, cross-dressing, and nymphomania—behaviors that, at that time, were deemed to be psychological disorders. It was employed by psychiatrists, psychoanalysts, and general practitioners, and it could be found as a therapeutic tool in large state mental institutions, in private hospitals, and at the local doctor's office. Some doctors even made house calls with their portable ECT machines (Kneeland & Warren 2008).

ECT was the gold standard of somatic treatments in the United States until the invention in the 1950s of new drug therapies such as chlorpromazine (CPZ), or Thorazine, for treating psychosis (Healy 2004). Following the development of pharmacological treatments for the management of schizophrenia and major and minor depressive episodes, ECT declined greatly in use. The marketing campaign mounted by drug manufacturers was directed to physicians, psychiatrists, and state legislatures. Chlorpromazine, only eight months after its introduction, was already being used on 2 million patients suffering a range of psychotic ailments. ECT's hegemony in state mental wards began a steady decline (Kneeland & Warren 2008).

Decline of ECT

Electroconvulsive therapy was further challenged when new medications to treat depressive illnesses, the tricyclid and monamine oxidase inhibators, were introduced (Healy 1999) for depression and anxiety. As a result of the new medications, psychoanalysts, psychotherapists, and psychologists suggested alternate treatments that employed prescription drugs together with occupational therapy, talk therapy, or behavior therapy. This undercut the use of ECT in private hospitals and private practice (Kneeland & Warren 2008).

Following on the heels of new medications in the 1950s, there was an outbreak of antipsychiatric writings in the 1960s. Intellectuals and academics such as Erving Goffman, David Rothman, and Michel Foucault challenged the entire field of psychiatry, which triggered a political and social backlash aimed at state mental institutions and their treatment of the mentally ill. Journalists began to publically expose institutions for malpractices, including the use of somatic treatments such as ECT as a form of punishment, and the physical and sexual abuse of patients by staff. Patients and their families began to challenge the institutions in court and to demand the right to refuse treatment as part of the basic civil rights guaranteed to all citizens. In response, new legislation was passed to provide for patients' rights, and federal policy moved away from building new institutions for the mentally ill to closing them down. The process, sometimes called deinstitutionalization, led to a steep decline in hospitalized patients and increased reliance on drug therapy (Grob 2011).

In the 1960s and 1970s, several former mental patients who had been treated with ECT claimed that they had permanent brain damage resulting from their experience. They attacked the practice of electroconvulsive therapy as barbaric and called for a complete ban on its use. Among the leading figures in this movement was Leonard Roy Frank, who published a thorough and impressive text attacking ECT and demonstrating its abuses entitled *The History of Shock Therapy*. In 1973 Frank and Wade Hudson founded the Network against Psychiatric Assault (NAPA), which organized to protest all forms of psychiatric abuse. At about the same time, Ted Chabinski, who received shock as a child, started the *Madness Network News*, a publication devoted to patient advocacy. In the late 1970s Marilyn Rice, a former employee with the Department of Commerce, experienced significant memory loss following treatment with ECT and founded the Committee for Truth in Psychiatry (CTIP) in the early 1980s, which sought, among other things, to have the FDA ban electroconvulsive shock machines. After Rice died in 1992, CTIP continued under the direction of another ECT survivor, Linda Andre (Andre 2009).

ECT was indicted in novels such as Ken Kesey's *One Flew over the Cuckoo's Nest* (1962), documentaries such as Richard Cohen's *Hurry Tomorrow* (1975), and the film version of *One Flew over the Cuckoo's Nest* (1975). As a result of growing antipathy to psychiatry and ECT, a growing number of patients were inspired to speak out about their treatment, which they said left them more damaged than when they were first admitted to the hospital (Shorter & Healy 2007). By the mid-1970s ECT was no longer viewed as a "cure," and psychiatric practice and training shifted away from somatic therapies to pharmacology and psychotherapy (Fink 2002).

Recent Changes and Critiques

ECT was considered disreputable in the media and popular culture through the 1970s and 1980s, but it was never wholly abandoned by practitioners. Led by Max Fink, Richard Abrams, Harold Sackheim, and Richard Weiner, the methods for employing ECT were revised and the treatment was restored and became a reputable treatment for mental illness at the end of the twentieth century. New machines and techniques were introduced in the 1970s to deliver the electrical current in a series of brief pulses, to send the electricity through one side of the brain (unilateral), to monitor seizure duration, and to provide patients with muscle relaxers and sedatives prior to the procedure. Given muscle relaxants, patients now remain practically motionless on the table. Medication inhibits their secretions, and only their twitching toes are visible to the naked eye. At one time, practitioners observed the convulsion to assess the effectiveness of the treatment, but now the seizure is unseen and is detected by a series of machines that monitor the patients and assess the effectiveness of the seizure (Fink 2002; Kneeland & Warren 2008).

In addition to the modifications to the practice of electroconvulsive therapy, the return of ECT was aided by the discovery that even as the United States became the "Prozac nation," the pharmacological treatment of mental illness was no magic bullet. Drug therapies have their own set of side effects, can create dependency, and do not work for all patients. Antidepressant drugs work well in only 60 to 70 percent of cases in ameliorating depression. Proponents of ECT claim an 80 to 90 percent response rate. Antidepressants such as Elavil caused blurred vision, dry mouth, intestinal discomfort, sexual dysfunction, weight gain, and sleep disturbance. Prozac may cause sexual dysfunction, and even when taking the prescribed regimen patients have reported having bouts of severe depression in an effect called "Prozac poop-out." Prozac may be addictive with the symptoms of withdrawal mimicking that of depression. Hence, the need for treatment inspired a renewed use of ECT. ECT is now commonly used on patients who did not respond to drug therapy, have suicidal ideation, or have conditions that counter indicate the use of medication. Currently, the most likely candidates for ECT include elderly patients and pregnant women. Thus ECT has returned and continues to be employed in a variety of mental disorders (Fink 2002).

One of the significant critiques of ECT has been the side effect of memory loss. There are four kinds of memory loss associated with ECT, running the gamut from very mild to significant memory impairment. All patients are subject to a postictal (i.e., postconvulsion) disorientation that lasts for a few hours. Patients are also likely to suffer anterograde amnesia and will not remember any new information received during or after their treatment. More troubling for patients is a short-term retrograde amnesia that may create memory gaps of a few days or weeks leading up to their treatment. The most serious memory damage occurs when patients suffer retrograde memory loss of months or years. The problem of memory impairment continues to generate controversy, and despite the milder procedures for employing ECT, critics of the practice remain unconvinced that "modified ECT" is any less barbaric or dangerous (Andre 2009; Payne & Prudic 2009).

In 2003, assessing the effectiveness of ECT in a series of depressed Israeli patients, Bernard ("Benny") Lerer (1948–), director of the Biological Laboratory of Hadassah University Hospital in Ein Karem, Israel, said to a journalist from the newspaper *Haaretz*, "Have you ever asked yourself how it is that a treatment with such a terrible stigma, a treatment that the public is afraid of and [that] is said to be primitive and unhelpful—has, despite all this, survived into the 21st century, and not in obscure little places but in the world's most advanced medical centers? The answer is simple. Because it works."

—Edward Shorter

Source: Edward Shorter, *A Historical Dictionary of Psychiatry* (New York: Oxford University Press, 2005), 95.

The mechanism for how exactly ECT remediates mental illness remains, even today, unknown. There have been hundreds of ideas suggested as to why ECT works. Ugo Cerletti, who created the practice, continued to believe Meduna's postulate regarding the difference between the brains of epileptics and those of schizophrenics. Believing that he could isolate the source of that difference, Cerletti himself abandoned ECT. Some have suggested that the memory defects created by ECT might be the mechanism of action. Lucio Bini, Cerletti's associate, advocated what he termed "annihilation therapy," or multiple, repeated, daily dosages of shock on psychotic patients to obliterate faulty neural pathways. Other ideas on the efficacy of ECT drew on psychology. Noting that even though patients do not recall their procedure, almost all patients in the 1940s and 1950s expressed dread at the thought of receiving it; one psychologist said that the fear of ECT would lead patients to escape to health rather than face more treatment. One physician suggested that it satisfied a patient's need for punishment, that the seizure released the patient's pent-up aggression and hostility through the violent muscular convulsions (Gordon 1948).

Physiological theories about electroshock have been nearly as speculative. One early theory was that the shock produced some slight brain damage that erased the most recent neurological structures of the high brain area and thereby erased chemical pathways, thus eliminating the cognitive and somatic circumstances that precipitated mental illness. Recent research has centered on the hippocampus, where there has been evidence that ECT encourages the growth of new neurons in this region of the brain. Studies have already shown that mental disorders attack and inhibit neuron growth in this region. Thus ECT might provide a respite and regeneration of neural mechanisms. Researchers have also hypothesized that the efficacy is due to the release of neuropeptides and hormones such as prolactin, thyrotrophin, and vasopressin, which are released following ECT. Studies have also discovered that the brain responds to electroshock by functionally suppressing the convulsive effects, and it has been speculated that the resulting suppression of neural activity may be the key element of the therapeutic effect of electroconvulsive therapy (Payne & Prudic 2009).

Conclusion

Despite current debates over its specific mechanism of action, controversies over its potentially harmful side effects, and the lingering stigma of shock treatment in popular culture, electroconvulsive therapy is increasingly being employed in the practice of psychiatry, not as a measure of last resort but as an alternative to other therapies. Potential clinical uses for ECT are regularly identified in the medical literature and by proponents of the treatment such as Max Fink, thus ensuring its continued and likely expansive use into the twenty-first century.

See also Chronic Mental Illness; Ethical Issues; History of Mental Health Care; Hospitalization; Involuntary Treatment; Memory and Disorders of Memory; Psychiatry; Rights of Patients with Mental Health Conditions; Stigma

Bibliography

Abrams, Richard. 1997. *Electroconvulsive Therapy* (3rd ed.). New York: Oxford University Press.

Andre, Linda. 2009. *Doctors of Deception: What They Don't Want You to Know about Shock Treatment*. Piscataway, NJ: Rutgers University Press.

Braslow, Joel. 1997. *Mental Ills and Bodily Cures: Psychiatric Treatment in the First Half of the Twentieth Century*. Berkeley: University of California Press.

Cohen, Richard, dir. 1975. *Hurry Tomorrow*. Richard Cohen Films. DVD.

Fink, Max. 2002. *Electroshock: Healing Mental Illness*. New York: Oxford University Press.

Forman, Milos, dir. 1975. *One Flew over the Cuckoo's Nest*. United Artists.

Foucault, Michel. 1964. *Madness and Civilization: A History of an Idea in the Age of Reason*. New York: Pantheon.

Frank, Leonard Roy. 1978. *The History of Shock Therapy*. San Francisco: Leonard Roy Frank.

Goffman, Erving. 1961. *Asylums: Essays on the Social Situation of Mental Patients and Other Inmates*. New York: Anchor Books.

Gordon, Hirch. 1948. "Fifty Shock Therapy Theories." *Military Surgeon* 103: 397–401.

Grob, Gerald. 2011. *The Mad among Us: A History of the Care of America's Mentally Ill*. New York: Basic Books.

Healy, David. 1999. *The Anti-Depressant Era*. Cambridge, MA: Harvard University Press.

Healy, David. 2004. *The Creation of Psychopharmacology*. Cambridge, MA: Harvard University Press.

Kesey, Ken. 1962. *One Flew over the Cuckoo's Nest*. New York: Viking Press.

Kneeland, Timothy. 1996. "The Use of Electricity to Treat Mental Illness in the United States, 1870–Present." Unpublished doctoral dissertation, University of Oklahoma.

Kneeland, Timothy, and Carol Warren. 2008. *Pushbutton Psychiatry: A Cultural History of Electroshock in America*. Walnut Creek, CA: Left Coast Press.

Payne, Nancy, and Joan Prudic. 2009. "Electroconvulsive Therapy: Part I: A Perspective on the Evolution of Current Practice of ECT." *Journal of Psychiatric Practice* 15: 346–348.

Rothman, David. 1971. *The Discovery of the Asylum*. Boston: Little. Brown.

Sackheim, Harold. 1985. "The Case for ECT." *Psychology Today* 19: 36–40.

Shorter, Edward. 1997. *A History of Psychiatry: From the Age of the Asylum to the Age of the Prozac*. New York: Wiley.

Shorter, Edward, and David Healy. 2007. *Shock Therapy: A History of Electroconvulsive Treatment in Mental Illness*. Piscataway, NJ: Rutgers University Press.

Valenstein, Elliot S. 1986. *Great and Desperate Cures: The Rise and Decline of Psychosurgery and Other Radical Treatments for Mental Illness*. New York: Basic Books.

Weiner, Richard. 2001. *The Practice of Electroconvulsive Therapy: Recommendations for Treatment, Training and Privileging* (2nd ed.). Washington, DC: American Psychiatric Publishing.

Emergency Services

Susan Stefan

People with psychiatric disabilities have the greatest need for caring mental health services during psychiatric crises and emergencies. Yet first responders to these crises—police, emergency medical technicians (EMTs), and emergency department personnel—rarely have substantial training in handling psychiatric issues, with unfortunate and unpredictable consequences, including traumatic experiences on all sides, and sometimes injuries and death (Avery 2003; Stefan 2006).

However, because police, EMTs, and emergency departments are often the only available service at night and on weekends, people in psychiatric crisis and their families and providers frequently have little choice but to call 911 in an emergency. In addition, because of the scarcity of traditional mental health resources, people with psychiatric disabilities sometimes use emergency services for nonemergency psychiatric needs. Emergency services are used during "off-hours" by people who are suicidal, but also by those who just want to talk, just as they are used by people with urgent medical needs, by those who need prescription refills, and, sometimes, by people who have nowhere to eat or sleep. Hospital emergency departments (EDs) serve millions of people with psychiatric disabilities every year, far more than state hospitals or even the correctional system, and yet people with psychiatric disabilities constitute a relatively small percentage of the total volume of an ED (Centers for Disease Control 2011; Substance Abuse and Mental Health Services Administration 2011). Consequently, most hospital ED staff do not develop expertise in serving people with psychiatric disabilities (Institute of Medicine 2007).

Hospital EDs are far from optimal settings for an individual in psychiatric crisis (Miccio 2011; Stefan 2006). There are much better (and far less expensive) alternatives that currently exist and succeed in serving people in psychiatric crisis. Overuse of hospital EDs by people with psychiatric disabilities is a key indicator that the state's mental health programs are failing to provide these necessary crisis services in the community (Catalano, McConnell, Forster et al. 2003; Stefan 2006).

This entry will describe different types of emergency services for people with psychiatric disabilities, and the underlying theories that drive each of them. The entry will give examples of a variety of crisis services across the country and will list the core components of an effective community psychiatric crisis system.

Psychiatric Emergency Service Settings: The Current Reality
Hospital Emergency Departments

Hospital emergency departments see more individuals with psychiatric disabilities than any other setting. In 2010, state hospitals held about 49,000 beds (National Association of State Mental Health Program Directors Research

Institute 2011). Hospital emergency departments, by comparison, saw more than 4 million people in 2008 whose primary diagnosis was "mental disorders" (Centers for Disease Control 2011).

Although people whose complaints primarily arise from "mental disorders" constitute only about 3.3 percent of all visitors to emergency departments, they present difficulties to emergency departments out of proportion to their numbers (Institute of Medicine 2007). People with psychiatric disabilities wait twice as long in emergency departments as people with medical issues, thus taking up beds at about twice their nominal rate of presentation. They are also far more likely to be assessed as needing inpatient admission than people who present with medical issues, which contributes substantially to the delay. There is some reason to believe that a substantial number of these admissions are unnecessary. Statistics show that emergency departments are more likely to institutionalize a patient than a community evaluator (i.e., a clinician not part of a hospital or ED). Unless an ED evaluator has a great deal of mental health experience, "finding a bed" is often seen as the best disposition, even for patients who are calm and want to go home. Sometimes people in psychiatric crisis actually deteriorate because of the long waits and the environment of the emergency department. Emergency departments are rushed, overloaded, and cannot offer the slow, quiet, calming environment or hours of time to listen and counsel a desperate or confused or agitated individual.

Emergency departments are most useful when the cause of apparently psychiatric symptoms is an underlying medical condition: urinary tract infections in elderly patients, thyroid imbalance in persons presenting with a first psychiatric break, toxicity due to kidney problems, intoxication with various substances (Cresswell, Riccio, & McCabe 2008). However, these situations are relatively rare and can often be determined without sophisticated tests. For the most part, EDs can offer little to people in psychiatric crisis beyond temporary containment, medication, screening, and assistance with dispositional alternatives. Their advantages in psychiatric emergencies are their ubiquity and the fact that all hospital emergency departments must, by federal law, provide assessment services to people in psychiatric emergencies.

Psychiatric Emergency Services

A new specialty of emergency psychiatry has emerged in the past two decades, in tandem with the growth of psychiatric emergency services (Allen 1999; American Psychiatric Association Task Force on Psychiatric Emergency Services 2002; Currier 2003). Some states and urban areas have specialized psychiatric emergency departments, called "C-PEPs" ("comprehensive psychiatric emergency programs") in New York and PES ("psychiatric emergency services") in other parts of the country. These emergency departments are sometimes attached to hospitals and are sometimes freestanding. Some have additional services, such as mobile outreach and crisis beds. Unlike traditional hospital emergency departments, they are characterized by having on-site psychiatric staffing available at least eight hours a day (Currier 2003). Unfortunately, they are generally available only in major urban areas, and they do not necessarily reduce wait times. The advantages of psychiatric emergency services are that, like emergency departments, they are generally open around the clock and can provide medical evaluations; unlike most hospital emergency departments, they have staff well versed in mental health conditions and treatment, are less likely to restrain patients, and are more likely to divert patients from inpatient admission.

Community Crisis Locations

Some states, such as Massachusetts, have statewide walk-in locations in the community where an individual in psychiatric crisis can speak to a trained professional or peer counselor. The Massachusetts Behavioral Health Partnership has an excellent description of the model for these services (Massachusetts Behavioral Health Partnership n.d.). Like psychiatric emergency services, community crisis locations often have mobile and respite components, and may also house a "warm line" service, which is telephone counseling for people who are not necessarily suicidal but would like to talk to someone in order to avert the development of a crisis. The most effective community crisis locations offer a variety of different services. The Mental Health Center of Dane County, Wisconsin, which has received international recognition, offers a multiplicity of services geared to children, the elderly, people from Southeast Asia, and people with substance abuse issues, and an ED diversion program where people in crisis are given a room in a house operated by trained volunteers (Mental Health Center of Dane County n.d.).

Community sites may not be open 24/7, which greatly undermines their effectiveness, and there are often eligibility requirements for services. Individuals, families, treatment providers, and police may be insufficiently aware of their existence to access them during a crisis. The advantages of community crisis locations is that they may divert or prevent unnecessary hospitalization, and frequently people can be seen more quickly than in many hospital settings, and more time can be spent understanding the nature of their problems. Staff are often less medical-model oriented and more oriented to solving social problems.

Peer-Run Crisis Services

Peer-run crisis services are crisis services developed and operated by people who have been diagnosed with a psychiatric disability, and who have experienced psychiatric crises of their own. These services can include respite houses, home visits, peer accompaniment or assistance in emergency department settings, and warm lines.

Peer-run crisis services are available in many states. The National Empowerment Center lists peer-run crisis services across the nation, describing different models of services (National Empowerment Center n.d.). The most sophisticated and comprehensive peer crisis services are found in upstate New York, where Steven Miccio operates a system including peers in emergency department settings, two respite houses, in-home peer companions, and peer advocates in community health clinics. In addition, he has written a manual to enable others to develop peer-run hospital diversion services (Miccio 2012).

The Rose House in Poughkeepsie, New York, offers stays of five days in a home setting, where the individual in crisis is referred to as a "guest" rather than a patient, and his or her strengths are emphasized. The individual is encouraged to engage in artwork and conversation. The individual rarely waits long to access this service. However, not everyone is eligible or appropriate: the respite house does not accept homeless people, and guests are expected to manage their own meals, hygiene, and medication management. (Miccio 2012). Independence and recovery are promoted, rather than the dependence fostered by institutional environments.

What Are the Key Components of an Effective Community-Based Emergency Services System?

A community-based psychiatric emergency service system must be accessible in every sense of the word: it must operate 24/7 and be easily accessed, in terms of both transportation and eligibility requirements. It should have a telephone line answered by a knowledgeable and trained person who can provide counseling, triage, and referrals, at all hours of the day and night. There should be capacity for any language that is spoken by a substantial proportion of the local population.

An effective community-based emergency services system must have 24/7 mobile capacity with a deadline for responding to calls in person and a respite or crisis bed component. It must be staffed sufficiently to provide assessment and evaluation, crisis intervention and counseling, medication assistance, case management, assistance with practical problems such as housing and health care, and, optimally, some follow-up. It must be able to maintain data on the services it provides in order to continually improve services and assure continued funding.

An effective community-based psychiatric emergency service system is well known within the community and coordinates with police, schools, and community- and hospital-based mental health providers. A number of standards for psychiatric emergency services exist (American Psychiatric Association 2002; Miccio 2012; Stefan 2006). Most of these standards underscore that providing effective psychiatric emergency services requires a culture that is understanding, empathic, and compassionate, and that understands the role of patience and collaboration in helping a person who is in crisis. A substantial number of programs have shown that

---

Types of Emergency Psychiatric Services

The **traditional theory of psychiatric emergency services** held by most emergency department staff is that

- The principal job of emergency department staff is to assess, triage, and contain the patient.
- Mental illness is a medical/biological condition best responded to by appropriate medication.
- Most patients in psychiatric crisis require inpatient hospitalization to receive needed treatment.

Community crisis intervention service principles and practices differ from hospital-based emergency services in the following ways:

- They attempt to problem solve social problems underlying psychiatric emergencies, including housing, insurance, domestic violence, and trauma.
- They place a stronger emphasis on psychiatric emergencies as triggered or mediated by psychosocial stressors as a supplement to or substitute for the medical model of illness.
- They understand that the role of a community crisis center is to help the individual avert hospitalization and stay in the community.

Peer run services differ across states but most embody the following values and principles:

- The principal goal of peer run crisis services is to promote recovery and empowerment and provide hope.
- Psychiatric crisis is seen as emotional distress.
- The role of the peer services is to provide a safe place for the crisis to be processed as an opportunity to grow, learn and change.

---

these services can be provided more effectively and at less cost in the community than in hospital emergency departments, which are "at the breaking point" (Institute of Medicine 2007). Replicating those models is hard work and requires organization, funding, and political will—but it can be done (Miccio 2011).

See also Community Mental Health; Homelessness and Mental Illness; Hospitalization; Involuntary Treatment; Peer Support Groups; Rural Mental Health Services; State Mental Health Agencies; Undiagnosed Mental Illness

Bibliography

Allen, Michael. 1999. "Level 1 Psychiatric Emergency Services: The Tools of the Crisis Sector." *Psychiatric Clinics of North America* 22: 713–734.

American Psychiatric Association Task Force on Psychiatric Emergency Services. 2002. *Report and Recommendations Regarding Psychiatric Emergency and Crisis*

Services: A Review and Model Program Descriptions. Washington, DC: American Psychiatric Press.

Avery, Michael. 2003. "Unreasonable Seizures of Unreasonable People: Defining the Totality of the Circumstances Relevant to Assessing Police Use of Force against Emotionally Disturbed People." *Columbia Human Rights Law Review* 2003: 261–332.

Catalano, Ralph, William McConnell, Peter Forster, Bentson McFarland, and Dorothy Thornton. 2003. "Psychiatric Emergency Services and the System of Care." *Psychiatric Services* 2003: 351–355.

Centers for Disease Control, National Center for Health Statistics. 2011. National Hospital Ambulatory Medical Care Survey: 2008 Emergency Department Summary Tables. Retrieved from http://www.cdc.gov/nchs/data/ahcd/nhamcs_emergency/nhamcsec.

Cresswell, Lawrence H., Dustin M. Riccio, and John B. McCabe. 2008. "Medical Evaluation of Behavioral Emergencies." In Rachel L. Glick, Jon S. Berlin, Avram B. Fishkind and Scott Zeller, eds., *Emergency Psychiatry: Principles and Practice* (pp. 45–57). Philadelphia: Lippincott, Williams & Wilkins.

Currier, Glenn. 2003. "Organization and Function of Academic Psychiatric Emergency Services." *General Hospital Psychiatry* 25: 124–129.

Institute of Medicine. 2007. *Hospital-Based Emergency Care: At the Breaking Point.* Washington, DC: National Academies Press.

Massachusetts Behavioral Health Partnership. n.d. "Draft Performance Specifications." Retrieved from http://www.masspartnership.com/provider/pdf/ESPRFRAppendices.pdf.

Mental Health Center of Dane County. n.d. "Services." http://www.mhcdc.org/Services/services.html.

Miccio, S. 2011. *Hospital Diversion Services: A Manual on Assisting in the Development of a Respite/Diversion Service in Your Area.* Poughkeepsie, NY: People Inc.

National Empowerment Center. n.d. "Directory of Peer-Run Crisis Respites." http://www.power2u.org/peer-run-crisis-alternatives.html.

Stefan, Susan. 2006. *Emergency Department Treatment of the Psychiatric Patient: Policy Issues and Legal Requirements.* Oxford: Oxford University Press.

Substance Abuse and Mental Health Services Administration. 2011. "Funding and Characteristics of State Mental Health Agencies 2009." Retrieved from http://www.store.samhsa.gov/product/Funding-and-Characteristics-of-State-Mental-Health-Agencies-2009/SMA11-4655.

Ethical Issues

Christian Perring

Abuse of the Mentally Ill: A History of a Maligned Group

It is important to understand current debates about the rights and moral status of people with mental illness in historical and cultural context. Setting out the history of the treatment of people with mental illnesses is difficult because much of it is not well recorded, it is often not clear what conditions in the past correspond with our current categories of mental illness, and judgments about the treatment of people with mental illness need to take into account the overall social conditions of the time. Furthermore, it is often debatable whether what now appears as abuse was simply due to mistaken theories about the causes of mental illness, or whether it was the result of malice toward people who are different. Nevertheless, despite these difficulties, it is clear that there have been many episodes where the mentally ill have been mistreated.

In fifteenth-century Europe, many people whose behavior was strange were judged to be possessed by devils, to be under a hex, or to be witches. To have their demons cast out, they would undergo exorcisms, give confessions, visit holy shrines, or participate in religious ceremonies (King, Viney, & Woody 2009). In the sixteenth and seventeenth centuries, there were witch hunts in Europe and in New England; those accused of witchcraft were subject to painful and harmful forms of questioning, to unfair trials, and to public execution by burning.

Naturalistic explanations of bizarre behavior, which had always been available, came to replace the supernatural explanations almost completely by the end of the eighteenth century. The first hospitals had admitted patients with mental illnesses as early as the fourteenth century, but psychiatric institutions really started in the eighteenth and nineteenth centuries in Europe and the United States. Inside them, however, much of the treatment of patients was dismal and inhumane.

The most famous episode of humane treatment in psychiatric history was when French physician Philippe Pinel (1745–1826), working at the Bicêtre hospital in Paris, improved the condition of patients at the end of the eighteenth century. They lived in overcrowded, dirty spaces, and were confined by chains. Pinel introduced treatment that freed them of their chains and gave them better living conditions. This has served as an example of the way that modern medical approaches can recognize the humanity of people who were previously treated as less than human. Pinel's treatment of his patients, which consisted of talk with a therapist and support, has been an inspiration for humanistic psychology (King, Viney, & Woody 2009).

Much of the history of psychiatry in the nineteenth and twentieth century replays the story of barbaric treatment or conditions for patients being improved by reformers; and yet these reforms are not permanent in their effects, nor do they, however well intentioned, result in the desired improvement in life experience for the mentally ill. In England, after the bad treatment and death of a Quaker woman suffering from melancholy at the York Asylum, William Tuke (1732–1822) started the York Retreat in 1796. This was based on principles of providing a pleasant environment, not restraining the patients, and giving them useful tasks to perform. However, this approach did not become widespread. In the United States, Benjamin Rush (1745–1813) is known both for his humanitarian attitude toward the treatment of mental illness and for his invention of treatments that strike us today as cruel—namely, the gyrator and the tranquilizing chair. The first was a contraption that spun patients around to push more blood into their heads, and the second was a restraining device meant to stop movement. Dorothea Dix (1802–1887) devoted decades of her life to reforming prisons and asylums in Massachusetts and other states, and her efforts helped to improve the public appreciation for treatment of mental illnesses. Unfortunately, the treatment provided by the mental institutions she helped to establish deteriorated after the Civil War.

In both the United States and the United Kingdom, the population of mental institutions grew steadily until the mid-1950s, when public awareness of poor conditions and political concerns about the cost of housing and the care of such a large number of patients led to policies of deinstitutionalization. Over several decades, large mental hospitals were closed, and the residents were moved to smaller facilities, halfway houses, or care in the community; many moved back with their families, or they became homeless. In the latter half of the twentieth century and at the start of the twenty-first, one of the most pressing questions faced by industrialized countries has been how much long-term care can be provided for the chronically mentally ill, and what forms of treatment are most effective and thus the best use of scarce resources.

In recent years, there has been growing awareness of ethical issues in the representation of people with mental illness: their depiction in drama, art, film, and TV; the words used to refer to them in everyday speech and official documents; and the ways in which psychological theory conceptualizes them. The main worry is that the images, plotlines, and words used fail to respect the dignity of people with mental illness and instead represent them in stereotypes or in demeaning ways. There therefore has been an increased focus on how to include people with mental illness in positive, three-dimensional ways that do not perpetuate stigma (Corrigan 2005).

The Rights of the Mentally Ill and When to Take Away Freedom, Force Treatment, or Break Confidentiality

In the second half of the twentieth century, there was increasing recognition that people with mental illness have rights, and increasing debate over which rights they should forsake as a result of their reduced competence to make rational decisions and the possible effects that their choices would have on themselves or others. There is general agreement that when people are clearly not competent as a result of mental illness and represent a danger to themselves or others, then society has the right and even the responsibility to override the individual's wishes and prevent him or her from causing harm. There is much less agreement as to what counts as competence and how to judge whether a person has it. There is no universal legal standard of competence in the United States, although there are some guidelines and precedents about how to assess competence. Furthermore, there is also dispute as to what counts as being a danger, and there is enormous difficulty in predicting who will be dangerous.

Debates over the nature of competence are complex: they analyze what it is to be able to understand one's choices and make decisions rationally, and whether we should have a set threshold for competence or some kind of sliding scale according to which the more competent a person is, the more control over his or her life is to be allowed (Saks 2002). In understanding rational decision making, we need to pay attention not only to a person's ability to foresee the possible consequences of the choices available to him or her and how such choices may affect his or her life and the lives of other people, but also to the person's ability to appreciate the meaning and significance of the various possibilities. In other words, people arguably need not only cognitive abilities but also appropriate emotional responses to be competent. At the same time, we respect people's abilities to form their own values in idiosyncratic ways, and we need to be careful about insisting that they must share our values in order for us to agree to their competence. On top of this, we need to remember that people *without* mental illness are far from being perfectly rational, and therefore it is important not to hold people *with* mental illness to an unrealistic standard.

If a person is judged incompetent, the next stage is working out what to do. If they pose no danger to themselves or to others, then it may not be necessary to do anything. Assessing whether a person is a risk to themselves or others is inevitably an imprecise judgment. Depriving people of freedom, by confining them or making them accept treatment, is a major step. Since there will always be errors in judgment, it means that there will always be competent people who are deprived of their rights, and there will be incompetent people whose behavior is unchecked. The policy decision will be in working out which sort of undesired consequence is worse. There are also issues of who should be making decisions for incompetent people with mental disorders: family members, doctors, judges, or social workers, for instance (Buchanan & Brock 1989).

Thus the debates about when to force mentally ill people into treatment or put them in hospitals or even prisons for the safety of society are complex and have important ramifications for the rest of society.

Working Out What Is Best for the Mentally Ill: Difficult Decisions and Controversial Treatments

We have already seen that in the past, treatments that were given to those with mental illness may have been well intentioned but they were nevertheless dangerous and abusive. The problem persists in the present day: in recent history, there have been controversial treatments such as lobotomy, induced insulin comas, antipsychotic medication with disabling side effects, electroshock treatments, antidepressants that have caused suicidal behavior, and a host of fringe approaches to treating mental illness, many or most of which have been considered problematic

(Valenstein 1986; Whitaker 2001). There is also a long-standing debate over the efficacy of medication versus psychotherapy and the comparative cost-efficiency of these two approaches (Kirsch 2010). Many of these debates are not settled, and it may turn out that the purportedly unhelpful or dangerous treatments are in fact helpful. However, one of the biggest ethical issues facing health care providers, policy makers, patients, and families of patients is what to do about treatment while these treatments remain controversial. Nearly all medical treatments carry some risk or cause some harm, and the decision cannot be based on avoiding all risk and harm. Rather, it must be concerned with how to minimize risk or harm and how to maximize the possible benefits. Sorting out the matter is made more difficult by the fact that questions have been raised about the neutrality of the scientific process that creates and tests treatments; the pharmaceutical industry, in particular, has come under sustained criticism for corrupting the scientific process (Angell 2004).

The ideal solution would be to have sound scientific backing for all psychiatric treatments—and, indeed, there is a trend toward making all treatment evidence based. However, there is still debate about whether this is the best way for medicine to proceed and what role this leaves for clinical judgment (Miles 2008; Parker 2002). While a complete scientific basis for psychiatry is an ideal goal, it is clear that we are not currently in a position to have fully tested treatments available, and this leaves room for judgment for clinicians in working out how to operate in the absence of complete information.

When to Hold Mentally Ill People Legally and Morally Responsible for Their Actions

One of the most difficult areas of psychiatric ethics concerns when to hold people with mental illnesses socially accountable for their actions, and how to respond to those who have hurt others or pose a danger to others. Courts have developed an insanity defense for people who were psychotic at the time of committing a crime, with the key elements being that a person does not understand what he or she is doing or cannot determine the wrongness or rightness of it. There is a long legal history of different formulations of this defense, and different approaches to placing the burden of proof on the defendant's side or the prosecution's side. Although there have been some attempts to extend the insanity defense to cases of compulsive action (as in those suffering from obsessive-compulsive disorder), they have not been successful (Robinson 1996).

While the insanity defense does not apply to compulsive action, or to substance abuse, sexual disorders, or personality disorders, there is still a great deal of discussion as to what extent people with these conditions should be blamed and punished when they harm others through their symptomatic actions. One of the issues is what we mean by compulsive action, and to what extent having a strong desire to do something takes away the person's responsibility for doing it. Often with addiction, for example, the action of consuming drugs or alcohol, or even the acts of theft, lying, and crime associated with obtaining drugs or alcohol, are put under a medical model: all are seen as symptoms of a disease of addiction. Thus one can debate the implications of seeing addiction as a disease in terms of holding the person responsible for his or her actions, and one can ask, further, whether the medical model is appropriate for addiction (Ross et al. 2010).

The diagnostic category of psychopath, along with a set of related personality disorders (antisocial, borderline, narcissistic, and histrionic), has been controversial since its inception, and there has been particular controversy as to whether it is reasonable to hold people who have been given one of these diagnoses morally responsible for actions that have harmed others. The Hare Psychopathy Checklist-Revised, now the standard tool for diagnosing psychopathy, emphasizes qualities such as lack of remorse and guilt, lack of empathy, glibness, irresponsibility, lack of self-control, and impulsivity. The moral question is whether a person who is good at manipulating others and who at best pays lip service to the social disapproval of their behavior, with no feelings for the plight of the people they harm, should be morally condemned or rather treated simply as someone with a disability (a lack of a conscience) or a moral monster. There has been no settled agreement on this issue, although in practical terms, legal systems treat psychopaths as accountable for their behavior (Malatesti & McMillan 2010).

Clearly, students of ethics have a rich and varied subject in the field of mental health, and they will be debating most or all of the topics noted here, and more, well into the future.

See also Disability Rights; Electroconvulsive Therapy; Forensic Psychology and Psychiatry; History of Mental Health Care; Hospitalization; Involuntary Treatment; Marketing of Drugs; Medical Model of Mental Illness; Neurodiversity; Prisons and Mental Health; Psychopathy and Antisocial Personality Disorder; Rights of Patients with Mental Health Conditions; Stigma

Bibliography

Angell, Marcia. 2004. *The Truth about the Drug Companies: How They Deceive Us and What to Do about It*. New York: Random House.

Bloch, Sidney, and Stephen Green, eds. *Psychiatric Ethics* (4th ed.). New York: Oxford University Press.

Buchanan, Allen E., and Dan W. Brock. 1989. Deciding for Others: *The Ethics of Surrogate Decisionmaking*. Cambridge: Cambridge University Press.

Corrigan, Patrick W., ed. 2005. *On the Stigma of Mental Illness: Practical Strategies for Research and Social Change*. Washington, DC: American Psychological Association.

King, D. Brett, Wayne Viney, and William Douglas Woody. 2009. *A History of Psychology: Ideas and Context* (4th ed.). Boston: Pearson.

Kirsch, Irving. 2010. *The Emperor's New Drugs: Exploding the Antidepressant Myth.* New York: Basic Books.

Malatesti, Luca, and John McMillan, eds. 2010. *Responsibility and Psychopathy: Interfacing Law, Psychiatry and Philosophy.* Oxford: Oxford University Press.

Miles, Andrew, Michael Loughlin, and Andreas Polychronis. 2008. "Evidence-Based Healthcare, Clinical Knowledge and the Rise of Personalised Medicine." *Journal of Evaluation in Clinical Practice* 14(5): 621–649.

Parker, Malcolm. 2002. "Whither Our Art? Clinical Wisdom and Evidence-Based Medicine." *Medicine, Health Care and Philosophy* 5(3): 273–280.

Robinson, Daniel. 1996. *Wild Beasts and Idle Humors: The Insanity Defense from Antiquity to the Present.* Cambridge, MA: Harvard University Press.

Ross, Don, Harold Kincaid, David Spurrett, and Peter Collins, eds. 2010. *What Is Addiction?* Cambridge, MA: MIT Press.

Saks, Elyn R. 2002. *Refusing Care: Forced Treatment and the Rights of the Mentally Ill.* Chicago: University of Chicago Press.

Valenstein, Elliot S. 1986. *Great and Desperate Cures: The Rise and Decline of Psychosurgery and Other Radical Treatments for Mental Illness.* New York: Basic Books.

Whitaker, Robert. 2001. *Mad In America: Bad Science, Bad Medicine, and the Enduring Mistreatment of the Mentally Ill.* New York: Basic Books.

Ethnic Issues

See African Americans and Mental Health; American Indian and Alaskan Native Mental Health; Asian American and Pacific Islander Mental Health Issues; Latinos and Mental Health

Evidence-Based Practice and Outcome Measurement*

Timothy A. Kelly

> America's mental health service delivery system is in shambles, ... [and] needs dramatic reform.
>
> —President's New Freedom Commission on Mental Health (2003)

Mental health providers work hard to treat their patients, those in need of care (mental health care "consumers") want to get better, and third-party payers intend for their funded services to lead to healing. But somehow, despite all these efforts,

*"Evidence-Based Practice and Outcome Measurement" is adapted from chapter 3 of *Healing the Broken Mind: Transforming America's Failed Mental Health System* by Timothy A. Kelly © 2009 New York University Press.

the outcome of mental health treatment in the United States is often bitterly disappointing. Consumers continue to experience the vicious cycle of clinical crisis, hospitalization, and discharge to less-than-optimal community services—where the cycle starts all over again (Kelly 2009; Mechanic 2008).

As a former state commissioner for Virginia's Department of Mental Health, Mental Retardation, and Substance Abuse Services, the present writer saw many examples of a system in shambles. Unfortunately, effective evidence-based treatment was rare and as a result too many of those who struggled with serious mental disorders were unable to recover well enough to go home.

What can be done? The current system of mental health care, overly reliant upon outdated treatments, quick to medicate and hospitalize, must be transformed into one that focuses on measuring and achieving the desired outcome, which is recovery for those with serious mental illness. Recovery does not mean perfect healing, but it does mean being able to live well in the home community—to have a real home, a fulfilling job, and deep relationships. For that to happen, the United States' mental health system must be transformed into one based on evidence-based practices and supported by clinical outcome data. This entry addresses what that involves.

An Outcome-Oriented System of Care

Managers have long noted that that which is measured improves, since no one wants to turn in a poor report card. Accordingly, measuring clinical outcomes tends to improve results by focusing on just how well those receiving care are doing. If such information were readily available on a routine basis, it would by definition make clear what is working well in the lives of consumers and what is not. By so doing, we would shed light on those areas of the mental health service system that are sorely in need of reform, or transformation. It would provide accountability for treatments and programs, improve quality of care, and keep costs competitive.

The question of clinical effectiveness has been the focus of much research and publication—especially over the last 15 years. Clinical outcome research has established, for example, the effectiveness of cognitive and interpersonal therapy and antidepressant medications for treating depression, the effectiveness of cognitive and systematic-desensitization therapy and antianxiety medication for treating anxiety disorders, and the importance of the therapeutic relationship (Bickman 2005; Seligman 1994; Shadish et al. 2000).

Since this research requires the use of clinical surveys, there is also a growing body of literature on standardized clinical outcome measures and their uses. Martin Seligman demonstrated in the mid-1990s what has since become widely accepted, namely, that a survey of those receiving care in the field is in fact the "gold standard" of data for establishing clinical effectiveness. Also, he pointed

Clinical Outcome Research

The science involved in studying clinical outcomes is known as either *efficacy research*, which is performed under controlled situations (usually through a university lab), or *effectiveness research*, which is performed in the field. Effectiveness research is more applicable, since it takes into account the multiple variables that providers must address when working with actual patients in the field. For instance, many patients have more than one diagnosis (such as depression and alcohol dependence) whereas efficacy research typically focuses on only one diagnosis at a time.

to the two primary focuses that a clinical outcome survey must cover: (1) symptom reduction and (2) functional life improvement (Seligman 1995).

Drawing on this growing body of clinical effectiveness literature, several teams of researchers have developed core outcome batteries of questionnaires that meet the needs of researchers, clinicians, consumers, insurers, and policy makers alike (e.g., Barkham et al. 1998, 2001; Borkovec et al. 2001). However, despite the availability of these scientifically proven and clinically useful outcome measures, many researchers "are struck by how slow the field has been to deal adequately with the subtleties of outcome measurement" (Jacobson et al. 1999, 306).

What is needed is for the field to adopt a scientifically credible and consumer-focused methodology with which mental health providers can assess and document their patients' clinical improvements. It must be based on the consumer's self-report since that is the most direct source of information, and it must be scientifically sound. (Of course, there are some exceptions to this rule. Some consumers may be incapable of accurate assessment due to severity of illness, hypochondria, having another agenda requiring the need to "fake bad," etc.) Thankfully, over the past 15 years, standardized, objective clinical outcome measures have been developed and tested for use with just about every population and treatment setting (child/adult, inpatient/outpatient/community-based, etc.), and for just about any diagnosis (e.g., Corcoran & Fischer 2000). These measures are basically questionnaires, or "instruments," designed to be minimally burdensome on those who fill them out, yet comprehensive enough to capture improvement in the most relevant areas. The questions, or "items," used on these instruments have been honed through research to be clear and concise, and to identify clinical improvements as well as areas where further needs must be addressed. For example, an item might read: "During the past week I have felt down or depressed: (a) all the time, (b) frequently, (c) daily, (d) occasionally, (e) never." Assuming careful and honest responses, items like this yield important information that, when taken together, produce an accurate profile of the consumer's mental health status.

Standardized Outcome Measures

The Treatment Outcome Package is a 37-item instrument for measuring adolescent and adult clinical status that meets all scientific criteria (Kraus, Seligman, & Jordan 2005). It is designed to be appropriate for anything from solo practice to large networks of providers, and takes approximately 20 minutes for the client to complete. The items primarily cover four areas of concern: depression, anxiety disorders, suicidality, and violence. It is available from Behavioral Health Labs (see http://www.bhealthlabs.com).

The CORE Outcome Measure has 34 items designed to measure common symptoms, subjective well-being, life/social functioning, and risk to self and others, and is scientifically sound (Barkham et al. 2001). The instrument is designed to generate a "global level of distress" that is calculated as the mean score of all 34 items. (There are also shorter versions available with 18, 10, or 5 items.) The mean score, as well as individual items, can be tracked over the course of therapy as measures of clinical improvement. The measure was developed in England by Britain's Department of Health and has been in use there since 1998 (see CORE System Group 1998; and http://www.coreims.co.uk).

There are currently many reliable and valid standardized mental health outcome measures available, such as the Treatment Outcome Package and the CORE Outcome Measure, both developed for use in outpatient mental health clinics, and both available free for use by mental health providers. These are sometimes referred to as "core batteries," or "core measures." Typically, they contain around 35 to 40 questions, and take about 10 to 15 minutes to complete. The categories they address are the same covered in any doctor's office—symptoms (symptomatology) and level of functioning (functionality). The items must cover the range of symptoms normally seen with a given population, as well as how well one is functioning (at home, at work, or at school).

Although symptomatology and functionality are usually sufficient for applied clinical outcome measurement, one other category is often included as well—the consumer's overall sense of satisfaction with services received. Satisfaction with care is of course a valid expectation for mental health consumers just as it would be with customers of any service, and should be fairly high from day one of treatment.

How often outcome measures are used depends upon the consumer's needs, the setting, and other factors. For instance, in an intense inpatient setting such as a psychiatric hospital acute ward, symptoms may need to be checked daily. In a typical outpatient setting where the consumer is coming for weekly services, once every other week (or even every four weeks) may be sufficient. In every setting the goal is to measure frequently enough to capture important changes early on, yet infrequently enough so as not to unnecessarily burden the consumer or the provider.

Scientifically sound and easy-to-use clinical outcome measures are readily available for just about any mental health service setting. Unfortunately, they are not yet widely used as a matter of course by either public sector or private sector providers. There is currently little fiscal incentive to do so, but that is changing. Public and private insurers are beginning to require clinical outcome data for continued funding. Consequently, a small but growing number of both mental health agencies and private organizations are experimenting with outcome measures. They are spurred on by the call for results-oriented mental health reforms, and the related call for "evidence-based practice."

Evidence-Based Practice

The history of mental health care is strewn with practices that now make one cringe when reading about them. Locking persons with serious mental illness away in closets or warehousing them without treatment in run-down "lunatic asylums," overmedicating them to keep them under control in a zombie-like state, lobotomies (as portrayed in the movie *One Flew over the Cuckoo's Nest*)—all these practices were commonly accepted at one time.

But, thankfully, there has been a steady and much-needed march toward the promotion of evidence-based practice, which by definition weeds out treatment practices that are ineffective. Throughout the 1980s and 1990s, a growing number of researchers and policy makers began calling for evidence-based practices, especially in the United Kingdom. For instance, the Cochrane Collaboration, based in Oxford since 1993, is dedicated to the promotion of evidence-based practices and maintains a library of current relevant research (e.g., Clarke & Oxman 1999; see http://www.cochrane.org). A British journal titled *Evidence-Based Mental Health* is also dedicated to the topic and to helping mental health providers stay abreast of the latest practice-relevant evidence (see http://ebmh.bmjjournals.com).

Over the last 15 years, a growing body of research literature has succeeded in establishing the definition, importance, and practical usefulness of evidence-based mental health practices (e.g., Corrigan, McCracken, & McNeilly 2005; Davies, Nutley, & Smith 2000; Dixon & Goldman 2003; Drake, Merrens, & Lynde 2005; Evans et al., 2000; Glicken 2004; Hillman 2002; Kelly 2003a, 2003b, 2009; Lambert, Hansen, & Finch 2001; Merrens 2005; Nathan & Gorman 2002; Roth & Fonagy 1996). As a result, an increasing number of policy makers and insurers are expecting that treatments or services offered for a person with mental illness will first be subjected to scientific outcome-oriented testing, and found to be effective. It is important to note that the testing involved for establishing evidence-based practices requires using clinical outcome data. In fact, they can be seen as two sides of one coin. It is not possible to determine which treatments are effective without collecting clinical outcome data, and the natural result of such data as it accumulates is to identify evidence-based practices—treatments that work well.

The hope is all mental health treatments will eventually be evidence based, and those that are ineffective will be weeded out. It is likely that in the not too distant future mental health insurers will require that all covered services consist of evidence-based practices. But that has not yet happened, and consequently many mental health providers continue to offer services that cannot claim to be evidence based, with questionable results. In fact, one study found that less than 15 percent of consumers currently receive evidence-based mental health services (Merrens 2005).

Unfortunately, it is possible to support the general need for providers to use evidence-based practices, even while rejecting the use of real-time case-by-case clinical outcome data to guide care for individual patients. In other words, some policy makers are comfortable with requiring evidence-based treatments but not with having consumers use outcome surveys on a regular basis, even though it was those surveys that identified the evidence-based practices in the first place. Outcome surveys are seen as too burdensome, too threatening, too expensive, or simply unnecessary. This is unfortunate, as it deprives the consumer of being able to determine to what extent he or she is truly benefiting from a particular treatment at a particular time. After all, even if a treatment is evidence based, that does not prove that it is the best selection for a given person with their particular array of needs and vulnerabilities. The only objective way to determine that is to use standardized clinical outcome measures on an individual, real-time basis to ensure that treatment is having its intended effect.

What's Wrong with Clinical Outcome Data?

If clinical outcome data is so important, why is not everyone calling for it? What could possibly be wrong with measuring the extent to which a person has been helped by mental health care? The answer depends on who you are, since providers, insurers, and consumers have very different concerns regarding this matter.

Providers

Many mental health providers see the value of clinical outcome data as a way to help them do their best with each consumer, and are willing to take reasonable steps in that direction. But there are others who feel that outcome measures constitute simply one more intrusion in the consumer-provider relationship, as well as an unpaid administrative drain on already-stretched time. They are simply not willing to administer, score, and track patient results unless and until third-party payers cover the time and effort required—a valid concern. Consequently, some researchers are pessimistic about how quickly the field will actually adopt outcome measures, since it would require a "major change in clinical practice patterns." Routinely measuring outcomes, according to some, "is not likely to become a practice standard in the foreseeable future" (Lambert, Hansen, & Finch 2001, 169).

Additionally, there is concern that the resultant data could be used punitively by reviewers who may not take into account differences among consumer populations. For instance, although significant functional improvement at work, school, or home is the expected outcome for most patients, that is not so for all consumers. For those with the most severe cases of mental illness (e.g., chronic paranoid schizophrenia) simple maintenance of current functioning may be an appropriate expected outcome. If these differences in consumer populations are not taken into account, then outcome data may make providers who work with the most severe cases of mental illness appear ineffective in contrast with other providers. Clearly, population and setting differences must always be carefully referenced when analyzing outcome data.

Furthermore, most mental health providers are very familiar with managed care procedures and utilization review, wherein application is made to insurance reviewers in order to authorize coverage for continued treatment. Consequently, some providers fear that outcome measures may simply be used to add to the complexity and burden of utilization review.

It is certainly understandable that some providers may fear the misuse of clinical outcome data, or that punitive actions could be taken (rather than remedial) if their patients did not improve. It is also understandable that some providers cringe at the idea of an additional unpaid administrative requirement. All of these concerns must be addressed. Indeed, it is critical that as outcome measures become required, the resultant data are used to support the good-faith clinical efforts of the mental health provider. If outcomes are not as expected, then remediation or referral, not punishment, is in order. If outcomes are consistently below expectations for a given provider or program, then perhaps further training would be in order. If further training is not successful, then and only then should consideration be given to shifting funds to a more effective program or provider.

It is also critical that the providers' administrative burden in managing the flow of outcome data be adequately reimbursed. If policy makers or insurers want to require the use of outcome measures, then they must realistically cover the cost of time and effort, without reducing pay for services. In other words, new funds will be required (e.g., from increase in insurance premiums). Otherwise compliance will be sporadic and begrudging at best. Thankfully these concerns are not insoluble. They can and must be resolved in a fair manner, with give-and-take from both sides.

Insurers

Third-party payers are very interested in the possibility of clinical outcome data improving the quality of funded care, as well as the opportunity to build results-oriented accountability into mental health services. Already some insurance companies and governmental agencies are requesting that providers use evidence-based practices whenever possible. The use of clinical outcome measures takes that one step further by making sure that the treatment offered is not just statistically proven, but that it also works well for each individual consumer. Third-party payers have a lot to gain by using outcome data. But at the same time, some insurers note that the collection of information is not without cost, and that the resultant data could be used to justify additional care beyond usual provisions. In other words, there is concern about having to pay for the cost of surveying, as well as for additional services if the data shows further need. Furthermore, there is concern that outcome instruments could yield inaccurate measures of the consumer's actual clinical needs, or could perhaps be gamed by either consumers or providers to indicate need for services ad infinitum.

Given the strong psychometric properties of state-of-the-art clinical outcome measures, which means that their results are reliable and valid, accuracy is not a concern so long as the questions are carefully and honestly answered. The items have been honed through painstaking research so that they yield an accurate view of the respondent's actual clinical status. Consumers, providers, and insurers alike are usually pleasantly surprised at the extent to which clinical surveys provide accurate and revealing profiles of the patient's needs. For example, I have had patients who were relieved to acknowledge what their clinical survey revealed— that they were in fact significantly depressed despite denying it to themselves and others.

At the same time, the potential for inaccuracies must be addressed. It is possible to imbed a "fake-bad scale" of improbable answers in the survey in order to detect those who may be trying to game the system (as is done with the MMPI). This is a group of questions that are designed to be sensitive to someone who is exaggerating difficulties. If the respondent is either unable or unwilling to provide careful, honest answers then the results are invalid and will be so indicated on the survey. Furthermore, a consumer who has difficulty with the reading level required or with the language (although most measures are available in multiple languages) may unintentionally provide inaccurate data. But this can usually be detected by the random nature of responses, and can be corrected by having someone verbally walk through the items with the consumer.

If the respondent is unwilling to provide honest and accurate information for any reason (e.g., not wanting to terminate care even though all treatment goals are met; or not wanting to be hospitalized despite the need for inpatient care), this will become clear by the pattern of data and by the fake-bad scale (if used). Thus it is possible to detect those who may try to game the system by carefully analyzing the survey data and noting the improvement trajectory. For instance, if a person initially struggling with major depression has actually improved but tries to fake-bad in order to continue receiving services, they will typically generate a pro-file showing satisfaction with current services yet without improvement. This would serve as a red flag since a consumer who is not getting better is usually (and understandably) dissatisfied with his or her current services. In such a case, the provider could be asked to resolve the discrepancy by carefully reviewing the consumer's clinical status. (As an additional administrative burden, the time required must be covered by the third-party payer.) Given the sophistication of software programs that are used to score and interpret clinical outcome measures, it is not difficult to screen for patterns of data that indicate possibly invalid questionnaires which can then be double-checked.

Insurers should welcome the use of outcome measures, since benefits would clearly outweigh costs. Costs include the fact that insurers must fund the administrative component, and must authorize additional services when so indicated per the outcome data. Benefits include confidence that the consumer (and insurer) are getting what they are paying for—effective, evidence-based care. Surely it is better for insurers to know that their funded services are working well, even if it costs something to find that out, than to continue to pour money into ineffective treatments.

Consumers

Most consumers of mental health services like the idea of their improvement being monitored, taken seriously, and based on their own feedback. After all, it means that their assessment of treatment will be helping to shape their own care. This is the ultimate consumer-oriented and individualized treatment approach, since the outcome data used for case management is actually the voice of the one receiving care. Nonetheless, some consumers worry that filling out the surveys could be burdensome, that information may not be kept confidential, or that the results could be used to prematurely terminate care (once they show improvement). These are understandable concerns, but they can all be resolved fairly easily.

Regarding the question of burden, it is critical that outcome measures are selected that take no more than 10–15 minutes to complete. This is a short enough time not to disrupt schedules, and may simply mean that the consumer comes in a little early, say, every fourth session. This author found that the vast majority of consumers in an outpatient setting in the Washington, DC, area willingly came early and completed their outcome measures, convinced that it meant they would receive better care. Indeed this was the case, as the outcome data often helped the provider fine-tune therapy. Persons with serious mental illness in inpatient settings will likely require more time, and perhaps some help, to complete the surveys. But this is time well spent, even if staff efforts are required.

Regarding confidentiality, it is of course imperative that all clinical outcome data be kept absolutely confidential, and that only aggregated data (which consists of averages and includes no identifying information) be used for program review. Individual data must only be used to authorize further care, and must always remain strictly confidential. As for using data to prematurely terminate care, significant reduction of the consumer's symptoms and return to a normal level of functioning provide a reasonable target for treatment termination, but only if relapse issues have been addressed as well. On-paper-only improvement is not acceptable—only real recovery as verified by both the provider and the consumer. Outcome data constitutes but one source of information among many (e.g., clinician's judgment, reports from family members or coworkers, etc.) to be included when considering termination, which is a decision point that should be reached collaboratively by both provider and consumer. Furthermore, appeals mechanisms and emergency measures must be in place so that consumers have options in cases where care is not meeting their actual needs.

In sum, although some providers, insurers and consumers resist embracing clinical outcome measures, their concerns (though understandable) can be addressed. It is well worth doing so, since the potential for outcome-oriented improvement in quality of care, and in real-life consumer recovery, will greatly benefit all parties.

Conclusion

Promoting effective, cost-efficient clinical outcomes is critical not only for mental health system reform but also for the success of national health care reform. Many of the topics discussed above apply to both. It is hoped that as national health care reform advances, so does mental health system transformation—in both cases guided by the actual outcome of clinical care in the life of the consumer.

If correctly implemented, outcome data will improve life for all parties—providers, consumers and third party payers alike. Social workers, psychologists, and psychiatrists will find that the initial frustration of having to do "one more thing" will be more than compensated for by the resultant improvement in case management and consumer satisfaction. Consumers will find that their feedback becomes a primary voice in determining care, and promotes rapid improvement. Third-party payers will find their funded services becoming more effective and cost efficient. Mental health providers would thus do well to become proficient in the use of clinical outcome measures, and the related use of evidence-based practices, and thereby be ahead of the curve.

Now is the time for the United States to roll up her sleeves and do what it takes to develop an outcome-oriented mental health care system—one that leads to recovery for our neighbors and family members who struggle with serious mental illness. At that point articles will be written not about a system in shambles, but about a mental health system that works—that enables those with mental illness to come home.

See also History of Mental Health Care; Medical Model of Mental Illness; Preventative Mental Health Programs; Public Policy Issues; State Mental Health Agencies

Bibliography

Barkham, M., C. Evans, F. Margison, G. McGrath, J. Mellor-Clark, D. Milne, and J. Connell. 1998. "The Rationale for Developing and Implementing Core Batteries in Service Settings and Psychotherapy Outcome Research." *Journal of Mental Health* 7: 35–47.

Barkham, M., F. Margison, C. Leach, M. Lucock, J. Mellor-Clark, C. Evans, L. Benson, J. Connell, K. Audin, and G. McGrath. 2001. "Service Profile and Benchmarking Using the CORE-OM: Toward Practice-Based Evidence in the Psychological Therapies." *Journal of Consulting and Clinical Psychology* 69: 184–196.

Bickman, L. 2005. "A Common Factors Approach to Improving Mental Health Services." *Mental Health Services Research* 7: 1–4.

Borkovec, T. D., R. J. Echemendia, S. A. Ragusea, and M. Ruiz. 2001. "The Pennsylvania Practice Research Network and Future Possibilities for Clinically Meaningful and Scientifically Rigorous Psychotherapy Effectiveness Research." *Journal of Mental Health* 10: 241–251.

Clarke, M., and A. D. Oxman. 1999. "Cochrane Reviewers' Handbook 4.0." In *Review Manager* [computer program], Version 4.0. Oxford: Cochrane Collaboration.

Corcoran, K., and J. Fischer. 2000. *Measures for Clinical Practice: A Sourcebook* (3rd ed.; 2 vols.). New York: Free Press.

CORE System Group. 1998. CORE System (Information Management) Handbook. Leeds, UK: CORE.

Corrigan, P. W., S. G. McCracken, and C. McNeilly. 2005. "Evidence-Based Practices for People with Serious Mental Illness and Substance Abuse Disorders." In C. Stout and R. Hayes, eds., *The Handbook of Evidence-Based Practices in Behavioral Healthcare: Applications and New Directions* (pp. 153–172). New York: Wiley.

Davies, H., S. Nutley, and P. Smith. 2000. *What Works? Evidence-Based Practice in Public Services*. Bristol, UK: Policy Press.

Dixon, L. B., and H. H. Goldman. 2003. "Forty Years of Progress in Community Mental Health: The Role of Evidence-Based Practice." *Australia and New Zealand Journal of Psychiatry* 37: 668–673.

Drake, R. E., M. Merrens, and D. Lynde, eds. 2005. *Evidence-Based Mental Health: A Textbook*. New York: Wiley.

Evans, C., J. Mellor-Clark, F. Margison, M. Barkham, K. Audin, J. Connell, and G. McGrath. 2000. "Clinical Outcomes in Routine Evaluation: The CORE-OM." *Journal of Mental Health* 9: 247–255.

Glicken, M. D. 2004. *Improving the Effectiveness of the Helping Professions: An Evidence-Based Practice Approach*. Thousand Oaks, CA: Sage.

Hillman, J. L. 2002. *Crisis Intervention and Trauma: New Approaches to Evidence-Based Practices*. New York: Kluwer Academic/Plenum.

Jacobson, N. S., L. J. Roberts, S. B. Berns, and J. B. McGlinchey. 1999. "Methods for Defining and Determining the Clinical Significance of Treatment Effects: Description,

Application, and Alternatives." *Journal of Consulting and Clinical Psychology* 67: 300–307.

Kelly, T. A. 1997. "A Wake-Up Call: The Experience of a Mental Health Commissioner in Times of Change." *Professional Psychology: Research and Practice* 28: 317–322.

Kelly, T. A. 2000. "Principled Mental Health System Reform." *The Heritage Foundation Backgrounder* 1341: 1–12.

Kelly, T. A. 2002a. "Dealing with Fragmentation in the Service Delivery System." Invited expert testimony presented to the President's New Freedom Commission on Mental Health, Arlington. Retrieved from http://www.mentalhealthcommission.gov/presentations/presentations.html.

Kelly, T. A. 2002b. "A Policymaker's Guide to Mental Illness." *The Heritage Foundation Backgrounder* 1522: 1–16.

Kelly, T. A. 2003a. "Clinical Outcome Measurement: A Call to Action." *Journal of Psychology and Christianity* 22: 254–258.

Kelly, T. A. 2003b. "Transforming the Mental Health System: Principles and Recommendations." Paper presented at the annual meeting of the American Psychological Association, Toronto.

Kelly, T. A. 2009. *Healing the Broken Mind: Transforming America's Failed Mental Health System.* New York: New York University Press.

Kraus, D. R., D. Seligman, and J. R. Jordan. 2005. Validation of a Behavioral Health Treatment Outcome and Assessment Tool Designed for Naturalistic Settings: The Treatment Outcome Package." *Journal of Clinical Psychology* 61: 285–314.

Lambert, M. J., N. B. Hansen, and A. E. Finch. 2001. "Patient-Focused Research: Using Patient Outcome Data to Enhance Treatment Effects." *Journal of Consulting and Clinical Psychology* 69: 159–172.

Mechanic, D. 2008. *Mental Health and Social Policy: Beyond Managed Care* (5th ed.). Boston: Allyn & Bacon.

Merrens, M. 2005. *Evidence-Based Mental Health Practice.* New York: Norton.

MHSIP Task Force. 1996. *The Mental Health Statistics Improvement Program Consumer-Oriented Mental Health Report Card.* Rockville, MD: Center for Mental Health Services.

Nathan, P. E., and J. M. Gorman, eds. 2002. *A Guide to Treatments That Work* (2nd ed.). New York: Oxford University Press.

President's New Freedom Commission on Mental Health. 2003. *Achieving the Promise: Transforming Mental Health Care in America.* Rockville, MD: President's New Freedom Commission on Mental Health.

Roth, A., and P. Fonagy. 1996. *What Works for Whom? A Critical Review of Psychotherapy Research.* New York: Guilford Press

Seligman, M. 1994. *What You Can Change and What You Can't.* New York: Knopf.

Seligman, M. 1995. "The Effectiveness of Psychotherapy." *American Psychologist* 50: 965–974.

Shadish, W. R., A. M. Navarro, G. E. Matt, and G. Phillips. 2000. "The Effects of Psychological Therapies under Clinically Representative Conditions: A Meta-Analysis." *Psychological Bulletin* 126: 512–529.

Family and Mental Illness

Michelle S. Hinkle, Emily Herman, and Victoria E. Kress

Mental illness uniquely affects each individual in a family. Parents, siblings, spouses, and children of those with mental illness are faced with feelings of grief and anger while trying to cope with the negative implications of mental illness on their loved one. Family members can play a role in causing, sustaining, and healing mental illness. Perhaps one of the most significant challenges is being able to persuade a family member who has a mental illness—along with members of the person's family—to seek the help and resources he or she needs to successfully manage the illness.

When a family member is struggling with a mental illness, the stability of the family is threatened. If a parent has a mental illness, his or her ability to attach to, communicate with, and care for children may be strained. In addition, such a parent is at higher risk of being away from the children if he or she is hospitalized for an episode of mental illness (Reupert & Maybery 2007). As a result, children of parents who have a mental illness often must care for themselves and their parents, a situation that has an effect on children's social and emotional well-being (Pakenham et al. 2006), and family finances and resources (Reupert & Maybery 2007). In two-parent homes, mental illness may result in marital discord as parents endure the stress of caretaking for children as well as each other and the household. When a child has a mental illness, the family experiences trauma and grief over the symptoms and behaviors associated with the mental illness, and family discord as the family adjusts to the needs of the child is common (Mohr & Regan-Kubinski 2001).

Although only one member of a family may have a diagnosable mental illness, the whole family is equally impacted by the strain in adjusting to the symptoms and behaviors that coincide with a mental illness. It is important that the whole family participate in counseling so as to ease the adjustment, make necessary changes in family dynamics, improve communication, and increase stability so that all family members can improve the mental health outlook of the family.

Family Theories and Techniques

Over the second half of the twentieth century, the idea that that mental illness could be rooted in, or at least sustained by, family system dynamics emerged. Both family therapy and systems theory are rooted in the idea that all members of a family are influenced by one another through communication patterns, dynamics, and family rules. The concept of cybernetics, in which systems are capable of self-regulation and the preservation of stability, is an important one in understanding family systems theory. Family therapists believe that families self-regulate by seeking a more or less constant homeostatic balance (i.e., emotional and behavioral evenness or predictability) based on dynamics of communications, family and member roles, and consistent patterns of approach toward distress. Families constantly strive to maintain a measure of homeostasis, even if the stability attained leads to dysfunction. They do so because it is comfortable to operate in this way and because it may be the only way the family knows how to exist.

As emerging problems arise and stressors occur, new information may come into a family system. As a result, family members must decide what to do with the new information. A feedback loop is the mechanism by which families can either incorporate new information into their existing patterns to make a change, or maintain homeostasis. A *first-order change* in the family system involves the avoidance of change in order to maintain homeostasis. On the other hand, families can choose to integrate information and alter their patterns, thus changing their level of homeostasis; the latter outcome is referred to as *a second-order change*.

A goal of family counseling is to increase the likelihood of second-order changes and increased family adaptability—or, in other words, challenging family homeostasis—by creating new patterns of communication, structures, and family rules. When conflict arises, the family will strive to maintain homeostasis. As the system struggles to maintain stability, one family member may experience problematic symptoms or mental illness. Oftentimes this family member, *the identified patient*, will seek help from a counselor. A family counselor will conceptualize this family member not as an individual but rather a person embedded in a family system. The family counselor believes that the identified patient is manifesting symptoms that represent the family's problem and signifies the need for systemic changes. By understanding the individual in the context of his or her family, the counselor will be able to identify problematic patterns or relationships within the family that can be altered in an effort to assist the family as a whole.

Specific Interventions

Over the past 60 years, various approaches to family counseling have emerged. All of these approaches have as their goal the challenging of family dynamics.

Psychodynamic and Bowen family therapy (Bowen 1966) began in the 1950–1960s and was based on the work of the psychodynamic theorist Sigmund Freud. Family history and development are integral to the therapeutic interventions under this approach, as are the concepts of conscious and subconscious thoughts. Psychodynamic and Bowen family therapy techniques focus on the effect that past events have had and continue to have in the family, especially events that deal with family connections and attachments. The techniques belonging to Bowen's approach focus on differentiation and realignment through the use of genograms (a pictorial display of family relations) and detriangulation (the process whereby a person removes him or herself from the emotional and behavioral patterns of others; Kerr & Bowen 1988).

Experiential therapy (Satir 1991; Whitaker 1989) focuses on allowing family members to acknowledge and express their suppressed feelings and emotions. Allowing individuals in families the chance to explore their personal spontaneity is a key aspect in experiential techniques. Examples of such techniques include play therapy, filial therapy (the parent becomes the child's ally), art therapy, puppet interviews (use of surrogates), family sculpting (redesigning of relationships), touch, humor, and choreography.

Behavior therapy and cognitive-behavioral therapy explore cognitions (thoughts, thinking patterns) and consequences. This family theory (Bandura 1969) implements change through behavior and thought modification. The goal of such alterations is to improve interactions between couples and families. Family therapy techniques under these approaches include education, operant and classical conditioning, social learning theory, and coaching.

Structural family therapy (Minuchin & Fisheman 1981) is based on the design and interaction of the family structure. Counselors working from this approach examine the relationship between family members by categorizing subsystems and boundaries. Further categorization focuses on family roles, rules, and distribution of power. Structural family techniques work to track, accommodate, reframe, *un*balance, and restructure the family.

Strategic family therapy (Erickson 1989; Haley 1973) refutes the idea that history and the past play a role in the counseling process. This approach provides quick and realistic modifications of particular behaviors present in families or couples. Techniques such as reframing, using directives, employing paradox, and positioning and repositioning are implemented in order to resolve problems.

Solution-focused theorists (e.g., Berg 1994; de Shazer 1985) believe that people have the solutions they need to resolve their problems. As such, this approach does not place a value on processing or analyzing problems but instead concentrates on addressing solutions. Counselors using this approach assume that people have the strengths and resources they need to resolve family conflicts, and they consider themselves, in essence, to be families' cheerleaders. Solution-focused counselors' primary tool is the use of "solution talk" (i.e., language that assumes change can and will occur).

Narrative family therapy (White 1989; White & Epston 1990) empowers families to assess their life experiences through cooperation. In doing so, families externalize their problems and "re-author their stories." Families' stories, in other words, begin to shift away from being problem-saturated and deficit-based and toward becoming a healthier, positive reality. Counselors who use this approach explore family problems and their effects, raise questions about how such problems fit into the family story (examining their meaning or significance), and encourage the rewriting of family and individual narratives to achieve more satisfying ends.

See also Elder Abuse and Neglect; Group Therapy; Marriage, Divorce, and Mental Health; Psychotherapy

Bibliography

Bandura, A. 1969. *Principles of Behavior Modification*. New York: Holt, Rinehart & Winston.

Berg, I. K. 1994. *Family-Based Services: A Solution-Focused Approach*. New York: Norton.

Bowen, M. 1966. "The Use of Family Theory in Clinical Practice." *Comprehensive Psychiatry* 7: 345–374.

de Shazer, S. 1985. *Keys to Solutions in Brief Therapy*. New York: Guilford Press.

Erickson, M. H. 1989. *February Man*. New York: Irvington.

Haley, J. 1973. *Uncommon Therapy: The Psychiatric Techniques of Milton H. Erickson*. New York: Norton.

Kerr, M. E., and M. Bowen. 1988. *Family Evaluation: An Approach Based on Bowen Theory*. New York: Norton.

Minuchin, S., and H. C. Fishman. 1981. *Family Therapy and Techniques*. Cambridge, MA: Harvard University Press.

Mohr, W. K., and M. Regan-Kubinski. 2001. "Living in the Fallout: Parents' Experiences When Their Child Becomes Mentally Ill." *Archives of Psychiatric Nursing* 15(2): 69–77.

Pakenham, K. I., S. Bursnall, J. Chiu, T. Cannon, and M. Okochi. 2006. "The Psychosocial Impact of Caregiving on Young People Who Have a Parent with an Illness or Disability: Comparisons between Young Caregivers and Non-caregivers." *Rehabilitation Psychology* 51(2): 113–126.

Reupert, A., and D. Maybery. 2007. "Families Affected by Parental Mental Illness: A Multiperspective Account of Issues and Interventions." *American Journal of Orthopsychiatry* 77: 362–369.

Satir, V. 1991. *The Satir Model: Family Therapy and Beyond*. Palo Alto, CA: Science and Behavior Books.

Whitaker, C. A. 1989. *Musings of a Family Therapist*. New York: Norton.

White, M. 1989. *Selected Papers*. Adelaide, Australia: Dulwich Centre Publications.

White, M., and D. Epston. 1990. *Narrative Means to Therapeutic Ends*. New York: Norton.

Forensic Psychology and Psychiatry

Steven K. Erickson

Forensic psychologists and psychiatrists are mental health professionals who provide expert analysis, and often testimony, regarding issues that implicate the legal system. Derived from the Latin word *forensis*, which means "forum," forensic psychology and psychiatry can be understood as the application of the behavioral sciences to legal questions about the capacity, culpability, and the mental state of people who are involved in the legal system. In this sense, forensic psychology and psychiatry are true interdisciplinary fields insofar as they require a comprehensive knowledge of both behavioral science and the various precepts, rules, and customs contained within legal codes.

In order to competently work in this interdisciplinary field, forensic psychologists and psychiatrists possess substantial knowledge about behavior, biology, human development, and psychopathology, as well as a robust understanding of the guiding substantive and procedure law in the jurisdictions in which they practice. Attainment of the former, often referred to as clinical knowledge, is what largely differentiates psychologist from psychiatrists. Psychologists obtain their knowledge about human behavior and psychopathology through graduate course work, research, and field training which usually culminates in the awarding of a doctoral degree in psychology. Psychiatrists attend medical school before entering a psychiatry residency program that involves additional years of clinical practice before graduation. In order to become a forensic psychologist or psychiatrist and obtain the requisite knowledge of the legal system, both professions generally require an interested clinician to complete specialized training which may be obtained by completion of an advanced fellowship or informal mentorship with an experienced colleague. While some forensic psychologists and psychiatrists also attend law school and are licensed attorneys, there is no requirement for this additional education, although the enhanced knowledge of the legal system obtained during formal legal education is often advantageous.

Historical Roots

In the United States, courts have employed the expertise of people knowledgeable about human behavior as far back as the mid-nineteenth century. But modern-day forensic psychology and psychiatry owes its birth to Hugo Münsterberg, a Harvard University professor and experimental psychologist. In 1908, Münsterberg published the first textbook of forensic psychology. In his now classic *On the Witness Stand*, a collection of chapters in which he recounted many of his own pioneering experiences as an expert witness in a number of celebrated trials, Professor Münsterberg asserted that the legal system would be vastly improved and more just outcomes assured if psychological expertise were broadly employed within the legal system (Münsterberg 1908).

Münsterberg's work was part of an incipient movement that used behavioral science data to advocate legal prescriptions. In 1908, Louis Brandeis—who would later become an influential member of the Supreme Court—authored a brief in the highly contested case of *Muller v. Oregon* (1908). The *Muller* case is highly regarded as one of the first instances in which social science data was heavily relied upon to urge a court toward a certain outcome. Since that time, the influence of the social sciences, including forensic psychology and psychiatry, on the law have waxed and waned. But it is unquestionable that within the past 50 years, most mature legal systems have broadly employed the social sciences within its normative framework of decision-making. It is now quite common for courts to use social science data in reaching decisions, including constitutional issues.

For forensic psychology and psychiatry, modernity has brought tremendous recognition to the field, although public perception is often inaccurate. Television shows such as *C.S.I.* and movies such as *Silence of the Lambs* portray forensic practice as highly glamorous, with forensic experts accompanying police to crime scenes and directly involved in the interrogation of suspects. Reality being less ostentatious, forensic practice nevertheless involves a keen knowledge by the expert of both science and law, with the expert often testifying in important cases involving serious legal issues, including capital cases, sexual predators, and child abuse.

Differences between Clinical and Forensic Work

Psychologists and psychiatrists are professionally trained to provide assessment, diagnosis, and treatment of mental disorders. Since the legal system is inherently a social system centered on the regulation of human conduct, the expertise that psychologists and psychiatrists possess makes them invaluable in many legal matters. Inasmuch as forensic work relies on the general skills and abilities of the clinician, it differs substantially from clinical practice in ways that are informative of the specialized nature of forensic work.

Perhaps most prominently to the novice, the role of the forensic psychologist or psychiatrist is quite different from that of the general clinician (Goldstein & Weiner 2003). When providing assessment and treatment in the clinical setting, the client is most often the patient and the clinician's role is rather straightforward insofar as the psychologist or psychiatrist evaluates the patient and provides treatment, usually in the form of psychotherapy or pharmacotherapy. In forensic practice, the psychologist or psychiatrist is usually retained by an attorney or appointed by the court and provides no treatment to the person subject to the evaluation. Rather, the sole focus lies on providing expert insight on key legal issues that are of concern to the parties who are usually involved in some type of litigation. These issues may involve whether the person is mentally competent, whether a child is best served by residing solely with one parent, or whether a person is likely to pose a danger to the community in the future.

Thus the different role reveals a difference between clinical and forensic work as it relates to the work itself. Within the clinical setting, the psychologist or

A forensic psychologist testifies in a courtroom, commenting on photographic evidence used in a case involving serial murder. (AP Photo/M. Spencer Green.)

psychiatrist is guided by his or her expert knowledge of behavior, mental illness, and therapeutic processes. The sole concern is the patient's emotional functioning and growth. In the forensic setting, the exclusive concern is the legal issue at hand. That issue directs the focus of interaction between the expert and person being evaluated and it does so in ways that fundamentally alters the doctor-patient relationship. Indeed, there is none.

The work of the forensic psychologist or psychiatrist is generally investigatory; hence, skepticism plays a significant part in the repertoire of skills possessed by the experienced forensic expert (Rogers 2008). Most people who are involved in litigation or issues relevant for forensic assessment have a vested interest in the outcome. For instance, a defendant who claims insanity for a crime has an incentive to appear psychologically infirmed; likewise, a plaintiff claiming psychology injury due to the negligent driving of another party may wish to appear more psychologically damaged in the hopes of recovering a larger settlement. These ulterior motives of the party being evaluated necessitate vigilance by the forensic expert and substantially modify the interaction between the mental health expert and the person subject to the evaluation. In traditional clinical practice it is not uncommon for the therapist to accept the patient's narrative at face value, but forensic practice requires rigorous questioning of the account provided by the person evaluated.

Similarly, forensic practice is almost always limited to a specific incident in time whereas customary clinical work is open-ended. For instance, a forensic expert may be requested by the court to provide testimony as to whether a particular defendant possesses a danger to the community if released from custody. In conducting the evaluation, the forensic expert must consider numerous factors that raise or lower the defendant's risk, which might include age, criminal history, and the drug and alcohol abuse (Heilbrum 2009). When experts provide testimony on this or other issues, they assist the court in rendering a decision that is fixed in time. Even if a defendant's risk to the community might change in future, such suppositions are outside of the realm of consideration because the factual findings of the court are guided by the legal doctrine of collateral estoppel, which provides finality to most legal decisions. In contrast, clinical practice focuses on the present functioning of the patient, which by definition can change from day to day.

By far, however, the most significant difference between forensic practice and clinical work is the integration of legal doctrine. Psychology and psychiatry are social sciences that rely on empirical methods to achieve broad-based theories of human behavior (Erickson & Erickson 2008). Law is inherently a normative construct subject to the social norms of the community. The legal issues that forensic experts often testify on are not subject to the scientific method; they are constructs constrained by communal beliefs about justice and fairness. For instance, the legal issue of insanity is not equivalent to mental illness or psychosis despite the strong belief by many that defendants who are mentally ill at the time of their offense should be deemed insane (Morse 1985). Rather, insanity is the legal embodiment of society's principle that it is unjust to punish those who are morally blameless. Since society's principles are subject to change depending on the values of those within it, the doctrine of insanity is not an empirical construct like anxiety, although it is subject to the same social forces that mold and form social constructs such as mental illness.

Forensic Assessment

Forensic psychologists and psychiatrists provide evaluations with the anticipation that they will be required to provide testimony in a court of law regarding their findings. Since forensic experts provide no treatment or therapy, the bulk of their activities involve assessment of individuals involved in litigation. Experts are treated uniquely by most legal systems insofar as they are the only witnesses who may offer opinions. In contrast, lay witnesses are usually permitted to testify only about facts of personal knowledge. For instance, a lay witness may testify that she observed a car speeding through an intersection; she may not testify that the driver was acting recklessly, which is an opinion about a legal issue.

Since forensic work usually involves rendering an opinion, the method by which the expert ascertains her opinion is of tremendous importance. Reliance upon reliable and valid methods is crucial and it is not uncommon for forensic psychologists and psychiatrists to use tests, structured interviews, and various other protocols to ensure that their opinions accurately answer the key issues involved in any particular case. Nonetheless, at the heart of forensic work is the judgment by the expert based on extensive education and experience that either supports or denies a fact being asserted by a party. The issue may make place in a civil suit for monetary damages or a criminal case where liberty is at stake, the realm of forensic psychology and psychiatry is vast given their expertise. Some of the most notable areas of forensic assessment are discussed below.

Criminal Responsibility

Although the Supreme Court has never held that there is a constitutional right to be free from punishment if one commits a crime while insane, there is a long-standing, shared belief that punishment is only morally permissible if a defendant was a rational agent at the time of his offense. Going back to old English common law, the insanity defense relieves a defendant from criminal culpability if, due to mental illness, he was unable to appreciate the quality of his actions or know that they were wrong. While the "test" for insanity has changed over the years and varies among the states, the essential thrust of the insanity doctrine is to forbid punishment for people who are suffering from severe mental illnesses at the time of their crimes. Forensic psychologists and psychiatrists are almost always employed when a defendant claims insanity and conduct an evaluation to determine whether or not the defendant meets the statutory criteria for the insanity defense.

Defendants who are successful in achieving an insanity verdict are not released back into the community, but almost always are civilly committed to psychiatric hospitals where they usually are confined for periods of time that exceed what their jail sentences would have been if convicted. Even when released, most defendants acquitted by insanity are intensely monitored for life.

Competence to Stand Trial

A criminal defendant has a constitutional right to be competent during every phase of a criminal proceeding. The idea of competency to stand trial rests on the notion that it is ultimately the defendant who must risk punishment, and therefore, the defendant must have sufficient awareness of the process and the ability to assist his or her attorney unimpeded by mental illness. Thus any time a defendant becomes substantially disoriented or unable to make rational choices due to mental illness from the time of her arraignment to imposition of sentence, she may be declared incompetent to proceed and required to undergo mental health treatment. Forensic experts often testify as to whether the defendant is indeed incompetent and in need of treatment. Once a defendant has been treated and restored to competency, the criminal proceedings resumes.

Capital Sentencing

In *Jurek v. Texas* (1976) the Supreme Court held that imposition of the death penalty is only appropriate for offenders who can be legitimately be segregated from other defendants convicted of homicide. Most jurisdictions rely upon a finding of future dangerousness as one of the criteria that justifies the sentence of death. That is, those offenders who would likely engage in violence if released receive the death penalty while those who would not receive a lesser punishment. Forensic psychologists and psychiatrists offer their opinions about whether a particular defendant is likely to be dangerous in the future. Likewise, in several cases, the Supreme Court has held that capital defendants are entitled to introduce any relevant mitigating evidence to avoid the death penalty. Forensic experts are often utilized to provide an evidence of a defendant's character or history that suggests reduced culpability.

Sexual Predators

Many states and the federal government provide for the civil commitment of people determined to be sexual predators. Sexual predators are usually defined as people who have engaged in sex acts with children who are likely to do so again if they are not confined. Most modern sexual predator statutes provide for commitment after the offender has served his or her prison sentence. Determining which sexual offender is likely to reoffend again the future is often left to the forensic expert who provides testimony at the commitment hearing.

Child Abuse

When a child is physically or sexually abused, it is often the case that the only witness to the crime is the child. All jurisdictions provide for the removal of a child who has been subjected to physical or sexual abuse. Likewise, criminal charges may be logged against any perpetrator of child abuse. However, determining whether child abuse has occurred is often not easily evident absent serious injury or the presence of a sexually transmitted disease. Even with these telltale signs, young children may be confused about the identity of the perpetrator or may be too afraid to be forthcoming. Forensic experts are used to ascertain whether abuse has occurred and to help identify the perpetrator. Additionally, in some cases, the child may be returned to the family once it has been determined that the child's safety is no longer in jeopardy. Forensic psychologists and psychiatrists assist the court and child protective agencies in determining when, and if, it is appropriate to reunite an abused child with his or her family.

Child Custody and Visitation

The guiding principle in most legal determinations of child custody is the "best interests" standard. This simple rule posits that when parents no longer reside with each other, a child should remain with the parent who serves the best interests of the child. Similarly, recognizing that in most situations, children benefit from frequent visitation by the non-custodial parent, courts often require divorced and separated parents to follow a visitation schedule that provides generous contact between the child and both parents. However, parents are often sharply in disagreement about who should have custody of a child, when and how much visitation should be permitted, and what decisions are in the best interests of the child. Forensic experts are broadly employed to help the courts arrive at decisions that maximize the best interests of the child.

Civil Commitment and Dangerousness

People who suffer from mental illnesses may be civilly committed for treatment if they pose a danger to themselves or others. A hallmark symptom of schizophrenia—a severe and persistent form of mental illness—is the denial that one is sick and in need of treatment. Known as anosognosia, this compromised ability of insight often leads to discontinuation of treatment by people with psychotic illnesses, which, in turn, leads to a worsening of symptoms. Feelings of persecution, delusions, and other disturbing symptoms may lead to violence or self-harm.

Personal Injury Claims

Injuries sustained in car accidents and other mishaps often result in litigation. In addition to physical injuries, plaintiffs often also claim that they suffer from emotional injuries. A devastating car accident may be followed by depression, anxiety, or cognitive impairment. Likewise, a plaintiff might claim that she suffers from depression due to unrelenting sexual harassment at her workplace. In these cases, forensic experts can provide useful testimony about the veracity and extent of the psychological injuries sustained by the plaintiff. Specialized psychologists with additional training in neuropsychology might also be helpful in determining whether neurological damage is present as well.

Future Directions

The rule of law knows few boundaries within civil society. Since law inherently operates to regulate human conduct, it is unsurprising that behavioral science experts are used to provide guidance within the normative framework of the legal system. Unlike physics or chemistry, psychology and psychiatry intersect at the crossroads of what is empiricism and what is uniquely the human experience. This is what makes it a challenging yet rewarding area of study. Forensic psychology and psychiatry take that endeavor one step further by employing social science to assist the legal system at achieving its ultimate end of justice and fairness.

As a practical matter, the questions that forensic psychology and psychiatry seek to answer are unknowable because they are rooted in the normative constructs of the law and human experience. Whether a person was insane at the time of a crime can never be known with absolute certitude because the legal standards for insanity implicitly recognize that defining insanity is a murky nexus between the objective and subjective. There is a limit to how law can define the human experience as a set of rules.

But as long as we have rules embodied within our legal codes, they represent opportunities for behavioral science experts to apply scientific knowledge to our social experience. Forensic psychology and psychiatry made their début by promising to elucidate the fine grain of entrenched legal doctrine by examining the behavior of the people who are subject to its regulatory framework. The profession has grown immensely because most people intuitively want to know why people obey and break the law.

See also Clinical Psychology; Criminalization and Diversion Programs; Disability Rights; Ethical Issues; Involuntary Treatment; Prisons and Mental Health; Psychiatry; Rights of Patients with Mental Health Conditions; Violence and Violence-Prone Individuals

Bibliography

Erickson, Patricia, and Steven Erickson. 2009. *Crime, Punishment, and Mental Illness: Law and the Behavioral Sciences in Conflict*. Piscataway, NJ: Rutgers University Press.

Goldstein, Alan, and Irvin Weiner. 2003. *Handbook of Psychology, Forensic Psychology*. New York: Wiley.

Heilbrum, Kirk. 2009. *Evaluation for Risk of Violence in Adults*. Oxford: Oxford University Press.

Jurek v. Texas, 428 U.S. 262 (1976).

Morse, Stephen. 1985. "Excusing the Crazy: The Insanity Defense Reconsidered." *Southern California Law Review* 58: 777–836.

Muller v. Oregon, 208 U.S. 412 (1908).

Münsterberg, Hugo. 1908. *On the Witness Stand: Essays on Psychology and Crime*. New York: Doubleday, Page.

Rogers, Richard. 2008. *Clinical Assessment of Malingering and Deception*. New York: Guilford Press.

G

Gambling Addiction

Thomas Broffman

Overview

Games of chance have been with us since the beginning of history. At about 3500 BC Babylonians were playing the game of hounds and jackals with knuckle bones from sheep or cattle, and six-sided dice were in use 500 years later in Egypt (Diagram 1995). The vesting of lots to deliver judgment is well documented in the Old Testament of the bible and in other religious texts from the Middle and Far East.

Over time gambling activities have been understood from moral, mathematical, economic, social, psychological, cultural, and biological perspectives. During the early part of the twentieth century, most types of gambling were considered criminal and legal gambling was highly restricted. In the last decade in the United States, an unprecedented growth of legalized gambling occurred within a new and expanded public policy framework. Today the person who wants to gamble has a multiplicity of choices. The primary driving force behind the explosion of gambling in has been the fiscal and economic needs of states and local governments. States have promoted the leisure and recreational aspects of gambling.

Since the 1970s, legalized gambling has spread geographically and is now legal in all but two states, Utah and Hawaii. Moreover, according to the National Gambling Impact Study Report (U.S. Senate 1999) legalized gambling has become one of the fastest growing industries. Casinos now operate in 27 states. Legalized gambling has never been more available or socially acceptable. On the Las Vegas strip alone, there are 42 casinos, which earned $4.7 billion in 2002 (Atchison 2003). Gambling on the Internet is also growing at a staggering rate, with 1,400 online wagering sites and over 400 sports betting sites, grossing over $1 billion annually (compared to inconsequential revenues a few years ago; U.S. Senate 1999). In 1999, Americans spent more on gambling ($50.9 billion) than they did on all other forms of recreation and leisure combined including cruise ships, sporting events, music, movies and amusement parks (U.S. Senate 1999). Gambling varies by venues: casino gambling accounts for 40.3 percent, lotteries 32.6 percent, tribal gambling 13.1 percent, pari-mutuel 7.5 percent, and charity gambling 6.5 percent. Amazingly, only 2.5 percent of bettors account for 15 percent of the wagering in America (U.S. Senate 1999).

Gamblers Anonymous on the Problem Gambler

"Most of us have been unwilling to admit we were real problem gamblers. . . . The idea that somehow, some day, we will control our gambling is the great obsession of every compulsive gambler. The persistence of this illusion is astonishing. Many pursue it into the gates of prison, insanity or death."

Source: Gamblers Anonymous. Retrieved from http://www.gamblersanonymous.org/ga/node/1.

Gambling has become much more accepted in recent years. Three primary forces appear to be motivating the growth in legalized gambling: (1) the desire of governments to identify new sources of revenue without invoking new or higher taxes; (2) tourism entrepreneurs developing new destinations for entertainment and leisure; and (3) the rise of new technologies and forms of gambling (i.e., video lottery terminals, Powerball mega-state lotteries, and computer offshore gambling on the Internet). State and local governments (counties and cities) often support such venues as casino gambling, lotteries, and video slot machines at racetracks because the governments receive part of the revenues (representing the third leading source of revenue in several states). Gambling revenues are seen as a painless form of taxation, one that adults support freely and enjoyably.

The growth of the gambling industry throughout the United States has not been without consequence. As the availability of gambling options and venues has increased, so have the associated problems. The 1999 National Gambling Impact Study Commission Report illustrated a number of health and social costs associated with gambling. Problem gamblers and those at risk of becoming problem gamblers face higher rates of depression, stress, family and peer relationship problems, financial strain, alcohol dependence, and poor health (U.S. Senate 1999). Gambling has not only become a high source of revenue for governments throughout the United States but also an important public health issue.

Gambling is one of the few activities that cuts across all barriers of race, gender, class, and culture. For the majority of people in the United States gambling is a form of recreation and entertainment, it provides an outlet for socialization and amusement at a reasonable price. One of the concerns relating to the increase in gambling opportunities is the potential rise in the number of problem gamblers. Associated with this phenomenon, there has been an increase in the prevalence of problem gambling (Korn & Shaffer 1999). Gambling disorders arise from an interaction and interplay between many factors, including biological or genetic predisposition, psychological constitution, social environment, and the nature of the activity itself.

A minority of gamblers have significant problems associated with gambling. Pathological gambling, as defined in the *Diagnostic and Statistical Manual of Mental Disorders* (*DSM-IV*), entails loss of control over one's gambling, a progression to more frequent and higher-stakes wagering, and gambling becoming a life focus in spite of adverse consequences (American Psychiatric Association [APA] 1994). Problem gambling implies a negative impact on one's life that falls short of pathological gambling. In evaluations of the costs versus the benefits of gambling to society, stories of ruined finances and destroyed relationships are balanced against stories of having the individual freedom to enjoy a harmless activity that supplants tax increases. What is rarely considered is the impact of a gambling culture on our society's values and measures to prevent the resulting harm.

Definitions

The words "game," "gamble," "gambler," and "gambling" are all derived from the Anglo-Saxon *gamen*, "game," and *gameman*, "to sport or play" (Wykes 1964). The way we define a problem determines what we do about it. To begin with, *gambling* (used interchangeably with the terms *gaming* and *wagering*) is defined as placing something of value at risk in order to win a prize of value if a chance event (or an event in some part determined by chance) occurs (Korn & Shaffer, 1999). The chance events are usually determined by the outcome of card hands or dice tosses, contests between players, or the drawing of lots. The legal definition of gambling requires three elements: consideration, chance, and prize (Atchison 2003). Gamblers Anonymous (2012) defines it as any betting or wagering, for self or for others, no matter how slight or insignificant, where the outcome is uncertain or depends upon chance or skill. The casino industry prefers the term *gaming*, as it sounds more acceptable to the general populace. "Wagering" is a term that generally applies to betting on horse races, dog races, or pari-mutuel events such as jai alai.

Gambling occurs on a continuum from nonproblem (i.e., social or recreational) gambling to problem gambling to compulsive or pathological gambling. A social or recreational gambler is a person who participates in gambling as a casual activity to fill time with friends or for excitement during leisure time (McGurrin 1994). The player may expect to incur some losses, but these are seen as the cost of the entertainment experience. The losses are monies that the player can afford to spend on recreation. A social gambler differs from a compulsive gambler in that he or she can quit gambling anytime. This seems due to three factors: (1) there is no self-esteem tied to winning or losing; (2) other aspects of the person's life are felt to be more important and rewarding; and (3) the social gambler rarely enjoys a big win (Blume 1997).

In the mental health and addictions field the most common terms used today are *problem* and *pathological gambling*. *Problem gambling* is defined as all patterns of gambling that compromises, disrupt or damages personal, family, or vocational pursuits and leads to adverse consequences (Volberg 2001). A problem gambler gambles excessively, usually more than he or she would like to gamble. Losses exceed the amount of money the gambler can easily afford to lose. The problem gambler maintains some control over his or her gambling activity, being able to stop and then avoid gambling activity. However, most pathological gamblers go through a stage of problem gambling. These gambling problems may be mild, moderate, or severe.

Problem gambling is not a well-defined concept. *DSM-IV* provides a diagnosis of gambling problems only at the "pathological" level. Currently, there is no diagnostic equivalent to substance abuse such as gambling abuse or problem gambling. In the sixteen states where prevalence studies were conducted beginning in 1986, the terms "problem," "compulsive," and "pathological gambling" have been used synonymously.

Pathological gambling is "persistent and recurrent maladaptive gambling behavior that disrupts personal, family or vocational pursuits" (APA 1994, 615). The pathological gambler has succumbed to a psychiatric impulse-control disorder. The disorder is evidenced by progression of gambling activity that cannot be controlled by the gambler, who becomes intolerant of losing and must keep betting to satisfy his or her inner drives. The gambling preoccupies the gambler's thinking to the point where the consequences of the gambling activity are completely disregarded. The gambler seems unable to stop; he or she suffers from urges and cravings similar to those of other addictions. Eventually, gambling interferes with functioning in almost every aspect of life.

Professional gamblers, in contrast, are persons who tend to be very skilled in the games they choose to play. They are almost always able to control the time spent gambling and the amount of money spent. In essence, they know when to quit. Usually they are not addicted to gambling. It is estimated that fewer than 3,000 people in the United States make a living as a professional gambler (McCown & Chamberlain 2000). These days, professional gamblers are largely confined to the games of blackjack, which can be beaten with much effort, and poker, which requires the development of a great deal of skill.

The distinction between problem and pathological gambling is a complex and important issue for clinicians. Problem gamblers do not meet the *DSM-IV* criteria for pathological gambling, but they do exhibit features of the disorder. Individuals who are problem gamblers would benefit from early diagnosis and treatment to reduce the risk of further deterioration into pathological gambling. Owing to their denial, an individual with a severe gambling problem may not appear to meet the diagnostic criteria for pathological gambling. However, on further scrutiny (e.g., on the basis of collateral information obtained from family members) the severity of the illness usually emerges.

Most commonly, pathological gamblers will seek help only at a time of crisis. The crisis may stem from mounting pressure to repay loans and debts to family, loan sharks, creditors, or banks, or it may, for example, follow an arrest on charges of gambling-related illegal activity such as embezzlement or fraud. Family and friends frequently make the initial contact with treatment providers because the affected individual typically denies the extent of his or her problem and is resistant to the idea of treatment. Pathological gamblers commonly report feeling under pressure to continue gambling in the hope of making a big win that will, they believe, alleviate their financial problems.

Gambling Treatment Interventions

Methods for treating pathological gambling include approaches that are psychoanalytic, psychodynamic, behavioral, cognitive, pharmacological, addiction-based, multimodal, and self-help (National Research Council 1999). Often these approaches are combined to varying degrees in most treatment programs or counseling settings. The discussion below briefly summarizes each method.

Psychoanalytic and psychodynamic treatment approaches seek to understand the basis of all human behavior by considering the motivational forces that derive from unconscious mental processes. Even the most destructive behaviors can serve a defensive or adaptive purpose. This approach suggests that pathological gambling is a symptom or expression of an underlying psychological condition. Psychoanalytic and psychodynamic therapy attempts to help the pathological gambler to understand the underlying source of his or her distress and confront it. Clinicians have considered psychodynamically oriented psychotherapy useful in treating some of the comorbid (co-occurring) disorders and character pathology observed among pathological gamblers, specifically the narcissistic and masochistic subtypes (Ladouceur Sylvian et al. 2002).

Behavioral treatment actively seeks to modify pathological gambling behavior on the basis of principles of classical conditioning or operant theory. Four variations of behavioral treatment methods are used today, often in combinations: (1) aversion treatment, (2) imaginal desensitization, (3) imaginal relaxation, and (4) in vivo exposure (McCown & Chamberlain 2000). Aversion treatment consists of applying an unpleasant stimulus, such as a small electrical shock, while the patient reads phrases that describe gambling behavior. Imaginal desensitization consists of getting patients to relax and then having them imagine an arousing gambling scenario. In this way they learn to relax while gambling opportunities present themselves, rather than submitting. An extension of imaginal desensitization is "in vivo exposure," in which relaxation techniques are applied while the patient is actually experiencing a gambling situation.

Cognitive-behavioral approaches address pathological gamblers' irrational beliefs about gambling risks, the illusion of control, biased evaluations of gambling outcomes, and the belief that gambling is a solution to their financial problems (Shaffer et al. 2003). Cognitive treatment aims to counteract underlying irrational beliefs and attitudes about gambling that are believed to initiate and maintain the undesirable behavior. Typical treatment involves teaching clients strategies to correct their erroneous thinking. The "illusion of control" over gambling outcomes, for example, is a core cognition that influences problem gamblers. This sense that one has the "omnipotence skill" necessary to beat the odds is an enduring characteristic of pathological gamblers. Moreover, cognitive-behavioral therapy attends to the effect of gambling on others and attempts to minimize impacts to family, work, and personal finances (Korn & Shaffer 2004).

Pharmacotherapy is a relatively new approach to the treatment of pathological gambling. Neurobiological studies suggest the involvement of serotonin, norepinephrine, and dopamine—neurotransmitter systems—in pathological gambling. The medications used target one or more of these systems. One of the most promising such medications involves agents that block the excitement or pleasure of gambling. The best known of these blocking agents is naltrexone, an opiate antagonist used in the treatment of alcoholism. Another avenue of approach is the use of medication to treat co-morbid conditions. In practice, this is the most commonly cited reasons for putting gamblers on medication. Co-morbid disorders for which medications are commonly prescribed include depression, bipolar disorder, and ADHD (National Research Council 1999).

See also Impulse Control Disorders; Internet Gaming Addiction; Peer Support Groups

Bibliography

American Psychiatric Association. 1994. *Diagnostic and Statistical Manual of Mental Disorders* (4th ed.). Washington, DC: American Psychiatric Publishing.

Atchison, E. 2003. *Joe Gambel's Hidden Secrets: Behavioral Control and Psychosocial Impact in Las Vegas*. Cheyenne, WY: Pioneer Printing.

Berman, L., and M. Siegel. 2001. *Behind the Eight Ball*. New York: Simon & Schuster.

Blume, S. 1997. "Pathological Gambling." In N. Miller, ed., *The Principles and Practice of Addictions in Psychiatry* (pp. 422–432). Philadelphia: Saunders.

Castelani, B. 2000. *Pathological Gambling: The Making of a Medical Problem*. Albany: State University of New York Press.

Diagram, G. 2004. *The Book of Gambling Games*. New York: Sterling.

Federman, E., C. Drebing, and C. Krebs. 2000. *Don't Leave It to Chance: A Guide for Families of Problem Gamblers*. Oakland, CA: New Harbinger Press.

Gamblers Anonymous. 2012. "Questions and Answers." Retrieved from http://www.gamblersanonymous.org/ga/content/questions-answers-about-gamblers-anonymous.

Korn, D., and H. Shaffer. 1999. "Gambling and the Health of the Public: Adopting a Public Health Perspective." *Journal of Gambling Studies* 15(4): 289–365.

Korn, D., and H. Shaffer. 2004. *Practice Guidelines for Treating Gambling-Related Problems: An Evidence-Based Treatment Guide for Clinicians*. Boston: Massachusetts Council on Compulsive Gambling.

Ladouceur, R., C. Sylvian, H. Letarte, I. Giroux, and C. Jacques. 2002. *Understanding and Treating the Pathological Gambler.* New York: Wiley.

McCown, W., and L. Chamberlain. 2000. *Best Possible Odds: Contemporary Treatment Strategies for Gambling Disorders.* New York: Wiley.

McGurrin, M. 1994. *Pathological Gambling: Conceptual, Diagnostic, and Treatment Issues.* Sarasota, FL: Professional Resource Press.

National Research Council. 1999. *Pathological Gambling: A Critical Review.* Washington, DC: National Academy Press.

North American Training Institute. 1997. *Gambling Away the Golden Years.* Duluth, MN: North American Training Institute.

Petry, N. M. 2005. *Pathological Gambling: Etiology, Comorbidity, and Treatment.* Washington, D.C.: American Psychological Association.

Shaffer, H., M. Hall, J. Vander Bilt, and E. George. 2003. *Futures @ Stake: Youth, Gambling, and Society.* Reno: University of Nevada Press.

Skolnik, S. 2011. *High Stakes: The Rising Cost of America's Gambling Addiction.* Boston: Beacon Press.

U.S. Senate, Committee on Indian Affairs. 1999. *National Gambling Impact Study Commission Final Report.* Retrieved from http://govinfo.library.unt.edu/ngisc/index.html.

Volberg, R. (2001). *When the Chips Are Down: Problem Gambling in America.* New York: Century Foundation.

Wykes, A. (1964). *Gambling.* London: Spring Books, 1964.

Gender Identity Disorder

Stephanie Brzuzy

Gender identity disorder (GID) is a hotly contested diagnostic category used by the American Psychiatric Association (APA) to label nonconforming gender identity expression as a mental illness. Activist groups are challenging the pathologizing of gender identity expression and claim that similar to the declassification of homosexuality as a mental illness in the 1970s, nonconforming gender identity expression, too, must be declassified and cease being labeled a mental illness. Supporters believe that gender is a biological fact and that lack of identification with the gender assigned at birth is a dysfunction.

Background: Gender Identity Disorder Diagnosis

GID is one of the most controversial categories of mental disorders in the *Diagnostic and Statistical Manual of Mental Disorders* (*DSM*). Those who believe it should be eliminated from the *DSM* contend there is little evidence to support its use and that gender roles and expectations are not binary categories as the *DSM* suggests. Gender identity is a social construction and its pathology has been created by the medical profession. Therefore the category should be dropped altogether from the next version of the *DSM* (*DSM-5*, which is now under discussion and targeted for a 2013 release date). Psychologist Daryl Hill argues that GID is not a mental disorder at all and that it is largely a diagnosis designed to alleviate the stress experienced by social institutions and parents who cannot accept a child's exploration of gender roles and expectations that do not fit prescribed categories (Hausman 2003).

Supporters of the diagnosis disagree with this analysis. They believe that gender is a biological fact and the diagnostic category is valid because gender-congruent roles and behaviors are an expectation of society. Thus if individuals do not identify with the gender they are "born into," it is a "dysfunction" and should be labeled and treated as such.

Gender Identity Disorder Diagnostic Criteria

A. A strong and persistent cross-gender identification (not merely a desire for any perceived cultural advantages of being the other sex). In children, the disturbance is manifested by four (or more) of the following:

1. Repeatedly stated desire to be, or insistence that he or she is, the other sex.

2. In boys, preference for cross-dressing or simulating female attire; in girls, insistence on wearing only stereotypical masculine clothing.

3. Strong and persistent preferences for cross-sex roles in make-believe play or persistent fantasies of being the other sex.

4. Intense desire to participate in the stereotypical games and pastimes of the other sex.

5. Strong preference for playmates of the other sex.

B. Persistent discomfort with his or her sex or sense of inappropriateness in the gender role of that sex.

C. The disturbance is not concurrent with a physical intersex condition.

D. The disturbance causes clinically significant distress or impairment in social, occupational, or other important areas of functioning (American Psychiatric Association 2000, 302.85).

Others argue for GID reform instead of complete removal of the category from the *DSM*. GID Reform Advocates is one group dedicated to keeping the diagnosis of "gender dysphoria" as a serious medical condition that can be treated with medical intervention but declassifying gender nonconformity and "cross-gender" identities that are legitimate expressions of gender. They argue the criteria for a mental disorder should rise to the level of a "clear therapeutic purpose" for intervention that is based on distress or impairment for the individual. It should not be based on socially defined gender nonconformity constructs. (The *DSM* criteria include mention of "significant distress or impairment" for the individual, but these advocates would rewrite or abandon the criteria altogether.)

The World Health Organization's International Statistical Classification of Diseases and Related Health Problems (10th revision, 2003) classifies gender identity variance in a similar fashion as the *Diagnostic and Statistical Manual of Mental Disorders* (*DSM-IV-TR*), published by the American Psychiatric Association (APA 2000). Gender identity variances are classified as diseases under the broader category of "gender identity disorders."

Who Needs a GID Diagnosis?

People who consider themselves gender variant encompass a wide range of perspectives on whether GID should be a disease and have a wide range of perspectives on body transformation from one sex to another. Some seek body modification surgeries; others do not. To pursue body-transforming procedures in the United States, such as sex reassignment or hormone therapies, however, an individual usually enters the mental health system and obtains a diagnosis of GID after seeing a mental health therapist for a certain amount of time. Often without this designation, an individual cannot proceed with surgical interventions to modify the body. Activist groups continue to challenge essentialist assumptions of gender identity expression that pathologizes individuals who do not align themselves with traditional binary sex/gender categories; males must be men and females must be women, for example. In addition, activists see the pathologizing of gender identity expression as a form of social control that the *DSM-IV-TR* legitimizes. Supporters of GID as a mental disorder argue that individuals who experience "gender distress" and "gender dysphoria" are in need of psychological and medical interventions to help them cope with their condition.

Conclusion

To date, the APA has supported the pathologizing of nonconforming, cross-gender, and gender-variant identities. Activists in and outside of the mental health profession continue to challenge this stance. Whether gender identity disorder will be declassified by the APA as a mental illness in the next revisions of the *DSM* will be one of the most hotly debated issues facing the association.

See also Lesbian, Gay, Bisexual, and Transgender (LGBT) Mental Health Issues; Mind and Body Approaches to Mental Health

Bibliography

American Psychiatric Association. 2000. *Diagnostic and Statistical Manual of Mental Disorders* (4th ed., text rev.). Washington, DC: American Psychiatric Publishing.

Bering, J. (2010). "The Third Gender." *Scientific American Mind* May/June: 60–63.

Bornstein, Kate. 1994. *Gender Outlaw: On Men, Women, and the Rest of Us*. New York: Vintage Books.

GID Reform Advocates. 2006. "What Is GID?" December 5. Retrieved from http://www.gidreform.org.

Hausman, Ken. 2003. "Controversy Continues to Grow over *DSMs* GID Diagnosis." *Psychiatric News* 38(14): 25.

Heath, R. A. 2006. *The Praeger Handbook of Transsexuality: Changing Gender to Match Mindset*. Westport, CT: Praeger.

Israel, Gianna, and Donald Traver. 1997. *Transgender Care: Recommended Guidelines, Practical Information and Personal Accounts*. Philadelphia: Temple University Press.

Lev, Arlene Istar. 2004. *Transgender Emergence: Therapeutic Guidelines for Working with Gender-Variant People and Their Families*. New York: Haworth Press, 2004.

Lothstein, Leslie M. 2006. "The Scientific Foundations of Gender Identity Disorder." In Thomas G. Plante, ed., *Mental Disorders of the New Millennium* (pp. 227–250). Westport, CT: Praeger.

Parker, James, and Philip Parker. 2004. *Gender Identity Disorder: A 3–1 Medical Reference*. San Diego: ICON Health Publications.

Run, Henry. (2003). *Self-Made Men: Identity and Embodiment among Transsexual Men*. Nashville, TN: Vanderbilt University Press.

Scholinski, Daphne. (1997). *The Last Time I Wore a Dress: A Memoir*. New York: Riverhead Books.

Genetics and Mental Health

Jay Joseph

Government leaders frequently argue that the social, political, and material conditions found in the United States provide the potential for the happiness and well-being of its citizens. Nevertheless, the mental health status of Americans is not good. As a case in point, Ronald Kessler and his colleagues published a 2005 study in a leading psychiatry journal, where they found that "about half of Americans will meet the criteria for a *DSM-IV* [mental] disorder sometime in their life, with first onset usually in childhood or early adolescence" (Kessler et al. 2005, 593; *DSM-IV* is the fourth edition of the American Psychiatric Association's *Diagnostic and Statistical Manual of Mental Disorders*). Moreover, owing to several potential biases in their research design, Kessler and colleagues emphasized that their findings "are likely to be conservative" (2005, 599). Indeed, a 12-month prevalence study suggests that the United States is the world leader in diagnosed mental disorders and that, for example, Americans are diagnosed with a psychiatric disorder twice as often as residents of Mexico (26% vs. 12%), three times as often as residents of Italy (26% vs. 8%), and five times as often as residents of Nigeria (26% vs. 5%; WHO World Mental Health Survey Consortium 2004).

Some observers have criticized the *DSM*'s tendency to label a wide range of subjective states, socially disapproved behavior, and even normal behavior as "mental disorders," and have questioned the validity and reliability of psychiatric disorders (see Kirk & Kutchins 1992). Furthermore, the "mental illness" concept itself has been questioned (Szasz 1987).

These issues aside, additional statistics illustrate the current level of psychological distress in the United States. According to Robert Whitaker, author of *Anatomy of an Epidemic*, by 2007 approximately 4 million Americans under the age of 65 received Social Security benefits for a mental disability. Americans spend $25 billion annually on antidepressant and antipsychotic drugs, and spend over $40 billion annually on all psychotropic drugs. All told, $170 billion is spent annually on mental health services in the United States, and one in every eight Americans takes a psychiatric drug on a regular basis (see Whitaker 2010).

Given these findings and statistics, it is clear that a sizable portion of Americans will experience some level of chronic or acute psychological dysfunction or distress during their lifetimes. Having established this, the question remains open whether the causes are due mainly to hereditary factors or whether they reflect the impact of a wide range of psychologically harmful environmental influences that people experience in American society.

The current consensus position in the field of psychiatry (and related fields) is that genetic factors play an important role in the overall mental health of Americans. The leaders of the field argue that the evidence shows conclusively that conditions such as depression, schizophrenia, bipolar disorder, autism, and attention-deficit hyperactivity disorder (ADHD) have an important genetic basis. These are often called "multifactorial complex disorders," which means that they are viewed as being caused by the effects of multiple genes in combination with multiple environmental factors. This idea is based on the earlier *predisposition-stress* theory of psychiatric disorders. Although they recognize a role for environmental factors, psychiatric genetic researchers and popularizers of their work tend to emphasize the centrality of perceived genetic factors, and focus their research in this area.

An alternative to currently ascendant biological/genetic explanations of psychiatric disorders is the perspective of psychological theories that emphasize the major role of childhood family environments in establishing a person's potential for healthy psychological functioning. Indeed, a team of psychiatric researchers, in a study spanning 21 countries, found that "childhood adversities have strong associations with all classes of [psychiatric] disorders at all life-course stages in all groups of" the countries under study (Kessler et al. 2010, 378).

There is also the larger sociological context, which impacts family environments both directly and indirectly. Researchers in this area emphasize the psychologically harmful effects of social conditions such as racism, chronic stress, living in poverty, sexism, social class status, discrimination against sexual minorities, diminished social networks (which may be a product of the culture and economic system), social inequality, divorce, unemployment, and the consumer-driven individualist culture promoted in advanced industrial societies. As the psychologist Philip Cushman puts it, the quest for corporate profit in the post–World War II era transformed the predominant American self into an "empty self," one that strives for "self-liberation through the compulsive purchase and consumption of goods, experiences, and celebrities" (Cushman 1995, 211). Clearly, an "empty" self is not a healthy self.

The Genetic Perspective

As one sociologist has stated, "Diagnostic psychiatry minimizes the importance of social causes of mental disorder. This orientation naturally results from its emphasis on internal, genetic causes of disorder" (Horwitz 2002, 158). Psychiatry does indeed emphasize genetics, but we will see that there are problems with the evidence supporting this position.

Genetic theories in psychiatry are based on the results of family, twin, and adoption studies, in addition to some claims that genes have been discovered at the molecular level. As a group of researchers looking for schizophrenia and bipolar disorder genes have written, "Twin and adoption studies during the 20th century firmly established a genetic basis for the major mental illnesses and numerous other common diseases" (Gershon, Alliey-Rodriguez, & Liu 2011, 253). However, there are problem areas in twin and adoption research that cast doubt on researchers' ability to provide evidence in favor of genetic influences on mental disorders. In addition, it can be argued that we are witnessing an ongoing failure to identify the genes that researchers believe underlie these disorders (Gershon, Alliey-Rodriguez, & Liu 2011; Joseph 2010, 2011; Wade 2010).

The main problems with family, twin, adoption, and molecular genetic research will be briefly summarized here (see also Joseph 2004, 2006, 2010). First, family studies are clearly unable to disentangle the potential role of genetic and environmental factors, because family members share a common environment as well as common genes. Most genetic researchers now agree that a trait or disorder identified as "running in the family" can be explained on the grounds of *either* genetic *or* environmental factors, and that family studies therefore prove nothing about genetics alone (Joseph 2010). This in itself is a significant point.

Moving on to twin research, which forms the basis of current arguments in support of genetics, the main technique (called the "twin method") compares the trait resemblance of reared-together monozygotic (MZ, i.e., identical) twin pairs to reared-together same-sex dizygotic (DZ, i.e., fraternal) twin pairs. (MZs show 100% genetic similarity, whereas DZs show on average 50% genetic similarity.) Because members of MZ pairs usually resemble each other more with respect to psychiatric disorders than do members of DZ pairs, twin researchers conclude that such disorders must have a genetic component.

In order to reach this conclusion, however, researchers must rely on several theoretical assumptions about twins. The most controversial is the assumption that MZ and same-sex DZ twin pairs experience roughly equal environments. This is known as the "equal environment assumption" or "EEA." The problem here is that despite twin researchers' claims to the contrary, the equal environment assumption of the twin method appears to be faulty. This is because most research finds that MZ twins experience much more similar environments than do DZ twins (Joseph 2004, 2010). Thus the greater resemblance of MZ versus DZ twin pairs with respect to psychiatric disorders can be explained by MZ pairs' more similar environment and closer psychological bond. This means that the twin method is confounded by environmental factors, and that researchers in this area seem no more able to disentangle the potential roles of genes and environment than those employing family studies. Even in studies of *reared-apart* twins, which usually focus on psychological traits such as IQ and personality, there are additional environmental confounds and methodological problems that arguably make researchers' results explainable on nongenetic grounds. (Moreover, few of these pairs qualify as being truly "reared apart"; see Joseph 2004, 2010.)

Some researchers have turned to adoption studies, which they view as being less vulnerable to environmental confounds than are twin and family studies. Adoption studies investigate people who have received the genes of their birth parents but are reared in the family environment of people with whom they share no genetic relationship. These studies are frequently cited in support of genetic influences on disorders such as schizophrenia, ADHD, and bipolar disorder. In particular, studies conducted in Denmark, which maintains an extensive genetics database, are widely cited as having established schizophrenia as a genetic disorder.

Like family and twin studies, however, adoption studies appear to contain their own unique set of environmental confounds and biases. Among these biases are the late separation of adoptees who have been studied, the nonrepresentativeness of adoptive families (versus the general population), and issues involving the way adoption agencies "selective place" adoptees according to the socioeconomic and perceived genetic status of their biological parent(s). All of these factors, along with others, would seem to seriously hinder the utility of psychiatric adoption studies (Joseph 2004, 2006, 2010).

The pervasive existence of environmental confounds means that, although the siblings and relatives in family, twin, and adoption studies are frequently diagnosed with psychiatric disorders in patterns predicted by genetic theories, these same findings can be said to follow, as well, the patterns of *non*genetic causation. It therefore is possible to conclude that these studies have been largely unable to disentangle the potential roles of genetic and environmental influences on mental disorders. Critics thus believe that the foundations of genetic theories in psychiatry and psychology rest, in fact, on rather shaky ground.

The Search for Genes

Given that psychiatric genetic researchers believe that the genetic basis of psychiatric disorders has already been established, the search for the genes (genetic variants) presumed to cause these disorders has been under way since the 1970s. Although researchers and their financial backers recognize that environmental factors play a role in the development of psychiatric disorders, their emphasis on genetics and on costly gene identification efforts are based on the principle of *genetic determinism*. As the evolutionary biologist Richard Lewontin describes it, genetic determinism is the "assumption that all-important variations in basic physiological and developmental processes are the direct result of genetic variation" (Lewontin 2009).

Despite well-funded international efforts carried out over the past few decades, however, and despite the completion of the Human Genome Project, the genes believed to underlie the major psychiatric disorders have not been found (Gershon, Alliey-Rodriguez, & Liu 2011; Wade 2010). Although most researchers in the field continue to believe that such genes exist and simply await discovery, one pair of (nonpsychiatric) researchers who have reviewed the data have concluded that "genetic predispositions as significant factors in the prevalence of [most] common diseases are refuted," and that "the dearth of disease-causing genes is without question a scientific discovery of tremendous significance" (Latham & Wilson 2010).

Such investigations continue, however. Instead of recognizing the possibility that decades of failed gene identification efforts show that the genes may not exist—a recognition that would necessitate a thorough reexamination of family, twin, and adoption research (as well as genetic determinism itself)—most investigators choose instead to assume an attitude of *optimism* and downplay the prospect of *failure*. As Latham and Wilson (2010) observe, "The history of scientific refutation ... is that adherents of established theories construct ever more elaborate or unlikely explanations to fend off their critics." This can be seen in recent attempts by researchers to explain failed gene identification efforts on the basis of "missing heritability" (e.g., Gershon et al. 2011; Manolio et al. 2009) rather than concluding that such genes likely do not exist.

But even if researchers were to discover genes that predispose some people to developing mental disorders, many observers believe it would do little to help us understand, treat, or prevent these disorders. Genetic determinist ideas, that is, tend to divert society's attention from psychologically damaging environments, shifting causes onto the brains and bodies of those who suffer the effects of living in those environments. Critics of this type of genetic research note that it is heavily funded and promoted by political and corporate entities that have an interest in promoting their own policies and products, not addressing environmental conditions. Even for medical disorders such as type 2 diabetes, where environmental conditions such as poverty and malnutrition are well-known causes, supporters of genetic determinism continue to press for research dollars to be directed toward genetic research as opposed to improvements in social conditions and human health (Chaufan 2007).

It could be argued that the time has come to institute a moratorium on psychiatric molecular genetic research and to redirect scientific attention toward a thorough reassessment of the family, twin, and adoption studies that inspired the search for genes in the first place. Upon the completion of this reassessment, it would conceivably become apparent that the genes currently believed to be "missing" may well not exist. Other research avenues could be developed instead.

If Kessler and colleagues' (2005) finding is correct and 50 percent of Americans indeed will develop a (presumably genetically based) mental disorder, then, according to current genetic theories, a sizable percentage of the *other* 50 percent—i.e., those who *do not* develop a mental disorder but are related to those who do so— must nevertheless carry pathological genes (Joseph 2006). That is, based on the logic of the *DSM*, and on currently ascendant theories of genetic causation, most Americans carry genes predisposing them to developing mental disorders. Critics of this view, on the other hand, believe that the environmental/psychological/sociological perspective offers a more realistic and beneficial approach to reducing mental suffering and dysfunction. According to the psychologist David Jacobs, for example, an alternative approach to currently popular genetic theories would "examine changes in the social-cultural environment, and not our relatively unchanging and permanent genetic heritage, for clues regarding widespread psychopathology" (Jacobs 1994, 9). In sum, while mainstream supporters of genetic determinism worry about the "societal burden of mental disorders" (Kessler et al. 2005, 601), from an environmental/sociological perspective it might be better to characterize the problem as that of the *mental burden of societal disorders*.

See also Autism Spectrum Disorders; Creativity and Mental Health; *Diagnostic and Statistical Manual of Mental Disorders* (*DSM*); Drug Companies; Family and Mental Illness; Medical Model of Mental Illness; Neurodiversity; Psychiatry; Schizophrenia

Bibliography

Chaufan, C. 2007. "How Much Can a Large Population Study on Genes, Environments, Their Interactions and Common Diseases Contribute to the Health of the American People?" *Social Science and Medicine* 65: 1730–1741.

Cushman, Philip. 1995. *Constructing the Self, Constructing America*. Reading, MA: Addison -Wesley.

Gershon, E. S., N. Alliey-Rodriguez, and C. Liu. 2011. "After GWAS: Searching for Genetic Risk for Schizophrenia and Bipolar Disorder." *American Journal of Psychiatry* 168: 253–256.

Higgins, Edmund S. 2008. "The New Genetics of Mental Illness." *Scientific American Mind*, June/July, 40–47.

Horwitz, Allan V. 2002. *Creating Mental Illness*. Chicago: University of Chicago Press.

Jacobs, D. 1994. "Environmental Failure—Oppression Is the Only Cause of Psychopathology." *Journal of Mind and Behavior* 15: 1–18.

Joseph, Jay. 2004. *The Gene Illusion: Genetic Research in Psychiatry and Psychology under the Microscope*. New York: Algora (2003 United Kingdom edition by PCCS Books).

Joseph, Jay. 2006. *The Missing Gene: Psychiatry, Heredity, and the Fruitless Search for Genes*. New York: Algora.

Joseph, Jay. 2010. "Genetic Research in Psychiatry and Psychology: A Critical Overview." In K. E. Hood, C. Tucker Halpern, G. Greenberg, and R. M. Lerner, eds., *Handbook of Developmental Science, Behavior, and Genetics* (pp. 557–625). Malden, MA: Wiley-Blackwell.

Joseph, Jay. 2011. "The Crumbling Pillars of Behavioral Genetics." *GeneWatch* 24(6): 4–7.

Kessler, R. C., P. Berglund, O. Demler, R. Jin, K. R. Merikangas, and E. E. Walters. 2005. "Lifetime Prevalence and Age-of-Onset Distributions of *DSM-IV* Disorders in the National Comorbidity Survey Replication." *Archives of General Psychiatry* 62: 593–602.

Kessler, R. C., M. A. McLaughlin, J. G. Green, M. J. Gruber, N. A. Sampson, A. M. Zaslavsky, S. Aguilar-Gaxiola, A. O. Alhamzawi, J. Alonso, M. Angemeyer, C. Benjet, E. Bromet, S. Chatterji, G. de Girolamo, K. Demyttenaere, J. Fayyad, S. Florescu, G. Gal, O. Gureje, J. M. Haro, C. Hu, E. G. Karam, N. Kawakami, S. Lee, J.-P. Lépine, J. Ormel, J. Posada-Villa, R. Sagar, A. Tsang. T. B. Üstūn, S. Vassiley, M. C. Viana, and D. R. Williams. 2010. "Childhood Adversities and Adult Psychopathology in the WHO World Mental Health Surveys." *British Journal of Psychiatry* 197: 378–385.

Kirk, S. A., and H. Kutchins. 1992. *The Selling of DSM: The Rhetoric of Science in Psychiatry*. New York: Aldine De Gruyter.

Latham, J., and A. Wilson. 2010. "The Great DNA Data Deficit: Are Genes for Disease a Mirage?" *The Bioscience Research Project*. Retrieved December 18, 2010, from http://www.bioscienceresource.org/commentaries/article.php?id=46.

Lewontin, R. C. 2009. "Where Are the Genes?" *GeneWatch*. Retrieved April 17, 2011, from http://www.councilforresponsiblegenetics.org/GeneWatch/GeneWatchPage.aspx?pageId=183&archive=yes.

Manolio, T. A., F. S. Collins, N. J. Cox, D. B. Goldstein, L. A. Hindorff, D. J. Hunter, M. I. McCarthy, E. M. Ramos, L. R. Cardon, A. Chakravarti, J. H. Cho, A. E. Guttmacher, A. Kong, L. Kruglyak, E. Mardis, C. N. Rotimi, M. Slatkin, D. Valle, A. S. Whittemore, M. Boehnke, A. G. Clark, E. E. Eichler, G. Gibson, J. L. Haines, T. F. C. Mackay, S. A. McCarroll, and P. M. Visscher. 2009. "Finding the Missing Heritability of Complex Diseases." *Nature* 461: 747–753.

Szasz, Thomas S. 1987. *Insanity: The Idea and Its Consequences*. Syracuse, NY: Syracuse University Press.

Wade, N. 2010. "A Decade Later, Genetic Map Yields Few New Cures." *New York Times*, June 12. Retrieved April 17, 2011, from http://www.nytimes.com/2010/06/13/health/research/13genome.html.

Whitaker, Robert. 2010. *Anatomy of an Epidemic: Magic Bullets, Psychiatric Drugs, and the Astonishing Rise of Mental Illness in America*. New York: Crown.

WHO World Mental Health Survey Consortium. 2004. "Prevalence, Severity, and Unmet Need for Treatment of Mental Disorders in the World Health Organization World Mental Health Surveys." *JAMA* 291: 2581–2590.

Group Therapy

Jerrold Lee Shapiro

Group psychotherapy, group therapy, and group counseling are forms of mental health treatment in which one or two professionals provide services simultaneously to a small group (characteristically 5–14) of clients. Generally, the prime notion is that group members gain therapeutic help both from the expert leaders and from each other. The group process (development of a trajectory and interpersonal interactions) is considered to be the central mechanism producing change both during the group and subsequently in the clients' back-home lives.

Types of Groups

There are many types of groups, and the identifying labels for them are used inconsistently. In order of increasing focus on group process and intensity of interpersonal interaction, there are task groups, psychoeducational groups, counseling groups, growth (training, encounter) groups, and psychotherapy groups.

Task groups are generally focused on completing a project, organizational need, or activity that could promote healthier functioning. There is far less focus on the process—i.e., what is occurring between the members—than on the outcome of the task or problem solving per se.

Psychoeducational groups are often used with people whose needs fall within a particular theme or category. These groups pair substantial information giving with individuals' reactions to these data. Often, people with similar skill-building needs and a lack of important information are best candidates for such groups. These groups tend to be structured heavily or "manualized," with a topic or agenda for each meeting. Assertiveness training, where one is encouraged to state one's point of view, is one successful form of psychoeducation.

In *counseling groups*, members deal with usual, often difficult problems in living. They tend to focus primarily on conscious processes and resolution of short-term problems. Counseling groups do have an interpersonal focus and encourage members to explore in the present the personal impact of each other's interactions. The group is seen as a social microcosm in which problems may be safely discussed and resolved. Counseling groups often have specific behavioral goals in mind. University counseling centers often run these groups regularly.

Therapy groups focus more in depth on intrapsychic issues and more debilitating symptoms (i.e., depression, anxiety, etc.). The leaders of therapy groups foster an environment in which members may better identify psychological blocks, gain insight, and work through them, coming to a more stable, less painful life experience. Often the groups involve symptom amelioration, behavior change, and personality reconstruction. In short, group psychotherapy is generally more intense, deals with greater pathology, and members characteristically have lower GAF scores (Global Assessment of Functioning) as defined by the American Psychiatric Association's *Diagnostic and Statistical Manual of Mental Disorders*.

Growth or *encounter groups* use similar techniques to the therapy and counseling groups in that they focus on both interpersonal and intrapsychic issues. However, the members of these groups are presumed to be functioning successfully in life and are exploring new directions, new insights, and personal change.

Support groups and open meetings such as 12-step methods are seen as different from any of the above. The do not require professional leaders, have varying and open enrollment, and often do not have the kind of pricing structure of the therapy groups. They are also more prone to promote a particular outcome based on circumscribed behaviors. These groups also have a quite useful role in people's lives and in society, but they are not considered groups for the current purposes.

Even within categories, groups come in a variety of forms. Some are brief, with closed membership. Others are long term and open to new members. Some therapists, for example, have a constant group going for years with members entering and leaving as there is space available or at junctures designated to replenish membership. These groups have the benefit of being more "lifelike" in that, as with life, significant people enter and leave at regular intervals. Closed groups have other advantages. Membership is stable and assured, leading to better interpersonal trust. The group process unfolds naturally rather than returning to earlier phases of development as new members have to be integrated. The goals in such groups are more defined and measurable, and data collection is far more likely.

A Brief History of Group Therapy

The history of group therapy and encounter is varied and multidimensional. No one person or single force can claim a primary influence. The origins are murky and multifaceted. Evidence of the first examples of groups designed for amelioration of symptoms and behavior change date back to prehistory and coexisted in many cultures. Natural groups were used for centuries to provide somewhat intangible, but very real benefits in diverse cultures such as the healing temple at Epidaurus in Greece from 600 BC to 200 AD and traditional Hawaiian *ho'oponopono* ceremonies. Witches' covens and primitive shamans employed similar techniques to those of modern group therapists albeit with different rationales.

In modern history, Franz Mesmer's experiments with groups and hypnosis in eighteenth-century Paris may be considered the first formal group treatment. The Marquis de Sade also made an attempt at group treatment while he himself was an inmate at the asylum at Charenton. He directed plays performed by the patients for the staff and visitors. These plays had the surprising effect on the players of lessening their symptoms.

Pratt's (1906) class method of treating tuberculosis patients was economically instigated, yet there were observed improvements in patients that were based on the intangible effects of meeting. Other early twentieth-century proponents of group treatment were Trigant Burrow, Paul Schilder, and Alfred Adler.

The advent of Jacob Moreno's psychodrama methods demonstrated how individuals in a group setting could influence each other in positive ways. Moreno claimed to be the creator of the term "group therapy," and he has also been credited as the first to use the term "encounter" in a therapeutic setting. Since the 1930s, the influence of Moreno's methods and techniques have seeped into a host of other approaches to group. The journal he founded, *Group Therapy*, remains the organ of dissemination of research and practice of psychodrama.

During the post–World War II years, S. H. Foulkes and Wilfred Bion underscored the importance of transference among members as part of the healing process. Many therapists extended the use of group methods to children and adolescents. Loretta Bender and others noted that these were the most natural settings for these populations.

Groups, especially those organized for growth rather than amelioration of pathology, got a large boost in popularity and interest by professionals in the late 1940s–1970s by the advent of BST (basic skills training) groups. T-group (training), followed quickly by sensitivity groups and encounter groups, had explosive growth through the late 1960s and early 1970s.

Two of the most prolific writers on groups counseling therapy from 1970 were Gerald Corey (counseling) and Irvin Yalom (psychotherapy). Yalom's (2005) curative (therapeutic) factors in group are most influential. These factors include (1) universality, (2) altruism, (3) instillation of hope, (4) imparting information, (5) corrective recapitulation of the family experience, (6) development of socializing behavior, (7) imitation, (8) cohesiveness, (9) existential factors, (10) catharsis, (11) interpersonal learning, and (12) self-understanding.

Shapiro, Peltz, and Bernadett-Shapiro (1998) have suggested that additional benefits of group therapy include enhancement of self-esteem, minimization of a personal sense of pathology, and opportunity for real-time feedback from peers.

Most other authors and clinicians agree with most or all of these factors, regardless of their theories or therapeutic approaches. For the therapist, one of the differences in group is that what the client does, says, or thinks is based on real-time observable actions and interactions. By dealing with observables rather than the clients' subjective reports, the therapist and fellow members may intervene quicker and more effectively. Finally, group sessions can be a crucible in which new behaviors and orientations can be tested, prior to transfer of training to back-home life.

Despite the rich history of group treatment, it has often been considered more dangerous than individual approaches. Fears of mob psychology, reenactment of the primal horde attacking and devouring the leader, and a lack of training and awareness of group methods have all played a significant role in group therapy being feared and subsequently, denigrated.

Group Process and Trajectory

With properly trained leaders, groups follow a predictable trajectory and traverse several stages. These stages are reliable for closed, process-oriented groups in which the group begins and ends together. Successful completion of a prior stage is prerequisite to psychological availability for subsequent stages, although the process is rarely linear.

Because this group trajectory is epigenetic in nature, interventions by the leader need to be geared to the current phase of group functioning. In time-limited groups, there are fewer opportunities for leaders to recover from ill-timed interventions. Thus it is incumbent on group leaders to be aware of group development and regressions and to intervene accordingly.

Phase I: Preparation

This phase encompasses everything it takes to bring a group together. This may include needs assessment; determination of the group goals and population; a host of logistical factors such as cost, location, and time of day; length and number of sessions; leader characteristics and credentials; cultural factors; the desired mix of clients; and member screening. In the case of mandatory groups, leaders need to get the members to work through their resentment and overt resistance to be at least nominal volunteers.

Screening is essential for groups in determining whether an individual is right for the group and the group is right for the individual. Group therapy is most effective when the ego strength (the inverse of pathology) of the members is roughly equivalent. Isolates in a group can diminish the value of the group for everyone, so it is best to avoid them in a group. Thus although group treatment has proven quite effective for addictions, having a single addict in a group can be quite deleterious.

Phase II: Transition

The transition phase of the group begins with the leaders' introduction in the first meeting and prepares members for treatment or intervention. It is a time often dominated by conflict and struggle, establishing trust, defining hierarchical roles, dealing with feelings of inclusion and anxiety. Members need to learn what kinds of issues can be dealt in the particular cultural island of this group. To do this they characteristically experientially test the leaders to determine both what is within the leaders' capabilities also what is outside the purview of the group.

Transition is a period of trust building primarily between members and the leaders, but also between members. When transition is effective, members have learned what help is available in the group, experientially discerned group norms and rules, developed sufficient trust to be more vulnerable, and are now primed to focus on their issues.

Phase III: Treatment (Working, Intervention)

Members come to the group seeking solutions to problems, behavior change, and/or intrapsychic insight. During treatment, members are able to internalize new thinking and behavior by both trial-and-error experimentation with immediate feedback and vicariously by observing others. They are able to do this in an environment that paradoxically offers higher intensity and lower threat. This combination opens opportunities for members to deal with difficult issues and interactions and to observe themselves while they are reacting.

During treatment, the problems discussed are far more likely to be solvable, in part because the aspects of the issues that occur in the group per se can be dealt with directly and personally. As for all forms of therapy, the problems may not go away, but the individual's reactions may well be altered. This focus on what can be changed is coincident with a far more internal focus for members. In the course of increasing disclosure, members discover the universality of "closet skeletons" and face them in new ways.

Group leaders intervene with members at three levels: intrapsychically, interpersonally, or group-as-a-whole. During this period, there is often intense emotional expression, and in the better groups, members take on the tasks of supporting and appropriately challenging each other. Techniques include role playing, role reversals, psychodrama, focusing, sensory awareness exercises, desensitization, guided fantasy, behavioral rehearsals, and others.

This is the time in group to address directly and help ameliorate presenting problems. However, for this phase to be effective, the challenges of prior stages must be surmounted.

In brief, closed groups, treatment is always truncated by the need for termination.

Phase IV: Termination

Unless postgroup follow-up sessions are scheduled, termination is the final phase of the group. Until this point, entry into each succeeding stage was facilitated by successful addressing of prior stages. Termination uniquely is determined by the end of the allotted time. This timing may be intrusive, inconvenient, and insensitive to the unfolding group process.

There are two mandatory goals of termination: saying goodbye and transfer of training. Because each is often difficult, most groups estimate that 25 to 35 percent of group time must be spent on termination. Saying goodbye to those to whom one has grown close is representative of all human losses, including the final one, death. Even though when they entered, members understood that the group was temporary, it may still be difficult to let go of the intimate contact with others.

Transfer of training is the goal of any therapy. Group leaders work with members to bring what they have learned in group to their back home lives and help members translate how they can use those skills in settings that do not emulate the cultural island of group.

Research on Effectiveness

Conyne (2011) among others have summarized research on group therapy. It is hard to find a psychiatric or growth-oriented population for whom group counseling or therapy has not been applied successfully. Essentially, the evidence for the efficacy of group is in and it is quite positive. Barlow, Burlingame, and Fuhriman (2000), in a review of over 700 studies, concluded that the variety of treatments using a group format consistently produced positive effects across diagnoses. In addition, groups have been shown to be as effective as individual therapy

As Shapiro (2011) has indicated, the vast majority of research has been done on closed, short-term groups and extrapolated to more open, longer-term entities. In well-controlled empirical studies using appropriate control groups, process-oriented groups show the most improvements. Psychoeducational groups have shown success, but comparatively less. Neither subjective nor objective measures indicate such improvement for (waiting list) control groups. Yet despite these data, spanning decades, group therapy continues to have second-class citizenship in the panoply of available therapies.

Although there is reason to be somewhat comfortable with outcome research, to date, little has been done to look carefully and experimentally inside the group "black box." Knowing the active ingredients in a group will go a long way toward understanding the phenomenon more thoroughly. This process research is the next logical step.

Another concern is that meta-analyses, combining the results of related studies using statistical regression and modeling, are used to deal with the nonequivalence across hundreds of studies. The resultant integrated average is expressed in a ratio of effect size: the higher the effect size, the greater confidence in the data.

Of course, meta-analyses are dependent on relatively well-designed original studies—which is not always the case for such studies.

Finally, the use of well-trained clinicians in experimental studies, particularly comparative approach studies, is quite limited to date.

Training

Despite the proven effectiveness of group treatment, increase in the number of groups offered, and the demands of managed care for more economical treatment, training in group therapy is for the most part limited to on the job. The modal number of mandatory classes in psychiatry and clinical psychology programs is zero. Most universities do not even offer an elective class for doctoral students. MFT (Marriage and Family Therapist), MSW (Master of Social Work), and LPC (Licensed Professional Counselor) master's programs typically have a single class required, but no specialty.

Excellent rubrics of appropriate training programs have been offered by the American Group Psychotherapy Association (2002) and the Association of Specialists in Group Work (2000). Yet few training programs have adopted these or similarly laddered approaches (i.e., Shapiro 2001).

Without well-trained group leaders and awareness of the impact of this modality in graduate programs, group therapy will continue to have a powerful, yet second-class impact.

See also Peer Support Groups; Psychotherapy; Recovery Movement

Bibliography

American Group Psychotherapy Association. n.d. "Group Therapy." Retrieved from http://www.agpa.org/group/consumersguide2000.html.

American Group Psychotherapy Association. 2002. *Guidelines for the Training of Group Psychotherapists*. New York: American Group Psychotherapy Association.

Association of Specialists in Group Work. 2000. "Professional Standards for the Training of Group Workers." *Journal of Specialists in Group Work* 25: 327–342.

Barlow, S., G. Burlingame, and A. Fuhriman. 2000. "Therapeutic Applications of Groups: From Pratt's 'Thought Control Classes' to Modern Group Psychotherapy." *Group Dynamics: Theory, Research, and Practice* 4: 115–134.

Barlow, S., A. Fuhriman, and G. Burlingame. 2004. "The History of Group Counseling and Psychotherapy." In J. DeLucia-Waack, D. Gerrity, C. Kalodner, and M. Riva, eds., *Handbook of Group Counseling and Psychotherapy* (pp. 3–22). Thousand Oaks, CA: Sage.

Conyne, Robert K., ed. 2011. *Oxford Handbook of Group Counseling*. New York: Oxford University Press.

Corsini, R. J. 1957. *Methods of Group Psychotherapy*. New York: McGraw-Hill.

Pratt, J. H. 1906. "The Home Sanitarium Treatment of Consumption." *Boston Medical Surgical Journal* 154: 210–216.

Shapiro, Jerrold. L. 1978. *Methods of Group Psychotherapy and Encounter.* Itasca, IL: Peacock.

Shapiro, Jerrold. L. 2001. *Training for Group Therapists and Counselors: Undergraduate, Master's Level, Doctoral Level and Post Doctoral Level.* Symposium presented at the annual meeting of the American Psychological Association, San Francisco.

Shapiro, Jerrold. L. 2011. "Brief Group Therapy." In R. K. Conyne, ed., *Oxford Handbook of Group Counseling* (pp. 487–510). New York: Oxford University Press.

Shapiro, Jerrold L., L. S. Peltz, and S. T. Bernadett-Shapiro. 1998. *Brief Group Treatment: A Practical Guide for Therapists and Counselors.* Pacific Grove, CA.: Brooks/Cole.

Yalom, Irvin D. (with M. Leszcz). 2005. *Theory and Practice of Group Psychotherapy* (5th ed.). New York: Basic Books.

H

History of Mental Health Care

Donna R. Kemp

People with mental illness have faced many problems from society throughout the ages. In the past, people with mental illness were often believed to be possessed by demons or the devil and were left in the care of their families or left to wander.

They were sometimes mistreated. Eventually, society chose to hospitalize people with mental illness, but their status was reflected in Pennsylvania, where the first mental hospital was placed in the basement of the general hospital. Mental health has continued to be the poor stepchild of the wider health care arena.

Early Period

Institutional care began in a few Arab countries; asylums were established as early as the eighth and ninth centuries to care for people with mental illness. Somewhat later in Europe, during the Middle Ages, the community began to seek confinement of people who were different. Some monasteries housed the mentally ill, usually treating them well. As societies became more urban and families became less able to care for persons with mental illness, eventually society chose to hospitalize people with mental illness.

In 1828, Horace Mann, an educational reformer, put forward a philosophy of public welfare that called for making the "insane" wards of the state. This philosophy was widely put into effect, and each state assumed responsibility for those with mental illness in that state. States often built their psychiatric hospitals in rural areas. Moral treatment and compassionate care were the main approach at this time, but with rapid urbanization and increased immigration, the state mental health systems began to be overwhelmed. Many elderly people who in rural areas would have been cared for at home could no longer be cared for when their families moved into the cities. Women, as well as men, frequently worked away from home, and there was no one to care for the elderly or see to their safety. Many people with brain-based dementias, probably caused by Alzheimer's or small strokes, became patients in mental institutions for the remainder of their lives. The institutions also had many cases of people in the last stages of syphilis. Many of those suffering from mental retardation, epilepsy, and alcohol abuse were also committed to the institutions; in hard economic times, the number of people admitted to the institutions increased.

By 1861, there were several state mental hospitals, and one federal hospital in Washington, DC. In the second half of the nineteenth century, attitudes changed and group and treatment practices deteriorated. Massive immigration to the United States led to a growing proportion of foreign-born and poor in the state hospitals. Most psychiatrists, community leaders, and public officials were native-born and generally well off and thus apt to be prejudiced against those who were neither (Rochefort 1993).

As more and more people were admitted to the institutions, the focus changed from treatment to custodial care. Commitment laws sent the dangerous and unmanageable to the state hospitals. More patients were alcoholic, chronically disabled, criminally insane, and senile. Treatment practices deteriorated. The institutions became overcrowded, and, by the late nineteenth century, the state hospitals were places of last resort, with mostly long-term chronic patients. Better treatment was found in small private psychiatric hospitals for those who could afford the care.

The Twentieth Century

As the nineteenth century drew to a close, a new idea, promoted by what is known as the eugenics movement, took hold. This movement held that insanity could be inherited. Professional conferences, humanitarian groups, and state legislatures increasingly identified insanity as a special problem of the poor. Insane persons were increasingly seen as possibly violent and incurable and as a threat to the community (Caplan 1969). These beliefs led to numerous state laws restricting the lives of people with mental disabilities, including involuntary sterilization laws and restrictive marriage laws. As a result, 18,552 mentally ill persons in state hospitals were surgically sterilized between 1907 and 1940. More than half of these sterilizations were performed in California (Grob 1983, 24).

Mental hospitals turned to the use of mechanical restraints, drugs, and surgery. Psychiatrists spent time diagnosing large numbers of patients rather than delivering individualized care. State legislatures did not increase budgets to meet the needs of the growing hospitals. Physical plants became overcrowded and deteriorated. Salaries were not adequate to attract good personnel. Superintendents no longer saw patients but spent their time on administrative tasks, and their influence declined as they became subordinate to new state boards of charity, which were focused on efficiency (McGovern 1985).

The first half of the twentieth century saw some promising new treatment developments and attempts to establish community-based systems of services. In 1909, Clifford Beers founded the National Committee for Mental Hygiene to encourage citizen involvement, prevention of hospitalization, and aftercare for those who left the hospitals. The custodial institutions remained the main site of care, but some institutions developed cottage systems that placed more able patients in small, more homelike structures on the hospital grounds, and family care programs were created to board outpatients. All these approaches, however, served only a small part of the population.

Although the Division of Mental Hygiene was created in 1930 in the U.S. Public Health Service, it did not address institutional or community mental health care in general but only narcotics addiction. During the Great Depression of the 1930s and World War II, few resources were available to psychiatric institutions, but they continued to grow anyway. Some hospitals had as many as 10,000 to 15,000 patients. From 1930 to 1940, the number of people in state mental hospitals increased five times faster than the general population to a total of 445,000 (Rothman 1980, 374).

Four new therapies arose in the 1930s: insulin coma therapy, metrazol-shock treatment, electroshock therapy, and lobotomy. These treatments were given to thousands of patients, in many cases with devastating results; nevertheless, they were widely used until the appearance of antipsychotic medications in the 1950s.

Shock treatments included electric shock and high doses of insulin and Metrazol (pentylenetetrazol), which were used to induce comas and were intended to jolt depressed or hallucinating patients out of their mental illness. Some patients were helped, but many suffered bone fractures, brain damage, and chemical poisoning.

Between 1936 and 1960, an estimated 50,000 lobotomies were performed in the United States. A Portuguese neurologist, Antonio Egas Moniz, developed the procedure. In 1936, he reported that he had cut into the brain lobes of psychiatric patients, including schizophrenics, to try to cure them. The most ardent supporter of lobotomies in the United States was Walter Freeman, a professor of neurology at George Washington University who was not a certified surgeon. By the late 1950s, however, owing to the lack of rigorous study and evaluation, the brutality of the surgery, the growing consumer and patients' rights movements, and the advent of neuroleptic (antipsychotic) drugs, the lobotomy procedure was on the wane.

The National Mental Health Act of 1946 brought the federal government into mental health policy in a significant way. The act created new federal grants in the areas of diagnosis and care, research into the etiology of mental illness, professional training, and development of community clinics as pilots and demonstrations. The act mandated the establishment of a new National Institute of Mental Health (NIMH) within the Public Health Service to encourage research on mental health.

The states moved toward reform when, in 1949, the Governors' Conference released a report detailing the many problems in public psychiatric hospitals, including obsolete commitment procedures; shortages of staff and poorly trained staff; large elderly populations; inadequate equipment, space, and therapeutic programs; lack of effective state agency responsibility for supervision and

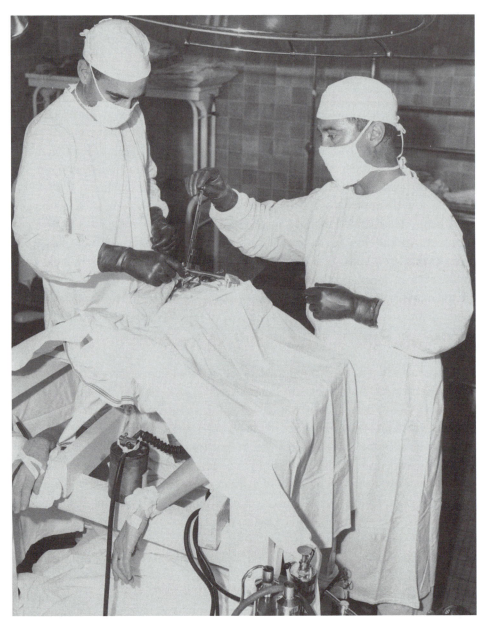

Two neurosurgeons are shown performing a prefrontal lobotomy on
August 17, 1951, at Eastern Oklahoma Hospital in Vinita, Oklahoma. (AP Photo.)

coordination; irrational division of responsibility between state and local jurisdictions; fiscal arrangements damaging to residents; and lack of resources for research. In 1954, a special Governors' Conference on Mental Health adopted a program calling for expansion of community services, treatment, rehabilitation, and aftercare.

During the 1950s, the states pursued both institutional care and expansion of community services. In the mid-1950s, major deinstitutionalization of hospitals began. The introduction of psychotropic medicines to reduce and control psychiatric symptoms created optimism that some mental illnesses could be cured and others could be modified enough to allow persons with mental illness to function in the community. Because of the apparent success of the drugs, more emphasis was placed on a biochemical view of mental illness. The discovery and use of psychotropic drugs in the 1950s had a profound impact on the treatment of the mentally ill. Tranquilizing drugs were widely used in the state institutions and played a major role in deinstitutionalization. Early discharge programs became common, and the inpatient census of public psychiatric hospitals continued to steadily decline.

In 1955, the Mental Health Study Act was passed, leading to the establishment of the Joint Commission on Mental Illness and Health, which prepared a survey and made recommendations for a national program to improve methods and facilities for the diagnosis, treatment, and care of the mentally ill and to promote mental health. The commission recommended the establishment of community mental health centers and smaller mental hospitals. It laid the groundwork for the Community Mental Health Centers Act of 1963. During the 1960s, the civil rights movement and public interest law strengthened mental health policy and encouraged community mental health treatment and the decline of the role of psychiatric hospitals. The belief that the community would be involved in care for the mentally ill became more widely accepted, and the passage in 1965 of Medicaid and Medicare stimulated the growth of skilled nursing homes and intermediate-care facilities. In 1971, Title XIX of the Social Security Act (Medicaid) was amended to require institutional reform and the meeting of accreditation standards by facilities in order to receive federal funding. But the fiscal erosion of the 1970s and the 1980s took a heavy toll on state and local mental health programs.

In 1990, only one in five of those with mental illness received treatment (Castro 1993, 59). The National Institute of Mental Health estimated the cost of treating mental illness at $148 billion, which included $67 billion for direct treatment (10% of all U.S. health spending) and $81 billion for indirect costs such as social welfare and disability payments, costs of family caregivers, and morbidity and mortality connected to mental disorders (Castro 1993, 60).

In the U.S. Department of Health and Human Services, from which federal funding still largely comes, mental health programs were organized in 1992 into the Substance Abuse and Mental Health Services Administration, consisting of the Center for Mental Health Services, the Center for Substance Abuse Prevention, and the Center for Treatment Improvement. The institutes on mental health, drug abuse, and alcohol and alcohol abuse were shifted to the National Institutes of Health and began to focus only on promotion of research in mental health and substance abuse. The Department of Veterans Affairs and the Bureau of Indian Affairs in the Department of the Interior provided community mental health services directly in a number of locations.

Once states became responsible for the distribution of the federal grant funds for mental health, many funds were shifted from the community mental health centers to community mental health services more responsive to the needs of the seriously mentally ill (Hudson 1983). The complex intergovernmental array of organizations involved made coordination difficult.

Mental health care continued to be both inpatient and community based, but the site of inpatient care shifted from state institutions to general acute care hospitals in the community, with many people seen in psychiatric units in general acute care hospitals or in short-term public or private community inpatient facilities. Children began to be able to receive services in special community or residential treatment centers for children. The cost of inpatient care rose at all sites, but most sharply in general hospitals. Total costs were held in check because the length of stay decreased. Most of the decrease occurred in state mental hospitals and Veterans Administration facilities, even though those facilities had the longest stays (Kiesler & Sibulkin 1987). Community inpatient services were complemented by community outpatient services, such as the private practices of mental health professionals, family services agencies, community mental health centers, social clubs, day hospitals, halfway houses, group homes, assisted housing, and foster care.

Mental Health Policy and Services Today

In the twenty-first century, the history of modern mental health care continues to be complex and cyclical. There is a tug and pull between many of the viewpoints about mental illness. Should people with mental illness be free to manage their lives as they see fit, or should there be social control by the government? Is mental illness physical, environmental, or both? Is mental illness a part of physical illness, a brain disease or disorder?

As was the case in the twentieth century, the United States continues to have no national mental health system. Each state has its own distinctive system. This approach allows for adjusting programs to the unique characteristics of different states and communities but has the disadvantage of creating disparities and differences in levels of community services. The private, nonprofit, and public sectors all play major roles in the delivery of services to people with mental illness. The system remains two-tiered, with lower-income people relying on the public sector and higher-income people on the private sector. People with insurance or sufficient income can access private mental health providers, from private psychotherapists, to general hospital psychiatric units in private and nonprofit hospitals, to private psychiatric facilities. The public mental health system remains the provider of last resort for people needing mental health services. However, there is a trend for more of these services being contracted out to the private sector rather than being provided by public agencies. The missions of most state mental health agencies focus resources on people with the most severe and persistent mental illnesses, such as bipolar disorder and schizophrenia.

The states remain the critical players in the development and maintenance of the public mental health system. "In fact, mental health more than any other public health or medical discipline, is singled out for exclusion and discrimination in many federal programs because it is considered to be the principal domain of the states" (Urff 2004, 84). In most states, the mental health system is administered by a state mental health agency. This agency may be an independent department but is most often an agency within a larger department, usually health or social services. As states downsize and close public psychiatric hospitals, services provided by private and nonprofit organizations take on increasing importance.

Conclusion

Mental health policy and services have traveled a long way from the days of the overcrowded state mental hospital. The civil rights movement brought many protections to people with mental illness. Yet the very deinstitutionalization of mental patients and the lack of funding for community care have led to new problems of homelessness and growing numbers of persons with mental illness in the criminal justice system. Although the stigma against people with mental illness is declining, many people with mental illness still have no access to treatment.

See also Hospitalization; Public Policy Issues; State Mental Health Agencies

Bibliography

Caplan, R. B. 1969. *Psychiatry and the Community in Nineteenth-Century America: The Recurring Concern with Environment in the Prevention and Treatment of Mental Disorder*. New York: Basic Books.

Castro, J. 1993. "What Price Mental Health?" *Time* (May 31): 59–60.

Frank, Richard G., and Sherry A. Glied. 2006. *Better but Not Well: Mental Health Policy in the United States since 1950*. Baltimore: Johns Hopkins University Press.

Grob, G. N. 1983. *Mental Illness and American Society, 1875–1940*. Princeton, NJ: Princeton University Press.

Grob, G. N. 1994. *The Mad among Us: A History of the Care of America's Mentally Ill*. New York: Free Press.

Hudson, C. G. 1983. "An Empirical Model of State Mental Health Spending." *Social Work Research and Abstracts* 23: 312–322.

Kemp, Donna R. 2007. *Mental Health in America: A Reference Handbook*. Santa Barbara, CA: ABC-CLIO.

Kiesler, C. A., and A. E. Sibulkin. 1987. *Mental Hospitalization: Myths and Facts about a National Crisis*. Newbury Park, CA: Sage.

McGovern, C. M. 1985. *Masters of Madness: Social Origins of the American Psychiatric Profession*. Hanover, NH: University Press of New England.

Rochefort, D. A. 1993. *From Poorhouses to Homelessness: Policy Analysis and Mental Health Care*. Westport, CT: Auburn House.

Rothman, D. J. 1980. *Conscience and Convenience: The Asylum and Its Alternatives in Progressive America*. Boston: Little, Brown.

Urff, J. 2004. "Public Mental Health Systems: Structures, Goals, and Constraints." In B. Lubotsky Levin, J. Petrila, and K. D. Hennessy, eds., *Mental Health Services: A Public Health Perspective* (2nd ed., pp. 72–87). New York: Oxford University Press.

Homelessness and Mental Illness

Dave Sells and Charles Barber

Persons with the dual problems of homelessness and mental illness within the United States might best be described as multiply burdened, in that they are among those most likely to also have alcohol and/or drug use disorders and significant physical maladies, and be the targets of domestic and street victimization. Correspondingly, addressing the psychiatric and housing needs of this population demands attention to associated burdens, often through the coordination of outreach and engagement services, suitably mediating client contact with large, dynamic, and often fragmented housing and health care delivery systems.

Prevalence and Recent History

Homelessness may be defined as the lack of "fixed, regular, and adequate nighttime residence" (U.S. Department of Education 1986) and may include living and sleeping on the streets, within shelters or other institutions, or under temporary arrangements with relatives or friends. There are no definitive estimates of homelessness within the United States, though an approximation published in *USA Today* in 2009 noted that 1.6 million persons made use of transitional shelters (Koch 2009). An updated source employing a broader definition estimated that over 3.5 million people within the United States may be homeless in any given year (National Law Center on Homelessness and Poverty 2011). With respect to mental illness, it is estimated that at any point in time, about 45 percent of those who are homeless also have a mental health problem, and that about 25 percent of those who are homeless have a serious mental illness, which often includes primary mood disorders (depression, bipolar disorder, etc.) and/or schizophrenia-spectrum disorders (National Alliance to End Homelessness 2011). With respect to causation, a survey completed in late 2010 by the U.S. Conference of Mayors across 27 U.S. cities identified mental illness as the second major cause of homelessness for unaccompanied persons.

While definitive data on homelessness are unavailable, most authorities agree that the proportion of persons within the U.S. population who are homeless with mental illness has substantially increased over the last 50 years. Explanations for this increase vary somewhat, though most identify the psychiatric deinstitutionalization movements beginning in the 1950s as a significant precursor. Deinstitutionalization within the United States was prompted by a number of factors including institutional overcrowding, popular dissatisfaction with the known inhumane conditions within asylums, and the advent of new psychiatric medications that promised to make more feasible the community-based management of persons with psychiatric illness. Correspondingly, resident populations within county and state mental hospitals in 1955 were estimated at about 339 per 100,000 in the population—by 1998, this number had dropped to 21 per 100,000 (Lamb & Bachrach 2001). The closing of longer-stay psychiatric institutions, however, was not met with a corresponding increase in resources for community-based care (Mowbray, Grazier, & Holter 2002), and several authors have identified this situation as a primary cause of the increased homelessness beginning in the 1950s, where a great many formerly institutionalized patients with preexisting serious mental illness suddenly became homeless (e.g., Lindblom 1991). More recent increases in homelessness among persons with mental illness have been attributed to social service funding cuts (National Coalition for the Homeless 2009), a growing scarcity of affordable housing, and a general increase of persons living below the national poverty line (O'Flaherty 1996).

Correlates of Homelessness and Mental Illness

While homelessness and mental illness are conditions that clearly influence one another, they are also typically joined by a host of other significant burdens. These burdens often include alcohol and drug use problems (Drake, Osher, & Wallach 1991), serious physical health problems (National Coalition for the Homeless 2009), and domestic and street-level victimization (Goodman et al. 2001). Alcohol and drug use problems are often initiated voluntarily, in part to temporarily allay the stress of surviving on the streets, and/or its associated social stigma. At other times, drug use is forced upon such vulnerable persons through promises of friendship and/or threats and acts of violence from drug dealers looking to cultivate new clientele (Sells et al. 2003).

Serious physical health problems may develop as a consequence of highly stressful living conditions and associated compromised personal judgment. Exposure to extreme cold, poor diet, use of injection drugs, and other factors leave persons with homelessness and mental illness vulnerable to diseases such as diabetes, tuberculosis, HIV, and a great variety of other skin and respiratory infections. Poor access to suitable medical care combined with inadequate resources for proper hygiene accelerates disease progression, which serves to compound stress, worsen psychiatric symptoms, and further impair judgment.

Vulnerabilities as to drug and alcohol abuse and/or addiction, impaired judgment, and loneliness may lead persons with homelessness and mental illness to forge and maintain relationships with abusive others. Often people in these situations, women and men alike, come from abusive upbringings, where young women in particular may become homeless in efforts to escape violent domestic situations. Unfortunately, homeless shelters and other transitional housing situations may expose these persons to still others who will exploit their vulnerabilities—often in violent ways—for sex, money, and other personal gain.

It is within this constellation of extreme hardships, often including substance dependency, poor physical health, and a history of victimization, that many persons with homelessness and mental illness are courted for possible housing and health care treatment. In terms of psychiatric treatment, a high percentage of these persons' experiences with psychiatric and drug abuse treatments is limited to repeated inpatient hospitalizations (Koegel, Burnam, & Farr 1988), where most do not make use of outpatient care. Outpatient alternatives to costly inpatient care are relatively inaccessible, however, as most persons with homelessness and mental illness are without health insurance, lack affordable transportation, are exhausted from trying to meet their basic daily needs, and expect as a consequence of most of their public interactions that they are unwanted and unwelcomed, anticipating similarly hostile receptions from potential caregivers.

Given the combination of hardships and basic distrust of healthcare providers, efforts toward successful outreach and engagement of persons with homelessness and mental illness within trusting relationships become a critical precondition to involvement in more comprehensive treatments (Rowe 1999). One of the ways to foster such relationships is through the provision of items addressing basic needs—offering food, clothing, blankets, and pocket money are relatively small but powerful ways to communicate understanding and compassion, thereby building a basis of trust for later considerations of housing and community-based mental health care.

Treatment Approaches

There exist a variety of approaches to treating people with homelessness and mental illness, some that are designed as primarily preventative, some that incorporate outreach and engagement strategies, and some that are intended primarily to maintain progress once people are suitably housed and engaged within outpatient care modalities. What the approaches described below share is that each has been subjected to some degree of empirical evaluation and found to help resolve homelessness, mental illness, or both.

Assertive Community Treatment

Assertive community treatment (ACT) originated in the 1960s as a team-based approach to addressing the needs of persons who are homeless with mental illness who also tend to be high users of inpatient psychiatric care. ACT teams are comprised of health care professionals from a variety of disciplines, often including outreach workers, case managers, social workers, and psychiatrists, where services are more direct and integrated, typically at the street level, than with more traditional case management approaches.

Veterans Administration Program

Veterans are overrepresented among persons who are homeless, where it has been estimated that 40 percent of homeless men have served in the military (Rosenheck et al. 1996), many of whom also have severe mental illnesses that may include posttraumatic reactions to combat-related events. To help address some of the special needs of this population, the U.S. Veterans Administration launched a program for homeless and chronically mentally ill veterans in the 1980s to provide outreach, case management, and residential services.

Mental Health Linkage Intervention

Developed by Mowbray and colleagues (1992), the Mental Health Linkage Intervention combines team-based street outreach for mental health care with programming for finding independent housing in communities. Once housing can be arranged, residential support is provided to help maintain housing and connection to community-based mental health care and social support services.

Critical Time Intervention

The Critical Time Intervention (CTI) is a structured nine-month case management approach to ensure continuous care for persons who are making the often challenging transition from shelter to community living. CTI makes use of existing services system resources for persons with homelessness and mental illness, integrating these resources in a manner that is manageable for clients, and helping to strengthen ties to any of clients' natural supports such as family and friends, all the while providing emotional and practical supports.

Choices

Introduced in New York, Choices is a program designed expressly to give clients an active role within their own treatments, with the aim of securing and maintaining independent community housing. The Choices approach is typically divided into the components of outreach and engagement, access to a treatment drop-in facility, respite housing, and community-centered rehabilitation services.

Integrated Treatment for Mental Health and Substance Abuse Disorders

Drake, Osher, and Wallach (1998) designed their long-term comprehensive integrated approach expressly for persons with co-occurring psychiatric and drug use problems, in part to better address the particularly stubborn problem of drug use in this population, as it tends not to improve much within other approaches. Integrated Treatment combines several components including outreach, motivational approaches, risk reduction, psychiatric services, and others, all within the context of the primary service and treatment relationships.

The Controversy over the "Dumping" of Patients

On the afternoon of March 20, 2006, a 62-year woman named Carol Ann Reyes was filmed by a street camera ambling aimlessly in a roadside within a Los Angeles neighborhood, dressed in little more than a hospital-issue gown. Reyes had been dropped off in the neighborhood just moments before, by a taxi service contracted with Kaiser Permanente Bellflower Hospital, where Reyes had been treated for three days for injuries related to a fall. Per hospital discharge instructions, the taxi driver dropped off Reyes in a neighborhood called "Skid Row," a profoundly impoverished section of Los Angeles known to have the highest concentration of persons who are homeless within the United States. As the film footage suggested, Reyes was disorientated, and it was later revealed that she suffered from dementia and was dressed in a hospital gown because during her admission the hospital had lost her clothes. Moreover, Reyes was discharged without any plan for follow-up care, which is contrary to stated hospital policy. Finally, Reyes was not from the Skid Row neighborhood but rather a neighborhood some 15 miles away, where she had been sleeping in a park. The footage of Reyes meandering along a Skid Row street made its way to law enforcement officials, who quickly leveled suit against the hospital. The topic was also picked up by the popular press, making city, state, and national headlines. Several other major Los Angeles hospitals were then similarly accused of discharging patients (or "dumping" them, with no suitable follow-up care) to Skid Row, even after the Reyes case had made headlines. The media attention culminated in a television news report by Anderson Cooper on the show *60 Minutes*, airing on CBS in 2007.

In contrast to the public shock and upset that followed from the news reports, residents and social service workers from the Skid Row neighborhood asserted that the practice of patient dumping was nothing new. In fact, so common was patient dumping that the camera that had filmed Reyes wandering Skid Row had been purposely set up as one of several "dumping cams" by local shelter workers, expressly to garner hard evidence of the practice. The full extent of "dumping" patients with mental illness and homeless in Los Angeles is unclear, though a rough estimate might be extrapolated from city officials' allegations that within the span of just two years, two major hospitals within the Los Angeles area had discharged approximately 150 patients to Skid Row.

The Growing Ranks of Homeless Families

Among the most alarming recent trends within the population of persons who are homeless with mental illness is the mounting rate of homeless families with children. To be sure, the rate of homelessness among families had been increasing since the early 1980s, though it has been somewhat unclear as to the precise rate and proportion. Prompted from the very beginnings of the recent economic recession and associated housing crisis, the rate of homelessness among families has been shown to be far steeper than expected, increasing at about 9 percent for 2009, and again in 2010, as reported by the U.S. Conference of Mayors and the Department of Housing and Urban Development. Moreover, an article in the *New York Times* in July of 2009 reported that people within homeless families then made up a third of the population known to use transitional housing and/or shelter services (Fuller 2009).

Homeless families tend to be comprised of single mothers in their 20s with two children under the age of 6 (Rosenheck, Bassuk, & Solomon 1999). Mothers in homeless families are particularly prone to serious mood, anxiety, and drug use disorders, which, combined with the conditions of homelessness, has a deleterious effect upon the children, who are in turn likely to develop serious emotional and behavior problems (Bassuk et al. 1996). Despite the increases in familial homelessness, existing transitional housing and shelter programs do not have adequate resources to address the particular and pressing needs of this vulnerable population.

Conclusion

All available measures show that persons with homelessness and mental illness represent a population that is growing within the United States, and as spurred by the recent economic recession and housing crisis, at a rate faster than could have been projected. This increase maintains despite the fact that we as citizens are aware of the problem and many of its causes, and have valid treatments to address it.

Our health care system's treatment of Carol Ann Reyes, the homeless woman with dementia who was discharged to the street, may be viewed as an example of an attempt at de facto institutionalization within the postpsychiatric deinstitutionalization era. That is, the Los Angeles neighborhood of Central City East, locally known as "Skid Row," now serves—and likely has been serving for some time—one of the social functions that historically had been performed by the psychiatric asylum, namely, a convenient though chaotic repository for containing persons with mental illness. The question of how quickly and effectively we move away from such practices and implement humane models of care depends largely on the social and political will of the citizenship, and how well we can collectively embrace a clear vision of homelessness and mental illness as a shared, and presently growing, social reality.

See also Community Mental Health; Criminalization and Diversion Programs; History of Mental Health Care; Mental Health Advocacy; Public Policy Issues; Undiagnosed Mental Illness; Veterans' Mental Health Care

Bibliography

Bassuk, E. L., L. F. Weinreb, J. C. Buckner, A. Browne, A. Salomon, and S. S. Bassuk. 1996. "The Characteristics and Needs of Sheltered Homeless and Low-Income Housed Mothers." *JAMA* 276(8): 640–646.

Drake, Robert E., Fred C. Osher, and Michael A. Wallach. 1991. "Homelessness and Dual Diagnosis." *American Psychologist* 46(11): 1149–1158.

Fuller, Andrea. 2009. "Homeless Families Increasing, U.S. Finds." *New York Times*, July 9. Retrieved from http://www.nytimes.com/2009/07/10/us/politics/10homeless.html.

Goodman, Lisa A., Michelle P. Salyers, Kim T. Mueser, Stanley D. Rosenberg, Marvin Swartz, Susan M. Essock, Fred C. Osher, Marian I. Butterfield, and Jeffrey Swanson. 2001. "Recent Victimization in Women and Men with Severe Mental Illness: Prevalence and Correlates." *Journal of Traumatic Stress* 14(4): 615–632.

Koch, Wendy. 2009. "Homelessness in Suburbs, Rural Areas Increases." *USA Today*, July 9. Retrieved from http://www.usatoday.com/news/nation/2009-07-09-homeless _N.htm.

Koegel, Paul, M. Audrey Burnam, and Rodger K. Farr. 1988. "The Prevalence of Specific Psychiatric Disorders among Homeless Individuals in the Inner City of Los Angeles." *Archives of General Psychiatry* 45(12): 1085–1092.

Lamb, H. Richard, and Leona L. Bachrach. 2001. "Some Perspectives on Deinstitutionalization." *Psychiatric Services* 52: 1039–1045.

Lindblom, Eric N. 1991. "Toward a Comprehensive Homeless-Prevention Strategy." *Housing Policy Debate* 2: 957–1025.

Mowbray, Carol T., Evan Cohen, Shirley Harris, Stuart Trosch, S. Johnson, and B. Duncan. "Serving the Homeless Mentally Ill: Mental Health Linkage." *Journal of Community Psychology* 20(3): 215–227.

Mowbray Carol T., Kyle L. Grazier, and Mark Holter. 2002. "Managed Behavioral Health Care in the Public Sector: Will It Become the Third Shame of the States?" *Psychiatric Services* 53(2): 157–170.

National Alliance to End Homelessness. 2011. "Mental/Physical Health." Retrieved from http:/www.endhomelessness.org.

National Coalition for the Homeless. 2009. "Why Are People Homeless?" Retrieved from http://www.nationalhomeless.org/factsheets/why.html.

National Law Center on Homelessness and Poverty. 2011. " 'Simply Unacceptable': Homelessness and the Human Right to Housing in the United States 2011." Retrieved from http://www.nlchp.org/content/pubs/SimplyUnacceptableReport1.pdf.

O'Flaherty, Brendan. 1996. *Making Room: The Economics of Homelessness.* Cambridge, MA: Harvard University Press.

Rosenheck, Robert, Ellen Bassuk, and Amy Salomon. 1999. "Special Populations of Homeless Americans." In Linda B. Fosburg and Deborah L. Dennis, eds., *Practical Lessons: The 1998 National Symposium on Homelessness Research* (pp. 2.1–2.31). Delmar, NY: National Resource Center on Homelessness and Mental Illness.

Rosenheck, Robert, Catherine A. Leda, Linda K. Frisman, Julie Lam, and An-Me Chung. 1996. "Homeless Veterans." In Jim Baumohl, ed., *Homelessness in America* (pp. 97–108). Phoenix, AZ: Oryx Press, 1996.

Rowe, Michael. 1999. *Crossing the Border: Encounters between Homeless People and Outreach Workers.* Berkeley: University of California Press.

Schutt, Russel K., with Stephen M. Goldfinger. 2011. *Homelessness, Housing, and Mental Illness.* Cambridge, MA: Harvard University Press.

Sells, David J., Michael Rowe, Deborah Fisk, and Larry Davidson. 2003. "Violent Victimization of Persons with Co-occurring Psychiatric and Substance Use Disorders." *Psychiatric Services* 54(9): 1253–1257.

U.S. Conference of Mayors. "A Status Report on Hunger and Homelessness in America's Cities: 2010." Retrieved from http://www.usmayors.org.

U.S. Department of Education. 1986. "McKinney-Vento Homeless Assistance Act" (Pub. L. 100-77, July 22, 1987, 101 Stat. 482, 42 U.S.C. § 11301 et seq.).

Hospitalization

Sarah C. Sitton

The classic asylum of the 1800s and the later mental hospital of the modern era were both designed to insulate the mentally ill from the pressures and community life. Each strove, to a greater or lesser extent, to provide something like a homelike environment in which rest, recreation, education, and religious expression took place alongside work and psychiatric treatment. When such institutions were small and rural, they often provided shelter and reasonably good care. It was as they became large and overcrowded, beginning in the late nineteenth century, that they became known for their poor conditions. As more and more people were admitted to these institutions, the focus changed from treatment to custodial care. Dangerous and unmanageable individuals increasingly were sent to state hospitals under loosened commitment laws. More patients were alcoholic, chronically disabled, criminally insane, and senile. By the early twentieth century, state hospitals were often regarded as places of last resort, with mostly long-term chronic patients.

The present entry provides a kind of snapshot of hospital life for the period extending roughly from the late 1800s to the mid-1900s. Obviously, there were many variations to the basic picture; yet there were strong similarities across institutions as well.

Wake Up

Residential mental institutions imposed schedules on occupants, which—while they varied by time period and patients' diagnoses—varied little by geographical location. Mental hospitals generally had specific times for rising. Friends' Asylum in Pennsylvania, supervised by Thomas Kirkbride (1809–83) who popularized the linear design for mental hospitals, required residents to rise by 5 a.m. (Rothman 1970). At the Texas State Lunatic Asylum in 1861 the timing of the morning bell changed with the seasons, sounding at 4:30 from May through August, at 5:00 in March, April, September, and October, and at 5:30 from November through February (*By-laws* 1861).

Proponents of the nineteenth century "cult of curability" believed that imposing a strict routine on persons with mental illness would result not only in more orderly behavior but also in more orderly thinking (Rothman 1970). In fact, recent research does indicate longer periods between bouts of mania for individuals diagnosed with bipolar disorder when a routine is maintained (Frank 2005). Not coincidentally, adherence to schedules also facilitated the running of institutions that might house several thousand patients.

Grooming

Following the wake-up bell (which later became a whistle) attendants, assisted by better-functioning patients, helped residents comb hair, wash hands and faces, and dress. A diagnosis of mental illness was often partially based on poor grooming, and mental institutions imposed strict standards of personal tidiness. Since longer hair styles for women necessitated more attention, once the "boyish bob" became fashionable in the 1920s some hospitals required women to adopt this style.

For males personal grooming included shaving, by either an attendant or a professional barber, since patients could not have razors. All mental institutions strove to prevent patient suicide, and even after the safety razor replaced the straight-edge blade such items remained banned to patients and kept carefully locked away when not in use. Daily grooming might also include mandatory change of socks (Lael, Brazos, & Margo 2007).

Attendants and other patients helped the most disturbed to dress, buttoning buttons and fastening hooks. Early on, mental hospitals supplied clothing for residents, primarily loose-fitting "Mother Hubbard" dresses for women and work shirts and pants for men. Material for the clothing might be denim or osnaburg (a course flax or flax-and-jute fabric), depending on which could be purchased more cheaply (Graham 1866). Tailor shops and sewing rooms made the clothes.

Uniformity of clothing facilitated the identification of any escaped patients. Hospital administrators stressed the need for vigilance in preventing escape, and attendants often personally forfeited the bounty paid to citizens for returning escapees. Most institutions had fences to deter escape, and one enterprising superintendent who could not afford the cost of a fence planted an osage orange hedge instead (Lael, Brazos, & Margo 2007). As institutions became less self-sufficient toward last third of the twentieth century, only the undergarments for large patients were sewn on site.

Medications and Meals

The morning ritual also included dosing of patients. Depending on the time period and the patient's specific diagnosis, medications included sedatives, lithium, or psychotropic drugs such as Thorazine (chlorpromazine). Nurses dispensed the drugs and watched to see that the patients actually swallowed rather than merely "cheeking" them and spitting them out later. In the days before psychotropic drugs, sedatives such as paraldehyde and chloral hydrate could be administered at bedtime to help patients sleep and to ensure a quiet night on the ward.

Dressed for the day, patients went to breakfast, with the men marching to the various dining halls. Women did not march, but followed attendants. Institutions often had rules regarding how much time could elapse between rising and breakfast, usually no more than two hours. A well-balanced diet was part of the treatment regimen. Breakfast typically consisted of oatmeal, fried eggs, biscuits, milk, and coffee. By the mid-twentieth century, many institutions provided free cigarettes to patients, with the first designated smoke break immediately following breakfast. The fear of fire meant that attendants supervised all patient smoking. Austin State Hospital programmed 11 smoking breaks into the patient's routine as well as two Coke breaks (Austin State Hospital 1950).

Following the morning's work, a whistle blew signaling the noon meal, which was generally called dinner. In the nineteenth and early twentieth century most institutions produced most of their own food, which included beef, chicken, mutton, and pork from state hog farms. At this time mental hospitals resembled plantations, slaughtering and curing their own meat and growing and preserving fruits and vegetables. In the time before refrigeration, meat did not keep and so animals were slaughtered as needed. The Texas State Lunatic Asylum had its own cattle brand, a short straight line (Graham 1866, 9).

A population of several thousand necessitated several dining rooms, which varied in quality. Typically, the best dining hall served the doctors and higher-level staff. Meals as well as housing, laundry, and medical care were part of the emoluments the hospitals provided in lieu of higher salaries. Dinner consisted of a main dish, usually meat, although beans and field peas might appear, along with vegetables, bread, iced tea, and dessert. Moving down the hierarchy of dining halls, the next level served attendants, other staff, and the better-functioning patients. At the bottom level seriously disturbed individuals, who in the nineteenth century were classified as the noisy or filthy insane, had their meals. These patients' table manners or lack thereof could be offensive to the more fastidious since they might take food from others' plates or gobble everything in sight. In some instances, this untoward behavior might include picking teeth with a fork, blowing noses at the table, or urinating in the corner (Dwyer 1987, 17).

At Austin State Hospital dining halls, patients dined at long wooden tables with benches. They ate off metal trays with spoons. Only a few received knives or forks, and these were carefully counted at the end of each meal. The most seriously disturbed or the criminally insane ate their meals on the wards. Fear of escape meant that residents of the maximum-security wards had few, if any, grounds privileges.

The final meal of the day, called tea in the nineteenth century and supper in the twentieth, appeared at six at the Texas State Lunatic Asylum as it did at Friends' Asylum in Pennsylvania. A much lighter meal than dinner, it sometimes consisted of only toast and fruit or leftovers from dinner.

Work

Following breakfast many patients reported for work, tending the vegetable gardens or caring for livestock in the nineteenth and early twentieth centuries. Mental institutions of the time strove for self-sufficiency, and most residents, having grown up on farms, knew how to perform these duties. In addition, men worked on carpentry or cement crews, on landscaping teams, or in the woodworking shop. Women performed household chores, cleaning, cooking, washing and ironing clothes, sewing, and even child care. Hospital employees who lived on the grounds in housing provided by the institution usually employed one or more patients. Institutional jobs varied in desirability, with attendants parceling out the better jobs to the most tractable patients. Work in the hot, steamy laundry and remilling soiled mattresses ranked at the bottom in terms of job desirability.

Although working patients might be granted special privileges such as eating at the attendants' table, they customarily received no pay for their labor. At Friends' Hospital in Pennsylvania, men had to work three to four hours each day for which they got extra rations of beer and tobacco (McGovern 1985, 10). Occasionally, patients who performed favors for attendants, for example carrying messages to other buildings, would receive small amounts of change as tips. They often spent this money on snacks at the canteen or nearby cafes.

Having a job alleviated some of the tedium of institutional life and may actually have had therapeutic value; for example, "atoning" for guilt by performing menial tasks. Certainly, patient labor greatly reduced the cost of running mental institutions. Patients performed most of the physical labor of the hospital including grave digging and the transport of bodies for burial if the cemetery was located off the grounds.

If a patient had worked at a trade such as blacksmith, brick mason, plumber, or mechanic, he might continue to practice his craft. Many of these men became essential to the daily operation of the institution and any attempts to discharge them met with opposition from their supervisors, who feared the loss of talented workers. However, patient employment came to an end when the Fair Labor Standards Act of 1973 prohibited unpaid labor in mental institutions.

Life on the back wards, reserved for custodial patients or the criminally insane, afforded few opportunities for recreation or treatment. These individuals did not have institutional jobs and rarely left the wards. After dressing and eating breakfast, they often sat all day in the dayroom. Few bothered to interact with others, and as long as they were quiet the attendants left them alone. They often went to bed immediately after the evening meal instead of the normal bedtime of 9:30.

Self-Sufficiency

Mental hospitals produced most of the vegetables and fruits consumed on their premises. In addition to fresh produce in season, excess fruits and vegetables were canned or dried for winter use. In Texas, Superintendent Beriah Graham' s annual report to the legislature in 1866 noted that the institution had dried 700 pounds of peaches and processed 350 additional pounds into preserves for winter use. A later superintendent reported that in addition to peaches, the asylum grew asparagus, beets, beans cucumbers, figs, grapes, lettuce, leeks, melons, onions, ears, Irish potatoes, plums, peas, radishes, squash, strawberries, and turnips (Wallace 1875, 26). Institutions purchased only a few staples, such as coffee beans and flour, from merchants in town. Since agricultural work depended on the labor of horses and mules, hay, fodder, oats, and corn were stored for their feed as well as that of the milk cows and chickens. Pigs received scraps from the dining rooms. The Willard Asylum in New York carried self-sufficiency to even greater extremes, maintaining its own fire department, a small hotel for visitors, and even a local train (Dwyer 1987, 25).

Treatment

Following dinner, patients might participate in various kinds of therapy. Often occupational or vocational therapy coincided with job assignments, so that someone who had expressed an interest in nursing might be placed in the medical facility to perform relatively easy tasks such as wrapping needles. As mental institutions moved toward deinstitutionalization in the 1970s, they began a concentrated effort to provide vocational training so that former patients would be able to support themselves after release. One of the more successful programs for women involved training as beauticians in the institution's beauty salons. Other successful programs included clerical training and training in vocational nursing, whose graduates often found jobs in nursing homes, which had replaced mental institutions in caring for the elderly.

Another common treatment, recreational therapy, included such sports as bowling, tennis, croquet, and baseball. Staff stressed the importance of baseball since it encouraged teamwork. Both men's and women's teams competed with community teams. Other forms of recreation involved walking or simply relaxing on the grounds, talking with other residents and staff or listening to music. Weekly dances, band concerts, and community sing-songs were common. Art therapy encouraged creative expression, and some patients sold their paintings, which could achieve renown as "outsider art." Ecumenical religious services occurred on Sundays, and holidays might occasion picnics or watermelon feasts.

Carefully chosen movies played in the auditorium as early as 1915 (Sitton 1999, 108). In the summer a screen was erected outside, which enticed local children to enter the grounds. Patients could also visit the hospital's library, which stocked recent fiction, nonfiction, and popular magazines.

Most early institutions employed some form of hydrotherapy, which ranged from "needle" showers whose high-intensity spray stimulated lethargic patients, to hot or cold baths for reducing agitation. Many had natatoria, or indoor swimming pools. Patients might also receive enemas or "colonic irrigation."

Before the development of antibiotics in the mid-twentieth century, a significant number of mental patients, perhaps a third, suffered from syphilis. An Austrian psychiatrist named Wagner-Juaregg (Grob 1994, 293) discovered that maintaining body temperature at 105–6°F for several hours killed the spirochetes and produced improved mental functioning. He had noticed that syphilitic patients who developed typhoid became less disturbed. American mental institutions adopted fever therapy quickly.

Sleep therapy, in which patients remained sedated for up to a month, might be prescribed for those diagnosed with mania. While this treatment did reduce manic symptoms temporarily, they soon reappeared. Sedatives such as paraldehyde calmed patients.

Before the development of psychotropic drugs such as Thorazine, not much could be done to reduce the symptoms of schizophrenia. Institutions tried various inventive therapies including spinning therapy in which patients spun in rotation swings until they were dizzy. Many saw electricity as a possible cure and purchased electrostatic shock devices that delivered electric shock to arms or legs. After Cerletti and Bini's observation in 1938 that applying the shock directly to the head improved mental functioning, mental institutions began the widespread use of electroconvulsive shock for treatment of a wide array of mental problems including schizophrenia (Valenstein 1986, 51). Therapeutic convulsions previously had been induced by the use of Metrazol or insulin. The advantage of electroshock was that the patients did not remember the experience as they did with the other methods, serving to lessen fear of the procedures. Electroconvulsive therapy became very controversial and is presently used only in cases of severe depression and risk of suicide.

Psychotherapy, "the talking cure," occurred rarely in mental institutions (Grob 1994, 136). Presently, in-patient care often consists of crisis stabilization and release. Longer stays may be necessary for psychotropic drugs to take effect. Self-help skills and social training may be provided.

Deinstitutionalization

Conditions in mental hospitals changed dramatically after psychotropic drugs became available, with many treated as outpatients or "deflected" to nursing homes. Currently, most institutions admit only the most disturbed or seriously suicidal, and the goal is to release them as soon as they are stable. Institutions for the criminally insane continue to provide long-term care, and these have always resembled prisons more than mental institutions. Prisons themselves now have wings devoted solely to the care of inmates with mental illness, and presently the largest mental institution in the country is the Los Angeles County jail, with as many as 2,000 residents (Sheriff's Department, Los Angeles).

See also Community Mental Health; Criminalization and Diversion Programs; Disability Rights; Electroconvulsive Therapy; History of Mental Health Care; Involuntary Treatment; Popular Remedies and Quackery; Rehabilitation Services; Residential Treatment for Young People; Rights of Patients with Mental Health Conditions; State Mental Health Agencies; Veterans' Mental Health Care

Bibliography

Austin State Hospital. *Daily Schedule, 7–3 Shift*. Austin State Hospital Archive, ca. 1950.

By-Laws, Rules and Regulations for the Government of the Texas State Lunatic Asylum. 1861. Austin, TX: Intelligencer Book Office.

Dwyer, Ellen. 1987. *Homes for the Mad: Life Inside Two Nineteenth-Century Asylums*. New Brunswick, NJ: Rutgers University Press.

Frank, Ellen, David J. Kupfer, Michael E. Thase, Alan G. Mallinger, Holly A. Swartz, Andrea M. Fagiolini et al. 2005. "Two-Year Outcome for Social and Interpersonal Rhythm Therapy for Individuals with Bipolar Disorder." *Archives of General Psychiatry* 62: 996–1004.

Graham, Beriah. 1866. *Superintendent's Report from the State Lunatic Asylum*. Austin, TX.

Grob, Gerald. 1994. *The Mad among Us*. New York: Free Press.

Kirkbride, Thomas. 1854. *On the Construction, Organization and General Arrangements of Hospitals for the Insane*. Philadelphia: Lindsay and Blackstone.

Lael, Richard, Barbara Brazos, and Margo Ford. 2007. *Evolution of a Missouri Asylum: Fulton State Hospital, 1851–2006*. New York: Macmillan.

McGovern, Constance. 1985. *Masters of Madness: Social Origins of the American Psychiatric Association*. Hanover: University of Vermont Press.

Penney, Darby, and Peter Stastny. 2008. *The Lives They Left Behind: Suitcases from a State Hospital Attic*. New York: Bellevue Literary Press.

Perry, John. 1857. *Superintendent's Report for the State Lunatic Asylum*. Austin, TX.

Rothman, David. 1970. *The Discovery of the Asylum.* Boston: Little, Brown.

Sheriff's Department, Los Angeles County. Retrieved from http://sheriff.org/divisions/corrections/mh/index.html.

Sitton, Sarah. 1999. *Life at the Texas State Lunatic Asylum, 1857–1997.* College Station: Texas A&M University Press.

Valenstein, Elliot S. 1986. *Great and Desperate Cures.* New York: Basic Books.

Wallace, David R. 1875. *Superintendent's Report for the State Lunatic Asylum.* Austin, TX: State Lunatic Asylum.

Humanistic Theories and Therapies

Gretchen Reevy

Humanistic psychology emerged in the 1940s and 1950s as a reaction to two movements in psychology—Freudianism and behaviorism—that came to be viewed by thinkers such as Carl Rogers and Victor Frankl as highly deterministic. Humanists see people differently than do Freudians or behaviorists. To a humanist, people are not products of their unconscious minds, their pasts, or their environments; rather, people possess free will and self-determination. People are naturally motivated to achieve their own unique potentials, possessing drives for self-actualization. Additionally, humanistic psychologists do not see people as component psychological processes such as cognitions, motives, and emotions. Instead, they perceive people as integrated wholes, unique human beings with intrinsic worth and dignity. Although many humanistic psychologists are scientists, they oppose the positivistic determinism of many approaches to science, with the nearly exclusive focus on laboratory experiments and the study of nonunified components of human experience and existence. The basic values of the humanist have been expounded by a number of psychologists, including Maslow (1962), Buhler (1971), and Buhler and Allen (1971).

Techniques used by humanistic psychotherapists vary with the particular form of psychotherapy. More precisely, compared to other psychotherapy approaches such as psychodynamic or cognitive-behavioral therapy, humanistic therapy is relatively nontechnique centered. Examples of therapies that include fundamental humanistic values are Carl Rogers's client-centered therapy, existential therapy, Victor Frankl's logotherapy, and Gestalt therapy.

Client-Centered Therapy

Client-centered therapy originated with the publication of several works by American psychologist Carl Rogers, including *Counseling and Psychotherapy* (1942) and *Client-Centered Therapy* (1951). In the earlier book, Rogers dubbed his approach the "new" psychotherapy. He emphasized four main tenets about the newer therapy. First, the psychotherapy patient (later called "client") is viewed as normally choosing to grow and develop. Psychotherapy involves freeing the client for this natural unfolding rather than giving him or her authoritative direction. Second, the newer therapy focuses more on emotional, feeling aspects of a client's experience rather than intellectual features. Third, the client's present experience is emphasized rather than memories and events from the past. Last, the therapeutic relationship is viewed as a potential situation for growth, a situation in which "the individual learns to understand himself; to make significant independent choices, to relate himself successfully to another person in a more adult fashion" (Rogers 1942, 30).

In *Client-Centered Therapy* and in an article published in 1957, Rogers further developed his theory of psychotherapy. He again emphasized that the therapist is not an authority figure; rather, the client is primarily responsible for the course of therapy. He argued that characteristics of the therapist are very important in determining the outcome for the client; in fact, these characteristics may be more important than specific therapy techniques. He identified three important characteristics of the therapist. First, the therapist must experience an "unconditional positive regard" for the client; that is, the therapist is fully accepting of the client, feels warmth, and is nonjudgmental. Second, the therapist must have an empathic understanding of the client. This involves, to a point, seeing things the way the client sees them and feeling what it must be like to be the client. Last, the therapist must be genuine, or honest with the client. The honesty does not have to be bluntness or brutality, but a certain level of truthfulness and forthrightness is necessary for the client to trust the therapist.

Although client-centered therapy is primarily about creating a certain type of climate in the psychotherapy room and not primarily about technique, Rogers did mention a couple of techniques for his new therapy. One such method is mirroring. In mirroring, the therapist rephrases what the client has said. This has at least two purposes. First, it shows the client that the therapist understands and is empathic. Second, it is a means of clarification for the therapist to ensure that she indeed understands the client. If the therapist's rephrasing seems to be inaccurate, the client may say so. Another method is to encourage experiencing; that is, the therapist encourages the client to feel his or her feelings in the present, deeply. The therapist will gently guide a client toward focusing on the present rather than the past and toward focusing on emotions rather than intellectual aspects of experience.

Client-centered therapy continues to be a popular as well as effective form of therapy. As discussed in Lambert's (2003) large volume, major types of therapy, including client-centered therapy and counseling, are effective overall. No one type of therapy stands out in terms of overall effectiveness, although some specific conditions are better treated by some particular types of therapy. Their book provides much detail about the research on efficacy of different types of therapy and different types of therapists.

Existential Psychotherapy

A fundamental idea behind existential psychology is free will, the freedom to choose. Existentialists and others representing the humanistic approach argued that neither Freudianism nor behaviorism made allowances for free will; according to Freudians, human behavior is largely controlled by unconscious factors, and according to behaviorists, much of human behavior is caused by external circumstances. From an existentialist point of view, contrariwise, humans are free to choose both what they think and how they will behave.

Existential psychology is rooted in existential philosophy, particularly the writings of Soren Kierkegaard (1813–55), Martin Heidegger (1889–1976), and Jean-Paul Sartre (1905–80), among others. A number of basic assumptions and principles form the foundation of existential philosophy. As noted, one principle is that humans have free will. Along with free will comes responsibility. A bad childhood does not excuse bad adult behavior; the individual has chosen the effects that the bad childhood has had on him or her. Another assumption is that life has no intrinsic meaning. Thus life puts us in a position where we must search for our own meaning. Life may be experienced as meaningful through many, diverse routes, and each person chooses unique meaning, which may transform from moment to moment. Another assumption is the importance of phenomenology, an individual's particular perception or experience. Each of us has our own way of viewing experiences. In a family with children of similar age who sit together with their siblings and parents at dinner and who all ride together in a car as they go on vacation, these children may nonetheless, despite that they may seem objectively similar in a number of ways, have very different perspectives on events—the parents' argument during dinner or the hysterical laughing that occurred in the car while on vacation. These differences in perspective are each child's unique phenomenology. To completely understand one another, people must be aware that life is experienced by each individual through his or her own, unique, selective filter. Understanding others requires an open-minded, nonjudgmental attitude.

The first existential psychotherapist was Swiss psychiatrist Ludwig Binswanger (Smither 2009), a student of Carl Jung and close friend of Sigmund Freud. In his book *Foundations and Knowledge of Human Existence*, published in 1942, Binswanger described different levels of existence and modes of interpersonal relations. The highest level is *Eigenwelt*. Individuals operating at this level are self-aware and self-actualizing. They experience life in relation to their own personal meanings; the norms of society and opinions and judgments of others are secondary to the individual's own values and perspectives. Binswanger believed that most people crave purpose in their lives, but many do not know their purpose.

Many people, in their search for meaning and direction, make decisions without thinking such as following an organized religion or joining a political cause. This lack of authenticity causes suffering.

Other existential therapists came after Binswanger, including Austrian psychiatrist Viktor Frankl, famous for inventing his own form of psychotherapy, *logotherapy* (*logos* means "meaning" in Greek). In logotherapy, the client is encouraged to find his own meaning in life. Frankl describes a number of ways that people experience meaning, including creating or accomplishing something, giving to others, and loving another. In logotherapy, the therapist presents the client with alternative ways of looking at events, in an attempt to reveal the client's unique meaning or purpose in life. Frankl eloquently describes his philosophy, in addition to his experience as a captive in a number of concentration camps in World War II, in his book *Man's Search for Meaning* (Frankl 1962).

Another noteworthy existential psychotherapist is American psychiatrist Irvin Yalom. Yalom sees existential anxiety as the root of most neurosis. In his book *Existential Psychotherapy*, published in 1980, he describes four causes of existential anxiety: fear of death, human freedom (which means that we are responsible for our choices), isolation (humans enter and exit this existence alone), and meaninglessness. Yalom is also well known as a group psychotherapist and applies his existential principles to both individual and group therapy.

Existential psychotherapy exists in the present day; however, it is not nearly as popular as other forms of psychotherapy such as cognitive-behavioral or behavioral psychotherapy. Additionally, existential psychotherapy is difficult to test empirically for a number of reasons, including that it assumes individual meanings rather than general laws of human nature. However, some research lends support to fundamental principles of existential psychology or psychotherapy. For instance, research indicates that most people value meaning in life more than they value wealth (King & Napa 1998). Additionally, therapy is more effective if the therapist recognizes the client's phenomenological perspective (e.g., Walsh, Perrucci, & Severns 1999).

Gestalt Therapy

Gestalt therapy is a type of existential therapy based on theories and techniques developed in the 1940s by Friedrich (Fritz) Perls (1893–1970), a German-born psychiatrist. Laura Perls (Fritz's wife) and Paul Goodman worked with Fritz Perls to refine the ideas and techniques of Gestalt therapy. Other theorists further developed the model in the 1970s, especially Joen Fagan and Irma Lee Shepherd (Gladding 2004).

Gestalt sprang from the early twentieth-century Gestalt movement founded by Czech psychologist Max Wertheimer (1880–1943), German psychologist Kurt Koffka (1886–1941), and German psychologist Wolfgang Köhler (1887–1967).

The Gestalt movement was based on the philosophical and psychological theories of Johann Wolfgang von Goethe (1749–1832), Immanuel Kant (1724–1804), and Ernst Mach (1838–1916). "Gestalt" means "the whole figure." The main idea of Gestalt is that the whole defines the parts of which it is composed. A Gestalt perspective maintains that objects (and people) are more than the sum of their parts; objects are perceived within an environment according to all their parts taken together. While influenced by Wertheimer's theories, *Gestalt therapy* is only peripherally linked to *Gestalt psychology.*

Gestalt therapy arose largely in reaction to what Perls perceived as the reductionist emphasis of other therapies at that time (e.g., psychoanalysis [Freudian psychotherapy] and behaviorism). Gestalt therapy operates on the premise that people strive for wholeness and completeness in their lives (i.e., people have a self-actualizing tendency) and emphasizes how people function in their totality (or whole). The self-actualizing tendency emerges through self-awareness and personal interaction with the environment. The Gestalt view places trust in people's inner wisdom and a belief that people seek to live in an integrated fashion and strive toward a healthy, unified whole. People are *actors* in the events around them, not just *reactors* (Gladding 2004).

Gestalt is an existential, phenomenological, and experiential therapy that emphasizes the present moment. According to the *existential* perspective, people form their lives by the choices they make. A *phenomenological* perspective maintains that a person's perception of reality or an event is more important than the event itself. *Experiential* learning is that which is derived from experience. Gestalt therapy utilizes a person's life experiences (and exercises and experiments in therapy) to help develop insight. The emphasis is on discovering different aspects of the self through experience rather than talk. Gestalt therapy purports that an overdependency on intellectual experience diminishes the importance of emotions and the senses, limiting a person's ability to respond to situations. The basic goal of Gestalt therapy is to attain awareness through self-knowledge, taking responsibility for choices, contact with the environment, and self-acceptance. Gestalt therapy does not aim to analyze internal conflicts but to integrate them. Conflicts include *unfinished business*—earlier thoughts, feelings, and reactions that still affect personal functioning and interfere with living. An example of unfinished business is not forgiving one's parents for their mistakes. The identification and resolution of conflicts allows an individual to grow and move forward in life.

The role of the Gestalt therapist is to create an atmosphere that promotes a client's exploration by being honest, exciting, energetic, fully human, and intensely and personally involved with clients (Gladding 2004). Maintaining focus on the present moment (the here and now) allows the therapist to help clients recognize patterns in their lives. Recognition of the immediacy of experience, a focus on verbal and nonverbal communication (e.g., body language), and a focus on the concept that life includes making choices all help the client to resolve the past and become integrated.

With an emphasis on action (more than analysis or interpretation), Gestalt therapy techniques utilize exercises and experiments. Exercises—designed to evoke certain responses from the client such as anger or frustration—include the enactment of fantasies, role playing, psychodrama, and dream work. Unlike dream work in psychoanalysis, the Gestalt therapist does not interpret dreams. Clients recount dreams and are directed to experience what it is like to be in each part of the dream. One Gestalt exercise is the *empty chair*, in which clients talk to various aspects of their personality; this helps clients deal with the dichotomies and conflicts within them. Gestalt experiments are unplanned activities that grow out of the interaction between client and therapist.

Perls challenged clients to see how they were avoiding feelings or avoiding responsibility using a confrontational, abrasive, and theatric style. A newer version—relational Gestalt therapy—shows more support, kindness, and compassion than Perls's original Gestalt therapy style (Corey 2008). While Gestalt therapy has been adapted for use in a group format, it was originally developed for use in individual therapy (Corey 2008). Gestalt therapy is suitable for individuals with mood disorders (e.g., major depressive disorder, bipolar disorder), adjustment disorders, somatoform disorders (e.g., physical symptoms with no known physical cause), and occupational or interpersonal problems (Gladding 2004). It is not a recommended treatment for individuals with severe emotional disturbance (e.g., schizophrenia).

Gestalt therapy is a flexible approach that helps people integrate all aspects of their lives. It considers the whole individual, in the present moment, within the context of their environment and relationships. Critics say that Gestalt therapy lacks a strong theoretical base. Some say that Gestalt therapy is too focused on technique (exercises) and the present experience to allow for passive insight and change, which may work better for some people. Others have said that Gestalt therapy is self-centered, focusing solely on feelings and personal discovery. A limitation of Gestalt therapy is that it does not utilize diagnosis or assessment techniques (Gladding 2004). This makes it difficult to monitor progress and change and could result in an individual receiving an inappropriate type of therapy. It is crucial for Gestalt therapists to be properly trained and supervised, lest they cause harm to clients (Gladding 2008).

Conclusion

Humanistic therapy still exists as a treatment alternative, although other approaches (e.g., cognitive-behavioral, behavioral) are now more popular. Humanism, as a philosophy in psychology, is alive and well. It has additionally enjoyed a rebirth in the (altered) form of positive psychology, which endeavors to understand the good life and the best in people through application of the scientific method. For example, evidence indicates that it is healthier to have a generally optimistic attitude in life than to have a pessimistic one, or even a realistic one. Compared to pessimists, optimists have better outcomes in a variety of domains, including better academic performance, greater satisfaction in interpersonal relationships, more productive work records, and even superior physical health (Snyder & Lopez 2007). Additionally, positive psychologists have already developed a number of applied programs that train people in positive traits such as optimism, resiliency, and forgiveness. Positive psychology was initiated as an academic field in 1999, when the first positive psychology course appeared at a university, and has grown rapidly in just a few years; by 2007 over 200 positive psychology course were offered, largely at American and European universities.

See also Behavioral Theories and Therapies; Psychoanalysis; Psychotherapy

Bibliography

Association for Humanistic Psychology. 2001. "Humanistic Psychology Overview." Retrieved from http://www.ahpweb.org/aboutahp/whatis.html.

Binswanger, L. 1942. *Foundations and Knowledge of Human Existence*. Zurich: M. Niehaus.

Buhler, C. 1971. "Basic Theoretical Concepts of Humanistic Psychology." *American Psychologist* 26: 378–386.

Buhler, C., and M. Allen. 1971. *Introduction to Humanistic Psychology*. Pacific Grove, CA: Brooks/Cole.

Corey, G. 2008. *Theory and Practice of Group Counseling* (7th ed.). Belmont, CA: Thomson Brooks/Cole.

Frankl, V. E. 1962. *Man's Search for Meaning*. New York: Washington Square.

Funder, D. 2010. *The Personality Puzzle* (5th ed.). New York: Norton.

Gestalt Therapy page. http://www.gestalt.org/.

Gladding, S. T. 2004. *Counseling: A Comprehensive Profession* (5th ed.). Upper Saddle River, NJ: Pearson Education.

Hartston, H. 2008. "The State of Psychotherapy in the United States." *Journal of Psychotherapy Integration* 18: 87–102.

King, L. A., and C. K. Napa. 1998. "What Makes a Life Good?" *Journal of Personality and Social Psychology* 75: 156–165.

Lambert, M. J., ed. 2003. *Bergin and Garfield's Handbook of Psychotherapy and Behavior Change* (5th ed.). New York: Wiley.

Latner, J. 1992. "The Theory of Gestalt Therapy." In E. C. Nevis, ed., *Gestalt Therapy: Perspectives and Applications* (pp. 13–56). Cleveland, OH: Gestalt Institute of Cleveland Press.

Maslow, A. H. 1962. *Toward a Psychology of Being*. Princeton, NJ: Van Nostrand.

Rogers, C. R. 1942. *Counseling and Psychotherapy*. Boston: Houghton Mifflin.

Rogers, C. R. 1951. *Client-Centered Therapy: Its Current Practice, Implications, and Theory*. Boston: Houghton Mifflin.

Smither, R. 2009. Existential and Humanistic Psychotherapies. In D. C. S. Richard and S. K. Huprich, eds., *Clinical Psychology: Assessment, Treatment, and Research* (pp. 309–328). Burlington, MA: Elsevier.

Snyder, C. R., and S. J. Lopez. 2007. *Positive Psychology: The Scientific and Practical Explorations of Human Strengths*. Thousand Oaks, CA: Sage.

Walsh, R. A., A. Perrucci, and J. Severns. 1999. "What's in a Good Moment: A Hermeneutic Study of Psychotherapy Values Across Levels of Psychotherapy Training." *Psychotherapy Research* 9: 304–326.

Yalom, I. D. 1980. *Existential Psychotherapy*. New York: Basic Books.

Hypnosis and Hypnotherapy

Gretchen Reevy

Hypnotherapy is a treatment modality utilizing specific techniques while the patient is in a state of hypnosis. Hypnosis, in turn, is a state of heightened concentration in which a motivated person may experience altered sensations and perceptions and may be more receptive to suggestions from a therapist. The term "hypnosis" comes from the Greek root *hypnos* (sleep). Self-hypnosis is a technique an individual can learn to reinforce desired emotional or behavioral changes. Hypnosis is a therapeutic tool, not a therapy in itself; it is often used in conjunction with other types of therapy (e.g., cognitive-behavioral therapy). Hypnotherapy has been used to treat a variety of conditions, including anxiety disorders (e.g., panic disorders, general phobias, social phobia, generalized anxiety disorder), posttraumatic stress disorder (PTSD), obsessive-compulsive disorder, Tourette's syndrome, depression, eating disorders, attention-deficit hyperactivity disorder, chronic pain, asthma, and irritable bowel syndrome. Hypnosis has been used as anesthesia, in both surgical and dental procedures.

Historical Roots

German physician and astrologer Franz Anton Mesmer (1734–1815) utilized a force he called *animal magnetism* to heal people. It was thought that all elements in the universe, including the human body, were interconnected through a magnetic fluid. Disease resulted from an imbalance of this fluid. The physician served as a conduit to channel animal magnetism from the universe into the patient's body. The process, known as mesmerism, was initially popular. In 1784, French King Louis XVI appointed commissioners from the Faculty of Medicine and the Royal Academy of Sciences to investigate animal magnetism. The commission concluded that any healing effects of mesmerism were due to imagination. Scottish neurosurgeon James Braid (1795–1860) is considered the father of hypnotherapy. Braid was influenced by the demonstrations of Mesmer. The term "hypnotism" (short for *neurohypnotism*)—as used in the sense of inducing a trance —was coined by Braid in 1843. French neurologist Jean-Martin Charcot (1825– 93) believed that hysteria (a neurosis of the brain or emotional disorder) was a neu-rological disorder. He performed experiments using hypnosis to induce a state of hysteria in patients. Charcot described the somatic (physical) effects of hypnosis as occurring in successive stages and claimed that somatic manifestations could be transferred from one side of the body to the other utilizing magnets. French physi-cian Hippolyte Bernheim (1840–1919) disagreed with Charcot's explanations. Bern-heim conceived of hypnosis as a normal state of mind in which suggestion plays an essential role (Wozniak 1995). While Charcot focused on the physical and neuro-logical aspects of hypnosis, Bernheim emphasized the power of suggestion. Mesmer believed that a force within the hypnotist was responsible for the effects of hypno-tism; however, Bernheim posited that the power of suggestion and expectation within both the patient and the hypnotist was responsible for hypnotic effects.

In the 1840s, hypnosis was used as surgical anesthesia in England and India. However, with the advent of chemical anesthesia, hypnosis fell out of favor with the medical establishment (James 2008). As a psychiatric treatment, hypnosis was used in World Wars I and II to treat battle fatigue (now known as PTSD) so that soldiers could return to battle (Zahourek 2002).

Hypnosis in the United States

American psychiatrist Milton Erickson (1901–80) practiced a unique form of hypnotherapy. Ericksonian hypnosis was based on three approaches he referred to as *naturalistic*, *utilization*, and *indirect*. His approach incorporated the waking trance. The *naturalistic* approach utilizes memories of early learning while in a trance state. The *utilization* approach accepts and appreciates the client where he is. The client may be as receptive to suggestion in a waking trance as in a deep trance state. Trance is a changed state of awareness or consciousness that varies naturally and continuously. A light trance is a common experience, for example, losing track of time and place when completely absorbed in a good book. A deep trance is not considered necessary in Ericksonian hypnotherapy (Zahourek 2002). The *indirect* approach is less authoritarian or directive as traditional forms of hyp-nosis. Using a directive approach, a hypnotherapist might suggest to a client "relax," "stop smoking now," or "remember a time when you felt in control." An indirect approach is framed positively and is less specific, allowing room for inter-pretation. For example, "you may find you are increasingly comfortable." Ericso-nian hypnotherapy influenced the development of many other therapeutic modalities and techniques, including family therapy and group therapy. Neurolin-guistic programming (NLP), which emerged in the 1970s, was an approach utiliz-ing Erickson's ideas. NLP, which was loosely based on Ericksonian hypnotherapy, has been used in employee training (Maron 1979).

Applications in Therapy

While similar in some ways to relaxation, imagery, and biofeedback techniques, hypnosis differs in the timing and manner with which suggestions are introduced (Zahourek 2002). Myths about hypnosis include a fear of loss of control, doing or revealing embarrassing things under hypnosis, or being under the control of the hypnotist. These are common misperceptions that are perpetuated by stage hypnosis, which tends to be sensationalist and is performed for entertainment. Being in a hypnotic trance cannot cause people to violate their values, morals, or ethical code or to reveal information against their will (Appel 2002).

In hypnotherapy, the therapist learns about the client's background, culture, learning style, strengths, goals, and desires. A diagnostic assessment is performed to determine which therapeutic techniques (including hypnosis) will be most effective. If the client is motivated to try hypnosis, the process is explained to the client. During hypnotic induction, the therapist observes the client's attention, focus, and breathing to assess the depth of the client's trance state. The therapist may introduce direct or indirect suggestions that are in line with the client's stated goals and values. Suggestions generally reinforce the client's internal resources, drawing on examples of past successes and positive interactions. Posthypnotic suggestions form a bridge so that the client can transfer feelings and states experienced during the trance state into future behaviors, thoughts, and feelings. The therapist's tone of voice, rhythm of speech, and body language can reinforce suggestions given during hypnosis (Zahourek 2002).

Research, often based on small sample sizes or case studies, has made it difficult to establish the effectiveness of hypnotherapy for mental health issues. There has been more research establishing effectiveness of hypnosis for treatment of physical issues such as pain and irritable bowel syndrome. Children seem to respond more readily to hypnosis than adults (Huynh, Vandvik, & Diseth 2008). As hypnotherapy seems to demonstrate beneficial effects in a shorter period of time (fewer sessions) than traditional psychotherapy, incorporating hypnotherapy into a treatment plan can save time and money—both for the patient and in the context of managed care (or limited health care resources). Many different types of professionals can be trained to utilize hypnotherapy, including psychologists, psychiatrists, clinical social workers, nurses, physicians, surgeons, and dentists.

See also Clinical Psychology; Cognitive-Behavioral Therapy; Dissociative Disorders; Mind and Body Approaches to Mental Health; Psychotherapy

Bibliography

Appel, P. R. 2002. "Clinical Hypnosis." In S. F. Wainapel, ed., *Alternative Medicine and Rehabilitation: A Guide for Practitioners* (pp. 213–243). New York: Demos Medical.

Barrett, D., ed. 2010. *Hypnosis and Hypnotherapy.* Santa Barbara, CA: Praeger.

Huynh, M. E., I. H. Vandvik, and T. H. Diseth. 2008. "Hypnotherapy in Child Psychiatry: The State of the Art." *Clinical Child Psychology and Psychiatry* 13: 378–393.

James, U. 2008. "Wake Up to Hypnotherapy." *New Scientist* 199(2678): 18.

Maron, D. 1979. "Neurolinguistic Programming: The Answer to Change?" *Training and Development Journal* 33(10): 68–71.

Wozniak, R. H. 1995. "Mind and Body: René Descartes to William James." *Bryn Mawr College, Serendip*. Originally published in 1992 at Bethesda, MD, and Washington, DC, by the National Library of Medicine and the American Psychological Association.

Zahourek, R. P. 2002. "Using Ericksonian Hypnosis in Psychiatric-Mental Health Nursing Practice." *Perspectives in Psychiatric Care* 38: 15–22.

I

Impulse Control Disorders

Kathryn H. Hollen

Also known as behavioral addictions, impulse control disorders (ICDs) are defined by compelling urges to perform acts that may give immediate pleasure but have negative consequences and cause remorse later. They are similar to obsessive-compulsive disorders (OCDs), but the latter represent an anxiety-driven need to quiet repetitive and troublesome thoughts by performing compulsive, irrational, ritualized acts. Impulsive behaviors like suddenly deciding to buy unneeded items, on the other hand, are usually associated with gratification of some kind, at least temporarily. When such behaviors become pathological—occurring to such a degree that an individual's ability to function or behave appropriately is impaired—they are considered impulse control disorders. Like those with obsessive-compulsive disorders (or children with conduct disorders), people with impulse control disorders are likely to have an anxiety disorder or depression, and are usually more susceptible to substance abuse.

In the fourth edition of its *Diagnostic and Statistical Manual of Mental Disorders*, the American Psychiatric Association (APA) describes individuals suffering from impulse control disorders as unable to resist impulsive behaviors that may be harmful to themselves or others. Their acts are usually not premeditated and can seldom be controlled by willpower because they are performed to relieve the increasing tensions or arousal which typically precede it.

Most experts agree that nine disorders meet the appropriate criteria: compulsive computer use (Internet addiction), compulsive shopping, self-injury (including cutting behaviors), intermittent explosive disorder (rage addiction), kleptomania (stealing), pathological gambling, pyromania (fire starting), sexual addiction, and trichotillomania (pulling out one's hair). Some mental health professionals do not agree that these behaviors are addictions even though they meet a principal diagnostic criterion—they are characterized by a repeated compulsion to engage in an activity despite the adverse consequences of doing so.

Differentiating ICDs from Other Categories of Illness

Some impulse control disorders that are not associated with addiction include attention-seeking behaviors or antisocial and narcissistic disorders. Eating disorders, including so-called food addictions, are complex and cannot be easily categorized; many experts feel they should be classified as anxiety or depressive disorders, although one form, bulimia nervosa, is regarded by some mental health professionals as an impulse control disorder. Some experts regard novelty seeking (or risk taking) as an impulse control disorder in which the individual engages in high-risk behaviors like bungee jumping or extreme sports for the rush they deliver. Kleptomania and other thrill-seeking behaviors are frequently seen in the same individual, and there is speculation that the neurotransmitter norepinephrine may be partly responsible. However, the APA has yet to include risky behavior or novelty seeking as symptoms of the mental disorder it has identified.

Most behavioral addictions start in childhood, although some emerge in late adolescence or adulthood. Even if children experience urges to steal, it is not until later that the urges become compelling and the older or grown children have the independent means to act on them. Despite earlier beliefs to the contrary, researchers are learning that impulse control disorders are not likely to have originated with a precipitating trauma or parental neglect or abuse. Instead, increasing evidence points to a combination of neurobiological factors that combine with genetic and environmental influences, and there is a clinically significant correlation between many of these disorders and alcoholism or other substance abuse.

Diagnosis can be difficult, principally because of patient reluctance to admit to certain behaviors. Furthermore, in adolescents, their youth already predisposes them to risky and impulsive behaviors that are part of the maturing process, and this can lead to misdiagnosis. Parents can help by being attuned to significant deviations from so-called normal levels of teenage behavior. Another factor complicating diagnosis is the fact that many health care professionals, unaware of the prevalence or manifestations of the diseases, view the symptoms as diagnostic of a manic-depressive illness (bipolar disorder), obsessive-compulsive disorder, major depressive disorder, or borderline personality disorder, and patients are frequently prescribed inappropriate medications or therapies that do little to treat the real problem. This has caused a significant portion of people to consider suicide as the only way to end the torment their disease has caused them and the people who care about them.

Treatment Considerations

Impulse control disorders are associated with the area of the brain that processes reward and pleasure. Research findings suggest that they may be related to low levels of serotonin, and the effectiveness of serotonin reuptake inhibitors and opioid antagonists in treating them tends to confirm this. Evidence for a genetic basis is also supported by studies showing that pathological gambling is more common in the identical twin of someone suffering from the disease than it is in unaffected identical twins. Unfortunately, even if patients can admit the nature of their addiction to others, many do not know that they are suffering from a treatable psychiatric disease.

Although some impulse control disorders are relatively uncommon, anywhere from 8 to 35 million Americans are afflicted with some form of them, and they create major problems for families. Once the disorders are properly diagnosed and assessed to determine the variables that apply in individual cases, they can be treated effectively with appropriate combinations of medication and cognitive behavioral therapy. Adolescents, whose developing brains leave them particularly susceptible to the influences that help foster impulse control disorders, respond well to early treatment. Since about half of the people diagnosed also have a history of substance abuse, it is essential that both disorders be treated at the same time.

Frequently Asked Questions about ICDs

- What causes impulse control disorders?

  There is no single cause; impulse control disorders are complicated illnesses that arise from biology, genes, and/or environment.

- Are impulse control disorders chronic?

  Although impulse control disorders do not simply disappear, the behavior may be arrested for long periods. After treatment ends and impulses have stopped, however, those afflicted must remain vigilant to avoid things that might trigger new urges. Most people resume the behavior at some point if the illness is not managed.

- Is there a genetic component to impulse control disorders?

  There is evidence to suggest that it is common to find several members of the same family with similar disorders.

- Once the disorder is treated, will another one take its place?

  Some people do shift from one addiction to another. Education, treatment, and counseling help control this tendency.

- Does an impulse control disorder indicate a failing of character?

  No, people do not lack willpower or moral character just because they suffer from an impulse control disorder. They are psychiatric illnesses of the brain and can be treated.

- How can someone with an impulse control disorder be helped?

  Most people with impulse control disorders do not think they need treatment and may need to suffer serious consequences of their behavior before they find or accept treatment. Presenting education and treatment options to the afflicted person can make a difference. Also, support groups for family and friends of those afflicted by impulse control disorders may have suggestions for urging the person into treatment.

Source: Adapted from Jon E. Grant and S. W. Kim. 2003. *Stop Me Because I Can't Stop Myself: Taking Control of Impulsive Behavior* (New York: McGraw-Hill).

See also Eating Disorders; Gambling Addiction; Internet Gaming Addiction; Obsessive-Compulsive Disorder; Self-Injury and Body Image

Bibliography

Aboujaoude, Elias, and Lorrin M. Koran, eds. 2010. *Impulse Control Disorders*. New York: Cambridge University Press.

American Psychiatric Association. 2000. *Diagnostic and Statistical Manual of Mental Disorders* (4th ed., text rev.). Washington, DC: American Psychiatric Publishing.

Davis, Caroline. 2001. "Addiction and the Eating Disorders." *Psychiatric Times*, February. Retrieved from http://www.psychiatrictimes.com/p010259.html.

Grant, Jon E. 2008. *Impulse Control Disorders: A Clinician's Guide to Understanding and Treating Behavioral Addictions*. New York: Norton.

Grant, Jon E., and S. W. Kim. 2003. *Stop Me Because I Can't Stop Myself: Taking Control of Impulsive Behavior*. New York: McGraw-Hill.

Hyman, S. E., and R. C. Malenka. 2001. "Addiction and the Brain: The Neurobiology of Compulsion and Its Persistence." *Nature Reviews Neuroscience* 2(10): 695–703.

Peele, Stanton. 2001. Is Gambling an Addiction Like Drug and Alcohol Addiction? *Electronic Journal of Gambling Issues*, February. Retrieved from http://www.camh.net/egambling/issue3/feature/index.html.

Potenza, Marc N. 2006. "Should Addictive Disorders Include Non-Substance-Related Conditions?" *Addiction* 101(Suppl. 1): 142–151.

Young, Kimberly S., and Cristiano Nabuco de Abreu, eds. 2010. *Internet Addiction: A Handbook and Guide to Evaluation and Treatment*. New York: Wiley.

Insurance and Parity Laws

Stacey A. Tovino

Since the inception of public and private health insurance in the United States in the middle of the twentieth century, stakeholders have debated whether individuals with mental illness should have the same health insurance benefits as individuals with physical illness. Traditionally, public health care programs and private health insurers have provided less comprehensive health insurance benefits for individuals with mental illness in both the inpatient and outpatient mental health care settings.

The Medicare program, a public health care program funded and administered by the U.S. government, provides health insurance for individuals who are 65 years of age or older, individuals under the age of 65 who have certain disabilities, and individuals with end-stage renal disease regardless of age. Both Medicare Part A, which provides hospital insurance benefits, and Medicare Part B, which provides physician and other supplementary medical insurance benefits, provide less comprehensive health insurance benefits for beneficiaries with mental illness. Medicare Part A restricts beneficiaries to a lifetime maximum of 190 inpatient days in a freestanding psychiatric hospital but places no lifetime maximum on the number of days a beneficiary may stay as an inpatient in a nonpsychiatric hospital (42 C.F.R. § 409.62). The federal government justifies the 190-day limitation as a cost-control measure. In addition to the Medicare Part A limitation on inpatient care provided in a freestanding psychiatric hospital, Medicare Part B also provides less comprehensive outpatient mental health benefits. In particular, Medicare Part B currently imposes a 45 percent beneficiary coinsurance on most outpatient mental health services, including individual, family, and group psychotherapy services, instead of the 20 percent beneficiary coinsurance traditionally applied to non-mental health outpatient services (42 U.S.C. § 1395l(c)). Although Medicare will phase out the disparate coinsurances by the year 2014, Medicare beneficiaries who receive outpatient mental health services before 2014 will be required to pay up to 45 percent of the cost of those services out of their own pockets, unlike Medicare beneficiaries who receive non-mental health outpatient services, who are required to pay only 20 percent of the cost of such services out of their own pockets.

The Medicaid Program, a public health care program jointly funded by the federal and state governments and administered by the states, provides health care to certain low-income individuals and families who fit into an eligibility group recognized by federal and state law. Like the Medicare Program, the Medicaid Program also has limited support for individuals who require mental health care in certain inpatient psychiatric settings. For example, Medicaid does not cover inpatient mental health care provided to individuals age 22 through 64 in an "institution for mental disease," defined as a hospital, nursing facility, or other institution of more than 16 beds that is primarily engaged in providing diagnosis, treatment, or care of persons with mental disease (42 C.F.R. § 435.1009(a)(2), 2011). Medicaid also does not cover mental health care provided in small residential facilities, including halfway houses, adult residential foster homes, and crisis centers.

Private health insurers also have a long history of providing less comprehensive insurance benefits for individuals with mental illness (Barry 2003). Traditionally, many private health plans did not provide any insurance coverage for mental health treatments (U.S. Department of Health and Human Services 1999). Prior to the enactment of mental health parity laws, private health plans that did cover mental health treatments frequently imposed more stringent cost-sharing and administrative requirements, including higher deductibles, higher copayments, and higher coinsurance amounts for mental health care, as well as lower numbers of covered inpatient days, lower numbers of covered outpatient visits, lower lifetime spending caps, and lower annual spending caps for mental health care (U.S. Department of Health and Human Services 1999). Frustrated with these public and private mental health insurance disparities, mental health parity advocates began lobbying Congress for mental health parity legislation in the early 1990s.

The Mental Health Parity Act of 1996

The federal government took its first step toward establishing mental health parity on September 26, 1996, when President Bill Clinton signed the Mental Health Parity Act (MHPA) into law (MHPA 1996). As originally enacted, MHPA regulated only insured and self-insured group health plans of large employers, including those that employed an average of 51 or more employees. MHPA thus did not apply to the group health plans of small employers. MHPA also did not apply to individual health plans, the Medicare Program, Medicaid non-managed care plans, or any self-funded, non-federal governmental plan whose sponsor opted out of MHPA. Finally, MHPA contained an "increased cost" exemption if the application of MHPA resulted in an increase in the cost under the plan of at least 1 percent. By November 1998, over two years following MHPA's enactment, only four plans across the United States had obtained exemptions due to cost increases of 1 percent or more.

In terms of its substantive provisions, MHPA was neither a mandated offer nor a mandated benefit law; that is, nothing in MHPA required a covered large group health plan to actually offer or provide any mental health benefits. As originally enacted, MHPA also was not a comprehensive parity law because it neither protected individuals with substance use disorders nor required parity between physical and mental health benefits in terms of deductibles, copayments, coinsurance, inpatient day limitations, or outpatient visit limitations.

What MHPA did do was regulate lifetime and annual spending limits that covered large group health plans applied to mental health benefits if such plans offered both physical health and mental health benefits. More specifically, if a large group health plan does not impose an aggregate lifetime or annual limit on physical health benefits, the plan may not impose an aggregate lifetime or annual limit on offered mental health benefits. If a large group health plan does impose an aggregate lifetime or annual limit on physical health benefits, either the plan must apply the applicable limit to both physical health and mental health benefits and not distinguish in the application of such limit between the two benefit sets; or the plan must not impose any aggregate lifetime or annual limit on mental health benefits that is less than the applicable lifetime or annual limit imposed on physical health benefits. MHPA thus prohibits a large group health plan from imposing a $20,000 annual cap or a $100,000 lifetime cap on mental health care if the plan had no annual or lifetime caps for physical health care or if the plan had higher caps, such as a $50,000 annual cap or a $500,000 lifetime cap, for physical health care.

The Paul Wellstone and Pete Domenici Mental Health Parity and Addiction Equity Act of 2008

Twelve years after President Clinton signed MHPA into law, President George W. Bush expanded federal mental health parity law by signing into law the Paul

Wellstone and Pete Domenici Mental Health Parity and Addiction Equity Act of 2008 (MHPAEA 2008). As originally enacted, MHPAEA (like MHPA) regulated only insured and self-insured group health plans of large employers, defined as those employers that employ an average of 51 or more employees. MHPAEA (like MHPA) thus did not apply to small group health plans, individual health plans, the Medicare Program, Medicaid non-managed care plans, or any self-funded, non-federal governmental plans whose sponsor opted out of MHPAEA. In terms of its substantive provisions, MHPAEA also was neither a mandated offer nor a mandated benefit law; that is, nothing in MHPAEA required a large group health plan to actually offer or provide any mental health benefits. Like MHPA, MHPAEA also contained an "increased cost" exemption for covered group health plans and health insurance coverage offered in connection with such plans, but under MHPAEA the amount of the required cost increase increased, at least for the first year. That is, a large group health plan that could demonstrate a cost increase of at least 2 percent in the first plan year and 1 percent in each subsequent plan year of the actual total costs of coverage with respect to medical and surgical benefits and mental health and substance use disorder benefits, would be eligible for an exemption from MHPAEA for that year. MHPAEA required determinations of exemption-qualifying cost increases to be made and certified in writing by a qualified and licensed actuary in good standing who belongs to the American Academy of Actuaries.

Notwithstanding these limitations and exemptions, MHPAEA built on MHPA by protecting individuals with substance use disorders and by imposing comprehensive parity requirements on covered group health plans. In particular, MHPAEA required financial requirements (including deductibles, copayments, coinsurance, and other out-of-pocket expenses) and treatment limitations (including inpatient day and outpatient visit limitations) that large group health plans imposed on mental health and substance use disorder benefits to be no more restrictive than the predominant financial requirements and treatment limitations imposed on physical health benefits. MHPAEA thus prohibited large group health plans from imposing higher deductibles, copayments, or coinsurances, or lower inpatient day and outpatient visit maximums, on individuals who were seeking care for conditions such as bipolar disorder, schizophrenia, alcohol abuse, and drug abuse compared to individuals who were seeking care for traditional physical conditions, such as pregnancy, cancer, and orthopedic injuries. On February 2, 2010, the U.S. Departments of Health and Human Services, Labor, and Treasury coreleased an interim final regulation implementing MHPAEA's requirements (U.S. Departments of Health and Human Services, Labor, and Treasury 2010a). The interim final rule clarified in favor of patients with mental health conditions several questions that MHPA and MHPAEA had left open, including the question of whether a covered group health plan could impose separately accumulating financial requirements or quantitative treatment limitations on mental health and substance use disorder benefits ("No"), and the question of whether a covered group health plan could impose a nonquantitative treatment limitation, such as a medical necessity limitation or an experimental-investigative limitation, only on mental health and substance use disorder benefits ("No").

The Affordable Care Act of 2010

Two years after President Bush signed MHPAEA into law, President Obama further expanded mental health parity law by signing into law the health care reform bill, formally known as the Patient Protection and Affordable Care Act of 2010 (PPACA) as reconciled by the Health Care and Education Reconciliation Act (HCERA)—or, as consolidated, the Affordable Care Act (ACA; ACA 2010). Perhaps best known for its controversial (and constitutionally challenged) individual health insurance mandate, ACA has buried deep within it several provisions that relate to mental health insurance and mental health parity. If upheld by the U.S. Supreme Court, these provisions will expand both mental health parity law and mandatory mental health and substance use disorder benefits to additional, but not all, groups of individuals with public and private health insurance.

The first provision within ACA relating to mental health insurance expands the application of MHPA and MHPAEA from just large group health plans to all of the health care reform bill's new "qualified health plans," defined as the health plans that will be offered on one of the new state- or regional health insurance exchanges beginning on or after January 1, 2014 (ACA § 1311(j)). Because individual and small group health plans will be offered on the health insurance exchanges then, the application of MHPA and MHPAEA will be expanded in 2014 to include not only large group health plans but also individual and small group health plans.

A second provision that protects individuals with mental illness prevents group health plans and health insurance issuers from establishing any lifetime as well as certain annual limits on the dollar value of "essential health benefits" for any participant or beneficiary (ACA § 1001). Although ACA reserves the right of a group plan or insurance issuer to impose annual and lifetime per-beneficiary limits on specific covered benefits that are not "essential health benefits," mental health and substance use disorder benefits, including behavioral health treatments, are considered such essential benefits and thus cannot be limited under the right of reservation (ACA § 1302). This second ACA provision builds on the original MHPA, which allowed lifetime and annual limits but only so long as such limits that applied to treatment of mental health conditions were not lower than those that applied to treatment of physical health conditions. Now, ACA prohibits all lifetime as well as most annual limits.

Perhaps most importantly, a third set of ACA provisions mandate that "essential health benefits" be covered by plans that operate in certain settings, including the individual health plan and small group health plan settings (ACA § 1201), the qualified health plan setting (ACA § 1301), and the Medicaid benchmark plan (and benchmark-equivalent) setting (ACA § 2001). ACA defines "essential health benefits" to specifically include "mental health and substance use disorder services, including behavioral health treatment[s]" (ACA § 1302). Read together, this third set of ACA provisions is quite significant. Federal law for the first time is mandating that mental health and substance use disorder benefits be covered in certain plan settings.

Under regulations copublished by the U.S. Departments of Health and Human Service, Labor, and Treasury on June 17, 2010, the departments clarified, however, that the "essential health benefit" requirement does not apply to "grandfathered health plans" (U.S. Departments of Health and Human Services, Labor, and Treasury 2010b). Such a plan is defined as a group health plan or health insurance issuer that was in effect on March 23, 2010, the day President Obama signed PPACA into law (U.S. Departments of Health and Human Services, Labor, and Treasury 2010b). Nongrandfathered health plans include group plans and insurance issuers established after March 23, 2010, as well as originally grandfathered health plans that subsequently lose their grandfathered status. Situations that will not cause a grandfathered plan to lose grandfathered status include: (1) the cessation of coverage by the plan of one or more or all of the individuals enrolled in the plan on March 23, 2010, so long as the plan has continuously covered someone since March 23, 2010; (2) the enrollment of new family members in the plan after March 23, 2010, so long as the family members are dependents of an individual who was enrolled in the plan on March 23, 2010; (3) the enrollment of newly hired employees and the enrollment of existing employees eligible for new enrollment after March 23, 2010; and (4) entering into a new policy, certificate, or contract of insurance (that is, changing insurance carriers) after March 23, 2010 (U.S. Departments of Health and Human Services, Labor, and Treasury 2010b). Activities that will cause a grandfathered plan to lose grandfathered status include: (1) the elimination of all or substantially all benefits to diagnose or treat a particular condition; (2) any increase in a percentage cost-sharing requirement; (3) certain increases in fixed-amount cost-sharing requirements, including deductibles and out-of-pocket limits but not copayments; (4) certain increases in fixed-amount copayments; (5) certain decreases in contribution rates by employers and employee organizations; and (6) certain changes in annual limits (U.S. Departments of Health and Human Services, Labor, and Treasury 2010b).

Understanding the distinction between grandfathered and nongrandfathered plans is the key to understanding the application of ACA's health insurance reforms, including its mandatory mental health and substance use disorder benefits provision. Grandfathered health plans are exempt from the vast majority of new insurance reforms required by ACA, including the "essential health benefits" provision. The result (in terms of mandated benefits) is that grandfathered health plans are regulated only by MHPA and MHPAEA, neither of which contains a mandated mental health or substance use disorder benefit, as well as state law, which may or may not contain a mandated mental health and substance use disorder benefit. Grandfathered health plans are not the only health plans that are exempt from the essential health benefits requirement. Large group health plans not offered on a health insurance exchange, self-insured Employee Retirement Income Security Act (ERISA) plans, and ERISA-governed multiemployer welfare arrangements also are exempt from the essential health benefits requirement.

Conclusion

Traditionally, individuals with mental illness were subject to a range of mental health insurance disparities, including a complete lack of insurance coverage and more stringent cost-sharing and administrative requirements. Typical mental health insurance disparities included higher deductibles, higher copayments, and higher coinsurance amounts for mental health care, as well as lower numbers of covered inpatient days, lower numbers of covered outpatient visits, lower lifetime spending caps, and lower annual spending caps for mental health care. By the 1990s, mental health parity advocates began to lobby Congress for mental health parity. Enacted in 1996, MHPA eliminated the ability of large group health plans to impose lower lifetime and annual dollar spending limits on mental health care. Enacted in 2008, MHPAEA eliminated the ability of large group health plans to impose higher deductibles, copayments, and coinsurance amounts on mental health care. Enacted in 2010, ACA requires individual and small group health plans, qualified health plans, and most Medicaid plans to provide mental health and substance use disorder benefits. ACA also requires qualified health plans to comply with the mental health parity requirements set forth in MHPA and MHPAEA. Notwithstanding these legislative developments, many public health care program beneficiaries and private health plan members, including Medicare beneficiaries and grandfathered health plan members, still will not have a federal legal right to mental health parity and mandatory mental health and substance use disorder benefits even after the full implementation of President Obama's health care reform bill.

See also Disability Rights; Evidence-Based Practice; Mental Health Advocacy; Public Policy Issues; Rights of Patients with Mental Health Conditions

Bibliography

Affordable Care Act [ACA], Pub. L. No. 111-148, 111th Cong., 2nd Sess. (2010), *as amended* Pub. L. No. 111-152, 111th Cong., 2nd Sess. (2010).

Barry, Colleen. 2003. "Design of Mental Health Benefits: Still Unequal after All These Years." *Health Affairs* 22: 127–137.

Mental Health Parity Act of 1996 [MHPA], Pub. L. No. 104-204, § 701 et seq., 110 Stat. 2944 (1996).

Paul Wellstone and Pete Domenici Mental Health Parity and Addiction Equity Act [MHPAEA], Pub. L. No. 110-343, Subtitle B, § 511 et seq., 122 Stat. 3756, 3881 (2008).

U.S. Department of Health and Human Services. 1999. *Mental Health: A Report of the Surgeon General.* Rockville, MD: U.S. Department of Health and Human Services.

U.S. Departments of Health and Human Services, Labor, and Treasury. 2010a. *Interim Final Rules under the Paul Wellstone and Pete Domenici Mental Health Parity and Addiction Equity Act of 2008*, 75 Fed. Reg. 5410–51 (2010).

U.S. Departments of Health and Human Services, Labor, and Treasury. 2010b. *Interim Final Rules for Group Health Plans and Health Insurance Coverage Relating to Status as a Grandfathered Health Plan Under the Patient Protection and Affordable Care Act*, 75 Fed. Reg. 34538-70 (2010).

42 C.F.R. § 409.62 (2011).

42 C.F.R. § 435.1009(a)(2) (2011).

42 U.S.C. § 1395l(c) (2011).

Intellectual Disability

Christine D. Cea and Celia B. Fisher

Intellectual disability—or mental retardation, as it was previously called—is a disorder affecting a person's ability to learn in a variety of contexts. Three essential criteria are necessary for a diagnosis of intellectual disability (American Association on Intellectual and Developmental Disabilities 2010; American Psychiatric Association 2000). First, an individual must have significant limitations in intellectual functioning, defined by an intelligence test score of 70–75 or below. Second, intellectual limitations must coexist with deficits in adaptive behavior in two or more of the following areas: communication, self-care, home living, social and interpersonal skills, community use, self-direction, health and safety, functional academics, leisure, and work. Finally, limitations in intellectual functioning and adaptive behavior must appear prior to an individual's 18th birthday.

Classification

People with intellectual disability (ID) can be classified into four overlapping levels of severity based upon their intelligence test scores: mild (IQ of 50–70), moderate (IQ of 35–55), severe (IQ of 20–40), and profound (IQ below 20–25) (American Psychiatric Association 2000). They can also be classified from higher to lower functioning by the type and intensity of supports needed to function in society: (1) intermittent (episodic, as-needed supports of high or low intensity); (2) limited (constant, but time-limited supports); (3) extensive (chronic long-term supports in some environments, e.g., home or work); and (4) pervasive (constant, high-intensity supports across environments). In recent years, there has been a growing interest in employing a multidimensional classification system that puts greater emphasis on adaptive behaviors and other factors in addition to intelligence tests and intensity of support needs (American Association on Intellectual and Developmental Disabilities 2010).

Etiology

Biological causes of ID may be hereditary (e.g., Fragile X, Down syndrome), prenatal (e.g., maternal drug and alcohol abuse), or perinatal (e.g., fetal malnutrition, prematurity, hypoxia, trauma); or they may involve disease or injury (e.g., encephalitis, meningitis, head trauma). Psychosocial causes include malnutrition and lack of nurturance, stimulation, or proper medical care. The cause of ID is unknown in 30 to 40 percent of the population.

Development

The developmental course of the disorder will vary with the level of ID. People with mild ID are often indistinguishable from children without mental retardation during the preschool years, and deficits in learning are often not diagnosed until school age. During the school years, expressive speaking skills and the ability for spontaneous play with peers develop. Adolescents with mild ID can achieve normal language ability and academic functioning up to a sixth-grade level, have the same kind of social interests as their typically developing peers, and show similar self-directed behavior. Adults functioning at the mild level are capable of social and vocational skills, and though they may need assistance when under stress, many can live and work independently in the community.

People classified with moderate ID are more likely to be identified during the preschool years because of delays in achieving developmental milestones (e.g., standing, walking). By school age, many acquire communication skills and can attend to personal care with some supervision. Individuals with moderate ID typically do not progress beyond second-grade level in academic subjects, but generally benefit from social and occupational skills training. As adolescents, their poor socialization skills may interfere with peer relations. Adults functioning at the moderate level do not commonly achieve independent social status, but with training, many adapt well to living in supervised community settings with supports.

People classified with severe ID are most often identified in infancy or the first two years of life, due to substantially delayed developmental milestones or the presence of congenital anomalies, or both. In early childhood, these individuals acquire little speech, often using a single word or gesture to communicate. During the school years, basic self-care skills such as feeding and dressing can be achieved with training, and some may develop language. When they reach adolescence, the academic and adaptive skills of people with severe ID are similar to

A counselor (center) discusses with a young man (right) with intellectual disability the prospect of his transitioning to independent living. (AP Photo/Carolyn Kaster.)

those of typical four- to six-year-olds. As adults, they may be capable of performing self-care skills and simple work tasks in highly supervised settings and adapting to community living with families or in small group residences.

People with profound ID are usually diagnosed as infants because of evident developmental delays and congenital anomalies. In early childhood, there is often significant impairment in sensory and motor functioning. They typically have life-long limited motor, self-care, and communication skills, which may continue to improve through training. Optimal development at all stages for people functioning at this level can only be achieved with consistent assistance in highly structured supervised contexts.

Social-Ecological Influences

The development of people with ID is largely dependent upon environmental factors such as education, appropriate supports, and opportunities for growth. Historically, it was believed that people with ID could not learn or contribute to society, and little was done to enhance their development. Labeled feebleminded and mentally defective, they were segregated from society and subjected to custodial care in large overcrowded institutions. Their prognosis was poor. Over the past 40 years, changes in public policies and societal expectations have led to great

Inclusive Education

"Over the past several decades . . . [an] almost universal consensus has emerged worldwide pertaining to the education of students with ID [intellectual disability]; that is, the expectation that every child has a fundamental right to education and that efforts should be made to educate them in inclusive classrooms with their nondisabled peers. The Salamanca Statement [UNESCO, 1994] calls upon all governments and the international community to (a) adopt as a matter of law or policy the principle of inclusive education, enrolling all children in regular schools, unless there are compelling reasons for doing otherwise and (b) endorse the approach of inclusive schooling and to support the development of special needs education as an integral part of all education programs. In summary, there is an emerging consensus that children and youth with ID be included in general education settings so that they have access to the same educational opportunities available to the majority of children."

—American Association on Intellectual and Developmental Disability (2010)

strides in the treatment and education of people with ID. Deinstitutionalization from congregate care facilities in the early 1970s and recognition of the positive influence of parenting led to community living with the family or in small-group home residences and the strengthening of parent and teacher advocacy. In 1975, the Education of All Handicapped Children Act (retitled the Individuals with Disabilities Education Act in 1990) and subsequent amendments ensured free and appropriate educational services in the least restricted environment for all children with ID from 3 through 21 years.

Today, advanced assessment techniques facilitate early identification of developmental disabilities, enabling infants who are days old to receive an array of support services intended to enhance their development to typical levels. In public schools, many students with disabilities attend regular classrooms, learning with peers their own age. A willingness of the business community to employ people with intellectual disabilities has enabled many adults to work and live in the community. Some are married, raising children, and experiencing full citizenship. With ongoing environmental opportunities and supports and the evolving expectations of those around them, the functioning of people with ID will continue to improve, enabling many more individuals to become more independent and productive members of the society in which they live.

See also Autism Spectrum Disorders; Children and Mental Health; Learning Disabilities; Rehabilitation Services

Bibliography

Ainsworth, Patricia, and Pamela Baker. 2004. *Understanding Mental Retardation.* Jackson: University of Mississippi Press.

American Association on Intellectual and Developmental Disabilities. 2010. *Intellectual Disability: Definition, Classification, and Systems of Supports* (11th ed.). Washington, DC: American Association on Intellectual and Developmental Disabilities.

American Psychiatric Association. 2000. *Diagnostic and Statistical Manual of Mental Disorders* (4th ed., text rev.). Washington, DC: American Psychiatric Publishing.

Carlson, Licia. 2010. *The Faces of Intellectual Disability: Philosophical Reflections.* Bloomington: Indiana University Press.

Harris, James C. 2006. *Intellectual Disability: Understanding Its Development, Causes, Classification, Evaluation, and Treatment.* New York: Oxford University Press.

Hodapp, R. M., M. A. Maxwell, M. H. Sellinger, and E. M. Dykens. 2006. "Persons with Mental Retardation: Scientific, Clinical, and Policy Advances." In T. G. Plante, ed., *Mental Disorders of the New Millennium: Vol. 3. Biology and Function* (pp. 25–53). Westport, CT: Praeger.

National Association on Intellectual and Developmental Disabilities. 2011. National Resources (listing). Retrieved from http://www.aamr.org/content_535.cfm?navID=146.

Switzky, Harvey N., and Stephen Greenspan, eds. 2006. *What Is Mental Retardation?: Ideas for an Evolving Disability in the 21st Century.* Washington, DC: American Association on Intellectual and Developmental Disabilities.

Trent, James. 1994. *Inventing the Feeble Mind: A History of Mental Retardation in the United States.* Berkeley: University of California Press.

UNESCO. 1994. *The Salamanca Statement and Framework for Action on Special Needs Education.* n.p.: UNESCO.

Internet Gaming Addiction

Kimberly Young

Internet gaming addiction is an addiction to online video games, role-playing games, or any interactive gaming environment available through the Internet that can create problems in the addict's daily routine, school performance, family relationships, or mood (Leung 2007; Ng & Wiemer-Hastings 2005). Games such as EverQuest, The Dark Age of Camelot, or Diablo II—dubbed "heroinware" by some players—tend to pose the most complex problems. Extensive chat features give such games a social aspect missing from offline activities, and the collaborative/competitive nature of working with or against other players can make it a hard habit to break (Ducheneaut & Moore 2004).

In the early days of the Internet, interactive online games were a take-off on the old Dungeons and Dragons games, often know as Multi-User Dungeons, or MUDs, that drew upon power, dominance, and recognition within a role-playing make-believe virtual world. Young men traditionally gravitated toward these role-playing games to assume a character role associated with specific skills, attributes, and rankings that fellow players acknowledge and treat accordingly (Turkle 1998). MUDs differed from traditional video arcade games in that instead of a player's hand-eye coordination improving, the actual strength, skills, and rankings of the character improved. MUD players earned respect and recognition from fellow players, and younger players, especially those with low self-esteem and weak interpersonal skills, were at greatest risk to get addicted if they developed a powerful persona within the game (Young 1998). Of late, online gaming addiction has reached epidemic proportions in China, Korea, and Taiwan (Associated Press 2007). Chinese authorities mandate therapy for those suspected of Internet gaming addiction and opened the first treatment center for adolescent Internet addicts in Beijing.

The Nature of the Problem

Online gaming addiction can be regarded as belonging to a broader set of Internet addictions that include compulsive Internet sexuality, compulsive Internet gambling, and compulsive Internet shopping and/or bidding on online auction house websites. The present entry focuses on Internet gaming, which has seen the most significant growth over the last few years. As billions of dollars have been poured into the gaming industry to develop more interactive and immersive gaming environments, the general population has seen a tremendous surge in addictions and other mental health issues (not to mention physical problems such as eye strain, back strain, and poor diet).

Women as well as men are likely to become addicted to online games. However, the focus has been on male players as they make up over two-thirds of the gaming market. Women are also likely to become addicted to social features such as chat rooms, Facebook, and Twitter, while men in general are likely to become addicted to Internet pornography and Internet gambling (poker and blackjack) as well as to gaming.

Among adolescents, Yee (2007) found that individuals who suffer from low self-esteem or other emotional problems are at greater risk for developing an addiction to online gaming. Yee's studies suggested that hard-core players have a tendency toward neuroticism or may suffer from emotional problems or low self-worth and esteem. In the game, these interactive environments allow young individuals to experiment with parts of their personality: they can be more vocal, try out leadership roles, and assume new identities. Problems emerge when players rely on these new online personas to the extent that the distinction between what is real and what is part of a fantasy role-play game becomes blurred.

Online gaming is a social activity. Most online games include copious amounts of chat activity, allowing players to interact with each other in the guise of the characters they represent. Many adolescents who have trouble with social relationships and feel lonely as if they have never truly belonged can develop a sense of belonging in the game (Leung 2007). In some cases, the game provides the only friends they interact with. Gamers can become hooked on the social aspect of the game-joining guilds that provide a great sense of community and accomplishment when they take out those big monsters or strategize about their next online session. Through these nightly quests, gamers form close bonds and friendships with fellow players that replaces the social contact missing in their lives.

Gaming provides players with an outlet for their imaginations (Yee 2007). Especially among adolescents who are academically bright and who feel under-stimulated in school, they turn to the game as a place for adventure and intellectual stimulation. Such games also lure players with complex systems of goals and achievements. Players are drawn into the virtual fantasy world of the game; they internalize the game as a real place, and other characters are seen as real people and not fictional characters. Especially in goal-oriented multiuser role-playing games, players engage in activities to develop their characters from one level to the next and compete to find valuable in-game elements such as armor and weapons. Players can find themselves wrapped up in the game for hours as they struggle to gain one more skill or weapon.

Signs of Internet Gaming Addiction

Gamers who become hooked show clear signs of addiction. Like a drug, gamers who play almost every day, play for extended periods of time (over four hours), get restless or irritable if they cannot play, and sacrifice other social activities just to game are showing signs of addiction (Griffiths, Davies, & Chappell 2003). Other warning signs are outlined below (see Young 2009).

Preoccupation with Gaming

The addiction process begins with a preoccupation with gaming. Gamers will think about the game when offline and often fantasize about playing the game when they should be concentrating on other things. Instead of thinking about the paper that needs to be completed for school, or going to class, or studying at the library, the gamer becomes completely focused on playing the game. Gamers start to miss deadlines and/or neglect work or social activities, as being online and playing the game becomes their main priority.

Lying or Hiding Gaming Use

Some gamers spend days and nights online. They do not eat, sleep, or take a shower because of the game. They lie to family and friends about what they are really doing on the computer. Students tell their parents that they are doing their homework, spouses tell their family that they are using the computer for work, and friends will make up excuses for why they cannot go out—all to find more time to play the game.

Loss of Interest in other Activities

As the addiction progress grows, gamers become less interested in hobbies or activities that they used to enjoy and more fascinated with the game. I had one mother tell me about her son who loved baseball and played varsity on his high school team until he discovered X-Box Live. "His grades plummeted after he discovered the game, but it wasn't until he quit the baseball team that I knew that something seriously wrong. He loved baseball too much. He even won a baseball scholarship for college and dreamed about playing professionally. Now, nothing else matters to him except the game."

Social Withdrawal

Some gamers experience personality changes the more addicted they become. A once outgoing and social daughter becomes withdrawn from her friends and family only to spend more time alone in front of the computer. A normally happy son becomes withdrawn only to prefer making friends in the game as the people that were once important in real life become less important. As one mother explained, "If no one else existed, he would play all day." If children do have real-life friends, they are usually fellow gamers. In some cases, gamers are introverts and have problems making social connections in real life and turn to the game for companionship and acceptance.

Disobedience with Respect to Time Limits

Because of their addiction, gamers become defensive about their need to play the game and angry when forced to go without it. Parents who try to put time limits on the game describe how their sons and daughters become angry, irrational, and even violent. In one case, a mother told me about her son who spent his nights gaming and his days sleeping. "When I took away his computer, he pushed me, slammed the door to his room, and wouldn't come out all night. When I came home from work the next day, he took a sledgehammer to my computer, which was off limits to him. This isn't my son. He was a good kid and never gave me a moment's trouble until I lost him to the game."

Psychological Withdrawal

Gamers who cannot access the game experience a loss. They want to be on the game and they miss playing the game. This feeling can become so intense that they become irritable, anxious, or depressed when they are forced to go without the game. They cannot concentrate on anything else except when they can go back online to play. Their minds become so fixated on the game that they can experience a psychological withdrawal from the game. Their feelings intensify and they stop thinking rationally and begin to act out toward other people in their lives. All that they can think about is getting back to the game, and they become angry and bitter at anyone who threatens taking it away.

Using Gaming as an Escape

Gaming addicts use the online world as a psychological escape. The game becomes a safe means to cope with life's problems. It is a legal and inexpensive way to soothe troubling feelings and can quickly become a convenient way to instantly forget whatever stresses and pains they are experiencing. Like a drug addict or alcoholic who uses drugs or alcohol as a way to escape problems that they are not able to deal with, gaming addicts use the game to avoid stressful situations and unpleasant feelings. They escape into the gratification of the game and the feelings they associated with playing it. Gamers who feel socially awkward, isolated, and insecure in real life can transform themselves into someone who feels socially confident, connected, and self-assured with others through the game. As the gamer progress deeper into the game, they make friends, or maybe their friends were the ones who first introduced the gamer to the game and these social relationships with other players become highly significant. While playing, they feel more accomplished, more accepted, and better about themselves, and through their characters, gamers live out a fictional life that is more satisfying and interesting than their own.

Continued Use Despite Its Consequences

Gamers often want to be the best at the game. In order to grow in the game, they need to play, especially in Quest type of games, where there is a shared activity, they hunt together for items, and it can take several hours to complete one quest. Gamers who become hooked become obsessed with the need to be the best at the game. They want to feel powerful and to be recognized by other players, and in order to do this they must spend time in the game. With that said, they continue to use the game despite consequences it may be causing in their lives. Among adolescents, they may fail school, lose a scholarship, break up with a girlfriend or boyfriend, neglect their diet, drop out of school, and ignore their basic hygiene just to be online.

Family Therapy

Recent studies in Taiwan suggest that family factors also increase risk for developing online gaming addiction (Yen et al. 2007). Adolescents from families from lower economic-level households, whose parents are separated or divorced, who have high parent-adolescent conflict, or who have a family history of addiction are at greater risk to develop gaming addiction. Many addictions stem from a history of addiction in the family as a way to cope with painful feelings and difficult situations. Seeing that this is how an aunt, uncle, or other relative copes with problems through drinking, drug use, gaming, or smoking might be a sign that this is the way to cope with all problems. Especially among adolescents, gamers who become addicted often use the game as way of escaping conflict or turbulence in their lives. Adolescents experiencing a traumatic transition such as divorce or family problems because the family is relocating or who have difficulty accepted a new stepparent face a personal crisis and learn to cope through the Internet.

Adolescent gaming addiction continues to be a major issue in our society as teen abuse is growing at an alarmingly high rate. Adolescence alone, regardless of the involvement in the Internet, is an extremely challenging and complex transition for young individuals. Exploring and attempting to discover one's identity as an adolescent can be an overwhelming stage in one's life. In the event that an adolescent is using online games, it is more than likely that many more obstacles will be encountered and as a result a teen will struggle with unmanageable physical and emotional consequences (Leung 2004).

Peer pressure and environmental distresses are chief influences for an adolescent becoming involved with gaming. Friends are often gamers, and as discussed, family dynamics can play a role in the development of online gaming addiction. Furthermore, children of substance-abusing parents are shown to have an increased risk of using gaming as a means to cope with problems such as developmental issues, school problems, health problems, delinquency, sexual problems, mental issues, and family problems.

It is much harder for teens to recover from gaming addiction, especially when the computer is often a necessary component of their home and school environments. Effective treatment requires that the dynamics of the family be assessed and that family members must also be helped to achieve health or relapse is much more likely.

Successful treatment must not only address the gaming behavior but also help an adolescent navigate the normal developmental tasks of identity formation that are often neglected while using gaming as a means of coping with life's problems. Treatment should focus on effective problem solving and the social skills necessary to build self-esteem. Many gamers lack a strong sense of self, using gaming as means to form their identities. However, self-esteem in real life is fragile or nonexistent. Family therapy must focus on ways to build or rebuild their identities within a nongaming environment.

Gamers often minimize the extent they game and avoid dealing with family issues that may be driving their desire to game. It is important to consider an adolescent's individual family situation when treating their addiction. Comprehending the teen's immediate environment in most cases enhances the understanding of why the addiction is taking place. It is necessary to look at family dynamics such as family history of addiction, background, communication dynamics, or conflict and how these factors may be impacting a teen's developmental stages, emotional well-being, and self-esteem.

Finally, family therapy needs to include educating the family on ways that they can help the addict whether or not he or she is in individual counseling or treatment. This may include counseling for family members, education on problem/compulsive gaming for the family, strategies on how to cope with anger and loss of trust from the addicted loved one, and education on the emotional costs of online gaming. Often, gaming addiction will be addressed as a part of a weekly family program. Each week topics related to addiction are addressed to help family members understand the process of recovery, relapse triggers, and the importance of keeping healthy boundaries. This is especially important for parents as they struggle to understand a son or daughter's compulsive need to game and the underlying dynamics associated with their addiction.

Conclusion

Online gaming is an emotionally draining and time-consuming activity, and to create more time for the computer, addicts neglect sleep, diet, exercise, hobbies, and socializing. The initial loss of online gaming means an increase in idle time or boredom, which only increases the temptation to surf, making it vital for clients to create positive lifestyle changes to fill the void created with the time now not spent at the computer. Given the dynamics involved with Internet addiction, family therapy is an ideal therapeutic framework to treat adolescents who suffer from the condition. While new techniques and refinements may need to be developed using family therapy with adolescent online gaming addicts, this entry helps us to focus on ways to deal with situational factors that may be playing an underlying role in the development of Internet gaming addiction. Having the family involved also enables members to serve as sponsors and support systems for the gaming addict providing a safe haven at home to recover.

See also Adolescence and Mental Health; Gambling Addiction; Impulse Control Disorders

Bibliography

Associated Press. 2007. "Beijing Ministers to Clinics for Online Addicts." Retrieved from http://www.msnbc.msn.com/id/8430811/.

Dongseong Choi, D., and Jinwoo Kim. 2004. "Why People Continue to Play Online Games: In Search of Critical Design Factors to Increase Customer Loyalty to Online Contents." *CyberPsychology & Behavior* 7(1): 11–24.

Ducheneaut, Nicholas, and Robert J. Moore. 2004. "The Social Side of Gaming: A Study of Interaction Patterns in a Massively Multiplayer Online Game." In Proceedings of the ACM Conference on Computer-Supported Cooperative Work (pp. 360–369). New York: ACM.

Griffiths, Mark D., Mark N. O. Davies, and Darrin Chappell. 2003. "Breaking the Stereotype: The Case of Online Gambling." *CyberPsychology & Behavior* 6(1): 81–91.

Leung, Louis. 2004. "Net-generation Attributes and Seductive Properties of the Internet as Predictors of Online Activities and Internet Addiction." *CyberPsychology & Behavior* 7(3): 333–348.

Leung, Louis. 2007. "Stressful Life Events, Motives for Internet Use, and Social Support among Digital Kids." *CyberPsychology & Behavior* 10(2): 204–214.

Ng, Brian D., and Wiemer-Hastings, Peter. 2005. "Addiction to the Internet and Online Gaming." *CyberPsychology & Behavior* 8(2):110–113.

Turkle, Sherry. 1998. *Life on the Screen: Identity in the Age of the Internet.* Cambridge, MA: MIT Press.

Yee, Nick. 2007. "Motivations of Play in Online Games." *CyberPsychology & Behavior* 9: 772–775.

Yen, Ju-Yu, Cheng-Fang Yen, Cheng-Chung Chen, Sue-Huei Chen, and Chih-Hung Ko. 2007. "Family Factors of Internet Addiction and Substance Use Experience in Taiwanese Adolescents." *CyberPsychology & Behavior* 10(3): 323–329.

Young, Kimberly S. 1998. "Internet Addiction: The Emergence of a New Clinical Disorder." *CyberPsychology & Behavior* 1: 237–244.

Young, Kimberly S. 2007. "Cognitive-Behavioral Therapy with Internet Addicts: Treatment Outcomes and implications." *CyberPsychology & Behavior* 10(5): 671–679.

Young, Kimberly S. 2009. "Online Gaming Addiction: Risk Factors and Treatment." In Andrea Browne-Miller, ed., *The International Collection on Addictions* (Vol. 4, pp. 217–234). Westport, CT: Praeger.

Involuntary Treatment

Melissa Floyd

Psychiatry has been called "virtually the only medical specialty that includes coerced, involuntary treatment" (Shore 1997, 325). Involuntary treatment in mental health generally refers to mandated services, both inpatient and outpatient, that are provided to consumers (or patients), often despite their wishes to the contrary.

Writers in the helping professions as well as consumer advocates (Taylor & Bentley 2005) have pointed out the incongruity—and perhaps, incompatibility—of involuntary treatment interventions and elements of professional codes of ethics. The latter codes generally call for restriction of self-determination in the case of consumers only when risk is "foreseeable and imminent" (National Association of Social Workers 1997). Other writers strongly disagree with this perceived incompatibility between helping values and involuntary or beneficent treatment interventions (Murdach 1996; Rosenson 1993); they cite the consumer's right to treatment, not just his or her right to *refuse* treatment, as an important consideration. Still others suggest that taking pro and con positions in this debate distracts the mental health community from more important questions about the state of service delivery in the mental health arena (Saks 2002).

Practical Aspects

Opinions aside, for many mental health practitioners, using coercive and involuntary treatments has become part and parcel of their job duties. These practitioners may regularly hospitalize consumers under involuntary orders or facilitate court orders for medication and outpatient treatment. At the least, many practitioners are increasingly faced with negotiating difficult practice decisions with consumers who present for treatment under court mandate. Likewise, since involuntary treatment of some sort for mental illness is probably as perennial as mental illness itself (Dennis & Monahan 1996), many mental health consumers with serious and persistent mental illnesses will experience such treatment at least once over the course of their illness.

Most commonly, involuntary mental health services may be provided as a "crisis stabilization" form of hospitalization when there is an imminent danger to the consumer him or herself or to others. Less common are ordered medications, as well as involuntary electroconvulsive therapy. Some states are increasingly utilizing outpatient mandated treatment that ideally provides "assisted treatment" with added resources as well as added consequences if treatment regimens are not adhered to.

Effects

While some individuals may feel a sense of gratitude for their diagnosis and treatment or understand retrospective need for involuntary treatment, many report feelings of fear, confusion, or anger and frustration with the process. At the extreme, some who experience restraint or have been given involuntary shock treatments look back on the experience as torture, a process where their rights were systematically deprived. Also alarming are the reports that past difficult treatment experiences pose a barrier to seeking treatment again. Clearly there is much ambivalence with which involuntary treatment is viewed by both consumers and providers alike (Brophy & Ring 2004).

To minimize harmful effects of involuntary treatment, authors have emphasized that one of the first steps on the part of professionals, family members, and others is recognizing the coercive aspects of such treatment. In other words, using terms that downplay or water down the coercion inherent in being placed against one's will in a psychiatric facility insults the intelligence of the service user and should be avoided. A term used by some, "negotiated coercion," recognizes that coercion is part of the process yet allows the patient to retain as much dignity as possible (Owen & Floyd 2010). Of course, terms mean little without some follow-up actions, so it is important to shore up the current practices with real supports to encourage patient autonomy.

While consumers in crisis may be in need of stabilizing treatment, they should still retain all other rights to the greatest extent possible. Too often, societal stigma plays a role as individuals requiring commitment are subject to the equivalent of a criminal response, practically ensuring a feeling of degradation. Even many professionals misunderstand the term "incompetent," which in the United States is actually a legal description for someone who has been determined by a court to be unable to make his or her own decisions, not someone who may be in a psychiatric emergency and requires, at that point, proxy decision making. Individuals in involuntary treatment situations should still be able to make decisions about what medications they most prefer to be treated with, and where and by whom they choose to be treated, including access to consults as needed. In other words, while the *fact of treatment* is not a choice, the *treatment process* should offer as much choice as possible for the benefit of all concerned. Recognizing the individual behind the diagnosis is the essential first step for any genuine person-centered plan of treatment.

Conclusion

Despite controversy on both sides of the issue, involuntary treatment continues to be utilized in current mental health service delivery. Indeed, in the current mental health climate of budget cuts and failing resources, more consumers yet may reach a crisis point before they can be treated under voluntary methods, leading to an overall rise in involuntary methods funded by the state. Being aware of the underlying issues of coercion and value mismatch for professionals may help to provide a more supportive environment for those mental health consumers involved in these more problematic modes of service.

See also Disability Rights; Emergency Services; Ethical Issues; Family and Mental Health; Hospitalization; Medical Model of Mental Illness; Rights of Patients with Mental Health Conditions; Stigma

Bibliography

Brophy, L., and D. Ring. 2004. "Efficacy of Involuntary Treatment in the Community." *Social Work in Mental Health* 2: 157–174.

Dennis, D. L., and J. Monahan. 1996. *Coercion and Aggressive Community Treatment: A New Frontier in Mental Health Law.* New York: Plenum Press.

Interlandi, Jeneen. 2012. "Love and Commitment: What It Takes To Put Your Father Away in a Mental Institution." *New York Times Magazine*, June 24. Retrieved from: http://www.nytimes.com/2012/06/24/magazine/when-my-crazy-father-actually-lost-his-mind.html?_r=1&pagewanted=all.

Murdach, A. D. 1996. "Beneficence Re-examined: Protective Intervention in Mental Health." *Social Work* 41: 26–31.

National Association of Social Workers. 1997. *Code of Ethics.* Washington, DC: National Association of Social Workers.

Owen, J. L., and M. R. Floyd. 2010. "Negotiated Coercion: Thoughts about Involuntary Treatment in Mental Health." *Ethics in Social Welfare* 4: 297–299.

Rosenson, M. K. 1993. "Social Work and the Right of Psychiatric Patients to refuse Medication: A Family Advocate's Response." *Social Work* 38: 107–112.

Saks, E. R. 2002. *Refusing Care: Forced Treatment and the Rights of the Mentally Ill.* Chicago: University of Chicago Press.

Shore, M. F. 1997. "Psychological Factors in Poverty." In L. M. Mead, ed., *The New Paternalism: Supervisory Approaches to Poverty* (pp. 305–329). Washington, DC: Brookings Institution Press.

Taylor, M. F., and K. J. Bentley. 2005. "Professional Dissonance: Colliding Values And Job Tasks in Mental Health Practice." *Community Mental Health Journal* 41: 469–480.

L

Latinos and Mental Health

Linda Wasmer Andrews

Latinos (or Hispanic Americans) are the largest ethnic minority in the United States, comprising 15 percent of the total population. Because this group is growing so rapidly, however, it is expected to make up nearly one-quarter of the U.S. population by 2050. Two-thirds of Latinos trace their ancestry back to Mexico. The rest have roots in Cuba, Puerto Rico, Central America, South America, or another Spanish culture. This diverse community is bound together by the Spanish language, sometimes still spoken by the current generation, and by shared traditions and cultural values.

In general, rates of mental illness for Latinos are similar to those for non-Hispanic whites. Studies of major depression, for example, have found that Latinos have similar or lower rates than non-Hispanic white individuals. But certain subgroups of Latinos—most notably, immigrants and youth—are at increased risk for serious emotional distress.

Although Latinos are vulnerable to the same mental health challenges as anyone else, they use mental health services less often than average. A large, national survey of U.S. adults who had experienced major depression within the last year found that just 52 percent of Latinos received treatment, compared to 73 percent of non- Hispanic whites. Among young people ages 12 through 17, the treatment rate was even lower—only 36 percent, compared to 41 percent for non-Hispanic white youth.

In part, this disparity may stem from cultural attitudes toward mental health disorders. Depression, for example, may be viewed as simply a passing case of nerves, tiredness, or physical illness. Rather than turning to a mental health professional for help, Latinos often reach out first to their family, friends, community, and church, or to a traditional healer.

At-Risk Groups

Ironically, some of the lowest rates of mental health care are found in high-risk subgroups. Among Latino immigrants with mental disorders, for example, fewer than 5 percent receive treatment from a mental health specialist.

Susto and Curanderismo

Susto ("soul loss") is a folk illness resembling depression that is prevalent among some Latino groups in the United States as well as in Mexico, Central America, and South America. Other names for susto include *espanto*, *pasmo*, *tripa ida*, *perdida del alma*, and *chibih*. The condition is thought to occur when a terrifying event causes the soul to leave the body. The resulting unhappiness and illness make it hard to get along in everyday life.

The first signs of susto may appear at any time from days to years after the frightening event. Many symptoms of susto are similar to those of depression, including sadness, lack of motivation to do anything, appetite disturbances, sleep problems, and feelings of low self-worth. Physical symptoms of susto include muscle aches and pains, headaches, stomachaches, and diarrhea. In extreme cases, it is believed that susto can lead to death.

Curanderismo is a Latino system of folk medicine that includes healing rituals, prayer, herbal remedies, and massage. People may seek help from specially trained healers, known as *curanderos* (men) or *curanderas* (women), whose knowledge of healing methods has been passed down from relatives or learned through apprenticeships. Many attribute their healing ability to divine energy channeled through their bodies.

Curanderos/as maintain that humans are physical, mental, emotional, and spiritual beings. The spiritual self, in the form of an energetic aura surrounding the body, is especially vulnerable to trauma. When the soul is lost due to a great fright, this aura is violated. The healing process aims to restore strength, health, and resilience to the damaged spirit. The techniques used may include ritual healings to call the soul back to the body. *Barridas* (ritual cleansings) may be performed to rebalance the body and soul.

Curanderismo exists outside mainstream medicine, so its effectiveness has not been established in scientific studies. However, proponents claim that it reduces symptoms and relieves stress. Believers who choose to use curanderismo along with, rather than instead of, conventional treatments may be getting the best of both worlds. They should inform their health care providers about any herbal remedies they are using, however, because some herbs can cause side effects or interact harmfully with medications.

Source: American Psychiatric Association, *Diagnostic and Statistical Manual of Mental Disorders*, 4th ed., text rev., Washington, DC: American Psychiatric Association, 2000; Avila, Elena, with Joy Parker, *Woman Who Glows in the Dark: A Curandera Reveals Traditional Aztec Secrets of Physical and Spiritual Health* (New York: Jeremy P. Tarcher, 1999); American Cancer Society, "Curanderismo," March 26, 2007, Retrieved from http://www.cancer.org/Treatment/Treat mentsandSideEffects/ComplementaryandAlternativeMedicine/HerbsVitaminsandMinerals/curanderismo.

Immigrants

Immigrants face many challenges. They must adapt to a new culture with foreign customs and often an unfamiliar language, and they must make this difficult transition without the support of loved ones left behind. Many also are faced with discrimination, financial hardship, and poor living conditions in their adopted country. It is little wonder that immigrants sometimes experience considerable stress, which may trigger or worsen depression in vulnerable individuals.

In addition, many immigrants from Central America are refugees who fled political turmoil and violence in their homelands. Over 90 percent of these immigrants arrived in the United States between 1970 and 1990. However, the traumatic events that brought them to this country may have lingering repercussions to this day, putting them at high risk for posttraumatic stress disorder and depression.

Youth

Latino youth are another subgroup with an increased risk for poor mental health outcomes. They have the highest rate of suicide attempts among all ethnic minorities in the United States. Plus, they are at greater risk for depressive symptoms, anxiety-related behaviors, delinquency, and drug use than non-Hispanic white youth.

Young Latinos may experience the same stress and discrimination as their parents, but without the secure grounding in traditional values. In addition, immigrant parents often invest high hopes for the American dream in their children. Although some youngsters are propelled to success, others buckle under the pressure.

Barriers to Care

Lack of access to appropriate, high-quality care is a problem for many Latinos with mental health problems. One hurdle is the language and culture gap between Latino patients and non-Hispanic treatment providers. Another hurdle is the disproportionately high number of Latinos in low-income, underserved communities.

Language

About 12 percent of Latinos speak Spanish at home. Lack of fluency in English is a major barrier for many of these individuals. Bilingual treatment providers and translators are in limited supply, making it difficult for Spanish speakers to get adequate assessment, treatment, and emergency care for pressing mental health problems.

Providers

Even Latinos who speak English fluently may have trouble finding culturally appropriate services. An individual's culture can influence such things as how depression is expressed, how symptoms are understood, and which treatments are most acceptable. Yet Latinos are underrepresented in the mental health field.

There are only 29 Latino mental health professionals per every 100,000 Latino individuals, compared to 173 non-Hispanic white professionals per 100,000.

Socioeconomic Factors

Low socioeconomic status is a well-established risk factor for depression and other forms of emotional disturbance. Although 8 percent of non-Hispanic whites live at the poverty level, the poverty rate for Latinos is 21.5 percent. A low income, and the poor living conditions that go along with it, may contribute to poor mental health directly by causing long-term stress. At the same time, people with limited social and financial resources are apt to have trouble accessing high-quality mental health care.

Insurance

Latinos have the nation's highest rate of uninsured individuals—37 percent, compared to 16 percent for the general population. Another 18 percent of Latinos rely on public health insurance. Only 43 percent have employer-based health coverage.

Protective Factors

Helping balance out these risks are protective factors that decrease the likelihood of succumbing to mental illness. For instance, the traditional Latino value of strong family ties may offer social support. This support, in turn, may promote resilience in the face of hardship or stress.

Interestingly, there is evidence that resilience may decrease as Latino individuals spend more time in the United States or become more fluent in English. Researchers have found lower rates of mental health disorders for Mexican-born immigrants and island-born Puerto Rican adults compared with those of Mexican or Puerto Rican descent who are born in the United States. The more acculturated these individuals become, the less protected they may be against mental health problems.

Therapeutic Issues

Traditional Western psychotherapies are based on an egocentric view of the world and focus their attentions on the individual as against the family, a view that fits well with American culture generally. Such is not the case for Latinos, however, who tend to look down on individualism, construing it as a kind of selfishness. For members of the Latino community, family is valued over and above the individual. It is thus inappropriate to assume that classic Euro-American therapies can be applied uncritically to persons from this community.

Another significant issue involving cultural competency in therapy is appreciating generational change in immigrant families. While, typically, the first generation remains bound to the culture of origin and does not assimilate, the second generation is often bicultural. That is, members of the parental generation tend to retain their original language, traditions, worldview, and beliefs, whereas subsequent generations speak English as well as their original language and begin to assimilate within American society.

In the context of mental health counseling, cultural competency means being aware of such biculturalism and being sensitive to the behavior known as codeswitching. The original language tends to be the seat of emotions; thus when a bilingual (and bicultural) client wants to avoid problematic thoughts and emotions, he or she may unconsciously switch to the second language. A good bilingual, bicultural counselor should take notice of such a change and gently encourage the client to go back to his or her original language to confront the issue.

Conclusion

The issue of Latino mental health, and, in particular, that of Latino immigrant mental health, will continue to pose questions for researchers and policy makers. Despite efforts made by the government and public agencies, a lack of funding for services remains a problem. Whenever there is competition for valuable resources, one group will have a smaller share of the financial pie. In this case, undocumented immigrants, especially, are likely to be excluded from the system, even while other members of the Latino community may retain limited access.

The number of immigrants will likely continue to increase, and the Latino population will grow in general. As the United States becomes increasingly diversified, the needs of its culturally diverse communities will become ever more apparent. There is a continuing need at present for the education of mental health professionals, legislators, and their constituencies in the matter of Latino mental health services and culturally competent care.

See also Culturally Competent Mental Health Care; Posttraumatic Stress Disorder; Poverty, Unemployment, Income Inequality, and Mental Health; Undiagnosed Mental Illness

Bibliography

Agency for Healthcare Research and Quality. U.S. Department of Health and Human Services. 2010. *2010 National Healthcare Quality and Disparities Reports*. Retrieved from http://www.ahrq.gov/qual/qrdr10.htm.

American Psychiatric Association. 2011. *Latino Mental Health*. Retrieved from http://healthyminds.org/More-Info-For/HispanicsLatinos.aspx.

Mendelson, Tamar, David H. Rehkopf, and Laura D. Kubzansky. 2008. "Depression among Latinos in the United States: A Meta-Analytic Review." *Journal of Consulting and Clinical Psychology* 76: 355–366.

National Latino Behavioral Health Association. http://www.nlbha.org.

Riolo, Stephanie A., Tuan Anh Nguyen, John F. Greden, and Cheryl A. King. 2005. "Prevalence of Depression by Race/Ethnicity: Findings from the National Health and Nutrition Examination Survey III." *American Journal of Public Health* 95: 998–1000.

U.S. Department of Health and Human Services, Office of Minority Health. 2009. *Hispanic/Latino Profile*. Retrieved from http://www.omhrc.gov/templates/browse.aspx?lvl=3&lvlid=31.

U.S. Department of Health and Human Services, Office of Minority Health. *Mental Health and Hispanics*. Retrieved from http://www.omhrc.gov/templates/content.aspx?lvl=3&lvlID=9&ID=6477.

U.S. Department of Health and Human Services. 2001. *Culture, Race, and Ethnicity: A Supplement to Mental Health: A Report of the Surgeon General*. Rockville, MD: U.S. Department of Health and Human Services.

Learning Disabilities

Amanda M. Marcotte

Learning disability (LD) is a pervasive condition in today's society, with 10 to 20 percent of the population affected by at least one type of LD (Council for Exceptional Children 2011), and over 50 percent of students receiving special education services due to an LD diagnosis. Since LD was designated as a disabling condition in the 1968 Americans with Disabilities Act, the number of people diagnosed with LD has grown by nearly 250 percent to almost 3 million children (U.S. Department of Education 2002). This rapid increase can be attributed to unreliable procedures for identifying individuals with LD, and requirements for struggling learners to have a disability diagnosis to receive the academic supports they need in the public education system.

Scholars have defined "learning disability" in one of two ways. Early researchers defined LD from a biophysical perspective. More recently, scholars have defined LD in behavioral terms. These approaches can be attributed to the two fields through which LD has been observed. The first historical records of individuals who were affected by LD were in the observational notes of physicians, thus the biomedical approach to defining the disability (Lyon, Fletcher, & Barnes 2003). The second field to play a pivotal role in defining LD was the field of education, where students who failed to make progress with typical instruction confound educators and challenge both general education and special education delivery systems.

Historical Perspectives on Learning Disability

The earliest researchers to record their perspectives on LD were physicians whose patients had suffered losses in their cognitive functioning due to brain injury. These doctors observed two consistent phenomena. First, they discovered a history of brain damage that appeared to cause a loss in cognitive functioning that was previously intact. Second, the deficits they observed were localized, affecting a specific function rather than more global brain damage.

In the mid-1800s, French neurologist and anthropologist Pierre Paul Broca conducted brain autopsies on individuals who had experienced speech dysfunction. Broca identified lesions in the brain's inferior left frontal lobe—now known as the Broca region. He hypothesized that these lesions resulted in expressive language deficits but did not affect receptive language or other cognitive functions. During the late eighteenth and early nineteenth centuries, German physician and phrenologist Franz Joseph Gall tested his theories of localized functions of the brain by examining soldiers who had suffered brain injury that resulted in the loss of their expressive language capabilities. These early researchers and others revealed evidence that specific cognitive deficits can occur due to damage to localized regions of the brain. However, they studied people for whom normal brain functioning was observed prior to an incident resulting in brain damage.

In 1895, ophthalmologist James Hinshelwood published a report about a teacher who had come to him because he was suddenly unable to read. Despite the teacher's ability to see the letters, he was unable to say what they were. Yet the man displayed no difficulty working with numbers, and exhibited no other apparent cognitive dysfunction. The report resonated with English physician W. Pringle Morgan, who was working with a bright seven-year-old boy who manifested similar symptoms. However, Morgan's case appeared to be of a congenital origin rather than from a specific incidence of brain injury. Morgan published his observations, rousing the attention of other doctors—including Dr. Hinshelwood—who encountered the same set of symptoms in children experiencing unexplained reading failure. Morgan and Hinshelwood can be credited with identifying a congenital disability of word-blindness. Because of previous research on brain damage and its effects on specific cognitive functions, they theorized that word-blindness resulted from congenital brain damage.

Into the mid-twentieth century terms such as "minimal brain injury" (MBI) were commonly used, but perspectives on LD shifted from this biophysical perspective to one that was more behavioral through, among other means, Samuel Kirk's use of the term "learning disability" in 1968. With this newly coined terminology and the perspective it reflects, research and policies shifted to a focus on LD as the inability to acquire specific academic skills. Importantly, this shift allowed researchers to investigate variables beyond static, individual-based characteristics to broader environmental variables that are malleable to intervention, such as educationally supportive environments and therapeutic interventions. This was an important catalyst for the advocacy of people with disabilities in the United States, specifically in terms of their access to public education.

Deemed uneducable or too disruptive, students with disabilities were historically excluded from public education. Advocates for disabled children were aware that public education was too often withheld from students with special needs and promoted the passing of the Education for All Handicapped Children Act in 1975. This law ensured free and appropriate public education for all children and codified procedures for delivering instruction in public education settings. In 1990, this law was reauthorized and renamed the Individuals with Disabilities Education Act (IDEA), and in 2004 it went through another iteration and was renamed the Individuals with Disabilities Education Improvement Act (IDEIA). Through these important federal regulations, students with LD were protected as educable, and their teachers were required by law to provide individual education plans to ensure that they made similar academic progress as their nondisabled peers. These federal requirements reflect the evolving perspective regarding the unique learning needs of students with congenital LD and the malleability of the disabling consequences.

Current Definitions of Learning Disability

To date, definitions of LD combine both the biophysical nature and behavioral features of LD. Leading sources that define LD contain four common characteristics. Each describes LD as a (1) heterogeneous disability (2) characterized by unexpected academic failure that is (3) due to localized cognitive deficits with (4) biophysical origins. For example, the definition provided by the National Joint Committee on Learning Disabilities (1990) states:

> Learning disabilities is a general term that refers to a heterogeneous group of disorders manifested by significant difficulties in the acquisition and use of listening, speaking, reading, writing, reasoning or mathematical abilities. These disorders are intrinsic to the individual, presumed to be due to central nervous system dysfunction, and may occur across the lifespan. (4)

The fourth edition of the *Diagnostic and Statistical Manual of Mental Disorders* (*DSM-IV-TR*; American Psychiatric Association [APA] 2000) divides the localization and heterogeneity characteristics of LD into four separate disabilities, namely, (1) reading disorder, (2) mathematics disorder, (3) disorder of written expression, and (4) learning disorder not otherwise specified (NOS). The *DSM-IV-TR* defines unexpected failure in procedural terms, stating the specified disorder exists if achievement in that skill area "as measured by individually administered standardized tests ... is substantially below that expected given the person's chronological age, measured intelligence and age-appropriate education" (53–55).

The third source provides the most common framework for identifying LD, because it is the source that guides educators who encounter students failing to acquire academic skills as expected. The present iteration of IDEIA (2004) defines a learning disability as

> a disorder in one or more of the basic psychological processes involved in understanding or in using language, spoken or written, that may manifest itself in an imperfect ability to listen, think, speak, read, write, spell, or do mathematical calculations, including conditions such as perceptual disabilities, brain injury, minimal brain dysfunction, dyslexia, and developmental aphasia. [However, learning disabilities do not include] learning problems that are primarily the result of visual, hearing, or motor disabilities, of mental retardation, of emotional disturbance, or of environmental, cultural, or economic disadvantage.

Use of the historical evidence of LD and these existing definitions allow us to broadly define the LD construct. At first glance, each definition appears comprehensive and diagnostic. However their components are complicated in their applications to the assessment and identification of individuals with LD.

LD Is a Heterogeneous Disorder

Because LD affects specific learning deficits, it can manifest itself as a reading disability, a math disability or a written or verbal communication disorder. Additionally, within each of these domains are specific areas of dysfunction.

Reading Disability

Reading disability is the most common learning disability both in the population and in research, and can be disaggregated into two types, word-level reading disability (WLRD) and reading comprehension disability. Students with LD represent the majority of people served by special education with approximately 80 to 90 percent of those children diagnosed with a reading disability. Researchers estimate that 10 to 17 percent of the population may be afflicted with WLRD and 5 to 10 percent with reading comprehension disabilities without word-level deficits (Fletcher et al. 2007).

WLRD is more commonly called dyslexia and is characterized by difficulties learning "accurate and fluent single word decoding skills" (Lyon 1995). The primary cause of dyslexia is a phonological processing problem. People affected with dyslexia are unable to convert the letters on the page to sounds those letters represent. Reading comprehension difficulties are a consequence of dyslexia, because fluent word-level reading is necessary for understanding. However, there are cases of individuals, who despite good word-level decoding, are still unable to understand what they read (Leach, Scarborough, & Rescorla 2003). Some people struggle with reading comprehension because their basic language skills are deficient, such as their grammar and vocabulary. Still others fail to understand what they read when decoding, grammar, and vocabulary are intact.

Math Disabilities

Math disabilities are less frequently observed in the population and less well understood than reading disabilities. It is estimated that 4.6 to 6 percent of school-age children experience some form of math disability (Lyon, Fletcher, & Barnes 2003). While some theorize that math disabilities have subtypes, little research exists to support the types as distinct disabilities. However, as with any disability, deficits will vary in how they manifest themselves for individuals. Dyscalculia is the inability to master basic arithmetic. Dyscalculia may be observed as difficulties attaining basic math fact fluency and conducting basic calculations. Math disability may include language-based difficulties in identifying the names of mathematical symbols and concepts. It may also include conceptual problems in understanding relationships between different math concepts.

Writing Disability

Writing disability is the least understood and substantiated of all the LDs. Most research supporting writing disability as a unique LD subtype is through case study research, and few studies have isolated writing LD from comorbid reading LDs. Writing disability has been associated with expressive language disorder. Aphasia is the inability to verbally express oneself; agraphia is the inability to express oneself via writing. Researchers have identified skill deficits that are common for people who fail to attain adequate writing abilities, including handwriting and spelling problems and generating ideas. When ideas are written, they are often incohesive, lacking proper grammar and organization.

LD Is an Innate Characteristic

Researchers who investigate the causes of LD have identified two sources that may account for learning failures, namely, congenital factors and environmental factors. Although studies typically focus on individual factors, most agree that LD is a consequence of the interplay between multiple factors.

There is evidence that LD is an innate characteristic with biophysical origins in brain structure, brain functioning and genetics (Lyon, Fletcher, & Barnes 2003). Modern technological advances have allowed researchers to test the theories of early physicians that LD results from variations in brain structure, and there is evidence that this may be the case. Some researchers have found variations in the sizes of specific brain structures in individuals with dyslexia when compared to individuals with typical reading development (Galaburda 1993).

Researchers have also revealed evidence that blood flow, electromagnetic activity, and chemistry of the brain functions of dyslexic individuals vary when compared to brain functioning of typical readers (B. A. Shaywitz et al. 2002). Using similar technology, researchers have also demonstrated that when individuals with reading disabilities receive intensive intervention, their brains begin to function more similarly to nondisabled readers (Simos et al. 2002). This evidence suggests that individuals with disabled brain functioning may in fact be remedied with instructional interventions. This also provides evidence for the significant interaction between congenital and environmental factors that may mediate a predisposed reading disability.

Genetics also appear to play a causal role in the development of LD. Children are eight times more likely to have a reading disability when one parent has a reading disability (Lyon, Fletcher, & Barnes 2003). Researchers also found that monozygotic twins are more likely to both experience dyslexia than if they were dizygotic twins (Grigorenko 2001). There is compelling evidence that genetics are an important causal factor in LD, but home environment also plays an important role. For example, parents experiencing reading disability may be less likely to read to their children and have fewer books or less reading material in the home.

In addition to home literacy environments, there are many environmental factors that influence the development of LD. Research shows weak oral language skills are a risk factor for later reading failure (Scarborough 2009). Children's vocabulary as they enter their first year of schooling has been identified as an important predictor of learning to read (National Research Council 1998), and the amount of talking that occurs in their households is directly related to their vocabulary development (Hart & Risley 1995).

Early instruction is the most powerful environmental mediator and has been found to prevent reading problems from becoming disabling conditions. There is evidence that the use of direct and systematic instruction in the areas of phonemic awareness, phonics and fluency can dramatically reduce the numbers of struggling readers (S. E. Shaywitz 2003). Though 10 to 17 percent of the population may be affected with dyslexia, when reading is taught systematically less than 2 to 6 percent of students continue to experience chronic reading failure (Torgesen 2004).

LD Is Unexpected Failure

A core characteristic of LD is that the cognitive deficits are unexpected, where the individual performs as expected in all other areas and has normal general intellectual functioning. There are two complications with this assumption. First, the term "unexpected" is difficult to operationally defined and procedurally identify. The second problem is that it assumes individuals with varying general intelligence will not also experience LD.

Early physicians were the first to note "unexpected failure" as a definitional characteristic of LD. Typically, they were presented with a few children from advantaged backgrounds for whom educational opportunities were carefully selected. When these children failed to learn, it was truly an unexpected phenomenon. However, even these early researchers noted the difficulties identifying LD in more typical populations (S. E. Shaywitz 2003).

With the onus of public schooling for all children, sorting LD as a disabling condition from the multitudes of explanations regarding why some children fail to learn proved a complicated endeavor. The most common procedure used is an IQ-achievement discrepancy model. In this model, expected achievement is estimated by using a standardized test of intelligence. Achievement is measured via a standardized test specific to the deficient domain. If the scores on the achievement test fall significantly below the results of the cognitive ability test, the inference is drawn that a disability exists. These procedures are embedded in APA's definition of LD and were once codified in IDEA, although they are fraught with problems.

Some criticize these procedures for their psychometric flaws. For example, whenever a test is administered, its score contains error. When the scores of two tests are compared the error is compounded in the difference score, resulting in unreliable conclusions. The tests have also been criticized for their lack of validity. Intelligence tests may underestimate the abilities for students who struggle in areas of literacy because of their reliance on verbal indices (Cunningham & Stanovich 1998), and standardized achievement tests do not necessarily assess content children have been taught, specifically when they lag behind in the curriculum.

The IQ-achievement procedures rely on the assumption that students who have low IQ scores will have low levels of achievement. When they struggle to learn, these procedures do not reveal a discrepancy between intelligence scores and achievement scores (Shinn, Good, & Parker 1999). Proponents of this model would suggest that their academic failure is expected, illustrating the second problem associated with the notion that LD is characterized by "unexpected failure." Individuals with low levels of intelligence may also be affected by specific learning disabilities. In schools, where often the only means for additional educational support is through a disability diagnosis, low-achieving students often do not receive the support they need. Without proper intervention they fall further behind and eventually exhibit such severe failure that a discrepancy will be found.

The 2004 reauthorization of IDEIA included amendments in response to criticisms of the IQ-achievement discrepancy procedures. Students who struggle to learn may now be evaluated using response-to-instruction (RTI) procedures. RTI is an education model through which all students receive instructional support to meet their specific needs. All students receive evidence-based instructional practices and are evaluated for their progress. Students who fail to make expected gains received modifications to their instructional program, and their progress is continually evaluated until the adequate achievement is observed. RTI is also based on a discrepancy model, but this model examines two discrepancies. A dual discrepancy is observed when there is a difference between a student's level of achievement when compared to his or her typical peers and his or her rate of learning as a function of instructional intensification (McMaster et al. 2002).

RTI methods are preferred because they make use of tests that directly assess performance on curriculum and are administered over multiple time points, consider instructional factors, and incorporate immediate instructional support. RTI is criticized because it too lacks standardized procedures. There is little consensus regarding which tests to use to measure learning trends and instructional methodology varies greatly across schools. Also, there is little evidence regarding how long to attempt instructional interventions before making a diagnosis.

However, since 2004 the rate of students identified with LD in the United States decreased for the first time in 30 years, dropping from 13.8 percent to 13.1 percent of the student population (Scull & Winkler 2011). Some warn that the decrease may not reflect real changes in the rates of disabled students. Because RTI practices do not necessitate disability diagnoses for instructional services, students with LD may be going undiagnosed. Others are optimistic that the prevention-oriented practices of RTI have eliminated the wait-to-fail scenario that was leading to an overdiagnosis of LD, and early instructional support is preventing disabling conditions from occurring.

See also Adolescence and Mental Health; Attention Deficit Hyperactivity Disorder; Autism Spectrum Disorders; Children and Mental Health; Disability Rights; Intellectual Disability; Neurodiversity; School Mental Health

Bibliography

American Psychiatric Association. 2000. *Diagnostic and Statistical Manual of Mental Disorders* (4th ed., text rev.). Washington, DC: American Psychiatric Publishing.

Council for Exceptional Children. 2011. "Identifying Learning Disabilities." Retrieved from http://www.cec.sped.org/AM/Template.cfm?Section=Identifying_ Learning _Disabilities&Template=/TaggedPage/TaggedPageDisplay.cfm&TPLID=11&ContentID=3543.

Cunningham A. E., and K. E. Stanovich. 1998. "What Reading Does for the Mind." *American Educator* 22: 8–15.

Education for all Handicapped Children Act of 1974. Pub. L. No. 94-142. Renamed the Individuals with Disabilities Education Act in 1990, 20 U.S.C. Chapter 33.

Fletcher, J. M., G. R. Lyon, L. S. Fuch, and M. A. Barnes. 2007. *Learning Disabilities: From Identification to Intervention*. New York: Guilford Press.

Galaburda, A. M. 1993. "The Planum Temporale." *Archives of Neurology* 50: 457.

Grigorenko, E. L. 2001. "Developmental Dyslexia: An Update on Genes, Brains and Environments." *Journal of Child Psychology and Psychiatry* 42: 91–125.

Hart, B., and T. R. Risley. 1995. *Meaningful Differences in the Everyday Lives of Young American Children*. Baltimore: Brookes.

Individuals with Disabilities Education Improvement Act of 2004. Pub. L. No. 108–446,118 Stat. 2647; 2004 Enacted H.R. 1350; 108 Enacted H.R. 1350. Final regulations implementing IDEA 2004 were published in the *Federal Register*, Monday, August 14, 2006, 46540–46845.

Leach, J. M., H. S. Scarborough, and L. Rescorla. 2003. "Late-Emerging Reading Disabilities." *Journal of Educational Psychology* 95(2): 211–224.

Lyon, G. R. 1995. "Toward a Definition of Dyslexia." *Annals of Dyslexia* 45: 3–30.

Lyon, G. R., J. M. Fletcher, and M. C. Barnes. 2003. "Learning Disabilities." In E. J. Mash and R. A. Barkley, eds., *Child Psychopathology* (2nd ed., pp. 520–586). New York: Guilford Press.

McMaster, K., D. Fuchs, L. S. Fuchs, and D. L. Compton. 2002. "Monitoring the Academic Progress of Children Who Are Unresponsive to Generally Effective Early Reading Intervention." *Assessment for Effective Intervention* 27(4): 23–33.

National Joint Committee on Learning Disabilities. 1991. "Learning Disabilities: Issues on Definition." *ASHA* 3: 18–20.

National Research Council. 1998. *Preventing Reading Difficulties in Young Children.* Washington, DC: National Academy Press.

Scarborough, H. S. 2009. "Connecting Early Language and Literacy to Later Reading (Dis)abilities: Evidence, Theory and Practice." In F. Fletcher-Campbell, J. Soler, and G. Reid, eds., *Approaching Difficulties in Literacy Development: Assessment, Pedagogy and Programmes* (pp. 23–38). London: Sage.

Scull, J., and A. M. Winkler. 2011. *Shifting Trends in Special Education.* Washington, DC: Thomas B. Fordham Institute.

Shaywitz, B. A., S. E. Shaywitz, K. R. Pugh, E. Mencel, R. Fulbright, P. Skudlarski, R. T. Constable, K. E. Marchione, J. M. Fletcher, G. R. Lyon, and J. C. Gore. 2002. "Disruption of Posterior Brain Systems for Reading in Children with Developmental Dyslexia." *Biological Psychiatry* 52: 101–110.

Shaywitz, S. E. 2003. *Overcoming Dyslexia: A New and Complete Science-Based Program for Reading Problems at Any Level.* New York: Knopf.

Shinn, M. R., R. H. I. Good, and C. Parker. 1999. "Non-categorical Special Education Services with Students with Severe Achievement Deficits." In D. J. Reschly, W. D. I. Tilly, and J. P. Grimes, eds., *Special Education in Transition: Functional Assessment and Noncategorical Programming* (pp. 81–106). Longmont, CO: Sopris West.

Simos, P. G., J. M. Fletcher, E. Bergma, J. I. Breier, B. R. Foorman, E. M. Castillo, R. N. Davis, M. Fitzgerald, and A. C. Papanicolaou. 2002. "Dyslexia-Specific Brain Activation Profile Becomes Normal Following Successful Remedial Training." *Neurology* 58: 1–10.

Torgesen, J. K. 2004. "Lessons Learned from Research on Interventions for Students Who Have Difficulty Learning to Read." In P. McCardle and V. Chhabra, eds., *The Voice of Evidence in Reading Research* (pp. 355–382). Baltimore: Brookes.

U.S. Department of Education. 2002. *Digest of Education Statistics 2001* (NCES 2002–130). Washington, DC: U.S. Government Printing Office.

Legal Issues

See Criminalization and Diversion Programs; Disability Rights; Emergency Services; Forensic Psychology and Psychiatry; Hospitalization; Insurance;

Involuntary Treatment; Prisons and Mental Health; Residential Treatment for Young People; Rights of Patients with Mental Conditions

Lesbian, Gay, Bisexual, and Transgender (LGBT) Mental Health Issues

Mária I. Cipriani

In 1973 homosexuality was eliminated as a diagnostic category by the American Psychiatric Association and in 1980 was removed from the *Diagnostic and Statistical Manual of Mental Disorders*. However, the word "homosexual" still connotes an implied pathology based on its origin as a medical term, and most people prefer to use "lesbian" or "gay man" to identify their sexual orientation. In 1990, the *International Statistical Classification of Diseases and Related Health Problems* (*ICD-10*) stated that "sexual orientation alone is not to be regarded as a disorder" (Kaplan & Sadock 1998, 682). This statement reflects a change in the classification of homosexuality from pathological disorder to a variation of human sexuality. In 1993, the statement was amended to read: "sexual preference *per se* is not necessarily problematic or abnormal" (*ICD-10* 1993, 138).

Historically, bisexuality has presented a different challenge for the field of mental health. Some see homosexuality as an anomaly to be corrected, but this assumes a unique category of people who are "homosexual" and contrasts it to another group who are "heterosexual," reducing questions of sexual orientation to an either/or proposition. In 1949, Alfred Kinsey reported that nearly 50 percent of all men and 25 percent of all women do not fit exclusively into either category, statistics that have since gone virtually unchallenged. Bisexuality has not been studied, perhaps because of the wide range and scope of its manifestations.

"Gender-variant" people, transsexual and transgender people, are typically seen from a treatment perspective as being interested in hormonal therapy and surgical sex change. This has ramifications for mental health concerns. A transgender identity does not constitute a mental disorder, though transgender individuals may experience distress because of gender confusion or gender-identity indecision. Current training programs for mental health professionals typically do not address the special counseling needs that transgender clients and their families may bring to counseling.

Outline of the Basic Issues

Overall LGBT mental health treatment includes specific issues, such as dealing with identity and self-esteem, homophobia, coming out, HIV/AIDS, relationships, dating, and substance abuse. Because of homophobic societal attitudes, the LGBT population faces the reality of being targets of hate or bias crimes. A 1999 study for the U.S. Department of Justice reported that lesbians and gay men may be the most victimized groups in the nation. Also, as in heterosexual relationships, the experience of battering or partner abuse is a risk within LGBT relationships.

LGBT people who have serious mental illnesses face many challenges in receiving responsive, high-quality mental health care. In addition to dealing with the variable quality and availability of services, lack of affordable housing, and social stigma against the mentally ill, they also face the same hostility and hetero-normativity (i.e., heterosexual bias) experienced by LGBT people in all walks of life, including stereotyping, ignorance, and disrespect. This disrespect also leads to one of the most significant medical risks for LGBT individuals: the avoidance of routine health care. Studies have shown that LGBT individuals avoid prevention and treatment services more than their straight counterparts; mental health professionals must be aware of this when treating LGBT clients.

Because many LGBT people keep their sexuality a secret, they lack the opportunities common to heterosexuals to discuss significant relationships with their families, friends, coworkers, or religious community. This lack of social support is a considerable stressor for LGBT individuals, and this stress manifests in a number of health-related ways, including higher rates of alcoholism and other substance abuse. Studies also show individuals with same-sex partners reported a higher risk for anxiety and for suicidal thoughts than individuals with partners of the opposite sex. The use of alcohol or other drugs may provide a sense of relief from distress as well as foster a sense of acceptance by self and others. Other factors may contribute to the documented increasing use of alcohol and other drugs by this population. Historically, many gays and lesbians have sought social contact in bars and clubs, which typically promote alcohol use. In our current society, these sites still often remain the initial social venue of choice for many LGBT individuals. Additionally, the misconception held by some religious groups that homosexuality is a choice and that homosexuals can be "cured" or "healed" poses another stressor for lesbians and gays, especially in locations where this belief is prevalent and antigay bias is high.

Youth, Drugs, Suicide, and HIV/AIDS

LGBT youth face unique issues because of their sexual orientation or gender identity. In addition, each segment of the LGBT population has different mental health issues unique to it, as well as physical health issues of which mental health practitioners must be aware. This population often lacks positive role models and community support, which means that they rely on the media to learn what it means to be lesbian, gay, or transgendered and often receive information that enforces stereotypes. One study showed that 80 percent of LGBT youth ages 14 to 17 believed common media stereotypes depicting gay men as effeminate and lesbians as masculine. LGBT youth often internalize negative societal messages regarding sexual orientation and suffer from self-hatred and social and emotional isolation. They may resort to substance use to attempt to deny same-sex sexual feelings, to manage stigma and shame, or to defend against ridicule and violence (Haffner 1995). They are often at risk for self-destructive behaviors: nearly 17 percent of bisexual adolescent females reported unprotected vaginal or anal sex with a man during the last two months (Garofalo et al. 1998); 41 percent of 15- to 22-year-old males who have sex with men reported engaging in unprotected anal sex (Valleroy et al. 2000).

Links have been established between suicide attempts and gender nonconformity, early awareness of sexual orientation, stress, violence, lack of support, dropping out of school, family problems, homelessness, and substance use. A 2000 survey found that 33 to 40 percent of lesbian, gay, and bisexual high school students reported attempting suicide in the previous year (a figure that is six times higher than the national average, according to the Report of the Secretary's Task Force on Youth Suicide), compared to 8 percent of their heterosexual peers (Centers for Disease Control and Prevention 2000).

Aging, loss of a long-term partner, and relationship issues are factors that often bring lesbians to psychotherapy. Beyond this, analysis of studies on lesbians is problematic because of problems in identifying this population. The medical establishment was forced to reevaluate gay men's health when AIDS appeared, but lesbians have lacked the same visibility. For example, any practitioner who works with lesbians should be aware that studies suggest an increased risk of various cancers based on childbearing status; that is, because fewer lesbians become pregnant than their heterosexual counterparts, they are at greater risk. It has also been reported that smoking is more prevalent in lesbians than in straight women, and lesbians are more likely to abuse alcohol. Lesbians are thus predicted to have a higher risk of breast, ovarian, lung, and endometrial cancers than their straight counterparts.

In a survey that compared women's use of preventive health measures, lesbians were nearly twice as likely as their heterosexual counterparts to have used illicit drugs in the past 30 days. Additionally, more than a third of lesbians 22 to 52 years old reported partner abuse, with alcohol or other drug use involved in most of the incidents. Further, lesbian victims of partner abuse are even less likely than their straight counterparts to seek help in shelters or from counselors, feeling that they may be stigmatized or treated inadequately. These factors must be of concern to the mental health professionals serving the lesbian population.

In addition to aging and loss of a long-term partner, health issues (e.g., recent HIV+ diagnosis) bring gay men to psychotherapy. Regarding health, epidemiological studies reveal relationships between specific behaviors and diseases. For example, gay men are at increased risk for certain medical conditions that are related to specific behaviors such as receptive anal intercourse and oral-anal sexual contact. These include an increased risk for gastrointestinal infections and sexually transmitted diseases, including HIV and hepatitis B and C viruses. Mental health professionals working with gay men must be aware of these risks and must be able to speak frankly with their gay clients about safe sex practices and health risks. In addition, gay men who seek long-term monogamous relationships, or who are facing the prospects of aging and illness, may find themselves without the support of their community and thus seek psychotherapy.

Issues for Bisexuals and Transgendered Individuals

Bisexuality undoes the rigid heterosexual-lesbigay dichotomy, opening a continuum of sexual choices that can be threatening to people—including mental health practitioners—who must have black-and-white categories of sexuality. Calling into question traditional social values and rules of relationships, bisexuals find themselves pushed to self-define as either straight or lesbigay. Often bisexuals must ask themselves more complex questions about short- and long-term relationships, monogamy and nonmonogamy, than their straight or lesbigay counterparts, and they must deal implicitly or explicitly with the assumptions of nonbisexuals that their lifestyle is "wrong," "unstable," or "uncommitted." Quality mental health care starts with a therapist who is nonjudgmental about the fluidity of a person's sexual identity, is willing to accompany the client through an evolution of sexual choices, and is willing to stand outside of personal preconceptions in order to meet the client at any point along his or her journey.

Often transgender individuals find that they are the first transgender clients with whom a psychotherapist has worked. Thus they are in the position of understanding more than the mental health professional from whom they are seeking counseling, and of therefore having to educate that professional. Transgender clients frequently come to therapy to engage in self-exploration and transpersonal issues (as do many nontransgender psychotherapy clients). Counselors who misdiagnose clients, push clients to identify as gay or lesbian, or assume that their services are required because of a client's transgender status, do more harm than good. Insensitive practitioners who use the wrong personal pronouns (e.g., referring to a transgender man as "she") add to the stress, rather than support the client. Support systems, which are very important in maintaining mental health, are often missing or strained for transgender clients; in many cases family relationships are ruptured, and other emotional and psychological stressors, including feelings of alienation and powerlessness, may lead a transgender person to psychotherapy. Affirmative practitioners must start with the premise that individuals have a right to self-determination and ask a client how he or she would like to be identified. Additionally, practitioners must learn to see gender as fluid with a view to accepting each individual where he or she is at any given moment.

See also Gender Identity Disorder; Mental Health Advocacy

Bibliography

Advocates for Youth. http://www.advocatesforyouth.org/PUBLICATIONS/factsheet/fsglbt.htm.

Alexander, Christopher J. 1998. *Working with Gay Men and Lesbians in Private Psychotherapy Practice*. Binghamton, NY: Harrington Park Press.

Bieschke, Kathleen, Ruperto M. Perez, and Kurt A. Deboard, eds. 2007. *Handbook of Counseling and Psychotherapy with Lesbian, Gay, Bisexual and Transgender Clients* (2nd ed.). Washington, DC: American Psychological Association.

Centers for Disease Control and Prevention. 2000. HIV Trends in U.S. Highlight Need for Expanded Prevention. Press Briefing at the Thirteenth International AIDS Conference, Durban, South Africa, July 10. Retrieved from http://www.thebody.com/content/whatis/art2355.html.

Garofalo, Robert, R. Cameron Wolf, Sharri Kessel, Judith Palfrey, and Robert H. DuRant. 1998. "The Association between Health Risk Behaviors and Sexual Orientation among a School-Based Sample of Adolescents." *Pediatrics* 101(5): 895–902. Retrieved from http://pediatrics.aappublications.org/cgi/content/abstract/101/5/895.

Gould, Madelyn S., Ted Greenberg, Drew Velting, and David Shaffer. 2003. "Youth Suicide Risk and Preventive Interventions: A Review of the Past 10 Years." *Journal of the American Academy of Child and Adolescent Psychiatry* 42(4): 386–405.

Haffner, Debra. 1995. "Facing Facts: Sexual Health for America's Adolescents." *Journal of Adolescent Health* 22: 453–59. Retrieved from http://fcs.osu.edu/hdfs/bulletin/volume.4/bull44f.htm.

Hellman, Ronald E., and Jack Drescher, eds. 2004. *Handbook of LGBT Issues in Community Mental Health*. Binghamton, NY: Haworth Medical Press.

ICD-10 International Statistical Classification of Diseases Diagnostic Criteria for Research. 1993. Geneva: World Health Organization, Division of Mental Health.

Kaplan, Irwin, and Benjamin Sadock. 1998. *Synopsis of Psychiatry: Behavioral Sciences/Clinical Psychiatry* (8th ed.). Baltimore: Williams & Wilkins.

Messich, Juan E., and T. Bedirhan Üstün. 2002. "Diagnostic Criteria for Research." *Psychopathology* 35: 59–61. Retrieved from http://content.karger.com/ProdukteDB/produkte.asp?Aktion=ShowPDF&ProduktNr=224276&Ausgabe=228600&ArtikelNr=65119.

National Alliance on Mental Health. 2011. "Gay, Lesbian, Bisexual, and Transgender (GLBT) Mental Health Resources." Retrieved from http://www.nami.org/Content/NavigationMenu/Find_Support/Multicultural_Support/Resources/GLBT_Resources.htm.

Silverstein, Charles, ed. 1991. *Gays, Lesbians, and Their Therapists*. New York: Norton.

Valleroy, Linda, Duncan A. MacKellar, John M. Karon, Daniel H. Rosen, William McFarland, Douglas A. Shehan, Susan R. Stoyanoff, Marlene LaLota, David D. Celentano, Beryl A. Kobin, Hanne Thiede, Mitchell H. Katz, Lucia V. Torian, and Robert S. Janssen. 2000. "HIV Prevalence and Associated Risks in Young Men Who Have Sex with Men." *Journal of the American Medical Association* 284: 198–204. Retrieved from http://jama.ama-assn.org/cgi/content/full/284/2/198.

Weinberg, Martin, Colin Williams, and Douglas Pryor. 1994. *Dual Attraction*. New York: Oxford University Press.

Literary Works and Mental Illness

Glenn Rohrer

Edgar Allan Poe wrote:

> Men have called me mad; but the question is not yet settled, whether madness is or is not the loftiest of intelligence—whether much that is glorious—whether much that is profound—does not spring from disease of thought—from moods of mind exalted at the expense of the general intellect. They who dream by day are cognizant of many things, which escape those who dream only by night. ("Eleonora," 1842)

Poe (1809–49) was writing about the narrow boundary between what we think of as sane or insane, normal or abnormal. The world's great writers have an amazing ability to bring their readers to the very brink of the elusive boundary between sanity and insanity. Sometimes they take us well beyond that line into the depths of insanity, into the world of those who dream by day.

Literature has always been a rich source of information related to human behavior. The subject of madness and genius, and the often finely drawn distinction between the two, has been a continuous theme in Western literature from its beginnings (Rohrer 2004). Myths and legends appear in symbolizations of delusions, mania, and other bizarre forms of thought and behavior (Vernon 1973).

Talented writers often capture the human experience in ways most of us simply do not have the capacity to articulate. Imaginative writers from the fifth century BCE to the present have been concerned with madness as a revelation of processes of the human mind (Feder 1980). Writers can offer superb insights into human conduct because often, in their own lives, they share a character's struggle or condition (Rohrer 2004). Strange, abnormal, and deviant actions of literary characters offer an indispensable resource for investigating personality (Rieger 1994).

Literature has many advantages over using artificially created "case studies" in the study of human behavior. A major problem with case studies is that they are often written to illustrate a diagnostic point. They lack the vitality of writings designed to develop characters without the limitations of a prescribed set on diagnostic criteria. As Rieger (1994) points out, from what better source could one learn about madness, violence, murder, deceit, betrayal, lust, greed, loneliness, and depression than from great writers? Charles Hartwell (1980) notes, "Editorial commentary places characters' lives in precise psychological categories, suggesting abnormal, clinical case histories rather than literature." More specifically, the use of labels from the *Diagnostic and Statistical Manual of Mental Disorders* ("the bible of psychiatry") "reduces the characters to one-dimensional clinical studies, forcing them to conform exactly to the current thinking regarding

Some Noted American Works on the Experience of Mental Illness

Fiction

Charlotte Perkins Gilman, *The Yellow Wallpaper* (1892)

F. Scott Fitzgerald, *Tender Is the Night* (1934) and *The Crack-Up* (1940)

John Steinbeck, *Of Mice and Men* (1937)

J. D. Salinger, *Catcher in the Rye* (1951)

Harper Lee, *To Kill a Mockingbird* (1960)

Ken Kesey, *One Flew Over the Cuckoo's Nest* (1962)

Sylvia Plath, *The Bell Jar* (1963)

Joanne Greenberg, *I Never Promised You a Rose Garden* (1964)

Marge Piercy, *Women on the Edge of Time* (1967)

Wally Lamb, *She's Come Undone* (1992) and *I Know This Much Is True* (1998)

Stephen King, *The Green Mile* (1996)

T. C. Boyle, *Riven Rock* (1998)

Annie Waters, *Glimmer* (1998)

Jonathan Franzen, *The Corrections* (2001)

James Frey, *A Million Little Pieces* (2003)

Mark Haddon, *The Curious Incident of the Dog in the Night-time* (2003)

Dennis Lehane, *Shutter Island* (2003)

Kristin Waterfield Duisberg, *The Good Patient* (2004)

Amanda Fillipacchi, *Love Creeps* (2006)

John Wray, *Lowboy* (2009)

Patricia Grossman, *Radiant Daughter* (2010)

Jeffrey Eugenides, *The Marriage Plot* (2011)

Memoir

William Styron, *Darkness Visible* (1990)

Susanna Kaysen, *Girl, Interrupted* (1993)

Lori Schiller, with Amanda Bennett, *The Quiet Room* (1994)

Elizabeth Wurtzel, *Prozac Nation* (1994)

Kay Redfield Jamison, *An Unquiet Mind* (1995)

Mary Karr, *Liar's Club* (1998)

Marya Hornbacher, *Wasted* (1999)

Andrew Solomon, *The Noonday Demon* (2001)

Rick Moody, *The Black Veil* (2002)

Andy Berhman, *Electroboy* (2003)

Floyd Skloot, *In the Shadow of Memory* (2003)

Jennifer Traig, *Devil in the Details* (2004)

Lauren Greenfield, *Thin* (2006)

Elyn Saks, *The Center Cannot Hold* (2007)

Allen Shawn, *Wish I Could Be There* (2007)

Michael Greenberg, *Hurry Down, Sunshine* (2008)

Siri Husvedt, *The Shaking Woman* (2010)

Mark Vonnegut, *Just Like Someone without Mental Illness Only More So* (2010) significant characteristics and labels. Such procedures can reduce literature's complexity to trite, simplistic observations."

Charles Dickens (1812–70) had never heard of dysthymic disorder when he wrote "The Bloomsbury Christening," yet he provides us with a remarkably accurate portrayal of the disorder (Dickens 2004). In his description of Nicodemus Dumps, Dickens writes, "He was never happy but when he was miserable; and always miserable when he had the best reason to be happy. . . . Mr. Dumps was the most miserable man in the world" (61). Dickens clearly understood the psychiatric disorder we call dysthymia today.

Literature also repeatedly challenges the simplistic motion of clear-cut distinctions between sanity and insanity. Literary characters, described as highly disturbed or handicapped, often provide us with profound insights. One excellent example comes to us from Jack London's story "Told on the Drooling Ward." The story is set in an institution for the mentally retarded in California and is narrated by a 25-year resident of the facility who we are told is "feeble minded," the term used at the time (1914) to describe the mentally retarded. Tom, the mentally retarded resident, provides us with some fascinating insights about state politics and the operation of the institution:

> My name is Tom. I'm 28 years old. Everybody knows me in the institution. This is an institution, you know. It belongs to the State of California and it is run by politics. I know. I've been here a long time. Everybody trusts me. I run errands all over this place, when I'm not busy with the droolers. I like droolers. It makes me think how lucky I am that I ain't a drooler.
>
> . . . there are fifty-five low-grade droolers in this ward, and how could they ever be fed if I wasn't around? I like to feed droolers. They don't make trouble. They can't. Something's wrong with most of their arms and legs, and they can't walk. They're very low-grade. I can walk, and talk, and do things. You must be careful with the droolers and not feed them too fast. Then they choke. Miss Jones says I'm an expert.
>
> Miss Kelsey says I talk too much. But I talk sense and that's more than the other feebs [i.e., feeble-minded persons] do. Dr. Dalrymple says I have the gift of language. I know it. You ought to hear me talk when I'm by myself, or when I've got a drooler to listen. Sometimes I think I'd like to be a politician, only it's too much trouble. They're all great talkers; that's how they hold their jobs.
>
> It's a snap to be a high-grade feeb. Just look at Dr. Dalrymple. He has troubles. He holds his job by politics. You bet we high-graders talk politics. We know all about it, and it's bad. An institution like this oughtn't to be run on politics. Look at Dr. Dalrymple. He's been here two years and learned a lot. The politicians will come along and throw him out and send in a new doctor who don't know a thing about feebs. (London 1990, 1762–1764)

These glimpses of lucidity, spoken by the characters of insightful writers serve to remind us that the distinction between illness and health is not as neatly drawn as we might like to think.

Literature also questions the concept that insanity rests solely within the individual. Feder (1980) reminds us that "madness as a theme of myth and literature has always dealt with personal responses to environmental influences, which include, political, social, and cultural pressures, or perhaps it would more correct to say which exclude nothing" (xi). Vernon (1973) adds, "The madman, like other people, does not exist alone. He or she both reflects and influences those around them. In the study of madness in literature, psychological theory provides but one discipline that, along with others, especially literary, religious, and social history, helps us elucidate the various symbolic forms into which the human mind transforms experience" (66). Literature has and continues to make a strong and vital contribution to our understanding of human behavior.

Types of Literary Contributions

Writers who capture mental health issues in their works may be divided into three types:

1. Many gifted writers have an enormous talent for observing, describing, and categorizing the behaviors they describe in their characters. Such writers accomplish these insights by the manner in which they develop the characters in their stories. These writers capture the nuances and quirks of the human behaviors they describe through the development of their characters. These writers do not obviously suffer from the conditions they so accurately observe and describe.

2. The second group of writers have suffered from the conditions they describe. Many of these individuals have overcome their difficulties through treatment and medications. Having suffered from mental or substance abuse difficulties themselves, they write about their experiences with the insight they have gained from their own life experiences. Having been there, they write from a unique perspective and provide tremendous insight to their readers. In some instances, writers are able to recover sufficiently to write of their difficulties during a period of remission but eventually slip back into their former difficulties.

3. Finally there are those writers who write about mental illness or addiction while actively in the throes of the condition itself. These writers capture the reader's attention by writing through the eyes of an affected person. These writers are not telling us about a condition; rather, they are writing through the eyes of one currently experiencing the condition.

Each of these types of writers approaches their writing about mental illness from their own perspective. Each writer provides us with information vital to the understanding of mental conditions. Whether the writer has directly experienced the mental condition and recovered, is writing from the throes of the condition, or is a talented observer of human behavior, each of these writers adds significantly to our understanding of mental illness.

Kate Chopin

One example of a writer who is a keen observer of behavior without suffering from the exact condition she describes is Kate Chopin (1851–1904). She was born Katherine O'Flaherty in St. Louis, Missouri. By the time she was 24 years old, her father, grandmother, best friend, and all of her brothers and sisters had died. When she graduated from the Academy of the Sacred Heart, she was known as a lonely student with a depressed manner who was a brilliant storyteller.

In 1870 she married Oscar Chopin, who died in 1883, leaving Kate with their six young children to raise alone. One year later her mother died. Her mother's death left Kate emotionally drained from the numerous losses in her life. When she turned to her family doctor for help he suggested that she begin to write as a way to express her anger and frustration about the losses in her life.

Chopin's works are filled with memorable characters and lives full of tragedy and heartbreak. Her ability to describe the loneliness and hopelessness of a life in despair is clearly evident in this selection from *The Awakening* (1899). The suicide of Edna Pontillier is the context in which the author describes the despondency and anguish of major depression, which results in the worst possible outcome.

The Awakening

An indescribable oppression, which seemed to generate in some unfamiliar part of her consciousness, filled her whole being with a vague anguish. It was like a shadow, like a mist passing across her soul's summer day. It was strange and unfamiliar; it was a mood.

. . . She was seeking herself and finding herself in just such sweet, half darkness which met her moods. But the voices were not soothing that came to her from the darkness and the sky above and the stars. They jeered and sounded mournful notes without promise, devoid even of hope.

In a sweeping passion she seized a glass vase from the table and flung it upon the tiles of the hearth. She wanted to destroy something. The crash and clatter were what she wanted to hear. But as she sat there amid her guests, she felt the old ennui overtaking her, the hopelessness which so often assailed her, which came upon her like an obsession, like something extraneous, independent of volition. It was something which announced itself; a chill breath that seemed to issue from some vast cavern wherein discords wailed.

Despondency had come upon her there in the wakeful night, and had never lifted. There was no one thing in the world that she desired. There was no human being whom she wanted near her.

Edna had found her old bathing suit still hanging, faded, upon its accustomed peg. She put it on, leaving her clothing in the bath-house. But when she was there beside the sea, absolutely alone, she cast the unpleasant, prickling garments from her, and for the first time in her life she stood naked in the open air, at the mercy of the sun, the breeze that beat upon her, and the waves that invited her.

How strange and awful it seemed to stand naked under the sky! how delicious! She felt like some new-born creature, opening its eyes in a familiar world that it had never known. The foamy wavelets curled up to her white feet, and coiled like serpents about her ankles. She walked out. The water was chill, but she walked on. The water was deep, but she lifted her white body and reached out with a long, sweeping stroke. The touch of the sea is sensuous, enfolding the body in its soft, close embrace.

She went on and on. She remembered the night she swam far out, and recalled the terror that seized her at the fear of being unable to regain the shore. She did not look back now, but went on and on, thinking of the blue-grass meadow that she had traversed when a little child, believing that it had no beginning and no end.

Her arms and legs were growing tired. She thought of Leonce and the children. They were a part of her life. But they need not have thought that they could possess her, body and soul. Exhaustion was pressing upon and overpowering her. "Good-bye - because, I love you." He did not know; he did not understand. He would never have understood if she had seen him—but it was too late; the shore was far behind her, and her strength was gone.

She looked into the distance, and the old terror flamed up for an instant, and then sank again. Edna heard her father's voice and her sister Margaret's. She heard the barking of an old dog that was chained to the sycamore tree. The spurs of the cavalry officer clanged as he walked across the porch. There was the hum of bees, and the musky odor of pinks filled the air. (Chopin 1899, 14 passim)

Charles Jackson

Charles Jackson (1903–1968) is a writer who has suffered from the disorder about which he writes. *The Lost Weekend* is Jackson's semiautobiographical tale of alcoholism. At the time of Jackson's landmark work (1944), alcoholism was portrayed in books, movies, and television primarily as a weakness in the drinker. Jackson's book became a bestseller, and Billy Wilder's film version (1945) initiated a new public perception of the alcoholic. Prior to *The Lost Weekend*, alcoholism was a hidden topic, but after its commercial success the topic began to be addressed more honestly and openly. While the Hollywood studios were reluctant to take on the subject of alcoholism, *The Lost Weekend* became a huge hit. The film won Academy Awards for Best Picture, Best Director, Best Screen Play, and Best Actor.

Jackson had conquered his own battle with alcoholism and thrived on the success of his first novel. However, in 1946, after almost 10 years of sobriety, he relapsed and slipped back into his own alcoholism. From that point onward his life and career spiraled downward, and he faded from the literary scene until his final book in 1967. In 1968, Jackson took his own life with an overdose of sleeping pills. At the time of his death he was working on a sequel to *The Lost Weekend*.

In this selection, Don Bernam has experienced repeated episodes of drinking. Jackson provides us an in depth account of what alcoholism feels like through the eyes of the alcoholic.

The Lost Weekend

He had awakened fully dressed on the couch in the living room. His feet burned. He reached down and unlaced his shoes and kicked them off as he rose to a sitting position and pulled off his coat and vest, untied his tie and loosened his collar. Automatically his hand groped beside the couch for the pint on the floor. His heart sank as he found it, and found it empty.

Had he been sleeping all night, or all the next day? There was no way of telling till the light changed outside, for better or worse if it were evening, thank Christ. He could go out and buy another, a dozen more. But if morning—He feared to find out; for if it were morning, dawn, he would be cut off till nine or after and so made to suffer the punishment he always promised himself to avoid. It would be like the dreaded Sunday, always (at these times) the day most abhorred of all the week; for on Sundays the bars did not open till two in the afternoon and the liquor stores did not open at all. Once again he had not been clever enough to provide a supply against this very thing; again he had lost all perspective and forgotten his inescapable desperation more urgent and demanding than any need of the evening before. Last night it had been merely drink. It was medication now. . . .

Though he hated this need of his, hated this dependency on the pick-up . . . all the same he had a profound and superior contempt for those who spurned liquor on the morning after, whose stomachs, shaken as they were by the dissipation of the night, turned and retched at the very thought of it. How often he had been dumbfounded—at first incredulous, then contemptuous—to hear someone say, after a night of drinking, "God, take it away, I don't want to smell it, I don't want to *see* it even, take it out of my sight!"—this at the very moment when he wanted and needed it most.

How different that reaction was from his own, and how revealing. Clearly it was the difference between the alcoholic and the non-. He was angry to know this, but he knew it; he knew it far better than others; and he kept the knowledge to himself. (Jackson 1944, 39–40)

Edgar Allan Poe

Edgar Allan Poe is a writer who writes from the heart of his own disorders. He was born in Boston in 1809. Both of his parents died before he was three years old, and he was taken into the home of John and Fanny Allan in Richmond, Virginia. The Allans lived in England from 1815 to 1820 where Edgar attended school. He also attended the University of Virginia and West Point unsuccessfully.

Poe's life is marked with several personal tragedies. The death of his wife, Virginia, who was his first cousin, and whom he married when she was only 13, was particularly difficult for him. Poe's life was marked by depression as a result of these losses. Throughout his life he experienced argumentative outbursts, suicidal thoughts, and well-documented alcohol and drug problems. His biological father reportedly died from alcoholic complications, and his stepfather was a heavy drinker. Drinking played a part in his expulsion from the University of Virginia and West Point and may have been a factor in his untimely death at the age of 40.

The narrators of Poe's stories are often "madmen," and his writings seem to capture the thoughts and feelings of seriously disturbed people with remarkable insight and understanding. Poe suffered serious emotional difficulties throughout his life. His writings often reflect the thoughts of a troubled individual. He is given credit for inventing the detective story, and his imaginative descriptions of his characters continue to provide us with excellent pictures of the troubled human mind. In these excerpts from *The Telltale Heart* (1843), Poe gives us a clear picture of the delusions and hallucinations of schizophrenia.

The Tell-Tale Heart

True!—Nervous—Very, very, dreadfully nervous I had been and am; but why will you say that I am mad? The disease had sharpened my senses—not destroyed—not dulled them. Above all was the sense of hearing acute. I heard all things in the heaven and in the earth. I heard many things in hell. How, then am I mad? Harken! and observe how healthily—how calmly I can tell you the whole story.

It is impossible to tell how first the idea entered my brain; but once conceived, it haunted me day and night. Object there was none. Passion there was none. I loved the old man. He had never wronged me. He had never given me insult. For his gold I had no desire. I think it was his eye! yes it was this!

One of his eyes resembled that of a vulture—a pale blue eye, with a film over it. Whenever it fell upon me, my blood ran cold; and so by degrees—very gradually—I made up my mind to take the life of the old man, and thus rid myself of the eye for ever.

. . . Presently I heard a slight groan, and I knew it was the groan of mortal terror. It was not a groan of pain or grief—oh no!—it was the low stifled sound that arises from the bottom of the soul when overcharged with awe. I knew the sound well. Many a night, just at midnight, when all the world slept, it has welled up from my own bosom, deepening, with its dreadful echo, the terrors that distracted me.

When I had waited a long time, very patiently, without hearing him lie down, I resolved to open a little—a very, very little crevice in the lantern. So I opened it—you cannot imagine how stealthily, stealthily—until, at length, a single dim ray, like the thread of the spider, shot from out the crevice and full upon the vulture eye. . . .

. . . The old man's hour had come! With a loud yell, I threw open the lantern and leapt into the room. He shrieked once—once only. In an instant I dragged him to the floor, and pulled the heavy bed over him. I then smiled gaily, to find the deed so far done. But, for many minutes, the heart beat on with a muffled sound. This, however, did not vex me; it would not be heard through the wall. At length it ceased. The old man was dead. I removed the bed and examined the corpse. Yes, he was stone, stone dead. I placed my hand upon the heart and held it there many minutes. There was no pulsation. He was stone dead. His eye would trouble me no more.

I then took up three planks from the flooring of the chamber, and deposited all between the scantlings. I then replaced the boards so cleverly, so cunningly, that no human eye—not even *his*—could have detected anything wrong. There was nothing to wash out—no stain of any kind—no blood-spot whatever. I had been too wary for that. A tub had caught all—ha! ha!

When I had made an end of these labors, it was four o'clock—still dark as midnight. As the bell sounded the hour, there came a knocking at the street door. I went down to open it with a light heart,—for what had I *now* to fear? There entered! three men, who introduced themselves, with perfect suavity, as officers of the police. A shriek had been heard by a neighbor during the night; suspicion of foul play had been aroused; information had been logged at the police office, and they (the officers) had been deputed to search the premises.

The officers were satisfied. My *manner* had convinced them. I was singularly at ease. They sat, and while I answered cheerily, they chatted familiar things. But ere long, I felt myself getting pale and wished them gone. My head ached, and I fancied a ringing in my ears: but still they sat and still chatted. The ringing became more distinct:—it continued and became more distinct: I talked more freely to get rid of the feeling: but it continued and gained definitiveness—until, at length, I found that the noise was *not* within my ears.

No doubt I now grew *very* pale;—but I talked more fluently, and with a heightened voice. Yet the sound increased—and what could I do? It was a *low dull, quick sound-much such a sound as a watch makes when enveloped in cotton*. I gasped for breath—and yet the officers heard it not. I talked more quickly—more vehemently; but the noise steadily increased. I arose and argued about trifles, in a high key and with violent gesticulations, but the noise steadily increased. Why *would* they not be gone? I paced the floor to and fro with heavy strides, as if excited to fury by the observation of the men—but the noise steadily increased. Oh, God! what *could* I do? I foamed—I raved—I swore! I swung the chair upon which I had been sitting, and grated it upon the boards, but the noise arose over all and continually increased. It grew louder—louder—*louder*! And still the men chatted pleasantly, and smiled. Was it possible they heard not? Almighty God!—no, no! They heard!—they suspected—they *knew*!—they were making a *mockery* of my horror!—this I thought, and this I think. But anything was better than this agony! Anything was more tolerable than this derision. I could bear those hypocritical smiles no longer! I felt that I must scream or die!—and now again!—hark! louder! louder! *louder*—

"Villains!" I shrieked, "dissemble no more! I admit the deed!—tear up the planks!—here, here!—it is the beating of his hideous heart!" (Poe 1982, 3–8)

Great writers have contributed significantly to our understanding of mental health issues. Literature has consistently provided us with insights based on writers' incredible powers of observation, their personal experiences with mental illness (and recovery), and their ongoing encounters with mental disorders. We can be thankful to those in the literary community who have done so, as these writings have been and are helpful in providing us with an enhanced understanding of mental illness.

See also Creativity and Mental Health; Recovery Movement

Bibliography

Chopin, Kate. 1899. *The Awakening*. Chicago: Stone.

Dickens, Charles. 2004 (1834). "The Bloomsbury Christening." In Dennis Denisoff, ed., *Broadview Anthology of Victorian Short Stories* (pp. 61–78). Peterborough, Ontario: Broadview Press.

Feder, Lillian. 1980. *Madness in Literature*. Princeton, NJ: Princeton University Press.

Hartwell, Charles. 1980. *Disordered Personalities in Literature*. New York: Longman.

Jackson, Charles. 1944. *The Lost Weekend*. New York: Farrar & Rinehart.

London, Jack. 1990 (1914). "Told on the Drooling Ward." In Earle Labor, Robert C. Leitz III, and I. Milo Shepard, eds., *Short Stories of Jack London* (pp. 1762–1770). New York: Macmillan, 1990.

Poe, Edgar A. 1982. *The Tell-Tale Heart and Other Writings*. New York: Bantam Books, 1982.

Rieger, Branimir. 1994. *Dionysus in Literature*. Bowling Green, OH: Bowling Green State University Press.

Rohrer, Glenn. 2004. *Mental Health in Literature: Literary Lunacy and Lucidity*. Chicago: Lyceum Books.

Vernon, John. 1973. *The Garden and the Map: Schizophrenia in Twentieth-Century Literature and Culture*. Urbana: University of Illinois Press, 1973.

Loss and Grief

Gretchen Reevy

Loss is associated with many life events and transitions, including illness, disability, infertility, miscarriage, loss of housing or employment, educational failure, war or natural disasters, abuse, relationship breakdown, divorce, addiction, migration, aging, and death of a loved one. Grief is a complex, often long-lasting reaction to a loss. Although the loss may be anything of central importance to a person, most research and theorizing about grief has focused on the aftermath of the death of a loved one.

Bereavement is a state of sorrow over a loss or death of a loved one; to be *bereft* is to be left alone or to experience a loss. *Grief* is the feeling of distress caused by bereavement (by experiencing loss).

The Grieving Process

There are many ideas about the grieving process, among them theories about grief occurring in phases or stages. In 1961, British psychiatrist John Bowlby described three stages of grief based on young children's reactions to separation from parents: protest, despair, and detachment. Later he refined his stages and added a fourth to his theory of grieving in adults: numbness and disbelief, yearning and searching, disorganization and despair, and finally reorganization or recovery from bereavement (see Bowlby 1980). In 1969, Swiss-born psychiatrist Elisabeth Kübler-Ross published *On Death and Dying*, which suggested that there are five stages when facing one's own terminal illness: denial, anger, bargaining, depression, and acceptance. Kübler-Ross's five-stage model has gained popularity, has been extended to dealing with any sort of loss (including death of a loved one), and has been incorporated into many mental health practitioners' treatment practices. However, most researchers now recognize that the five-stage model lacks empirical support.

Responses to loss may include many different reactions, including those in the five-stage model. Reactions may occur in many orders or combinations and may vary depending on the bereaved person's mental state and circumstances (Archer 1998).

Grieving is a normal process; it is an individual, unique, and highly personal experience. Depending on social context and personal experience, grief has potential for both personal deterioration and personal growth. Unless symptoms of grief become debilitating, causing significant distress over a prolonged period of time, grief will resolve on its own, without the need for intervention from a mental health practitioner. Complicated grief, on the other hand, does benefit from therapy. According to Australian psychologist Judith A. Murray (2001), complicated grief is more likely when the bereaved individual loses a child (including an unborn child), has an intellectual disability or other mental health disorder, sustains multiple losses simultaneously, sustains losses that occur through trauma or violence, or experiences a sudden loss (without time to prepare). Circumstances surrounding a loss—including cultural, social, and family contexts—influence the stress accompanying the grief reaction. For example, the response to a suicide may be different among members of cultures or religions that consider suicide a sin versus those that consider suicide an honorable action. Loss may threaten a person's sense of safety, security, and control (Murray 2001).

Grief may be accompanied by many symptoms, including depressions, somatic symptoms (physical illness), and a higher risk for suicide. John Bowlby's work on attachment theory showed that even people who cannot fully understand the finality of death (e.g., young children and individuals with intellectual disabilities) are capable of experiencing grief. Individuals with intellectual disabilities may have a more complex grieving process, with a higher risk for emotional disturbance (e.g., sadness, anger, anxiety) and behavioral disturbance (e.g., irritability, lethargy, hyperactivity; Brickell & Munir 2008). Multiple losses, which can complicate the grieving process, may affect individuals' health, marriages, employment, finances, and emotions (Mercer & Evans 2006).

Ambiguous loss—such as when a loved one is missing or is presumed to be dead but no body has been found—freezes the grieving process. This can occur in the context of an abduction or a soldier who is missing in action. It can be especially difficult if some family members are still holding out hope that their missing loved one will be found, while other family members want to accept the loss to move forward with their lives. This type of ambiguity can be emotionally devastating for individuals as well as putting a great strain on families and relationships. Closure is impossible; family members have no choice but to live with uncertainty (Boss 2007). An extended period of preparation for an expected loss is known as *anticipatory loss*. For example, caregivers of family members with dementia or terminal illness know that their loved one is expected to die but may not know how soon. Anticipatory loss may be accompanied by a complex mix of emotions, including sadness, anger, and feeling overwhelmed, tired, trapped, guilty, frustrated, and relieved. Individuals anticipating loss may feel powerless in the face of the inevitability of the loss (Green 2006).

Therapeutic Directions

Psychotherapist J. William Worden wrote *Grief Counseling and Grief Therapy* (2008), a handbook for mental health professionals who treat grief. He discussed four tasks that constitute grieving, which are to accept that the loss is real, to feel the pain of the loss, to adjust to the new circumstance and environment without the lost person or object, and to withdraw one's emotional energy from the lost person/object and attach the energy to a new person/object. Knowledge of these four tasks can help the mental health professional identify areas of grieving in which the client is having difficulty.

As Bonanno, Goorin, and Coifman (2008) note, grief may be associated with a variety of emotions, notably sadness (along with anger, fear, and guilt), but some positive emotions may also be present at points during the grieving process, including happiness, pride, and amusement. The event that precipitated the grief state is felt to be a blow to one's understanding, either of oneself or of the world, or both. Grieving therefore involves a re-creating of meaning; identity may become restructured and/or worldviews may transform. In that sense, grief involves extensive, long-term efforts at coping. Bonanno, Goorin, and Coifman (2008) and other researchers suggest that the occurrence of positive emotions during grief is healthy. Experiencing positive emotions punctuating the negative emotions makes it less likely that the individual will slip into a downward spiral of negative emotion that could become a dysfunctional state such as clinical depression.

Conclusion

Grief has engaged the interest of researchers and thinkers from diverse fields such as psychology, philosophy, anthropology, and others. Anthropologists have observed grief reactions across cultures, noting both similarities and differences. For instance, in mainstream American culture, a death is typically followed by a single funeral. In some other cultures, deaths may be commemorated in several ceremonies over several years. Grief is a popular theme in the arts. For centuries, novelists, musicians, and poets have described or represented grief in eloquent and moving fashion. This universal and profound experience is sure to continue as a common theme in art and an intriguing field of inquiry in science.

See also Depression; Disasters and Mental Health; Peer Support Groups; Religion, Spirituality, and Mental Health; Self-Help

A young girl participates in a grief counseling exercise, putting a clipping representing what she feels about the death of her uncle (who was killed in war) into a brown bag for safekeeping. (AP Photo/Al Grillo.)

Bibliography

American Cancer Society. 2010. "Coping with the Loss of a Loved One: Grieving, Mourning, and Bereavement." Retrieved from http://www.cancer.org/acs/groups/cid/documents/webcontent/002826-pdf.pdf.

Archer, J. 1998. *Nature of Grief: The Evolution and Psychology of Reactions to Loss.* Florence, KY: Brunner-Routledge.

Bonanno, G. A., L. Goorin, and K. G. Coifman. 2008. "Sadness and Grief." In M. Lewis, J. M. Haviland-Jones, and L. F. Barret, eds., *Handbook of Emotions* (3rd ed., pp. 797–810). New York: Guilford Press.

Boss, P. 2007. "Ambiguous Loss Theory: Challenges for Scholars and Practitioners." *Family Relations* 56: 105–111.

Bowlby, J. 1980. *Attachment and Loss: Vol. 3. Loss: Sadness and Depression.* New York: Basic Books.

Brickell, C., and K. Munir. 2008. "Grief And Its Complications in Individuals with Intellectual Disability." *Harvard Review of Psychiatry* 16: 1–12.

Green, S. 2006. " 'Enough Already!': Caregiving and Disaster Preparedness—Two Faces of Anticipatory Loss." *Journal of Loss and Trauma* 11: 201–214.

GriefNet. http://www.griefnet.org/.

Hughes, V. 2011. "Shades of Grief: When Does Mourning Become a Mental Illness?" *Scientific American*, June/July. Retrieved from http://www.scientificamerican.com/article.cfm?id=shades-of-grief&page=2.

Kübler-Ross, E. 1969. *On Death and Dying.* New York: Macmillan.

Mercer, D. L., and J. M. Evans. 2006. "The Impact of Multiple Losses on the Grieving Process: An Exploratory Study." *Journal of Loss and Trauma* 11: 219–227.

Moffat, M. J. 1992. *In the Midst of Winter: Selections from the Literature of Mourning.* New York: Vintage.

Murray, J. A. 2001. "Loss as a Universal Concept: A Review of the Literature to Identify Common Aspects of Loss in Diverse Situations." *Journal of Loss and Trauma* 6: 219–241.

Parkes, C. 1997. *Death and Bereavement across Cultures.* New York: Routledge.

Worden, J. W. 2008. *Grief Counseling and Grief Therapy: A Handbook for the Mental Health Practitioner.* New York: Springer.

M

Manic-Depressive Disorder

See Bipolar Disorder

Marketing of Drugs

Fred Leavitt

More than 70 percent of office visits to a U.S. physician (including psychiatrists) end with prescription of at least one drug. Given the more than 20,000 known diseases and more than 13,000 approved drug products (with about 100 new ones approved annually), it is unrealistic to expect physicians to always prescribe optimally. In fact, prescribing is in some ways further from optimal than might be expected. Conservative estimates are that about 7,000 annual hospital deaths in the United States are attributable to drug errors, and about 17 percent of hospital admissions are for conditions *caused by* prescription drugs. Improvement might require substantial changes in how physicians initially learn and then keep current about drugs. At present, drug company marketing plays an enormous role in this. The Pharmaceutical Research and Manufacturers of America (PhRMA), a U.S. lobbying group for research-based drug companies, contends that drug firms spend more on research and development than on marketing. However, Gagnon and Lexchin (2008) questioned the accuracy of the data used by PhRMA, and their reanalysis led to very different estimates. These researchers concluded that, in 2004, U.S. drug companies spent approximately $31.5 billion for research and development and $57.5 billion on marketing.

Medical School

Most physicians are introduced to pharmacology in medical school, and drug company marketing starts there. When residents at one teaching hospital were checked, 97 percent had items bearing drug company brand names in their pockets (Sigworth, Nettleman, & Cohen 2001). The companies offer consulting and other business relationships to medical school instructors, which potentially introduces conflicts of interest that can influence the information they provide. The *New York Times* (2009) reported that 1,600 of Harvard's 8,900 professors and lecturers

The Case for Printed Drug "Fact Boxes"

Some advocates have argued that drug makers should be required to print fact boxes on packaging for prescription drugs in order to allow consumers to understand how well a drug works and how common are its side effects. For example, Steven Woloshin and Lisa M. Schwartz in the *New York Times* ("Think Inside the Box," July 6, 2011, A19) noted that Abilify, an antipsychotic drug with domestic sales of $4.5 billion in 2010 and approved for a variety of disorders, including depression, is advertised as a drug that will help people with depression symptoms, if those symptoms are only partly responsive to another drug they are taking. The ad tells people to ask their doctors about adding Abilify.

> But, as is generally the case, the ad doesn't tell them how well the drug works. And the professional label for doctors says only that the drug was "superior to placebo," not by how much [in this case, only 3 points higher on a 60-point scale—a small difference]. (Woloshin & Schwartz 2011)

A fact box, according to Woloshin and Schwartz, "would quantify the benefits and side effects of Abilify."

—Editor

admitted to having some kind of business link to drug companies. Nearly two-thirds of academic leaders surveyed at U.S. medical schools and teaching hospitals had financial ties to the drug or medical-device industry (Campbell et al. 2007).

Marketing practices can limit the usefulness of even unbiased information about specific drugs. The reason is that drugs have an effective patent life of about 13 to 15 years, after which inexpensive generics may become available. Thus in order to maximize their profits, companies constantly seek to develop and promote new drugs even if such drugs have no clear advantage over existing ones. By the time medical students have graduated and finished their internships and residencies, many of the drugs they had learned about are no longer in vogue. Compounding the problem is the fact that many adverse effects do not show up until after a drug has been approved. Thus from a medical standpoint, the best strategy might be to introduce new drugs gradually to a limited number of patients. Yet drug companies market their drugs widely as soon as they are approved and while they are still protected by patent. For example, the antidepressant Paxil (paroxetine) was launched in 1992 and subsequently subject to a series of FDA warnings regarding potentially dangerous side effects, including severe withdrawal symptoms and suicidality. Numerous civil law suits were filed against the manufacturer, GlaxoSmithKline, claiming that users of the drug were not sufficiently warned of the side-effects (Harris 2004; http://www.drugrecalls.com).

Experiences and Colleagues

Once licensed to practice, physicians continue to learn about drugs from their experiences, and they adjust their prescribing habits accordingly. But mere experience is less useful than it might seem. For one thing, the experiences are invariably much smaller in scope than the variety of medical conditions and drugs. For another, each patient can be considered an uncontrolled experiment; even if a drug seems to have helped, a different drug might have been even more effective, or the patient might be responding on the basis of other factors (including the placebo effect). This is particularly true in psychiatry, where definitive biological sources of illnesses remain elusive. If a drug does *not* work, the physician might never know—some patients improve despite ineffectual treatments, and others do not return for follow-up. Physicians, therefore, seek information from other sources. Marketing plays a role in all of them.

Social networks such as Facebook, LinkedIn, and Twitter allow physicians to organize professional online communities that exchange information. One free online MD-only community, for example, has more than 100,000 members and is rapidly growing (http://www.sermo.com; see also, e.g., http://www.imedexchange.com). But the same reasons that limit personal experiences as an educational tool also limit the value of the experiences of colleagues. Furthermore, many of the online "colleagues" are employees of drug companies whose job is to promote the company's drugs; and many of the companies become clients of the online sites, which enables them to follow the discussions and promote their brands.

Key Opinion Leaders

Given the impossibility of reading even a modest portion of the medical literature (see below), many physicians rely on the lectures or writings of experts to teach them about topics outside their fields of expertise. Key opinion leaders (KOLs or OLs) are prominent physicians such as distinguished medical school faculty whose celebrity status makes them highly effective in influencing their peers. Although they try to appear independent from industry, some KOLs earn more money from drug companies than from their academic institutions. One former drug company sales representative said that she had paid KOLs $2,500 for individual lectures, based largely on slides supplied by the company. She said that the experts were considered company salespeople; if prescriptions for the company's drugs did not increase after the presentations, the experts would not be invited back (Moynihan 2008). (The experts typically claim that payments from drug companies do not affect their presentations.)

KOLs are usually hired early in the drug development process so they can proclaim the forthcoming arrival of the drug as a tremendous pharmacological breakthrough. They are often retained until and even beyond the time that the patent on the drug expires. While on the company payroll, they consult, give grand-rounds lectures, conduct clinical trials, publish articles in prestigious journals (often ghostwritten by company writers—see below), and make presentations at regulatory meetings and hearings. Their goals are to make side effects appear trivial, encourage off-label uses (i.e., uses other than those for which the drug has been approved), and disparage the comments of critics.

KOLs sit on FDA committees that help determine whether new drugs should be approved and on panels that write treatment guidelines for various medical conditions. Eighteen of the 20 psychiatrists on panels who wrote the 2009 guidelines for treating depression, bipolar disorder, and schizophrenia had financial ties to drug companies affected by their guidelines (Cosgrove et al. 2009). Fifty-six percent of the 498 people who helped write guidelines for the American Heart Association and American College of Cardiology from 2003 through 2008, and 81 percent of the chairs of the groups, had financial ties to drug companies (Mendelson et al. 2011).

Although federal law forbids committee members from having a direct financial interest in drugs under evaluation, waivers are frequently granted. The reason given is that most experts have ties to the drug industry, so completely unbiased panelists are unlikely to be sufficiently knowledgeable. Most drugs available today were evaluated by FDA committees packed with industry-funded scientists. However, in the study of cardiology guideline writers cited in the previous paragraph, the authors found that 44 percent had no financial interests in the area they reviewed. That rebuts the argument that independent, experienced experts cannot be found.

Businesses have emerged to identify, recruit, train, and manage KOLs. The businesses coach aspiring KOLs on public speaking and provide slides likely to be used in presentations. For example, one Internet site (http://www.kolonline .com/services-development.asp) has posted such advice as: "Everyone recognizes the value of opinion leaders (OL), or thought leaders. . . . It is imperative that you know the OLs in your market at a national, regional and local influence level as well as [the] 'rising stars.' We can help you understand the needs and interests of your OLs, and hence align your strategy."

Medical Journals

Diligent physicians subscribe to medical journals that publish original research. Yet even the most dedicated professional cannot possibly read more than a small fraction of the medical literature. Each year more than 6 million articles are published in scientific journals. The Medline database contains more than 12 million articles and adds more than 2,000 daily. On May 12, 2011, Medline listed 31,131 articles about bipolar disorder. Assuming 20 minutes on average to read each article, reading all would take more than 10,000 hours—almost 1,300 eight-hour days for just that one condition.

Virtually all medical journals take advertising, without which they could not survive. Although physicians typically claim that ads have minimal influence on their prescribing habits, the evidence indicates otherwise. In one study, journal subscribers were randomly assigned to receive low, medium, or high frequencies of exposure to advertisements for a specific drug. During the year-long study, physicians exposed to the most ads increased the number of their prescriptions for that drug the most (Matalia 1994).

Drug company ads frequently cite references to the company's own research, which is typically off-limits to outsiders. Othman, Vitry, and Roughead (2009) reviewed ads from 26 countries and found that about two-thirds of the claims were unsupported by a systematic review, a meta-analysis, or a randomized control trial.

Even when factually correct, the ads can mislead. For example, Abilify is an antipsychotic drug approved to treat depression when the condition only partly responds to another drug (an antidepressant). According to an Abilify advertisement, "approximately two out of three people being treated for depression still have depression symptoms." People with depression are thus encouraged to ask their doctor about prescribing Abilify in addition to their antidepressant. The ad, however, does not say anything about how well the drug might be expected to work based on data from clinical trials. The label for physicians says only that Abilify was "superior to placebo"; it does not state that the drug came out only 3 points higher on a 60-point scale—a very small difference (Woloshin & Schwartz 2011).

Even more insidious, the biggest advertisers can influence journal content. A leading journal rejected an editorial questioning the value of a particular treatment because it feared losing advertising. The journal editor wrote the author saying he had been overruled by the marketing department (Dyer 2004). Furthermore, there is ample proof that many companies have persuaded researchers to forgo submitting unfavorable study results to journals. The negative studies are never made public. (Journal editors have been changing their policies to deal with this problem. The International Committee of Medical Journal Editors [ICMJE] proposed comprehensive trials registration and announced that all 11 ICMJE member journals, which includes some of the most prestigious journals, will adopt a trials-registration policy. The ICMJE member journals will require, as a condition of consideration for publication, registration in a public trials registry. Trials must register at or before the onset of patient enrollment. At least one journal, the *Journal of Negative Results in BioMedicine*, publishes negative data.)

Many drug companies pay professional writers to write articles that portray their products favorably. The company then seeks a respected scientist to put his or her name on the manuscript and submit it to an appropriate journal. Any requested revisions are handled by the ghostwriter. The eminent psychiatrist David

Healy, in 2004 testimony to a House of Commons Select Committee, claimed that "at least half of articles on drug efficacy that appear in the *BMJ*, the *Lancet*, and *NEJM* [leading medical journals] are ghost-written by drug companies." Healy wrote that "the most distinguished authors from the most prestigious universities put their names to them without ever seeing the raw data" (Kmietowicz 2004).

Direct-to-Consumer Advertising

Marketing strategists also target laypeople, by promoting prescription drugs through newspaper, magazine, television, and Internet marketing. (The United States and New Zealand are the only two developed countries that allow direct-to-consumer advertising.) Patients tend to ask for the most heavily marketed drugs. Physicians may try to dissuade them, but only by lengthening office visits and straining physician-patient relationships. Thus they frequently grant patients' requests even when more effective drugs or nondrug treatments are available.

A more subtle form of marketing to both physicians and laypeople involves promoting or creating diseases out of nonpathologic physical conditions. The widely used *Diagnostic and Statistical Manual of Mental Disorders*, the diagnostic manual of the American Psychiatric Association, was first published in 1952 and listed 112 psychiatric disorders. Each subsequent edition has added more. The most recent, published in 1994 (with textual revisions in 2000), lists 297 disorders including stuttering, spelling disorder, and written expression disorder. The trend will almost surely continue with publication of the 2013 edition. Critics have observed that many of the diagnoses, like social phobia, seem tailormade to create a market for drugs. More than 50 percent of the psychiatrists who developed the revised DSM had financial ties to drug companies (Cosgrove et al. 2006).

Continuing Medical Education Courses

Most physicians must complete accredited continuing medical education (CME) programs to maintain their medical licenses and hospital privileges. A substantial proportion of CME funding comes from drug companies that skew content in various ways to match their goals. The sponsoring company's drugs are generally portrayed more favorably than drugs manufactured by competitors. Furthermore, CME programs typically devote much more time to drug treatment of diseases than to prevention or nondrug treatments. Physicians spend more hours in industry-supported CME programs than in either medical schools or professional societies (Sufrin & Ross 2008).

Formularies

Many physicians are affiliated with health maintenance organizations (HMOs). HMOs develop formularies—lists of prescription drugs that the HMO will pay for.

The plan does not pay for unlisted drugs unless the prescribing physician requests and is granted an exemption. The rationale for formularies is sound: Participating physicians can evaluate efficacy, safety, and cost-effectiveness of all the drugs in a particular class and then pick the best one. They can share their experiences as they learn about optimal doses, contraindications, and so forth. But, unfortunately, drugs may be listed in formularies for business rather than for medical reasons. Some companies have offered HMOs substantial discounts to list their drugs; some have offered substantial discounts on a drug already listed if the HMO also lists a different company drug in another category.

Drug Company Representatives

Drug companies hire young, attractive people to promote drugs to physicians. Formerly called "detail men" and now called drug sales representatives, about 90,000 of them visit physicians' offices to dispense free samples, dinner invitations, tickets to ball games, and various other gifts. The drug industry agreed in 2002 to limit marketing gifts to less than $100 in value, but sales reps still give meals and tickets. They sometimes offer physicians lecturing or consulting fees to encourage the physicians to prescribe certain drugs.

To help sales reps build relationships, the companies provide them with information about the physician's personal life, such as names of family members and entertainment and clothing preferences. The trade journal *Drug Representative* offers tips such as how to sell to a stubborn physician and how to flatter a physician. Most drug sales reps meet with 5 to 10 physicians a day and try to see each one every few weeks. Drug companies spend about $5 billion annually on sales reps and their gifts and judge them by their success in getting the physicians to prescribe the company's drugs. There is a strong relationship between gifts given by sales reps to physicians and the physicians' subsequent prescribing habits. The *New York Times* reported that "doctors who have close relationships with drug makers tend to prescribe more, newer and pricier drugs regardless of the drug's efficacy over less expensive brand name or generic medications" (Harris & Roberts 2007). The companies claim that their sales force provides a service by keeping physicians updated on the newest and best drugs. But Ziegler, Lew, and Singer (1995) analyzed statements made by sales reps and reported that 11 percent were false; all the false statements favored the drugs of the sales reps' companies.

Drug manufacturers can legally promote drug use only for indications that have been FDA approved. However, physicians can prescribe approved drugs to any patient for any medical condition. Nonapproved use, called off-label prescribing, is sometimes justified. For example, after carbamazepine was approved as an anticonvulsant, physicians observed that it is also effective in treating bipolar disorder. So it was prescribed off label for that condition. But off-label prescribing should be relatively rare and is not. Radley, Finkelstein, and Stafford (2006) found that 21 percent of prescriptions of 160 common drugs were off label, and 73 percent of the off-label uses had little or no scientific support. Drug sales representatives play a major role in promoting off label uses to physicians.

In recent years, sales reps have become an endangered species. Thousands have been laid off as companies slashed costs. They are no longer needed to distribute free samples, because physicians can order samples through the Internet.

Free Drug Samples

Gagnon and Lexchin (2008) estimated that, in 2004, sales representatives gave U.S. physicians free samples totaling nearly $16 billion in retail value—approximately half of the drug industry's marketing budget. Today, sales reps can be bypassed—physicians can order free samples online.

Drug companies claim that samples enable physicians to provide low-income and uninsured patients with otherwise unaffordable drugs. But the most disadvantaged patients are less likely than others to receive free samples. Cutrona and colleagues (2008a) found that people with health insurance and the more affluent were more likely than poor, uninsured people to receive free samples. Many samples are kept by drug reps or physicians for personal or family use.

Free samples are almost always of expensive, brand-name drugs. Physicians with access to samples of a particular drug are more likely to prescribe that drug, primarily because patients had been started on it. As a result, expensive drugs are prescribed even when more effective ones or generics or lower priced brand drugs are available. The drugs generally require high copayments for prescriptions, so free samples *increase* rather than reduce drug costs. Patients started on free samples may be forced to discontinue their treatments when the samples run out.

The most expensive drugs are those still protected by patent, so they are relatively new and their safety has not yet been firmly established. Free samples rarely come with information about potential side effects, interactions, information about what to do in the event of an overdose, or instructions on how the drug should be taken or special instructions for children. New drugs are unlikely to have been tested in large numbers of children. In 2004, more than 500,000 children received samples of four drugs that were later the subject of serious safety warnings. Cutrona and colleagues (2008b) reported that 2 of the 15 most frequently distributed drug samples have a high potential for misuse and abuse; 4 others received new safety warnings since 2004.

Copycat Drugs

After the FDA approves a drug, its manufacturer holds patent rights for about 13 to 15 years. But a patent does not ensure that a drug will be profitable, and most radically new drugs are not. Therefore companies spend the bulk of their research money developing drugs that differ only marginally from the successful drugs of competitors—differ only enough to avoid patent issues. These copycat drugs, or mimics, are sufficiently like the existing drugs that they generally have similar effects and are approved by the FDA. From 1998 through 2003, 379 of the 487 drugs approved by the FDA were classified as having therapeutic qualities similar to those of one or more already marketed drugs. Only 67 of the 487 were new drugs considered likely improvements over older ones.

Once a drug is approved, sales depend at least as much on marketing as on the drug's effectiveness. (Head-to-head comparisons between competing drugs are relatively rare.) And that is why drug company marketing budgets are generally considerably greater than research and development budgets.

See also Drug Companies; Ethical Issues; Medical Model of Psychiatric Illness; Psychiatry; Psychopharmacology

Bibliography

Angell, M. 2004. *The Truth about the Drug Companies*. New York: Random House.

Campbell, E., J. Weissman, S. Ehringhaus, S. Rao, B. Moy, S. Feibelmann, and S. Goold. 2007. "Institutional Academic-Industry Relationships." *JAMA* 298:1779–1786.

Carlat, D. 2007. "Dr. Drug Rep." *New York Times Magazine*, November 25. Retrieved from http://www.nytimes.com/2007/11/25/magazine/25memoir-t.html.

Cosgrove, L., H. Bursztajn, S. Krimsky, M. Anaya, and J. Walker. 2009. "Conflicts of Interest and Disclosure in the American Psychiatric Association's Clinical Practice Guidelines." *Psychotherapy and Psychosomatics* 78: 228–232.

Cosgrove, L., S. Krimsky, M. Vijayaraghavan, and L. Schneider. 2006. "Financial Ties between *DSM-IV* Panel Members and the Pharmaceutical Industry." *Psychotherapy and Psychosomatics* 75: 154–160.

Cutrona, S., S. Woolhander, K. Lasser, D. Bor, D. McCormick, and D. Himmelstein. 2008a. "Characteristics of Recipients of Free Prescription Drug Samples: A Nationally Representative Analysis." *American Journal of Public Health* 98: 284–289.

Cutrona, S., S. Woolhander, K. Lasser, D. Bor, D. Himmelstein, W. Shriank, and N. LeLeiko. 2008b. "Free Drug Samples in the United States: Characteristics of Pediatric Recipients and Safety Concerns." *Pediatrics* 122: 736–742.

Drugrecalls.com. n.d. "Paxil and Other Antidepressants." Retrieved from http://www.drugrecalls.com/paxil.html.

Dyer, O. 2004. "Journal Rejects Article after Objections from Marketing Department." *British Medical Journal* 328: 244.

Gagnon, M., and J. Lexchin. 2008. "The Cost of Pushing Pills: A New Estimate of Pharmaceutical Promotion Expenditures in the United States." *PLoS Med* 5: e1.

Harris, G. 2004. "Spitzer Sues a Drug Maker, Saying It Hid Negative Data." Retrieved from http://www.nytimes.com/2004/06/03/business/spitzer-sues-a-drug-maker-saying-it-hid-negative-data.html.

Harris, G., and J. Roberts. 2007. "Doctors' Ties to Drug Makers Are Put on Close View." Retrieved from www.nytimes.com/2007/03/21/us/21drug.html?pagewanted=print.

Kmietowicz, Z. 2004. "Consumer Organisations Criticise Influence of Drug Companies." *British Medical Journal* 329: 937.

Leavitt, J., and F. Leavitt. 2011. *Improving Medical Outcomes: The Psychology of Doctor/Patient Visits*. Lanham, MD: Rowman & Littlefield.

Matalia, N. 1994. "Journal Advertising Works! Three Studies Say So!" *Medical Marketing and Media* 5: 12–14.

Mendelson, T., M. Meltzer, E. Campbell, A. Caplan, and J. Kirkpatrick. 2011. "Conflicts of Interest in Cardiovascular Clinical Practice Guidelines." *Archives of Internal Medicine* 171: 577–584.

Moynihan, R. 2008. "Key Opinion Leaders: Independent Experts or Drug Representatives in Disguise?" *British Medical Journal* 336: 1402–1403.

Othman, N., A. Vitry, and E. Roughead. 2009. "Quality of Pharmaceutical Advertisements in Medical Journals: A Systematic Review." *PLoS One* 4(7): e6350.

Peterson, M. 2009. *Our Daily Meds: How the Pharmaceutical Companies Transformed Themselves into Slick Marketing Machines and Hooked the Nation on Prescription Drugs*. New York: Macmillan.

Radley, D., S. Finkelstein, and R. Stafford. 2006. "Off-Label Prescribing among Office-Based Physicians." *Archives of Internal Medicine* 166: 1021–1026.

Sigworth, S., M. Nettleman, and G. Cohen. 2001. "Pharmaceutical Branding of Resident Physicians." *JAMA* 286: 1024–1025.

Sufrin, C., and J. Ross. 2008. "Pharmaceutical Industry Marketing: Understanding Its Impact on Women's Health." *Obstetrical & Gynecological Survey* 63: 585–596.

Wilson, D. 2009. "Harvard Medical School in Ethics Quandary." Retrieved from http://www.nytimes.com/2009/03/03/business/03medschool.html.

Woloshin, S., and L. M. Schwartz. 2011. "Think Inside the Box." *New York Times*, July 7, A19.

Ziegler, M., P. Lew, and B. Singer et al. 1995. "The Accuracy of Drug Information from Drug Sales Representatives." *JAMA* 273: 1296–1298.

Marriage, Divorce, and Mental Health

Melanie Kautzman-East, Sherdene Simpson, and Victoria E. Kress

The positive effects of marriage are well documented, with much of the research literature suggesting a symbiotic relationship between marital status and positive health, including mental health (Gove, Style, & Hughes 1990; Wood, Goesling, & Avellar 2007). In this entry, the relationship between marriage, divorce, and mental health will be reviewed.

Marriage and Mental Health

A happy marriage may provide substantial emotional benefits. For many people, marriage creates an important sense of identity and self-worth (Gove, Style, & Hughes 1990; Wood, Goesling, & Avellar 2007). Additionally, having a spouse may provide emotional intimacy and support, fulfilling an essential human need for interconnectedness in interpersonal relationships (House, Umberson, & Landis 1988; Wood, Goesling, & Avellar 2007). As a result, married people may be happier, more satisfied, and less depressed than those who are unmarried. These emotional benefits may improve physical health, by reducing the impact that stress, depression, and other mental health problems can have on physical well-being (Wood, Goesling, & Avellar 2007).

Taking a more in-depth look at the explanation of advantages of the married, one sees that several common indicators emerge. One significant factor contributing to this phenomenon is socioeconomic status. Married individuals may have resources such as education, income, and work status, all of which are critical in affecting mental health—mostly for the better. Regarding education, research suggests that higher education levels result in a greater likelihood that an individual will enter into and maintain a marriage, which in turn can result in greater mental health (Bierman, Fazio, & Milkie 2006). Additionally, employment appears to have an effect on the marital relationship. Men with full-time employment positively affect the marital relationship, whereas women working full time may increase the risk of divorce (Bierman, Fazio, & Milkie 2006).

Although socioeconomic status is a contributor to marital satisfaction, psychosocial resources also play a vital role in the mental health advantages of the married. Social support, including social integration and a perceived sense of personal control contribute to marital satisfaction as well (Bierman, Fazio, & Milkie 2006). For those who are married, the factors contributing to mental health are confounded by gender, remarriage, and other variables. However, contemporary research consistently finds that, for both men and women, being married reduces the prevalence of depressive symptoms (Wood, Goesling, & Avellar 2007).

Impact of Divorce on Mental Health

In considering the divorce rate, although some states do not report divorce as a vital statistic, and although some couples are permanently separated while not being technically divorced, the common estimate that about half of all marriages end in voluntary dissolution seems logical. Common risk factors for divorce include marrying as a teenager, cohabitation, having a premarital pregnancy/birth, having children from a previous marriage, marrying someone of a different race, and growing up in a home with unmarried parents (Amato 2010). Current research suggests that divorced individuals exhibit more mental health symptoms—specifically, depression and anxiety—more health problems, and more substance abuse, and have a greater risk of mortality (Amato 2010).

Research has shown that women tend to be more strongly affected economically by divorce than men (Holden & Smock 1991), possibly because in the case of divorce, women more often retain custody of the children, and children generally limit a mother's ability to cultivate resources (Duncan & Hoffman 1985). Although more divorced women suffer financial hardship than divorced men, both men and women who need financial help from others have poorer adjustment than those who do not (Kitson & Holmes 1992).

Adjustment to divorce among adults varies in relation to its strain and other effects. A divorce following a severely distressed marriage results in improvements in happiness, whereas divorce after a nondistressed marriage generally decreases happiness. Spouses who initiate the divorce may display improved postdivorce adjustment. Other moderating factors on adjustment include motherhood, higher-order divorces (e.g., second or third divorces), single parenthood, coparenting, and race. Such moderating factors affect both the intensity and the severity of the impact of divorce on individuals. Research suggests that the consequences of divorce influence both short-term and long-term adjustment (Amato 2010).

Preexisting mental health problems also impact marital disruption. Research by Butterworth and Rodgers (2008) suggests that in couples where one partner reported poor mental health, greater rates of marital disruption occurred. Strohschein, McDonough, Monettec, and Shaob (2005) propose that losing a marital partner has a greater impact on psychological distress than gaining one; they postulate that mental health responses to marital change are similar for men and women in the short term, but at some point diverge such that men recover at a more rapid rate than women. Factors that may contribute to this difference in acclimation tend to be secondary in nature, such as socioeconomic status, single parenthood, etc., as opposed to internal, psychological resources. That is, resources that lessen the negative impact of divorce might reside within the individual (e.g., self-efficacy, coping skills, social skills), in interpersonal relationships (e.g., social support), and/or in structural roles and settings (employment, community services, supportive government policies). Divorce often brings about an initial decline in emotional support, and people vary in their ability to reconstruct social networks following divorce, including how quickly they are able to form new, supportive intimate relationships (Amato 2000).

Researchers have acknowledged the presence of social support as a major determinant of an individual's adjustment to stressful life events, but have reached different conclusions regarding the precise role played by social support in divorce situations (Buehler & Legg 1993). For instance, it has been demonstrated that the divorced tend to have smaller and less dense social networks (Gerstel, Kohler, & Rosenfield 1985), However, the divorced also have been shown to have a higher degree of informal social integration (Umberson, Chen, House, Hopkins, & Slaten 1996), possibly because a lack of a partner means that the divorced have more time to devote to contacts with friends and relatives.

Overall, most researchers agree that marriage has a positive influence on mental health and that marital dissolution has a negative effect. Although there are moderating factors effecting mental health both pre- and postdivorce, at some point following divorce most individuals adjust well to their changed life circumstances (Amato 2010).

See also Family and Mental Illness; Loss and Grief; Stress and Stress Management

Bibliography

Amato, P. R. 2000. "The Consequences of Divorce for Adults and Children." *Journal of Marriage and the Family* 62: 1269–1287.

Amato, P. R. 2010. "Research on Divorce: Continuing Trends and New Developments." *Journal of Marriage & Family* 72(3): 650–666.

Bierman, A., E. M. Fazio, and M. A. Milkie. 2006. "A Multifaceted Approach to the Mental Health Advantage of the Married." *Journal of Family Issues* 27(4): 554–582.

Buehler, C., and B. H. Legg. 1993. "Mothers' Receipt of Social Support and Their Psychological Well-Being Following Marital Separation." *Journal of Social and Personal Relationships* 10: 21–38.

Butterworth, P., and B. Rodgers. 2008. "Mental Health Problems and Marital Disruption: Is it the Combination of Husbands and Wives' Mental Health Problems That Predicts Later Divorce?" *Social Psychiatry & Psychiatric Epidemiology* 43: 758–763.

Duncan, G. J., and S. D. Hoffman. 1985. "A Reconsideration of the Economic Consequences of Marital Dissolution." *Demography* 22: 485–497.

Gerstel, N., C. Kohler, and S. Rosenfield. 1985. "Explaining the Symptomatology of Separated and Divorced Women and Men: The Role of Material Condition and Social Network." *Social Forces* 64: 84–101.

Gove, W. R., C. B. Style, and M. Hughes. 1990. "The Effect of Marriage on the Well-Being of Adults: A Theoretical Analysis." *Journal of Family Issues* 11: 4–35.

Holden, K. C., and P. J. Smock. 1991. "The Economic Costs of Marital Dissolution: Why Do Women Bear a Disproportionate Cost?" *Annual Review of Sociology* 17: 51–78.

House, J. S., D. Umberson, and K. R. Landis. 1988. "Structures and Processes of Social Support." *Annual Review of Sociology* 14: 293–318.

Kitson, G., and W. M. Holmes. 1992. *Portraits of Divorce*. New York: Guilford Press.

Strohschein, L., P. McDonough, G. Monettec, and Q. Shaob. 2005. "Marital Transitions and Mental Health: Are There Gender Differences in the Short-Term Effects of Marital Status Change?" *Social Science & Medicine* 61: 2293–2303.

Umberson, D., M. D. Chen, J. S. House, K. Hopkins, and E. Slaten. 1996. "The Effect of Social Relationships on Psychological Well-Being: Are Men and Women Really So Different?" *American Sociological Review* 61: 837–857.

Williams, K., A. Frech, and D. L. Carlson. 2009. "Marital Status and Mental Health." In T. L. Scheid and T. N. Brown, eds., *A Handbook for the Study of Mental Health: Social Contexts, Theories, and Systems* (2nd ed., pp. 306–320). New York: Cambridge University Press.

Wood, R. G., B. Goesling, and S. Avellar. 2007. *The Effects of Marriage on Health: A Synthesis of Recent Research Evidence*. Washington, DC: Mathematica Policy Research.

Media Portrayals of Mental Illness

Danny Wedding

Mental illness is routinely portrayed in the mass media, but this portrayal is often misleading. Unfortunately, this contributes directly to the stigma associated with mental disorders. Likewise, television shows like HBO's *In Treatment* and films like *Good Will Hunting* show mental health professionals at work, and the public's beliefs about psychologists, psychiatrists, and other mental health professionals are directly shaped by television, film, and other media.

Films and television can educate the public in very positive ways. For example, millions of people who had never heard of autism learned a great deal about the disorder by watching Dustin Hoffman's portrayal of Raymond, a man with autism spectrum disorder, in the film *Rainman*. Likewise, *A Beautiful Mind* introduced an even larger number of people to the diagnosis of paranoid schizophrenia, making the important point that even very brilliant and successful people can be affected by this disorder. Films based on true life stories (e.g., *The Story of Adele H.* and *Camille Claudel*) are more likely to be accurate portrayals of mental illness.

Specific Disorders

Anxiety disorders in all of their many forms are portrayed in hundreds of films. Some salient examples include *Patton*, *The Aviator*, *Born on the Fourth of July*, *Inside Out*, *Falling Down*, *Full Metal Jacket*, *Glengarry Glen Ross*, *Apocalypse Now*, and *The Killing Fields*. Nicholas Cage accurately plays the role of a man suffering from profound obsessive-compulsive disorder in *Matchstick Men*. Likewise, Jack Nicholson offers a convincing portrayal of a misogynistic, homophobic man obsessed with cleanliness in *As Good as It Gets*. Panic attacks are illustrated in the film *Dirty Filthy Love* and *Something's Gotta Give*, and Robert De Niro plays a mob boss with panic disorder in *Analyze This* and *Analyze That*. Sean Connery is cast as William Forrester, an extremely agoraphobic man, in *Finding Forrester*. Posttraumatic stress disorder (PTSD) is a staple theme in contemporary cinema; in addition to the war films mentioned above, characters with PTSD are found in *Saving Private Ryan*, *Reign over Me*, *The Human Stain*, and *The Pawnbroker*.

While usually accurate, some portrayals of mental illness are misleading and only confuse the public; one example is the 1991 film *The Fisher King* in which Robin Williams plays the role of a college professor who becomes homeless and psychotic after seeing his fiancée murdered in a restaurant. While this is certainly a traumatic event, Williams's character develops symptoms (e.g., paranoia, vivid hallucinations) much more characteristic of schizophrenia than posttraumatic stress disorder.

Dissociative identity disorders are a staple in the genre of "mental illness films," and there are numerous examples such as *Sybil*, *The Three Faces of Eve*, and *Primal Fear*. In *Primal Fear*, an alter boy murders an archbishop and then feigns a dissociative identity disorder in order to avoid prosecution. The murderer, played by Edward Norton, is presented as someone who is smart, manipulative, and totally effective in outwitting his attorney, played by Richard Gere. Films of this type support the public's misconception that criminals commonly pretend to be mentally ill in order to avoid punishment for their behavior.

Alfred Hitchcock's *Psycho* is a classic movie shown in most classes devoted to the history of cinema. Unfortunately, this movie enhances the stigma associated with mental illness and perpetuates the myth that people with mental illness are almost inevitably dangerous. In addition, many people who have seen this movie associate Norman Bates with general and common psychotic disorders like schizophrenia and not with a specific dissociative identity disorder (multiple personality disorder), a very uncommon disorder. Films that illustrate dissociative amnesias include *The Return of Martin Guerre*, *Paris, Texas*, *Sullivan's Travels*, *Dead Again*, *Spellbound*, and *Suddenly Last Summer*. Other films illustrating dissociation include *Sisters*, *Persona*, *Raising Cain*, *3 Women*, *The Dark Mirror*, *Steppenwolf*, and any of the *Dr. Jekyll and Mr. Hyde* films.

The 2010 film *Peacock* is an interesting movie that portrays a character with a split personality—but one personality is feminine while the other is masculine, and the lead character is able to maintain a double life until a derailed train crashes into his Nebraska home.

Literally hundreds of films and television scripts portray one or more characters dealing with depression, and suicide is a staple element in television and film dramas. For example, Nicole Kidman plays the role of a depressed Virginia Woolf in *The Hours*. Al Pacino is cast as a dejected, depressed, and suicidal lieutenant colonel in *Scent of a Woman*. Pacino's character can be used as a pedagogical tool to introduce students to the warning signs for suicidal risk—he is depressed, old, unemployed, and alcoholic. He is also estranged from his family, and he is comfortable, as a retired army officer, handling guns. All of these factors put him at high risk for suicide. Other examples of films that portray depression are *Dead Poets Society*, *Night Mother*, *Ordinary People*, *The Last Picture Show*, *It's a Wonderful Life*, *The Deer Hunter*, *The Field*, *The Tenant*, *Mishima*, *Network*, *The Last Emperor*, *Elvira Madigan*, *The Hairdresser's Husband*, and *Harold and Maude*. *Ordinary People* is sympathetic in its portrayal of an effective psychiatrist, Judd Hirsch, treating a depressed and suicidal teenager who feels responsible for his brother's death by drowning.

Mr. Jones presents a fairly accurate portrayal of borderline disorder; regrettably, Mr. Jones, played by Richard Gere, winds up having an affair with his psychiatrist. This film perpetuates the false belief that therapists commonly violate sexual and professional boundaries.

Electroconvulsive therapy (ECT) is commonly portrayed in films that have characters who are markedly depressed or hospitalized on psychiatric wards (e.g., *An Angel at My Table*, *One Flew over the Cuckoo's Nest*, and *Chattahoochee*). These films, and similar misleading television programs, are largely responsible for the very negative opinions abut ECT found in the general public as well as the false belief that psychiatrists routinely use ECT to punish disagreeable and unpleasant patients.

Personality disorders are complicated, overlapping conditions that present myriad diagnostic challenges. However, these disorders are routinely presented on television and in films, although most often without precise labels. The classic example is Glenn Close's role as Alex Forrest in *Fatal Attraction*. This film presents a compelling and unforgettable portrayal of a deeply troubled woman who fits all the diagnostic criteria for borderline personality disorder. Another film depicting the same disorder, though this time based on a published memoir, is *Girl, Interrupted*, with Winona Ryder playing the memoir's author, Susanna Kaysen (and Angelina Jolie playing a friend with antisocial personality disorder).

Personality disorders are lumped into three diagnostic categories. Cluster A includes paranoid, schizoid, and schizotypal personality disorders; cluster B includes antisocial, borderline, histrionic, and narcissistic personality disorders; cluster C captures avoidant, dependent, and obsessive-compulsive disorders.

Humphrey Bogart, playing Captain Queeg in *The Caine Mutiny*, is a powerful illustration of paranoid personality disorder. George C. Scott presents an equally compelling illustration of the same disorder in *Dr. Strangelove*. The schizoid personality is illustrated by Jack Nicholson's character in *Five Easy Pieces*, and a schizotypal personality is seen the cult classic *Pi*.

Antisocial personality is a cluster B diagnosis illustrated in hundreds of films dealing with murder and violence; some examples include *Henry: Portrait of a Serial Killer*, *Silence of the Lambs*, *A Clockwork Orange*, *In Cold Blood*, *The Boston Strangler*, *Cape Fear*, *Reservoir Dogs*, *Peeping Tom*, *Strangers on a Train*, *Helter Skelter*, *Natural Born Killers*, *Widows' Peak*, and *Blue Velvet*. Histrionic personality disorder is seen in films like *A Streetcar Named Desire*, *La Cage aux Folles*, *Long Day's Journey into Night*, and *Blue Sky*. Narcissistic personality disorder is convincingly portrayed in the movies *Sunset Boulevard*, *Bugsy*, and *What Ever Happened to Baby Jane?*

The cluster C avoidant personality is typified in the film adaptation of Tennessee Williams's play *The Glass Menagerie*, and the dependent personality is almost perfectly captured by Bill Murray's character in *What about Bob?* The character of Felix Unger in *The Odd Couple* is a vivid example of someone with an obsessive-compulsive personality disorder, as is Major Frank Burns in *M*A*S*H*.

Hundreds of films and television series like *Breaking Bad* and *The Wire* present compelling illustrations of substance use disorders. Billy Wilder's film *Lost*

Weekend is a classic movie presentation of alcoholism, and the scene in which Ray Milland experiences delirium tremens and hallucinates being attacked by bats is unforgettable. Some other memorable films dealing with alcoholism include *Clean and Sober, The Verdict, Ironweed, Hoosiers, Under the Volcano, Barfly, Who's Afraid of Virginia Woolf?, The Days of Wine and Roses, Come Back Little Sheba*, and *Key Largo*; more recent films include *When a Man Loves a Woman, Leaving Las Vegas, 28 Days, Trees Lounge*, and *Drunks*. Unfortunately, movies like *Arthur* trivialize the problem of alcoholism and suggest that driving under the influence is more likely to be comical than lethal.

Long Day's Journey into Night and *The Man with the Golden Arm* offer dramatic illustrations of the power of addiction and its influence on life and behavior. *Spun* is a powerful film showing how methamphetamine addiction can come to dominate all of the addict's time and energy.

Opium addiction is found in dozens of excellent film; two examples are *Indochine* and *The Last Emperor*. Other memorable films portraying drug addiction include *The French Connection, Christiane F., Trainspotting, Mona Lisa, Chappaqua, Drug Store Cowboy, Naked Lunch, The Bad Lieutenant, Goodfellas, Scarface*, and *Lady Sings the Blues*.

The 1999 film *Boys Don't Cry* stars Hilary Swank playing the role of a Nebraska transsexual teen trying to find her way in a rural and hostile Nebraska community. Some other films that illustrate gender identity disorders include *Myra Breckinridge, Dog Day Afternoon, The World According to Garp, Come Back to the Five and Dime, Jimmie Dean, Jimmie Dean, La Cage aux Folles, To Wong Foo, M. Butterfly, The Ballad of Little Jo, The Crying Game*, and *Hedrick and the Angry Inch*.

There is widespread public interest in the paraphilias (sexual disorders) in general and in fetishes in particular. Films like *Claire's Knee, Breaking the Waves*, and *Tie Me Up! Tie Me Down!* all deal with fetishes, and sexual sadism is a significant theme in David Lynch's *Blue Velvet*. Incest is portrayed in films like *Angels and Insects*, and there are classic portrayals of pedophilia in Peter Lorre's lead role in *M* and in James Mason's role as Humbert Humbert in *Lolita*. Some other films addressing psychosexual themes include *Cabaret, Chinatown, The Collector, Fellini Satyricon, Female Perversions, The Good Mother, Henry & June, Ju Dou, Jules and Jim, Kiss of the Spider Woman, Matador, Midnight Cowboy, Murmur of the Heart, Peeping Tom, Pretty Baby*, and *The Sergeant*.

Both movies and television are increasingly presenting gay men and women in positive and role-enhancing ways. Recent examples are found in the characters of Keith and David in the HBO series *Six Feet Under*, and in shows such as *Queer as Folk* and *Queer Eye for the Straight Guy*. This shift can be traced to the very positive portrayal of Will, a gay attorney, in *Will & Grace*, a television show that was watched by more than 17 million viewers each week at the turn of the twenty-first century. *Will & Grace* ran from 1998 to 2006, and it continues to be watched by millions of viewers in reruns. Similarly, movies like *The Kids Are All Right*, a movie about two lesbian mothers, normalize homosexuality and suggests that the family issues confronting lesbian parents are pretty much those confronted by all parents.

Disorders of childhood and adolescence are now as routinely portrayed in movies and television as adult disorders, perhaps because the diagnostic labels used for childhood disorders are often less precise and well defined than those used for adult disorders. Some of the films that illustrate childhood psychopathology include *The Butcher Boy, Forbidden Games, Fanny and Alexander, The 400 Blows, The Best Little Girl in the World, Lord of the Flies, The Tin Drum, The Wild Child, Every Man for Himself and God against All*, and *We Have to Talk about Kevin*. The psychological sequelae associated with childhood poverty are documented in *Slumdog Millionaire, El Norte, Pixote*, and *Salaam Bombay*.

The general public is fascinated by schizophrenia and other psychotic disorders, and movies like *Spider, Angel Baby, Benny and Joon, Birdy, Clean Shaven, The Fisher King, Shine, Sweetie, Taxi Driver*, and *A Beautiful Mind* include main characters who are suffering from schizophrenia or a similar psychosis. *Lars and the Real Girl* is a 2007 film about a young man (played by Ryan Gosling) with a delusional disorder who believes that a lifelike blowup doll is a real girlfriend. The film, which is better than expected, based on the description, shows Lars living in a supportive family and community structure that eventually enables him to let go of his delusion. *Aguirre, the Wrath of God*, is a classic Werner Herzog film in which the title character is a Spanish conquistador with profound delusions of grandeur.

Conclusion

It is clear that both television and films perpetuate myths about people with mental illness. These myths include the belief in a schizophrenogenic parent, the association between the onset of mental illness and repressed childhood experiences, the presence of a ubiquitous link between trauma and mental illness, the belief that love will conquer mental illness, and, perhaps most pernicious of all, the belief that people with mental illness are violent and dangerous. While there are truths upon which these stereotypes build (parents can be poisonous, repression is a real psychological phenomenon, being loved does help someone with mental illness, and people with mental illness are sometimes dangerous), films and television massively overstate the case, exaggerate these links, and in doing so help justify the discrimination and prejudice commonly experienced by people with mental illness. At the same time, when viewed critically, media portrayals can be useful tools for students (as when compared and contrasted with real-life situations), and in some cases they have led to greater public awareness and understanding.

See also Literary Works and Mental Illness; Popular Remedies and Quackery; Public Awareness and Public Education

Bibliography

Harper, Stephen. 2009. *Madness, Power, and the Media: Class, Gender, and Race in Popular Representations of Mental Distress*. New York: Palgrave Macmillan.

Horsley, Jason. 2009. *The Secret Life of Movies: Schizophrenic and Shamanic Journeys in American Cinema*. Jefferson, NC: McFarland.

Wahl, Otto F. 1997. *Media Madness: Public Images of Mental Illness*. New Brunswick, NJ: Rutgers University Press.

Wedding, Danny, Mary Ann Boyd, and Ryan M. Niemiec. 2005. *Movies and Mental Illness: Using Films to Understand Psychopathology* (2nd ed.). Cambridge, MA: Hogrefe & Huber.

Zimmerman, Jacqueline Noll. 2003. *People Like Ourselves: Portrayals of Mental Illness in the Movies*. Lanham, MD: Scarecrow Press.

Medical Model of Mental Illness

Christian Perring

Health care professionals, like all professionals, need a model for how to go about their practice. The medical model aims to provide this.

Historical and Philosophical Overview

Doctors have existed at least since the time of Imhotep in ancient Egypt in the twenty-seventh century BCE, and we know that since the era of Hippocrates in ancient Greece, in the fifth century BCE, they have had their own codes of practice. These codes have of course changed over the years, but the central idea is that when there is something wrong with a person, a doctor can help. The doctor has professional standards of conduct and expert knowledge that enables him or her to offer help that nondoctors are not able to offer. Medical expertise has long been associated with knowledge of biomedical science. The doctor's goal is to help the patient; therefore the doctor must set aside personal agendas and apply the knowledge of the profession in an unbiased way.

There has long been a contrast between treating problems as medical and treating them as moral, spiritual, social, or religious. If someone is behaving erratically, it is one thing to treat his or her problem as a result of a vitamin deficiency, defective organ, or traumatic experience and quite another to treat it as the result of demonic possession (as was done in previous centuries). With the rise of modern medicine, it has proven useful to treat many problems as medical. Indeed, it is often held to be a mark of Western progress that we have given up superstitious attitudes about human misfortune and see problems for what they are, the results of biomedical diseases.

This has been especially true for problems in thought, emotion, and behavior. Our society has in the past taken psychological problems to be the result of supernatural problems such as possession or the result of dabbling in the dark arts, or as moral failings. We are generally proud to have risen above these attitudes and now understand such problems as the result of illness or disability. Today, our approach toward those who are suffering is far more humane.

Nevertheless, there are worries that taking a medical stance toward people's problems is not always appropriate, and that we may be going too far in the direction of medicalizing different parts of life. Often, there are problems that are not medical at all but instead genuinely moral, social, religious, or in some other way nonmedical. This is particularly important in cases where a medical approach does not or cannot identify a particular internal failure of the body and address that failure or repair a broken part of the body. Indeed, in most cases of mental illness or problematic behavior, it is debatable to what extent it is possible to identify a specific malfunction as opposed to simply pointing to a cluster of problematic actions. This has led to a greater need to spell out exactly what it is to treat a problem as medical, and to set out clear criteria for when it is appropriate to do so.

Models in Psychiatry

Within medicine, there has been exploration of what exactly a medical model is. The main debate has been between the biomedical model and the biopsychosocial model. In mental health, the biomedical model tends to see all psychological problems as fundamentally related to the brain. Although no connection has yet been established between problem thoughts, emotions, and behaviors on the one hand, and brain pathology on the other, it is assumed that such a connection eventually will be established. Specifically, it is assumed that the most promising avenue of research today is to investigate mental disorders as brain disorders involving neurotransmitters, or the substances (such as norepinephrine and serotonin) that transmit nerve impulses across synapses (Guze 1992). Thus the biomedical model guides the direction of both research and treatment, with many medicines (such as those known as selective serotonin reuptake inhibitors, or SSRIs) being developed to address presumed problems with neurotransmitters.

In contrast, the biopsychosocial model, primarily associated with George Engel (1980), is far more holistic and argues that all psychological problems can be understood simultaneously at different levels—biological, psychological, and social—and that these levels interact. On this view, no problem is solely biological, psychological, or social; rather, each problem can be understood as involving multiple levels. Further, it is understood that an intervention aimed at one level can have effects at the other levels. Therefore it might be possible to solve biological problems with social changes, and it might be possible to address social problems biologically. The advantage of the biopsychosocial approach, then, is that it is far more inclusive and holistic. The disadvantage is that it is far less distinctive, and it provides little guidance in distinguishing medical approaches from others approaches.

In any case, it is clear that our current approaches to understanding disease and disorder in mental health are very much governed by considerations of human value. For example, the decision-making process of the American Psychiatric Association in creating the different editions of the *Diagnostic and Statistical Manual of Mental Disorders* (*DSM*) has been subject to intense scrutiny and criticism. The debates over whether to include homosexuality in the *DSM* in the early 1970s, to cite a notable case, were intensely political; and in recent years, debates over the classification of childhood disorders such as attention deficit/hyperactivity disorder (ADHD), Asperger syndrome, and pediatric bipolar disorder have likewise been weighed in terms of their wider social effects. In general, there has been a clear trend toward expanding the range of conditions that count as medical disorders: increasing proportions of the population have been diagnosed and treated for depression, ADHD, and social anxiety disorder, to name a few examples. The worry among commentators has been that this trend involves the illegitimate extension of the medical model to problems that are not really medical. (Indeed, this is what is meant by the term "medicalization.") Defenders of the process say that it is scientifically legitimate to do so and leads to more individuals being helped for the problems they experience.

Disease, Illness, and Disability

The terms "illness" and "disease" are not always well defined. The difference between them is standardly stated as follows: illness is the experience of disease, and disease is the biomedical condition of dysfunction (see Boorse 1975). Thus it is not possible to be ill without feeling ill, but one can have a disease without knowing it. Many diseases take a long time to manifest themselves and do not cause discomfort or disability until they are far along in their progression. One becomes ill from these diseases only once they manifest themselves. But they exist for a long time, and if it is possible to detect them and cure them, one might be able to rid a person of a disease before he or she ever becomes ill. The common view is that disease is a more fundamental concept than illness, and therefore we should start by defining disease; once we have done that, we can define illness simply as the experience of disease. However, not all theorists have taken this view; others have argued that illness is the more fundamental concept, and we should define it first, then define disease as the condition that can lead to illness (Fulford 1989).

It should be noted that while some diseases and illnesses are disabling, there is a difference between a disease and a disability. The difference is not absolute as there is an overlap between the two, but still it is important to appreciate the difference. A disease is a process, whereas a disability is a relatively stable condition. A disease is always a medical condition, whereas a disability is not: some people with disabilities have no special need for medical treatment. Of course there can be chronic diseases that are permanently disabling, and conditions that count as disabilities are rarely completely stable; they may change in subtle or dramatic ways. Nevertheless, the distinction is important.

Consider the political movement involving people with disabilities who have protested the medicalizing of disability (i.e., the labeling of it as a medical problem). Such activists have insisted that it is a mistake to see their disabilities as intrinsic to themselves rather than as something they live with (in much the same way others live with different sets of differences; see Barnes, Mercer, & Shakespeare 1999). They want to argue that while their bodies or minds may be different from those of people without disabilities, the disability is caused by social conditions: if social conditions were different, more accepting, they would not be at a disadvantage. This social model of disability is controversial, because it calls into question what kind of people we should call normal and what principles we should have when designing society or defining job fairness, equality of opportunity, and discrimination. Yet the basic point that a disability need not be a medical condition is far less controversial.

Crime and Mental Illness

It seems to be an assumption in setting out a medical approach to a person that we should not blame him or her for behavior that is symptomatic of a disease. Yet when people with severe mental illness commit crimes, the legal and moral reaction in most Western societies is to hold the individual responsible, except in cases of demonstrable psychosis where the person has no real understanding of what he or she is doing. In cases of crimes by psychopaths and addicts, and crimes involving compulsive sexual behavior that harms others, we still hold the individual responsible for his or her actions, although the extent to which we do so may be affected by the extent of the person's mental illness. This raises doubts as to whether there is any good reason for the medical model to preempt our holding of mentally ill people responsible for their harmful actions. Recent discussion has suggested that the medical model is in fact compatible with holding people morally and legally responsible for criminal actions. While such a view fits with current practice, it raises additional questions about what is meant by saying that a problem is a medical one (Zachar & Potter 2010).

Looking Deeper: When Is a Disease a Disease?

Finally, there are debates as to whether disease is itself a purely scientific concept. There is no doubt that particular diseases such as cancers, viruses, or malfunctioning hearts can be studied scientifically. But the question is whether disease is a value-laden concept, and whether we need to make normative assumptions (i.e., judgments relating to social norms) in identifying diseases. To give an example, what makes schizophrenia a disease? Is it the fact that it causes disturbance in the cognitive processes and emotions of the people with it, or do we have also to include the fact that we do not socially *value* those disturbances? Those who defend a purely biomedical approach to understanding the nature of disease argue that diseases are diseases whatever our values. On the other side of the argument are those who argue that the normativity (valuation) in our understanding of disease is essential to the concept, and that to make the statement that a person has a disease is thereby to make a value judgment (Sadler 2005).

Thus the question becomes one of whether there is any scientifically credible way to judge what is normal that does not impose human values. Many have argued that there is such a way, namely, evolutionary success (see Wakefield 1992). Researchers involved in this project seek to define health as evolutionary success and disease as conditions that reduce evolutionary success. The claim has led to debate over the coherence of the project: it seems that evolutionary success should be applied to whole species, not individuals; it therefore becomes less clear to what extent this approach can give us a notion of individual disease. Further, some have argued that evolutionary theory applies not really to species but rather to types of gene, an argument that results in an even more foreign notion of disease. If this sort of approach can indeed provide a basis for a concept of disease that is independent of human value, it could prove significant. Yet however interesting it may be to find a scientifically respectable concept of disease, it does not follow that such a concept will inevitably be employed by physicians in their clinical practices.

Conclusion

Generally, when people get ill, they are treated by doctors. The doctors find out what disease or medical condition the person is suffering from and then try to cure it or at least alleviate its symptoms. This has led to a need to spell out exactly what it is to treat a problem as medical, and to set out clear criteria for when it is appropriate to do so. The current consensus in mainstream psychiatry centers on the biomedical model (or, more specifically, the *neuro* biological model). Yet the broader biopsychosocial model and various other models remain competitive and should be of interest to all students in the mental health field.

See also Diagnostic and Statistical Manual; Disability Rights; Ethical Issues; History of Mental Health Care; Mind and Body Approaches to Mental Health; Neurodiversity; Neuropsychiatry; Popular Remedies and Quackery; Psychiatry; Psychopharmacology

Bibliography

Barnes, Colin, Geoffrey Mercer, and Tom Shakespeare. 1999. *Exploring Disability: A Sociological Introduction*. Oxford: Blackwell.

Bentall, Richard P. 2009. *Doctoring the Mind: Is Our Current Treatment of Mental Illness Really Any Good?* New York: New York University Press.

Boorse, Christopher. 1975. "On the Distinction between Disease and Illness." *Philosophy and Public Affairs* 5: 49–68.

Engel, George L. 1980. "The Clinical Application of the Biopsychosocial Model." *American Journal of Psychiatry* 137: 535–544.

Fulford, K. W. M. 1989. *Moral Theory and Medical Practice*. Cambridge: Cambridge University Press.

Ghaemi, S. Nassir. 2010. *The Rise and Fall of the Biopsychosocial Model: Reconciling Art and Science in Psychiatry*. Baltimore: Johns Hopkins University Press.

Guze, Samuel B. 1992. *Why Psychiatry Is a Branch of Medicine*. New York: Oxford University Press.

Reznek, Laurie. 1987. *The Nature of Disease*. New York: Routledge.

Sadler, John. Z. 2005. *Values and Psychiatric Diagnosis*. Oxford: Oxford University Press.

Small, Meredith. 2006. *The Culture of Our Discontent: Beyond the Medical Model of Mental Illness*. Washington, DC: Joseph Henry Press.

Wakefield, Jerome C. 1992. "The Concept of Mental Disorder: On the Boundary between Biological Facts and Social Values." *American Psychologist* 47(3): 373–388.

Zachar, Peter, and Nancy Nyquist Potter. 2010. "Personality Disorders: Moral or Medical Kinds—or Both?" *Philosophy, Psychiatry, & Psychology* 17(2): 101–117.

Memory and Disorders of Memory

Tessa Lundquist and Rebecca Ready

Memory is the acquisition and retention of information (Loring 1999). It is an integral part of cognitive functioning and daily life. Memory lends continuity, richness, and meaning to our experiences. The scientific study of memory began in the late 1880s, and tremendous strides have been made in understanding memory subtypes and the neuroanatomy of memory, particularly over the past 50 years. It is clear that memory is not a unitary phenomenon; rather, it can be broken down into subtypes. The present entry will discuss three common and useful classification systems for memory based on duration, content, and time as well as common disorders of memory, clinical neuropsychological assessment of memory, and how the normal aging process affects memory systems.

Subtypes of Memory
Duration of Memory Trace

Sensory Memory   The briefest memory trace is sensory memory; it is also the first stage of memory processing (Loring 1999). Information is encoded from each of the five senses (i.e., sight, smell, touch, taste, hearing); each sense has its own

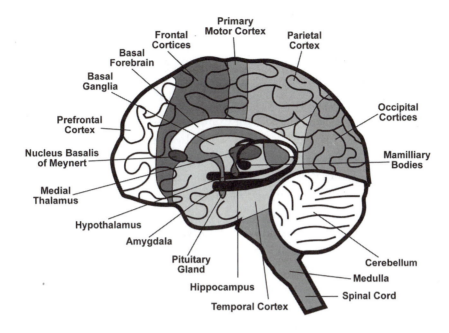

Cross section of the human brain, including areas associated with memory functions.

sensory memory. For example, visual sensory memory is called iconic memory while auditory information is encoded in echoic memory (Loring 1999). Sensory memory stores a perceptual record of sensory information. There are vast amounts of data processed by our sensory systems but we consciously attend to only a small fraction of this information; most is fleeting and erased from memory within hundreds of microseconds. The sensory information to which we attend (rather than allow to be immediately erased) is processed further and may enter into short-term memory stores.

Short-Term Memory   Short-term memory traces last from a few seconds to a few minutes (Kolb & Wishaw 2009; Loring 1999). Such memory has a limited capacity and can hold about five to nine pieces of information at a time. Short-term memory is useful for participating in conversation; humans must briefly hold and attend to incoming information in order to maintain the stream of a conversation.

Long-Term Memory   Long-term memory holds memories for hours, days, weeks, years, and potentially for a lifetime (Breedlove, Rosenzweig, & Watson 2007).

The storage capacity of long-term memory is unknown. If information goes through elaborative processing, wherein it is rehearsed and organized, or if information in particularly meaningful, it is likely to be encoded in long-term storage.

Working Memory   Memories in long-term or short-term storage can be pulled into working memory when needed—for example, to solve problems, recall a fact, perform tasks, find a location, or tell a story (Loring 1999). Of note, working memory is not a subtype of memory; rather, it is the brain's sketchpad or workspace. Working memory actively processes information to facilitate goal-directed behavior. It is thus a subtype of *executive functions* and not of memory per se. Working memory is subserved by prefontal-subcortical circuitry.

In short, memory trace duration is a useful way to classify memories and to understand how new information travels from sensory and short-term memory stores before potentially being encoded into long-term memory. It also helps us appreciate how information can be temporary activated for processing in working memory. However, there is another useful classification system for memory that is based on the type of information, or content, to be remembered.

Content of Memory

Declarative Memory   Declarative memory holds facts and information that are consciously recalled or recognized. This type of memory has two subdivisions: (1) *episodic memory*, which is embedded in a context and often is autobiographical (Loring 1999), and (2) *semantic memory*, which is knowledge about the world, including sets of ideas, facts, words, and symbols associated with an individual's culture; semantic memories are not context dependent.

The neuroanatomical basis for consolidating declarative memory is the diencephalic-medial-temporal lobe system, which has been extensively mapped. The process of consolidation involves transferring information to long-term storage; once memories are consolidated, they are stored in other cortical regions. The diencephalic-medial-temporal lobe system involves several interconnected structures, including the hippocampus and surrounding tissue as well as the medial thalamus, the basal forebrain, the mammillary bodies, the amygdala, and the frontal cortices (Saykin & Wishart 2010). A lesion anywhere along this pathway can cause varying degrees of memory impairment, or amnesia, in declarative memory functions. Most commonly, deficits will involve reduced capacity to form new long-term memories.

Nondeclarative Memory   Nondeclarative memory is the second major subdivision of memory based on content. Nondeclarative memories are demonstrated in nonverbal behavior and performance (Saykin & Wishart 2010), and because learning occurs in this case without conscious mediation, nondeclarative memory is sometimes called implicit memory (Loring 1999). There are three major subtypes of nondeclarative memories. First, procedural memory involves skill learning, such as riding a bike or learning to play the guitar; such learning is demonstrated through performance. The basal ganglia, motor cortex, and the cerebellum are integral for skill learning.

A second subtype of nondeclarative memory is priming, which is the process by which a response to a stimulus is learned based on prior exposure to a different stimulus. For example, if someone is shown the word "stamp" and, sometime later, asked to complete the word stem "STA__," he or she will be more likely to respond "stamp" than someone who did not see the word previously (Breedlove, Rosenzweig, & Watson 2007). The neuroanatomical regions believed to facilitate priming are the occipito-temporal and frontal cortices, which may show reduced activity with implicit learning due to priming (Breedlove, Rosenzweig, & Watson 2007). The third subtype of nondeclarative memory is conditioning, which occurs when associations between two stimuli are formed as a result of temporal pairing (Breedlove, Rosenzweig, & Watson 2007). Different neuroanatomical regions are involved in the acquisition of conditioned responses depending on the type of conditioning, but the hippocampus and cerebellar regions often are involved. The amygdala is centrally involved in fear conditioning (Kolb & Wishaw 2009).

Time Frame

Memories also can be differentiated as to *when* the memory was acquired relative to a particular event or time. Memories that have been formed before the occurrence of an injury or event are called retrograde memories (Loring 1999). Information that has been learned after an event or particular time is called anterograde memory. This distinction is useful when, for example, a person suffers a head injury that might cause memory impairment. Medical personnel will try to determine if memories for events before or after the injury are impaired in order to gauge, in part, the severity of the injury.

Memory Disorders

Some of the greatest discoveries about the neuroanatomical bases of learning and memory and about dissociations between subtypes of memory occurred through the study of persons with amnesia, or memory disorders. The case of the patient known as H.M. is arguably the most famous in the neurosciences (Ogden 2005). In 1953, in order to control epileptic seizures, H.M. had his amygdala, hippocampus, and surrounding temporal cortex removed. He was 27 years old at the time. After the surgery, H.M. lost the ability to recall events that happened 10 years before his surgery and was unable to form new declarative memories.

Hence, he suffered anterograde and limited retrograde amnesia. However, H.M.'s short-term memory and procedural learning remained intact (Breedlove, Rosenzweig, & Watson 2007). His unique and initially perplexing constellation of memory impairments stimulated decades of research, which led to the eventual discovery of the medial temporal lobe memory system and to ideas about dissociations between memory subtypes.

Several neurologic injuries and disease processes cause memory impairment, or amnesia. Some of the most common causes are described below. First, clinical neuropsychological assessment of memory is described to provide a context for understanding different constellations of memory impairments in different disorders.

Amnesic Action Heroes

In the popular film series featuring the fictional character Jason Bourne (played by Matt Damon), because of an accident the character loses his memory of who he is (his identity); and yet physically, bodily, he "remembers" how to defend himself—for he had been trained as a CIA assassin before the accident. He is able to fight—and to escape harm—when needed, but he is not exactly sure why he is able to do so (until later in the film series when he learns of his past).

In the film *Unknown*, starring Liam Neeson, the main character, Dr. Martin Harris, similarly loses his memory following an accident. In this case, however, the character takes on, unwittingly, the persona of the man he had been impersonating prior to the accident, for Harris/Neeson too had been trained as an assassin before the accident and had assumed a false identity to perform his duties. In *Unknown*, however, unlike in the Bourne series, the character *forgets* he has martial arts skills, which leaves him defenseless until, later on, he comes to suspect his past and thus to "remember" his physical training.

The question may be asked: Which film is truer to the science of memory? Would a person who has lost his or her identity because of an accident retain "bodily" or "physical" memory, particularly in threatening situations where self-defense is called for; or would the person likely lose this sort of memory as well?

In fact, both movies are a bit off the mark. It is exceedingly rare to lose one's autobiographical memory completely. Sometimes there is limited or partial loss of personal memory after a head injury (the most recent past is lost) or in cases of dementia (including Alzheimer's, where, again, more recent rather than distant memories are lost first). More often, it is learning new information that is impaired.

That said, if one does have amnesia for some personal information, one can still hold on to prior skill learning or a "bodily" memory (like martial arts). In this case, the Bourne movies are closer to reality.

Memory is not unitary. Persons with some memory impairments can hold onto other memory abilities. The dissociation between personal memory and skill memory is classic and indeed is illustrated in famous neurologic cases, including that of H.M. (Ogden 2005).

—Rebecca Ready and Michael Shally-Jensen

Clinical Assessment of Memory

Neuropsychologists test multiple aspects of memory. In classic learning and memory tasks, new information is presented to a patient. This new information can be verbal, such as a word list or story, or nonverbal, such as abstract diagrams or pictures. The patient is exposed to the new information and asked to remember it. Performance in the learning, or encoding, phase of the task can provide information about the patient's ability to efficiently acquire and organize new information. After time passes, usually about 15 to 30 minutes, the patient is asked to recall the information again. He or she is asked to freely recall the information, without being provided any cues or hints by the examiner. Free recall assesses the patient's access to newly learned information. Next, the patient is provided with cues, such as a multiple-choice task, to determine if they can recall more information when provided with a hint, otherwise known as recognition testing. If a patient performs poorly on recall and recognition testing, he or she likely has a true amnesia and an inability to learn little, if any, new information. If a patient performs poorly in recall but better on recognition testing, he or she likely has a retrieval deficit. A retrieval deficit is a type of memory impairment in which it is difficult to recall information that is stored in memory. Neuropsychologists also will assess for older memories by testing vocabulary knowledge, for example, and for accuracy in autobiographical recall when there is information against which to measure the accuracy of the patient's statements (e.g., historical documents, informants' reports).

Traumatic Brain Injury

Amnesia often occurs following traumatic brain injury (TBI), which can occur after a blow to the head or when a foreign object (e.g., a bullet) enters into the brain tissue (Loring 1999). The patient may experience retrograde amnesia, in which they fail to remember events that occurred prior to the trauma. Over time, the duration of retrograde memory loss may decrease but there may be permanent memory loss for events immediately preceding injury (Loring 1999). Retrograde amnesia often is due to disrupted consolidation of memories acquired prior to neurologic injury. Anterograde amnesia, which is more common than retrograde amnesia, occurs when the patient is unable to recall events that happened after the trauma (Breedlove, Rosenzweig, & Watson 2007). Anterograde amnesia is usually due to lesions in the diencephalic-medial-temporal lobe memory system (Loring 1999). The duration of anterograde amnesia is a gauge of the severity of head trauma.

Korsakoff's Syndrome

Korsakoff's syndrome is a neurologic disorder accompanied by memory impairment that commonly occurs in persons with chronic alcoholism and extreme malnutrition (Kolb & Wishaw 2009). In this syndrome, severe thiamine deficiency can damage the medial thalamus, a critical component of the declarative memory system. The anterior area of the thalamus can also be damaged and general cerebral atrophy is observed. There are six core symptoms of Korsakoff's syndrome: anterograde amnesia, time-limited retrograde amnesia, confabulation, meager content in conversation, lack of insight, and apathy.

Stroke

A stroke occurs when there is disruption of blood supply to neural tissue due to an occlusion (an ischemic stroke) or bleed (hemorrhagic stroke) (Loring 1999). Stroke will cause focal neurologic symptoms based on the affected neuroanatomical region. Posterior cerebral artery (PCA) stroke will most likely cause amnesia because it is the primary vascular supply to many structures of the diencephalic-medial-temporal lobe memory system. Stroke that causes damage to subcortical structures, such as the basal ganglia, might cause memory impairment characterized by a retrieval deficit, but with relatively better recognition memory. Learning of new information also can be inefficient with subcortical neuropathology, but once information is learned, recognition memory is relatively intact.

Anoxia

Anoxia occurs when there is lack of oxygen supply to neural tissue (Loring 1999). The most common cause is cardiac arrest; other causes are stroke, carbon monoxide poisoning, and birth and delivery complications. Some cells of the hippocampal region are particularly sensitive to lack of oxygen. Consequently, damage to this region can cause amnesia.

Neurodegenerative Diseases and Dementia

Neurodegenerative diseases, such as Parkinson's disease or Huntington's disease, often result in a deterioration of cognitive functioning, including memory. In Huntington's disease, progressive neurodegeneration occurs in the caudate and putamen. Parkinson's disease is a neurodegenerative disease due to cell loss of dopamine-producing neurons in the substantia nigra. Huntington's and Parkinson's diseases are characterized by motor impairments; specifically, excess movement in the case of the former and loss of movement in the case of the latter. Both disorders also are commonly characterized by executive dysfunction and retrieval deficits. Both can lead to dementia, which is defined by functional decline, memory impairment, and impairment in at least one other cognitive domain (American Psychiatric Association 2000).

However, the most common cause of dementia is Alzheimer's disease (AD; Kolb & Wishaw 2009). AD is characterized by early atrophy of the area known as the nucleus basalis of Meynert, which is rich in acetylcholine, a neurotransmitter involved in learning and memory. Early neurodegeneration also occurs in the temporal lobes, including the hippocampal formation. Beta-amyloid plaques, neurofibrillary tangles, and neuronal degeneration cause atrophy in these and other frontal and parietal cortical regions. The hallmark feature of AD is an amnesia characterized by a deficit in new learning.

The second most common cause of dementia is vascular dementia, which can be caused by a single stroke, repeated cerebral infarction, or chronic ischemia. The latter two are characterized by greater retrieval than recognition memory deficits, similar to memory loss in Parkinson's disease and Huntington's disease. If a stroke or vascular disease causes a lesion in the diencephalic-medial-temporal lobe memory system, amnesia may result.

Mild Cognitive Impairment

Persons with mild cognitive impairment (MCI) experience some cognitive decline, often in memory, but do not meet diagnostic criteria for dementia (Broder et al. 2008). Persons with MCI may have other cognitive deficits but usually have minimal or no functional impairment. MCI is estimated to affect 17 to 34 percent of older adults over the age of 60 (Hill 2005). Persons with MCI are likely to convert to dementia, usually dementia due to AD or to cerebrovascular disease, at a rate of about 10 to 15 percent per year (Broder et al. 2008; Risacher et al. 2010). Neuroimaging has shown progressive neural atrophy in the medial temporal lobe and in the hippocampal region in persons with MCI. In addition, MCI is accompanied by cerebral atrophy and loss of cortical thickness and density (Risacher et al. 2010).

Memory and Aging

Older adults experience changes in neural function and cognition that are part of normal aging. Contrary to notions that aging is accompanied by widespread and deleterious changes in memory, there are only two primary changes in memory that tend to occur with age. Memory retrieval and learning are less efficient. For example, the frontal lobes are less efficient with age (Craik 2008), which contributes to difficulty with self-initiated processing, such as is required for memory retrieval (Moulin & Gathercole 2008). Further, the hippocampus and medial temporal lobes function less efficiently in older adults, which contributes to less efficient learning of new declarative information. Imaging data reveal less general cortical activation in older adults in comparison to younger adults during encoding or retrieval tasks (Breedlove, Rosenzweig, & Watson 2007).

Some aspects of memory change very little with age. Perceptual and semantic memory are best preserved in the aging mind, both of which involve habitual tasks and general knowledge (Craik 2008). When tested on measures of crystallized memory, such as vocabulary, older participants demonstrate similar or superior ability to younger adults (Christensen et al. 1994). The assumptions of the past that older persons are senile and disabled by memory impairment have been replaced with knowledge that whereas memory goes through some changes in aging, much is preserved and functions normally.

Conclusion

Memory is not a unitary phenomenon but rather a constellation of systems with different neuroanatomical underpinnings. Memory can be categorized based on duration of the memory trace, content of the memory, and when information was acquired. These distinctions are useful to dissociate neuroanatomical underpinnings of memory and to determine which aspects of memory are impaired or preserved after neurologic injury or disease. Memory capabilities change with age but only to a limited degree. The study of memory continues to advance at a rapid pace, thanks to technological advances in neuroimaging and brain mapping and to careful study of patients with circumscribed lesions and memory impairment (Saykin & Wishart 2010).

See also Alcohol Abuse, Alcoholism, and Mental Health; Alzheimer's Disease and Other Dementias; Dissociative Disorders; Hypnosis and Hypnotherapy; Neuropsychiatry; Post-traumatic Stress Disorder

Bibliography

American Psychiatric Association. 2000. *Diagnostic and Statistical Manual of Mental Disorders* (4th ed. text. rev.). Washington, DC: American Psychiatric Publishing.

Breedlove, S. M., M. R. Rosenzweig, and N. V. Watson. 2007. *Biological Psychology* (5th ed.). Sunderland, MA: Sinauer Associates.

Broder, A., A. Herwig, S. Teipel, and K. Fast. 2008. "Different Storage and Retrieval Deficits in Normal Aging and Mild Cognitive Impairment: A Multinomial Modeling Analysis." *Psychology and Aging* 23: 353–365.

Christensen, H., A. Mackinnon, A. F. Jorm, A. S. Henderson, L. R. Scott, and A. E. Korten. 1994. "Age Differences and Interindividual Variation in Cognition in Community-Dwelling Elderly." *Psychology and Aging* 9: 381–390.

Craik, F. I. M. 2008. "Memory Changes in Normal and Pathological Aging." *The Canadian Journal of Psychiatry* 53: 343–345.

Gillings, Annabel. 2008. *How Does Your Memory Work?* (DVD). Princeton, NJ: Films for the Humanities and Sciences.

Kolb, B., and I. Q. Wishaw. 2009. *Fundamentals of Human Neuropsychology* (6th ed.). New York: Worth.

Lezak, M. D., D. B. Howieson, and D. W. Loring. 2004. *Neuropsychological Assessment* (4th ed.). Oxford: Oxford University Press.

Loring, D. W. 1999. *INS Dictionary of Neuropsychology*. Oxford: Oxford University Press.

Moulin, C. J. A., and S. E. Gathercole. 2008. "Memory Changes across the Lifespan." In G. Cohen and M. A. Conway, eds., *Memory in the Real World* (pp. 305–326). New York: Psychology Press.

Ogden, J. A. 2005. *Fractured Minds: A Case Study Approach to Clinical Neuropsychology.* Oxford: Oxford University Press.

Risacher, S. L., L. Shen, J. D. West, S. Kim, and A. J. Saykin. 2010. "Longitudinal MRI Atrophy Biomarkers: Relationship to Conversion in the ADNI Cohort." *Neurobiology of Aging* 31: 1401–1418.

Saykin, A. J., and H. A. Wishart. 2010. "fMRI of Memory in Aging and Dementia." In S. H. Faro and F. B. Mohamed, eds., *BOLD fMRI: A Guide to Functional Neuroimaging for Neuroscientists* (pp. 161–182). New York: Springer Science and Business Media.

Mental Health Advocacy

Dave Sells, Charles Barber, and Michele Klimczak

The roots of mental health advocacy the United States are long and varied, and are inextricably bound to the stigma, discrimination, and almost complete lack of power and larger societal influence faced by individuals suffering from mental illness. Public policies in the United States, and internationally, have historically failed people with mental illnesses (Bloche 1990). In the last 25 years, however, the mental health advocacy movement has strengthened considerably, which has led to at times increased support for community mental health services and initiatives, greater public understanding of brain-based psychiatric illnesses, and more enlightened public policy, such as the President's New Freedom Commission on Mental Health (2003), which placed consumer issues at the core of mental health policy. As a result, the mental health advocacy movement in recent decades can be viewed in the tradition of earlier influential human rights movements such as civil rights, women's rights, and gay rights.

History

There have been three broad historical trends in mental health care in the United States: the asylums of the nineteenth century, the mental hygiene movement and inpatient care of the early to mid-twentieth century, and community-based and outpatient care in the latter half of the twentieth century. While each era ultimately resulted in more progressive, less restrictive, and in large part more effective treatments, each period was also diminished by abuses and misguided treatment, creating the need for vocal and often courageous advocates. During the era of the asylum, patients were routinely institutionalized for life based on the recommendations of family members or one or two doctors. Prior to the development of asylums, the mentally ill were arbitrarily subjected to confinement in prisons, workhouses, and sometimes imprisonment in their own homes. It was not uncommon for individuals to be chained, caged, and whipped into submission. Unfortunately, the institutionalization of care for the mentally ill through the development of asylums did not result in better outcomes for patients. Conceptions of mental illness at the time, based in misunderstanding and steeped in fear, resulted in care that was custodial at best, and more often than not, deplorable and inhumane. During the asylum era, patients, particularly those who suffered from psychotic disorders, were considered at times subhuman and were often not accorded basic human rights. This mind-set lingered well into the twentieth century.

In the 1948 book *The Shame of the States*, Alfred Deutsch wrote that state psychiatric facilities were like "Nazi concentration camps Belsen and Buchenwald ... buildings swarming with naked human beings herded like cattle and treated with less concern, pervaded by a fetid odor so heavy, so nauseating, that the stench seemed to have almost a physical existence of its own" (42). Patients were often sterilized, under the rationale that the practice would halt the moral contagion of their conditions. In 1927, the U.S. Supreme Court approved of "the sterilization of moral defectives" (Whitaker 2002). Other remarkably cruel treatments, all considered at one point best practices of their day, included, literally, the freezing of patients (such that their body temperatures fell 10 to 20 degrees below normal); insulin therapy; and the lobotomy, to which 20,000 American psychiatric patients were subjected between 1935 and 1950 (Eisenberg 2000). Current psychiatric practice is rarely so outwardly abusive, although there are, to be sure, isolated instances of coercion, punishment, extreme and at times fatal overuse of medications, and physical and sexual abuse of patients.

Key Advocates

Early advocates such as Dorothea Dix, Elizabeth Packard, and Clifford Beers drew much-needed public attention to the plight of the mentally ill in the United States in the nineteenth and early twentieth centuries. Dix (1802–87) was an influential advocate, lobbyist, and crusader on behalf of the mentally ill, both in the United States and abroad. While volunteering at a Massachusetts prison, she discovered women chained and confined in filthy conditions whose only crime was mental illness. Investigations of other prisons revealed a strikingly similar pattern of cruel and punitive treatment. Thus began her lifelong crusade for the improvement of conditions for the mentally ill, by exposing the rampant abuse and enlisting the support of the government to create specialized hospitals and to improve conditions in existing institutions.

Elizabeth Packard (1816–97) of Illinois was institutionalized in the 1800s against her will at her husband's behest. While in the asylum she collected patient's stories and kept a journal. After she was released it took her nine years to regain custody of her children. Packard fought for the rights of people who were accused of being mentally ill until her death, and inspired a law passed in Illinois in 1869 requiring a jury trial before someone was committed (Langworthy 2007).

Clifford W. Beers (1876–1943), a native of New Haven, Connecticut, was educated at Yale. He suffered from severe depression and underwent numerous hospitalizations in Connecticut state hospitals, where he was psychically assaulted. After leaving the asylum, Beers became an advocate for more humane treatment of people suffering from mental illness, writing a highly influential autobiographical account of his experiences, *A Mind That Found Itself*, and became known as the founder of the mental hygiene movement in the United States. "A pen rather than a lance has been my weapon of offense and defense; with its point I should prick the civic conscience and bring into a neglected field men and women who should act as champions for those afflicted thousands least able to fight for themselves," Beers wrote of his calling (Beers 1908, 88). In 1909 Beers founded the National Committee for Mental Hygiene, currently known as Mental Health America, a now thriving organization dedicated to advocacy and education. Beers also founded the first outpatient psychiatric facility in New Haven in 1913, which operates to this day.

As a result of misguided and at times cruel hospital treatments, as well as their expense, starting in the 1960s the state hospital system began to gradually empty. According to Goldman and Morrissey (1985), "between 1950 and 1980 . . . the resident population of state mental hospitals was reduced from approximately 560,000 to less than 140,000" (278). In the 1960s and 1970s, as American society as a whole underwent social change movements such as civil rights and women's liberation, the consumer movement also grew and held similar goals, which included liberation from state institutions, and empowerment for people with mental health diagnoses (Jacobson 2000).

The U.S. courts assisted in the processes of deinstitutionalization and consumer empowerment. The Supreme Court ruled in 1975 in *O'Connor v. Donaldson* that a person who was not a danger to themselves or others could not be confined against their will (Odegaard 2007). In *Lessard v. Schmidt* in 1976 held that Wisconsin had to get rid of existing civil commitment laws (Odegaard 2007). Further, in 1999 the Supreme Court ruled in *Olmstead v. L.C.* that states had to give consumers the option of community-based treatment programs as well as psychiatric hospitals.

Contemporary advocates include Moe Armstrong, a decorated Vietnam veteran who developed a psychotic illness on the battlefield. After years of hospitalizations, homelessness, and rampant drug abuse, Armstrong turned around his life around in 1980. Since that time he has received two master's degrees and founded Vet to Vet, a peer counseling service for the Veterans Administration. Other influential advocates include well-known figures who have gone public with their struggles with psychiatric illness. Examples are former U.S. Representative Patrick Kennedy, the writer William Styron (who died in 2006), newscasters Mike

Wallace and Jane Pauley, and actresses Carrie Fisher and Patty Duke. In addition, prominent mental health professionals have disclosed their own personal histories of mental illness. Kay Redfield Jamison, a leading researcher of bipolar disorder, revealed her own history with the illness in *An Unquiet Mind* (1995); and Marsha Linehan, who developed an innovative treatment for bipolar disorder, recently shared her experiences with that disorder when she was a young woman (see Carey 2011).

Obstacles to the Advocacy Movement

The stigma of mental illness, although somewhat diminished in recent decades, remains profound. According to Byrne, "Stigma is defined as a sign of disgrace or discredit, which sets a person apart from others. The stigma of mental illness, although more often related to context than to a person's appearance, remains a powerful negative attribute in all social relations" (Byrne 2000, 65). The adaptive response to stigma is shame and secrecy due to public ignorance, scapegoating, and discrimination. The historical depth and intensity of stigma against people diagnosed with psychiatric illnesses has also served to thwart efforts that call for the full social inclusion of people suffering from mental illness, and, along with maltreatment has created the need for ongoing advocacy.

In recent decades, the media, and particularly film and television, have had a powerful effect in reinforcing stigma and in shaping common stereotypes of people with mental illnesses as violent and uncontrollable. Alfred Hitchcock's highly influential *Psycho* (1960) depicts a killer suffering from a dissociative disorder. The relatively recent *Primal Fear* (1996), *Fight Club* (1999), *The Number 23* (2007), and *Black Swan* (2010) all depict violent behavior as a product of having a mental illness. It is the rare Hollywood movie that features a main character with a mental illness who is heroic. A notable exception is the Oscar-winning *A Beautiful Mind* (2001), the story of Nobel Prize winner John Nash's experience with schizophrenia. Negative depictions of people with mental illnesses feed society's fear and ignorance and prevent forward progress in the mental health field.

Mixed Progress

In 1999, Otto Wahl, with the assistance of the National Alliance for the Mentally Ill, conducted a large study of mental health consumers' experience of stigma and discrimination. Respondents felt stigmatized from a variety of sources, including communities, families, churches, coworkers, and mental health caregivers. Most respondents hid their mental health issues and lived in a psychiatric "closet" of fear and stress. "They reported discouragement, hurt, anger, and lowered self-esteem as results of their experiences, and they urged public education as a means for reducing stigma. Some reported that involvement in advocacy and speaking out when stigma and discrimination were encountered helped them to cope with stigma" (Wahl 1999, 467). Eighty percent of respondents reported overhearing hurtful comments made by individuals. The study also showed that mental health professionals are also implicated in helping to stigmatize mental health consumers.

In recent years, there has been, at least superficially, an increase in acceptance of psychiatric illness by Americans. A significant factor in the change in attitudes has certainly been the widespread use of psychotropic medications (which are taken by 10–20% of the American public in a given year) and the increasing influence and popularization of neuroscientific explanations of behavior. If psychiatric illnesses are thought to brain-based, "physiological" disorders, rather than expressions of human frailty or a characterological defect, then they are regarded with a much higher degree of sympathy and acceptance. As a result of this sea change in how Americans conceive of the causes of mental illness, there has been a significant increase in the tolerance and to some degree understanding of psychiatric disorders. This has led to the occasional depiction of mental illness in the media in positive terms, or at least as something that may be adaptive or provide some utility. An example would be the popular television show *Monk* (USA Network 2002–9), which depicts a detective who uses his obsessive-compulsive tendencies as a resource to solve crimes. The new, friendlier environment to mental illness has resulted in the passing of mental health parity legislation in many states, and continued support for public mental health funding even in recent, economically challenged, years.

Antistigma and advocacy efforts in recent years have been successful for certain illnesses, particularly depression and bipolar disorder. However, advocacy efforts for arguably the most severe disorders, psychotic illnesses, have made less progress in broader society. Patient advocates suffering from severe mood and psychotic disorders, such as Will Hall, have used the media and in particular the Internet to make their voices heard. Often these advocates use the language with which they have been labeled as part of their armamentarium. Hall calls his web-based radio show "Madness Radio," and the movement generally has been described as "the Mad Pride" movement (see http://www.madnessradio.net/). The movement in general is ambivalent, at best, about mainstream psychiatry, and members often express anger at the way they have been treated in that system.

Where Do We Go from Here?

The World Health Organization (WHO) identified mental health advocacy as one of the four pillars of the global mental health strategy (Funk 2006). World Mental Health Day is October 10, a designation started by the WHO in 2008 to promote mental health advocacy all over the world (World Federation for Mental Health, http://www.wfmh.org). In the United States, May is designated as Mental Health Month.

Finally, the recovery movement plays a vital role in mental health advocacy. The key aspects of a recovery orientation are: (1) recovery is a process—there is not necessarily a "cure" for some mental illnesses; (2) no two recovery processes are alike and different people will need different supports; (3) a consumer is empowered to take an active role in his or her own recovery with a multitude of choices and the support of family, friends, and professionals; and (4) the mental health consumer will be supported in finding a deep sense of hope and meaning—fulfillment for his or her life (Jacobson 2000). Community-based nonprofits in the United States are increasingly adopting a recovery approach to mental health care and advocacy. Organizations such as Mental Health America (with 320 nationwide partners) and the National Alliance for the Mentally Ill (with 210,000 members in 1,200 affiliates across the country) are leading advocacy organizations for public education and research (http://www.mnha.org; http://www.nami.org). Although there still needs to be more evidence collected regarding the effectiveness of the recovery method, initial studies have shown that, at the very least consumers have more positive feeling regarding their treatment as a result of this approach (Jacobson 2000).

Conclusion

Mental health advocacy has grown out of a need for justice, empowerment, and liberation for mental health consumers who were once subject to the whims of their family members and unsympathetic courts. Through the recovery movement and the work of ex-patients, consumers are taking a more active role in their treatment and in advocacy in general. It is imperative that mental health advocates conduct more empirical research, support educational opportunities, and contribute to positive media depictions of people with mental illnesses.

See also Disability Rights; History of Mental Health Care; Hospitalization; Literary Works and Mental Illness; Media Portrayals of Mental Illness; Neurodiversity; Peer Support Groups; Recovery Movement; Rights of Patients with Mental Health Conditions; Stigma

Bibliography

Beers, Clifford. 1908. *A Mind That Found Itself: An Autobiography.* New York: Longmans, Green.

Bloche, M. G., and F. Cournos. 1990. "Mental Health Policy for the 1990s: Tinkering in the Interstices." *Journal of Health Politics, Policy and Law* 15: 387–411.

Byrne, P. 2000. "Stigma of Mental Illness and Ways of Diminishing It." *Advances in Psychiatric Treatment* 6: 65–72.

Carey, B. 2011. "Expert on Mental Illness Reveals Her Own Fight." *New York Times*, June 23, p. A1.

Deutsch, Albert. 1948. *The Shame of the States.* New York: Harcourt, Brace.

Eisenberg, L. 2000. "Is Psychiatry More Mindful or Brainer Than It Was a Decade Ago?" *British Journal of Psychiatry* 176: 1–5.

Funk, M., A. Minoletti, N. Drew, J. Taylor, and B. Saraceno. 2006. "Advocacy for mental Health: Roles for Consumer and Family Organizations and Governments." *Health Promotion International* 21: 70–75.

Goldman, H. H., and J. P. Morrissey. 1985. "The Alchemy of Mental Health Policy: Homelessness and the Fourth Cycle of Reform." *American Journal of Public Health* 75: 1–5.

Gruskin, S., E. J. Mills, and D. Tarantola. 2007. "History, Principles, and Practice of Health and Human Rights." *Lancet* 370: 449–455.

Jacobson, N. 2000. "Recovery as Policy in Mental Health Services: Strategies Emerging from the States." *Psychosocial Rehabilitation Journal* 23: 333–341.

Jamison, Kay Redfield. 1995. *An Unquiet Mind*. New York: Knopf.

Langworthy, D. 2007. "Elizabeth Packard Biography." Mrs. Packard: A McCarter Theater Production. Retrieved from http://www.mccarter.org/education/mrs-packard/html/4.html.

Mental Health America (formerly the Mental Health Association). http://www.nmha.org.

Milner, N. 1986. "The Symbols and Meanings of Advocacy." *International Journal of Law and Psychiatry* 8: 1–17.

National Alliance for the Mentally Ill. http://www.nami.org/.

Odegaard, A. M. 2007. "Therapeutic Jurisprudence: The Impact of Mental Health Courts on the Criminal Justice System." *North Dakota Law Review* 83: 225–259.

President's New Freedom Commission on Mental Health. 2003. *Achieving the Promise: Transforming Health Care in America*. Washington, DC: U.S. Government Printing Office.

Saraceno, B., M. van Ommeren, R. Batniji, A. Cohen, O. Gureje, J. Mahoney, D. Sindhar, and C. Underhill. 2007. "Barriers to Improvement of Mental Health Services in Low-Income and Middle-Income Countries." *Lancet* 370: 1164–1174.

Wahl, O. F. 1999. "Mental Health Consumers' Experience of Stigma." *Schizophrenia Bulletin* 25: 467–478.

Whitaker, Robert. 2002. *Mad in America: Bad Science, Bad Medicine, and the Enduring Mistreatment of the Mentally Ill*. New York: Perseus.

Wolff, G., S. Pathare, C. Craig, and J. Leff. 1996. "Public Education for Community Care: A New Approach." *British Journal of Psychiatry* 168: 441–447.

Mental Health Counseling

Nicole Bradley, Laura Shannonhouse, and Victoria E. Kress

Counselors are trained professionals who, in the mental health field, work to address and treat mental health issues. According to the American Counseling Association (2011), "counseling is a professional relationship that empowers diverse individuals, families, and groups to accomplish mental health, wellness, education, and career goals." All 50 states, the District of Columbia, Puerto Rico, and Guam now license professional counselors (National Board for Certified Counselors). This licensure serves to protect the public by regulating who can (and cannot) use the title of licensed counselor and thus provide counseling services in a given jurisdiction/state (National Board for Certified Counselors). Although there may be differences among licensure requirements for each state, most states require a combination of the following in order to become a counselor: a master's degree in counseling, counseling experience (including supervision), and a passing score on a state-required examination (National Board for Certified Counselors).

Mental Health Counseling Settings

Counseling is employed in many different settings and applied to many different situations. Mental health counselors can work in community mental health agencies, hospitals, private practices, employee assistance programs, substance abuse treatment programs, school settings, college/university counseling centers, or disaster response environments, to name a few.

Counseling sessions can involve individuals (one on one), families (parents, siblings, or other relatives who are part of the family system), couples (relationship issues), or groups (individuals struggling with similar problems).

Counselors at community mental health agencies may provide outpatient counseling services or services in the community, such as in schools, or they may provide intensive in-home counseling. The latter is often used when the client needs more intensive care than outpatient services can provide or when the family as a whole needs counseling services. Counselors in hospitals can work in inpatient treatment, where clients remain in the hospital for a period of time to manage their symptoms. During this time the client receives intensive counseling, medication monitoring (as necessary), and a referral for services after he or she is released from inpatient treatment (Gladding & Newsome 2010). In addition to such treatment, hospitals also provide partial hospitalization programs (PHPs), or intensive outpatient programs (IOPs), where clients may receive intensive treatment but do not require 24-hour supervision (Gladding & Newsome 2010).

Counselors working in private practices handle a variety of issues and are generally reimbursed through a variety of funding sources. Employee assistance programs (EAPs), for example, are employment benefits programs intended to help individuals deal with any personal struggles that may adversely impact their work performance, well-being, or health. EAPs tend to include assessment, short-term counseling, and referral services for both employees and their household members.

Substance abuse treatment programs involve a skilled team of certified physicians, psychiatrists, and licensed clinical psychologists and counselors. Various techniques such as individual counseling, 12-step programming (a standard method), yoga, meditation, tai-chi, peer recovery support group, life-skills training, music/art therapy, hope and faith-based support groups, stress reduction, and codependency education are utilized in such programs.

Looking for a Few Good Men

There is growing concern that there are not enough male mental health counselors in the field, and that as a result, men are less likely to seek therapy, especially those who have never had therapy.

Men earn only one in five of all master's degrees awarded in psychology, down from half in the 1970s. They account for less than 10 percent of social workers under the age of 34, according to a recent survey. And their numbers have dwindled among professional counselors—to 10 percent of the American Counseling Association's membership today from 30 percent in 1982. (Carey 2011).

Source: Benedict Carey, "Need Therapy? A Good Man Is Hard to Find," *New York Times*, May 22, 2011, A1, A4.

University counseling centers serve the college student community. Students are usually offered between 6 and 12 sessions a year, as covered by their student fees. University counseling centers have a range of services from psychiatric (medication), biofeedback (anxiety), crisis and on-call services, referral services (if students needs surpass what a center can provide), and group therapy (e.g., for social anxiety, eating disorders, substance abuse, low academic performance, LGBT issues, and ethnicity/race-related issues).

The Essence of Change in Counseling

Four major factors account for a client's improvement under mental health counseling (Hubble, Duncan, & Miller 2006; Lambert 1992):

1. The counselor's theoretical orientation and the techniques applied
2. The quality of the therapeutic relationship
3. The clients' hopes and expectations for change
4. Extratherapeutic factors (matters outside the counselor's direct control)

The power of the therapeutic relationship accounts for a significant portion of clients' change (30% or more). Many in the field argue that the relationship is the single most important factor and that the trust established through the relationship can impact clients' hopes, expectations, belief in the process, and level of motivation. Thus the consensus is that it is critical to foster a good counselor-client relationship.

The Counseling Process

Early Steps in the Counseling Process

The counseling relationship begins with rapport building. Microskills on the counselor's part such as active listening, reflecting feelings, paraphrasing, encouraging, summarizing, and asking open- and closed-ended questions are useful tools (Ivey & Ivey 2003). Ideally, such tools help the counselor to understand his or her clients' problem issues, goals, and needs phenomenologically—that is, through the clients' lens as opposed to the counselor's own (Clarkson 1999; Korb et al. 2007). In addition, building rapport fosters the trust that is essential to have if the client is to feel safe and be comfortable with taking risks in the counseling process (e.g., by revealing personal information and perceptions).

The counseling process also begins with informed consent and an intake assessment. It is important to start by providing general information about the theoretical approach the counselor uses and any potential risks associated with it so that the client can make an informed decision about whether or not to participate (Archer & McCarthy 2006). Once consent is given, the counselor will conduct an intake consisting of a structured set of questions that allow him or her to collect specific information from the client, information that aids in the understanding of the problem issues, the goals of the client, and what may or may not have worked before.

The application or use of a specific diagnosis—also referred to as diagnostic coding—can be helpful in understanding problem issues, in communicating with other helping professionals, and in treatment planning and is often required for insurance billing purposes (American Psychiatric Association 2000). The multiaxial system that forms the basis of the American Psychiatric Association's *Diagnostic and Statistical Manual of Mental Disorders* also enables clinicians to organize information: Axis I includes clinical disorders typically treated with psychological therapy/counseling and psychopharmacology (Preston, O'Neal, & Talaga 2010); Axis II includes personality disorders and mental functioning issues; Axis III includes general medical conditions; Axis IV includes psychosocial and environmental problems; and Axis IV concerns global assessment of functioning (GAF).

Many clinicians center their interventions on the clients' diagnosis and presenting symptoms. Counselors include this in their work and also consider the client's environment, family, and culture as necessary elements to the conceptualization of the client's case. It is said that counseling is wellness centered, and the ultimate goal is to help the client not to be functional but well—that is, somewhat beyond mere functioning.

The establishment of goals is an important early step in the counseling process. A goal is a broad statement addressing a desired outcome given the client's diagnosis and problem issues. Goals need to be directly related to the diagnosis and have realistic objectives (statements concerning how the goal will be met). For instance, a goal for someone diagnosed with depression might be for him or her to reduce feelings of sadness and isolation and to increase social activities. Potential objectives might include readings from the book *The Feeling Good Handbook* (Burns 1999) and utilizing particular strategies learned in the reading (e.g., client will use "turning a negative into a positive" thought pattern and report three times that this was used prior to the next session).

Addressing Clients' Concerns

The counselor must understand not only the problem issues and diagnosis but also the treatment of choice for particular symptoms (e.g., cognitive-behavioral therapy for depression). The counselor may begin with referrals to a primary care physician to rule out any medical conditions or to a psychiatrist to obtain (if appropriate) a prescription for medication. Through goal planning the counselor and client can work together to move in the direction of improved mental health and wellness. Working toward such goals may involve problem solving, generating alternatives for problem areas, and exploring the client's personal dynamics (Ivey & Ivey 2003).

There are many different theoretical approaches and therapeutic interventions that can lead to similar outcomes of health and wellness (Smith, Glass, & Miller 1980). However, there are common pathways to change for the better what happens both within and between counseling sessions. Positive change occurs through a series of stages, and at each stage the individual can apply a beneficial process in order to progress to the next stage (DiClemente & Prochaska 1982). Another way of stating this is to say that counselors help clients move from a place of inaction to a place of action (Ivey & Ivey 2003).

The six most commonly accepted stages of change are:

1. Precontemplation (not intending to change or to take action within the next six months)
2. Contemplation (intending to change within the next six months)
3. Preparation (intending to take action in the immediate future)
4. Action (have made specific lifestyle or other modifications within the past six months)
5. Maintenance (working to prevent relapse)
6. Termination (experience zero temptation and 100% self-efficacy) (Hubble, Duncan, & Miller 2009)

The same stages-of-change model can be applied at each phase of the counseling process, including recruitment, retention, progress, process, and outcome. As a general rule, it is important to invite clients to move to the next stage as opposed to skipping stages or jumping around. In order to help clients progress through the stages, the positive aspects of personal change must be highlighted and shown to be valuable, the negative aspects must be stated yet kept in perspective, and, throughout, the particular processes of change need to be matched to specific stages of change (Hubble, Duncan, & Miller 2006).

Once the final goals are met, the counselor can begin the termination process by helping the client to explore themes from the course of the counseling work. The counselor can ask, for example, what the client would like to take away from the experience and how he or she might do so. Thus the termination process involves getting the client to generalize what he or she has learned in counseling to other areas of his or her life.

See also Behavioral Theories and Therapies; Campus Life and Mental Health; Cognitive-Behavioral Therapy; Culturally Competent Mental Health Care; Disasters and Mental Health; Family and Mental Illness; Group Therapy; Humanistic Theories and Therapies; Marriage, Divorce, and Mental Health; Peer Support Groups; Recovery Movement; School Mental Health; Workplace Issues in Mental Health

Bibliography

American Counseling Association. 2011. Retrieved from http://www.counseling.org/resources/.

American Psychiatric Association. 2000. *Diagnostic and Statistical Manual of Mental Disorders* (4th ed., text rev.). Washington, DC: American Psychological Publishing.

Archer, J., and C. J. McCarthy. 2006. *Counseling Theories: Contemporary Applications and Approaches*. Upper Saddle River, NJ: Prentice-Hall.

Burns, David D. 1999. *The Feeling Good Handbook* (rev. updated ed.). New York: Plume.

Clarkson, P. 1999. *Gestalt Counseling in Action* (2nd ed.). London: Sage.

DiClemente, C. C., and J. O. Prochaska. 1982. "Self-Change and Therapy Change of Smoking Behavior: A Comparison of Processes of Change in Cessation and Maintenance." *Addictive Behavior* 7: 133–142.

Gladding, S. T., and D. W. Newsome. 2010. *Clinical Mental Health Counseling in Community and Agency Settings* (3rd ed.). Upper Saddle River, NJ: Pearson.

Hubble, M. A., B. L. Duncan, and S. D. Miller. 2009. *The Heart and Soul of Change* (2nd ed.). Washington, DC: American Psychological Association.

Ivey, A., and M. Ivey. 2003. *Intentional Interviewing and Counseling: Facilitating Client Development in a Multicultural Society*. Pacific Grove, CA: Brooks Cole.

Korb, M. P., J. Davenport, A. Martin, and J. Korb. 2007. *iContact: A Gestalt Guide to Skilled Communication*. Gouldsboro, ME: Gestalt Journal Press.

Lambert, M. 1992. "Implications for Outcome Research for Psychotherapy Integration." In J. C. Norcross and M. R. Goldstein, eds., *Handbook of Psychotherapy Integration* (pp. 94–129). New York: Basic Books.

National Board for Certified Counselors. http://www.nbcc.org.

Preston, J. D., J. H. O'Neal, and M. C. Talaga. 2010. *Handbook of Clinical Psychopharmacology for Therapists* (6th ed.). Oakland, CA: New Harbinger.

Smith, M. L., G. V. Glass, and T. I. Miller. 1980. The Benefits of Psychotherapy. Baltimore: Johns Hopkins University Press.

Mental Retardation

See Intellectual Disability

Milieu Therapy

See Therapeutic Community and Milieu Therapy

Mind and Body Approaches to Mental Health

Stanley Krippner, Cheryl Fracasso, and Harris Friedman

Defining the field of mind and body medicine is challenging since there are no clear-cut boundaries that differentiate many of the modalities that fall within its domain. In fact, mind and body medicine is a subfield of the larger umbrella referred to as complementary and alternative medicine (CAM), which encompasses a diverse group of modalities and health care systems that are not considered to be part of conventional medicine. According to the National Center for Complementary and Alternative Medicine (NCCAM website 2011), a branch of the National Institutes of Health (NIH), CAM consists of fields that fall under the broad category of holistic health and natural approaches, including phytochemicals, mind and body medicine, manipulative and body-based practices, integrative medical systems, energy medicine, exercise and movement therapies, expressive art therapies, and a broad array of other practices that do not fit neatly into one category. Complementary practices "complement" mainstream practices (e.g., exercise and movement therapies) while alternative practices are "alternatives" to mainstream practices because they are based on different premises (e.g., homeopathic theory, which simply does not make sense under conventional ways of thinking about the relationship between dose and effect of medicines). Some practices fall under both categories (e.g., Chinese traditional medicine, some aspects of which are complementary, such as massage, and some of which are alternative, such as moxibustion—the burning of herbs on segments of the patient's body).

According to NCCAM, the main premise behind mind and body medicine is that a focus on the interactions between the mind and body (i.e., brain, and behavior) will impact physical and mental well-being and promote health. The historical roots of integrating the mind and body as an important element in the treatment of illness dates back over 2,000 years ago to traditional Chinese medicine, ancient Greek medicine, Ayurvedic medicine, and similar holistic approaches. In the past few decades, CAM has gained increasing popularity in Western cultures, as indicated in the 2007 National Health Interview Survey (NHIS). which revealed that 38 percent of Americans used some type of CAM (NCCAM website 2011).

The modalities that fall under the domain of mind and body medicine include yoga, meditation, acupuncture, guided imagery, hypnotically facilitated psychotherapy, progressive muscle relaxation, QiGong, Tai Chi, and biofeedback, to name a few. However, it could be argued that all healing modalities fall under the mind and body domain to some extent, since at a deeper level there is no justifiable way to delineate mind from body. However, CAM approaches are geared toward integrating what a culture considers "body" and what that culture considers "mind" (including "emotions" and "spirit") to improve health, whereas more conventional medical approaches segment these into separate domains. For example, Reiki— which also falls under the "energy medicine" domain—is geared toward the movement of the hypothetical construct of some sort of "energy" to remove mind and body blockages to promote health. While this technique does not use physical touch, its clients are typically passive recipients of its treatment. Clients do not have to meditate, visualize, or relax. The hoped for result is that the effects of this treatment will impact the mind and body by at least inducing relaxation and perhaps by more deeply affecting other mechanisms that remain unknown.

Since these mind and body modalities are so diverse, for purposes of this entry we will overview some of the most widely used modalities as reported by adults in the 2007 NHIS survey. For example, the survey found that 12.7 percent of adults practiced some sort of deep breathing, 9.4 percent practiced some form of meditation or self-regulated attention (ranging from mindfulness meditation to guided imagery), 6.1 percent practiced yoga, 1.4 percent had used acupuncture, with smaller percentages reporting employing other practices, such as Reiki. The 2007 NHIS survey showed that utilization of mind and body modalities substantially increased as compared with the previous NHIS survey in 2002 (NCCAM website 2011). We have selected four of these modalities for our overview, namely yoga, guided imagery, acupuncture, and Reiki.

Four Popular Modalities

Yoga

Yoga consists of a variety of techniques but in the West is usually seen as a set of relatively gentle stretching postures that purport to increase flexibility, balance, and strength, invoke relaxation, as well as provide cardiovascular benefits when practiced vigorously over a long period of time (Kabat-Zinn 1990). Physical yoga (i.e., Hatha yoga) can also be performed strenuously as an athletic event (e.g., Bikrim yoga), or it can be devoid of a physical emphasis, such as in a focus on good deeds (i.e., Karma yoga) or sharpening the intellect (i.e., Agni yoga). The procedures behind most physical yogas involve a focus on breathing while relaxing into various postures and holding them for a few minutes, and for some types of yoga, then holding each posture for a period of at least five minutes. According to Kabat-Zinn (1990), being mindful of how the body feels during each of these stretches invokes the feeling of being comfortable in the body, as well as realizing "wholeness" and "connectedness" through disciplined practice. Some yogas, however, focus on increasing discomfort to alter consciousness, such as "breath of fire" movements involving rapid hyperventilation combined with strenuous movement, such as deep knee bends. This can be done for several hours in some forms of kundalini yoga practice.

Research has shown that yoga can help patients suffering from cardiovascular disease, osteoporosis, multiple sclerosis, back and neck pain, as well as the recovery of patients who have suffered a stroke (Butler et al. 2008). Studies also showed that yoga can improve cholesterol readings, lower blood pressure, lower the pulse rate, as well as reduce stress, anxiety, and chronic pain (Wahbeh, Elsas, & Oken 2008). Likewise, Schure, Christopher, and Christopher (2008) pointed out that the practice of Hatha yoga has been able to decrease mood disturbances, lower rates of depression, as well as increase immune system functioning by decreasing psychological distress and physical discomfort.

Guided Imagery

Guided imagery is a consciously guided cognitive process that may utilize all the major senses (i.e., sight, hearing, touch, kinesthesia, smell, taste), which can have a profound impact on the body's physiology and biochemistry (Lynn et al. 2000). Uses of this technique can be found in hypnosis and biofeedback, along with various forms of meditation to invoke relaxation and manage stress (Leon-Pizzaro et al. 2007). Guided imagery has been used to treat many disorders ranging from phantom limb syndrome (MacIver et al. 2008), breast cancer (Nunes et al. 2007), stroke, posttraumatic stress disorder in survivors of sexual assault (Krakow et al. 2001), anxiety and depression in hospitalized patients (Toth et al. 2007), and even to increase breast milk production in women with premature infants (Feher et al. 1989). Additional applications of guided imagery include pain management for many types of cancers, tension and/or migraine headaches, diabetes, severe burn trauma, as well as for reducing pain and inflammation caused by arthritis (Freeman 2004). Overall, guided imagery has been used to treat many disorders within many specialties of behavioral medicine and is employed adjunctively with many other forms of CAM.

Acupuncture

Acupuncture operates from the assumption that there are various energy centers (acupuncture points) and pathways (meridians) located throughout that body. Originating from the practice of traditional Chinese medicine (Brown 2009), meridians reside on the various acupuncture points located throughout the body. They are thought to channel the body's flow of energy or "life force" (Eden & Feinstein 2008). Meridians allegedly impact and "feed" the body's metabolism, major organs, and physiological systems, and even are thought to impact changes at the cellular level. Key systems of meridians are allegedly connected to "the immune, nervous, endocrine, circulatory, respiratory, digestive, skeletal, muscular, and lymphatic systems" (Eden & Feinstein 2008, 3). Moreover, practitioners of this approach suggest there are hundreds of acupuncture points. Consequently, the theoretical assumption is that if a meridian is "blocked," it will impact the corresponding organ/physiological system to which it is supposedly connected. Hence, practitioners of acupuncture inserts tiny needles into these various acupuncture points to clear any meridians that may be blocked to promote increased health in any corresponding organs to which these meridians may be connected. Variants of acupuncture include massaging these points (as in Japanese shiatsu), stimulating or tonifying them with heat (as in moxibustion), or even directing a laser beam to specific acupuncture points in more contemporary approaches.

Acupuncture has been used to treat a number of disorders ranging from depression, drug/alcohol addiction, and anxiety, to managing chronic pain and reducing stress in patients diagnosed with chronic diseases, such as fibromyalgia, cancer, and asthma (Ainsworth 2009). While the studies on the results of its long-term effectiveness are mixed, acupuncture seems to show promising results for managing pain and treating various stress disorders. Often sham treatments, in which stimulation is not given to the designated points but to points not on so-called meridians, have been found to be as effective as real acupuncture (Harris et al. 2009). However, most of these investigations fail to realize that classical acupuncture was only one part of traditional Chinese medicine; a fair research study would include the other elements (such as nutrition and movement) as well.

Reiki

The term "Reiki" is derived from two Japanese characters that can be translated as *rei* (universal) and *ki* (life energy) (NCCAM website 2011). In short, practitioners of this method place their hands above a client's hypothetical energy fields (such as the chakras that are an integral part of yoga and Ayurvedic medicine) to help stimulate the client's own natural healing mechanisms, while supposedly unblocking any restricted energy (Baldwin, Wagers, & Schwartz 2008; Bossi, Jane, & DeCristofaro 2008).

There are two main types of Reiki, referred to as traditional Japanese Reiki and Western Reiki, which both consist of three levels of knowledge (Herron et al. 2009). Level 1 practitioners are able to heal both themselves and others; level 2 practitioners can perform healing from a distance (often using standard symbols); and level 3 practitioners (the so-called Master's level) are able to teach others.

According to NCCAM (2011), Reiki is used in various types of health care settings and has shown promising results for treating various diseases and disorders. For example, Reiki has been shown to reduce anxiety among cancer patients (Bossi, Jane, & DeCristofaro 2008; Mansky & Wallerstedt 2006), reduce stress in children and adults (Barnett 2005), reduce chronic headaches (Sutherland et al. 2009), reduce phantom limb pain (Leskowitz 2009), increase healing following coronary bypass surgery (MacIntyre et al. 2008), increase problem-solving abilities among stressed-out nurses (Raingruber & Robinson 2007), and reduce chronic pain associated with fibromyalgia (Assefi et al. 2008), as well as other applications. In a review of 1,321 studies done on the use of Reiki in various health care settings, the practice was often found to have overall positive effects on both physical and psychological health (Herron-Marx et al. 2008).

More recently, Morse and Beem (2011) found that Reiki was effective in improving a patient's absolute neutrophil (or white blood cell) count (ANC). The patient was a 54-year-old male who was severely ill with hepatitis C types 1 and 2 who did not respond to conventional treatments. The patient was administered an experimental high dose of interferon/riboviron therapy, which resulted in extreme anemia and neutropenia (i.e., low red and white blood cell count). Reiki therapy was administered to increase the patient's well-being and to reduce anxiety associated with these side effects, and was found not only to improve his ANC count but to assist him in tolerating the interferon treatment. Initially, the patient had only a 5 percent chance of being free of the virus, but in this case he was free of the virus when followed up after one year.

Conclusion

While the above offers a brief overview of a few modalities that fall within the field of mind and body medicine, along with mention of some promising research showing its possible effectiveness for treating various disorders, there is still much to be learned—and the jury is not yet out regarding the efficacy or inefficacy of any of these approaches. Consequently, we caution potential consumers that although research data from the utilization of these modalities preliminarily have shown mixed results, there is little research in regard to their long-term effectiveness. For example, one of the drawbacks with acupuncture is that some studies

Mind over Matter

American psychiatrist and psychoanalyst Elio Frattoroli, author of *Healing the Soul in the Age of the Brain*, offers a provocative view of the relationship between mind and body. He notes that seasoned psychiatrists like himself know well that treating the mind produces benefits for the disordered brain. Frattoroli describes how, before the era of managed care, a patient hospitalized for a major mood disorder or psychosis might, in fact, go several days without being administered a drug while doctors worked with him or her to understand the nature of the problem. Doctors typically were able to do so, says Frattoroli, because the mere act of hospitalization, wherein the patient came into contact with professional caretakers, had salutary effects. "Experience showed," he writes, "that even the most dramatic biological symptoms of mental illness often disappear quite rapidly once the patient feels he is in a safe, nonstressful, and caring environment." So does this mean that the psychiatric patients he examined were not actually suffering from chemical imbalances in the brain—the contemporary conception of illness? No, says Frattoroli, in many cases they likely were; but, as he also came to appreciate over the length of his career, such neurophysiological disturbances "occurred and had meaning within a psychological context and [were] triggered, at least in part, by psychological stressors."

Frattoroli goes on to condemn the nearly exclusive focus in contemporary psychiatry on biological causes and presents his own case for understanding *anxiety* as an emotion or experience that plays a central role in the connection between mind and body:

> The proposition that mental illnesses are merely brain disorders is not a scientific fact but an unprovable and implausible philosophical prejudice, an attempt to evade the awareness of existential anxiety by simply defining it out of existence. . . . Denying the existence of the Spirit will not make the anxiety go away. It remains as ineradical evidence of the mind-body problem [or relationship]. In fact, I would go so far as to say that anxiety *is* the mind-body problem. It is an uneasy combination of physiological response and dawning awareness; an unconscious feeling trying to become conscious, something that has existed only in physiological form in the body, now beginning to emerge painfully into psychological form in the mind. (Frattoroli 2001: 95, 100)

—*Editor*

Source: Elio Frattoroli, *Healing the Soul in the Age of the Brain: Becoming Conscious in an Unconscious World* (Viking, 2001).

indicate that clients must repeatedly use acupuncture in order for it to remain effective, while sham acupuncture can give effects as robust as traditional acupuncture in brief trials. These data suggest that expectation, belief, and other elements of placebos may have much to do with the outcome. In regard to other practices, such as meditation, yoga, Tai Chi, and QiGong, it should be noted that ongoing practice under qualified guidance is thought to be required in order to maintain any beneficial effects of these modalities. Thus these modalities are generally geared toward lifestyle change, rather than a "quick fix" that can be used in short-term emergencies.

See also Culturally Competent Mental health Care; Humanistic Theories and Therapies; Hypnosis and Hypnotherapy; Nutritional Therapies; Stress and Stress Management

Bibliography

Ainsworth, Steve. 2009. "Acupuncture: What Are We to Make of It?" *Practice Nurse* 38: 31–32.

Assefi, Nassim, Andy Bogart, Jack Goldberg, and Dedra Buchwald. 2008. "Reiki for the Treatment of Fibromyalgia: A Randomized Controlled Trial." *Journal of Alternative and Complementary Medicine* 14: 1115–1122.

Baldwin, Ann L., Christina Wagers, and Gary E. Schwartz. 2008. "Reiki Improves Heart Rate Homeostasis in Laboratory Rats." *Journal of Alternative and Complementary Medicine* 14: 417–422.

Barnett, Deborah. 2005. "The Effects on Well-being of Parents Who Learn and Practice Reiki." Ph.D. dissertation, Institute of Transpersonal Psychology, Palo Alto, CA.

Bossi, Larraine M., Mary Jane Ott, and Susan DeCristofaro. 2008. "Reiki as a Clinical Intervention in Oncology Nursing Practice." *Clinical Journal of Oncology Nursing* 12: 489–494.

Brown, Daniel. 2009. "The Energy Body and Its Functions: Immunosurveillance, Longevity, and Regeneration." In William C. Bushnell, Erin L. Olivio, and Neil D. Theise, eds., *Longevity, Regeneration, and Optimal Health: Integrating Eastern and Western Perspectives* (pp. 312–337). New York: Wiley-Blackwell.

Butler, L. D., L. C. Waelde, T. A. Hastings, X. H. Chen, B. Symons, J. Marshall, A. Kaufman, T. F. Nagy, C. M. Blasey, E. O. Seibert, and D. Spiegel. 2007. "Meditation with Yoga, Group Therapy with Hypnosis, and Psychoeducation for Long-term Depressed Mood: A Randomized Pilot Trial." *Journal of Clinical Psychology* 64: 806–820.

Eden, Donna, and David Feinstein. 2008. "Principles of Energy Medicine." Retrieved from http://www.energymed.org/hbank/handouts/principles_ener_med.htm.

Feher, Stephen D. K., Lawrence R. Berger, John D. Johnson, and Judith B. Wilde. 1989. "Increasing Breast Milk Production for Premature Infants with a Relaxation/Imagery Audiotape." *Pediatrics* 83: 57–60.

Freeman, Lynn. 2004. *Mosby's Complementary & Alternative Medicine: A Research-Based Approach* (2nd ed.). St Louis, MO: Mosby.

Harris, Richard E., Jon K. Zubieta, David J. Scott, Vitaly Napadow, Richard H. Gracely, and Daniel J. Clauw. 2009. "Traditional Chinese Acupuncture and Placebo (Sham) Acupuncture Are Differentiated by Their Effects on Mu-Opioid Receptors (MORs)" [abstract]. *Neuroimage* 47: 1077–1085.

Herron-Marx, Sandy, Femke Price-Knol, Barbara Burden, and Carolyn Hicks. 2008. "A Systematic Review of the Use of Reiki in Health Care." *Alternative & Complementary Therapies* 14: 37–42.

Kabat-Zinn, Jon. 1990. *Full Catastrophe Living: Using the Wisdom of Your Body and Mind to Face Stress, Pain, and Illness.* New York: Dell.

Krakow, Barry, Michael Hollifield, Lisa Johnston, Mary Koss. 2001. "Imagery Rehearsal Therapy for Chronic Nightmares in Sexual Assault Survivors with Posttraumatic Stress Disorder: A Randomized Controlled Trial." *JAMA* 286: 537–545.

Leon-Pizarro, Concha, Ignasi Gich, Angeles Rovirosa, Blanca Farrus, Francesc Casas, Eugenia Verger, Albert Biete, Bartle J. Craven, Jordi Sierra, and Angeles Arcusa. 2007. "A Randomized Trial of the Effect of Training in Relaxation and Guided Imagery Techniques in Improving Psychological and Quality-of-Life Indices for Gynecologic and Breast Brachytherapy Patients." *Psycho-Oncology* 16: 971–979.

Leskowitz, Eric. 2009. "Energy Medicine Perspectives on Phantom Limb Pain." *Alternative & Complementary Therapies* 15: 59–63.

Lynn, Steven J., Irving Kirsch, Arreed Barabasz, Etzel Cardeña, and David Patterson. 2000. "Hypnosis as an Empirically Supported Clinical Intervention: The State of Evidence and a Look to the Future." *International Journal of Clinical and Experimental Hypnosis* 48: 239–259.

MacIntyre, Barb, Jane Hamilton, Theresa Fricke, Wenjun Ma, Susan Mehle, and Matt Michel. 2008. "The Efficacy of Healing Touch in Coronary Artery Bypass Surgery Recovery: A Randomized Clinical Trial." *Alternative Therapies* 14: 24–32.

MacIver, K., D. M. Lloyd, S. Kelly, N. Roberts, and T. Nurmikko. 2008. "Phantom Limb Pain, Cortical Reorganization and the Therapeutic Effect of Mental Imagery." *Brain: A Journal of Neurology* 131: 2181–2191.

Mansky, P. J., and D. B. Wallerstedt. 2006. "Complementary Medicine in Palliative Care and Cancer System Management." *Cancer Journal* 12: 425–431.

Morse, Melvin L., and Lance W. Beem. 2011. "Benefits of Reiki for a Severely Neutropenic Patient with Associated Influences on a True Random Number Generator." *Journal of Alternative and Complementary Medicine* 17(11): 1181–1190.

National Center for Complementary and Alternative Medicine. http://nccam.nih.gov.

National Institutes of Health, National Organization for Complementary and Alternative Medicine. 2011. *CAM Basics: What Is CAM?* Retrieved from http://nccam.nih.gov/health/whatiscam/.

Nunes, Daniela, Adriane L. Rodriguez, Hernanda da Silva, Clarice Luz, Aroldo Filho, Marisa C. Muller, and Moises E. Bauer. 2007. "Relaxation and Guided Imagery Program in Patients with Breast Cancer Undergoing Radiotherapy is not associated with Neuroimmunomodulatory Effects." *Journal of Psychosomatic Research* 63: 647–655.

Raingruber, Bonnie, and Carol Robinson. 2007. "The Effectiveness of Tai Chi, Yoga, Meditation, and Reiki Healing Sessions in Promoting Health and Enhancing Problem Solving Abilities of Registered Nurses." *Issues in Mental Health Nursing* 28: 1141–1155.

Schure, M. B., J. Christopher, and S. Christopher. 2008. "Mind-Body Medicine and the Art of Self-care: Teaching Mindfulness to Counseling Students through Yoga, Meditation, and Qigong." *Journal of Counseling & Development* 86: 47–56.

Sutherland, Elizabeth, Cheryl Ritenbaugh, Susan J. Kiley, Nancy Vuckovic, and Charles Elder. 2009. "An HMO-Based Prospective Pilot Study of Energy Medicine for Chronic Headaches: Whole-Person Outcomes Point to the Need for New Instrumentation," *Journal of Alternative and Complementary Medicine* 15: 819–826.

Suzuki, Shunryu. 2004. *Zen Mind, Beginner's Mind: Informal Talks on Zen Meditation and Practice* (7th ed.). New York: Weatherhill.

Toth, Maria, Peter M. Wolsko, Judy Foreman, Roger B. Davis, Tom Delbanco, Russell S. Phillips, and Peggy Huddleston. 2007. "A Pilot Study for a Randomized, Controlled Trial on the Effect of Guided Imagery in Hospitalized Medical Patients." *Journal of Alternative and Complementary Medicine* 13: 194–197.

Wahbeh, H., S. M. Elsas, and B. S. Oken. 2008. "Mind-Body Interventions: Applications in Neurology." *Neurology* 70: 2321–2328.

Mood Disorders

See Bipolar Disorder; Depression